Kings
A new translation with commentary

Cover illustration: Siege and plunder of a city

From A.H. Layard, A Second Series of the Monuments of Nineveh *(London: John Murray, 1853), plate 40. Public domain image available at the New York Public Library Digital Collections:*
`/https://digitalcollections.nypl.org/items/510d47dc-4738-a3d9-e040-e00a18064a99`

Kings

A new translation with commentary

Translated with comments by William Whitt

The
Cutting Horse
Press

Weatherford, Texas

First published in 2025
by The Cutting Horse Press
Weatherford, Texas

Typeset in pdfLaTeX by the author
© 2025 by William Whitt

Print edition: ISBN 978-1-959-4870-5-0
Digital edition: ISBN 978-1-959-4870-4-3

Table of contents

Translator's note to the reader	vii
The book of Kings	1
Notes and comments	113
The composition history of Kings	333
Schema for the composition history of Kings	401
Appendix: Chronology of the kingdoms of Israel and Judah	407

Translator's note to the reader

> "Whoever wishes to translate, and purposes to render each word literally, and at the same time adhere slavishly to the order of the words and sentences in the original, will meet with much difficulty; his rendering will be faulty and untrustworthy. This is not the right method. The translator should first try to grasp the sense of the subject thoroughly, and then state the theme with perfect clearness in the other language. This, however, cannot be done without changing the order of words, putting many words for one word, or *vice versa*, and adding or taking away words, so that the subject be perfectly intelligible in the language into which he translates."
> Moses Maimonides, Letter to His Translator Samuel ibn Tibbon
> Cited from *Miscellany of Hebrew Literature*, vol. 1 (1872), p. 222.

This book is the culmination of a larger project that I have undertaken to translate the Torah and the Former Prophets—the first nine books of the Tanakh (or what Christians call the Old Testament).[1] These books, which present a chronicle of the people who came to call themselves "Israel" and which begin with the world's creation and end with the destruction of Yahweh's temple in Jerusalem and the exile of Judah's citizenry to Babylonia, have indisputably had an outsized impact on human history. Through the act of their writing in the centuries spanning the first millennium BCE, their authors laid the groundwork for a new type of religion, one in which study of and adherence to "the book" ultimately displaced animal sacrifice as the primary avenue for humans to access the divine realm. These nine books, as they grew and came to take their current form over a period of centuries, provided a framework out of which the religion of Judaism emerged, and then, centuries later, shaped and inspired Christian theology. Yet despite these books' impact on human history, they are—with the possible exception of Genesis—barely read today.

One reason why they are unread is simply that most people today find them unreadable. This is true not only for the typical university-educated person, but even many devout Jews and Christians view them as such. One of the primary goals I have in this larger translation project, then, is to make these books readable—or at least less unreadable—for the modern-day audience.

---

[1] All the books that I have published for this project are freely available to read and download at the Internet Archive and on my webpage at researchgate.net.

**

The book of Kings[2] presents itself as a chronicle of the reigns of the kings of Israel and Judah and spans a period of roughly four hundred years, from the mid-tenth century BCE to the mid-sixth century BCE. The book begins with Solomon's installment as David's successor and it concludes with King Jehoiachin's release from prison in 560 BCE, some three decades after the destruction of Yahweh's temple in Jerusalem and the exile of the people of Judah to Babylonia.

Of the nine books of the Torah and Former Prophets, Kings is the longest[3] and, uniquely among those books, it has numerous connections to historical events and individuals that are known from extra-biblical sources from ancient Assyria and Babylonia, Egypt, Aram, and the Levant. The sheer length of Kings and its many references to actual events and people known from history make the book especially challenging for modern-day readers. Even professional biblical scholars can feel overwhelmed by the dozens of kings and prophets in the cast of characters, the different theologies and obscure politics that shape the narrative, and the confusing chronological system employed by the book's authors.

Separate from the difficulty of following the twists and turns of Kings' narrative, there is also the challenge of identifying and understanding the different authors of the book and their motivations. The book of Kings in its current form is a composite work that, like the books of the Torah and the other books of the Former Prophets, was

---

2   Throughout this translation and commentary, I refer to Kings as a single book and not in the more familiar form by which it is known today, First Kings and Second Kings. In the Masoretic tradition, Kings is written as a single book, as is the book of Samuel. The division of Kings into two books has its origins in the earliest Greek translations of the books of the Former Prophets in the second century BCE; in those translations, the books of Samuel and Kings were each split into two parts, and the four parts were collectively known as the books of Kingdoms. Thus Samuel became First and Second Kingdoms, and Kings became Third and Fourth Kingdoms. This is how the books appear in Jerome's translation of the Christian Old and New Testaments into Latin, the Vulgate. This division of Kings into two books has carried on in Christian tradition down to the present day, and the two-part division even made its way into Jewish tradition in the sixteenth century CE, when the medieval Christian chapter divisions of the Old Testament were adopted in printed Hebrew Bibles.

3   In the Leningrad Codex, which is the oldest complete manuscript of the Tanakh, the text of Kings occupies 217 columns of the manuscript, which displays three columns per page. The next longest book in the Torah and the Former Prophets is Samuel, which is written in 203 manuscript columns in the Leningrad Codex. By comparison, Genesis is the longest of the books of the Torah, and its text covers just 181 columns in the Leningrad Codex.

written over a period of centuries, with dozens of authors and editors adding to, revising, and commenting on the original work. A full appreciation of Kings requires the reader to give close consideration to the different literary layers present in the book, and to the question of how they might relate to one another.

**

In seeking to understand the book of Kings, many scholars have viewed the book's original composition as closely connected to the writing of the so-called Deuteronomistic History.[4] Scholars generally agree that this work consists of the books of Joshua, Judges, Samuel and Kings, plus the addition of a narrative framework to Deuteronomy to which Joshua was then attached. There is also general agreement that this work represents an attempt by individuals associated with the royal court of Judah and/or Yahweh's cult on Mount Zion to explain the history of the Israelite people through the lens of Deuteronomy and the treaty obligations imposed on the people in that book.[5] There is, however, a fair amount of disagreement over the specific circumstances behind the composition of the Deuteronomistic History, including when it was written, whether it was the work of one or multiple authors, whether there was more than a single "edition" of it, and to what extent it involved a revision of pre-existing books versus the composition of entirely new books.

In fact, in recent decades, these points of disagreement have led a number of scholars to question the entire concept of a Deuteronomistic History.[6] At the most general level, the primary problem with such

---

4 The idea of a Deuteronomistic History was first proposed by the German scholar Martin Noth in 1942, and since then has served as a foundation for much scholarship on the Former Prophets. Noth's work devoted to this proposal has been translated into English and published as *The Deuteronomistic History*, Sheffield: JSOT Press, 1981. For a good concise overview of scholarly approaches to the idea of a Deuteronomistic History, see T. Römer, "Deuteronomistic History," EBR 6 (2013), cols. 648-653. For a more detailed discussion of scholarship on the Deuteronomistic History, see S. McKenzie, *The Trouble with Kings: The Composition of the Book of Kings in the Deuteronomistic History*, Leiden: E.J. Brill, 1991.

5 For Deuteronomy's presentation of itself as a treaty document, see the introductory comments to my translation of Deuteronomy.

6 See, for example, K. Noll, "Deuteronomistic History or Deuteronomistic debate? (A thought experiment)," *Journal for the Study of the Old Testament* 31 (2007), pp. 311-345 and G. Knoppers, "Rethinking the relationship between Deuteronomy and the Deuteronomistic History: the case of Kings," *The Catholic Biblical Quarterly* 63 (2001), pp. 393-415. See also K. Schmid, "The Emergence and Disappearance of the Separation between the Pentateuch and the Deuteronomistic

a history is that the books ascribed to it can't really be considered a unified work. The books are only loosely connected by theme and, most importantly, the so-called Deuteronomistic elements differ from book to book—and in some books, these elements barely appear at all. A close reading of the individual books of the history reveals the presence of multiple "Deuteronomistic" authors and editors, to say nothing of the many other "non-Deuteronomistic" authors whose works the so-called Deuteronomists utilized, sometimes revising and editing and other times leaving practically untouched. The messiness of the material in the history, the lack of internal inconsistency both within and across the books of the history, and the absence of Deuteronomic themes in large sections of these books thus create almost insurmountable challenges for the traditional proposal for a Deuteronomistic History represented by Joshua - Kings.

Prior to 2023, when I began work on my translation of Judges, my views about the Deuteronomistic History were by and large within the older mainstream of scholarly thinking. In brief, my views were: that the earliest "edition" of the work was composed in the decades immediately following the destruction of the Jerusalem temple in 586 BCE; that the work as a whole was sponsored by leaders within Yahweh's cult and the former royal court of Judah, some of whom also served as lead editors of the work; that these sponsors commissioned a number of individuals to write the books that comprise the history; and that the books' authors drew on and incorporated pre-existing written documents and oral traditions, but shaped these materials in their own individual ways to express the larger themes of their books and of the overall history. The one place where my views differed from those of most other scholars was that I also ascribed the earliest edition of Exodus-Numbers (originally a single book in my view) to the Deuteronomistic History.[7] Over the course of my work on Judges, however, I came to see that my views on the composition of

---

History in Biblical Studies," in T. Dozeman, T. Römer, and K. Schmid (eds.), *Pentateuch, Hexateuch, or Enneateuch: Identifying Literary Works in Genesis through Kings* (Atlanta: Society of Biblical Literature, 2011), pp. 11-24.

7   My rationale for this was that, as I argue in my translation of Joshua, the narratives of the early layers of Numbers and Joshua assume one another and are inextricably linked. Thus, if the earliest edition of Joshua was part of the Deuteronomistic History, then the earliest edition of Numbers must be as well. Likewise, because the early layers of Numbers and Exodus are inextricably linked and in fact seem to comprise a single work, then the earliest version of Exodus must also belong to the Deuteronomistic History. For additional thoughts on Exodus-Numbers as part of the Deuteronomistic History, see the introductions to my translations of Joshua, Exodus, and Numbers.

the books associated with the Deuteronomistic History—and the very idea of a "Deuteronomistic" history itself—would need to be modified significantly to explain the material that we find in Judges. My work on Kings has further solidified in my mind the views that I initially developed working on Judges.

**

A close examination of the book of Kings with respect to Deuteronomy and the key concepts in that book helps make clear the problems for the traditional theory of a Deuteronomistic History as a unified work of the sixth century BCE. Most important in my view is that Yahweh's treaty with the Israelites, which is the entire focus of the book of Deuteronomy, plays an extremely limited role in Kings. If we accept that there was a "Deuteronomistic" author or group of authors who conceived of and wrote a "history" of the Israelites, we would expect to see these authors express their opinion about historical events in terms of whether or not the Israelites kept the obligations imposed on them by their treaty with Yahweh. For the authors of Deuteronomy, it is the people's adherence to the treaty obligations—the commandments and laws that Yahweh gave them through Moses—that determine whether they will be blessed with success or cursed with suffering and destruction. In Deut 28.1f, they introduce a series of blessings the Israelites will receive by keeping true to the obligations of their treaty with Yahweh:

> And it will happen that if you really do obey your god Yahweh, being careful to follow all his commandments which I am giving you today, then your god Yahweh will place you in a position above all nations on earth. Then all these blessings will come your way and overtake you, for you will have obeyed your god Yahweh.

Likewise, in Deut 28.15, they introduce a long list of curses the Israelites will be subjected to if they do not fulfill their treaty obligations:

> And it will happen that if you do not obey your god Yahweh by being careful to follow all his commandments and laws which I am giving you today, then all these curses will come at you and overtake you.

It is within this framework of the treaty blessings and curses that the authors of Deuteronomy express their own views about the destruction of Israel and Judah and the exile of their peoples. These events occurred because the people forsook their treaty with Yahweh (Deut 29.21ff):

> When they see the blows the land has suffered and the diseases that Yahweh has inflicted on it... all the nations will ask, "Why did Yahweh act like this toward this land? What was the reason for this great burning anger?" And they'll answer, "It's because they forsook the treaty with their ancestors' god Yahweh, which he made with them when he brought them out of Egypt...." So Yahweh's anger was kindled against that land, bringing upon it the curse in its entirety, as written on this scroll. Yahweh rooted them out from their land in his anger, in his fury and in his great wrath, and then flung them away to another land, as is the case today.

However, the people's treaty with Yahweh and the attendant blessings and curses are not the framework of judgement that we see in Kings. Rather, for the authors of Kings, what is most important—what drives historical events and explains why the nations of Israel and Judah were ultimately destroyed—are the actions of the king himself. The authors of Kings evaluate all kings of Israel and Judah in terms of whether their actions were "pleasing to Yahweh" or "displeasing to Yahweh." It is the king's own actions, which are displeasing to Yahweh, that lead Yahweh to inflict punishment and suffering on the Israelites. Whether or not the people were true to their treaty obligations plays no real role in Yahweh's decision to destroy Israel and Judah and to drive the peoples of both nations out of the land he gave their ancestors.

The most striking example of this frame of judgement is how the authors of Kings explain Yahweh's destruction of Judah and Jerusalem ("this town that I chose") and the temple on Mount Zion ("the house that I said would be my very own").[8] These disasters were not due to the people's violation of their treaty obligations, but rather to the crimes of a single king—Manasseh. The authors state this in three places. In 2 Kings 21.11ff, they write:

---

[8] The phrase that I translate as "that I said would be my very own" is traditionally rendered "where I said my name would be." The use of the word "name" in this fashion is an idiomatic way to express possession in ancient Hebrew. On this idiomatic use of "name," see S. Richter, "Does YHWH's Name Dwell in the Temple?" at the website thetorah.com.

"Because Manasseh King of Judah has done these abominable things, doing things more despicable than anything the Amorites did before his time," Yahweh said through his servants the prophets, "and because he also caused Judah to err with his useless gods: Therefore, thus says Yahweh God of Israel: 'Know that I'm going to bring disaster upon Jerusalem and on Judah—something that anyone who hears about it will be astounded by.'"

Even more forceful is the statement in 2 Kings 23.26f:

However, Yahweh didn't relent from his great burning anger—the anger that burned against Judah because of all the outrageous things that Manasseh did to provoke his anger. "I'm going to remove Judah from my presence also," thought Yahweh, "just as I removed Israel, and I'm going to reject this town that I chose, Jerusalem, and I'm going to reject the house that I said would be my very own."

And finally, in 2 Kings 24.3f, the authors of Kings note that:

Indeed, it was at Yahweh's command that Judah suffered these attacks, in order to remove it from his presence on account of Manasseh's wrongdoing, as was fitting for everything that he did (including also the innocent blood that he shed and the fact that he filled Jerusalem with the blood of the innocent—crimes Yahweh was unwilling to forgive).

Likewise, the authors of Kings attribute the destruction of the northern kingdom, the kingdom of Israel, to the crimes of King Jeroboam. In explaining Israel's destruction—as with the explanations for Judah's destruction—the authors of Kings never mention the people's treaty with Yahweh, nor their obligations under the treaty, nor the treaty curses. Instead, the authors repeatedly cite Jeroboam's crimes[9] as the reason for Yahweh's displeasure with the kingdom of Israel; indeed, it was Jeroboam's actions that "caused Israel to do wrong."

---

9   The principal crime of Jeroboam was installing gold statues of Yahweh in the form of a bull calf in the Yahwistic shrines in Bethel and Dan, and then causing the people of Israel "to err" through veneration of the two bull calves. The people's veneration of these calves, which are "useless gods," contributes to Yahweh's rage against Israel, but it is Jeroboam's actions that cause his rage.

The later kings of Israel likewise are condemned because they "perpetuated" Jeroboam's error by supporting the cults in Bethel and Dan and thus "caused Israel to do wrong" through its veneration of the bull calves. The key passage attributing Israel's destruction to Jeroboam's actions is found in 1 Kings 14.15f:

> Yahweh will strike down Israel like a reed fluttering in the water, uprooting Israel from this good land which he gave to their ancestors and scattering them east of the Great River... doing this to Israel on account of the many wrongs that Jeroboam committed and that he caused Israel to commit.

**

It is the king, then, who drives the course of events in Kings. And what is most important to the authors of Kings are the king's actions with respect to the cult of Yahweh: if those actions please Yahweh, the king's family and the nation prosper; but if they displease Yahweh, the king's family and the nation suffer disaster. This attitude of the authors of Kings is best understood as a reflection of the concept of sacral kingship, which was the dominant way of understanding the world in ancient Near East.[10] Documents and inscriptions from ancient Mesopotamia, Egypt, and the Levant frequently portray the king as the earthly representative of the national god and as the chief intermediary between the god and the people.[11] One of the principal roles of the king in this capacity as intermediary between the god and his people was to serve as the head of the god's cult.

This idea of the king as head of the cult is central to the conception of kingship that we find in Kings. Thus, the authors of Kings consistently portray the kings of both Israel and Judah as the head of Yahweh's cult in their respective nations. The kings build and renovate temples and shrines to Yahweh, receive visions from him, appoint and remove his priests, proclaim and lead religious festivals in his honor, perform offering rites to him, direct the design, construction, and use of the equipment used in his cult, and oversee the administration of

---

[10] On the concept of the king and his role in the ancient Near East, see the classic study, H. Frankfort, *Kingship and the Gods: A Study of Ancient Near Eastern Religion as the Integration of Society and Nature*, Chicago: The University of Chicago Press, 1948.

[11] In some societies of the ancient Near East, the king himself was also a god; however, this was not the case for most societies, and it was not the case for the kingdoms of Israel and Judah.

taxes collected by his priesthood. This is the context for understanding the statements by the authors of Kings that a king's actions were either "pleasing" or "displeasing" to Yahweh. The king's administration of justice and his domestic and international policies are of relatively minor importance—what matters above all else is that he support Yahweh's cult in a fashion that pleases Yahweh. The dozens of statements in Kings about "displeasing" Yahweh or "pleasing" him are always about the kings' actions with respect to the cult, and nothing else.

Consistent with the conception of kingship in the ancient Near East, the authors of Kings—whose views reflect a Judean perspective on the world—understood there to be a special relationship between Yahweh and the Davidic kings who ruled Judah. I will argue below that this theme is especially important for understanding the circumstances surrounding the original composition of Kings. For that reason, a close look at Judean royal ideology is in order.

**

At the core of the Judean royal ideology is the binding agreement or "treaty" (*berīt* in Hebrew) between Yahweh and David. The clearest expression of this binding agreement and the special relationship between Yahweh and the Davidic king appears in Psalm 89. The psalm contains much material that is late—its second half is a lament over the destruction of the Davidic dynasty and thus must date to the exile or Persian period. However, two sections—verses 4-5 and verses 20-37—reflect in great detail the royal ideology that must have existed during the period of the monarchy.

In Ps 89.4-5, Yahweh states he has made a binding agreement (*berīt*) with David, which includes an oath to David that he will make his dynasty last forever:

> "I made a binding agreement with my chosen one—
>   yes, I swore to my servant David:
> 'I shall sustain your offspring for all eternity—
>   I shall establish your throne across the ages.' "

It is especially interesting that Yahweh declares he will remain true to his binding agreement with David, even if future Davidic kings fail in their obligation to lead and support the cult in accord with Yahweh's demands. This idea—that Yahweh will remain true to the Davidic king despite previous kings' failure to please him—in essence describes the narrative of the earliest version of Kings, as I will argue below. The relevant passage for this aspect of Judean royal ideology is Ps 89.31-37:

> "If his sons forsake my directions—[12]
>> if they don't follow my customs—
>> if they profane my rules—
>> if they don't observe my commandments—
> I shall punish their offenses with the rod—
>> raining blows upon them for their wrongdoing.
>
> "But I won't violate my agreement with him—
>> nor turn my loyalty into a lie.
> I won't defile the agreement [*berīt*] I made—
>> nor change the words that came from my lips.
> Once and for all I swore on my own sanctity
>> that I wouldn't be false to David.
> His descendants will endure forever—
>> like the sun, his throne will endure before me—
>> steadfast for all time, like the moon—
>> a sure witness among the clouds."

The other aspect of Judean royal ideology that is important to the authors of Kings is the close relationship between Yahweh's temple and the throne of the Davidic kings. The temple—the place where Yahweh's "presence" can be experienced by humans—is physically located in the same place where the Davidic king sits on his throne.[13] Moreover, there is a supernatural sense to this connection, in which the temple somehow shares its identity with the Davidic throne. For the authors of Kings, because of the shared identity between the Davidic throne and Yahweh's temple, the destruction of one implies the destruction of the other. The clearest expression of this shared identity is in Psalm 132.[14] The psalm contains a number of other

---

12   The terms in this stanza all relate specifically to the cult. The term for "directions" is *tōrāh*, which is the set of rules that Yahweh has provided regarding management of the cult and offerings to him. The other three terms—customs, rules, and commandments—are used practically synonymously and in connection with *tōrāh* throughout Exodus, Leviticus, Numbers, and Deuteronomy.
13   It is interesting to note that there was not a similar ideology in the kingdom of Israel. There the seat of the king's power was the city of Samaria, and the leading royal cult center was in Bethel, a full day's journey away.
14   There is a debate among scholars about the age of this psalm, with some dating it to the ninth or tenth centuries BCE (two or three centuries before the earliest version of Kings was composed) and others treating it as a Persian period

interesting aspects of Judean royal ideology, and for that reason I quote the psalm in its entirety:

A song for processing up to Yahweh's house:

"Remember David, O Yahweh—
    and all the troubles that afflicted him!
He who swore to Yahweh—
    who vowed to the Mighty One of Jacob:
'I won't enter the comfort of my home—
    nor climb into the bed where I recline—
I won't let my eyes have a moment's rest—
    nor my eyelids a wink of sleep—
until I find a place for Yahweh—
    yes, a dwelling for the Mighty One of Jacob.'

" 'We heard the news in Ephrathah—
    we found out about it in Ya'ar's countryside.
Let's go to the place where he dwells—
    let's bow down in worship before his footrest.'[15]

" 'Rise up, Yahweh, to your place of repose![16]
    You and your mighty battle chest!

---

composition. I personally view the psalm as early, perhaps dating to the ninth century, and see it as a composition celebrating three related things: the founding of Yahweh's cult in Jerusalem, the founding of the Davidic monarchy, and the inseparable link between Yahweh and the Davidic king. Regardless of whether the psalm is early or late, however, I think it is clear that the royal ideology expressed in it is characteristic of the era of the Judean monarchy.

15 The term "footrest" is a reference to Yahweh's battle chest, which was the chief object of veneration of Yahweh's cult in Jerusalem. It is this object that occupied the inner sanctum of Yahweh's temple there. It should be noted that during the period of the Judean monarchy, the battle chest had no association with Yahweh's treaty with his people. The transformation of Yahweh's battle chest into the "treaty chest" was an invention of the late exilic era or early Persian period. It was during those decades that the leaders of Yahweh's cult replaced the concept of the treaty between Yahweh and the Davidic king with the idea of a treaty between Yahweh and his people. To promote this new understanding of the relationship between Yahweh and his people, I believe that the cult leadership composed—or sponsored the composition of—the earliest versions of the books of Deuteronomy, Exodus-Numbers (then a single book) and Joshua.

16 Yahweh's "place of repose" is his temple in Jerusalem. Note that both Yahweh and his battle chest go to the "place of repose."

Let your priests be clothed in victory—[17]
    and your devotees cry out in exultation!
For the sake of your servant David—
    do not refuse your anointed one's request!'[18]

"Yahweh swore an oath to David—
    truly, may he not renege on it:
'From the fruit of your loins, I shall establish a throne for you.
[*If your sons honor my agreement with you—*
    and their treaty obligations to me that I teach them—
    then their sons too for all time
    shall occupy this throne of yours.][19]
[*For Yahweh has chosen Zion—*
    for himself he has desired a place to stay!][20]
This shall be my place of repose for all time—
    here I shall stay, because I want to!
The meals served at its table I certainly shall bless—
    those in want who visit it I shall stuff with food.
Its priests I shall clothe in victory—
    and its devout ones most certainly will cry out in exultation!'[21]

---

17 I translate צדק here as "victory" and not "righteousness." The parallel statement later in the psalm where Yahweh states he will clothe the temple's priests in victory (ישע) makes it clear that this is the intended nuance here. For צדק with the sense of "victory," see BDB, p. 842, top of first column.

18 The psalmist uses idiomatic language in this line. The phrase "to turn aside the face [of another person]" means to refuse or to deny that person (see BDB, p. 999, def. 5). This stanza states the threefold request of the psalmist: (1) that Yahweh and his battle chest take up residence in the place David has chosen for them, (2) that Yahweh's priests don their priestly garments and begin service to their god in his new home, and (3) that Yahweh's devotees—the common people—come to their god's new home to sing their praises of him (which includes the presentation of offerings to their god).

19 I view the material that I place in brackets as a late addition to the text. This material expresses the view that Yahweh's binding agreement with the Davidic king is conditional. Such a view is entirely at odds with the early royal ideology of Judah, where Yahweh's commitment to the Davidic monarchy is unconditional. (Note, for example, the unconditional aspect of this agreement in the passage from Psalm 89 quoted above).

20 This sentence interrupts Yahweh's oath to David, and for that reason I see it as a late addition to the text. Yahweh's oath to David has two parts: (1) that he will establish a dynasty for David and (2) that he will make his permanent home in the place that David has chosen for him and his battle chest.

21 Note that Yahweh's oath in this stanza fulfills each of the three requests that David made of him in the previous stanza. (For these requests, see note 18 above.)

> " 'There I shall make a horn sprout for David—
>   there I have set up a lamp for my anointed one!
> His enemies I shall clothe in shame—
>   while above him his crown blossoms forth!' "

The royal ideology expressed in the psalm is fascinating. The psalm tells us of the dynastic promise that Yahweh made to David: in return for David and his descendants establishing a permanent home for Yahweh (who previously was a wandering god without a fixed home), Yahweh will grant David a dynasty. This promise, which is at the core of the books of Samuel and Kings, seems to have existed within Yahweh's cult in Jerusalem from very early on.

The psalm is also full of language alluding to the king's role as military leader alongside whom Yahweh fights and to whom Yahweh grants victory. The military language is expressed most clearly in the first two couplets of the third stanza, which begins "Rise up, Yahweh" (vv. 8-9).[22] I understand these two couplets originally to have been part of an ancient chant or song welcoming the return of the king and Yahweh's battle chest after a military victory. The psalmist of Ps 132, who is celebrating the long-ago establishment of Yahweh's cult, has repurposed this old chant to be about Yahweh and the battle chest taking up residence in the temple for the first time.

The final stanza of the psalm (vv. 17-18), which begins "There I shall make a horn," is especially interesting because it expressly connects the temple and the Davidic throne: it is there—in the temple—that Yahweh will make a horn sprout for David. The Hebrew word used here is *qeren*, which is the term for an animal horn such as that of a bull or a ram, and it is frequently used to signify power and strength. For the psalmist, the temple in a supernatural sense is the source of the Davidic king's military and political power. The stanza additionally connects the Davidic king and the temple in alluding to the king's role as head of the cult. The psalmist tells us that there is a physical object inside the temple associated with the Davidic king: a lamp that has been set up by Yahweh (presumably to provide light for the king when he is performing rites in the temple).[23] The connection between the Davidic king and the temple cult is also present in the

---

22 See also v. 16, which repeats v. 9.
23 The rites likely would have involved the incense altar in the temple's great hall. Other scholars interpret the lamp metaphorically as a reference to the descendants of David succeeding him on the throne. However, if the psalm is early (as I believe), it seems more likely to me that the psalmist is simply alluding to a special royal lamp that has been set up inside the temple.

final line of the stanza. The image of the king's crown "blossoming" is reminiscent of the headgear worn by Aaron (Yahweh's head priest).[24] Here the psalmist may be alluding to the special headgear worn by the king when conducting rites in the temple, or he may be alluding more generally to the king's role as head of the cult.

**

It is clear, I believe, that the authors of Kings have structured their book around the idea that the king's actions with respect to the cult ultimately determine the success or failure of the nation as a whole. This concept is entirely alien to Deuteronomy. Indeed, the authors of Deuteronomy viewed the king as of minor importance; the most important things to them were the treaty between Yahweh and his people, and the people's requirement to uphold the treaty obligations in order to remain in their god's favor.

There are a number of similarities between Kings and Deuteronomy, but in no place is the direction of dependence clearly from Deuteronomy to Kings. The most important similarity is the view expressed in both books that there is a single place that Yahweh has chosen to be his very own.[25] In Kings, however, this place has a special connection to the king, reflecting Yahweh's special relationship (or binding agreement) with the Davidic king. This connection to the king is entirely absent in Deuteronomy.[26] Kings and Deuteronomy do indeed share the idea that Yahweh has chosen a place to be his very own, but the context around that choice in the two books is entirely different. Here we see that Kings is adjacent to Deuteronomy, but it cannot be called Deuteronomistic.

Other similarities between Kings and Deuteronomy show no evidence that the latter has influenced the former. For example, the authors of Kings repeatedly condemn the people's use of open-air

---

24   See Exodus 28.36ff and 39.30f for a description of Aaron's headgear, which consists of a turban to which a golden flower has been attached. The word for "blossoming" in Ps 132 is from the same root (צוץ) as the word in Exodus used to describe the golden flower; moreover, in Exodus the golden flower itself is called a "crown."

25   In Hebrew, "the place that Yahweh has chosen for his name." On this phrase, see note 8 above.

26   The authors of Deuteronomy, who I believe were writing long after the initial composition of Kings, reinterpret Yahweh's choice of a place that will be his own in the context of his treaty with his people. Under the terms of the treaty, there is only one legitimate altar on which Yahweh's people may make offerings to their god. The choice of place has nothing to do with the Davidic king.

shrines (called "high places" in many translations) to make offerings to Yahweh and other gods. This has some similarity to Deuteronomy's demand that the people make offerings only at the place Yahweh chooses, and that they destroy any altars used by Canaan's native peoples. However, there is no reason to suppose that the authors of Kings here have been influenced by Deuteronomy. It is noteworthy that the word for open-air shrine (*bāmāh*) appears more than thirty times in Kings, but the word is never used in Deuteronomy with this meaning.[27] The authors of Kings repeatedly condemn Jeroboam and the kings of Israel after him for supporting the cults of Bethel and Dan, which venerated an image of Yahweh in the form of a gold bull calf; likewise, the authors of Deuteronomy express abhorrence over the image of Yahweh in the form of a gold bull calf that Aaron made at Mount Sinai.[28] However, there is no reason to think that Deuteronomy influenced the authors of Kings in their condemnation—indeed, there is no reason even to suppose that the authors of Kings knew of a story about a gold bull calf at Mount Sinai.

One final example: statements in both Kings and Deuteronomy reflect the idea that Yahweh demands the people acknowledge only him and none of the gods of the surrounding peoples. In many cases these condemnations use identical language. But the terms used are commonplace verbs and idioms—"worship," "walk after," "serve," etc. Moreover, the authors of Kings typically condemn gods by name—they most frequently condemn the Baal and the Asherah, but they also condemn Milkom, Kemosh, Ashtarte, and others. By contrast, the condemnations by Deuteronomy's authors are almost always generic; they never mention the Baal and instead speak simply of "other gods." Thus, here too, there is no reason to believe that Deuteronomy has influenced the authors of Kings.

While the examples above show that the ideas expressed in Kings are adjacent to Deuteronomy, in each case there are sufficient differences to suggest that the authors of Kings have not been influenced by Deuteronomy. Given this, given the radically different views that Deuteronomy and Kings have about the role of the king, and given the absence of a treaty between Yahweh and his people in Kings, I think it is clear that the book of Kings cannot be characterized as "Deuteronomistic."

---

27 The word *bāmāh* appears once in the Song of Moses (Deut 32) and once in the Blessing of Moses (Deut 33), and in both instances it has the meaning of "elevated place, ridge."
28 See Deut 9.12-21.

**

If the overarching narrative frame of Kings shows no influence of Deuteronomy, that is not to say the book lacks material that has been influenced by Deuteronomy. However, this material is always secondary to the overall narrative, and it typically comments on or corrects pre-existing material.[29] At most, the material influenced by Deuteronomy represents just one thread—and a relatively slender one at that—in the book of Kings. I elaborate on this idea in the comments to the translation and in my essay on the composition history of Kings toward the end of this book. But for the purposes of this introductory note, I think it will be useful to the reader to see two examples of how material influenced by Deuteronomy functions as commentary and correction to the material in an older version of Kings.

One of the most significant passages showing the influence of Deuteronomy, as has been pointed out by all scholars who have studied Kings, is Solomon's prayer to Yahweh at the inauguration of the temple in 1 Kgs 8. The first part of the prayer (verses 22-26) reflects the Judean royal ideology discussed above and shows no influence of Deuteronomy; these verses represent the older layer of Kings that the material influenced by Deuteronomy comments on and corrects. The entire remainder of the prayer (verses 27-53) and the blessing that follows (verses 54-61) reflect the influence of Deuteronomy. In these verses we see many themes that are fundamental to Deuteronomy, including Moses and the exodus from Egypt, Yahweh's treaty with his people, and the people's obligations under that treaty. Most importantly, this material serves to correct the older view about the temple: it shifts the focus away from Yahweh's promise to the Davidic king and toward Yahweh's treaty with his people.

A second important passage showing the influence of Deuteronomy is the lengthy commentary on the reasons for the downfall of

---

[29] We see this even in the account Josiah's reforms in 2 Kings 23. As I discuss in the notes following my translation and in my essay on the composition history of Kings, I believe that the original version of Kings concluded with the death of Amon (Josiah's father), and that authors writing in the exilic period brought the narrative down to their own time in the sixth century BCE. The original account of Josiah's reign composed by these authors focused on Josiah's abolition of the open-air shrines, the eradication of the cults of non-Yahwistic gods in the temple, and the destruction of the cult at Bethel. But there was no account of the discovery of the Torah scroll, no ratification of a treaty between Yahweh and the people, and no passover celebration. These elements are secondary to the original account of Josiah's reign, and they were added by authors in the Persian period who were influenced by Deuteronomy.

the kingdom of Israel in 2 Kgs 17.7-17. As with the material in 1 Kgs 8, in this passage we also see several themes that are fundamental to Deuteronomy—in particular, the exodus from Egypt, Yahweh's treaty with the people, and the treaty obligations. This material serves to correct the rationale for Israel's downfall that is given in the older version of Kings, which appears in 2 Kgs 17.18-23. The older version of Kings attributes the downfall to Israel's breaking from Davidic rule by making Jeroboam king, who then "drove Israel away from Yahweh" and "caused them to commit a very great wrong." The material influenced by Deuteronomy corrects this view by shifting the blame away from Jeroboam and placing it entirely on the people's actions in forsaking their treaty with Yahweh.[30]

**

All scholars who have studied Kings have recognized that the book contains several compositional threads or "layers." In the sections above, I have presented evidence of two of these layers: one that uses Judean royal ideology as its frame of reference and another that uses ideas found in Deuteronomy as its frame of reference. Moreover, we saw that the layer employing Judean royal ideology must be earlier, for the layer influenced by Deuteronomy typically comments on and corrects it. In addition to these two compositional layers, through my work translating Kings I have identified five others.[31] Of the seven layers that I have found, it is the layer associated with Judean royal ideology that serves as the base narrative and that therefore must represent the earliest version of Kings.

This brings us to the question of the original composition of Kings. What were the circumstances surrounding the book's creation? Who wrote it, and who was the book intended for?

**

Two important clues that help us answer these questions can be found in this early layer's account of the reign of Jeroboam, the first king of Israel in the era of the divided monarchy. In this account, Yahweh makes a promise to Jeroboam about his own dynasty, and in this promise, Yahweh states that he will make the Davidic line suffer,

---

30 See 2 Kgs 17.15: "They rejected his laws and the treaty he made with their ancestors, including the treaty terms which he had invoked against them."

31 I provide detailed thoughts on these other five layers in the section below beginning on page xxvii.

although "not for all time."[32] That is, one day Israel will come back under Davidic rule and the Davidic line's suffering will end. The second clue appears at the beginning of story of the holy man who delivers the oracle against the altar in Bethel in 1 Kgs 13. This story presents King Josiah, who ruled Judah from 641 to 609 BCE, as the Davidic king who will eradicate the abhorrent cult practices of Jeroboam. He will destroy Yahweh's cult in Bethel, defile its altar, and slaughter the priests who serve in the open-air shrines that Jeroboam established. The key passage is found in 1 Kgs 13.2f, which is an oracle proclaimed by the holy man from Judah:

> "Altar, altar!" he cried. "Thus says Yahweh: 'A son shall be born to the Davidic line whose name will be Josiah. On you he shall slaughter the priests of the open-air shrines, who burn their offerings on you. Yes, human remains will be burned on you!' On that day, the following sign shall be given. Here's the sign that Yahweh foretold: the altar is going to split into pieces, and the fat on it will pour off."

Because of the unusual stature of Josiah in this early layer—he is the sole Davidic king of the divided monarchy who is portrayed as asserting his authority over Yahweh's cult in the north—I locate the original composition of Kings to his reign.[33] This gives us a date for the original composition of Kings as sometime in the period 641 - 609 BCE. In turn, this date—if we accept it—helps us narrow down the options for how to answer the questions about the circumstances leading to the book's creation, and who its authors and intended audience were.

**

Although I place the earliest composition of Kings to Josiah's reign, the account of his reign in 2 Kgs 22 - 23 is not part of the early narrative thread associated with Judean royal ideology; rather, the account of his reign is full of language and ideas from Deuteronomy and cannot have

---

[32] Yahweh's promise to Jeroboam is delivered in an oracle by the prophet Ahiyyah the Shilonite. See 1 Kgs 11.29-39; the statement that the Davidic line's suffering will not last for all time is in v. 39.

[33] That the original composition of Kings was associated with Josiah's reign is a very common view among scholars. The most influential early proponent of this view was Frank Moore Cross, who proposed a pre-exilic version of the so-called Deuteronomistic History that dated to the reign of Josiah. Cross first published his proposal in "The Structure of the Deuteronomistic History," *Perspectives on Jewish Learning*, Annual of the College of Jewish Studies 3 (Chicago, 1968), pp. 9-24.

been part of the original version of Kings. That is to say, in the original version of Kings, the narrative must have ended prior to Josiah's reign. I argue in the notes below and my essay on the compositional history of Kings that the original version of the book ended in 2 Kgs 21 with the account of the reign of Josiah's father and predecessor, Amon.

In my work on Judges, I proposed that the earliest versions of Judges, Samuel, and Kings were originally composed during the reign of Josiah to support his radical cult reforms and his expansionist political policies that aimed to bring the former lands of the northern kingdom under the rule of the Davidic king. As such, I argued that the earliest versions of these three books should be considered a "Josianic History." I also proposed in my work on Judges that these three books may have been written to educate the young king Josiah (he assumed the throne at the age of nine) about the roles and responsibilities of the ideal king. This would include instruction on the qualities of a great military leader (the stories in Judges and Samuel) and education about the importance of the king "pleasing" Yahweh in his actions as head of Yahweh's cult (the material in Kings). In my work on Judges, I had assumed the Josianic History's version of Kings included an account of Josiah's reign. But now I believe that is not the case. Ending the Josianic History's version of Kings with the reign of Amon makes perfect sense, however, if the Judges-Samuel-Kings "trilogy" were composed specifically for the education of the young king Josiah.

My work on Kings has strengthened my views that the original composition of Kings (and of Samuel and Judges) must have been connected to the boyhood education of King Josiah. Based on how I understand these three books to have been put together and the various literary threads I have detected in them, I speculate there were two groups working in partnership to compose these books and to educate the young king. For these two groups, the young king was the vehicle to realize their own political ambitions with respect to Yahweh's cult and the Davidic monarchy. One group must have been officials within the royal palace; possibly some members of Yahweh's cult who opposed Manasseh's cult reforms belonged to this group as well. The individuals in this group most likely were from prominent Judean families and would have been ardent believers in the traditional Judean royal ideology. They would have understood that if the young king were truly loyal to Yahweh, Yahweh would remove the "suffering" he had inflicted on the Davidic line and would fulfill his promise to raise the Davidic king to greatness. I believe the second group consisted of northern families who had fled to Judah after the fall of Israel and who had become influential at the royal court. One can imagine them as having won over Josiah's regent and/or his mother Jedidah (if she was not regent) to their views and as having convinced both to allow them to assist with, if not lead, the education of the young king. I believe it is this second group that composed the earliest version of the book of Judges, which consisted of stories about the legendary military "champions" of the northern tribes of ages long ago. This second group may have been ardent proponents of the idea of the exclusive worship of Yahweh, which is an idea that runs through Kings.[34] Although I don't believe there is a true "Deuteronomic" thread in the earliest version of Kings, we did see in the discussion above that the early thread contains ideas that are adjacent to Deuteronomy. After Josiah's reign—and especially after the fall of Jerusalem and the destruction of the temple—these northern ideas about the exclusive worship of Yahweh influenced practices in the southern cult and ultimately were foundational to the composition of Deuteronomy in the exilic era and Persian period.[35]

---

34 That Yahweh alone should be worshipped is also one of the principal ideas of Deuteronomy. Many scholars hold the view that the ideas found in Deuteronomy originated in the north and were brought to Judah in the eighth century by refugee families fleeing the Assyrian conquest of Israel. While I view Deuteronomy as an exilic era and Persian period composition, it is reasonable to suppose that many of the ideas in the book, which has numerous connections to the northern prophet Hosea, may indeed have northern roots. The proposal for a northern origin for Deuteronomy (or the ideas in it) goes back to the early twentieth century; the most influential proponent of the idea was E. W. Nicholson in his book *Deuteronomy and Tradition*, Philadelphia: Fortress Press, 1967. (See in particular his discussion on pp. 94-106, especially p. 94 and p. 102.) For a recent review of the history of scholarship on this proposal, see C. Edenburg and R. Müller, "A Northern Provenance for Deuteronomy? A Critical Review," *Hebrew Bible and Ancient Israel* 4 (2015), pp. 148-161.

   It should be noted that Edenburg and Müller are critical of the sort of speculations engaged in by myself and other scholars regarding the origins and life setting of the various biblical books. In their view, rather than speculate on a book's origins, it is more productive to investigate why different audiences found that book significant, how they used the book to reinforce identity, and what characteristics of the book allowed for "multivalent" readings by competing groups. While I agree that the questions posed by Edenburg and Müller provide productive avenues for research, I firmly believe that there is also much value in addressing questions about the origins and composition history of the different biblical books. For even if we can never move beyond the realm of speculation, examining these questions helps sharpen our thinking about the complexities and inconsistencies in these books and—most importantly—they can deepen our understanding of the text by offering plausible and historically-grounded explanations for these books' themes, structure, and content.

35 As an example of the way in which the original northern ideas might have evolved under the influence of ideas from the south, consider the idea of "cult centralization," which all scholars recognize as a core principle of Deuteronomy. This is an idea that almost certainly did not originate in the north. Worship of

In my work on Judges, I had assumed that an early version of the book of Deuteronomy was composed in support of Josiah's reforms. This was in large part because I had thought the account of Josiah's reign must be part of the earliest version of Kings. After working through Kings, as I state above, I now believe that Kings originally ended with the reign of Amon. And if this work did not include an account of Josiah's reign, then there is no compelling reason to think that Josiah's reforms were necessarily based on an early version of the book of Deuteronomy. I think it is better to say that his reforms were based on ideas that later became key principles of Deuteronomy. In my work on Leviticus, I argued that there were cult rule books in circulation in the northern kingdom that served to instruct (or remind) priests and worshippers of the rules for presenting offerings to Yahweh.[36] In several places Deuteronomy reflects the structure of these rule books.[37] It may have been the case that Josiah's reforms were in part based on cult rule books that the northern families had brought to Judah, and that some of these rule books were adopted by Yahweh's cult in Jerusalem, which later revised and expanded them and which included pieces of them in their composition of the book of Deuteronomy during the exile and early Persian period.

**

Kings, like the other books of the Torah and Former Prophets, shows very clear signs of a long composition process covering several centuries. In my work in translating these nine books over the past decade, I have found my own understanding of each book significantly enriched through the effort of trying to untangle the complex com-

---

Yahweh in the kingdom of Israel was conducted in numerous open-air shrines, many of which were supported by the king, who was head of the cult. Northern families coming to the south would have been comfortable with the idea of multiple legitimate altars to Yahweh. What these families opposed were the worship of other gods alongside Yahweh in shrines and altars they shared with him; they also opposed the creation of any images of Yahweh. Under the influence of Judean royal ideology, which believed that Yahweh had "chosen" a place to reside alongside the Davidic king, the ideas about the problematic way the open-air shrines were used may have morphed into a belief in cult centralization, where the manner in which Yahweh is worshipped can be strictly controlled.

36 See the introduction to my translation of Leviticus for a detailed discussion of this idea.
37 See note 24a to my translation of Leviticus, where I identify the passages in Deuteronomy that reflect the use of older cult rule books.

position process in order to identify the different authorial layers that comprise the book.[38] Because my notes and comments—and even my translation—reflect my understanding of Kings' compositional history, it will be helpful here to provide an overview of my views on this topic.[39] My comments so far have focused on two important literary threads in Kings—a thread associated with Judean royal ideology that I date to the reign of Josiah, and a thread reflecting some of the ideas of Deuteronomy that I date to the Persian period. In addition to these threads, I have identified five others in my work on Kings.

One thread—the oldest thread—contains matter-of-fact statements about kings, the length of their reigns, the key events of their reigns, the manner of their death, and who succeeded them. This thread is best thought of as a "pre-compositional" stage, for it represents source documents that were used by the authors of the earliest versions of Kings. The material that I attribute to this pre-compositional stage comes primarily from two documents, a book called *The Chronicles of the Kings of Israel* and a second book called *The Chronicles of the Kings of Judah*. These documents would have belonged to the official records in the royal palaces of each kingdom; they recorded important events of each king's reign, including the regnal years in which each event occurred.[40] We know that the earliest authors of Kings used these documents as sources for their accounts of the reigns of each king, because they repeatedly cite the two documents by name. We should imagine these two royal chronicles as living documents that would have grown in a piecemeal fashion across the reigns of successive kings, with palace scribes attaching a new section to the end of the existing scroll in order to record the events of the current king's reign. A third document that the authors of Kings cite as a source is *The Acts of Solomon*. Although some scholars believe this document was fictional, I see no reason to question its historicity—there are numerous administrative details about Solomon's reign in Kings that likely came from this document. The three source documents cited by the authors

---

38 The attempt to understand a book's evolution and how it came to have its present form is referred by by scholars as a "diachronic" understanding. Scholars traditionally have employed diachronic approaches to their study of the biblical books; however, this approach has come under criticism in recent decades because it is highly speculative and is based primarily on conjecture. See note 34 above for my thoughts on the value of informed speculation.

39 A detailed discussion of Kings' compositional history can be found below following the notes and comments.

40 Similar documents are known from Mesopotamia and Egypt. The standard study of the Mesopotamian documents is A. K. Grayson, *Assyrian and Babylonian Chronicles*, Winona Lake: Eisenbrauns, 2000.

of Kings spanned a very long period: the earliest material in them dates to Solomon's reign (the second half of the tenth century BCE) and the latest material dates to the beginning of the sixth century BCE, when the final citation of one of these documents is given. Numerous scholars have speculated that the authors of Kings may have used other source documents as well, such as documents from the temple archives; however, I am less sure of this proposal and I do not include these other sources in this "pre-compositional" stage.

A second literary thread in Kings shows a strong interest in the idea of the Davidic kingship and its unique relationship to Yahweh. At the core of this relationship is Yahweh's unconditional promise to David that his dynasty will last forever. The material belonging to this thread judges each king on whether his actions with respect to Yahweh's cult pleased or displeased Yahweh; this thread is also interested in the cause of the split between Judah and Israel, and in the reasons for the fall of the northern kingdom. I believe the material in this thread represents the earliest version of Kings and was composed in the 630s BCE as part of the educational program of the young king Josiah. As discussed above, I believe this early version of Kings was one of three books composed as part of Josiah's education (the others being the early versions of Samuel and Judges). I speculate that two groups of authors collaborated on these educational works—a group of palace officials imbued in Judean royal ideology and individuals from northern families who had gained influence in the palace and/or with Josiah's mother. These two groups shared a political and religious program that included the elimination of the worship of any god but Yahweh, and the expansion of the Davidic king's control to the lands of the former kingdom of Israel. Through the books they wrote, they aimed to inculcate the principles of their program into the young king. Because this thread represents the earliest version of Kings, I refer to it as the book's "first compositional stage."

Pharaoh Necho's execution of Josiah in 609 BCE must have led to a great deal of doubt and questioning among those who supported Josiah's program and who believed that once the cult had been purified, Yahweh would again bestow greatness on the Davidic king. These doubts would have been greatly magnified some two decades later when Nebuchadnezzar's army burned Jerusalem, destroyed the temple, and exiled much of Judah's citizenry to Babylonia. These events provide the background for the third literary thread in Kings. This thread, which is closely related to the second thread, seeks to explain the exile to Babylonia and Yahweh's "rejection" of his temple and of Jerusalem in terms of Yahweh's relationship with the Davidic kings. In particular, these authors have reinterpreted Yahweh's promise to

David as conditional on the loyalty of David's descendants to Yahweh. The material belonging to this thread represents what I call the second compositional stage of Kings, and it must have been composed between the 580s and 550s BCE. This compositional stage consists of a relatively small amount of material—the account of Josiah's reign, the accounts of the reigns of the kings after him, the account of the destruction of Jerusalem and the temple, and the account of the exile, including the release of Jehoiachin from prison at the end of the book. The Davidic kingship remained the primary frame of reference for the authors of this material, and their additions to Kings represent an early attempt to explain the horrible events that the people of Judah had suffered. In their view, the destruction of Jerusalem and the temple and the exile of Judah's people were due to the crimes of Manasseh, who violated the terms of the binding agreement between Yahweh and the Davidic king and who thus caused Yahweh to reject his promise to David.

A fourth literary thread in Kings introduces the theme of Yahweh's treaty with the Israelites and of the Torah given by Moses. This thread also has a special interest in the reforms of Josiah, which it presents as connected to the Torah of Moses. The material in this thread represents what I call the third compositional stage of Kings, and it is the first material in the book that is clearly influenced by Deuteronomy. I believe the authors of this material were active during the middle and late decades of the Persian period (ca. 500-350 BCE). These authors added material to Kings that harmonized the book with the new theological ideas developed during the exile and the early Persian period. It was during those years that the leaders of the Jerusalem-based cult abandoned the old Judean royal ideology and a belief in Yahweh's binding agreement with the Davidic king. They replaced these concepts with the idea of a treaty between Yahweh and his people, the Israelites. To provide a basis for this radical reimagination of Yahwism, these cult leaders conceived of and wrote a series of works examining Yahweh's relationship with his people and his people's duties towards him. These works included the earliest version of Deuteronomy, followed some time later by the earliest versions of Exodus-Numbers and Joshua and expansions to Deuteronomy. As a result of these efforts, the earliest version of the books of the Torah was complete by roughly 500 BCE. In the decades that followed, successive authors within the cult added material to the books in the temple library that reflected the new theology behind the initial creation of the books of the Torah. In relation to the books of the Former Prophets, this editorial work included very minor additions to Judges, and small but significant additions to Samuel and Kings. It is the additions made to Kings that represent what I call the book's third compositional stage.

A fifth literary thread in Kings is focused on the great prophets of old—especially the two northern figures Elijah and Elisha—and on the role of the prophet and his relationship to the king. The material in this thread, which I call Kings' fourth compositional stage, shows many signs of being relatively late. It knows Deuteronomy, and so must be later than (or contemporaneous with) the third stage discussed above. It has no interest whatsoever in the reasons for the destruction of Israel and Judah and the Babylonian exile—those events were far in the past for its authors. Moreover, the material contains numerous statements that reflect ideas from the Persian period, most particularly the monotheistic view of Yahweh as the sole god of the universe. For these reasons, I date the material in this stage to the middle and late decades of the Persian period and the early years of the Hellenistic period (ca. 450 - 300 BCE). Unlike other compositional stages, the material from this stage does not seek to correct or comment on the material from other stages. Rather, the authors of this stage composed stories with their own independent themes, and they used the book of Kings simply as a vehicle for promulgating their views. The authors of these stories would have had the option of creating stand-alone literary works about Elijah and Elisha, but they instead chose to insert their stories into Kings. We can only speculate about the reasons for their choice; perhaps they felt their stories would gain in stature and authority as part of Kings, which by the time they were writing was an important document in the temple library.

A sixth literary thread in Kings is especially interested in the construction of Yahweh's "house" (or temple) and in the great king responsible for its construction, Solomon. This thread, which I call Kings' fifth compositional stage, shows a strong interest in priestly matters, as can be seen its focus on Yahweh's temple and in the additions it makes to material from Kings' earlier compositional stages. The material in this stage also shows an interest in Solomon's greatness, and includes several stories about his great wisdom and wealth. I date the material in this compositional stage to a broad swathe of the Persian and Hellenistic periods—some of this material may have been contemporaneous with material from the third and fourth stages, but the majority of it likely was composed after the material from those two stages.

Finally, there is a seventh literary thread in Kings that consists almost entirely of editorial comments and glosses on the material found in the first six threads. I assign the material in this thread to the sixth compositional stage, which I view as spanning a very long period from late in the monarchy to late in the Hellenistic period. I view only a small amount of the activity in this sixth stage as contemporaneous with the first and second stages. Nearly all the material in the sixth stage is from the late Persian period and the Hellenistic period, when the institution of the synagogue was first established and when the books of the Torah and the Prophets and some of the Writings began circulating in the Babylonian and Egyptian diasporas. In my view, the editorial activity of the sixth stage primarily took place against the background of the emergence of Judaism, the adoption of a quasi-standardized collection of holy writings, and the recitation and study of these holy writings in the early synagogue within the diaspora communities. To support the use of these books in the synagogue, the individuals responsible for this stage added numerous comments, glosses, and harmonizations to Kings, thus giving the book the form it has today.

**

Some scholars who hold to the traditional idea of a Deuteronomistic History go so far as to treat the book of Kings as a work of historiography, and they speak of a "historian" or "historians" as the author(s) of the book.[41] Over the course of the past three years in studying and translating Joshua, Judges, and now Kings, I have come to see this terminology as unhelpful if not downright misleading in the effort to understand the books of the Former Prophets. Because there is fairly broad acceptance among scholars of the idea that Kings and the other books of the Former Prophets are in some way a "history,"[42] I think it would be useful here to take a small detour to discuss this topic.

As I hope is clear from the composition history sketched out above, the composition of Kings was a complex process involving dozens of authors and spanning several centuries. These authors—unlike the early Greek historians Herodotus and Thucydides—were not writing to inform the world about great events of the past in order to keep these events from being forgotten.[43] Nor do the authors of

---

41 The most influential proponent of this idea is John Van Seters, who made the case for viewing Kings and the other books of the Former Prophets as works of history in his book, *In Search of History: Historiography in the Ancient World and the Origins of Biblical History*, New Haven: Yale University Press, 1983.

42 Indeed, in my own work on Joshua and Judges, I accepted this terminology and used it throughout my books.

43 Note, for example, Herodotus' introduction to his *Histories*: "Here are presented the results of the enquiry carried out by Herodotus of Halicarnassus. The purpose is to prevent the traces of human events from being erased by time, and

Kings—unlike Herodotus and Thucydides—show evidence of critical evaluation of their sources.[44]

The book of Kings in its original form was not a work of historiography. It appears to have been originally put together as a "study book" (or textbook) for the education of a king. The authors of this textbook were concerned with educating their student about what a king must do to please Yahweh. These authors show little interest in historical events except insofar as they reinforce the idea that a king should strive to please Yahweh. Indeed, the authors of this textbook effectively admit that historical events are not their primary interest: they repeatedly refer the reader to their source documents in order to read the full details of each king's accomplishments.[45] In making these statements, they implicitly acknowledge that they were selective in what they included and that their goal was not to provide a full account of each king's reign.

In proposing that Kings and the other books of the Former Prophets were composed by a "historian" who intentionally set out to write a "history," Van Seters uses the definition of history proposed by the Dutch historian Johan Huizenga: "History is the intellectual form in which a civilization renders account to itself of its past."[46] But this is not what is going on in Kings—this is not what the book's authors were attempting to do in their work. In the book's earliest incarnation during Josiah's reign, it simply served as a textbook. Initially it was used in the education of the young king Josiah, but one can also imagine it being used in the education of Josiah's own sons. In any case, the book must have been one of the documents taken to Babylonia by palace officials or by priests in Yahweh's cult, or by the members of the royal family, when they were exiled from Judah. The book was first edited during the exile—this is the "second compositional stage" discussed above. The exilic authors used the book as a vehicle to

---

to preserve the fame of the important and remarkable achievements produced by both Greeks and non-Greeks; among the matters covered is, in particular, the cause of hostilities between Greeks and non-Greeks." Cited from R. Waterfield (trans.), *Herodotus: The Histories* (Oxford 1998), p. 3.

44 Herodotus, for example, frequently makes comments to the effect that even though he has included a story as it was told to him, he does not find the story credible. And, as every reader of *The Peloponnesian War* is aware, Thucydides applied an astonishing amount of rigor to his researches. See for example, his famous description of his research methodology in *The Peloponnesian War* 1.22.

45 These statements are given for nearly all kings of Israel and Judah. To cite just one example, see 1 Kgs 16.27: "The rest of Omri's acts—what he did and the valorous deeds he accomplished—are recorded in the book *The Chronicles of the Kings of Israel.*"

46 Van Seters, *op. cit.*, p. 1.

reflect on the cause of their own predicament, but in the conclusion of their work they also express some hope for the restoration of the Davidic king.[47] After this first series of edits, the book likely remained unchanged for many years. Completely separate from Kings, towards the end of the exile and early in the Persian period, authors associated with Yahweh's cult transformed the idea of a binding agreement (or "treaty") between Yahweh and the Davidic king by removing the king and replacing him with the people Israel. This treaty between Yahweh and his people then became the governing principle of Yahwism. To support this new framework for Yahwism, they composed the book of Deuteronomy, and some years later, the books of Exodus-Numbers and Joshua. When Kings was next edited and expanded—what I refer to above as the book's third compositional stage, which spanned the fifth century and first half of the fourth century BCE—the changes made to it were simply for the purpose of introducing the new framework of Yahwism into this old book which was kept in the temple library. The book remained confined to the cult; at this stage in its compositional history, it is difficult to imagine it had any readers outside the cult, and even within the cult, it may have been little read. It certainly did not qualify as a "history" in Huizenga's terms—it did not address a broad audience, nor did it attempt to render to any audience an account of its past.

Parallel to these additions to Kings, these same authors added comments to the other two "study books" composed for Josiah—Judges and Samuel—that introduced the new framework of Yahwism into them as well. The result of the various editorial iterations made by dozens of authors over the course of more than four centuries was a collection of books that gave the appearance of a continuous narrative spanning the period from the Egyptian captivity to the Babylonian exile. This collection certainly had points of connection with Huizenga's definition of "history," but these connection points came about by happenstance over many years and were not created intentionally. It is thus a mistake, in my opinion, to think that the authors who worked on this larger collection of books (Exodus, Numbers, Deuteronomy, and the Former Prophets) during the Persian period were acting as historians and engaging in an activity that can legitimately be called "historiography."

**

---

47   See 2 Kgs 25.27-30.

Modern translation theory speaks of two types of translation—translation that aims for "formal" equivalence and translation that aims for "functional" (or what is sometimes called "dynamic") equivalence. Formal equivalence is concerned with fidelity to the text and aims to produce a translation that accurately reflects the meaning of the source text, preserving wherever possible word order and sentence structure, and seeking to maintain one-for-one correspondences in vocabulary. Robert Alter's translation of the Tanakh, published in 2018, is an example of a translation that emphasizes formal equivalence over functional equivalence. By contrast, functional (or dynamic) equivalence is concerned with fluency; the aim here is to produce a natural-sounding translation that recreates for the reader the same experience of the text as that of a native speaker of the source language. Such a translation by necessity breaks with one-to-one correspondences in vocabulary and word order in order to express a specific thought or idea in the most natural way in the target language.

From antiquity, one of the fundamental debates among translators has been whether translations should strive for formal equivalence or for functional equivalence. The early Church father Jerome, who spent the better part of two decades translating the Christian Old and New Testaments (the translation known as the Vulgate), discusses this issue at length in his "Letter to Pammachius on the Best Method of Translating." In this letter, Jerome defends his decision to translate "sense for sense and not word for word" and points out the absurdities that result in translating word for word. For Jerome, then, functional equivalence is the superior method of translation for all texts, including the Bible. Jerome develops his argument with numerous examples and quotes from authorities such as Cicero and Horace in which they argue in favor of what we today call functional equivalence.[48]

/https: //www.tertullian .org/fathers2/ NPNF2-06/Npn f2-06-03.h tm#P2314_581746

---

48   Cicero's comments are excellent and are worth quoting at length: "I have translated the noblest speeches of the two most eloquent of the Attic orators... I have rendered them not as a translator, but as an orator, keeping the sense but altering the form by adapting the metaphors and the words to suit our own idiom. I have not deemed it necessary to render word for word but I have reproduced the general style and emphasis. I have not supposed myself bound to pay the words out one by one to the reader but only to give him an equivalent in value." And "I shall be well satisfied if my rendering is found, as I trust it will be, true to this standard. In making it I have utilized all the excellences of the originals, I mean the sentiments, the forms of expression and the arrangement of the topics, while I have followed the actual wording only so far as I could do so without offending our notions of taste. If all that I have written is not to be found in the Greek, I have at any rate striven to make it correspond with it."

Today, outside translators of the Bible, the debate has largely been settled in favor of functional equivalence. With translations of the Bible into English, however, it is a different story. Perhaps because of the undue influence of the King James translation (which emphasized formal equivalence), or perhaps out of the (conscious or unconscious) belief that the exact Hebrew and Greek words in the Tanakh and the Christian New Testament are divinely inspired, many English-language translators of the Bible employ approaches that strive for formal equivalence and that reject functional equivalence outright.

I began this note with an epigraph from Moses Maimonides on the translator's task because it sums up succinctly the technique that I believe produces the most successful translations. Along with Maimonides, I come down firmly on the side of functional equivalence. In this and my other translations, I have put special effort into trying to convey the authors' meaning in natural English—in particular, I have written what I imagine the authors would have written had they been native speakers of modern-day English. My priorities are always to try to express the ideas in the text in the most natural way in English, and at the same time to capture the energy and rhythm of the original. When a Hebrew passage is awkwardly phrased, repetitive, or confusing, the English translation should reflect that; likewise, when a passage is written in a fluid or a highly literary style in the original, the English translation should be written that way as well.

Hebrew is very different from English—its vocabulary is limited, it is sparing in its use of particles and adverbs, its sentence structure and verb tenses are simpler, and the logical connections between successive sentences or actions are typically implied and rarely expressed as explicitly as in English. Translations which carry over these features into English—as translations that aim for formal equivalence inevitably must—produce a wooden, lifeless prose (or poetry) that fails to do justice to the energy and vibrancy of the original Hebrew. In this and my other translations, bringing the Hebrew over into natural English and prioritizing functional equivalence have required me to break significantly from literal renderings in nearly every sentence. I have frequently added particles and adverbs, inserted logical connections where lacking, omitted words that are superfluous in translation, introduced word variety consistent with English usage, altered verb tenses and pronouns, changed word order, and, on occasion, added short phrases and clarifying clauses when needed to produce natural English. Following Maimonides' advice to his own translator quoted in the epigraph at the beginning of this note, I have relied on my understanding of the text and of what I believed to be the authors' intent to guide my many departures from the literal text. My goal in the translation here was always to be faithful to the ideas that the authors of Kings were expressing in Hebrew—but to express those ideas in English in the most natural way.

**

One place where I make a major departure from nearly all other present-day English translations of the Tanakh is that I do not follow the familiar chapter divisions, which are based on a scheme introduced by Archbishop of Canterbury Stephen Langton in the thirteenth century CE. Rather, my translations follow the division of the text into literary units—or *parashot*—as preserved in the Masoretic traditions.[49] We know that most of the *parashot* in the Masoretic text reflect very ancient traditions, for they agree broadly with textual divisions found in the biblical texts that were recovered from Qumran and that date between the third century BCE and the first century CE.[50] Moreover, the *parashot* are marked in an identical fashion in the Masoretic text and in the texts from Qumran—space breaks where the text resumes in the middle of a line are used to indicate the beginning of smaller literary units, and space breaks where the text resumes at the beginning of a new line are used to indicate the beginning of major literary units. The general agreement of the *parashot* in the texts from Qumran with the Masoretic text can be seen in numerous textual fragments from Qumran, but it is most easily and convincingly seen in a simple visual comparison of the *parashot* in the Great Isaiah Scroll from Qumran and the Book of Isaiah in the Aleppo Codex and the Leningrad Codex.

/http://dss.collections.imj.org.il/isaiah

Although the evidence from Qumran clearly demonstrates that the *parashot* have ancient roots, that is of little help in answering the questions of how old they are and whether they might have been part of the earliest "editions" of the books of the Tanakh. It is of course impossible to answer these questions definitively, but it is reasonable to suppose that the ultimate source for most of the *parashot* might indeed be the original composition itself. We know, for example, that

---

49 An excellent overview of this system of dividing the biblical text into literary units can be found in Wikipedia in the article "*Parashah*."

50 For detailed discussions of this topic, see the articles by E. Tov: "The Background of the Sense Divisions in the Biblical Texts," in M. Korpel and J. Oesch (eds.), *Delimitation Criticism: A New Tool in Biblical Research*, Pericope 1 (Assen 2001), 312-350 and "Sense divisions in the Qumran texts, the Masoretic text, and ancient translations of the Bible," in J. Krosovec (ed.), *Interpretation of the Bible: International symposium on the interpretation of the Bible* (Sheffield 1998), 121-146.

textual divisions were regularly employed in ancient texts.[51] And perhaps more important, once the medieval chapter divisions are stripped away and the *parashot* highlighted, it is striking to see how the *parashot* contribute to and enhance the flow of the narrative. I have seen this in all nine of the translations that I have now completed—the five books of the Torah and the four books of the Former Prophets.

Because the *parashot* are sometimes employed in ways that modern-day readers do not expect, it is worth providing some comments on their usage in the Tanakh. There are two types of *parashot*—the *parashah petuhah* (or "open *parashah*") typically marks the beginning of a major literary unit, while the *parashah setumah* (or "closed *parashah*") typically marks the beginning of a smaller literary unit.[52]

In the prose books of the Tanakh, both the *parashah petuhah* and the *parashah setumah* are frequently used to indicate a change in compositional layer, a change in the author's source material, a change of subject matter, or a change of scene. Both types of *parashot* are also used to draw attention to important speeches and to alter the pace of the narrative for dramatic effect. In addition, both types of *parashot* are often used to organize related content and to facilitate the reader's navigation of repetitive text. The best example of this in Kings is the use of a *parashah petuhah* before and after the account of each king's reign to separate it from the accounts of the preceding and succeeding kings. Finally, it should be noted that the "closed" blank space associated with the *parashah setumah* has two special uses: to separate items in a list and to separate lines of songs. In 1 Kings 4, for example, there are two lists—one of Solomon's "chief officials" and one of his twelve "tax commissioners"—and both lists separate the individuals' names with a *parashah setumah*.

In my translation, I have indicated each *parashah petuhah* with a triple line break and a double asterisk (**), while I have indicated each *parashah setumah* with a single line break and an em-dash (—). Because I have found the use of *parashot* in the Aleppo Codex to be superior overall to their use in the Leningrad Codex, the *parashot* in

---

51 For examples predating the biblical texts, see those cited in E. Tov, "Background of the Sense Divisions," pp. 334f.

52 The *parashah petuhah* is indicated by a blank space in the text where the text resumes at the beginning of a new line. This type of *parashah* gets its name from the fact that the blank space before it is "open" (*petuhah* in Hebrew) and not bounded by text on the left side. The *parashah setumah* is indicated by a blank space in the text where the text resumes in the middle of a line; it gets its name from the fact that the blank space in the text is "closed" (*setumah* in Hebrew)—that is, it is bounded by text on both the left and right sides.

my translation follow it and not the Leningrad Codex.[53]

As a convenience to readers, I have noted the Masoretic literary units (the "open" and "closed" *parashot*) and the familiar chapter divisions of the Christian Bible in the margins of my translation. Although the Masoretes did not number the *parashot*, I have taken the liberty of numbering them in order to make it easier for readers to keep track of their place in the text, and to move back and forth between the text and the notes and comments. In the margins of the translation, I indicate the *parashot petuhot* with the prefix "P" followed by a number (P1, P2, P3, etc.). In my numbering system, I treat the *parashot setumot* as subunits of the *parashot petuhot*—thus P20,1 and P20,2, for example, indicate the first and second "closed" *parashot* after P20. In addition, I indicate the more familiar chapter divisions by placing the book and chapter number within brackets—for example, [2.17] denotes 2 Kings 17. Lastly, I also use the margins to indicate places in the text that are discussed in the notes and comments that follow the translation; for each *parashah*, these are marked in lowercase letters—a, b, c, etc.—and are hyper-linked in the pdf version of this book.

**

A few final comments about my translation that the reader should be aware of: in translating names of people and places, I have not employed the traditional anglicized spelling, but have chosen instead to use transliterations that approximate how scholars believe ancient Hebrew was pronounced. Thus, I write Shelomo rather than Solomon, Yoshiyyahu instead of Josiah, and Yarov'am in place of Jeroboam.[54]

---

53 It is worth noting here that Maimonides used the Aleppo Codex as his source for the identification of all the *parashot petuhot* and *parashot setumot* within the books of the Torah. His mention of the Aleppo Codex and his listing of the *parashot* in the Torah can be found in chapter eight of the "Laws Governing Torah Scrolls, Tefillin, and Mezuzot" in the Sefer Avahah within the *Mishneh Torah*. Moreover, there is a consensus among scholars of Masoretic studies that the Aleppo Codex is superior to the Leningrad Codex and all other Masoretic manuscripts; in the words of Israel Yeivin in his *Introduction to the Tiberian Masorah* (Scholar's Press: 1980), p. 16f: "A thorough study of the oldest MSS (A, L, B, S, S¹) and their Masorah...shows conclusively that A [that is, the Aleppo Codex] is superior to any other MS in spelling, in the writing of the songs in the Bible, and in its Masorah. Not only this, but A is the only one of these MSS in which the presentation of these features is almost everywhere flawless."

54 I employ this spelling practice in the translation and in the notes and comments. However, in the other sections of this book—the essay on Kings' composition history and the appendix—I revert to the traditional anglicizations for the most common names, such as Solomon and David, and I use a simplified transliteration for the other names.

Another unusual feature of my translation of names is that I have chosen in many places to replicate one of the principal quirks of Hebrew spelling: the occasional use of the letters *yodh* ("y") and *he* ("h") to indicate specific vowels. In Kings, this results in my writing Eliysha rather than Elisha, and Hiyram instead of Hiram. Such an approach to translating names, I believe, removes much of the theological baggage that many of the biblical names have taken on over the centuries, thus helping modern-day readers look at the text with fresh eyes.

Lastly, I have chosen in this translation to reproduce the majority of the notes that the Masoretes wrote in the margins of their manuscripts to correct errors in the text and replace words they viewed as indecent or obscene.[55] In my translation, I reflect the error or the indecent term in the text and I show the corrected term in the margin. While at times this may be distracting, it has value for readers in replicating an essential part of the experience of reading the Hebrew manuscript. More importantly, it gives readers a glimpse into the complex transmission history of the text, in which errors inevitably have crept in, and it helps readers appreciate the fanatical devotion of the Masoretes to preserving and maintaining the text passed down to them.

**

Kings is an exceptionally rich and complex book, with a cast of more than one hundred characters from all walks of life—good kings and bad kings, rulers of great empires and of petty kingdoms, prophets and priests, holy men and miracle workers, queens and wealthy women, impoverished widows and prostitutes, lepers and sickly children, great generals and common foot soldiers, assassins and executioners, and servants and lackeys and slaves. It mixes fantastic stories and folk tales with contemporary accounts of real events known from history. It contains great literature written in the most polished prose, but also matter-of-fact government records and mundane administrative lists.

The ideas in the book are almost as diverse as its content and its literary styles. Some of its authors were ardent proponents of Davidic kingship and the Davidic king's unique relationship to Yahweh; other authors upheld the Davidic ideal, but qualified this by making it conditional on the king's exclusive loyalty to Yahweh. Still other

---

[55] Scholars use the terms *qere* and *ketiv* to refer to these corrections. The *ketiv* ("what is written") is the word as received in the consonantal text, and the *qere* ("what is read") is the word that should be read or pronounced. For readers interested in more detail, there is a very good overview of the Masoretic system of making corrections in this fashion in the article "Qere and Ketiv" in Wikipedia.

authors rejected outright the idea of the king's special role. They removed the king from the picture entirely and promoted the idea that it is the people who have a special relationship with—and obligations to—their god Yahweh. Interwoven into the evolving ideas about the king and the people are separate threads of ideas about the role of the prophet and the nature of prophecy, and about Yahweh as a universal and all-powerful god. These threads, while subordinate to the ideas about kingship, further enrich and complicate the book.

The diversity of content, ideas, and styles in Kings reflects the book's composition history: the book came together over a period of centuries, evolving in fits and starts as material was added, rearranged, altered, and corrected by dozens of authors and editors in ways that promoted their own biases and addressed problems that they and their contemporaries faced. Kings began as a textbook for a young king and later became part of the temple library, where it must have had only a small number of readers. Only toward the end of its composition process, when the holy writings from the temple library began circulating in the synagogues across the diaspora, did the book come to serve a wider audience, who were entertained by its stories but who also drew from it lessons about their relationship to their god and their obligations to him. It is my hope that through my work here—both in the translation that strives to express the ancient authors' ideas in natural modern-day English and in the notes and comments that follow—readers may gain a deeper appreciation of the richness and complexity of this fascinating book and how it came to be.

Kings   מלכים

WHEN KING DAWID WAS OLD AND ADVANCED IN YEARS, even when he was covered with layers of clothes, he couldn't keep warm.

"Let a marriageable girl be sought for my lord the king," his officials proposed to him. "Someone who will wait on the king and personally attend to him, someone who will snuggle with you and keep my lord the king warm."

They searched everywhere throughout the territory of Yisra'el for a beautiful girl—and then they found Aviyshag the Shunammite. They brought her to the king, and indeed, the girl was extraordinarily beautiful. She served as the king's personal attendant and tended to his needs. (The king did not, however, have sexual intercourse with her.)

Now around this time Adoniyyah Haggiythsson was accumulating power for himself, with the intention of becoming king. As a result, he acquired a chariot and some chariot horses, as well as a royal guard of fifty men who would run ahead to clear the way for him. At no point during this period, however, did his father give him any grief by asking him why he was doing such things. (Two other things to know about him: he was exceptionally good looking, and he was born after Avshalom.) He had shared his plans with Yo'av Tzeruyahsson and Evyathar the Priest, and they actively supported his efforts. However, Tzadoq the Priest, Benayahu Yehoyadasson, Nathan the Prophet, Shim'iy, Re'iy, and the military officers in Dawid's service did not ally themselves to Adoniyyahu.

Adoniyyahu put on a feast at Serpent Rock next to Fuller's Spring, slaughtering sheep, cattle, and fatlings. To this feast he invited all his brothers [*the king's sons*] and all Yehudah's leading men [*the king's senior officials*], but he didn't invite Nathan the Prophet, Benayahu, and the military officers—nor did he invite his brother Shelomo.

"I know you've heard that Adoniyyahu Haggiythsson is now acting as king," Nathan said to Bath-Sheva Shelomosmother. "And that our lord Dawid seems clueless about it. So now, come, I'd like to give you some advice, if I may. You need to save your life and the life of your son Shelomo. Here's what you must do: go to King Dawid and say to him, 'Didn't you yourself, my lord and king, swear to your maidservant that my son Shelomo would be king after you and that he would be the one to sit on your throne? So why is Adoniyyahu now acting as king?' And here's what I'll do: while you're still speaking with the king, I'll come in behind you and confirm what you just told him."

So Bath-Sheva went to see the king in his chambers. (Now the king was very old at this time, and Aviyshag the Shunammite was tending to the king's needs.) Bath-Sheva bowed low and prostrated herself to the king.

"What brings you here, Bath-Sheva?" asked the king.

"My lord," she replied, "you yourself swore by your god Yahweh to your maidservant that my son Shelomo would be king after you and that he would be the one to sit on your throne. But now it turns out that Adoniyyah is acting as king and my lord the king may not be aware. He has just put on a feast, slaughtering large numbers of cattle and fatlings and sheep.

**

"To this feast he invited all the king's sons and Evyathar the Priest and General Yo'av. However, he didn't invite your servant Shelomo. But you, my lord, are still the king: all of Yisra'el is looking to you to tell them who will occupy my lord the king's throne after him. It's likely that when my lord the king lies down with his ancestors, me and my son Shelomo will be treated as criminals!"

Now while she was still speaking with the king, Nathan the Prophet arrived. His arrival was announced to the king, and then Nathan entered the king's presence and prostrated himself to the king, putting his face to the ground.

"My lord and king," said Nathan, "it seems that you must have said Adoniyyahu would be king after you and that he would be the one to sit on your throne. For he went today and put on a feast, slaughtering large numbers of cattle and fatlings and sheep. He invited all the king's sons and the generals of the army and Evyathar the Priest, and right now they're eating and drinking with him. They even said, 'Long live King Adoniyyahu!' However, as for me—me, your servant!—and Tzadoq the Priest and Benayahu Yehoyadasson and your servant Shelomo, he didn't invite us. Surely, it can't be that this thing would have happened with my lord the king's approval and you not have made it known to your servant regarding who would occupy my lord the king's throne after him!"

———

King Dawid answered by saying, "Summon Bath-Sheva for me!"   P2,1   a
She entered the king's presence and stood in front of the king.

"As Yahweh lives," swore the king, "the god who saved me from all my troubles, I swear that exactly as I swore to you by Yahweh God of Yisra'el when I said your son Shelomo would be king after me and would be the one to sit on my throne in my place, so I'm going to make that happen this very day!"   b c

Bath-Sheva bowed low, bringing her face to the ground, and prostrated herself to the king. "May my lord King Dawid live forever!" she exclaimed.   d

**

"Summon Tzadoq the Priest for me," King David ordered, "along with Nathan the Prophet and Benayahu Yehoyadasson."   P3   a

They entered the king's presence.

"Take your lord's officials with you," he said to them, "and put my son Shelomo on one of my mollies, and then lead him down to Gihon Spring. Tzadoq the Priest and Nathan the Prophet will anoint him as king of Yisra'el there. Sound the ram's horn and proclaim, 'Long live King Shelomo!' Follow him back up here, and then he'll come in and sit on my throne. He shall rule as king in my place, for he's the one I've chosen to be supreme leader over Yisra'el and Yehudah."   b

   c

"May it ever be so!" replied Benayahu Yehoyadasson to the king. "So says my lord the king's god Yahweh! Just as Yahweh was with my lord the king, so may he be with Shelomo and make his reign even greater than my lord King Dawid's reign!"

may he be: read "shall he be"

Tzadoq the Priest, Nathan the Prophet, and Benayahu Yehoyadasson departed the royal residence with the king's personal guard. They had Shelomo mount King Dawid's molly and led him down to Gihon Spring. Tzadoq the Priest anointed Shelomo there with a horn of oil he had taken from Yahweh's tent. Then they sounded the ram's horn.   d

   e

"Long live King Shelomo!" cried the people. Everyone followed him back up to the royal residence, and along the way everyone was blowing pipes and making merry in a huge celebration—in fact, the ground beneath them split open from all the noise they made!   f

Adoniyyahu and all of his guests heard the commotion just as they had finished eating. "What's the reason for the uproar in town?" asked Yo'av when he heard the blast of the ram's horn. He was in the middle of saying these words when Yonathan Evyatharsson the Priest showed up unexpectedly.

"Come in," Adoniyyahu said, "for you are an excellent man, and I trust you bring good news!"   g

h	"Unfortunately," replied Yonathan, "our lord King Dawid has made Shelomo king. The king sent Tzadoq the Priest and Nathan the Prophet to go with him, along with Benayahu Yehoyadasson and the king's personal guard. They put him on the king's molly, and Tzadoq the Priest and Nathan the Prophet anointed him king at Gihon Spring. From there they went back up to the royal residence, celebrating all the way. And the town's in an uproar—that's the noise you hear. Moreover, Shelomo is now seated on the royal throne, and the king's officials have already given their congratulations to our lord King Dawid. 'May your god make Shelomo more famous than you,' they said, 'and may he make his reign greater than yours.' Then the king prostrated himself on his bed, and he also said something like this: 'Blessed be Yahweh God of Yisra'el, who today has granted me a successor to sit on my throne while I'm still alive to see it!'"

your god: read "God" i

j

All Adoniyyahu's guests were seized with fear, and every single one of them left for home at once. Now, as Adoniyyahu was terrified

k   of Shelomo, he went straight away to the altar and grabbed hold of its horns.

When Shelomo was informed that Adoniyyahu was terrified of him and that he had grabbed hold of the altar's horns and had specifically pled, "Let King Shelomo swear to me today that he won't put his servant to death," Shelomo said, "If he proves himself worthy, not a hair on his head will be harmed. But if I ever find out he's guilty of some wrong, he shall die." Then King Shelomo sent some men and they brought him down from the altar. He went to the royal residence and prostrated himself to King Shelomo. Only then did Shelomo allow him to go home.

∗∗

P4 [1.2]   When the time of Dawid's death was approaching, he gave orders to his son Shelomo. "I am going the way of all the earth," he said.

a   "You must be strong and be a man. You must keep the service due to
b   your god Yahweh by staying true to his ways in order to adhere to his
c   laws, his commandments, his precepts, and the obligations under his treaty, exactly as written in Mosheh's Torah, in order that you might have success in all that you do and wherever you turn, in order that
d   Yahweh might fulfill the promise he made about me, that if my sons
e   were careful about their ways, walking before him in truth, with all their heart and with their entire being, 'then,' he said, 'none of your descendants will be removed from Yisra'el's throne.'

"In addition, you do know what Yo'av Tzeruyahsson did to me—what he did to the two heads of Yisra'el's armies, Avner Nersson and Amasa Yethersson, murdering them and committing war crimes during peace time—yes, staining the sash around his loins and the sandals on his feet with the blood-guilt of his war crimes. You must act according to your best judgment, but don't let a peaceful death in his old age be the way he enters She'ol.

"As for Barzillai the Gil'adite's descendants, be kind to them—they should join those taking their meals with you, for they provided me with similar support when I was fleeing from your brother Avshalom. One more thing: Shim'iy Gera'sson the Binyaminite from Bahuriym is with you. He cursed me with a noxious curse when I was on my way to Mahanayim. When he came down to the Yarden to meet me, I swore to him by Yahweh that I wouldn't put him to death. So now, don't let him go unpunished. For you are a wise man, and you know what you must do to him, sending the old man on a bloody road to She'ol."

Dawid then lay down with his ancestors and was buried in Fort Dawid.

∗∗

Dawid's reign over Yisra'el lasted forty years. He ruled for seven years in Hevron and in Yerushalem he ruled for thirty-three years. Shelomo succeeded his father Dawid on the throne, and his hold on it was unassailable.

—

Adoniyyahu Haggiythsson went to see Bath-Sheva Shelomosmother.
  "You had no problems in your journey here, I trust?" she asked.
  "None at all," he said. "But I have a matter to discuss with you."
  "Tell me."
  "You yourself know that the kingship was mine," he said, "and that all Yisra'el expected me to become king. But then the kingship passed out of my hands and became my brother's, for it was Yahweh's decision that it be his. So now I'd like to make one request of you. I hope you won't refuse me."
  "Go on."
  "Please speak to King Shelomo—for he won't refuse you—so that Aviyshag the Shunammite might be given to me for a wife."
  "I shall speak favorably about you to the king," she replied.
  Bath-Sheva went to see King Shelomo to speak to him about Adoniyyahu. The king rose to greet her, bowed to her, and sat down on his throne. Now a throne had been set up for the king's mother, and she sat down to his right.

i "I'd like to make one small request of you," she said. "I hope you won't refuse me."
"Ask me, mother," the king replied, "for I won't refuse you."
"Let Aviyshag the Shunammite be given to your brother Adoniyyahu for a wife."
"Why are you the one making the request of Aviyshag the Shunammite for Adoniyyahu?" the king answered to his mother. "Go ahead and request the kingship for him too, for he's my oldest brother—yes,
j ask it for him and for Evyathar the Priest and Yo'av Tzeruyahsson!"

**

P6 a "So may God do to me, and so may he do again," swore Shelomo in Yahweh's name, "for Adoniyyahu has said this at the cost of his life! So now, as Yahweh lives—the one who secured my position and sat
b me down on my father Dawid's throne, and who gave me a dynasty, just as he promised—I swear that Adoniyyahu shall be put to death this very day!"
c King Shelomo sent a message for Benayahu Yehoyada'sson to carry out his order. He went and attacked him, and so Adoniyyahu died.

———

P6,1 a "Go to Anathoth, to your properties," the king said to Evyathar the Priest, "for you deserve to die. However, I won't put you to death
b today, because you carried my lord Yahweh's battle chest in advance
c of my father Dawid, and because you suffered all the travails that my father suffered." Shelomo banished Evyathar from serving as priest
d to Yahweh, in order to fulfill the promise Yahweh made concerning Eliy's family in Shiloh.

**

P7 a Now when the report of these events came to Yo'av, because he had
b been in league with Adoniyyahu [*though he hadn't been in league with*
c *Avshalom*], he fled to Yahweh's tent and grabbed hold of the altar's horns.
When King Shelomo was informed that Yo'av had fled to Yahweh's tent and that presently he was there beside the altar, he sent Benayahu Yehoyadasson with orders to go attack him.
Benayahu made his way to Yahweh's tent. "By order of the king,"
d he said, "come out!"
"No," Yo'av replied. "I intend to die right here."
Benayahu sent back word to the king regarding what Yo'av said and how he answered Benayahu.

"Do exactly as he said," the king replied. "Attack him and put him in the grave. You must rid me and my father's family of the pointless blood-guilt that Yo'av brought upon us. Then Yahweh will have put the blood-guilt he caused back on his own head, because he attacked and violently murdered two men more upstanding and better than him (though my father Dawid didn't know about it in advance) [*the head of Yisra'el's army, Avner Nersson, and the head of Yehudah's army, Amasa Yethersson*]. Their blood will go back on Yo'av's head, and on the heads of his descendants, for all time. Then for Dawid and his descendants, and for his family and his throne, there shall be peace forever, granted by Yahweh."

So Benayahu Yehoyada'sson went up to the altar and attacked and killed Yo'av. He was buried in his house in the desert.

The king appointed Benayahu Yehoyadasson to replace Yo'av as head of the army, and he appointed Tzadoq the Priest to replace Evyathar. The king then sent a message summoning Shim'iy. "Build yourself a house in Yerushalem," he said to him, "where you shall live. You mustn't leave there under any circumstances. For on the day that you leave and cross the Wadi Qidron, know for certain that you shall surely die—and it will be entirely your own fault."

"Your decree is a good one," Shim'iy said to the king. "Exactly as my lord the king has said, so shall your servant do." And so Shim'iy lived in Yerushalem for a long time.

Three years later, it so happened that two of Shim'iy's slaves ran away to Akiysh Ma'akahsson King of Gath. When Shim'iy learned that his slaves were in Gath, he immediately saddled his donkey and went to Gath to see Akiysh and ask for his slaves. Shim'iy then went on his way, bringing back his slaves with him from Gath.

When Shelomo was informed that Shim'iy had left Yerushalem for Gath and then returned, he sent a message summoning Shim'iy.

"Didn't I make you swear an oath in Yahweh's name—and didn't I warn you—that on the day you left and went anywhere at all," the king said to him, "you should be certain to know that you shall surely die? And didn't you say to me that the decree you heard was a good one? Why didn't you keep your oath to Yahweh, and the decree that I gave concerning you?

"You yourself know the harmful things that your mind contemplated," the king continued, "which you did to my father Dawid. And now Yahweh will put the harm you did back on your head."

"Blessed be King Shelomo! May Dawid's throne be secure in front of Yahweh for all time!"

		The king gave the order to Benayahu Yehoyada'sson. He made his exit and attacked Shim'iy, resulting in his death. And so the kingship was secure in Shelomo's hands.

[1.3] e Shelomo made a marriage alliance with Phar'oh King of Egypt. He took Phar'oh's daughter and brought her to Fort Dawid until he had finished building his palace and Yahweh's house, as well as the wall surrounding Yerushalem. However, the people continued to make sacrificial offerings in the open-air shrines, for no house that was Yahweh's own had yet been built during those days.

f
g

**

P8 a Shelomo loved Yahweh, abiding by his father Dawid's practices—
b except he would regularly make his sacrificial offerings and burn his incense offerings in open-air shrines. In particular, the king went to
c Giv'on to make his sacrificial offerings there, for that was the most prominent open-air shrine. In fact, Shelomo used to make a thousand whole offerings at a time on that altar.

It was in Giv'on that Yahweh appeared one night to Shelomo in a dream. "Ask what I should give you," said God.

"You yourself acted with great kindness toward your servant, my father Dawid," Shelomo replied, "because he walked before you with honesty and rectitude, keeping his heart perfect with you. You performed for him this great act of lovingkindness, giving him a son who would succeed him on the throne, as is the case today. And now, O Yahweh my god, you have set your servant as king in place of my father Dawid, though I am but a mere boy with no experience of life.

d As your servant lives among your people (the people you chose, a vast people so populous they can be neither counted nor numbered), so may you give your servant a discerning mind, in order to render judgements for your people and to distinguish right from wrong—
e for otherwise, how would one be able to judge this great people of yours?"

The Lord was pleased in this matter, because Shelomo had asked specifically for this thing. "Because you asked for this specifically," God said to him, "and you didn't ask for a long life, nor did you ask for great wealth, nor for your enemies' lives—yes, because you asked for the discernment to judge legal disputes, know this: I hereby do as you ask. Yes, I now grant you a wise and discerning mind, the like of which has never been seen before and will never be seen again. Moreover, those things that you didn't ask for, I now also give you: wealth and fame both, the likes of which will not be equalled by any king during your lifetime. And if you walk in my ways, adhering to my laws and commandments, just as your father Dawiyd did, then I will give you a long life."

Shelomo woke up and realized at once it was a dream. He went back to Yerushalem and stood in front of the Lord's treaty chest, following which he offered up whole offerings and prepared welfare offerings and held a feast for all his officials.

P8,1 a

b

**

Now at that time, two prostitutes had been making their way to see the king.

P9 a

"I beg you, my lord," the first woman said when they stood before him. "This woman and I live in the same house, and I gave birth when she was home with me. Then, two days after I gave birth, this woman also gave birth. It's just us together—there isn't anyone else in the house with us. Only the two of us live in the house. This woman's son died in the night as a result of her accidentally lying on him. She got up in the middle of the night and took my son from beside me while your maidservant was sleeping, putting him on her breast and laying her dead son on my breast. When I got up in the morning to nurse my son, he was dead. I looked at him closely in the morning light and saw right away that he wasn't the boy I'd given birth to."

b

c

"No!" exclaimed the other woman. "My son is that one that's alive! Yours is dead!"

"No!" the other woman was saying. "Yours is dead! My son is the one that's alive!"

And so they argued in front of the king.

"This woman is saying, 'The one that's alive is my son right here. Yours is dead,'" the king repeated, "and that woman is saying, 'No—your son is dead. Mine is the one that's alive.'"

**

"Get a sword for me," the king said. So they brought a sword into the audience with the king. "Now cut the baby that's alive into two, and give half of him to one woman, and half to the other woman."

P10

Then the woman whose son was alive addressed the king, for she was overcome with love for her son. "I beg you, my lord, give the baby that's alive to her!" she cried. "Don't kill him!"

"He won't be mine or yours!" the other woman was saying. "Cut him in half!"

		"Give the baby that's alive to her," said the king in response. "Don't kill him. She's the mother."
	a	—
P10,1		When Yisra'el heard the decision that the king had made, they were in awe of the king, for they saw there was a divine wisdom within him for adjudicating legal disputes.
		—
P10,2 [1.4]	a	King Shelomo was king over all of Yisra'el.
		—
P10,3	a	These were his chief officials:
		Azaryahu Tzadoqsson: chief priest
		—
P10,4		Eliyhoreph Shiyshasson and Ahiyyah Shiyshasson: secretaries
	a	—
P10,5	a	Yehoshaphat Ahiyludsson: chief recorder
	b	—
P10,6		Benayahu Yehoyadasson: head of the army
	a	—
P10,7	a	Tzadoq and Evyathar: priests
		—
P10,8	a	Azaryahu Nathansson: head of the tax commissioners
	b	—
P10,9	a	Zavud Nathansson: priest [*confidante to the king*]
	b	—
P10,10	a	Ahiyshar: palace chamberlain
	b	—
P10,11	a	Adoniyram Avda'sson: head of the labor gangs
		—
P10,12	a	Shelomo had twelve tax commissioners over the whole of Yisra'el. They would provide food to the king and the palace. One month each year one of the was responsible for provisioning food.

the: read "them"

P10,13		These were their names:
		Hursson: taxes in the Ephrayim hill country.

Deqersson: taxes in Maqatz and in Sha'alviym, and Beyth Shemesh; Eylon, Beyth Hanan

P10,14 a

Hesedsson: taxes in Arubboth. He was also responsible for Sokoh and the entire Hepher region.

P10,15 a

Aviynadavsson: all of Dor Heights. Taphath Shelomosdaughter was his wife.

P10,16 a

Ba'ana Ahiyludsson: Ta'nak and Megiddo, plus all of Beyth She'an [*which is adjacent to Tzarethanah just south of the Yizre'el Valley*]—that is, the region from Beyth She'an to Dancing Meadow to just beyond Yoqme'am.

P10,17 a

b

Geversson: taxes in Ramoth Gil'ad. He was responsible for Ya'iyr Menashshehsson's hamlets, which are in Gil'ad; he was also responsible for the Argov district, which is in the Bashan region [*sixty large towns with walls and with gates secured by bronze bars*].

P10,18 a

b

Ahiynadav Iddo'sson: Mahanayim and vicinity

P10,19 a

b

Ahiyma'atz: taxes in Naphtaliy. In addition, he took Bosmath Shelomosdaughter for a wife.

P10,20

a

Ba'ana Hushaysson: taxes in Asher and in Aloth

P10,21

Yehoshaphat Paruahsson: taxes in Yissakar

P10,22

Shim'iy Ela'sson: taxes in Binyamin

P10,23

Gever Uriysson: taxes in the Gil'ad region [*the land of Siyhon King of the Amorites and Og King of the Bashan*]—an additional tax commissioner who collected taxes in that territory.

P10,24

a

	b	Yehudah and Yisra'el were large in population—as numerous as the sand on the seashore—all of them eating and drinking and living cheerfully. At that time Shelomo was suzerain over all the kingdoms between the Perath River [*including the Philishtines' country*] and Egypt's border, regularly bringing tribute and performing forced labor for Shelomo for his entire life.
[1.5]		
	c d	

**

P11	a	The food consumed at Shelomo's court each day amounted to thirty *kor* of fine flour and sixty *kor* of course meal, ten head of fatted cattle, twenty head of grass-fed cattle, and one hundred sheep, apart from rams, gazelles, roebucks, and fatted *barburim*. For he had dominion over the entire region of Beyond-the-River, from Tiphsah to Azzah [*that is, over all the kings in the Beyond-the-River region*], and he had peaceful relations with his neighbors on all sides.
	b c	
	d	
	e f g	
	h	
	i	
	j k	For Shelomo's entire life, Yehudah and Yisra'el lived peacefully, each person enjoying the fruit of his own land, from Dan in the north to Be'er Sheva in the south.

P11,1	a	Shelomo had forty thousand stalls [*horses*] for his chariotry and twelve thousand chariot horses. These tax commissioners supplied King Shelomo and all those who sat at the king's table—each commissioner for one month, ensuring there was never a shortfall of anything. In addition, they would bring the barley and straw for the horses and steeds to each location where they were customarily stationed.
	b	
	c	

P11,2	a	God endowed Shelomo with extraordinary amounts of wisdom and discernment and with a breadth of intelligence as vast as the sand on the shore of the sea. Shelomo's wisdom was greater than that of all the men of the eastern lands and greater than all the wisdom found in Egypt. He was wiser than any human being—wiser than Eythan the Native, wiser than Heyman, and wiser than Kalkol and Darda the Maholites—and his fame extended to all the peoples around him. He was the author of three thousand proverbs and one thousand and five songs. He discoursed on all the trees, from the mightiest cedars of Levanon to the hyssop that shoots out from the cracks in a wall, and he discoursed on all the animals—those that fly, those that live on land, and those that live in water. People from everywhere would come to hear Shelomo's wisdom, including all the kings in the world who had heard of his wisdom.
	b	
	c	

P11,3	Hiyram King of Tzor sent an official delegation to Shelomo, for he

had heard that he had been anointed king in place of his father (for Hiyram had been a close friend to Dawid his entire life).

—

Shelomo sent the following message to Hiyram: "You yourself know regarding my father Dawid that he wasn't able to build a house that would belong to his god Yahweh because of the constant warfare with those surrounding him—until Yahweh brought them to heel under him. And now my god Yahweh has given me respite from all the neighboring peoples. I have no adversaries anywhere, and nothing harmful is threatening me. Given my situation, I intend to build a house that will belong to my god Yahweh, just as Yahweh promised my father Dawid. 'Your son whom I shall place on your throne in your stead,' he told him, 'he's the one who will build the house that will be my very own.' So now, give orders that cedars from the Levanon mountains be cut down for me. My workers will be with your workers, and I will pay you whatever wages that you specify for your workers, for you know that among us there is no one who is as skilled in felling trees as the Tzidonians."

Hiyram was exceedingly glad when he heard Shelomo's message. "Blessed be Yahweh today," he thought, "because he gave Dawid a wise son to rule over such a populous nation!" Hiyram then sent Shelomo the following message: "I received the message you sent me. I shall do all that you desire—with both cedar trees and cypress trees. My workers will take them from the Levanon mountains down to the shore, and I shall make them into rafts and float them on the sea to the location that you specify for me. I will break them up there, and then you may take them away. And you yourself can do me the favor of providing the food required for my palace operations."

And so it came about that Hiyrom was regularly providing Shelomo with cedar trees and cypress trees—as much as he wanted—and Shelomo in turn paid Hiyram twenty thousand *kor* of wheat as food for his palace operations, and twenty *kor* of freshly-pressed oil. This is the amount Shelomo would pay Hiyram each year.

✳✳

[*Now as Yahweh had given Shelomo wisdom, just as he had promised him,*] There was peace between Hiyram and Shelomo, and the two of them made a treaty with each other. King Shelomo conscripted labor gangs from all parts of Yisra'el—the labor gangs numbered thirty thousand men total. He sent them to Levanon in shifts of ten thousand each month. They would be in Levanon for one month and then two months at home. Adoniyram supervised the labor gangs.

under him: read "under me"

P12,1 a   Shelomo employed seventy thousand men to carry loads and eighty thousand men to quarry stone in the mountains. Besides Shelomo's chief tax commissioners who supervised this work project, there were thirty-three hundred men who directly managed the gangs doing the work.

      b   —

P12,2   The king ordered that large stones—stones of excellent quality—be quarried to serve as the foundation for Yahweh's house, stones that had been hewn into shape. Shelomo's construction workers and Hiyrom's construction workers and the Gevalites finished the stones, and then they fixed the timber and the stones in place so that the house could be built.

      a b
      c

**

P13 [1.6] a   *[In the four hundred and eightieth year after the Yisra'elites left Egypt]* In the fourth year that Shelomo ruled Yisra'el, in the month of Ziw [*that is, the second month*], he built a house for Yahweh.

      b
      c   The house that King Shelomo built for Yahweh was sixty cubits in length, twenty cubits in width, and thirty cubits high. The porch
      d   in front of the house's great hall was twenty cubits wide along the façade, and it extended ten cubits from the front of the house. Narrow

corniche: read "cornice"   framed windows were made for the house; a corniche was built atop the house's wall on all sides [*that is, the walls of the house on all sides,*
      e   *for both the great hall and the cella*]; and side chambers were made on

corniche: read "cornice"   all sides. The lower corniche was five cubits wide, the middle one six
      f   cubits wide, and the third one seven cubits wide, for ledges had been put on the outside of the house on all sides so that the side chambers would not need to be secured to the house's walls.

      When the house was built, it was constructed with quarried stones
      g   of a uniform size; as a result, neither hammers, nor saws, nor any sort of iron tool were heard in the house during its construction. The door
      h   to the middle side chambers was on the south side of the structure, and by means of winding staircases one could go up to the middle level, and from the middle level to the third level.

      Once construction on the house was complete, it was paneled in
corniche: read "cornice"   cedar planks arranged in rows and semi-circles. A corniche that was five cubits in height was built atop the entire house and it was attached to the house with cedar planks.

**

The following oracle of Yahweh was given to Shelomo: "As for this house that you are building: if you walk in my laws and carry out my precepts, and if you follow all my commandments by walking in them, then through you I shall fulfill the promise that I made to your father Dawid—I shall dwell among the Yisra'elites and never abandon my people Yisra'el."

P14 a

**

b

Shelomo built the house and completed it. He constructed the house's interior walls with cedar planks, from the floor to the ceiling, overlaying the exterior stone with wood on the inside and covering the floor with cypress planks. Using cedar planks, he constructed a space extending twenty cubits from the back of the house, from the floor to the walls and ceiling, inside of which he built the cella [*the most holy place*]. Forty cubits was the length of the remaining structure—that is, the great hall in front. Inside the house was cedar wood carved with gourds and flower garlands. The entire inside was cedar—none of the exterior stone could be seen. He prepared the interior of the cella inside the house in order to plasce Yahweh's treaty chest there. The area in front of the cella—an area measuring twenty cubits deep, twenty cubits wide, and twenty cubits high—he overlaid with *sagur*-gold, and likewise he overlaid the cedar altar.

P15 a

b

c

d
e

Shelomo overlaid the house on the inside with *sagur*-gold, and he hung gold chaines across the front of the cella, and overlaid it with gold. The entire structure he overlaid with gold until the entire structure was completely covered, and the cella's altar he overlaid entirely with gold.

f
chaines: read "chains"

g

Inside the cella he made two winged sphinxes out of wild olive wood. The one was ten cubits in height, and each of its wings measured five cubits—ten cubits from wingtip to wingtip. The second sphinx was also ten cubits. The two sphinxes were the same size and shape—the first sphinx was ten cubits in height, and so was the second sphinx. He placed the sphinxes in the inner structure; when the sphinxes' wings were extended, one sphinx's wing touched one wall, and the other's wing touched the opposite wall, and their interior-facing wings touched each other. He then overlaid the sphinxes with gold.

h

i

On all the house's walls on all sides, he carved depictions of winged sphinxes and date palms and flower garlands, on both the inner room and the outer room. Likewise, he overlaid the house's floor with gold—both the inner room's floor and the outer room's floor. On the front of the cella he made doors of wild olive wood, with

j
k

	the wall joist serving as a fifth door post. As for the two doors of wild olive wood: on them he carved depictions of winged sphinxes and date palms and flower garlands, overlaying them with gold and then beating the gold onto the carvings of the sphinxes and the date palms.
l	
m	He did the same thing for the entrance to the great hall, making
n	door frames of wild olive wood square in shape and making two
o	doors of cypress wood—each door consisting of two folding panelqs— and carving on them winged sphinxes and date palms and flower garlands, and then overlaying them with gold placed exactly over the engraving.
p	Next he built the inner courtyard—three courses of hewn stone and one course of milled cedar.
q	In the fourth year of Shelomo's reign, in the month of Ziw, the foundation of Yahweh's house was laid. And in the eleventh year, in the month of Bul [*that is, the eighth month*], the house was completed according to all its specifications and all its plans, its construction taking seven years.
[1.7]	Shelomo then built a house for himself, taking thirteen years to
r	finish his house in its entirety. He constructed the Levanon Forest House: it was one hundred cubits long, fifty cubits wide, and thirty
s	cubits high, and it was supported by four rows of cedar pillars, with
t	cedar beams on top of the pillars; it was paneled with cedar on the
u	ceiling—panels laid over the ribbing that sat atop the pillars (forty-five,
v	or fifteen per row); there were three rows of cased windows, aperture facing aperture three times; all the doorways and door posts were set
w	in square frames, aperture directly facing aperture three times.
	He constructed a porch of columns measuring fifty cubits deep and thirty cubits wide. To the east of the columns was another porch,
x	and further east were more columns and an *av*.
y	He constructed the throne porch where he would decide legal cases—that is, the Judgement Porch; it was paneled in cedar from the
z	floor to the floor.
aa	His personal quarters where he was to live (the hindmost court on the inside of the porch) were of similar design, and the quarters that were to be made for Phar'oh's daughter whom Shelomo married were like this porch.
	All of these structures were constructed with costly stone of the
ab	standard quarried size and finely chiseled on both the interior and the exterior, from the foundation to the coping, and on the exterior
ac	extending to the Great Court. The foundation was constructed with costly stones—stones that were quite large, measuring either ten cubits in length or eight cubits in length. Above the foundation, the construction was of costly stones of the standard quarried size and

of cedar wood. Great Court on each side had three rows of quarried stone and one row of milled cedar, after the design of the inner court of Yahweh's house and the house's porch.

ad

ae

**

King Shelomo sent envoys and summoned Hiyram from Tzor. He was the son of a widow from the tribe of Naphtaliy, and his father was a Tzorian bronzesmith. He possessed the wisdom, skill, and knowledge to make all sorts of things in bronze. He went to see King Shelomo and carried out all his metalwork. He fashioned two pillars in bronze—each was eighteen cubits in height and twelve cubits in circumference. He made two capitals to be placed atop the pillars, cast in bronze and each five cubits in height.

The capitals that were on top of the pillars were ornamented with lattice-work and twisted cordage—each capital had seven cords. He made the pillars: two surrounding rows of pomegranates on the first lattice work, for covering the capitals that were on top of the, with the same being done for the second capital. The capitals atop the pillars were shaped as flower petals [*in the porch*] four cubits in height. The capitals atop the two pillars also were ornamented above: alongside the bulb that is next to lattice work were two hundred pomegranates, arranged in rows around the second capital.

He erected the pillars in the porch of the great hall—he set up one pillar on the south side and named it Yakiyn, and he set up the other pillar on the north side and named it Bo'az. [*On top of the pillars was a flower design.*] The work on the pillars was then complete.

Next he made the Sea of cast bronze. It was circular in shape and had a diameter of ten cubits; it was five cubits in height and its circumference was thirty cubits. There were knobs below its rim going all around and surrounding it, ten cubits in circumference, going entirely around the Sea. The knobs were arranged in two rows and cast in the same mold as the Sea. Standing atop twelve head of cattle, three facing north, three facing west, three facing south, and three facing east—the Sea was on top of them and their hindquarters faced to the inside. Its thickness measured one hand-breadth, and its rim was shaped like a flower blossom rim on a cup. Its capacity was two thousand *bath*.

P16

a

b

c
d
e

f
lattice: read "the lattice"

g

h i

j

k

l
m

**

He next made ten bronze stands, each measuring four cubits square and three cubits in height. Here is the design of the stands: they had

P17

a

    b plating—specifically, they had plating between their lateral ribs. On the plating between the ribs were lions, cattle, and winged sphinxes.
    c Likewise on the ribs, both above and below: hanging wreaths of lions and cattle. Each stand had four bronze wheels, bronze axles, and
   d e on their four feet they had supports. The supports were beneath the lavers and were cast in bronze, with wreaths alongside each support.

      Each stand had an opening inside the capital that extended one cubit above it; each opening was circular, of the same design, one-and-
    f a-half cubits. In addition, on each opening were carvings, and the
    g plating for the openings was square, not round.
    h As for the four wheels below the stands' plating: the axle-trees for the wheels were fixed in the stand; the height of each wheel was one-and-a-half cubits. The design of the wheels was similar to that of a chariot wheel. Their axle-trees, their rims, their spokes, and their hubs were all made of cast bronze.

    i Each stand had a support on each of its upper corners, with the supports sticking up from the stand.

      On top of the stand was a circle one-half of a cubit in height. The vertical ribs were fixed to the top of the stand, and the stand's plating extended down from the top of the stand.

    j Engraved on the plates [*its vertical ribs*] [*that is, on the stand's plating*] were winged sphinxes, lions, and date palms, filling the blank space on each plate and surrounded by engravings of wreaths.

      The ten stands were made in this fashion, cast from a single mold and all of them of a uniform size and shape.

P17,1 a Next he made ten lavers of bronze. The capacity of each laver was
    b forty *bath*, and each laver was four cubits. One laver sat atop each of the ten stands. He placed five stands on the right side of Yahweh's house and five stands on the left side. At the same time he placed the Sea on the right side of Yahweh's house, just to the southeast.

P17,2 a Lastly, Hiyram made the lavers, the shovels, and the bowls for the blood.

     And so Hiyram completed the work that he did for King Shelomo on Yahweh's house:

    —Two pillars and the bulbs of the capitals atop the pillars

    —The two lattice-work pieces covering the two bulbs of the capitals atop the pillars

    —The four hundred pomegranates for the two lattice-work pieces, with the pomegranates arranged in two rows on each lattice-work
    b piece, serving to cover the two bulbs of the capitals that are on the front side of the pillars

— The ten stands and the ten lavers on the stands
— The one Sea and the twelve cattle under the Sea
— The caldrons, the shovels, and the bowls for the blood

All of the aforenemtioned items which Hiyram fashioned for King Shelomo for Yahweh's house were made of polished bronze.

aforenemtioned: read "aforementioned"

The king cast them in the Yarden district in the clayey ground between Sukkoth and Tzarethan. Shelomo put all these items in place; because of the extraordinary quantity of them, the weight of the bronze used was not measured.

c

Shelomo made all the equipment associated with Yahweh's house:

d

— The golden altar
— The table for the presentation of the bread offering: gold
— The lampstands (five on the south side and five on the north side) in front of the cella: *sagur*-gold
— The flower bud, the lamps, and the pair of tongs: gold
— The bowls, the snuffers, the basins, the dishes, and the fire-pans: *sagur*-gold
— The sockets for the doors of the inner house [*that is, the most holy place*] and for the doors of the house [*that is, the great hall*]: gold.

✳✳

Once all the work that King Shelomo did on Yahweh's house was complete, Shelomo transferred the cult equipment belonging to his father Dawid, placing the silver, the gold, and the vessels in the storerooms of Yahweh's house.

P18   a

b

✳✳

Then King Shelomo summoned Yisra'el's elders [*that is, all the heads of the tribes*]—the Yisra'elites' ancestral chiefs—to meet with him in Yerushalem, in order to bring up Yahweh's ~~battle~~ *treaty* chest from Fort Dawid [*that is, Tziyyon*]. All the Yisra'elites gathered together, joining King Shelomo in the month of Ethaniym for a great feast [*that is, the seventh month*]. All Yisra'el's elders came, and the priests carried the chest. They brought Yahweh's chest [*and the Meeting Tent*] and all the consecrated vessels that were in the tent. [*The priests and the Lewites brought them.*]

P19 [1.8] a

b

c

King Shelomo and the whole congregation of Yisra'el who had assembled there with him in front of the chest were making sacrifices of sheep and cattle in such large quantities that they couldn't be numbered or counted. The priests brought Yahweh's ~~battle~~ *treaty* chest to its place in the cella [*the most holy place*] beneath the wings

d

e

f	of the sphinxes. Because the sphinxes' wings were extended toward the spot where the chest was, the sphinxes served as a screen for the chest and for its staves from above. As the staves were quite long, the
g	stave ends could be seen from the great hall in front of the cella [*but*
h	*they could not be seen from the outside*], where they have been down to
i	the present day. There was nothing in the chest except the two stone tablets that Mosheh put there at Horev, which Yahweh ratified with
j	the Yisra'elites after they left Egypt. And when the priests emerged from the great hall, a smoke cloud filled Yahweh's house, and the priests weren't able to remain to perform their service because of the smoke cloud, for Yahweh's radiant splendor filled his house.

**

P20	a	Then Shelomo spoke: "As Yahweh intended to live in a storm cloud, I have now built a mountain house for you, a secure place for you to live for eternity."
		The king turned around and blessed the entire congregation of Yisra'el while the congregation was standing. "Blessed be Yahweh God of Yisra'el," he said, "who made a personal promise to my father
	b	Dawid and who installed him as king, saying to him, 'From the time I brought my people Yisra'el out of Egypt, I didn't choose a town from
	c	any of Yisra'el's tribes where a house might be built that would be my very own. Then I chose Dawid to be responsible for my people Yisra'el.'
	d	"Now as it was my father Dawid's deepest wish to build a house
	e	that would be Yahweh God of Yisra'el's very own, Yahweh said to my father Dawid, 'Because it's been your deepest wish to build a house that would be my own, you have done very well—indeed, it's been your deepest wish! However, you won't be the one to build that house. Rather, your son—one who is your very own offspring—is the one who will build the house that will belong to me.' And Yahweh has made that which he promised come true: I succeeded my father Dawid and occupied Yisra'el's throne, just as Yahweh promised, and I built the house belonging to Yahweh God of Yisra'el. Moreover, I
	f	made a place there for the chest that holds Yahweh's treaty, which he entered into with our ancestors when he brought them out of Egypt."

P20,1	a	Shelomo stood before Yahweh's altar in front of the entire congregation of Yisra'el and spread his hands out to the sky. "Yahweh God of Yisra'el," he proclaimed, "there are no gods like you in the skies above,
	b	nor on the earth below, you who honor the binding agreement with and show lovingkindness toward your servants who walk before you

with all their heart. For you upheld for your servant, my father Dawid, that which you promised him. You made a personal promise, and today through your actions you have fulfilled that promise! So now, Yahweh God of Yisra'el, uphold for your servant, my father Dawid, the other part of your promise to him—that no one occupying Yisra'el's throne would be cut off from you so long as his descendants were careful to walk before you, just as he walked before you. So now God of Yisra'el, please, may that which you promised your servant, my father Dawid, be confirmed!

"But can God truly live on earth? Certainly not: neither the skies, nor the skies above the skies, can contain you! Nor indeed, moreover, this house that I have built! May you give your attention, O Yahweh my god, to your servant's prayer and to his petition, hearkening to the plea and to the prayer that your servant is making before you right now: that your eyes be on this house day and night, that they be on the place that you said would be yours alone—yes, hearkening to the prayer that your servant is directing toward this place!—so that you give heed to your servant's plea, and to your people Yisra'el's plea which they also are directing toward this place, so that when our prayers reach you in your dwelling place in the skies, you will give heed to them and forgive us.

"Should a man accused of wronging his colleague be subjected to an oath that he must swear to—an oath sworn in front of your altar in this house—then may you from your dwelling place in the sky hear it, taking action and giving justice to your servants by pronouncing the one in the wrong to be wrong and holding him accountable for his actions, and by pronouncing the one in the right to be right and providing him just compensation.

"And should your people Yisra'el suffer defeat at the hands of an enemy because they do wrong to you, then when they come back to you, lauding your great name and praying to you and seeking your compassion here in this house, may you from your dwelling place in the sky hear their plea, forgiving the wrongdoing of your people Yisra'el and returning them to the land that you gave their ancestors.

"And should the skies be shut up and there be no rain because they wrong you in some way, then when they direct their prayers to this place, lauding your great name, and they repent of their wrongdoing because of the suffering you're causing them, may you from your dwelling place in the sky hear their plea and forgive the wrongdoing of your servants and your people Yisra'el—yes, may you teach them the best way for them to live and may you then give rain to your land, which you have given to your people as their own possession.

P20,3 "Should there be famine in the land, should there be plague, should there be blight or pestilence, or desert locusts or tree locusts, should one's enemy afflict one in one's own homeland—or there be any disease, or any outbreak—then any prayer, any plea of any person at all belonging to your people Yisra'el who is experiencing pain and suffering, when such a one spreads out his hands towards this house, may you from your dwelling place in the sky, from your secure habitation, hear his plea and forgive him, taking action and rewarding that person in accord with how he lives his life, for you know what is in his heart—indeed, you alone know what's in the heart of each and every human being—in order that they might give reverence to you all the days they're alive on the land that you gave our ancestors.

"So too the foreigner who is not of your people Yisra'el, one who comes from a distant land on account of your fame—because they hear of your great fame, your immense power, and your overwhelming might—should such a one come and direct his prayer to this house, may you from your dwelling place in the sky, from your secure habitation, hear his plea and then do all that this foreigner requests of you, in order that all the world's peoples might know of your name, to give reverence to you as your people Yisra'el does, and so that they might know that this house which I built belongs to you.

a

b

you built: read "I built"   c

d

"When your people march out to battle against their enemies in the direction you send them on, and they pray to Yahweh in the direction of the town you have chosen and of the house that you built as your very own, then may you from your dwelling place in the sky hear their prayers and their pleas and carry out justice for them. Should they do wrong to you—for there's no human being who doesn't wrong you in some way—and you become angry at them and deliver them over to their enemies, and their captors take them captive to a hostile land, whether it be near or far, then when they recall their wrongdoing in the land where they've been taken captive and they turn back to you, seeking your favor in the land of their captors, saying 'We've gone astray, we've caused harm, we're in the wrong'"—yes, turning back to you with all their heart and with their entire being in the land of their enemies who took them captive—and they pray to you in the direction of their land, which you gave their ancestors, in the direction of the

e

town that you chose and of the house that I built as your very own—yes, when they do all these things—may you from your dwelling place in the sky, from your secure habitation, hear their prayer and their plea, and carry out justice for them, forgiving your people who wronged you, forgiving all the transgressions they committed against you, and

f

making their captors have compassion on them so that they show them compassion—for they are your people, whom you personally possess, and whom you took out of Egypt, from the flames of an iron furnace—keeping your eyes open to your servant's plea and to your people Yisra'el's plea, and listening to them whenever they call out to you. For out of all the peoples in the world, you selected them for yourself as your very own possession, just as you said you would through your servant Mosheh when you took our ancestors out of Egypt, O my lord Yahweh."

**

Once Shelomo had finished delivering this prayer and this plea in their entirety to Yahweh, he rose from his kneeling position in front of Yahweh's altar with his hands spread out to the sky. In this standing position he blessed the congregation of Yisra'el in a loud voice: "Blessed be Yahweh who has given safety and security to his people Yisra'el, just as he promised—every single thing out of all the good things that he promised through his servant Mosheh has come to pass! May our god Yahweh be with us, just as he was with our ancestors, and may he never abandon or forsake us! May he turn our hearts toward him, so that we walk in his ways and keep his commandments, his laws, and his precepts, which he gave to our ancestors! May these words of mine by which I beseech Yahweh for his favor be near to our god Yahweh day and night, in order that he carry out justice for his servant and justice for his people Yisra'el, each and every day, so that all the world's peoples might know that Yahweh is the supreme god—there is none besides him! And then your hearts shall be perfect with our god Yahweh, living out his laws and keeping his commandments as you do now today."

At this time, the king along with all of Yisra'el were offering up sacrifices to Yahweh. Shelomo slaughtered the animals for the welfare offering which he made to Yahweh—twenty-two thousand head of cattle and one hundred and twenty thousand sheep—and then the king and all the Yisra'elites dedicated Yahweh's house. On that day, the king consecrated the interior of the court in front of Yahweh's house, for it was there he made the whole offering and the grain offering and offerings of fat from the welfare offerings, for the bronze altar that was in front of Yahweh was too small to hold the whole offering and the grain offering and the fat parts from the welfare offerings.

At that time, Shelomo held a festival, and all Yisra'el joined him—a huge congregation extending from Hamath's Gateway in the north to the Egypt Wadi in the south—celebrating in the presence of our

	h	god Yahweh for seven days and then seven days again, or fourteen days total. On the eighth day he dismissed the people; after bidding farewell to the king, they journeyed home cheerful and happy because of all the good things that Yahweh had done for his servant Dawid and for his people Yisra'el.
	i	
[1.9]	j	Now it so happened that once Shelomo had finished building Yahweh's house and the royal palace, as well as any other luxurious buildings that he fancied to make…

**

P22	a	[*Yahweh showed himself to Shelomo a second time, similar to when he appeared to him in Giv'on.*]
	b	…Yahweh spoke to him: "I have heard your prayer and your plea by which you sought my favor. The house that you built I have now consecrated, marking it as my own for all time, and my eyes and my heart will be there always. Now as for you: if you walk before me just as your father Dawid did, with integrity and rectitude, doing exactly what I command you to do while also observing my laws and precepts, then I will secure your kingship over Yisra'el for all time, in keeping with my promise regarding your father Dawid that none of his descendants would be removed from Yisra'el's throne. But if you and your descendants turn away from me, and if you don't keep my commandments—that is, my laws which I have placed before you—
	c	
	d	
	e	and if you go and give service to different gods and worship them,
	f	then I shall wipe Yisra'el off the face of the land that I have given them,
	g	and at the same time I shall reject the house that I consecrated as my
	h	own. With the result that the name Yisra'el shall become a proverbial insult and a taunt among every people on earth—and with the result
	i	that this house shall be high. All who pass by it will be astounded and will give out a hiss, wondering why Yahweh did such a thing
	j	to this land and this house. And then they'll think that it must be because they forsook their god Yahweh, who brought their ancestors out of Egypt, and because they latched onto different gods whom they worshippd and gave service to—yes, they'll think that's why Yahweh brought all this misfortune down on them."

worshippd: read 'worshipped'

**

P23	a	At the end of the twenty years that it took for Shelomo to build the two houses (Yahweh's house and the royal palace)—during which time Hiyram King of Tzor supplied Shelomo with all the cedar trees and cypress trees and gold that he wanted—King Shelomo paid Hiyram

with twenty towns in the Galiyl region. When Hiyram came from Tzor to inspect the towns that Shelomo had given him, he found them dissatisfactory. "Brother," Hiyram said, "what's with these pathetic towns that you've given me?" He called them 'Good-for-Nothing Land,' which they are still called today.

**

Hiyram sent the king one hundred and twenty *kikkar* of gold. P24 a

Here is the record of the forced labor that King Shelomo conscripted to build Yahweh's house, the royal palace, the citadel, and Yerushalem's wall, as well as the towns of Hatzor, Megiddo, and Gezer. (Phar'oh King of Egypt had campaigned in the north and captured Gezer, burning it to the ground and slaughtering the Kena'anites who were living in the town; he then gave it as a parting gift to his daughter when she became Shelomo's wife.) b / c

Shelomo built:

—Gezer, Lower Beyth Horon, and Ba'alath

—Tamar out in the desert in the land of   *Tamar*: read "Tadmor" d

—All the fortified storehouses that Shelomo possessed, as wells as forts for his chariotry and forts for his war horses e

—Various luxurious buildings that struck Shelomo's fancy to build in Yerushalem, in the Levanon mountains, and everywhere in his kingdom

All the remaining descendants of the Amorites, Hethites, Perizzites, Hiwwites, and Yevusites who were not descended from the Yisra'elites—that is, their descendants who remained in the land after them, whom the Yisra'elites were unable to put to the ban devotion: it was these peoples whom Shelomo conscripted for forced labor, as they remain in the present day. Shelomo did not, however, place any Yisra'elites into servitude, for they served as his soldiers, his government officials, his army chiefs and his military officers, and the captains of his chariotry and his cavalry. f / g / h / i

The chief managers overseeing Shelomo's work projects numbered five hundred and fifty—men who directed the gangs doing the work. (Only after Phar'oh's daughter left Fort Dawid to go to the house that was built for her was the citadel built.) P24,1

Three times each year Shelomo would offer up whole offerings and welfare offerings on the altar that he built to Yahweh, and at the same a / b

    c   time he would make incense offerings at the companion altar that was
    d   in front of Yahweh, and so he would fulfill his annual obligations at Yahweh's house.

    e   In addition, King Shelomo built a fleet of ships in Etzyon Gever, which is near Eloth on the coast of the Reed Sea in Edom. Hiyram sent some of his own officers—seamen who knew the ways of the sea—to serve in the fleet with Shelomo's officers. They went to Ophiyr, where
    f   they procured four hundred and twenty *kikkar* of gold and brought it back to King Shelomo.

    **

P25 [1.10] a   Now when the Queen of Sheva heard the report about what Shelomo did to honor Yahweh, she came to test him with riddles. She arrived in Yerushalem with a very large retinue, including camels loaded with balsam, great quantities of gold, and precious stones.

She went to see Shelomo and she told him everything that she was curious about, and Shelomo in turn told her everything she wanted to know—there wasn't a single thing beyond the king's ken which he couldn't tell her. The Queen of Sheva thus saw the full extent of
    b   Shelomo's wisdom, as well as the house he had built, the food at his
thos: read "those"   table, the assembly rooms used by his officials, the stations of thos who served him and their uniforms, and his cup-bearers (not to mention
    c   the whole offerings that he would offer up at Yahweh's house)—and her breath was completely taken away.

"It's true what I heard back in my country about the things you've done and your wisdom!" she exclaimed to the king. "I didn't believe those things until I came here and saw them with my own eyes, and now I realize that what I'd been told wasn't even the half of it! Your wisdom and excellence far exceed the report that I heard! How lucky are your men! How lucky these officials of yours who stand in your presence every day listening to your wise decisions! Blessed be your god Yahweh, who has taken such delight in you as to place you on
    d   Yisra'el's throne [*because of Yahweh's eternal love for Yisra'el*] and to make
    e   you king, so that you might render justice and vindicate those in the right!"

    f   She gave the king one hundred and twenty *kikkar* of gold, great quantities of balsam, and precious stones—never since has so much balsam come here as that which the Queen of Sheva gave to King
    g   Shelomo. [*In addition, Hiyram's fleet which had carried back gold from Ophiyr also brought back from Ophiyr precious stones and large quantities of*
    h i   *mpingo wood. With the mpingo wood the king made balusters for Yahweh's house and the royal palace, and lyres and harps for the royal singers—never*

has so much mpingo wood come here or been seen down to the present day.] King Shelomo in turn gave the Queen of Sheva every item striking her fancy that she asked for, apart from what was given her out of the king's own generosity. And then she and her retinue made ready and returned to their country.

**

The gold coming to Shelomo each year weighed six hundred and sixty-six *kikkar*—this was separate from what came in from the bands of explorers, the goods brought by the traders, and the tribute from all the Arabian kings and the country's satraps.

King Shelomo made two hundred body shields of beaten gold, each shield being plated with six hundred sheqels of gold, and three hundred warrior's shields of beaten gold, each shield being plated with three *maneh* of gold. The king put them on display in the Levanon Forest House.

**

The king made a large ivory throne and plated it with *muphaz*-gold. The throne had six steps and a circular headrest in back; there were armrests on each side of the seat, with two lions standing beside the armrests, and on the six steps stood twelve lions, six on each side. Such a throne was unique among all the world's kingdoms.

All King Shelomo's drinking cups were made of gold, and all the utensils in the Levanon Forest House were made of *sagur*-gold—there was no silver at all, as it wasn't considered to be worth anything in Shelomo's time. For the king's fleet of Tarshiysh-ships were in the sea with Hiyram's fleet. Once every three years the fleet of Tarshiysh-ships would arrive carrying gold and silver, and ivory and *qophiym* and *tukkiyyiym*.

King Shelomo was greater than any of the world's kings with respect to wealth and wisdom, and the entire world would come seeking an audience with Shelomo, to hear the wisdom that God had bestowed on him. All those who came would bring a gift—silver utensils and gold utensils, garments, weapons, and balsam, and horses and mules—in fulfillment of their annual obligation.

Shelomo accumulated chariotry and horses for chariotry—he had fourteen hundred chariots and twelve thousand chariot horses; they were stationed in forts designated for chariotry and in Yerushalem with the king himself. In Yerushalem, the king made silver as common as stones, and he made cedar wood as abundant as the sycamores

| | | in the lowlands. Egypt was the source for Shelomo's horses, and the company of men serving as the king's traders would procure each drove at fair prices. Chariots were imported from Egypt for six hundred sheqels of silver each, and horses for one hundred and fifty each—the same prices they would pay when importing on behalf of Aram's kings or any of the Hethites' kings. |

b

**

P28 [1.11] King Shelomo loved a great many foreign women—[*Phar'oh's daughter,*] Mo'avite women, Ammonite women, Edomite women, Tzidonian women, and Hethite women—women from the nations regarding which Yahweh told the Yisra'elites, "You mustn't go among them, nor they go among you, for they assuredly will turn your hearts after their gods." [*Yet these were who Shelomo was attached to and loved.*] He had seven hundred princesses as wives and three hundred concubines (and his wives did in fact pervert his heart). Now it so happened that when Shelomo had grown old, his wives turned his heart after other gods, and his heart was no longer wholly with his god Yahweh as his father Dawid's heart was. Shelomo observed rites for Ashtoreth Goddess of Tziydonians and for the Ammonites' abominable god Milkom. And so Shelomo did what was displeasing to Yahweh—he didn't exclusively carry out rites for Yahweh as his father Dawid did.

a

b

c

d e
f
g

P28,1 a At that time Shelomo built an open-air shrine on the mountain opposite Yerushalem dedicated to Mo'av's abomination, Kemosh, and to the Ammonites' abomination, Molek. He did likewise for all his foreign wives, as they would regularly make incense offerings and animal sacrifices to their gods.
b
c d

Yahweh became enraged with Shelomo, because his heart had turned away from Yahweh God of Yisra'el, who had twice shown himself to him—he had warned him about this matter so that he wouldn't follow the ways of other gods, but he didn't honor Yahweh's commandment.

e

f

**

P29 a "Because of this thing associated with you," Yahweh said to Shelomo, "and because you didn't keep the binding agreement with me, nor the laws that I commanded you to follow, know this: I shall tear the kingdom away from you and give it to one of your officials. However, I won't do this while you're still living, on account of your father Dawid—rather, I'll tear it out of your son's hands. But I won't tear the
b

entire kingdom away—I'll give your son one tribe, on account of my servant Dawid and on account of Yerushalem, the place I've chosen as my very own."

—

Then Yahweh raised up an adversary for Shelomo—Hadad the Edomite, who was descended from the royal line in Edom. Now when Dawid was with Edom, when General Yo'av went to bury those fallen in battle, he also killed every male in Edom—indeed, Yo'av and all Yisra'el's forces stayed there for six months, until they had cut down every male in Edom. But Adad along with some Edomite men who had served under his father took flight and headed toward Egypt. (Hadad was a young boy at the time.) They left Midyan and traveled to Paran, and after picking up some men from Paran, they went to Egypt to seek an audience with Phar'oh King of Egypt. He gave them shelter and ordered that they be supplied with food; he also gave them some land.

Now Phar'oh came to be very fond of Hadad, and he gave him a wife—the sister of his own wife, the sister of Queen Tahpeneys. Tahpeneys's sister bore him a son, Genuvath, and Tahpeneys arranged for him to be broughd up in Phar'oh's household—and so Genuvath stayed in Phar'oh's household with Phar'oh's children. When Hadad (who was still in Egypt) heard that Dawid had died and joined his ancestors in the grave, and that General Yo'av was dead, he asked Phar'oh to release him so that he could return to his home country.

"But what is it that you lack here with me," Phar'oh asked him, "that makes you want to go back to your home country?"

"Not a thing," he replied, "but nonetheless, I beg you to release me."

God raised up an adversary to him—Rezon Elyada'sson, who had deserted his lord Hadad'ezer King of Tzovah. Rezon had gathered some men to follow him and he was the leader of a bandit gang when Dawid killed them. They went to Dammeseq and stayed there, and they ruled over Dammeseq. He was an adversary to Yisra'el for Shelomo's entire reign, in addition to the harm associated with Hadad. He felt a deep hatred against Yisra'el, and he ruled as king over Aram.

**

Yarov'am Nevatsson was an Ephrathite from the town of Tzeredah; his mother, who was a widow, was named Tzeru'ah. one of Shelomo's officials, and he led an insurrection against the king. Here is the account of how he incited an insurrection against the king:

  Shelomo had built the citadel and closed the breach in Fort Dawid. Now this man Yarov'am was a very capable officer. Shelomo took notice of the young officer, for he was very industrious, and he gave him responsibility for all forced labor in the nation of Yoseph.

One day around that time, it so happened that Yarov'am left Yerushalem on a journey and the prophet Ahiyyah the Shiylonite chanced to meet him on the road. He was wearing a new tunic, and the two of them were alone out in the countryside. Ahiyyah grabbed hold of the new tunic that he was wearing and ripped it into twelve pieces.

  "Pick up ten of those pieces," he said to Yarov'am, "for thus says Yahweh God of Yisra'el: 'I'm going to rip the kingdom out of Shelomo's hands and give ten tribes to you. Only one tribe will be his, on account of my servant Dawid and on account of Yerushalem, the town that I've chosen for myself out of all Yisra'el's tribes. Because they've abandoned me and begun worshipping Ashtoreth Goddess of Tziydonians, Kemosh God of Mo'av, and Milkom God of the Ammonites. They haven't followed in my ways—not to mention my laws and my precepts—by doing what pleases me like his father Dawid did. I won't take the entire kingdom from him, for I made him supreme leader for his entire life, on account of my servant Dawid whom I chose and who kept my commandments and my laws. I shall take the kingship from his son's possession and give it to you along with ten tribes. And to his son I shall give just one tribe, so that there might always be a lamp belonging to my servant Dawid that is present with me in Yerushalem, the town that I've chosen to claim as my very own.

  "'Whereas I shall take you and you may rule howsoever you desire—you will be king over Yisra'el. And if you obey all that I command you and walk in my ways, doing what is pleasing to me—that is, observing my laws and my commandments just as my servant Dawid did—then I shall be with you and I shall establish a lasting dynasty for you, just as I did for Dawid, giving you Yisra'el so that I might make Dawid's line suffer on account of this, although not for all time.'"

Shelomo attempted to have Yarov'am killed, but Yarov'am fled straight away to Egypt, to Shiyshaq King of Egypt, and he stayed there until Shelomo's death.

The rest of Shelomo's acts—including everything he did and his great wisdom—are recorded in the book *The Acts of Shelomo*. Shelomo reigned in Yerushalem over all Yisra'el for a period of forty years. Shelomo lay down in death with his ancestors, and he was buried in his ancestral fortress, Fort Dawid. His son Rehav'am succeeded him as king.

—

Rehav'am travelled to Shekem, for all Yisra'el had gone to Shekem to install him as king. When Yarov'am Nevatsson heard the news, he was still in Egypt, where he had remained after fleeing from King Shelomo.

He was summoned by messenger, and then Yarov'am and the full assembly of Yisra'el went to speak to Rehav'am. "Your father yoked us with hard labor," they said. "Now you must reduce your father's hard labor and lighten the heavy yoke that he placed on us if you want us to serve you."

"Go away for two days," he replied, "and then come back to me."

Once the people had gone, King Rehav'am conferred with the elders who had stood in service under his father Shelomo when he was alive. "How would you advise me to respond to the people's demand?" he asked.

"If you present yourself right now as a servant to the people," he replied, "and if in your answer you say pleasing things to them, then they will be your servants for as long as you live."

he: read "they"

But he ignored the advice that the elders gave him and conferred with his childhood buddies, who were then standing in service to him. "What would you advise that we say in response to the people who told me to lighten the yoke that my father put on them?" he asked.

"Here's what you should say to the people who told you that your father yoked them with hard labor and that you should lighten it," his childhood buddies advised. "You should say this to them: 'My little pinky is fatter than my father's prick. So know this: if my father made you carry a heavy yoke, I'm going to add even more to your yoke. And if my father kept you in line with whips, I'm going to keep you in line with scorpions.'"

Yarov'am and all the people cam back to see Rehav'am two days later, in keeping with the king's request that they return after two days. But the king answered the people harshly, ignoring the advice that the elders had given him and speaking to them as his buddies had advised. "My father yoked you with hard labor," he declared, "and I shall add even more to your yoke. My father kept you in line with whips, but I shall keep you in line with scorpions."

The king didn't heed the people's demands, for this turn of affairs was Yahweh's doing, in order to fulfill the promise he made to Yarov'am Nevatsson through Ahiyyah the Shiylonite. When the people of Yisra'el saw that the king hadn't listened to their demands, they answered back to him: "We have no territory with Dawid! Nor

<table>
<tr><td></td><td>i</td><td>any property with Yishaysson! Return to your homes, Yisra'el! Look on your nation now, Dawid!"
And so Yisra'el returned to their homes. (But as for the Yisra'elites who were living in Yehudah's towns, Rehav'am ruled over them as king.)</td></tr>
</table>

**

P31	a	King Rehav'am sent Adoram Boss of the Labor Gangs to confront the Yisra'elites. When they stoned him to death with rocks, the king somehow found the courage to get on his chariot and flee to Yerushalem.
	b	And so Yisra'el rebelled against the Dawidic dynasty, as is the case today.

P31,1	a	When the people of Yisra'el heard that Yarov'am had returned, they
	b	sent messengers to summon him to the assembly at Shekem and made
	c	him king over all Yisra'el. No one remained under Dawidic rule except the tribe of Yehudah alone.
	d	Once Rehav'am arrived in Yerushalem, he marshaled the entire
	e	nation of Yehudah as well as the tribe of Binyamin—one hundred and eighty thousand excellent warriors—intending to go to war with the nation of Yisra'el in order to restore the kingship to Rehav'am Shelomosson.

**

P32	a	Shema'yah the Holy Man received the following oracle from God: "Say this to Rehav'am Shelomosson, King of Yehudah, and to the
	b	entire nation of Yehudah, to Binyamin, and to the people who remain: 'Thus says Yahweh: 'Don't march north, and don't wage war with
	c	your kinsmen the Yisra'elites. Everyone should return home, for what has happened is my doing.''" Upon hearing Yahweh's oracle, they returned home as Yahweh instructed.

P32,1		Yarov'am built Shekem in the Ephrayim hill country and lived there.
a	b	He ventured out from there and also built Penu'el. "As things are now, the kingdom might return to Dawidic rule," Yarov'am reasoned
	c	to himself. "For if the people go make welfare offerings at Yahweh's house in Yerushalem, their hearts might turn back to their lord Rehav'am King of Yehudah. Yes, then they might kill me and go back to Rehav'am King of Yehudah!" After conferring with his advisors, the king made two gold bull calves. He then addressed the people. "There's no need for you to go

up to Yerushalem," he announced. "Here are your gods, Yisra'el! The ones that brought you up out of Egypt!" He installed one of them in Beyth-El, and the other he placed in Dan. What he did turned into a great error, with the people processing in front of the latter one all the way to Dan. He also established open-air shrines, and he designated people everywhere as priests [*none of whom were Lewites*].

Yarov'am organized a festival on the fifteenth day of the eighth month similar to the festival in Yehudah, including making offerings on the altar. And that is what he did in Beyth-El, making a great number of welfare offerings to the bull calves that he had made and stationing there the priests of the open-air shrines whom he had appointed.

On the fifteenth day of the eighth month, he offered up whole offerings on the altar that he had made in Beyth-El—in a month that he had invented apart from. And so he held a festival for the Yisra'elites, offering up and burning whole offerings on the altar.

apart from: read "all on his own"

**

One day out of the blue, a holy man from Yehudah showed up in Beyth-El at Yahweh's command. At the time Yarov'am was standing beside the altar preparing to burn an offering. At Yahweh's command, the holy man addressed the altar.

"Altar, altar!" he cried. "Thus says Yahweh: 'A son shall be born to the Dawidic line whose name will be Yoshiyyahu. On you he shall slaughter the priests of the open-air shrines, who burn their offerings on you. Yes, human remains will be burned on you!' On that day, the following sign shall be given. Here's the sign that Yahweh foretold: the altar is going to split into pieces, and the fat on it will pour off."

When the king heard the oracle that the holy man pronounced against the altar in Beyth-El, he stretched out his hand from atop the altar and yelled "Seize him!" But then the hand Yarov'am had stretched out against the altar shriveled up, and he couldn't bring it back to his body. [*That's when the altar split into pieces and the fat poured off it, just like the sign that the holy man gave in Yahweh's oracle.*]

"Please, entreat your god Yahweh and pray for me," the king said to the holy man, "so that I get my hand back." So the holy man entreated Yahweh, and the king got his hand back and it was normal again.

"Come with me to my house and have a bit of food," the king said to the holy man. "I'd like to give you something as a reward."

"Even if you gave me half of everything you owned, I still wouldn't go with you," replied the holy man. "And I'm certainly not going to g eat any food or drink any water in this place! For that's what I was ordered in a message from Yahweh—that I mustn't eat any food or drink any water, and that I couldn't go back the way I came."

And then he left, going down a different road and not traveling back on the road on which he had come to Beyth-El.

**

P34 a Now there was an old prophet living in Beyth-El at the time. When his son arrived home, he recounted to him everything that the holy man had done that day in Beyth-El, including the words he had spoken
b to the king. Once they had recounted all this to their father, he asked them which road the man had taken, and his sons in fact had noticed the road taken by the holy man who had come from Yehudah.

"Saddle a donkey for me," he said to his sons.

After his sons saddled a donkey for him, he got on and went after
c the holy man. He found him sitting beneath a terebinth tree.

"Are you the holy man who came from Yehudah?" he asked.

"Yes, I am."

"Then come with me to my house and have some food."

"I can't go back with you—or go anywhere at all with you. I certainly won't eat any food or drink any water with you in this place. For I was told in a message from Yahweh that I mustn't eat any food or drink any water here. And that I couldn't go back the way I came."

"Like you, I'm also a prophet. A divine messenger spoke to me at Yahweh's direction," he lied. "It said to take you back with me to my house so that you could have some food and water."

So he went back with him and ate some food in his house, and he also drank some water. Then, while they were sitting at the table...

d **

P35 a An oracle from Yahweh came to the prophet who had brought him back to Beyth-El. "Thus says Yahweh," he pronounced to the holy man who had come from Yehudah. " 'Because you disobeyed what Yahweh said and you didn't follow the orders that your god Yahweh gave you, and you instead came back and ate food and drank water in the place where he told you not to eat any food or drink any water—because of
b that, your remains won't join your ancestors in their grave!' "

After he had eaten some food and after he had drunk, a donkey belonging to the prophet who had brought him back was saddled for
c him. But on his journey back, a lion encountered him along the road and killed him. His body was lying sprawled in the road, and the

donkey was standing beside it. (The lion too was standing beside the dead body.)

Now it happened that some men were passing by, and they noticed that a body was lying sprawled in the road and that there was a lion standing beside it. They went on their way and reported what they had seen in the town where the old prophet was living. When the prophet who had brought him back from the road heard this, he thought, "That's the holy man who disobeyed Yahweh's orders! Yahweh gave him to a lion, and it tore him to pieces and killed him." [*Just like Yahweh's oracle that he had spoken to the holy man.*]   d

"Saddle a donkey for me," he told his sons.

They saddled a donkey and he went on his way. He found the holy man's body sprawled in the road, with the donkey and the lion standing beside it. The lion hadn't eaten the body, nor had it attacked the donkey. The prophet picked up the holy man's body, laid it on the donkey, and took it back, going to the old prophet's home town to perform lamentation rites and bury it. He laid the holy man's body in its grave as they performed the lamentation rites, wailing "Alas, dear brother!"   e

After he buried him, he made a request of his sons. "When I die," he said, "bury me in the grave where the holy man is buried. Lay my remains next to his, for what he proclaimed at Yahweh's command against the altar in Beyth-El and against all the open-air shrines in Shomeron's towns shall certainly come to pass!"   f

g

**

But after these events, Yarov'am didn't change his wrongful ways. He continued designating people from all over as priests of the open-air shrines—he would carry out the priestly installation rite for anyone who wanted it, so that they could serve as priests in the open-air shrines. It was this action that turned into the great error of Yarov'am's royal line, resulting in its annihilation and its obliteration from the face of the earth.   P36

a

b

**

Now around that time Yarov'am's son Aviyyah fell ill.   P37 [1.14] a

"Please, go and put on a disguise," Yarov'am said to his wife. "No one must know thine identity. Go to Shiloh—that's where Ahiyyah the Prophet is. He's the one who told me I'd become king over the people here. Take along ten loaves of bread and some biscuits and a

thine: read "your" b

flask of honey, and go pay him a visit. He'll tell you what will happen to the boy."

Yarov'am's wife did as he said. She went at once to Shiloh and made her way to Ahiyyah's house. Now Ahiyyahu was unable to see, for his eyes had frozen due to his old age.

**

"You should know," Yahweh said to Ahiyyahu, "Yarov'am's wife is coming to ask you for an oracle regarding her son, for he's fallen ill. Now here's what you should say to her...."

When she arrived to see Ahiyyah, she was making like she was a foreigner. Nonetheless, when Ahiyyah heard her footsteps as she was making her entrance, he said, "Come in, Madam Yarov'amswife. Why in the world are you pretending to be a foreigner? Anyway, I've been given a difficult message for you. Go and say this to Yarov'am: 'Thus says Yahweh God of Yisra'el: 'On account of the fact that even though I selected you out of all the people and made you supreme leader over my people Yisra'el, tearing dominion over Yisra'el from Dawid's line and giving it to you, you didn't behave like my servant Dawid who kept my commandments and who followed after me with all his heart, doing only what was pleasing to me—rather, you've done terrible things through your actions, worse than anyone who preceded you, going and making for yourself different gods and statues of gods to provoke my rage, and throwing me behind your back—therefore I'm going to bring misfortune to Yarov'am's line. I shall cut down Yarov'am's last remaining descendant, pissing himself against a wall—yes, every last one of them, wherever they are in Yisra'el—and then I shall incinerate the remains of Yarov'am's line like someone burning manure until it's completely gone. Those of Yarov'am's family who die in town will be eaten by dogs, and those who die in the countryside by the birds!'' For Yahweh has spoken.

"As for you, go back home at once. The moment you step foot in town, your boy will die. All Yisra'el will mourn for him when he's buried. For he alone of Yarov'am's family will go to the grave, but only because out of all Yarov'am's family there happened to be something in him that was pleasing to Yahweh God of Yisra'el. Then Yahweh will raise up for himself a king over Yisra'el who will cut down Yarov'am's family all at once. What more is there to say? Yahweh will strike down Yisra'el like a reed fluttering in the water, uprooting Yisra'el from this good land which he gave to their ancestors and scattering them to the east of the Perath River [*because they made Asherahs for themselves, thus enraging Yahweh*], doing this to Yisra'el on account of the many wrongs that Yarov'am committed and that he caused Yisra'el to commit."

Yarov'am's wife left immediately and went to Thirtzah. She had just crossed the threshold of her house when the boy died. He was buried and all Yisra'el performed mourning rites for him, as foretold by the oracle that Yahweh had spoken through his servant Ahiyyah the Prophet.

The rest of Yarov'am's acts, including the wars he fought and how he ruled, are recorded in the book *The Chronicles of the Kings of Yisra'el*. Yarov'am reigned for a period of twenty-two years; then he lay down in death with his ancestors, and his son Nadav became king in his place.

**

Rehav'am Shelomosson ruled as king in Yehudah. He was forty-one years old when he became king, and he ruled for seventeen years in Yerushalem, the town that Yahweh chose out of all Yisra'el's tribes to claim as his own. His mother's name was Na'amah the Ammonite.

Yehudah did what was displeasing to Yahweh, provoking him through the many wrongs they committed—provocations beyond anything that their ancestors did. Moreover, on top of every high hill and beneath every leafy tree they built for themselves open-air shrines with sacred pillars and Asherah posts. There was also *qedesh*-prostitution practiced in the land—the things the people did were just like all the abominable practices of the nations that Yahweh cleared away from the Yisra'elites.

**

In the fifth year of Rehav'am's reign, Shiyshaq King of Egypt campaigned against Yerushalem. He carried off the storerooms in Yahweh's house and the storerooms in the royal palace. In fact, he carried off everything in them and he took all the gold shields that Shelomo made. In their place King Rehav'am made bronze shields, which he placed in the care of the chiefs of the royal guard who protected the entry to the royal palace. Each time the king would enter Yahweh's house, the royal guard would pick them up and put them back in the guards' room.

The rest of Rehav'am's acts and everything that he did are recorded in the book *The Chronicles of the Kings of Yehudah*. During Rehav'am's reign, there was perpetual war between him and Yarov'am. Rehav'am lay down in death with his ancestors and was buried with his ancestors in Fort Dawid. [*His mother's name was Na'amah the Ammonite.*] His son Aviyyam became king in his place.

**

P41 [1.15] a In the eighteenth year of King Yarov'am Nevatsson's reign, Aviyyam became king over Yehudah. He ruled for three years in Yerushalem,
b and his mother's name was Ma'akah Aviyshalomsdaughter. He con-
c tinued all the erroneous practices that his father had done prior to him, and his heart was not wholly with his god Yahweh as his ancestor
d Dawid's heart was. (For it was on account of Dawid that his god
e Yahweh placed a lamp for him in Yerushalem, in order to raise up his son after him and in order to sustain Yerushalem, because Dawid did what was pleasing to Yahweh and didn't depart from anything that
f Yahweh commanded him his entire life, except in the affair regarding Uriyyah the Hethite.)
g During Rehav'am's reign, there was perpetual war between him and Yarov'am. The rest of Aviyyam's acts and everything that he did are recorded in the book *The Chronicles of the Kings of Yehudah*. There
h was war between Aviyyam and Yarov'am. Aviyyam lay down in death with his ancestors and was buried in Fort Dawid. His son Asa became king in his place.

**

P42 In the twentieth year of the reign of Yarov'am King of Yisra'el, Asa King of Yehudah became king. He ruled for forty-one years in Yeru-
a shalem, and his mother's name was Ma'akah Aviyshalomsdaughter.
b Asa did what was pleasing to Yahweh, like his ancestor Dawid. He
c eradicated *qedesh*-prostitution from the land and he removed all the
d statues of the worthless gods that his ancestors had made. That includes his mother Ma'akah—he deposed her from serving as queen
e mother because she made a horrid thing for the Asherah. Asa chopped down her horrid thing and burned it in the Wadi Qidron. Although the
f open-air shrines weren't removed, Asa's heart was otherwise wholly with Yahweh for his entire life.
g —

P42,1 a He restored the cult equipment that had belonged to his grandfather
equopment: read "equipment" and the cult equopment used in Yahweh's house—silver items, gold items, and various vessels.
b There was perpetual war between Asa and Ba'sha King of Yisra'el during the time that both reigned. Ba'sha King of Yisra'el campaigned
c against Yehudah and built HaRamah so as to prevent Asa King of
d Yehudah from making any military maneuvers. In turn, Asa took all
e the silver and gold that remained in the storehouses of Yahweh's house
royal palace: read "the royal palace" and in the storehouses of royal palace and entrusted it to the care of

his officials. King Asa then sent them to Hadadsson Tavrimmonsson Hezyonsson King of Aram whose royal seat was Dammeseq with the following message: "You and I have a treaty with one another, as did my father and your father. Here with these envoys I have sent you this incentive of silver and gold. Now go break your treaty with Ba'sha King of Yisra'el so that he might withdraw his forces."

Hadadsson heeded King Asa's request, and he sent some of his generals to attack Yisra'el's towns. They struck Iyyon, Dan, and Avel Beyth-Ma'akah, and the entire Kinroth district—everything in the territory of Naphtaliy. Once Ba'sha heard reports of this, he ceased building HaRamah and stayed put in Thirtzah. King Asa meanwhile issued a proclamation to all Yehudah under which no one was exempt: accordingly, they carried off the stones and wood that Ba'sha had used to build HaRamah, and with them King Asa built Geva in Binyamin and HamMitzpah.

All the rest of Asa's acts—all his valorous deeds and everything that he did, including the towns that he built—are recorded in the book *The Chronicles of the Kings of Yehudah* (except it doesn't mention that he suffered from a foot disease when he was old). Asa lay down in death with his ancestors, and he was buried with his ancestors in his ancestral fortress, Fort Dawid. His son Yehoshaphat became king in his place.

**

Nadav Yarov'amsson became king over Yisra'el in the second year of the reign of Asa King of Yehudah, and he ruled Yisra'el for two years. He did what was displeasing to Yahweh, following in the footsteps of his father and perpetuating the error which his father caused Yisra'el to commit.

Ba'sha Ahiyyahsson of the tribe of Yissakar conspired against him. Ba'sha struck him down in Gibbethon of the Philishtines when Nadav and Yisra'el were besieging Gibbethon. Ba'sha assassinated him in the third year of the reign of Asa King of Yehudah and became king in his place.

Once Ba'sha became king, he slaughtered Yarov'am's entire family. He didn't spare a single living soul belonging to Yarov'am's family—he exterminated them completely, as foretold by the oracle that Yahweh delivered through his servant Ahiyyah the Shiylonite. This was on account of the errors that Yarov'am committed and that he caused Yisra'el to commit through his outrageous actions by which he enraged Yahweh God of Yisra'el.

g | The rest of Nadav's acts and everything that he did are recorded in the book *The Chronicles of the Kings of Yisra'el*. There was perpetual war between Asa and Ba'sha King of Yisra'el during the time that both reigned.

**

P44 a | In the third year of the reign of Asa King of Yehudah, Ba'sha Ahiyyahsson ruled as king over Yisra'el in Thirtzah for twenty-four years. He did what was displeasing to Yahweh, following in the footsteps of Yarov'am and perpetuating the error that he caused Yisra'el to commit.

—

P44,1 [1.16] a | An oracle of Yahweh came to Yehu Hananiysson condemning Ba'sha as follows: "On account of the fact that even though I raised you up out of the dirt and made you supreme leader over my people Yisra'el, you followed in the footsteps of Yarov'am and caused my people Yisra'el to do wrong so that they would enrage me with their errors—

b | therefore, I'm going to send a conflagration to chase after Ba'sha and
c | his family, and I'll make your family just like Yarov'am Nevatsson's family: those of Ba'sha's family who die in town will be eaten by dogs, and those who die in the countryside by birds!"

The rest of Ba'sha's acts and what he did, including his valorous deeds, are recorded in the book *The Chronicles of the Kings of*
d | *Yisra'el*. Ba'sha lay down in death with his ancestors and was buried in Thirtzah. His son Elah became king in his place.
e | In addition, Yahweh delivered an oracle through Yehu Hananiysson the Prophet about Ba'sha and his family because of all the things
f | he did that displeased Yahweh, enraging him with the cult objects that he made for other gods—the oracle saying that he would be like Yarov'am's family, and on account of which he killed him.

**

P45 a | In the twenty-sixth year of the reign of Asa King of Yehudah, Elah Ba'shasson ruled as king over Yisra'el in Thirtzah for two years. His officer Zimriy, the chief of half of the chariotry, carried out a plot against him when he was in Thirtzah having a drinking bout at Artza
b | the Chamberlain's house: Zimriy went inside and assassinated him—it was the twenty-seventh year of the reign of Asa King of Yehudah— and then he became king in his place. Once he became king, as soon as he occupied the throne, he slaughtered Ba'sha's entire family, not
c | even sparing for him one pissing himself against a wall (this includes
d | his kinsmen and his associates). Zimriy exterminated Ba'sha's entire

family, as foretold by the oracle that Yahweh delivered about Ba'sha through Yehu the Prophet on account of all the errors that Ba'sha and his son Elah committed, and because they caused Yisra'el to err in their provoking Yahweh God of Yisra'el with their useless gods.   e

The rest of Elah's acts and everything that he did are recorded in the book *The Chronicles of the Kings of Yisra'el*.

**

In the twenty-seventh year of the reign of Asa King of Yehudah, Zimriy ruled as king in Thirtzah for seven days. At the time, Yisra'el's forces were in position to attack Gibbethon of the Philishtines. When the Yisra'elite forces involved heard the news that Zimriy had conspired against the king and also assassinated him, they unanimously made their commanding general, Omriy, king over Yisra'el that same day while they were still in camp.   P46 / a

Omriy and all the Yisra'elite forces then withdrew from Gibbethon and besieged Thirtzah. Once Zimriy realized the town had been captured, he went to the royal palace's citadel and set fire to the palace around him. And so he died on account of the errors he committed, having done what was displeasing to Yahweh—to wit, following in the footsteps of Yarov'am and perpetuating the error that he committed in causing Yisra'el to err.   b / c

The rest of Zimriy's acts and the conspiracy that he instigated are recorded in the book *The Chronicles of the Kings of Yisra'el*.   d

**

At that time, the people [Yisra'el] split into two, with half the people following Tivniy Giynathsson and making him king, and half following Omriy. However, the people following Omriy prevailed over those following Tivniy. Tivniy died and Omriy ruled as king.   P47 a / b

**

In the thirty-first year of the reign of Asa King of Yehudah, Omriy ruled as king over Yisra'el for twelve years. He ruled in Thirtzah for six years. He purchased the hill Shomeron from Shemer for two *kikkar* of silver, and he built up the hill. He gave the town that he built the name Shomeron, after the name of the hill's previous owner, Shemer.   P48 a / b / c

Omriy did what was displeasing to Yahweh, committing greater errors than any of his predecessors. He followed exactly in the footsteps of Yarov'am Nevatsson and in the errors that he caused Yisra'el   d e

errors: read "error"

to commit [*that is to say, provoking the rage of Yahweh God of Yisra'el with their useless gods*].

The rest of Omriy's acts—what he did and the valorous deeds he accomplished—are recorded in the book *The Chronicles of the Kings of Yisra'el*. Omriy lay down in death with his ancestors and was buried in Shomeron. His son Ah'av became king in his place.

**

P49 a Ah'av Omriysson became king over Yisra'el in the thirty-eighth year of the reign of Asa King of Yehudah. Ah'av Omriysson ruled over Yisra'el in Shomeron for twenty-two years. Ah'av did what was displeasing to Yahweh—more so than any of his predecessors.

b As if following in the errors of Yarov'am Nevatsson wasn't enough, he took as his wife Iyzevel, the daughter of Ethba'al King of the Tziydonians, and he went and gave service to the Ba'al and worshipped him. He erected an altar to the Ba'al [*that is, the Ba'al's temple which he built in Shomeron*]. Ah'av made an Asherah post as well. Again and again Ah'av did things to provoke the rage of Yahweh God of Yisra'el, more so than any of Yisra'el's kings who preceded him. (In his time, Hiy'el the Beyth-elite rebuilt Yeriyho, establishing its foundation at the cost of his oldest son Aviyram and installing its gate doors at the cost of his youngest son Segiyv, in keeping with the oracle that Yahweh delivered through Yehoshua Nunsson.)

c
d

e

Segiyv: read
'Seguv'

P49,1 [1.17] "As Yahweh God of Yisra'el, before whom I stand, lives," Eliyyahu the Tishbite [*from the residents of Gil'ad*] said to Ah'av, "I swear that these years there shall be neither rain nor dew unless it's at my say-so!"

a b

P49,2 A message from Yahweh came to him as follows: "Get away from here, making your way eastwards, and hide in the Wadi Kariyth just east of the Yarden River. For water, you can drink from the wadi, and I've told the ravens to support you there in the meantime with food."

He went and did just as Yahweh said: he went off and took up residence in the Wadi Kariyth just to the east of the Yarden River. Ravens would bring him bread and meat in the mornings and again in the evenings, and he would drink from the wadi. After some period of time, however, the wadi dried up, for there hadn't been any rain in the region.

P49,3 a Then a message from Yahweh came to him as follows: "Go at once to Tzarephath (the one in Tziydon's territory) and take up residence

b

there. You should know that I've told a widow there to provide you with food."

So he went at once to Tzarephath. When he arrived at the entrance to the town, he noticed a widow there collecting some kindling and he called to get her attention.

"Please put a little water in this jug for me to drink," he said.

As she came over to get him some water, he added, "Please get out a bit of food for me from what you've got."

"As your god Yahweh lives," she said, "I swear I don't have even a piece of bread—only a handful of bread flour in the jar and a little oil in this jug. Look, I'm just collecting a couple pieces of kindling and then I'm going to go and make something to eat for myself and my son before we die."

"Don't be afraid," Eliyyahu said to her. "Go and do like you said. However, first make me a small flatbread from what's there and bring it out to me. After that you can make something for yourself and your son. For thus says Yahweh God of Yisra'el: 'The flour jar won't become empty, and the oil jug won't need to be refilled until the day Yahweh allowes rain to fall on the ground.'"

So she went and did as Eliyyahu said. He as well as she and her family ate for several days, yet the flour jar didn't become empty and the oil jug didn't need to be refilled, as foretold by the oracle that Yahweh delivered through Eliyyahu.

allowes: read "allows"

He as well as she: read "She as well as he"

**

After these events, the son of the woman who owned the house fell ill. His illness was quite severe—to the point that he was barely breathing.

"What's your problem with me, mister holy man?" the woman wailed to Eliyyahu. "You only came here to find fault with me and to make my son die!"

"Give me your son," he demanded as he took him from her breast. He took him up to the room on the roof where he was staying and laid him down on his bed. Then he called out to Yahweh.

"O Yahweh my god," he said, "have you really decided to harm the widow with whom I'm staying by making her son die?"

Then he stretched himself out on top of the child three times while calling out to Yahweh. "O Yahweh my god," he cried each time, "please let this child's life-force go back into his body!"

Yahweh heeded Eliyyahu's demand—the child's life-force went back into his body and he was revived. Eliyyahu took the child and brought him back down into the house from the room on the roof, and he gave him to his mother.

"Look—your son is alive!" he said.

d "Now I really do know that you're a holy man!" she exclaimed. "And that the oracles you speak from Yahweh are true!"

**

P51 [1.18] a Many days later, in the third year of the drought, a message from Yahweh came to Eliyyahu as follows: "Go make an appearance to Ah'av, for I'm now going to make it rain." So Eliyyahu went to make an appearance to Ah'av. At the time, the famine in Shomeron was quite severe.

Ah'av summoned Ovadyahu the palace chamberlain. (Now Ovadyahu was especially devoted to Yahweh. When Iyzevel had Yahweh's prophets killed, Ovadyahu took one hundred prophets and hid them, fifty men to a cave, and then supplied them with food and water.)

"Go out into the land," Ah'av said to Ovadyahu, "to all the springs and all the wadis. Perhaps we'll find some grass, and then we can keep the horses and mules alive and not have to kill any livestock."

So they divided up the land for each of them to traverse—Ah'av went in one direction by himself and Ovadyahu went in the other direction by himself. While Ovadyahu was on the road, he by chance
b happened to see Eliyyahu, who coincidentally was coming his way. He recognized him at once and threw himself flat on his face. "My
c lord Eliyyahu," he called, "is that really you?"

"Indeed it is! Go tell your lord I'm here."

d "What have I done wrong? For in making your request, all you're doing is delivering your servant up to Ah'av, who'll kill me! As your god Yahweh lives, I swear there's not a nation or a kingdom in existence to which my lord didn't send someone to look for you! And when they would say you weren't there, he would make that kingdom or that nation swear an oath that it hadn't found you. And now here you are saying, 'Go tell your lord that Eliyyahu's here'!
e But the moment I leave you, a wind from Yahweh's going to carry you off to who knows where. And I'll go tell Ah'av about you, but then he won't find you and he'll kill me, even though your servant's been devoted to Yahweh from when I was a boy! Do you think my lord wasn't informed about what I did when Iyzevel killed Yahweh's prophets and how out of all his prophets I hid a hundred men, fifty men to a cave, and supplied them with food and water?! And now here you are saying, 'Go tell your lord that Eliyyahu's here'! He'll kill me for sure!"

———

P51,1 a "As Yahweh of Armies, before whom I stand, lives," replied Eliyyahu,

"I swear that I'll show myself to him today."

So Ovadyahu went to see Ah'av and told him the news, whereupon Ah'av went to meet Eliyyahu.

"Is that really you, the biggest trouble-maker in Yisra'el?!" Ah'av exclaimed to Eliyyahu upon seeing him.

"I haven't caused Yisra'el any trouble. Rather, it's you and your family who have! Because all of you have forsaken Yahweh's commandments, and you yourself have followed after the Ba'als! So now, here's what I propose: send out messengers and have all Yisra'el gather at Mount Karmel with me, including the four hundred and fifty prophets of the Ba'al and the four hundred prophets of the Asherah who take their meals at Iyzevel's table."

So Ah'av sent messengers out among all the Yisra'elites and had the prophets gather at Mount Karmel. Then Eliyyahu approached the people gathered there. "How long are you going to be hopping over two branches?" he asked. "If Yahweh is the supreme god, then follow him, and if the Ba'al is, follow him instead."

But the people didn't answer him with even a single word.

"I'm Yahweh's last remaining prophet," Eliyyahu declared to the people, "whereas the Ba'al's prophets are four hundred and fifty in number. Let two bulls be given to us. Let them choose one bull for themselves, butcher it into pieces, and then set the pieces on some wood, but not set fire to the wood. I'll prepare the other bull likewise and set its pieces on some wood, but not start a fire. Then you all can call out in the name of your god, and I'll call out in Yahweh's name. The supreme god will be the god that answers with fire!"

"Your proposal is a good one!" said the people in response.

"Choose one bull for yourselves," Eliyyahu said to the Ba'al's prophets, "and prepare it first, for you are many in number. Call out in the name of your god, but don't start a fire."

They took the bull that had been given to them and prepared it. Then they called out in the Ba'al's name from morning till noon, crying "O Ba'al, answer us!" But there wasn't a sound and there wasn't anyone answering, even though they were continually hopping up and down on the altar that had been built there.

When it turned noon, Eliyyahu began mocking them mercilessly. "Call out in a really loud voice! He's a god after all, and he might be daydreaming. Or maybe he's running an errand or went on a trip. I know—perhaps he's napping and just needs to wake up!"

They called out in a loud voice and cut themselves (as was their custom) with swords and spears until they were dripping with blood. Once it turned afternoon, they performed their ecstatic chants, culminating in the presentation of the grain offering. Still, there wasn't a sound, there wasn't anyone answering, nor was there any sign of life.

"Now come close to me," Eliyyahu said to everyone there. The people approached him, and then he worked to repair Yahweh's ruined altar: Eliyyahu took twelve stones, equal to the number of the Ya'aqovites' tribes [*whose ancestor received an oracle from Yahweh saying that his name would be Yisra'el*], and with the stones he built an altar dedicated to Yahweh. Next he dug a trench around the altar about the size of a two-*se'ah* container for seeds. He arranged the wood on the altar, butchered the bull and placed the pieces on the wood.

"Now fill four jugs with water," he said, "and pour them over the whole offering and the wood." And so they did.

"Now do it again," he said. And they did it again.

"Do it a third time." And they did it a third time. Water ran down the altar on every side, and it even filled up the trench.

When Eliyyahu the Prophet presented the grain offering, he approached the altar and cried, "Yahweh, god of Avraham, Yitzhaq, and Yisra'el, let it be known today that you are god in Yisra'el and that I am your servant! It is through your commands that I have done all these things! Answer me, Yahweh! Answer me, so that the people here may know that you, Yahweh, are the supreme god, and that it was you who made their hearts turn backwards!"

Then Yahweh's fire fell from the sky—it consumed the whole offering and the wood, as well as the stones and the dirt, while vaporizing the water that was in the trench. When everyone saw what was happening, they threw themselves flat on their faces. "Yahweh is the supreme god!" they cried. "Yahweh is the supreme god!"

"Seize the Ba'al's prophets!" Eliyyahu demanded. "Don't let anyone escape!" Once they had seized them, Eliyyahu took them down to the Wadi Qiyshon and slaughtered them there.

"Go now and have some food and drink," Eliyyahu said to Ah'av, "because the rain's going to roar." So Ah'av went to have some food and drink.

Meanwhile, Eliyyahu climbed to the top of Mount Karmel and crouched on the ground, putting his head between his knee. "Please go and look out to the sea," Eliyyahu said to his attendant. So he went and looked. "There isn't anything," he said.

Seven times he told him to go back and have another look. On the seventh time, he said, "There's a small cloud about the size of someone's hand coming up out of the sea."

"Go tell Ah'av to harness his chariot and proceed to. And tell him the rain's not going to slow him down."

After a little while, the sky turned black with clouds and wind—the downpour was tremendous. Ah'av mounted his chariot and proceeded to Yizre'el. Meanwhile, Yahweh's hand protected Eliyyahu. He tied his belt tight and took off at a run, keeping ahead of Ah'av all the way to Yizre'el. ab

After Ah'av told Iyzevel everything that Eliyyahu had done and the details of how he slaughtered all the Ba'al's prophets, she sent a messenger to Eliyyahu with this message: "So may the gods do, and so may they do again, for tomorrow I swear I'm going to make you just like one of them!" [1.19] ac ad

When he saw the messenger, he immediately fled for his life. He went to Be'er Sheva in Yehudah and left his attendant there. After he had gone a day's journey into the desert, he went and sat beneath a lome broom-shrub, wishing he would die. "Yahweh, enough already!" he thought. "Take my life, for I'm not any better than my ancestors!" He lay down and fell asleep under the lone broom-shrub. ae

lome: read "lone"

All of a sudden, a divine envoy was touching him. "Get up," it said. "Eat." af

He looked and noticed there was a griddle cake and a jug of water beside his head. He ate and drank and then lay back down. Yahweh's envoy returned and touched him again. "Get up. Eat," it said, "for you have a big journey ahead of you." ag

He got up and ate and drank. With the strength gained from that food, he travelled forty days and nights until reaching Horev, the mountain of God. He came to a cave there, where he spent the night. Suddenly, a message from Yahweh came to him: "What has brought you here, Eliyyahu?" ah ai

"I've fought zealously for Yahweh God of Armies, for the Yisra'elites have abandoned your treaty with them—they've knocked down your altars and slaughtered your prophets. I alone remain. And now they're trying to take my life!" aj ak

"Go outside and stand on the mountain in front of Yahweh." al

All of a sudden, Yahweh was passing right by—and in front of Yahweh a tremendously strong wind was shattering rocks and ripping the mountain apart. But Yahweh wasn't in the wind. am

After the wind was an earthquake. But Yahweh wasn't in the earthquake.

After the earthquake was a fire. But Yahweh wasn't in the fire.

Then after the fire was a slight, almost imperceptible sound.

When Eliyyahu heard it, he wrapped his cloak around his face and then went outside and stood in front of the cave. It was a voice addressing him. "What has brought you here, Eliyyahu?" it said.

"I've fought zealously for Yahweh God of Armies, for the Yisra'elites have abandoned your treaty with them—they've knocked down your altars and slaughtered your prophets. I alone remain and now they're trying to take my life!"

—

P51,2 a "Go, make your way back through the desert to Dammeseq," Yahweh said to him. "Go and anoint Haza'el as king over Aram. In addition, you must anoint Yehu Nimshiysson as king of Yisra'el. Furthermore,
b anoint Eliysha Shaphatsson from Dancing Meadow as prophet in place of you. Then whoever escapes Haza'el's sword will be killed by Yehu, and whoever escapes Yehu's sword will be killed by Eliysha. I'm
c going to spare just seven thousand people in Yisra'el—all those whose knees didn't kneel down to the Ba'al, and all those whose mouths didn't kiss his statue."

d Eliyyahu departed from there and found Eliysha Shaphatsson
e when he was ploughing twelve acres of land in front of him. As he was working the twelfth acre, Eliyyahu went over to him and tossed him his cloak. Eliysha abandoned the oxen and ran after Eliyyahu.

"Please let me kiss my father and mother goodbye and then I'll follow you," he said.

f "Go on. But hurry back because of what I've done for you."

Eliysha left him and went back. He then took his two oxen and
g h slaughtered them. After he cooked them [*the meat*] in a cattle pot, he gave the portions to the people in his village and they ate. Then he left at once, following Eliyyahu and serving him as his deputy.

**

P52 [1.20] a Now Hadadsson King of Aram had marshaled his entire army. Accompanied by thirty-two kings, along with a great many horses and chariots, he embarked on a campaign during which he laid siege to Shomeron and waged war against it. He sent envoys into the town to deliver this message to Ah'av King of Yisra'el: "Thus says Hadadsson: 'Your silver and gold belong to me now. And your wives and your pretty little children are mine also.'"

"As you say, my lord the king," the king of Yisra'el replied. "I and everything that I have are now yours."

Then the envoys returned with this message: "Thus says Hadadsson: 'Although I sent you a message ordering you to give me your silver and gold and your wives and children, sometime tomorrow I will send my officers to see you. They will make a thorough search of your palace and the houses of your officials. Anything that their eyes fancy they shall collect and take away.'"

Yisra'el's king summoned all the elders in the country. "You realize,
b don't you, that this jerk simply wants to humiliate me," he said. "For

he already ordered me to hand over my wives and children and my silver and gold, and I didn't withhold anything from him."

"Don't obey him," the elders and the people unanimously advised. "Do not under any circumstances consent to what he says."

So he said this to Hadadsson's envoys: "Say this to my lord the king: 'Everything that you demanded of your servant in your first message, I shall do. However, I am unable to comply with this latest message.'"

The envoys left and brought back to Hadadsson word of what he said. Hadadsson then sent him this message: "I swear, so may the gods do to me, and so may they do again, if even handfuls of Shomeron's dirt suffice for all the troops who are following me.'"

"Tell him that a man dressing before battle ought not make boasts like someone removing his gear afterwards," the king of Yisra'el answered.

Hadadsson was drinking with the allied kings in their huts when he heard the king's response. "Set your battle lines," he said to his officers. And so they set their battle lines against the town.

Meanwhile, out of the blue, a lone prophet approached Ah'av King of Yisra'el. "Thus says Yahweh," he said. "'Do you see this vast army? Here's what I'm going to do: I'm going to deliver it into your hands today, and then you shall know that I am Yahweh!'"

"Through whom?" Ah'av asked.

"Thus says Yahweh," he replied. "'Through the deputies of your provincial chieftains.'"

"Who will initiate the battle?"

"You will."

He mustered his provincial chieftains' deputies—there were two hundred and thirty of them. Behind them, he mustered all his military forces [*all the Yisra'elites*]: seven thousand men in total. They marched out at noon while Hadadsson was getting drunk in the huts along with the thirty-two kings fighting as his allies. The provincial chieftains' deputies advanced first.

Hadadsson sent out scouts and they informed him that some men had marched out from Shomeron. "If they've come out to make peace," he ordered, "capture them alive. And if they've come out for battle, take them alive also."

Once these men had marched out from town [*that is, the provincial chieftains' deputies followed by the army*], they attacked, with each man striking down his opponent. Aram took flight and Yisra'el chased in pursuit. Hadadsson King of Aram escaped on horseback with some of the cavalry. The king of Yisra'el marched out and attacked horses and chariotry, carrying out a great slaughter among Aram's forces.

The prophet then approached Yisra'el's king. "Go, strengthen your forces. Consider and see what you should do, for when spring comes the king of Aram is going invade again."

j

**

P53 "Their god is a mountain god," the king of Aram's officers said to him. "That's why they prevailed over us. However, if we do battle with them in the plains, we'll surely prevail. Here's the plan you must carry out: remove each of the allied kings from his position, and appoint captains in their place. At the same time, you should reconstitute your forces to replace those that you lost—the same number of horses as before, and the same number of chariots. Then we'll fight them in the plains. This way we'll surely prevail!"

The king of Aram gave heed to what they said and carried out their plan.

**

P54 When spring came, Hadadsson mustered Aram's forces and marched
a   over to Apheq to engage Yisra'el in battle. Now the Yisra'elites had mustered their own forces and were well prepared. They marched out to engage them, establishing a position opposite them at a dis-
b   tance roughly equal to two strips of goats. Aram's forces, meanwhile, entirely filled the land thereabouts.

     A holy man approached and addressed the king of Yisra'el. "Thus
c   says Yahweh," he declared. " 'On account of the fact that Aram claimed Yahweh is a mountain god and not a valley god, I shall deliver
d   this entire vast army into your hands, and then you all will know that I am Yahweh!' "

     The armies maintained their positions opposite each other for seven days. Then on the seventh day, the battle started: the Yisra'elites defeated Aram, killing one hundred thousand infantry in a single
e   day. The remaining forces fled to Apheq [*that is, to the town*], but the town wall fell on all twenty-seven thousand of them. Hadadsson
f   meanwhile fled and took refuge deep in the bowels of the town.

     "Consider this, please," Hadadsson's officers said to him. "With regard to the kings of the nation of Yisra'el, we've heard that they are
g   merciful kings. We beg you, let's put sackcloth around our waists and cords on our heads and go out to see Yisra'el's king. Perhaps he will spare your life."

     So they tied sackcloth around their waists and cords on their heads and went to see Yisra'el's king. "Your servant Hadadsson says, 'Please allow me to live,' " they declared.

"If he's still alive," the king answered, "I shall consider him my kinsman."

The men meanwhile had been taking augurs about the situation. They seized upon the king's answer at once and replied, "Hadadsson is indeed your kinsman!"

"Go summon him."

Then Hadadsson came out to see him and had him step up onto his chariot. "The towns that my father took from your father, I shall return to you," he said. "And you may establish streets for yourself in Dammeseq just as my father did for himself in Shomeron. I shall send you off with a treaty." Then he made a treaty with him and sent him off.

—

"As Yahweh has directed," one of the prophets said to his companion, "please hit me!" But the man refused to hit him.

"On account of the fact that you didn't obey Yahweh," he said, "when you leave here, a lion's going to kill you!" And when he left there, a lion found him and killed him.

Then he found another man and told him the same thing—"Hit me, please!" And that man hit him and bruised him all over. The prophet then went and waited by the roadside for the king, having disguised himself with a bandage on his eyes.

When the king passed by, he called out to get the king's attention. "Your servant had gone right into the thick of the battle," he said, "when someone suddenly turned aside and brought me a man. He told me to guard the man. And if he went missing, it would be my life instead of his, or I could hand over a *kikkar* of silver. Your servant continued going about his business, when all of a sudden he was gone."

"Well, it appears you got what you deserved," the king of Yisra'el replied.

He quickly removed the bandage from his eyes, and the king of Yisra'el immediately recognized him as one of the prophets. "Thus says Yahweh," he said to the king. " 'On account of the fact that you let go free a man subject to my ban devotion, it will be your life instead of his and your people's life instead of his people's!' "

The king of Yisra'el then made his way toward home, sullen and upset all the way back to Shomeron.

**

P55 [1.21] a After these events, it so happened there was a vineyard owned by Navoth the Yizre'elite that was located in Yizre'el next to the palace of Ah'av King of Shomeron.

"Give me your vineyard," Ah'av said to Navoth, "so that it can be turned into a pleasure garden for me, for it's right next to my house. I'll give you a better vineyard in its place. Or if you prefer, I'll pay you a fair price for it in silver."

"May I be damned by Yahweh if I'm going to give you my ancestral property!" Navoth replied.

d So Ah'av went home, sullen and upset because of what Navoth the Yizre'elite had said to him, telling him he wouldn't give him his ancestral property. He lay down on his bed and turned over, and didn't take any food.

e His wife Iyzevel went in to see him. "Why the sullen mood?" she asked. "Why don't you feel like eating anything?"

"It's because I was speaking with Navoth the Yizre'elite," he said to her. "I told him to sell me his vineyard, or if he wanted, that I could give him another vineyard in its place. But he said he wouldn't give me his vineyard."

f "For now, you should just concern yourself with carrying out your duties as king over Yisra'el," his wife Iyzevel said to him. "Get up and have some food—that'll make you feel better. As for me, I'll take it upon myself to get you Navoth the Yizre'elite's vineyard."

them: read "some" g h She wrote some letters in Ah'av's name, sealed them with his seal, and then sent them to the elders and nobles in his town [*that is, who lived with Navoth*]. This is what she wrote in the letters: "Call for a fast, and have Navoth sit at the head of the people. Have two scoundrels sit opposite him and accuse him of 'blessing' God and the king. Then take him outside and stone him to death."

k l The leading men of his town [*that is, the elders and the nobles who lived in his town*] did just as Iyzevel had sent to them [*that is, exactly as was written in the letters she sent them*]. They called a fast and had Navoth sit at the head of the people. Two scoundrels went and sat opposite him, whereupon they publicly accused Navoth of 'blessing' God and the king. Then they took him outside town and stoned him to death with rocks.

n They sent a message to Iyzevel that Navoth had been stoned and was dead. When Iyzevel heard that Navoth had been stoned and was dead, she said to Ah'av, "Quick, take possession of the vineyard that Navoth the Yizre'elite refused to sell you—for Navoth is no longer alive, but dead."

o Upon hearing that Navoth was dead, Ah'av made ready to go down to Navoth the Yizre'elite's vineyard and take possession of it.

**

A message from Yahweh came to Eliyyahu the Tishbite as follows: "Go at once to confront Ah'av King of Yisra'el who in Shomeron—right now he's in Navoth's vineyard, where he's gone to confiscate it for himself. This is what you must say to him: 'Thus says Yahweh: 'Did you really commit murder just to seize some property?' Then say this to him: 'Thus says Yahweh: 'The place where dogs lapped up Navoth's blood is where dogs will also lap up your blood!'"

"Enemy, why are you here?" Ah'av asked Eliyyahu.

"I'm here," he replied, "because you sold yourself to do what is displeasing to Yahweh. 'And now I'm going to brin disaster to you, and I will utterly annihilate you. I shall cut down Ah'av's last remaining descendant, pissing himself against a wall—yes, every last one of them, wherever they are in Yisra'el! I'm going to make your family just like Yarov'am Nevatsson's, and like Ba'sha Ahiyyahsson's because of how you provoked me and made Yisra'el err in its ways.' (In addition, this is what Yahweh says about Iyzevel: 'The dogs will eat Iyzevel on Yizre'el's ramparts.') Anyone in Ah'av's family who dies in town will be eaten by the dogs, and anyone who dies out in the country will be eaten by the birds!" (Indeed, there's never been the like of Ah'av—a man who sold himself to do what is displeasing to Yahweh, a man who was corrupted by his wife Iyzevel, and who performed especially abhorrent rites in honor of the worthless gods he followed, similar to all the rites practiced by the Amorites whom Yahweh drove away from the Yisra'elites.)

**

When Ah'av heard these words, he tore his clothes in anguish. He put sackcloth on his body and fasted—he even slept in the sackcloth and he was always very quiet when walking around.

**

A message of Yahweh came to Eliyyahu the Tishbite as follows: "Have you seen how Ah'av has humbled himself on account of me? Because he has humbled himself on account of me, I won't brin disaster during his reign—instead, I'll bring disaster on his family during his son's reign."

Conditions remained peaceful for three years, during which there was no war between Aram and Yisra'el...

✳✳

P59 a It so happened that during the third year, Yehoshaphat King of Yehudah went to see the king of Yisra'el.

"You do realize, don't you, that Ramoth Gil'ad belongs to us," the king said to his officials. "Yet we've done nothing to take it back from the king of Aram's control." Then he addressed Yehoshaphat: "Will
b you go with me into battle at Ramoth Gil'ad?"

"I'll be your partner in full," Yehoshaphat replied. "My troops will fight alongside your troops, and my cavalry alongside your cavalry."
c Then Yehoshaphat respectfully asked the king of Yisra'el to seek an oracle that day from Yahweh.

So the king of Yisra'el gathered the prophets—around four hundred in total—and asked them if he should go attack Ramoth Gil'ad or hold off.

d "You should go," they answered, "so that lord Adonay may deliver it up to the king!"

e "Isn't there any prophet of Yahweh still here from whom we can seek an oracle?" asked Yehoshaphat.

"There is still one man from whom we can seek an oracle from
f Yahweh," the king of Yisra'el replied, "but I despise him. Because when he enters a trance, he never prophesies good things about me, but only bad things—Miykayehu Yimlahsson."

"The king ought not talk like that," Yehoshaphat said.

So the king of Yisra'el summoned one of his senior officers and told him to be quick and fetch Miykayehu Yimlahsson. At the time,
g the king of Yisra'el and Yehoshaphat King of Yehudah were sitting on their own special chairs, decked out in their royal finery, in the threshing area in front of Shomeron's town gate, while all the prophets were chanting in trances in front of them. Tzidqiyyah Kena'anahsson fashioned some iron horns for himself and then proclaimed, "Thus says Yahweh: 'With these you're going to gore Aram again and again
h until you finish them off!'" And all the prophets were chanting similarly, saying "Go to Ramoth Gil'ad and prevail! Yahweh's going to deliver it into the king's hands!"

Meanwhile, the officer who had gone to summon Miykayehu informed him of the situation. "Please be aware," he said. "The prophets are all saying the same thing, giving agreeable oracles to
i the king. Please, your oracles ought to be like one of theirs—say something agreeable."

"As Yahweh lives," replied Miykayehu, "I swear that the only thing I'm going to say is what Yahweh tells me to say."

So he went to see the king. "Miykayehu," the king asked, "should we go to Ramoth Gil'ad to do battle, or should we hold off?"

"Go and prevail!" he replied. "Yahweh's going to deliver it into the king's hands!"

"How many times exactly must I make you swear that you will only speak truthfully in Yahweh's name to me?" the king said to him.

"I now see all Yisra'el scattering to the mountains like sheep without a shepherd. Yahweh says that they don't have a master and that each and every one should go safely back home."

"Didn't I tell you," said the king of Yisra'el to Yehoshaphat, "that he wouldn't prophesy something good about me, but rather something bad?"

—

"Now hear Yahweh's oracle," said Miykayehu. "I see Yahweh sitting on his throne, with the entire army of the sky standing in attendance to his right and to his left. 'Who will trick Ah'av,' Yahweh asks, 'so that he'll go and die in Ramoth Gil'ad?' They're all discussing this back and forth, and then the Wind steps out and stands in front of Yahweh.

" 'I'm the one who will trick him,' it says.

" 'How?' asks Yahweh.

" 'I'll go and be a deceitful Wind in the speech of all his prophets.'

" 'Yes, you shall trick him—and get the better of him too! Go and do so!'

"So now, know this: Yahweh has put a deceitful wind in the speech of all these prophets of yours. Meanwhile, Yahweh has in fact pronounced doom upon you!"

Tzidqiyyahu Kena'anahsson went up to Miykaheyu and smacked him on the jaw. "When the hell did Yahweh's wind leave me to go speak to you?" he bellowed.

"It's when you had a vision of how in the future you'd run off in a panic and go hide in a closet!" retorted Miykayehu.

"Seize Miykayehu," the king of Yisra'el ordered, "and take him to Amon the Town Chief and Prince Yo'ash. Tell them the king said to put this bastard in prison and to give him meager rations of food and water until I return safe and sound."

"If you really do return safe and sound," Miykayehu said, "then Yahweh hasn't spoken through me." Then he added, "Listen up, all them people here!"

So the king of Yisra'el and Yehoshaphat King of Yehudah went to Ramoth Gil'ad. The king of Yisra'el told Yehoshaphat he was going to disguise himself before going into battle, but he advised Yehoshaphat to wear his usual clothes. Then the king of Yisra'el disguised himself and went into battle.

g   Now the king of Aram had given orders to the thirty-two chiefs of his chariotry not to engage with any of the enemy, regardless of their rank, but to engage only with the king of Yisra'el. When the chiefs of the chariotry saw Yehoshaphat, they thought that it surely was the king of Yisra'el. But as they turned to engage him, he gave a loud

h   cry. The chiefs of the charioty then realized that he wasn't the king of Yisra'el, and they ceased their pursuit. Meanwhile, someone had drawn his bow at random and hit the king of Yisra'el on the seam of

i   his armor between the breastplate and the shoulder flaps.

"Turn around and get me out of the fighting," the king groaned to his chariot driver. "I've been wounded."

j   The battle continued throughout the day, and the whole time the king was propped up in a standing position in his chariot opposite Aram. He died that evening, the blood from his wound having seeped out all over the inside of the chariot. Around sunset, a proclamation was issued in camp ordering everyone to return to his home town and district. After the king died, he was taken to Shomeron and he was buried there in Shomeron. His chariot was rinsed off next to Shomeron

k   Pond—and while the town prostitutes bathed in the pond, the dogs lapped up his blood, just as Yahweh's oracle foretold.

l
m   The rest of Ah'av's acts and everything he accomplished, including the ivory house that he built and all the towns he established, are recorded in the book *The Chronicles of the Kings of Yisra'el*. Ah'av lay

n   down in death with his ancestors, and his son Ahazyahu ruled as king in his place.

**

P60   Yehoshaphat Asasson became king over Yehudah in the fourth year of the reign of Ah'av King of Yisra'el. Yehoshaphat was thirty-five years old when he became king, and he reigned for twenty-five years in Yerushalem. His mother's name was Azuvah Shilhiysdaughter.

He followed in his father Asa's footsteps and didn't deviate from them, doing what was pleasing to Yahweh. However, the open-air shrines weren't abandoned—the people were still regularly making animal sacrifices and burning incense offerings in the open-air shrines.

a   Yehoshaphat made a peace agreement with the king of Yisra'el.

The rest of Yehoshaphat's acts and the mighty things he accomplished, including the wars he waged, are recorded in the book *The Chronicles of the Kings of Yehudah*.

b   The remainder of the *qedesh*-prostitutes who were left over from his father Asa's time he eradicated from the land. As there was no king in Edom, he made himself king there. Yehoshaphat mare Tarshiysh-ships for voyaging to Ophiyr to obtain gold; however, the voyage didn't happen because some ships founderd at Etzyon Gever. (At the time Ahazyahu Ah'avsson had proposed to Yehoshaphat that his own officers make the voyage on the ships with Yehoshaphat's, but Yehoshaphat wouldn't give his consent.)

Yehoshaphat lay down in death with his ancestors, and he was buried with them in his ancestral fortress, Fort Dawid. His son Yeho-ram ruled as king in his place.

mare: read "made" c

founderd: read "foundered" d

———

Ahazyahu Ah'avsson became king over Yisra'el in Shomeron in the seventeenth year of the reign of Yehoshaphat King of Yehudah, and he ruled Yisra'el for two years. He did what was displeasing to Yahweh—he followed in his father's and his mother's footsteps, and in the footsteps of Yarov'am Nevatsson who caused Yisra'el to do wrong. He gave service to the Ba'al and worshipped him, thus provoking Yahweh God of Yisra'el to anger, similar to all the things his father had done.

P60,1

a

b

After Ah'av's death Mo'av rebelled against Yisra'el. Ahazyah fell through the window lattice in his roof chamber in the palace in Shomeron and was severely injured. He sent some messengers off, telling them to go seek an oracle from Lord Horse Fly God of Eqron inquiring whether he would survive his injury.

[2.1]

c

———

"Go at once to meet the king of Shomeron's messengers," Yahweh's envoy said to Eliyyah the Tishbite. "Say this to them: 'Is it because there aren't any gods in Yisra'el that you have to go get an oracle from Lord Horse Fly God of Eqron? Therefore, thus says Yahweh: 'You won't get down from the bed you climbed into, for you shall certainly die.'' " And off Eliyyah went.

P60,2 a

b

"Why in the world are you back already?" the king asked when the messengers returned.

"A man came to meet us," they said. "He told us to go back to the king who sent us and to give him this message: 'Thus says Yahweh: 'Is it because there aren't any gods in Yisra'el that you're sending men to get an oracle from Lord Horse Fly God of Eqron? Therefore, you won't get down from the bed you climbed into, for you shall certainly die.' ' "

"What was the man like who came to meet you and who said those things to you?" the king asked.

"He was quite hairy, and he had a leather skirt wrapped around his waist."

"That's Eliyyah the Tishbite."

_c
_d The king then dispatched a battalion captain and his battalion of fifty men to summon Eliyyah. The captain went up to see him when he was sitting on top of a mountain.

_e "Holy man, the king said for you to come down."

"If I'm a holy man," Eliyyahu answered the battalion captain, "then may a fire come down from the sky and obliterate you and your battalion!"

Then a fire came down from the sky and obliterated him and his
_f battalion. So another battalion captain and his battalion of fifty men were dispatched to summon him again.

_g "Holy man," the captain answered and said to him. "Thus says the king: 'Come down right now!'"

_h "If I'm a holy man," Eliyyah said in reply to them, "then may a fire come down from the sky and obliterate you and your battalion."

Then a divine fire came down from the sky and obliterated the
_i captain and his battalion. So a third battalion captain and his battalion of fifty men were dispatched to summon him yet again.

The third battalion captain went up the mountain, went over and kneeled in front of Eliyyahu, and begged for mercy.

"Holy man," he pleaded, "please treat my life as precious, as well as the lives of these fifty servants of yours. I know fire came down from the sky and obliterated the two previous battalion captains and their battalions. So now, I beseech you, treat my life as precious."

—

P60,3 "Go with him," Yahweh's envoy said to Eliyyahu. "Don't be afraid of him." So he went with him at once to see the king.

"On account of the fact that you sent messengers to seek an oracle from Lord Horse Fly God of Eqron," Eliyyahu said to him, "thus says Yahweh: 'Is it because there aren't any gods in Yisra'el that you seek an oracle from him? Therefore, you won't get down from the bed you climbed into, for you shall certainly die!'"

_a And so he died, just as foretold by Yahweh's oracle that Eliyyahu delivered. Yehoram became king in his place...

_b **

P61 _a ...in the second year of the reign of Yehoram Yehoshaphatsson King of Yehudah, for he had no son.

_b —

P61,1 The rest of the things that Ahazyahu did are recorded in the book *The Chronicles of the Kings of Yisra'el*.

**

At the time that Yahweh took Eliyyahu up into the sky in a whirlwind, Eliyyahu and Eliysha had left Gilgal on a journey.

"Please stay here," Eliyyahu said to Eliysha, "for Yahweh has sent me on to Beyth-El."

"By the life of Yahweh—and by your life—I swear I won't leave you!" exclaimed Eliysha.

So they proceeded on to Beyth-El. Some prophets who were at Beyth-El came out to meet Eliysha. "Do you know that today Yahweh's going to take your lord from you?" they asked.

"Yes, I do know that," he said. "So quit talking."

"Eliysha," said Eliyyahu, "please stay here, for Yahweh has sent me on to Yeriyho."

"By the life of Yahweh—and by your life—I swear I won't leave you!"

So they proceeded on to Yeriyho. Some prophets in Yeriyho approached Eliysha. "Do you know that today Yahweh's going to take your lord from you?" they asked.

"Yes, I do know that," he said. "So quit talking."

"Please stay here," Eliyyahu said to him, "for Yahweh has sent me on to the Yarden River."

"By the life of Yahweh—and by your life—I swear I won't leave you!"

So the two of them traveled on. Fifty of the prophets had come along with them, and they were standing opposite them some distance away while the two of them were standing beside the Yarden.

Eliyyahu took his cloak, folded it, and then struck the water with it, whereupon the water split and went in opposite directions. The two of them then crossed over on dry ground.

"Ask me what I may do for you before I'm taken from you," Eliyyah said to Eliysha as they were crossing over.

"Please," replied Eliysha, "I wish that a double portion of your power might be given to me!"

"You've asked a difficult thing. If you see me taken from you, then may your wish be granted! But if not, then it won't happen."

As they were walking along and talking, a fiery chariot drawn by flaming horses suddenly appeared and separated the two of them, and just as suddenly Eliyyahu shot up into the sky in a whirlwind.

As this was happening Eliysha was looking on and crying out, "Master! Master! Yisra'el's chariotry and cavalry!"

He never saw him again, but he did grab hold of his clothes, tearing them into two pieces. He picked up the cloak that had fallen off Eliyyahu and went back and stood on the bank of the Yarden. Then, taking the cloak that had fallen off Eliyyahu, he struck the water and cried, "Where is Eliyyahu's god Yahweh? Where is he?"

He struck the water again, and it split and went in opposite directions. Then Eliysha crossed back over.

When the prophets from Yeriyho standing on the other side saw him coming over, they thought, "Eliyyahu's power has settled onto Eliysha!" They went to meet him and made obeisance to him, prostrating themselves on the ground.

"Please know," they said to him, "that with your servants here are fifty excellent men. Please, we'd like them to go and look for your lord in case Yahweh's wind picked him up and threw him down on one of the hills or in one of the vallys."

vallys: read "valleys"

"Don't send anyone," he replied.

But they pressed him to the point of embarrassment, and he told them they could send out a search party. They sent fifty men, and they searched for three days but didn't find Eliyyahu. When they returned to Eliysha, he was staying in Yeriyho.

"Didn't I tell you not to go?" he said.

———

"Look here," Yeriyho's leading townsmen said to Eliysha, "the town is well situated, as my lord can see. However, the water is unhealthy and the land is always killing off the young."

"Get me a new jar and put some salt in there," he said.

They brought him a jar with salt in it, and he went out to the source of the water. "Thus says Yahweh," he declared as he threw some salt down at that spot. " 'I hereby cure these waters. Neither death nor fatal disease shall ever come again from this spot.' " And so the waters were cured, as they still are today, just as promised by the oracle that Eliysha delivered.

**

From there he went up to Beyth-El. As he ascended the road, some little boys came out from town and began making fun of him, calling out, "Climb baldy, climb! Climb baldy, climb!"

He turned around and looked at them—then he uttered a curse on them in Yahweh's name, whereupon two bears emerged from a thicket and mauled forty-two of the children in the group. From there he proceeded to Mount Karmel, and then from there he returned to Shomeron.

**

Yehoram Ah'avsson became king over Yisra'el in Shomeron in the eighteenth year of the reign of Yehoshaphat King of Yehudah, and he ruled for twelve years. He did what was displeasing to Yahweh, although not to the extent of his father and mother. He removed the sacred pillar to the Ba'al which his father had made; however, he persisted in the errors of Yarov'am Nevatsson who made Yisra'el do wrong, not deviating from them at all.

**

Meysha King of Mo'av was a breeder of sheep; he used to pay the king of Yisra'el as tribute the wool from one hundred thousand ram lambs and one hundred thousand rams. When Ah'av died, the king of Mo'av rebelled against the king of Yisra'el. In response, King Yehoram left Shomeron and embarked on a military campaign, marshalling troops from all parts of Yisra'el. He also went and sent a message to Yehoshaphat King of Yehudah. "The king of Mo'av has rebelled against me," he said. "Will you join my campaign against Mo'av?"

"Yes, I will campaign with you," he replied. "I'll be your partner in full—my troops will fight alongside your troops, and my cavalry alongside your cavalry. Which road," he added, "will we take on our campaign?"

"We'll take the Edom Desert Road."

And so the king of Yisra'el, the king of Yehudah, and the king of Edom got going, marching in this roundabout direction for seven days. But there was no water to be had for the army, nor any for the animals that were following them. "Ugh," groaned the king of Yisra'el (because he thought that Yahweh had called the three kings together in order to deliver them into Mo'av's hands).

—

"There isn't a prophet to Yahweh present, is there?" Yehoshaphat asked. "One from whom we can seek an oracle from Yahweh?"

"Eliysha Shapatsson is here," one of the king of Yisra'el's officers answered. "The guy who was Eliyyahu's handwasher."

"He can definitely give us an oracle from Yahweh," Yehoshaphat suggested. So the king of Yisra'el, Yehoshapahat, and the king of Edom went to see him.

"Why should I have any business with you?" Eliysha asked the king of Yisra'el. "Go consult your father's prophets, or your mother's prophets!"

"No, dammit!" insisted the king of Yisra'el (for he thought that Yahweh had called the three kings together in order to deliver them into Mo'av's hands).

"As Yahweh of Armies, before whom I stand, lives," Eliysha answered, "I swear if it weren't for the fact that I'm partial toward Yehoshaphat King of Yehudah, I wouldn't pay you any regard or even glance at you! So then, get me a musician."

As the musician plucked the lyre's strings, Yahweh's hand came down on Eliysha. "Thus says Yahweh," he declared. " 'Make lots and lots of ditches in this wadi.' For thus says Yahweh: 'You won't see any wind, and you won't see any rain, yet this wadi is going to be full of water.' Then you and your livestock and your cattle may drink. And Yahweh considers this but a trifle—he's also going to deliver Mo'av into your hands. You'll defeat every fortified town and every town worth having; you'll fell every good tree and stop up every spring; and every good plot of land you'll ruin with stones."

The next morning during the presentation of the grain offering, water suddenly appeared—it was coming from the direction of Edom, and before long the land filled up with water.

Now as Mo'av had heard that the kings were coming to wage war on them, troops from all the men of fighting age were marshalled and they stood guard along the border. As they went to their stations in the morning, the sun rose over the water. Mo'av saw the water some distance away—it was red like blood.

"That's blood," they concluded. "Indeed, the kings must have attacked one another, and comrades killed comrades in a free-for-all. Now to the spoils, Mo'av!"

When they came to Yisra'el's camp, Yisra'el leapt up and attacked Mo'av, who fled for their lives. They depeated them by it, defeating Mo'av. At the same time, they despoiled their land: they were demolishing their towns, each and every man was throwing stones and filling all the good plots of land with them, they were stopping up all the springs, and they were felling all the healthy trees. Finally, all that was left of the land's stones was in Qiyr Hareseth. Then the slingers surrounded the town and attacked it.

Once the king of Mo'av saw that the battle was going against him, he took seven hundred warriors with him to attempt to break through the King of Edom's battle lines, but they failed. Then he took his first-born son, who was to succeed him as king, and offered him up as a whole offering on the town wall. This resulted in a tremendous rage against Yisra'el, whereupon they picked up and left him and returned to their own land.

**

depeated: read "defeated"

One of the prophets' wives cried to Eliysha for help. "Your servant my husband has died," she said. "You yourself know that your sèrvant was devoted to Yahweh, and now the man we owe money to is coming to take my two children to be his servants."

"What shall I do for you?" asked Eliysha. "Tell me what youe have in the house."

"Your maidservant doesn't have anything in the house except a small jug of oil."

"Go ask for some jars from around here, from all youre neighbors—empty jars. Don't stop at just a few. Then go inside and shut the door behind you and your two sons. Pour oil into all those jars, stopping only when each is full."

She then left him and shut the door behind herself and her sons. They would bring the jars to her and she would peour oil into them. When all the jars were full, she asked her son to bring her another jar. "There aren't any more jars," he said. And then the oil stopped.

When she went and informed the holy man, he told her to go sell the oil. "Repay what youe owe, and then you both youre sons can live on what's left."

P66 [2.4] a

youe: read "you"
b

youre: read "your"

c

peour: read "pour" d

e

youe: read "you"
both youre: read "and both your"

**

One day on his travels Eliysha happened to pass through Shunem. There was a prominent woman there, and she insisted that he come dine with her. As a result, every time he passed through, he would make a detour to dine there.

"Look here, darling," she said to her husband. "I know that this holy man is very special. He passes by our way all the time. Wouldn't it be nice if we made a little walled room on the roof and put a bed for him there, and a table and chair and a lamp? Then when he comes to see us, he can retire there for the night."

And so the next time he went there, he retired to the roof chamber and slept there.

"Call the Shunammite woman up here," he said to his attendant Geyhaziy. So he summoned her and she stood in front of him.

"Please say to her, 'We can see that you've gone through a great deal of bother for us. What may we do for you in return? Is there something you'd possibly like us to speak with the king about on your behalf, or with the head of the army?' "

"I'm content just living here among my people," she replied.

"Then what can we do for her?" Eliysha asked Geyhaziy.

"In fact," Geyhaziy replied, "she doesn't have a son, and her husband is quite old."

P67 a

b

c

d

e

"Call her up here." So he summoned her and she stood in the doorway.

"Nine months from now in the spring," he said to her, "youe'll be cuddling a son."

"No, my lord Mr. Holy Man, don't tell lies to your maidservant!"

The woman became pregnant and gave birth to a son nine months later in the spring, as Eliysha had told her would happen. One day after the child had reached boyhood, he went out to see his father, who was with the field hands working the harvest.

"My head! My head!" he cried to his father. His father told a servant boy to carry him back to his mother. So he picked him up and took him back to his mother. He sat in her lap until noon and then he died. She took him up to the roof chamber and laid him on the holy man's bed. Then she shut the door to keep him safe and left.

"Please send me one of the servant boys and one of the jenny asses," she called to her husband. "I have to run to see the holy man and then I'll come right back!"

"Why are youe going to goe see him now? It's not the new moon or the Shabbath."

"Good-bye!" she said. She saddled the jenny and told her servant boy to get the jenny moving. "Don't interfere with my riding unless I tell you to!"

So off she went, going to Mount Karmel to see the holy man.

"Look—there's that Shunammite woman," the holy man said to his attendant Geyhaziy when he saw her in the distance. "Please run to her and ask her if she's okay, and if her husband and child are okay."

She told him things were fine, and then she went to see the holy man on the mountain. She immediately grabbed hold of his feet, and Geyhaziy approached to push her away.

"Leave her alone," the holy man said. "She's in distress about something. But Yahweh's hidden it from me and hasn't told me what it is."

"Did I ask my lord for a son?" she said. "Didn't I say you shouldn't mislead me?"

"Put on your belt and take my staff and go," he said to Geyhaziy. "If you happen to meet anyone, don't greet him, and if someone greets you, don't answer him. Put my staff on the boy's face."

"By Yahweh's life and by your own life," the boy's mother said, "I swear I'm not leaving without you!" So he followed her back right away. Now Geyhaziy had gone before them. When he placed the staff on the boy's face, there were no sounds,

f *youe'll*: read "you'll"

g

youe going to goe: read "you going to go" h

i

j

k

l

nor any signs of life. He went back to the holy man and told him that the boy didn't wake up.

Eliysha arrived and went inside the house—and there the boy was, laid out on his bed, dead. He entered the room and shut the door behind the two of them. He said a prayer to Yahweh, and then he got on the bed and lay down on top of the boy, placing his mouth on the boy's mouth and his eyes on the boy's eyes, and putting his palms on the boy's palms. As he crouched over the boy, the boy's body grew warm.

He went back down into the house and puttered around for a bit. Then he went back up, got on the bed and crouched over the boy. The boy sneezed seven times—and then the boy opened his eyes!

He summoned Geyhaziy. "Call the Shunammite woman up here!" he said.

So he summoned her, and she went up to Eliysha. "Pick up your son," he said, whereupon she went and threw herself at his feet, prostrating herself on the ground. Then she picked up her son and left the room.

**

After Eliysha had returned to Gilgal, the prophets happened to be in audience with him one time when there was a famine in the land.

"Put the big pot on the fire," he said to his attendant, "and cook some stew for the prophets."

One of them went out to the fields to pick some greens. He found a wild vine, picked some wild gourds from it, and loaded them onto his tunic. Then he went back and sliced them up into the pot of stew, unbeknownst to the others. The stew was poured for the men to eat, but as soon as they ate some of it, they cried out in disgust—"There's poison in the pot, Mister Holy Man!" They couldn't stand eating it.

"Get some barley meal," the holy man said. They did, and he threw it in the pot. "Now pour the stew for the group and let them eat." And then there was nothing in the pot that tasted bad.

—

Once a man arrived from Ba'al Shalishah, bringing some harvest bread for the holy man—twenty barley loaves—along with some garden produce in his knapsack.

"Give this food to the group and let them eat," said the holy man to his head servant.

"How can I put this in front of a hundred men?" his servant objected.

"Give it to the group and let them eat. For thus says Yahweh: 'Eat c and there'll be leftovers.'"

So he put the food in front of them, they ate, and they left some leftovers, just as Yahweh said.

**

P69 [2.5] a Na'aman, who was the head of the King of Aram's army, was an important man at his lord's court and much favored, for through him
b Yahweh had given Aram great military success. The man was an excellent warrior, but he suffered from a skin condition.

Now once when Aram had gone out making raids, they took captive a little girl from Yisra'el, and she became a servant to Na'aman's wife.

"How I wish my lord could visit the prophet who's in Shomeron!" she said to her lady. "Then he could get rid of his skin condition for him!"

An account of what the girl from Yisra'el had said made its way to Na'aman's lord. "Come now," the king said to Na'aman. "Make the journey—I'll send a letter of introduction for you to the king of Yisra'el."

c So he made the journey, taking with him ten *kikkar* of silver, six thousand sheqels of gold, and ten changes of clothes. He then took the letter to the king of Yisra'el; it read, "With the arrival of this letter to you, know that I have sent you my servant Na'aman so that you may rid him of his skin disease."

Upon reading the letter, the king tore his clothes in protest. "Am I God Almighty with the power of life and death," he objected, "that
d this jerk's asking me to rid some guy of his skin condition? Really now,
e if you just think about it, you'll realize he's simply trying to create a quarrel with me."

When Eliysha the Holy Man heard that the king had become upset and had torn his clothes, he sent him a message. "Why did you tear your clothes?" he asked. "Please let the man come to see me—then
f he'll see that there really is a prophet in Yisra'el!"

horse: read "horses"
g Na'aman arrived with his horse and chariot and stood at the entrance to Eliysha's house. Eliysha sent a messenger out to him with this message: "Go and bathe seven times in the Yarden. Then your skin will return to normal and won't be impure anymore."

h Na'aman stormed off in anger. "I really expected he would come out to meet me," he fumed, "and stand there and call in the name of his god Yahweh. And then wave his hand at where I'm diseased
i and get rid of my skin condition! How are the Avanah and the Parpar [*Dammeseq's rivers*] not better than any body of water in Yisra'el?

Can't I just wash in them and be clean?" He turned around and left, consumed with rage.

His servants approached and spoke to him. "Master, the prophet said something important to you. Won't you do it? He simply told you to wash, and then you wouldn't be impure anymore."

So he went down to the Yarden and dipped himself in it seven times, just as the holy man had advised. And his skin was restored, just like the skin on a young boy, and it was no longer impure. He and his entire retinue went back to see the holy man, and then he went and stood in front of him.

"Now I realize there are no gods anywhere on earth except in Yisra'el!" Na'aman declared. "So now, please accept a gift from your servant."

"As Yahweh lives, before whom I stand," he replied, "I won't accept any such thing."

He pressed him to accept something, but he still refused.

"If not," Na'aman said, "then please let your servant be given two mule-loads of dirt, for your servant will never again make a whole offering or welfare offering to any gods but Yahweh. For this incident may Yahweh forgive your servant: when my lord went to Rimmon's temple to worship there, because he had put his trust in me, I too was worshipping in Rimmon's temple. The fact that I was worshipping in Rimmon's temple: it is for this that I ask Yahweh to forgive your servant."

"Go on your way and don't give it another thought," he replied.

He left him and had only gone a short distance...

—

"Look here," thought Eliysha the Holy Man's attendant Gehaziy, "my lord has withheld from Mr. Na'aman the Aramean the kindness of accepting from him what he brought for a gift. As Yahweh lives, I'm going to run after him and get something from him." And so Gehaziy chased after Na'aman.

When Na'aman saw him running after him, he dismounted from his chariot to greet him. "Is everything okay?" he asked.

"Yes, things are fine," he replied. "My lord sent me with a message. It turns out that two young men came to see him—some prophets from the Ephrayim hill country. Please, he would like you to give them a *kikkar* of silver and two changes of clothes."

"Be so kind as to accept two *kikkar* of silver," Na'aman said. Pressing him with some insitsence, he secured two *kikkar* of silver into two bags along with two changes of clothes, and then gave the bags to his two attendants, who carried them in front of him. When they reached Shomeron's upper town, Geyhaziy took the bags from them and stored them in the house. He then dismissed the men and they left.

Wher: read "Where"

"Wher did you just get back from, Gehaziy?" asked Eliysha once Gehaziy had come back and was waiting on his lord.

"Your servant didn't go anywhere," Gehaziy replied.

g

"I didn't like it when a man turned from his chariot to greet you. Was that the time for accepting silver or accepting clothing? Why not olive groves and vineyards, or sheep and cattle, or manservants and maidservants also? May Na'aman's skin condition stick on you and your offspring forever!"

h
i

And so he left him, stricken with a disease that made his skin white as snow.

[2.6] j

"Look here now," the prophets said to Eliysha, "the place where we're living with you is too cramped for us. Please, we'd like to go to the Yarden, where each of us can get some lumber so we can make ourselves a place to live there."

"Of course," he said, "go on and do that."

"Please be so kind as to come along with your servants," one of them said.

"Yes, I'd be happy to go with you."

And so he went with them. Once they reached the Yarden, they

k
l
m

began cutting wood into planks. One of them was felling a piece of lumber when the head of his ax dropped into the water. "Oh no, my lord!" he exclaimed. "God knows where it went!"

"Where did it it fall?" asked the holy man.

n

He showed him the place. The holy man then cut off a stick and threw it to that spot, causing the ax-head to float up.

"Pick it up," he said, and the man reached out and grabbed it.

**

P70 a

Once when the king of Aram was waging war in Yisra'el, he consulted with his officers about locating his army's encampment at a particular place.

b

"Be careful not to pass by that place," the holy man messaged the king of Yisra'el, "because that's where Aram is capming." The king of Yisra'el then sent a message to the place that the holy man had spoken about to him when he warned him to be careful not to pass by

c
d

there—and not just one or two messages.

The king of Aram became enraged over the situation and summoned his officers. "Can't you tell me who from our side defected to the king of Yisra'el?" he asked.

"No, my lord the king, we can't," answered one of his officers. "Because Eliysha the Prophet, even though he's in Yisra'el, can tell the king of Yisra'el things you say in the privacy of your bedroom."

"Go and see where he is so I can send some men and take him."

Once he was informed that Eliysha was in Dothan, he sent horses and chariots there, along with a large army. They arrived during the night and surrounded the town. Early in the morning the holy man's attendant rose and went outside, where he was surprised to see an army surrounding the town, along with horses and chariots.

"Oh no, my lord!" his servant fretted. "What are we going to do now?"

"Don't be scared, for those with us are stronger than those with them." Then Eliysha prayed: "Yahweh, please open his eyes and let him see!"

Yahweh opened the servant's eyes and he saw right away that while the hills were full of horses and chariots, there were flames all around Eliysha.

When they descended on Eliysha, he again prayed to Yahweh. "Please strike these people blind!" he cried. And then he struck them blind, just as Eliysha had asked.

"This isn't the right road, and this isn't the right town," Eliysha told them. "Follow me, and I'll lead you to the man you're looking for." Then he led them to Shomeron.

"Yahweh, open these men's eyes and let them see!" Eliysha said once they had reached Shomeron. Yahweh then opened their eyes, and they saw right away that they were in the center of Shomeron.

"Master, shall I kill them?" the king of Yisra'el asked Eliysha when he saw Aram's troops.

"Don't kill them. Do you strike down with your sword or bow those whom you've taken captive? Put some food and water in front of them so they can eat and drink. Then let them go back to their lord."

He put on a big feast for them, and they ate and drank. Then he dismissed them and they went back to their lord. And Aram's raiding parties never again entered Yisra'el's territory.

**

After these events, Hadadsson King of Aram marshalled his entire army and then marched out and besieged Shomeron. As a result, there was a tremendous famine in Shomeron—in fact, the siege continued for so long that donkey's heads were going for eighty sheqels of silver and a fourth of a *qav* of dove shit for five sheqels.

shit: read "droppings"

Once as the king of Yisra'el was walking along on top of the town wall, a woman cried out to him—"My lord and king, save me!"

("If Yahweh can't save you," thought the king, "how can I? Does she think there's any food in the granaries, or any wine in the vats?")

"What's troubling you?" the king asked.

"This other woman said to me, 'Hand over your son and we'll eat him today. Then we can eat my son tomorrow.' So we boiled my son and ate him. Then the next day I said to her, 'Hand over your son so we can eat him,' but she hid her son."

When the king heard what the woman said, he became upset and tore his clothing. (He was walking along on top of the town wall at the time, and the townspeople noticed he was wearing sackcloth on his loins underneath his clothes.) "So may God do to me, and so may he do again," he swore to himself, "if by the end of today Eliysha Shaphatsson's head is still attached to his body!"

At the time Eliysha was sitting in his house and the town elders were sitting there with him. A man had been dispatched on the king's orders, and before the king's agent arrived, Eliysha said to the elders, "Do you realize that goddamn mass murderer has sent somebody to take off my head? Look here, when the king's agent arrives, shut the door and block him out. Isn't that the sound of his lord's henchmen coming right behind him?"

He was still speaking with them when the king's agent suddenly showed up, coming down to get him. "This misfortune can only be Yahweh's doing," he thought. "I certainly can't wait for Yahweh any longer!"

**

"Hear Yahweh's oracle!" Eliysha said. "Thus says Yahweh: 'This time tomorrow in Shomeron's market, a *se'ah* of fancy flour will go for a sheqel, and two *se'ah* of barley meal will go for the same.'"

A deputy of the king—the one he trusted most—responded incredulously to the holy man. "You think Yahweh's going to make sluices in the sky?" he asked. "Could something like that really happen?"

"I promise you, you'll see it with your own eyes—but you won't eat any of what's sold there!" retorted Eliysha.

**

Four men who had been stricken with leprosy were outside the entrance to the town gate and were talking with one another.

"Are we just going to sit here until we die?"

"Well, if we say we'll go into town, there's a famine in town, and we'll die there."

"But if we stay here, we'll also die."

"Come on then. Let's switch over to Aram's camp. If they let us live, we'll live. And if they kill us, we'll die like we would've anyway."

So at twilight, they made ready to go to Aram's camp. But when they got to the edge of the camp, there wasn't anyone there. _b

Now the Lord had made Aram's army imagine the sounds of chariots and the sounds of horses—sounds of an enormous army. "Yisra'el's king must've hired the Hethites' kings and Egypt's kings to attack us!" exclaimed the troops to one another. They fled at once—it was the twilight hour—leaving behind their tents, their horses, and their donkeys. The camp was like normal, except the troops had fled for their lives. _c

So when these lepers got to the edge of the camp, they went into one of the tents and ate and drank. They carried off silver and gold and clothing from there and went and hid them. Then they went back and entered another tent. From there too they carried off valuables and then went and hid them. But they started talking with one another: _d

"What we're doing isn't right."

"Yes—now's the time to share the news, but instead we're being silent."

"Well if we wait till first light, we'll be found out and punished."

"So come on, let's go give the news to the palace!"

So they went and called out to the guard at the town gate. "We went to Aram's camp," they told them. "And you know what, there wasn't anyone there. Not a sound of a human being—only horses and donkeys that were still tied up, and the tents like normal." _e

The guards at the gate gave a loud cry, and the news reached inside the royal palace, causing the king to get up in the middle of the night.

"Let me tell you what I think Aram's done to us," he said to his officials. "They know we're starving, so they left camp and hid out inthe the fields. They're thinking that we'll come out from the town, and then they can take us alive and enter the town."

inthe: read "in" _f

"May I suggest fetching five of the remaining horses that are still here?" replied one of his officials. "I think they must be about the entire the fighting strength of Yisra'el that's left here—yes, they're about all of Yisra'el's fighting strength that's still intact. Let's send them so we can see what's going on." _g

the fighting: read "fighting"

So two chariots with horses were fetched. The king sent them after Aram's army, telling them to go and see what was going on. They followed them as far as the Yarden—the road all the way there was littered with clothes and equipment that Aram had abandoned _h

in the their panic. When the men on reconnaissance returned and reported what they had seen to the king, the townspeople came out and ransacked Aram's camp. And so it happened that a *se'ah* of fancy flour went for a sheqel, and two *se'ah* of barley meal went for the same, just as Yahweh's oracle foretold.

Now the king had given his most trustworthy deputy responsibility for the town gate, and he died when the people trampled him as they were running through the gate, exactly as foretold by the holy man who said it when the king came down to execute him.

It was just as the holy man had said to the king: "Two *se'ah* of barley meal for a sheqel, and a *se'ah* of fancy flour for the same—that will be the price this time tomorrow in Shomeron's market." And then the king's deputy answered the holy man by saying, "You think Yahweh's going to make sluices in the sky? Could something like that really happen?" Prompting the holy man to respond, "I promise you, you'll see it with your own eyes—but you won't eat any of what's sold there." And that's what happened to him: the townspeople trampled him in the gate and he died.

—

P73,1 [2.8]
youe: read "you"

"Leave at once—youe and your family," Eliysha said to the woman whose son he had brought back to life. "Stay in whatever place you're able to stay, for Yahweh has proclaimed a famine. Moreover, it'll be in the land for seven years."

The woman immediately did as the holy man suggested: she and her family left and stayed in the Philishtines' country for seven years. At the end of the seven years, the woman returned from the Philishtines' country and made a trip to plead for the king's help with her personal property and her family farm. At the time, the king was speaking with the holy man's attendant Gehaziy. "Please tell me all the great things that Eliysha's done," he said.

—

P73,2

He was in the middle of telling the king how he had brought the dead boy back to life when the woman whose son he had revived suddenly showed up, pleading for the king's help regarding her personal property and her family farm.

"My lord and king," said Gehaziy, "that's the woman, and that's her son who Eliysha brought back to life!"

The king asked the woman about this, and she told him the story of what happened. The king then assigned one of his senior officials to her, telling him to return to her everything that was hers, including all the production from her family farm from the time she left the country until now.

**

Eliysha arrived in Dammeseq when Hadadsson King of Aram was ill. When the king was informed that the holy man had arrived there, he told Hazah'el to take a gift in hand and to go meet the holy man. "Ask him for an oracle from Yahweh about whether I'll survive this illness," he said.

So Haza'el went to meet the holy man, and he took a gift with him: an enormous load of all the excellent things that Dammeseq was known for, carried by forty camels.

Upon arriving, he presented himself to him. "Your dear friend Hadadsson King of Aram sent me here," he said. "He wants to know if he'll survive his illness."

"Go back and tell him he definitely won't live," Eliysha replied. "Yahweh's shown me that he'll definitely die." He fixed his face in a frozen position, holding it like that so long it made one uncomfortable to look at him. Then the holy man began crying.

"Why is my lord crying?" asked Haza'el.

"Because now I know the harm you're going to do to the Yisra'elites: you're going to burn down their forts, slaughter their young men, run their babies through, and slice open their pregnant women."

"Then what is your servant but a dog," said Hazah'el, "that he would carry out acts of such enormity?"

"And Yahweh showed me you as king over Aram," Eliysha added.

He then left Eliysha and went back to his lord.

"What did Eliysha say to you?"

"He told me you would definitely live."

The very next day he took a cloth, dipped it in water, and spread it over his face. And so he died and Hazah'el became king in his place.

P74 a

b

c

d

won't: read "will" e

f

g

h

**

In the fifth year of the reign of Yoram Ah'avsson King of Yisra'el and Yehoshaphat King of Yehudah, Yehoram Yehoshaphatsson ruled as king of Yehudah. He was thirty-two years old when he became king, and he ruled as king for eight year in Yerushalem. He followed in the footsteps of the kings of Yisra'el (exactly as Ah'av's family did, for he was married to Ah'av's daughter) and he did what was displeasing to Yahweh. But Yahweh wasn't willing to destroy Yehudah on account of his servant Dawid, in keeping with his promise to him to give him a lamp [*for his descendants*] that would last forever.

During Yehoram's reign, Edom rebelled against Yehudah's rule and chose a king for themselves. Yoram procceded to Tza'iyr with

P75 a

year: read "years" b

c

d

e

f
g
h
i

his entire chariotry. It happened during this campaign that he rose one night and attacked Edom when they had surrouwnded him along with the leaders of his chariotry, resulting in Edom's forces fleeing back to their homes. (And Edom has remained in rebellion against Yehudah's rule down to the present day.) After that, Livnah was also in open rebellion at that time.

The rest of Yoram's acts and everything he did are recorded in the book *The Chronicles of the Kings of Yehudah*. Yoram lay down in death with his ancestors, and he was buried with his ancestors in Fort Dawid. His son Ahazyahu became king in his place.

**

P76

a
b
c
d
e
f

In the twelfth year of the reign of Yoram Ah'avsson King of Yisra'el, Ahazyahu Yehoramsson ruled as king of Yehudah. Ahazyahu was twenty-two years old when he became king, and he ruled as king for one year in Yerushalem. His mother's name was Athalyahu Omriysdaughter, the daughter of Yisra'el's king. He followed in the footsteps of Ah'av's family, doing what was displeasing to Yahweh, just like Ah'av's family, for he was Ah'av's maternal grandson.

He went with Yoram Ah'avsson to fight against Haza'el King of Aram in Ramoth Gil'ad, and the Arameans defeated Yoram. King Yoram went back to recover in Yizre'el from the beating that the Arameans had given him in Ramah when he fought with Hazah'el King of Aram.

Now around the time that Ahazyahu Yehoramsson King of Yehudah had gone to see Yoram Ah'avsson in Yizre'el because he was wounded...

**

P77 [2.9] a

Eliysha the Prophet summoned one of the prophets in his company. "Put on your belt," he told him. "Then take this jug of oil with you and go to Ramoth Gil'ad. When you get there, look for Yehu Yehoshaphatsson Nimshiysson there. Go to him and separate him from his associates, and then take him to a private room. Take the jug of oil and pour some on his head. Then say, 'Thus says Yahweh: 'I hereby anoint you as king to Yisra'el.'' Then open the door and get out of there. Don't wait around."

b

So the young man went [*the young man is the prophet*] to Ramoth Gil'ad. When he arrived, he noticed some army officers sitting together.

"I have a matter to speak about with you, general," he said.

"Which one of us?" asked Yehu.

"With you, general."

He got up and went inside. The young man then poured oil on his head and said, "Thus says Yahweh God of Yisra'el: 'I hereby anoint you king to Yahweh's people, to Yisra'el. You shall strike down your lord Ah'av's family, and so I will avenge the murder of my servants the prophets [*and the murder of all Yahweh's servants*] by Iyzevel. Ah'av's entire family will perish. I shall cut down Ah'av's last remaining descendant, pissing himself against a wall—yes, every last one of them, wherever they are in Yisra'el. I'm going to make Ah'av's family like Yarov'am Nevatsson's family, and like Ba'sha Ahiyyahsson's family. The dogs are going eat Iyzevel in her property in Yizre'el and there won't be anything left of her to bury." Then he opened the door and got out of there.

Yehu went out to rejoin his lord's officers.

"Is everything okay?" asked one. "What did that crazy guy want with you?"

"You know that man and his mental state."

"Not true," they replied. "Please tell us what he said!"

"Okay, here's what he said to me: 'Thus says Yahweh: 'I hereby anoint you king to Yisra'el!'' "

Each man quickly took his coat and placed it at Yehu's feet on the center of the stairs. Then they blew the ram's horn, jesting "Yehu is king!"

Yehu Yehoshaphatsson Nimshiysson conspired against Yoram. (Recall that Yoram had been keeping watch in Ramoth Gil'ad—he and Yisra'el's entire army—on guard against Haza'el King of Aram; recall furthermore that King Yehoram had gone back to recover in Yizre'el from the beating that the Arameans had given him in his battle with Haza'el King of Aram.)

"If you value your life," Yehu said to them, "don't let anyone leave town, lest he make a run for it and tak news of my plans to Yizre'el."

Yehu got in his chariot and went to Yizre'el, for Yoram was recuperating there. (At the time, Ahazyahu King of Yehudah had gone to see Yoram.) A watchman who was stationed on top of the fortress in Yizre'el saw Yehu's patrol as it was approaching. "I see 's patrol," he said.

"Summon one of the cavalry," Yehoram ordered. "Send him to meet them and ask if there's anything wrong."

So a cavalryman went to meet him. "The king wants to know if there's anything wrong," he said.

"What do you care if there's anything wrong?" Yehu replied. "Get out of my way!"

tak: read "take"

"The messenger went to them, but he's not coming back," the watchman reported.

So he sent a second cavalryman. "The king wants to know if anything's wrong," he said when he got to them.

"What do you care if anything's wrong?" Yehu replied. "Get out of my way!"

"He got to them, but he's not coming back either," the watchman reported. "The driving is just like how Yehu Nimshiysson drives. Really, he's driving like a madman!"

"Get my chariot ready," Yehoram ordered. When his chariot had been readied, Yehoram King of Yisra'el and Ahazyahu King of Yehudah each left the fortress in his chariot, heading out to meet Yehu. They came upon him when he was on the property belonging to Navoth the Yizre'elite.

q

"Is everything okay, Yehu?" Yehoram asked when he saw him.

r

"How could things be okay while your mother Iyzevel is whoring around and carrying on her incessant hocus-pocus?"

Flipping the reins in his hands, Yehoram turned the chariot and made a getaway. "It's a trap, Ahazyah!" he cried to Ahazyahu.

Yehu meanwhile readied his bow and shot, striking Yehoram between the shoulders. As the arrow came out from his chest, he crumpled over in his chariot.

"Pick him up and throw him in a section of Navoth the Yizre'elite's farm," Yehu said to his adjutant Bidqar, "for both you and I remember the teams of riders following his father Ah'av and how Yahweh delivered that oracle against him: 'Because I witnessed the murders of Navoth and his children yesterday,' oracle of Yahweh, 'I swear I shall pay you back on that same plot of land'—oracle of Yahweh. So then, pick him up and throw in that plot, just as Yahweh said."

s

When Ahazyahu King of Yehudah saw what was happening, he fled down Gardenville Road. But Yehu went in pursuit. "Him too," he ordered. "Hit him in the chariot when he's at Gur's Pass [*which is near Yivle'am*]."

t

He fled as far as Megiddo and died there. His officers had him taken back to Yerushalem in his chariot. He was buried in a grave with his ancestors in Fort Dawid.

u

**

P78   a   In the eleventh year of the reign of Yoram Ah'avsson, Ahazyah ruled as king over Yehudah.

b
c
Yehu proceeded on to Yizre'el. When Iyzevel heard he was coming, she put black eyeliner on her eyes, prettied up her face and hair, and

then stood by the window and looked out.

"Did things work out for Zimriy when he killed his lord?" she called to Yehu as he entered town through the gate.

He looked up to the window and shouted, "Who's with me? Who?"

Two or three royal officials looked down at him from the palace windows.

"Throw hre down here!" he demanded.

So they threw her down. When she hit the ground, some of her blood splattered on the wall and on the horses nearby, which trampled her in their fright.

Yehu went inside and had something to eat and drink. "Please go deal with that cursed woman and bury her," he said. "For she is the daughter of a king after all."

So they went to bury her, but they didn't find any of her except the skull, the feet, and parts of her hands. When they returned and informed Yehu, he thought, "This is Yahweh's oracle, which he spoke through his servant Eliyyahu the Tishbite—'In a section of Yizre'el, the dogs will eat Iyzevel's body.' [*And 'Iyzevel's corpse wil be like manure spread on a field in a section of Yizre'el, so that the words 'There lies Iyzevel' shall never be uttered.'*]"

—

Now Ah'av had seventy sons in Shomeron. Yehu wrote letters and sent them to Shomeron, to the leaders of Yizre'el [*that is, the elders*] and to those who remained loyal to Ah'av. This is what the letters said: "When this letter reaches you, your lord's sons will be with you, and you'll have at your disposal chariots and horses, as well as the town's fortifications and armory. So give consideration to which of your lord's sons is the best and most satisfactory, place him on his father's throne, and then prepare to go to war in defense of your lord's family."

They were terrified when they heard the letters, thinking "It's a fact that two kings couldn't survive his assault. So how could we?" The palace chamberlain, the mayor of the town, the elders, and the loyalists sent back the following message to Yehu: "We are your servants. We shall do whatever you tell us. We won't make anyone king. Do as you see fit."

Then he wrote them a second letter. This is what it said: "If you're going to be subject to me and follow my orders, then get the heads of the men who are your lord's sons, and come to me here in Yizre'el sometime tomorrow."

Now the king's sons—all seventy of them—were with the town's leading men, men who had been their childhood mentors. But when

hre: read "her"

wil: read "will"

P78,1 [2.10]

g they received this letter, they took the king's sons and slaughtered all seventy of them. They then placed their heads in clay jars and sent them to Yehu in Yizre'el. When the messenger arrived and informed him that they had brought the heads of the king's sons, he said, "Put h them in two piles in front of the town gate until morning."

i In the morning, Yehu went out and stood at the gate. "You all bear no responsibility for this crime," he said to the people there. "It's true I conspired against my lord and killed him. But who has killed all j these men? Know therefore that not a single word of Yahweh's oracle which he spoke in condemnation of Ah'av's family will fail to come true. Yahweh has done what he said through his servant Eliyyahu he would do."

Yehu then killed all of Ah'av's remaining family in Yizre'el along k with all his important allies—those involved with him and his priests—not leaving a single person surviving. Immediately after that he left and went to Shomeron. On the way there, he was at a shepherds' binding station when he chanced to meet kinsmen of Ahazyahu King of Yehudah.

"Who are you?" he asked.

l "We're kinsmen of Ahazyahu. We've come to see if the king's children and the queen mother's children are safe."

"Seize them alive," he ordered. They seized them alive, and then they slaughtered them beside the binding station's cistern—forty-two m men in all. Not a single one of them was spared.

—

P78,2 a He proceeded from there and happened upon Yehonadav Rekavsson, b who was coming to meet him. Yehu greeted him and said, "Does it c please you when you and I agree on things?"

"Indeed, it does," replied Yehonadav.

d "Well if so, then give me your hand."

e Yehonadav offered his hand, raising it up to Yehu in the chariot. f "Come with me and see my zeal for Yahweh," Yehu said as they pulled him into the chariot. Then he proceeded to Shomeron and killed all the remaining members of Ah'av's family in Shomeron, eliminating g every last one, just as Yahweh foretold in the oracle that he spoke to Eliyyahu.

**

P79 Yehu gathered all the people together.

a "Ah'av gave service to the Ba'al in small measures," he said to them. "But Yehu will give service to him in great measures! So then, summon here to me all the Ba'al's prophets, all his devotees, and all his priests! No one must be absent! For I'm going to hold a great welfare offering in honor of the Ba'al. Anyone who misses it shall lose his life!" (Now Yehu did this as a trick, in order to destroy all those who participated in the Ba'al's cult.)

Yehu then gave the order to prepare an assembly sanctified to the Ba'al, and the summonses went out: Yehu sent messengers everywhere in Yisra'el, and all those who participated in the Ba'al's cult came—there wasn't a single person who didn't come. They entered the grounds of the Ba'al's temple, filling them from end to end.

"Bring out clothes for all the Ba'al's devotees," Yehu said to the manager of the temple vestry, who then brought out the clothing for them.

Yehu and Yehonadav Rekavsson arrived at the grounds of the Ba'al's temple. "Make a thorough search and look around," Yehu said to the Ba'al's devotees, "in case some of Yahweh's servants are here with you, not only the Ba'al's devotees by themselves."

As they proceeded with the preparation of the welfare offerings and the whole offerings, Yehu stationed eighty men in the street outside. "If any of the men I'm making you responsible for escape," he told them, "it will be one's own life instead of his!"

Once they had finished preparing the whole offering, Yehu gave the order to the royal guard and the army captains: "Go inside! Attack them! Don't let anyone get outside!"

And so they slaughtered them. After the royal guard and the army captains disposed of the dead bodies, they went to the citadel on the temple grounds, brought out the sacred pillars belonging to the Ba'al's temple, and burned down the citadel. They then knocked down the Ba'al's sacred pillar and demolished the Ba'al's temple, and they turned the place into a shit-hole, which it still is today.

shit-hole: read "latrine"

And so Yehu eradicated the Ba'al's cult from Yisra'el. However, with respect to the errors of Yarov'am Nevatsson, by which he caused Yisra'el to do wrong, Yehu didn't abandon them [*that is, the gold bull calves which were in Beyth-El and in Dan*].

✼✼

"On account of the fact that you've excelled in doing what pleases me, doing to Ah'av's family exactly as I wished," Yahweh said to Yehu, "four generations of your descendants will occupy Yisra'el's throne." (Yehu, however, didn't take care to wholeheartedly follow the Torah of Yahweh God of Yisra'el—he didn't abandon Yarov'am's errors by which he made Yisra'el do wrong.)

It was in this period that Yahweh began to carve up Yisra'el's territory. Haza'el attacked them in every part of Yisra'el's territory, beginning east of the Yarden River with all of the Gil'ad region [*the territory of the Gadites, the Re'uvenites, and the Menashshehites—that is, from Aro'er on the Wadi Arnon in the south, the Gil'ad region itself, and the Bashan region in the north*].

The rest of Yehu's acts—everything that he did and all his valorous deeds—are recorded in the book *The Chronicles of the Kings of Yisra'el*. Yehu lay down in death with his ancestors, and he was buried in Shomeron. His son Yeho'ahaz became king in his place. Yehu's reign over Yisra'el in Shomeron lasted twenty-eight years.

**

P81 [2.11] a
and saw: read "saw"

When Ahazyahu's mother Athalyah and saw that her son had died, she immediately eliminated all the males of royal descent. However Ahazyahu's sister, Yehosheva KingYoramsdaughter, grabbed Yo'ash Ahazyahsson and stole him away from the king's sons as they were being execututed, taking him and his wet nurse when they were in the dormitory. They hid him from Athalyahu, and so he escaped being killed. For six years he remained in hiding with her in Yahweh's house while Athalyah ruled the country as queen.

execututed: read "executed" b

c

**

P82 a
militarie: read "military" b

In Athalyah's seventh year, Yehoyada sent messengers to summon the officers of the militarie [*those of the Karian guard and the royal guard*] and have them meet him at Yahweh's house. He bound them to an oath of secrecy, making them swear to it in Yahweh's house, and then he showed them the king's son.

c
d
e
f

"Here's what you must do," he ordered them. "A third of you will come in on the Shabbath and assume the palace watch. The rest of you will be on the palace watch when the guard changes at that time, one third at the Sur Gate and one third at the gate behind the Royal Guards Gate. The two-thirds of you leaving your posts on the Shabbath will then assume the watch at Yahweh's house at the king's side. You must surround the king, each of you armed with his weapons. Anyone who tries to enter your ranks must be killed, and whenever the king enters or leaves a place, you must be right there at his side."

militarie: read "military"

The officers of the militarie did exactly as Yehoyada the Priest ordered: each man took his men—the group that would start watch on the Shabbath along with the two groups that would leave watch on the Shabbath—and went to see Yehoyada the Priest. The priest gave the officers of the militarie the spears and shields that had belonged to King Dawid that were stored in Yahweh's house. The royal guard took their stations, each man armed with his weapons, extending from the right side of Yahweh's house to the left side [*that is, including both the altar and the house itself*], thus surrounding the king.

    Yehoyada brought out the king's son and put the crown and the ar-bands on him. Then they made him king and anointed him with oil, clapping their hands and shouting, "Long live the king!"

militarie: read "military"   g

h

i

j

———

When Athalyah heard all the commotion [*the people*], she went to observe the crowd at Yahweh's house. She was stunned by what she saw: there was the king, standing beside the pillar like normal, with the leaders of the army and the cult trumpeters alongside the king and people from all over celebrating and blowing horns!

    "Conspiracy!" shrieked Athalyah as she ripped her clothes. "Conspiracy!"

    Yehoyada the Priest gave orders to [*the officers of the militarie*] those who oversaw the army. "Get her out of here, and keep her inside your ranks," he said. "Kill anyone who follows her." (For the priest was thinking that she mustn't be killed on the grounds of Yahweh's house.)

    They took her into custody, and then she proceeded down Horse Parade Road to the royal palace, where she was put to death.

P82,1   a

b

c

militarie: read "military"

d

———

Yehoyada made a treaty between Yahweh and the king [*and the people, to become Yahweh's people*] and between the king and the people. People from everywhere went to the Ba'al's temple—they tore it down along with the altar to him, they smashed every single image of him to pieces, and then they killed his chief priest Mattan in front of the ruined altars.

    Yehoyada the Priest set up a new system of oversight for Yahweh's house. He summoned the officers of the military, the Karian guard, the royal guard, and the people at large. They escorted the king out from Yahweh's house and proceeded down Royal Guards Gate Road to the palace, whereupon the king took his seat on the royal throne. The entire citizenry was filled with joy, and the town was free from disturbance—Athalyahu had been put to death in palace.

P82,2   a

b
altar: read "altars"

c

d

in palace: read "in the palace"

———

Yeho'ash was seven years old when he became king.

P82,3   [2.12]
a

**

In the seventh year of Yehu's reign, Yeho'ash became king. He ruled as king in Yerushalem for forty years, and his mother's name was

P83   a

Tzivyah of Be'er Sheva. Yeho'ash did what was pleasing to Yahweh for his entire life, doing things that Yehoyada the Priest directed him to do. However, the open-air shrines weren't abandoned—the people were still regularly making animal sacrifices and burning incense offerings in the open-air shrines.

"At our disposal," Yeho'ash said to the priests, "are all the consecrated items of silver that are regularly brought to Yahweh's house: tax contributions in silver [*that is, each person's annual poll tax*] plus all the silver that people bring to Yahweh's house of their own volition. Now each priest ought to recruit one of his customers—those men will work on repairing the structural problems in Yahweh's house—any place where a problem is found."

**

Now, as it happened that in the twenty-third year of King Yeho'ash's reign, the priests still hadn't gotten around to repairing the structural problems in Yahweh's house, King Yeho'ash summoned Yehoyada the Priest and the priests under him. "What possible reason do you have for not repairing the problems in Yahweh's house?" the king asked. "From now on, don't take any of your customers' money for yourselves—you must allocate that for the house's problems."

But the priests had agreed among themselves not to take money from the people, so as not to repair the house's structural problems. So Yehoyada the Priest took a chest and drilled a hole in its lid. He put it next to the altar, in the south of where one enters Yahweh's house, and the priests who guarded the house's entrance would put in it all the silver that was brought to Yahweh's house. Once they saw that there was a large amount of silver in the chest, the king's secretary along with the high priest went up to Yahweh's house, secured the chest, and counted all the silver that was there at Yahweh's house.

They entrusted the silver that had been counted t the workmen who had been give oversight of the work on Yahweh's house. They in turn used it to pay the carpenters and the construction men who were working on Yahweh's house, as well as to pay the stonemasons and the stone-cutters, and to purchase wood and blocks of cut stone for repairing the structural problems in Yahweh's house, and to pay anyone who would come out to assist in the repair of the house. However, no silver thresholds were to be made for Yahweh's house from the money that was brought there, nor tongs, nor bowls, nor trumpets, nor any gold or silver vessels. For they would give that money to the workmen overseeing the work, who in turn would use it to carry out the repairs on Yahweh's house. They didn't demand strict accountability from

in the south: read "to the south"

t the: read "to the"
give: read "given"

the men who were entrusted with the money to pay the workmen, for they were men who acted honestly. (Money from guilt offerings and money from error offerings would not be brought to Yahweh's house—those funds are for the priests' maintenance.)

i

**

At that time Haza'el King of Aram embarked on a military campaign. He waged war on Gath and captured it, and then he decided to march on Yerushalem.

P85

Yeho'ash King of Yehudah took all the consecrated items that his ancestors Yehoshaphat, Yehoram and Ahazyahu the kings of Yehudah had dedicated to Yahweh, plus the consecrated items he had dedicated, plus all the gold in the storerooms of Yahweh's house and the royal palace, and he sent them to Haza'el King of Aram, who then withdrew his forces from Yerushalem.

The rest of the Yo'ash's acts and everything that he did are recorded in the book *The Chronicles of the Kings of Yehudah*. His officials instigated a coup against him, and they killed Yo'ash in the citadel as he was coming down a ladder. His officials Yozavad Shim'athsson and Yehozavad Shomersson were the ones who assassinated him. He was buried with his ancestors in Fort Dawid, and his son Amatzyah became king in his place.

a
b

**

In the twenty-third year of the reign of Yo'ash Ahazyahusson King of Yehudah, Yeho'ahaz Yehusson ruled as king over Yisra'el in Shomeron for seventeen years. He did what was displeasing to Yahweh: he maintained the support for the errors of Yarov'am Nevatsson, who caused Yisra'el to do wrong—he didn't waver from this in any way. Yahweh burned with anger at Yisra'el and he made them vassals of Haza'el King of Aram and of his son Hadadsson Haza'elsson for Yeho'ahaz's entire reign.

P86 [2.13]

a

But Yeho'ahaz beseeched Yahweh, and Yahweh gave heed to his plea, for he saw Yisra'el's suffering, for the king of Aram was oppressing them. So Yahweh gave Yisra'el a liberator, and they were freed from Aram's control. And so the Yisra'elites remained in their homes as previously. However, they didn't abandon the errors of Yarov'am's family, who caused Yisra'el to err; in fact, they actively supported them. Moreover, the cult of the Asherah persisted in Shomeron.

b
c
d
e
f

Indeed, Yeho'ahaz had no military forces remaining except fifty cavalrymen, ten chariots, and ten thousand infantry, for the king of Aram destroyed them and trampled them like dirt. The rest of Yeho'ahaz's acts—everything he did and all his valorous deeds—are recorded in the book *The Chronicles of the Kings of Yisra'el*. Yeho'ahaz lay down in death with his ancestors and was buried in Shomeron. His son Yo'ash became king in his place.

**

P87

In the thirty-seventh year of the reign of Yo'ash King of Yehudah, Yeho'ash Yeho'ahazsson ruled as king over Yisra'el in Shomeron for sixteen years. He did what was displeasing to Yahweh: he didn't deviate from any of the errors of Yarov'am Nevatsson, who caused

a Yisra'el to do wrong—rather, he continued supporting them.

b The rest of Yo'ash's acts—everything he did and all his valorous deeds, including how he fought with Amatzyah King of Yehudah—are recorded in the book *The Chronicles of the Kings of Yisra'el*. Yo'ash lay

c down in death with his ancestors, and Yarov'am occupied the throne.

d Yo'ash was buried in Shomeron with the kings of Yisra'el.

**

P88

When Eliysha fell mortally ill, Yo'ash King of Yisra'el went to visit

a him and began weeping over him. "Master! Master!" he lamented. "Yisra'el's chariotry and cavalry!"

"Get a bow and some arrows," Eliysha said to him. A bow and some arrows were then procured for him.

"Now get a good grip on the bow," he said to the king. He gripped

b the bow. Then Eliysha put his hands over the king's.

c "Open the east window," he said. He opened it.

"Now shoot!" Eliysha said. He shot.

"That's Yahweh's victory arrow. The victory arrow against Aram. You'll ravage Aram in Apheq until they are no more."

He continued: "Now grab the arrows." He grabbed them.

"Strike the ground with them!" he said to the king. He struck the ground three times and then stopped, prompting the holy man to become angry with him.

"If you had struck the ground five or six times," he said, "then you would have ravaged Aram until they were no more. But now it's only three times that you'll defeat Aram."

d

**

Eliysha died and was buried. At this time, raiding parties from Mo'av were encroaching into the land (it was the beginning of the year). One time when a man was being buried, a raiding party suddenly came into view, and they threw the man into Eliysha's tomb. The man's body tumbled forward and bumped into Eliysha's skeleton, whereupon it came to life and stood on its feet.

P89

a

b

**

Haza'el King of Aram oppressed Yisra'el for Yeho'ahaz's entire reign. But Yahweh had mercy on them and showed them compassion, turning his regard to them on account of his binding agreement with Avraham, Yitzhaq, and Ya'aqov—he wasn't willing to destroy them, and he didn't cast them from his presence until now.

Haza'el King of Aram died and his son Hadadsson became king in his place. Yeho'ash Yeho'ahazsson took back from Hadadsson Haza'elsson the towns that Haza'el had taken from his father Yeho'ahaz in their war. Yo'ash defeated him three times and regained Yisra'el's towns.

P90 a

b

c

**

In the second year of the reign of Yo'ash Yo'ahazsson King of Yisra'el, Amatzyahu Yo'ashsson ruled as king of Yehudah. He was twenty-five years old when he became king, and he ruled in Yerushalem for twenty-nine years. His mother's name was Yeho'addayn of Yerushalem. He did what was pleasing to Yahweh [*not, however, like his ancestor Dawid*], doing exactly as his father Yo'ash had done. However, the open-air shrines weren't abandoned—the people were still regularly making animal sacrifices and burning incense offerings in the open-air shrines.

As soon as the kingship was securely in his control, he killed the officials under him who had killed his father the king. (However, he didn't put to death the children of his father's assassins, in keeping with what is written in the book *The Torah of Mosheh*—specifically the law in which Yahweh commanded: "Parents mustn't be put to death on account of their children, nor children put to death on account of their parents; rather, a person should only die for his own crime.")

He defeated Edom in Salt Valley, killing ten thousand men. During the battle, he seized control of Cliffville and renamed it Yoqthe'el, which is still its name in the present day.

P91 [2.14]

a

b

c

d

e

die: read "be put to death"

f

**

P92   Shortly thereafter, Amatzyah sent a delegation to Yeho'ash Yeho'ahazsson Yehusson King of Yisra'el to propose that they meet in combat. Yeho'ash King of Yisra'el sent back this response to Amatzyahu King of Yehudah: "A brierbush in the Levanon sent a message to a cedar in the Levanon proposing the cedar give its daughter as a wife to the brierbush's son. But then a wild animal living in the Levanon passed by and trampled the brierbush. Now that you've smashed Edom, you're really full of yourself. Go on thinking you're a big shot, but you really ought to stay where you are. Why do want to stir up trouble for yourself? You're only going to lose, and Yehudah will lose with you."

But Amatzyahu paid no heed to the message. So Yeho'ash King of Yisra'el marched into Yehudah and he and Amatzyahu King of Yehudah met in combat at Beyth Shemesh in Yehudah. Yehudah was routed by Yisra'el, and its men fled back home. Meanwhile, Yeho'ash King of Yisra'el seized Amatzyahu King of Yehudah Yo'ashsson Ahazyahusson at Beyth Shemesh. They then proceeded to Yerushalem and breached Yerushalem's wall at the Ephrayim Gate, with the breach continuing all the way to the Corner Gate, a distance of four hundred cubits. He took all the gold and silver and all the equipment that could be found in Yahweh's house and in the royal palace's storerooms, plus a number of hostages, and then he returned to Shomeron.

The rest of Yeho'ash's acts—the things he accomplished and his valorous deeds, including how he fought with Amatzyahu King of Yehudah—are recorded in the book *The Chronicles of the Kings of Yisra'el*. Yeho'ash lay down in death with his ancestors and was buried in Shomeron with the kings of Yisra'el. His son Yarov'am became king in his place.

They: read "He"

**

P93   Amatzyahu Yo'ashsson King of Yehudah lived fifteen years after the death of Yeho'ash Yeho'ahazsson King of Yisra'el. The rest of Amatzyahu's acts are recorded in the book *The Chronicles of the Kings of Yehudah*. A conspiracy was perpetrated against him in Yerushalem, and he fled to Lakiysh. A gang was sent in pursuit to Lakiysh and they killed him there. He was carried back with an escort of horses and he was buried in Yerushalem with his ancestors in Fort Dawid.

e was: read "he was"

The people of Yehudah took Azaryah (e was sixteen years old at the time) and made him king in place of his father Amatzyahu. He rebuilt Eylath and returned it to Yehudah's possession after the king had lain down in death with his ancestors.

**

In the fifteenth year of the reign of Amatzyahu Yo'ashsson King of Yehudah, Yarov'am Yo'ashsson ruled as king of Yisra'el in Shomeron for forty-one years. He did what was displeasing to Yahweh, not deviating at all from the errors of Yarov'am Nevatsson, who caused Yisra'el to do wrong.

He restored Yisra'el's territory from Hamath's Gateway in the north to the Desert Sea in the south, in fulfillment of Yahweh God of Yisra'el's oracle, which he spoke through his servant Yonah Amittaysson the Prophet from Diggers Winepress. For Yahweh had seen that Yisra'el's suffering was growing especially wretched, there being no one anywhere at all who could come to Yisra'el's aid. As Yahweh had no intention of obliterating the memory of Yisra'el from the world, he saved them through Yarov'am Yo'ashsson.

The rest of Yarov'am's acts—all that he did and his valorous deeds, including the battles he fought and how he restored Dammeseq and the town of Hamath in Yisra'el that had been under Yehudah's control—are recorded in the book *The Chronicles of the Kings of Yisra'el*. Yarov'am lay down in death with his ancestors [*that is, with the kings of Yisra'el*], and his son Zekaryah became king in his place.

P94

a

b

c d
e

f

g

**

In the twenty-seventh year of the reign of Yarov'am King of Yisra'el, Azaryah Amatzyahsson ruled as king of Yehudah. He was sixteen years old when he became king, and he ruled for fifty-two years in Yerushalem. His mother's name was Yekaleyahu of Yerushalem. He did what was pleasing to Yahweh, similar to all that his father Amatzyahu had done. However, the open-air shrines weren't abandoned—the people were still regularly making animal sacrifices and burning incense offerings in the open-air shrines.

Yahweh struck the king with disease, and he remained afflicted with a skin condition until the day he died. He lived in quarantine in a separate house, and his son Prince Yotham, who served as the palace chamberlain, assumed responsibility for adjudicating the citizenry's legal disputes.

The rest of Azaryahu's acts and all that he did are recorded in the book *The Chronicles of the Kings of Yehudah*. Azaryah lay down in death with his ancestors. He was buried with his ancestors in Fort Dawid, and his son Yotham became king in his place.

P95 [2.15] a

b

**

P96 In the thirty-eighth year of the reign of Azaryahu King of Yehudah,
a   Zekaryahu Yarov'amsson ruled as king over Yisra'el in Shomeron
     for six months. He did what was displeasing to Yahweh, just as
b   his ancestors had done—he didn't abandon the errors of Yarov'am
     Nevatsson, who caused Yisra'el to do wrong.
c   Shallum Yaveshsson conspired against him, attacking him *en plein
     jour* and assassinating him, and then he became king in his place.
        The rest of Zekaryah's acts are recorded in the book *The Chronicles
d   of the Kings of Yisra'el*. This was in fulfillment of the oracle that Yahweh
     delivered to Yehu that four generations of his descendants would
e   occupy Yisra'el's throne. And that's exactly what happened.

**

P97 a   Shallum Yaveyshsson became king in the thirty-ninth year of Uziyyah
        King of Yehudah, and he ruled for one month in Shomeron. Mena-
b   hem Gadiysson departed from Thirtzah and went to Shomeron. He
        attacked Shallum Yaveyshsson in Shomeron and assassinated him,
        and then he became king in his place.
            The rest of Shallum's acts and the conspiracy that he perpetrated
c   are recorded in the book *The Chronicles of the Kings of Yisra'el*. After
d   that, Menahem used Thirtzah as a base to carry out attacks on Tiphsah
e   and everyone there, and on its territory. When he didn't succeed
f   in opening the town, he slaughtered all the pregnant women in its
        territory by slicing open their bellies.

**

P98   In the thirty-ninth year of the reign of Azaryah King of Yehudah, Mena-
        hem Gadiysson ruled as king over Yisra'el for ten years in Shomeron.
        He did what was displeasing to Yahweh—during his life, he never
        deviated from the errors of Yarov'am Nevatsson, who caused Yisra'el
        to do wrong.
            Phul King of Ashshur invaded the country. Menahem paid Phul
a   one thousand *kikkar* of silver to gain his support and secure the king-
        dom firmly in his grasp. Menahem imposed a tax of silver on Yisra'el
b   [*that is, a tax on all the soldiers in the army*] to give to the king of Ashshur—
c   fifty sheqels of silver per soldier. The king of Ashshur then withdrew
        his forces and they didn't remain stationed anywhere in the country.
            The rest of Menahem's acts and all that he did are recorded in the
        book *The Chronicles of the Kings of Yisra'el*. Menahem lay down in death
        with his ancestors, and his son Peqahyah became king in his place.

**

In the fiftieth year of the reign of Azaryah King of Yehudah, Peqahyah Menahemsson ruled as king over Yisra'el in Shomeron for two years. He did what was displeasing to Yahweh: that is, he didn't abandon the errors of Yarov'am Nevatsson, who caused Yisra'el to do wrong.

Peqah Remalyahusson, the deputy head of his army, conspired against him and attacked him in Shomeron in the citadel of royal palace, along with Argov and 'the Lion.' (He had the help of fifty Gil'adites.) He assassinated him and became king in his place.

The rest of Peqahyah's acts and all that he did are recorded in the book *The Chronicles of the Kings of Yisra'el*.

P99

of royal: read "of the royal"

a

**

In the fifty-second year of the reign of Azaryah King of Yehudah, Peqah Remalyahusson ruled as king over Yisra'el in Shomeron for twenty years. He did what was displeasing to Yahweh: that is, he didn't abandon the errors of Yarov'am Nevatsson, who caused Yisra'el to do wrong.

During Peqah King of Yisra'el's reign, Tiglath Pil'eser King of Ashshur invaded and took possession of Iyyon, Avel at Beyth Ma'akah, Yanoah, Qedesh, Hatzor, the Gil'ad region, and the Circle region [*that is, the entire territory of Naphtaliy*], exiling their inhabitants to Ashshur.

Hoshea Elahsson perpetrated a conspiracy against Peqah Remalyahusson. He attacked and assassinated him, and he replaced him as king in the twentieth year of Yotham Uziyyahsson's reign.

The rest of Peqah's acts and all that he did are recorded in the book *The Chronicles of the Kings of Yisra'el*.

P100

a

b

c

d

**

In the second year of the reign of Peqah Remalyahusson King of Yisra'el, Yotham Uziyyahsson ruled as king of Yehudah. He was twenty-five years old when he became king, and he ruled for sixteen years in Yerushalem. His mother's name was Yerusha Tzadoqsdaughter.

He did what was pleasing to Yahweh, in keeping with all that his father Uziyyahu had done. However, the open-air shrines weren't abandoned—the people were still regularly making animal sacrifices and burning incense offerings in the open-air shrines. He built the upper gate to Yahweh's house.

The rest of Yotham's acts which he accomplished are recorded

P101 a

b

	c	in the book *The Chronicles of the Kings of Yehudah*. (In those times, Yahweh started sending Retziyn King of Aram along with Peqah Remalyahusson to make raids on Yehudah.) Yottam lay down in death with his ancestors. He was buried with his ancestors in his ancestral fortress, Fort Dawid, and his son Ahaz became king in his place.
	d	

**

P102 [2.16]	a	In the seventeenth year of the reign of Peqah Remalyahusson, Ahaz Yothamsson ruled as king of Yehudah. Ahaz was twenty years old when he became king, and he ruled for sixteen years in Yerushalem. He did not do what was pleasing to his god Yahweh, unlike his ancestor Dawid: he followed in the footsteps of Yisra'el's kings [*he even made a fire-offering of his son, similar to the abominable practices of the nations which Yahweh drove out from the Yisra'elites*], and he made animal sacrifices and burned incense offerings in the open-air shrines [*and also on the hills and underneath every leafy tree*].
	b	
	c	

In those years Retziyn King of Aram and Peqah Remalyahusson King of Yisra'el marched on Yerushalem, intending to attack it. They hemmed Ahaz in, but they were unable to engage him in battle. At that time Retziyn King of Aram took back control of Eylath, and he cleared the Yehudeans entirely out of Eyloth. [*It was then Arameans arrived at Eylath, where they have remained down to the present day.*]

Arameans: read "Edomites"

	d	
	e	
	f	Ahaz sent a delegation to Tiglath Peleser King of Ashshur. "I shall be your servant and subject," he said. "Come and save me from the clutches of the kings of Aram and Yisra'el, who are now attacking me." Ahaz then took whatever silver and gold he could find in Yahweh's house and in the palace storerooms and sent it to the king of Ashshur as a bribe.
	g	
	h	

The king of Ashshur heeded his request: he marched on Dammeseq and seized control of it, and then he exiled its citizens to Qiyr and executed Retziyn.

When King Ahaz went to meet Tiglath Pil'eser King of Ashshur at Dummeseq, he took notice of the altar that was in Dammeseq. King Ahaz sent a picture of the altar and the details of how it was constructed to Uriyyah the Priest. Uriyyah the Priest then built a replica of the altar—he made it similar in every detail that King Ahaz had sent from Dammeseq, finishing it prior to the king's arrival back from Dammeseq.

	i	When the king arrived from Dammeseq and saw the altar, he approached the altar and went up onto it. He burned a whole offering and a grain offering, and poured out a drink offering, following which
	j	

he splashed the blood of his welfare offerings against the altar. As for the old bronze altar located in front of Yahweh, he removed it from the front of Yahweh's house, where it sat between the new altar and Yahweh's house, and he placed it on the north side of the new altar.

"On the big altar," King Ahaz ordered him Uriyyah the Priest, "burn the morning whole offering, the evening grain offering, the king's whole offering and the associated grain offering, and the citizens' whole offering and the associated grain offering and drink offerings. Splash the blood from any whole offerings and from any welfare offerings on it as well. Then I'll use the bronze altar for haruspicy."

Uriyyah the Priest did exactly as King Ahaz ordered. Then King Ahaz cut the rims off the bronze stands and removed the lavers from them. He took the Metal Sea down from the bronze cattle under it and set it on paving stones. At the same time, the Shabbath *miysak* that had been constructed inside Yahweh's house and the king's outer entry he surrounded with walls in Yahweh's house, so that the king of Ashshur wouldn't see them.

The rest of Ahaz's acts which he accomplished are recorded in the book *The Chronicles of the Kings of Yehudah*. Ahaz lay down in death with his ancestors. He was buried with his ancestors in Fort Dawid, and his son Hizqiyyahu ruled in his place.

ordered him: read "ordered"

miysak: read "musak"

**

In the twelfth year of the reign of Ahaz King of Yehudah, Hoshea Elahsson ruled over Yisra'el in Shomeron for nine years. He did what was displeasing to Yahweh—however, not like the kings of Yisra'el who preceded him.

Shalman'eser King of Ashshur invaded and targeted him, and so Hoshea became his vassal and paid annual tribute to him. But then the king of Ashshur accused Hoshea of treachery, because he sent a delegation to So King of Egypt and he didn't send his annual tribute to the king of Ashshur. As a result, the king of Ashshur arrested him and locked him up in prison. Then the king of Ashshur carried out a military campaign throughout the country. He marched on Shomeron and laid siege to it for three years. In the ninth year of Hoshea's reign, the king of Ashshur captured Shomeron and exiled Yisra'el to Ashshur. He made them live in Helah, in Havor on the Gozan River, and in towns in Maday.

**

P104 a   And so it happened that the Yisra'elites wronged their god Yahweh, who had brought them out of Egypt and freed them from the clutches of Phar'oh King of Egypt—they revered other gods, and followed the customs of the nations that Yahweh had driven from the Yisra'elites' path [*and the customs that the kings of Yisra'el had practiced*]. The Yisra'elites secretly did things that were improper, in opposition to their god Yahweh: they built open-air shrines for themselves in all their settlements, from the smallest military outposts to the largest fortified towns. They set up for themselves cult pillars and Asherah posts on every lofty hill and under every leafy tree. There in all the open-air shrines, they made burnt offerings like the nations that Yahweh had exiled from them. They did terrible things that provoked Yahweh's rage, giving service to worthless gods even though Yahweh forbade them to do such things.

b

c

d
e

his prophet: read "the prophets of"

Yahweh warned Yisra'el and Yehudah through all his prophet [*every seer*], telling them to abandon their improper practices and to keep his commandments and laws, in keeping with all the teaching which he commanded to their ancestors and which he sent to them through his servants the prophets.

f g

But they didn't listen—they were as recalcitrant as their ancestors who didn't trust their god Yahweh. They rejected his laws and the treaty he made with their ancestors, including the treaty terms which he had invoked against them. They followed gods that were nothing and so they became nothing themselves, following in the ways of the nations around them, nations whose practices Yahweh forbade them to adopt. They abandoned all their god Yahweh's commandments—they made for themselves two metal statues bull calves, they made an Asherah, they prostrated themselves to the stars in the sky, they did service to the Ba'al, they sacrificed their sons and daughters as fire offerings, they practiced divination and observed signs—yes, they enslaved themselves to doing things that displeased Yahweh, thereby provoking his rage.

h i

statues: read "statues of"

j

k

Yahweh had grown furious with Yisra'el, and so he removed them from his presence. None remained except the tribe of Yehudah alone. [*But Yehudah didn't observe their god Yahweh's commandments either—they followed the customs that Yisra'el had practiced.*] Yahweh rejected everyone of Yisra'elite descent and brought them low, delivering them into the hands of people who terrorized them until they had been cast from his presence. For Yisra'el broke away from Dawid's family and made Yarov'am Nevatsson king, and Yarov'am drave Yisra'el away from Yahweh and caused them to commit a very great wrong. The Yisra'elites followed all the errors which Yarov'am committed, not abandoning that path until Yahweh removed Yisra'el from his

l

drave: read "drove"

presence, just as he had threatened through his servants the prophets. And so Yisra'el was exiled from its land to Ashshur, as is still true today.

**

The king of Ashshur brought people from Bavel, from Kuthah, from Awwa, and from Hamath and Sepharwayim and settled them in the towns of Shomeron in place of the Yisra'elites. They took possession of Shomeron and inhabited its towns.

Now when they first started living there, they didn't acknowledge Yahweh. So Yahweh sent lions to attack them, and the lions began killing them off one by one. When the king of Ashshur was told that the nations he had exiled and resettled in the towns of Shomeron didn't know the customs of the local god, and that as a result, the god had sent lions to attack them, and that the lions were presently killing them, as it wasn't possible that any of them could know the customs of the local god, he gave the following order: "Have one of the priests who was exiled from there go back there, so that they can continue living there. Let him teach them the customs of the local god."

So one of the priests who had been exiled from Shomeron went back and took up residence in Beyth-El, and he began teaching them how they should acknowledge Yahweh. Each people had been making statues of its own gods, placing the gods in the open-air shrines that the Shomeronians had made, each people doing so in the towns where they were living. The Bavelites made statues of the god Sukkoth Benoth, the Kuthians made statues of the god Nergal, the Hamathians made statues of the god Ashiyma, the Awwites made statues of the gods Nivhaz and Tartaq, and the Sepharwites made fire offerings of their children to Adrammelek and Anammelek [*the Sepharites' god*].

But then they began acknowledging Yahweh. They appointed shrine priests for themselves in every place they lived, and the priests made offerings for them in the shrines. They would regularly give honor to Yahweh, but they continued doing service to their gods, similar to the customs of the peoples that had been exiled from there.

(Even in the present day, they continue doing things in keeping with their former practices—none of them give honor to Yahweh, nor do any of them act in keeping with their laws and customs, nor in keeping with the Torah and the law code that Yahweh commanded the descendants of Ya'aqov [*whose name he changed to Yisra'el*], and with whom Yahweh made a treaty, commanding them as follows: "You mustn't acknowledge other gods, nor worship them, nor do service to them, nor make sacrifices to them. Rather, Yahweh—who took you

Sepharites' god: read "Sepharwites' gods"

out of Egypt with his mighty strength and his outstretched arm—is the one you must acknowledge. He is the one you must worship and make sacrifices to. The laws and the precepts—that is, the Torah and the law code that he wrote down for you—you must always be careful to observe, and you mustn't acknowledge other gods. You mustn't forget the treaty that I made with you, and you mustn't give honor to other gods. For if you do give honor to your god Yahweh, he shall surely rescue you from the clutches of your enemies.")

n   So they didn't really pay heed. Rather, they continued doing things in keeping with their former customs: these peoples would regularly acknowledge Yahweh, but at the same time, they would always give service to the statues of their gods. Moreover their descendants and the descendants of their descendants continued doing exactly as their ancestors did, as is still the case today.

**

P106 [2.18] In the third year of the reign of Hoshea Elahsson King of Yisra'el, Hizqiyyah Ahazsson ruled as king of Yehudah. He was twenty-five years old when he became king, and he ruled for twenty-nine years in Yerushalem. His mother's name was Aviy Zekaryahsdaughter.

a   He did what was pleasing to Yahweh, similar to all that his ances-
b c   tor Dawid had done: he removed the open-air shrines, he smashed the sacred pillars, he cut down the Asherah, and he bashed into
d   pieces the bronze snake that Mosheh had made. [*For up until that time the Yisra'elites would regularly make burnt offerings to it. They called it*
e   *'Bronzey.'*] He put his trust in Yahweh God of Yisra'el. After him, there hasn't been another like him among all Yehudah's kings [*including*
f   *those who were before him*].

    He held fast to Yahweh, never turning away from him and keeping
g   his commandments [*that is, those which Yahweh had given Mosheh*]. And so Yahweh would be with him—he would have success in whatever he
h   ventured to do: thus he rebelled against the king of Ashshur and didn't pay tribute to him, and he defeated the Philishtines as far as Azzah
i   and the entirety of its territory, from the smallest military outposts to the largest fortified towns.

**

P107 a   In the fourth year of King Hizqiyyahu's reign (this was the seventh year of the reign of Hoshea Elahsson King of Yisra'el), Shalman'eser King of Ashshur marched on Shomeron and laid siege to it. He cap-
b   tured it at the end of three years. In the sixth year of Hizqiyyah's reign

(this was the ninth year of Hoshea King of Yisra'el's reign), Shomeron was captured.

The king of Ashshur sent Yisra'el into exile to Ashshur, depositing them in Helah, in Havor on the Gozan River, and in the towns of Maday. [*Because they didn't obey their god Yahweh and because they violated the terms of his treaty—in fact, they neither gave heed to, nor did, anything that Mosheh Yahwehsservant had commanded.*]

**

In the fourteenth year of King Hizqiyyah's reign, Sanheriyv King of Ashshur embarked on a campaign against all of Yehudah's fortified towns and seized control of them. Hizqiyyah King of Yehudah sent a delegation to the king of Ashshur at Lakiysh with this message: "I have done wrong. Withdraw your forces. Whatever obligation you impose on me I shall pay."

The king of Ashshur then imposed on Hizqiyyah King of Yehudah three hundred *kikkar* of silver and thirty *kikkar* of gold. Hizqiyyah paid him all the silver that could be found in Yahweh's house and in the royal palace's storerooms. It was at that time that Hizqiyyah chopped up the doors to the great hall of Yahweh's house [*and the door pillars that Hizqiyyah King of Yehudah had plated with gold*] and gave them to the king of Ashshur.

**

The king of Ashshur sent his general darmay, a chef descadron, and a minister detat from Lakiysh, accompanied by a large and imposing army, to King Hizqiyyahu in Yerushalem. They proceeded to Yerushalem and, upon arriving, stood at the conduit to the Upper Pool, which is located on Fuller's Field Road. When they called for the king, Elyaqiym Hilqiyyahusson the Chamberlain came out to see them, along with Shevnah the Secretary and Yo'ah Asaphsson the Recorder.

"Please give this message to Hizqiyyahu," the minister detat said. "Thus says the greatest king, the king of Ashshur: 'What is this puny thing that you've put your trust in? The words that came from your lips spoke of military strategy and courage in battle. So now, who have you put your trust in that you've rebelled against me? Actually, it's obvious: you're hoping that Egypt—that pitiful crushed reed—will keep you standing upright. A reed that, when a man leans on it, pierces his hand. That's what Phar'oh King of Egypt is to all those who put their trust in him.' And if you all tell me that you've put

^g your trust in your god Yahweh, wasn't it his open-air shrines and his altars that Hizqiyyahu removed, telling Yehudah and Yerushalem that they must worship in front of that altar in Yerushalem? So now, please pledge your fealty to my lord the king of Ashshur. In return I'll give you two thousand horses, assuming you're able to put riders on them. How could you refuse even a single subaltern, the lowliest of my lord's officers? But you've put your trust in Egypt for chariots ^h and horses for your cavalry. Now do you think that my marching up against this place to lay it to waste isn't Yahweh's doing? Yahweh said to me, 'March forth against that country and lay waste to it.'"

"Please speak Aramaic to your servants," Elyaqiym Hilqiyyahusson, Shevnah, and Yo'ah said to the minister detat, "for we understand it. Don't speak Hebrew with us within earshot of the people on the town wall."

"Is it just for the benefit of your lord that my lord sent me to you to say these things?" the minister detat replied. "Isn't it also for the ⁱ benefit of the men sitting on the wall, who will soon be eating their own shit and drinking their own piss alongside you?"

shit: read "feces"
piss: read "urine"

Then the minister detat stood up and called out in a loud voice in Hebrew: "Hear what the greatest king, the king of Ashshur, says! Thus says the king: 'Don't let Hizqiyyahu deceive you.' For he can't save you from my lord's hand. Hizqiyyahu ought not make you put your trust in Yahweh by claiming that Yahweh will save you and that this town won't be delivered into the king of Ashshur's hands. Don't listen to Hizqiyyahu, for thus says the king of Ashshur: 'Make a peace ^j treaty with me and escape to me. Every one of you—eat your own grapes and figs, and drink water from your own wells until I come ^k back and take you to a land like yours—a land of grain and fresh wine, a land of cereals and vineyards, a land of fresh olive oil and honey. So live! You don't have to die. Don't listen to Hizqiyyahu, for he's deceiving you when he says that Yahweh's going to save you. Did any of the other nations' gods save their countries from the king of Ashshur? Where are Hamath's and Arpad's gods, and where are ^l Sepharwayim's and Hena's and Iwwa's gods? For they should have saved Shomeron from me! Of all the gods in the world, who are the ones that saved their countries from me, if you think that Yahweh could save Yerushalem from me?'"

The people remained silent and didn't say a word in answer, for there was an order from the king not to answer him. Elyaqiym Hilqiyyahusson the Chamberlain, Shevna the Secretary, and Yo'ah ^m Asaphsson the Recorder—each having ripped his clothes to show his distress—went to see Hizqiyyahu and reported to him what the minister detat had said.

When King Hizqiyyahu heard the report, he too ripped his clothes [2.19] in distress; then he covered himself in sackcloth and went to Yahweh's house. He sent Elyaqiym the Chamberlain, Shevna the Secretary, and the elders of the priests—all of whom had covered themselves in sackcloth—to Yesha'yahu the Prophet Amotzsson.

"Here's Hizqiyyahu's message," they said to him. " 'Today is a distressful, chastising, and hateful day, for fetuses are now crowning, but there's no strength to give birth. Perhaps your god Yahweh will take note of everything the minister detat said, who was sent by his lord the king of Ashshur to insult the living God, and then your god Yahweh will rebuke the words that he heard, should you raise up a prayer on behalf of the faithful ones who are still here.' "

King Hizqiyyahu's officials went to see Yesha'yahu. "Here's what you should say to your lord," Yesha'yahu told them. " 'Thus says Yahweh: 'Don't be afraid of the things you heard, which the king of Ashshur's lackeys said to taunt me. Be assured, I'm going to make him change his plans—he'll hear a report that will prompt him to return to his country, and then I shall cause him to die a violent death in his own country.' ' "

When the minister detat returned, he found the king of Ashshur as he was assailing Livnah, for he had heard that the army had moved on from Lakiysh. But then the king heard a report about Tirhaqah King of Kush, that he had marched out to go to war with him. So he again sent envoys to Hizqiyyahu, instructing them as follows: "This is what you should say to Hizqiyyahu King of Yehudah: 'Don't let your god whom you're pinning your hopes on deceive you when he tells you that Yerushelem won't be delivered into the king of Ashshur's hands. You're certainly aware of what the kings of Ashshur have done to every country they've fought, annihilating them completely. Yet you think somehow you're going to slip away? Did the gods of the nations destroyed by my ancestors save their peoples? Either Gozan or Haran, or Retzeph, or the Edenites in Telassar? Where is the king of Hamath or the king of Arpad now? Where is any king of Sepharwayim City, or Hena, or Iwwah?' "

Hizqiyyahu took the letters from the envoys and read them. Then he went up to Yahweh's house and spread them out in front of Yahweh.

**

Hizqiyyahu prayed in front of Yahweh. "Yahweh God of Yisra'el, Who Sits Astride the Winged Sphinxes," he said, "you alone are God for all the world's kingdoms. You are the one who made the skies and the earth. Bend your ears, Yahweh, and hear! Open your eyes, Yahweh,

	and see! Hear Sanheriyv's words, which he sent to insult the living God. Indeed, Yahweh, the kings of Ashshur have laid waste to nations and their lands, and they incinerated those nations' gods. For they weren't gods—rather, they were the handiwork of humans, made of wood and stone, and so they were destroyed. So now, Yahweh our god, I beg you, save us from him—then all the world's kingdoms shall know that you alone, Yahweh, are God."
e	
f	

P110,1 Yesha'yahu Amotzsson sent this message to Hizqiyyahu: "Thus says Yahweh God of Yisra'el: 'I have heard what you prayed to me in regard to Sanheriv King of Ashshur.' Here is what Yahweh said about him: 'Tziyyon's lovely daughter snubs you, mocks you even—yes, Yerushalem's girl wags her head at you behind your back!' and 'Who did you insult, who did you taunt? Who did you raise your voice against, who did you eye with impudence? None other than the Holy One of Yisra'el! You insulted the Lord through your envoys, boasting that you climbed high into the mountains with your chariot of chariotry, into the remotest parts of Levanon, cutting down its tallest cedars, its finest cypresses, and making your way to the most distant campsites in its abundant forests. Boasting that you bored wells and drank waters in foreign lands, boasting that you dried up all Egypt's watercourses with just the soles of your feet. Didn't you hear in that faraway land where you live what I did in ancient times, the thing I devised? When I brought it about, it made fortified cities crash into ruin heaps, their feeble inhabitants broken and humiliated—they were nothing more than vegetation in the fields, or shoots of green grass, or rooftop plantings, that had been blighted before ripening. I know everything you do: when you sit down, when you go outside, when you come in—and also how you get worked up over me. Because you get so worked up over me, because reports of your arrogance have come to me, I shall set a nose band around your snout and a bridle bit in your mouth, and I shall lead you back the way you came.'

a *b*

c *d*

e *chariot of*: read "vast"

f
g

h

i
j

k

Read "of Armies" in the blank space

"And here's the sign by which you'll know that it's happening: 'The first year volunteer plants will be eaten, and in the second year the volunteers of volunteers—then in the third year, sow and harvest, plant vineyards and eat their produce. The faithful ones remaining in the nation of Yehudah shall once again put down roots below ground, and bear fruit above it.' For, 'A steadfast remnant shall come forth from Yerushalem—yes, a faithful band of survivors emerge from Mount Tziyyon!' The zeal of Yahweh　　　　　shall make this happen.

P110,2 *a* *b* "Therefore, thus says Yahweh to the king of Ashshur: 'This town won't be entered. Arrows won't be fired into it, nor shields confront it, nor siegeworks be thrown up against it. The road anybody arrives by is the road he'll return on. This town won't be entered'—oracle of Yahweh. 'I will shield this town and rescue it, for my own sake as well as for the sake of my servant Dawid.'"

That very night Yahweh's emissary ventured out and killed one hundred and eighty-five thousand men in Ashshur's camp. When they got up in the morning, they were stunned to see all of them lying on the ground, dead corpses.

So Sanheriyv King of Ashshur decamped and left, returning home and staying put in Niyneweh. And it so happened that when he was worshipping in the temple of his god Nisrok,   Adrammelek and Sar'etzer attacked him and stabbed him to death. They escaped to the Ararat region, and his son Esar-Haddon became king in his place.

Read "his sons" in the blank space f

**

Around that time, Hizqiyyahu fell mortally ill, and Yesha'yahu Amotzs-son the Prophet went to see him. "Thus says Yahweh," he said to him. "'Get your affairs in order, for you're going to die. You won't survive this illness.'"

Turning his face to the wall, he prayed to Yahweh. "Alas, Yahweh! Please, I beg you, remember how I have lived my entire life in your presence with honesty and integrity, doing things that were pleasing to you!" Then Hizqiyyahu began sobbing very loudly.

—

Yesha'yahu hadn't even exited the middle town when an oracle of Yahweh came to him. "Go back," he said, "and say this to Hizqiyyahu, the supreme leader of my people: 'Thus says Yahweh, god of your ancestor Dawid: 'I have heard your prayer and I've seen your tears. Rest assured, I'm going to cure you. Two days from now, you should go up to Yahweh's house. I shall add fifteen years to your life, and I shall save you—and this town also—from the hands of the king of Ashshur. I'm going to shield this town, for my own sake as well as for the sake of my servant Dawid.'''"

town: read "courtyard"

"Get a fig-cake," Yesha'yahu said. They got a fig-cake and placed it on the infected area, and Hizqiyyahu recovered.

"What proof is there that Yahweh's going to cure me," he asked Yesha'yahu, "so that two days from now I can go up to Yahweh's house?"

"This is how Yahweh will prove to you that he's going to do what he said he would," answered Yesha'yahu. "Ten steps are now in shadow. If the shadow leaves the steps, that's your proof."

"It's too easy for a shadow to move across ten steps," objected

Hizqiyyahu. "That's not proof of anything. Proof would be if the shadow moved ten steps backwards."

So Yesha'yahu the Prophet called out to Yahweh, and he then made the shadow on the steps that had crept down Ahaz's Stairs move backwards ten steps.

**

P112 a At that time, Berodak Bal'adan Bal'adansson King of Bavel sent letters and a gift to Hizqiyyahu, for he had heard that Hizqiyyahu was ill.

b When Hizqiyyahu heard what was written on them, he showed the envoys his entire treasure-house—including the silver, the gold, the spices, and the fine oil there—and his armory and everything that was kept in his storerooms. There wasn't a thing in his palace or in any of his royal facilities that Hizqiyyahu didn't show them.

Yesha'yahu the Prophet went to see King Hizqiyyahu. "What did those men say," he asked, "and where are they coming from to see you?"

"They've come from a far away country," Hizqiyyahu said. "From Bavel."

"What did they see in your palace?"

"They saw everything in my palace," Hizqiyyahu replied. "There wasn't anything that I didn't show them in my storerooms."

c "Hear Yahweh's oracle," Yesha'yahu said. " 'Soon the days will come when everything in your palace and everything that your ancestors accumulated down to the present day will be carried off to Bavel. Not a single thing will remain.' So says Yahweh. 'And some of your descendants—those who are your offspring, whom you have fathered—will be taken, and they will serve as officials in the king of Bavel's palace.' "

d "Yahweh's oracle that you spoke to me is a good one," Hizqiyyahu
e said to Yesha'yahu. Then he added, "Isn't it, so long as there'll be peace and security during my lifetime?"

f The rest of Hizqiyyahu's acts and all his valorous deeds—how he built the pool and the watercourse, and how he supplied the town with water—are recorded in the book *The Chronicles of the Kings of Yehudah*. Hizqiyyahu lay down in death with his ancestors, and his son Menashsheh became king in his place.

**

P113 [2.21] a Menashsheh was twelve years old when he became king, and he ruled in Yerushalem for fifty-five years. His mother's name was Hephtziy-
b c Vah. He did things that were displeasing to Yahweh [*similar to the*

abominable practices of the nations that Yahweh drove out of the Yisra'elites' path]: he rebuilt the open-air shrines that his father Hizqiyyahu had destroyed; he erected altars to the Ba'al and made an Asherah (just as Ah'av King of Yisra'el did); he worshipped the stars in the sky and did service to them [*He was always building altars in Yahweh's house, about which Yahweh said, "Yerushalem is the place that I shall claim as my very own."*]; and he built altars to the stars in the sky in the two courtyards of Yahweh's house. [*He would regularly make his son pass through fire, and he was always practicing soothsaying and divination, as well as consulting ghosts and spirits.*] He went to great lengths to do things that displeased Yahweh, thus provoking his rage. He placed the statue of the Asherah that he had made in Yahweh's house—the place about which Yahweh said to Dawid and Dawid's son Shelomo, "This house and Yerushalem, which I have chosen out all the tribes of Yisra'el, are the places I shall claim as my own for all time. [*I shall no longer make Yisra'el wander about on foot, away from the land that I gave their ancestors—however, on the condition that they take care to do exactly what I have commanded them and in keeping with the entirety of the Torah that my servant Mosheh commanded them." But they didn't heed Yahweh's words—Menashsheh led them astray, causing them to do things worse than the nations which Yahweh obliterated from the Yisra'elites' path.*]

"Because Menashsheh King of Yehudah has done these abominable things, doing things more despicable than anything that the Amorites did before his time," Yahweh said through his servants the prophets, "and because he also caused Yehudah to err with his useless gods…

—

"…therefore, thus says Yahweh God of Yisra'el: 'Know that I'm going to bring disaster on Yerushalem and on Yehudah—something that all those who hear about it will be astounded by. I will measure Yerushalem with the plumb line used on Shomeron, yes with the plumb bob used on Ah'av's royal line. Then I will wipe Yerushalem clean just like a dish is wiped clean [*it is wiped and then flipped over*]. I shall abandon those who remain in my land and deliver them into their enemies' hands—they'll be nothing more than spoils and plunder for their enemies. [*Because they did what was displeasing to me, and because they were constantly provoking my anger, from the time their ancestors left Egypt down to the present day.*]"

In addition, Menashsheh killed a great many innocent people, literally filling Yerushalem from end to end with their corpses, completely separate from his wrongdoing by which he caused Yehudah to err and to do what was displeasing to Yahweh.

The rest of Menashsheh's acts and everything he did—including the wrongdoing that he committed—are recorded in the book *The*

P113,1 a
all those who hear: read "anyone who hears"

      Chronicles of the Kings of Yehudah. Menashsheh lay down in death with
  f his ancestors. He was buried in a garden in his palace, in Uzza's
      Garden, and his son Amon became king in his place.

**

P114 a Amon was twenty-two years old when he became king, and he ruled in Yerushalem for two years. His mother's name was Meshullemeth Harutzsdaughter of Yatevah. He did what was displeasing to Yahweh, just as his father Menashsheh had done: he maintained all the practices that his father had followed, doing service to and worshipping the useless gods that his father had done service to. He abandoned his ancestors' god Yahweh and didn't follow Yahweh's ways.

      Amon's officials conspired against him and assassinated the king in his palace. But the citizenry killed all those who had conspired against King Amon, and they made his son Yoshiyyahu king in his place.

      The rest of the things that Amon accomplished are recorded in the
  b book *The Chronicles of the Kings of Yehudah.* He was buried in his grave
  c in Uzza's Garden, and his son Yoshiyyahu ruled as king in his place.

**

P115 [2.22] a Yoshiyyahu was eight years old when he became king, and he ruled
    b in Yerushalem for thirty-one years. His mother's name was Yediydah Adayahsdaughter of Batzeqath. He did what was pleasing to Yahweh— he followed wholly in the footsteps of his ancestor Dawid and didn't deviate from them in any way.

**

P116 a In the eighteenth year of King Yoshiyyahu's reign, the king sent Shaphan Atzalyahusson Meshullamsson the Secretary to Yahweh's house. "Go to Hilqiyyahu the Chief Priest," he said, "so that a count can be made of the silver that has been brought to Yahweh's house, which the door-keepers have collected from the people. They should

give i: read "give it" b give i to the workmen hired to oversee the work on Yahweh's house, so that they can pay the workmen who are now in Yahweh's house repairing the cracks in the structure—the carpenters, the construction men, and the stonemasons—and also to purchase wood and blocks of cut stone for repairing the structure. However, there's really no need for the silver entrusted to the overseers to be counted out in their presence, for they are men who act honestly."

"I found the Torah scroll in Yahweh's house," Hilqiyyahu the Chief Priest said to Shaphan the Secretary. Hilqiyyah gave the scroll to Shaphan, who then read it.

Shaphan the Secretary went to see the king and reported back to him that they had dumped out the silver found in Yahweh's house and entrusted it to the workmen hired to oversee the repairs on the house. "Furthermore," Shaphan the Secretary informed the king, "Hilqiyyah the Priest gave me a scroll." He then read the scroll aloud to the king.

When the king heard the words contained in the Torah scroll, he grew distressed and tore his clothes. The king charged Hilqiyyah the Priest, Ahiyqam Shaphansson, Akbor Miykayahsson, Shaphan the Secretary, and Asayah the Royal Officer with the following order: "Go seek an oracle from Yahweh on behalf of me, on behalf of the people, and on behalf of all Yehudah in regard to the things contained in this scroll that's been found. Indeed, Yahweh's anger that now burns against us must be very great on account of the fact that our ancestors didn't heed the words contained in this scroll by acting in accord with all the obligations written down for us."

So Hilqiyyahu the Priest, Ahiyqam, Akbor, Shaphan, and Asayah went to see Huldah the Prophetess Shallumswife (that is, the wife of Shallum Tiqwahsson Harhasson Chief of the Vestry). At the time, she was living in District Two in Yerushalem. They spoke with her, and she replied, "Thus says Yahweh God of Yisra'el: 'Say this to the man who sent you to me: 'Thus says Yahweh: 'Know that I'm going to bring disaster to this place, and upon its citizens—everything contained in the scroll that the king of Yehudah read—because they have abandoned me, making offerings by fire to other gods in order to provoke me to anger with all the statues they made of those gods. My anger has now been sparked against this place, and it won't be extinguished.''"

"And to the king of Yehudah who sent you to seek an oracle from Yahweh, here is what you should say to him: 'Thus says Yahweh God of Yisra'el: 'In regards to the things that you have heard, because there is humility in your heart and because you humbled yourself before Yahweh when you heard what I said regarding this place and regarding its citizens—that they would become an object of horror and a curse—and because you tore your clothing in distress and wept before me, and furthermore because I myself heard you'—oracle of Yahweh—'therefore, know that when I have you join your ancestors, you shall go peacefully to join them in your graves and your eyes won't see any of the disastrous things that I'm going to bring down on this place.'''"

After they reported back to the king, the king sent out messengers, [2.23] and all of Yerushalem's and Yehudah's elders gathered to meet him. The king went up to Yahweh's house, accompanied by all the people of Yehudah, by all Yerushalem's citizens, and by the priests and the prophets—everyone, from the lowliest to the most important—and then he read out to them everything contained in the treaty scroll that had been found in Yahweh's house. The king stood beside the pillar and agreed to the treaty in Yahweh's presence—to follow Yahweh and to keep his commandments, his treaty's obligations, and his laws with his whole heart and his entire being—thus putting into effect the treaty's stipulations that were written on that scroll. And so the entire people became subject to the treaty.

The king ordered Hilqiyyahu the Chief Priest, the senior-ranking priests, and the door-keepers to bring out from the great hall of Yahweh's house all the items that had been fashioned for the Ba'al, for the Asherah, and for all the stars in the sky. He burned those things in the Qidron Fields outside Yerushalem, and then he disposed of their ashes in Beyth-El.

He put an end to the *komer*-priests whom the kings of Yehudah had appointed to make burnt offerings in the open-air shrines in Yehudah's towns and the area around Yerushalem; he also put an end to those who made burnt offerings to the Ba'al, to the sun god Shemesh, to the moon god Yareah, to the constellations, and to all the stars in the sky.

He removed the Asherah from Yahweh's house and took it to the Wadi Qidron outside Yerushalem. He burned it there in the wadi, pulverizing it into fine ash and scattering its ashes on the commoners' graveyard. He demolished the *qadeshim*-structures located on the grounds of Yahweh's house, where women wove household shrines for the Asherah.

He removed all the priests from Yehudah's towns, and he defiled the open-air shrines where priests from all over—from Geva to Be'er Sheva—made burnt offerings. Then he knocked down the gate shrines that were in front of the Town Chief Yehoshua Gate, which were on the left side as one enters the town gate. [*However, the shrine priests would never go up to Yahweh's altar in Yerushalem except when they ate unleavened bread among their kinsmen.*] He defiled the Topheth located in Hinnomssons' Valley in order to prevent people from making fire offerings of their sons and daughters to Molek. He put an end to the horses that the kings of Yehudah had dedicated to the sun god Shemesh, so that they would no longer enter the grounds of Yahweh's house to go to Nathan-Melek the Royal Official's room in the colonnade, and he also incinerated the sun god Shemesh's chariots.

At the same time, the king demolished the altars on the roof [*that is, the roof of Ahaz's Upper Chamber*] that the kings of Yehudah had made, and also the altars that Menashsheh had made in the two courtyards on the grounds of Yahweh's house. He then hurried from there and scattered their ashes in the Wadi Qidron.

The king defiled the open-air shrines east of Yerushalem that were located south of "Mount Destruction" and that Shelomo King of Yisra'el had built for the Tzidonians' detestable Ashtoreth, for Mo'av's detestable Kemosh, and for the Ammonites' abhorrent Milkom. He smashed their sacred pillars and cut down their Asherah posts, and filled their sites with human remains.

In addition, the altar that was located in Beyth-El (that is, the open-air shrine that Yarov'am Nevatsson who caused Yisra'el to do wrong made)—that altar too and the shrine platform he demolished. He burned the platform until it had become fine ash and he incinerated its Asherah post. Next, having noticed the graves that were there on the mountain, Yoshiyyahu sent men to fetch the bones from the graves and then he defiled the altar by burning the bones on it. This was in fulfillment of the oracle of Yahweh that the holy man had proclaimed (who had proclaimed these things specifically).

"What's this grave marker that I'm looking at?" he asked.

"The grave is the holy man who came from Yehudah," the townspeople answered him. "He proclaimed the exact things that you did on the altar here in Beyth-El."

"Leave him alone," he said. "No one should disturb his remains." And so they spared his remains, along with the remains of the prophet who had come from Shomeron.

In addition, at this time Yoshiyyahu forced the abandonment of the open-air shrines that were in Shomeron's towns and that the kings of Yisra'el had constructed to provoke Yahweh's anger, doing to them the exact same things that he had done in Beyth-El. He slaughtered all the priests who were attached to the open-air shrines there on the shrines' altars and burned human remains on them. Then he returned to Yerushalem.

"Observe the passover in honor of your god Yahweh," the king ordered the people, "in keeping with what is written in this treaty scroll." For nothing like that passover rite had been observed since the days of the champions who championed Yisra'el—nor at any time during the days of the kings of Yisra'el and the kings of Yehudah. Not until the eighteenth year of the reign of King Yoshiyyahu was this passover rite observed in Yahweh's honor in Yerushalem.

In addition, at this time Yoshiyyahu eradicated the practice of consulting ghosts and spirits of the dead and the practice of consulting *teraphim* and divine figurines—all the detestable objects that were commonly seen in Yehudah and in Yerushalem. This was in order ao to carry out the stipulations of the Torah that were recorded in the document that Hilqiyyahu the Priest found in Yahweh's house.

ap Never before was there a king like him who returned to Yahweh with all his heart, with all his strength, and with his entire being, in keeping with Mosheh's Torah. And after his time likewise, never was there anyone like him.

aq However, Yahweh didn't relent from his great burning anger—the anger that burned against Yehudah because of all the outrageous things that Menashsheh did to provoke his anger. "I'm going to remove Yehudah from my presence also," thought Yahweh, "just as I removed Yisra'el, and I'm going to reject this town that I chose,

ar Yerushalem, and I'm going to reject the house that I said would be my very own."

as The rest of Yoshiyyahu's acts and all that he did are recorded in the book *The Chronicles of the Kings of Yehudah*.

at During his reign, Phar'oh Neko King of Egypt campaigned against the king of Ashshur near the Perath River. King Yoshiyyahu went to meet him, and when Phar'oh Neko saw him, he had him killed in Megiddo. His officials carried him away from Megiddo in his chariot, dead, and brought him to Yerushalem. After he was buried in his tomb, the country's citizens took Yeho'ahaz Yoshiyyahusson and anointed him, making him king in place of his father.

**

P117 Yeho'ahaz was twenty-three years old when he became king, and he ruled as king in Yerushalem for three months. His mother's name

a was Hemutal Yirmayahusdaughter of Livnah. He did what was displeasing to Yahweh, similar to all that his ancestors had done. Phar'oh

b Neko imprisoned him in Rivlah in the district of Hamath, deposing
when: read "from"
c him when serving as king in Yerushalem. He imposed a levy on the country of one hundred *kikkar* of silver and one *kikkar* of gold.

d Phar'oh Neko then made Elyaqiym Yoshiyyahusson king in place of his father Yoshiyyahu, and he changed his name to Yehoyaqiym.

e At that time, Yeho'ahaz was taken away—he went to Egypt, where he died.

Yehoyaqiym did pay the levy of the silver and gold to Phar'oh.

f However, he had to impose a tax on the land in order to pay the money demanded by Phar'oh, exacting silver and gold from the citizenry at

g each man's usual assessed rate in order to pay Phar'oh Neko.

—

P117,1 Yehoyaqiym was twenty-five years old when he became king, and he ruled as king in Yerushalem for eleven years. His mother's name was

Zeviydah Pedayahsdaughter of Rumah. He did what was displeasing to Yahweh, similar to all that his ancestors had done.

During his reign, Nevukadnetztzar King of Bavel invaded. Yehoyaqiym was his vassal for three years, but then he changed his mind and rebelled against him. Yahweh sent marauders from Kasdiym, from Aram, Mo'av, and from the Ammonites, sending them into Yehudah to destroy it, in keeping with the oracles that Yahweh had spoken through his servants the prophets. Indeed, it was at Yahweh's command that Yehudah suffered these attacks, in order to remove it from his presence on account of Menashsheh's wrongdoing, as was fitting for everything that he did (including also the innocent blood that he shed and the fact that he filled Yerushalem with the blood of the innocent—crimes Yahweh was unwilling to forgive).

The rest of Yehoyaqiym's acts and all that he did are recorded in the book *The Chronicles of the Kings of Yehudah*. Yehoyaqiym lay down in death with his ancestors, and his son Yehoyakiyn became king in his place.

The king of Egypt didn't leave his land on a campaign again, for the king of Bavel had taken control of the lands from Egypt Wadi to the Perath River—all of which had previously belonged to the king of Egypt.

**

Yehoyakiyn was eighteen years old when he became king, and he ruled as king in Yerushalem for three months. His mother's name was Nehushta Elnathansdaughter of Yerushalem. He did what was displeasing to Yahweh, similar to all the things that his father had done.

At that time, Nevukadnetztzar King of Bavel's officers marched on Yerushalem and the town entered a state of siege. Nevukadnetztzar King of Bavel came to the town while his officers were besieging it. Yehoyakiyn King of Yehudah went out to meet the king of Bavel, accompanied by his mother, his personal staff, his military officers, and his high government officials. And so the king of Bavel in the eighth year of his reign arrested Yehoyakiyn.

He then brought out from Yerushalem everything in the storerooms on the grounds of Yahweh's house and in the storerooms of the royal palace. He cut into pieces all the gold items that Shelomo King of Yisra'el had made in the great hall of Yahweh's house, just as Yahweh had said would happen. He sent all of Yerushalem into exile—all its leaders and all its soldiers, ten thousand exiles total, as well as all its skilled workers and smiths. No one remained except

Zeviydah: read "Zevudah" a

[2.24] b

c

d
e

f

g

h

P118

a

b

c

d
e

f

leoding: read "leading"	the poorest of the citizenry. He sent Yehoyakiyn into exile in Bavel; likewise, he made the king's mother, the king's wives, his high officials, and the country's leoding citizens leave Yerushalem and go into exile in Bavel. So too all the capable men (seven thousand total) and the skilled workers and the smiths (one thousand total) [*all of them valiant warriors*]—the king of Bavel made them go into exile in Bavel. To replace Yehoyakiyn, the king of Bavel installed Yehoyakiyn's uncle Mattanyah as king; he then changed his name to Tzidqiyyahu.
g	

**

P119 a	Tzidqiyyahu was twenty-one years old when he became king, and he ruled as king in Yerushalem for eleven years. His mother's name was Hemiytal Yirmayahusdaughter of Livnah. He did what was displeasing to Yahweh, similar to all that Yehoyaqiym had done, for it was on account of Yahweh's anger that things had turned against Yerushalem and Yehudah, until he had cast them from his presence.
Hemiytal: read "Hemutal"	
b c	

And so Tzidqiyyahu rebelled against the king of Bavel…

―――

P119,1 [2.25]	In the ninth year of his reign, on the tenth day of the tenth month, Nevukadnetztzar King of Bavel along with his entire army arrived to attack Yerushalem. After establishing a position against the town, they built siege-works threatening the town on all sides. The town remained in a state of siege until the eleventh year of King Tzidqiyyahu's reign. By the ninth day of the month, the famine in town had become severe, and there was no food for the citizens. When the town's defenses were breached, all Yerushalem's soldiers by night down the gate road that runs between the double wall next to the royal garden as the Kasdians attacked the town on all sides.
a	
b	
c	
d	

e	The king made his way east toward the desert steppes. The Kasdians' army went in pursuit and caught up with him in the steppe lands around Yereho, by which time his entire army had scattered and abandoned him. After they seized the king, they took him to the king of Bavel at Rivlah, where they rendered judgement against him. They slaughtered Tzidqiyyahu's children before his eyes and then blinded him. Afterwards he was bound with bronze shackles and taken to Bavel.
f	
g	

―――

P119,2 a	On the seventh day of the fifth month—that is, the nineteenth year of the reign of King Nevukadnetztzar King of Bavel—Nevuzar'adan the Captain of the Royal Guard [*an officer of the king of Bavel*] entered Yerushalem. He burned down Yahweh's house and the royal palace; he also burned down all the houses in Yerushalem and all the large

buildings. The Kasdian army that was with the captain of the royal guard demolished Yerushalem's walls on all sides. At the same time, the rest of the people who were still in the town—the defectors who had defected to the king [*that is, the king of Bavel*] as well as all those from the general mass of citizens who remained—Nevuzar'adan the Captain of the Royal Guard sent into exile. (However, the captain of the royal guard let some of the poor among the populace stay to work in the vineyards and the fields.)

As for the bronze pillars that were on the grounds of Yahweh's house—and also the bronze stands and the bronze Sea that were on the grounds—the Kasdians broke them into pieces and took the bronze from them to Bavel. The pots and the shovels and the snuffers and the pans—all the bronze implements that were used in service of the cult—were taken as well. At the same time, the captain of the royal guard took the fire-pans and the basins, some of which were gold and some of which were silver. [*The two pillars, the one Sea, and the stands that Shelomo made for Yahweh's house: the weight of the bronze in these items is unknown. Each pillar was eighteen cubits in height; moreover, the capital on each was bronze and was three cubit in height. Plus the netting and pomegranates surrounding both capitals—which had identical netting—were made entirely of bronze.*]

cubit: read "cubits"

The captain of the royal guard took Serayah the Head Priest, Tzephanyahu the Deputy Priest, and the three door-keepers; from town he took one senior officer who had been given oversight of the soldiers, five of the king's personal attendants who were found in town, the secretary [*the army general*] responsible for marshalling the citizenry, and sixty men from the citizenry who were found in town. Nevuzar'adan the Captain of the Royal Guard took these men and brought them to the king of Bavel at Rivlah. The king of Bavel then slaughtered them, putting them to death in Rivlah in the district of Hamath. And so Yehudah was exiled from its land.

As for the people who remained in Yehudah (those whom Nevukadnetztzar King of Bavel had left behind), he appointed Gedalyahu Ahiyqamsson Shaphansson as their overseer. When the leaders of the army as well as some other men heard that the king of Bavel had appointed Gedalyahu overseer, they went to Mitzpah to see him; these included Yishma'el Nathanyahsson, Yohanan Qareahsson, Serayah Tanhumethsson the Netophathite, and Ya'azanyahu Ma'akathitesson, as well as their followers.

"Don't fear the Kasdian officials," Gedalyahu swore to them and their men. "Stay here in the land and serve the king of Bavel, and it will go well for you."

But then in the seventh month, Yishma'el Nathanyahsson Eliyshamasson who was of royal descent came with ten men and attacked Gedalyahu. He died, as did the Yehudites and the Kasdians who were with him in Mitzpah. Immediately after that, all the people—from the least to the most important—along with the leaders of the army went to Egypt, for they feared the Kasdians.

—

In the thirty-seventh year of Yehoyakiyn King of Yehudah's exile, on the twenty-seventh day of the twelfth month, Ewiyl Merodak King of Bavel in the first year of his reign showed favor to Yehoyakiyn King of Yehudah and released him from prison. He spoke agreeably with him, and he put him in a situation preferable to that of the other kings who were with him in Bavel. And so he changed out of his prison garb, and for the remainder of his life, he took his daily meals in the king's presence. As for his maintenance, a daily maintenance was given to him by the king each and every day, for his entire life.

Total sentences in the book:
One thousand five hundred and thirty-six

Notes and comments

This book, like the others I have written, is first and foremost a translation. Because I am employed outside the academy and have access only to resources freely available on the internet, I have consulted few sources apart from the Masoretic text and online versions of the standard Hebrew-English lexicon and Hebrew grammar. As I discuss in my introductory note, I have focused principally on how best to bring the prose of the authors of Kings over into English, striving to produce a fluent translation that is also faithful to the meaning of the Hebrew. My approach here is similar to that taken in my other translations. As with those translations, my intention was not to write a traditional biblical commentary, nor a work of literary or historical criticism. Because my personal circumstances practically forced me to engage with the text solely on my own, I did not consult other translations or make use of commentaries in writing this translation, and I relied on only a small number of academic studies and scholarly papers in developing my understanding of the book and its background.

As with the notes in my other translations, I focus many of my comments below on passages that will give readers some understanding of how I employed "functional equivalence" in crafting this translation and how it departs from a more literal rendering of the text. Although biblical scholars might find such notes of little interest, the notes can help those who don't know Hebrew understand what is involved in producing a translation that is functionally equivalent to the source text. In addition, I frequently use the notes to comment on my translation choices when dealing with unusual, idiomatic, or difficult prose. While my comments on these topics are relatively extensive, I have not aimed to be comprehensive and have not necessarily commented on every idiomatic, unusual or difficult passage. Finally, because the act of translation often required me to consider the composition history of Kings—and because there is such scholarly interest in this topic—I comment extensively in the notes on places where I see indications of different authors and different compositional layers. As I discuss in my essay at the end of the book, my comments on composition history are, by necessity, speculative; their value lies primarily in helping the reader appreciate the complexities in the text and in presenting a plausible scenario that explains those complexities.

Because of the sheer diversity of language and prose styles employed by the authors of Kings, the book can be quite challenging for the translator. As I discuss in the notes, the authors of the text drew from a wide range of sources, including official government records, administrative documents, and folk legends about famous holy men, and in many cases they appear to quote these documents verbatim. The source documents themselves seem to exhibit dialectical differences, and the literary skill of the authors of both the source documents and the many authors who contributed to Kings over the centuries was of widely varying quality. It was not always possible to represent these differences in a functionally equivalent translation in English, and in many cases the meaning of the terms and idioms used by the authors is unclear.

Complicating matters is that there is a great deal of uncertainty about the "original" text of Kings, as there are significant differences between the Masoretic text, the Septuagint, and the fragments of Kings found at Qumran. I do not attempt in my work to reconstruct an original text; rather, I have limited my translation to the Masoretic text, even when it is obviously imperfect. Where there do appear to be errors, I typically reflect the error in my translation and I do not attempt to correct the Hebrew that has been transmitted to us. (And as discussed in my introductory note, I also show the Masoretes' corrections to the errors that they perceived in the text.) Consequently, there is no place in this translation where I have intentionally emended the Masoretic consonantal text.

As mentioned in the notes to my previous translations, I did not consult the Biblia Hebraica Stuttgartensia in my translation work, but instead relied on the excellent iPhone app Tanakh for All as my main source for the Masoretic text. In general, I find the Tanakh for All app superior for the purposes of translation, as the line lengths are similar to those in the Aleppo Codex and the Leningrad Codex, and the *parashot petuhot* are prominently marked in the text. My translation process was to translate an individual *parashah* from Tanakh for All and then to read that *parashah* in the Aleppo Codex (or in the Leningrad Codex for the material missing from the Aleppo Codex) and adjust the translation as needed. In my translation work, I relied on the excellent photographic copies of the Aleppo Codex and Leningrad Codex that can be found at the Internet Archive. Because I have generally found the Aleppo Codex superior to the Leningrad Codex, the placement of the *parashot* in my translation follow the former and not the latter.

In the notes and comments, I frequently refer to specific lines in the Aleppo Codex and the Leningrad Codex. The citation system that I use is the codex abbreviation "A" or "L" followed by the leaf number, an indication of the recto or verso side, and then the column and line numbers. For example, A77 r.2.24 indicates line 24 of the second column on the recto of leaf 77 in the Aleppo Codex, and L190 v.3.4 indicates line 4 of the third column on the verso of leaf 190 in the Leningrad Codex.

The lexicon and grammar that I used were the 1906 edition of Wilhelm Gesenius' *Hebrew and English Lexicon of the Old Testament*, as edited and updated by Francis Brown, S.R. Driver, and Charles Briggs and the 2nd English edition of *Gesenius' Hebrew Grammar*, as edited and enlarged by E. Kautsch and A.E. Cowley (abbreviated below, respectively, as BDB and GKC).

/https://archive.org/details/hebrewenglishlex00browuoft/page/ii

/https://archive.org/details/geseniushebrewgr00geseuoft/page/n4

**

1a WHEN KING DAWID WAS OLD AND ADVANCED IN YEARS...: The book of Kings begins with the story of how Shelomo succeeded Dawid to the throne. The story, which is found in P1 - P7,2, assumes the events of Dawid's reign that are narrated in Sam P82,2 - P101,1. Most scholars view these two blocks of material—Kgs P1 - P7,2 and Sam P82,2 - P101,1—as a unified composition by a single author, and they commonly refer to this work as the "succession narrative."

Notes to P1

The author of the succession narrative is considered by many scholars to be one of the great literary artists of the ancient Near East, if not the entire ancient world. As a stylist of ancient Hebrew prose, he is unequalled by anyone except the author of the Joseph narrative in Genesis. And—in my opinion—he is superior to the latter with respect to his skill in characterization, his understanding of human psychology, and his ability to portray complex motivations and emotions.

There is some debate among scholars regarding where the succession narrative fits in the composition history of Samuel and Kings. The majority of scholars and commentators believe it was part of the earliest version of the two books. However, the view of kingship expressed in the succession narrative is not consistent with the view of kingship that we see in the early layer of Kings and in the early material about Dawid's reign in Samuel. In particular, the author of the succession narrative views the Dawidic promise as conditional, which is completely at odds with the unconditional Dawidic promise as expressed in traditional Judean royal ideology, in the long speech stating the Dawidic promise in Sam P80,2 (part of the early layer of Samuel), and in the early layer of Kings. For this reason, I believe that the succession narrative was not part of the earliest version of Kings. Rather, I understand it as a work of the Persian period that was most likely composed in the early fifth century BCE and that was authorized by the leadership of Yahweh's cult in Yerushalem.[1] I believe this composition had two primary purposes. First, it connected the narrative of Kings with that of Samuel. (Previously the two books were not truly connected—

---

1   John Van Seters is the most noteworthy proponent of a late date of the succession narrative; his arguments for this can be found in his works *In Search of History: Historiography in the Ancient World and the Origins of Biblical History* (New Haven, 1983), *The Biblical Saga of King David* (Winona Lake, 2000), and "The Court History and DtrH," in A. de Pury and T. Römer (eds.), *Die sogenannte Thronfolgegeschichte Davids* (Freiburg, 2000), pp. 70-93.

the earliest version of Samuel had no account of Dawid's death, and made only one brief mention of Shelomo.) Second, and most importantly, it served to critique the idea of the future revival of the Dawidic monarchy—an idea which had gained popularity among some factions within Yahweh's cult in Yehud after the return from exile and the reestablishment of the cult in Yerushalem. In adding the succession narrative to Samuel and Kings, the leadership of the Yerushalem cult made a conscious decision to radically change the portrait of their great founder: Dawid is no longer the perfect king to whom Yahweh has unconditionally promised an everlasting dynasty; rather, he is a flawed figure who was incapable of living up to the ideals of the "just" king known from Judean royal ideology. Moreover, as authors writing during the exile first proposed, Yahweh's promise to Dawid was not unconditional, but was conditioned on his descendants pleasing Yahweh by following his rules, commandments, and precepts. Dawid's descendants did not keep their obligations, thus invalidating the Dawidic promise. The Persian period leaders of Yahweh's cult replaced the Dawidic promise and the "binding agreement" (ברית) between Yahweh and the Dawidic king with the idea of the binding agreement (or "treaty") between Yahweh and his people—an idea that ultimately grew to become the single most important principle of Yahwism during the Persian period and that found its expression in the books of the Torah. The composition of the succession narrative should be understood simply as part of this Persian period effort to replace the binding agreement between Yahweh and the Dawidic king with a treaty between Yahweh and his people.

1b even when he was covered with layers of clothes: Literally, "they covered him with clothes." The subject of the verb is indefinite. Ancient Hebrew speakers typically avoided the passive voice. They often expressed the passive with an active verb governed by an indefinite subject ("he" or "they"), as is the case here. I have frequently commented on this quirk of Hebrew in my other translations. See for example, notes 9b and 17b in my translation of Leviticus.

1c he couldn't keep warm: Literally, "it wouldn't be warm for him." The Hebrew is idiomatic, and I have translated with the equivalent idiom in English.

1d a marriageable girl: The phrase used here is נערה בתולה. It refers to a girl who has reached puberty and is of marriageable age, typically her mid- to late teens. Sometimes בתולה is used with the meaning "virgin" or "virginity," but the more typical use of the word is simply a girl who is sexually mature and who is now of marriageable age.

1e and keep my lord the king warm: The author uses the identical idiom discussed above in note 1c. A literal translation is "and [then] it would be warm for my lord the king."

1f the territory of Yisra'el: Note that the term Yisra'el here denotes all tribal territories, including Yehudah. I believe the author of the succession narrative composed his work early in the Persian period, when the term Yisra'el in a geographic sense had come to denote all the territories of the former kingdoms of Yisra'el and Yehudah rather than just the territory of the northern tribes.

1g Aviyshag the Shunammite: Aviyshag is from Shunem, a town in the tribal territory of Yissakar. The town is mentioned in Jos P40 (the tribal allotment to Yissakar), in Sam P60 (where the Philishtines camp prior to fighting Sha'ul at Gilboa), and also later in Kings, in P67 (in one of the Eliysha stories).

1h Adoniyyah Haggiythsson was accumulating power for himself: Adoniyyah is mentioned only once in Samuel, in Sam P71,2, which lists the first six sons born to Dawid when he lived in Hevron, before becoming king. Adoniyyah was the fourth son born to Dawid, and thus fourth in line to the throne. What happened to Dawid's first three sons? The earliest version of Samuel—the version I associate with the Josianic "study books"—ended with Sam P82,1, with Dawid at the height of his powers; this version contained no information about his death or who succeeded him or what became of his sons. These topics, however, are addressed in the succession narrative. With respect to Dawid's sons, the author of the succession narrative tells us in Sam P88,1 that Dawid's eldest son Amnon was killed by Avshalom's retainers in revenge for his rape of Avshalom's sister Tamar. The succession narrative says nothing about Dawid's second-born Kil'av; nothing is known about him except that his mother was Aviygayil. (However, from the statement in Kings P5,1 that Adoniyyah is Shelomo's oldest brother, we can infer that the author of the succession narrative viewed Kil'av as already deceased by the time the book of Kings begins.) Dawid's third-born, Avshalom, plays a central role in the succession narrative in Samuel: he led a rebellion against his father and was killed by Dawid's general, Yo'av.

With respect to the narrative in Kgs P1, as the eldest surviving son of Dawid, Adoniyyah was the natural heir to the kingship after his father's death. Thus, it makes sense that the author of the succession narrative would portray him as taking action to strengthen his position vis-à-vis his other brothers prior to his father's death. Note that Adoniyyah's rival, Shelomo, is very far down in the order of succession to the throne. He is Dawid's tenth son overall, preceded by six sons born to Dawid in Hevron and three sons born to Dawid in Yerushalem (see Sam P75,1 for the sons born in Yerushalem).

It is interesting that Adoniyyah is referred to with a matronym ("Haggiythsson") as his surname. Royal children were sometimes referred to by their matronyms as a way to distinguish where they stood within the hierarchy of the royal family. As we will soon see, although Adoniyyah is older than Shelomo, Shelomo's mother Bath-Sheva is the favored wife and she holds considerable influence with Dawid. Haggiyth seems to have been a relatively unimportant wife (there are no stories preserved about her); moreover, by the time the story in P1 takes place, it is possible that she was dead, as she must have been much older than Bath-Sheva.

On the topic of surnames, it is worth noting that in many contexts, it would be more usual to use the patronym when referring to a child of the king—for example, Adoniyyah must have often been referred to as Adoniyyah Dawidsson.

1i a royal guard of fifty men who would run ahead to clear the way for him: With this statement, the author of the succession narrative implicitly compares Adoniyyahu's behavior with Avshalom's behavior in the period prior to his attempted coup against his father. Note that in Sam P94,1, which is part of the succession narrative in Samuel, Avshalom "equipped himself with a chariot and some horses, with a band of fifty men who would run before him" (in the Hebrew, the two passages are identical). Compare also Gen P37, which gives a similar picture of how Yoseph traveled after being made vizier by Phar'oh: "He [Phar'oh] had him ride in one of the second-rank chariots in his possession, with his servants calling out before him 'Vizier'!"

The author of the succession narrative models his depiction of Adoniyyahu on his depiction of Avshalom in Samuel (see Sam P92,3 and P94,1): both are unusually handsome, both make themselves prominent by traveling in a chariot preceded by a royal guard of fifty men, and both take on aspects of the kingship behind Dawid's back and build support among the people.

There are two types of royal guards mentioned in Samuel and Kings: the "Kerethite and Pelethite guard" (הכרתי והפלתי, which was sometimes shortened to הכרי) and "the Runners" (הרצים). In my translation, I typically use the generic terms "personal guard" and "royal guard" to refer to these guards rather than a literal translation of their names. The name of the Runners presumably reflects their role in running before the king as he traveled from one place to the next. The guard mentioned here in P1 is the Runners. In addition to the reference here and in Sam P94,1, the guard known as the Runners is also mentioned in Sam P51,5, where they accompany Sha'ul to the town of Nov and disobey his order to kill the priest Ahimelek. Finally, the Runners are mentioned in Kgs P40, where the author specifies that their role was to guard the entrance to the palace. It seems then that the Runners had two roles: to escort the king on his travels when he is out of the palace, and to guard the palace entrance when the king is in the palace.

1j At no point during this period, however did his father give him any grief: Even though Adoniyyahu is first in line to succeed Dawid, his actions in taking on the trappings of the king before assuming the throne are highly presumptuous. Dawid, however, does not rebuke him. This brief sentence provides a good example of the literary artistry of the author of the succession narrative, who—as mentioned above in note 1a—was one of the two great prose authors of ancient Hebrew. Note how with just a few words, the author characterizes Dawid in his old age as passive, weak and feeble-minded—providing a striking contrast to the savvy young Dawid portrayed in the earliest version of the book of Samuel, and heightening the drama of the palace intrigues that follow, when Bath-Sheva and Nathan the Prophet exploit Dawid's mental decline to secure the kingship for her son Shelomo.

1k (Two other things to know about him: he was exceptionally good looking... born after Avshalom.): The author of the succession narrative draws an explicit parallel between Adoniyyahu and Avshalom. Note that in Sam P92,3 (by the same author), it is said that "there was no man in Yisra'el who was more celebrated for being handsome than Avshalom."

With respect to the translation here, I have departed further from a literal rendering than usual to capture the sense of the Hebrew; where I have written "two other things to know about him," the Hebrew reads simply "and also" (וגם). It is also worth noting the author's use of an active verb with an indefinite subject to represent the passive—the clause translated as "he was born after Avshalom" in Hebrew reads "she bore him after Avshalom." It is quite common to express the passive in Hebrew in this fashion, but the indefinite subject almost always takes the third person masculine form. Here, because the verb is ילד ("bear, give birth to"), the author must use the third person feminine form of the verb.

1l Yo'av Tzeruyahsson and Evyathar the Priest: The author assumes the reader is familiar with these characters, both of whom play important roles in the earliest version of the book of Samuel as well as in the part of the succession narrative found in Samuel. Yo'av was the head of Dawid's army and the man who killed Avshalom in the battle between Avshalom's forces and Dawid's. Yo'av is a complex character in Samuel; in both the original version of Samuel and in the succession narrative, he is portrayed in a mostly positive light, although he creates problems for Dawid because he is rash and extremely violent. For a list of all the major stories involving him, see the index of characters in my translation of Samuel.

Evyathar is an important character in Samuel and played critical roles throughout Dawid's career. He was from the priesthood at Nov, and joined Dawid's band of outlaws after Sha'ul's slaughter of the priesthood there. During Dawid's kingship, he was one of the two chief priests in Yahweh's cult in Yerushalem, and in the aftermath of Avshalom's rebellion, he convinced the Yehudean elders to return their fealty to Dawid. For a list of all the major stories involving him, see the index of characters in my translation of Samuel.

1m Tzadoq the Priest, Benayahu Yehoyadasson, Nathan the Prophet, Shim'iy, Re'iy, and the military officers in Dawid's service: With the exception of Re'iy, all these individuals appear in the book of Samuel, some in important roles. Tzadoq the Priest was the nephew or second nephew of Evyathar (see note 1l directly above) and he was also from the priesthood at Nov. In the earliest version of Samuel, he appears only in a list of officials (Sam P82,1); however, he has a relatively important role in the succession narrative. With Evyathar, he was one of the two chief priests in Yahweh's cult in Yerushalem, and he partnered with Evyathar at critical moments when Dawid was under threat, including helping convince the Yehudean elders to return their fealty to Dawid in the aftermath of Avshalom's rebellion. For a list of the stories involving him, see the index of characters in my translation of Samuel.

Benayahu does not appear in any major stories in Samuel; he is mentioned in Sam P82,1 as the head of Dawid's personal guard and in Sam P106,6 as the chief of works and as the head of Dawid's personal guard. He was famous for a number of violent exploits mentioned in Sam P106,6.

Nathan the Prophet appears three times in Samuel, twice at critical junctures. In the earliest version of Samuel, his only appearance is in Sam P80, when he delivers an oracle telling Dawid not to build a temple in Yerushalem. In the portion of the succession narrative in Samuel, he appears twice; most importantly, he delivers an oracle to Dawid in Sam P85 promising that disaster will befall him because of his taking of Bath-Sheva. For the mentions of him in Samuel, see the index of characters in my translation of Samuel.

Shim'iy is a minor character in Samuel who appears only in the material belonging to the succession narrative. He is from Binyamin and belongs to Sha'ul's clan. He appears in Sam P96,4 - P96,6, where he quite comically curses Dawid as Dawid is fleeing Yerushalem to escape Avshalom. He reappears in P99,18 - P99,20 when he meets Dawid at the Yarden River to beg Dawid's forgiveness as Dawid is returning to Yerushalem after Avshalom's death.

Re'iy is not mentioned in Samuel, so the mention of him here in Kgs P1 is somewhat surprising.

The military officers in Dawid's service (הגברים אשר לדוד) are listed in Sam P106 - P106,7; of those listed, the only one who plays a major role in Samuel is Aviyshai, who was Yo'av's brother and a great military leader. He appears in both the original version of Samuel and in the succession narrative in Samuel; for the stories involving him, see the index of characters in my translation of Samuel.

It's worth noting that the succession narrative portrays the palace factions as dividing families—Yo'av supports Adoniyyahu but his brother Aviyshai does not; and Evyathar supports Adoniyyahu but his nephew and close partner Tzadoq does not.

1n Adoniyyahu put on a feast...slaughtering sheep, cattle, and fatlings: I have added language to make explicit that Adoniyyahu is holding a feast. The author uses the verb זבח ("slaughter"), which in the context of the cult may mean "sacrifice," "make a sacrificial offering," or "make a welfare offering." Here, however, there is no cultic rite implied—there is no shrine or altar to Yahweh at Serpent Rock—and Adoniyyahu is simply holding a large feast in an attempt to build political support for his claim to the throne.

1o Fuller's Spring: Fuller's Spring lies on the border between Binyamin and Yehudah and is quite close to Yerushalem; it is mentioned in Jos P30 and Jos P36.

1p Adoniyyahu Haggiythsson... Bath-Sheva Shelomosmother: In ancient Hebrew, it was most common to refer to individuals with their given name followed by a patronym ("son of PN" or "daughter of PN"), with the patronym functioning as the surname. It was also common for surnames to be based on occupations ("the Prophet," "the Priest," and "King of GN" are three very common surnames appearing in the book of Kings) or to be gentilics (such as Aviyshag the Shunammite, who is from the town of Shunem). The two surnames here—Haggiythsson and Shelomosmother—are quite unusual, and reflect the special practices of surnames within the royal family. As discussed above in note 1h, Adoniyyahu is given the matronym Haggiythsson as a way to reflect his status in the royal family, which is tied to the status of his mother Haggiyth. Similarly, Bath-Sheva is given the surname Shelomosmother, in reflection of her special status as mother of the (future) king. The use of surnames in ancient Hebrew was quite fluid, and depending on context, different surnames would be used for the same individual. For example, sometimes a king is referred to with a patronym and other times with an occupational surname ("King of Yehudah"). And sometimes two surnames are used together in a way that seems strange to an English speaker: in P110, for example, Yesha'yahu is referred to as Yesha'yahu the Prophet Amotzsson.

1q "Didn't you yourself... swear to your maidservant that my son Shelomo would be king: There is no record of this oath in either Samuel or Kings, and the author of the succession narrative would have expected his readers to know this. We should understand that the author is implying Nathan and Bath-Sheva have fabricated this oath as a way to trick the feeble-minded king into placing Shelomo on the throne instead of the natural successor, Adoniyyahu.

1r I'll come in behind you and confirm what you just told him: That is, he will confirm to Dawid that Dawid did in fact swear to Bath-Sheva that Shelomo would succeed him as king. Here Nathan and Bath-Sheva are exploiting Dawid's cognitive decline and failing memory. There is no record in the succession narrative or elsewhere of Dawid making this promise.

1s Bath-Sheva went to see the king in his chambers...: It is interesting to compare the characterization of Bath-Sheva in the succession narrative in Samuel with the characterization of her in Kings, especially since the same author was almost certainly responsible for both depictions of her. In both books, Bath-Sheva is presented as a mostly passive figure, but it is possible to infer that she actually has quite a bit of agency and that she takes action to influence events toward the outcomes she desires. It is unclear, however, whether the author intended the reader to make that inference. In Kings, for example, it is Nathan who initiates the scheme to trick Dawid to name Shelomo as his successor. But once Nathan informs Bath-Sheva of the plan, she actively partakes in Nathan's plot and plays her role flawlessly, effectively advocating for herself and Shelomo to the king. Her words at the end of P2,1, when the scheme has succeeded, are very powerful, as she takes satisfaction in her victory while Dawid remains unaware that he has been "played." Her actions in P5,1, when Adoniyyahu has an audience with her, are more ambiguous. Is Bath-Sheva naive in agreeing to take Adoniyyahu's request to Shelomo, not realizing Shelomo's likely reaction? Or is she deviously "playing" Adoniyyahu, agreeing to take his request to Shelomo because she knows that in so doing she will ensure Adoniyyahu's death and remove any remaining threat he poses to Shelomo?

Bath-Sheva appears in Samuel only in P84,1, P84,3, and at the end of P85,5. In these *parashot*, Bath-Sheva barely seems to be a character, and on the surface she appears to lack agency. Just as was the case in Kings, however, it is possible to infer from her actions in Samuel that she has quite a bit of agency, and that she was intentional in her actions to entice Dawid to take her. Again, it is unclear whether the author wanted the reader to make this inference. That said, the author of the succession narrative shows a very sophisticated understanding of human behavior and motivation. And the obvious way to understand her bathing on the roof is that she is putting herself on display, hoping to attract the king's attentions. It hardly seems credible that she wouldn't be aware that the roof of her house, which is opposite the palace, is visible from the roof where Dawid was pacing. Moreover, she puts herself on display to the king near the time of her peak fertility. She has just purified herself from her menstrual uncleanness, which on average would be thirteen days into her menstrual cycle—and it must have been common knowledge among women that they were most fertile shortly after the purification period (which according to Lev P33,1 lasts eight days after a woman is "free of discharge").

1t **: The Aleppo Codex has a *parashah petuhah* at this point in the text (see A71 v.2.4). The Leningrad Codex, however, does not show a *parashah* break here (see L184 v.1.21).

2a all of Yisra'el: Note again the expansive use of the term Yisra'el by the author of the succession narrative. Here the term is used not in a geographic sense, but as the name of a people. It no longer exclusively referred to the people (or the tribes) of the northern kingdom; instead, it denoted the people belonging to the tribes of both former kingdoms. This usage of the term is characteristic of the Persian period and offers some support for viewing the succession narrative as a late composition. See note 1f above.

Notes to P2

2b when my lord the king lies down with his ancestors: In ancient Hebrew, the phrase "lie down with one's ancestors" was a euphemism for "to die."

2c "My lord and king," ...: It is interesting to note Nathan's strategy in his speech to Dawid. He and Bath-Sheva are playing Dawid and taking advantage of his feeble-mindedness. Nathan seeks to confuse Dawid by feigning ignorance that Dawid has accepted Adoniyyahu—who is his oldest living son—as his successor. Nathan claims that Dawid didn't tell him this in order to create doubt in Dawid's mind about what decision he really made—whether he has agreed his eldest son Adoniyyahu would succeed him or whether he has instead chosen Shelomo even though he is far down in the line of succession. Once the seed of doubt was planted, it is then easy for Nathan and Bath-Sheva to convince Dawid that in fact it was Shelomo whom he chose as his successor.

It is interesting to compare the action here—where the younger son (Shelomo) usurps the position of the older son (Adoniyyahu) through the conniving of the mother—with the stories in Genesis where the mother connives to win a favored position for the younger son. In Gen P19,2, Sarah convinces Avraham to banish the older son Yishma'el and his mother Hagar, and in Gen P27,2, Rivqah orchestrates a trick in which in Ya'aqov receives a blessing reserved for the eldest son from Yitzhaq.

2d Surely, it can't be that this thing would have happened...: By "this thing" Nathan means Adoniyyahu's acting as king. Nathan is telling Dawid that he can't believe Adoniyyahu's acting as king has Dawid's approval, because if Dawid did approve, he is certain that Dawid would have told him of his decision to name Adoniyyahu his successor.

2,1a "Summon Bath-Sheva for me!": Note the incongruity in the narrative. Bath-Sheva was present in P2 during Nathan's audience with the king. Yet now, here in P2,1, she is portrayed as not being present during Nathan's audience with the king. We often see such incongruities in ancient Hebrew narrative. Ancient Hebrew authors prioritized dramatic and emotional impact over narrative consistency, and

Notes to P2,1

they often introduced inconsistencies in the narrative in order to achieve greater dramatic impact. This is clearly the case here in P2,1. The author of the succession narrative has temporarily removed Bath-Sheva from the proceedings in order to create a dramatic scene in which she enters the king's presence and he grants her wish, followed by her prostrating herself to him in gratitude. Note also how the author manipulates the action to heighten the drama: it would be customary for Bath-Sheva to prostrate herself upon entering the king's presence. Instead, the author has her remain standing so that he can create a dramatic conclusion to the scene in which she prostrates herself to the king.

This phenomenon of ancient Hebrew authors abandoning narrative consistency in order to achieve dramatic or emotional impact is something that I have frequently commented on in my other translations. See, for example, notes 21b and 23,1y in my translation of Genesis.

2,1b I swear that exactly as I swore to you…so I'm going to make that happen: It should be emphasized that there is no record of any such oath of Dawid. Nathan and Bath-Sheva have tricked the senile old king into believing he made such an oath and have now succeeded in their plot to place Shelomo on the throne.

2,1c Yahweh God of Yisra'el: The phrase "God of Yisra'el" should be understood as Yahweh's surname. In my previous translations, I treated the phrase as an epithet rather than a surname, and consequenty I mistranslated it as "Yisra'el's god." Yahweh has other surnames, such as "God of Armies" (אלהי צבאות, which is often shortened to "of Armies"), but God of Yisra'el is his most common surname.

In the Persian period, when the author of the succession narrative is writing, the surname God of Yisra'el would have been understood to mean "god of the people Yisra'el." The surname, however, is very old, and in the era of the monarchy God of Yisra'el would have been understood to mean god of a geographic territory. Originally, the term "Yisra'el" in Yahweh's surname likely referred only to the core of the tribal territories of Ephrayim, Menashsheh, and Binyamin. It is conceivable that even during the era of the monarchy, the term "Yisra'el" in Yahweh's surname would have retained this more limited territorial association.

It is important to recognize that, as Yahweh's surname implies, he was originally the local god of (some of) the tribal territories of Yisra'el, but not of the tribal territory of Yehudah. While it seems doubtful that there is much in the book of Samuel that reflects real historical events, its presentation of Dawid as the founder of Yahweh's cult in Yerushalem probably preserves a kernel of an actual historical event. It is tempting to speculate that Dawid may have first adopted worship of Yahweh God of Yisra'el after entering service to Sha'ul Qiyshsson King of Yisra'el, and that it was only after Dawid established the cult of the neighboring god Yahweh God of Yisra'el in Yerushalem that veneration of Yahweh became common in Yehudah.

When ancient authors and prophets from Yehudah used the phrase Yahweh God of Yisra'el, they would have understood God of Yisra'el as a surname. It seems likely to me that they further would have understood Yisra'el in the surname to refer to the tribal territories in the north. Viewing the phrase God of Yisra'el in this way also helps us understand the names Yahweh Shomeron and Yahweh Teman, both of which appear in inscriptions from Kuntillet 'Ajrud. Yahweh Shomeron is a shortened form of Yahweh God of Shomeron and Yahweh Teman is a shortened form of Yahweh God of Teman. We should understand both God of Shomeron and God of Teman as surnames of Yahweh. In the former surname, Shomeron is an alternate name for the kingdom of Yisra'el—it should not be understood as referring to the name of the royal seat where the king had his palace. As for the latter surname, Teman is a term meaning "south" or "southern region;" it is also the name of a region of Edom. The surname God of Teman may also have some association with the Paran and Siynai regions, which are in the vicinity of Edom and both of which are closely associated with Yahweh in ancient tradition.

One final comment on the Kuntillet 'Ajrud inscriptions: when these were written (ninth/eighth century BCE), "God of Yisra'el" may still have had the limited association with the areas of Ephrayim, Menashsheh and Binyamin; if so, then the author of the Kuntillet 'Ajrud inscriptions would have understood the surname "[God of] Shomeron" to be more expansive than the surname "God of Yisra'el," and this may explain why he chose to use that surname in his inscription rather than the surname familiar to us from the Tanakh.

2,1d "May my lord King Dawid live forever!": This short *parashah* is a good example of this author's mastery of prose narrative. The image the author has painted is exceptionally powerful: Bath-Sheva lies prostrate on the ground in front of the aged king, and from her prone position exclaims a phrase which signals her obeisance to the king, but which also is a cry of exultation at securing the kingship for her son. Following this sentence with a *parashah petuhah* further heightens the drama, for it forces readers to pause and reflect on the scene that they have just read.

3a Summon Tzadoq the Priest...along with Nathan the Prophet and Benayahu Yehoyadasson: Note once more the incongruity in the narrative. Nathan spoke to the king in P2, and the reader would assume he was still present in the scene with Bath-Sheva in P2,1. But now the author has the king ask that Nathan be summoned with Tzadoq the Priest and Benayahu Yehoyadasson. The author likely has chosen to include Nathan in the initial summons because the narrative is more effective this way—it would disrupt the flow of the storyline to summon only Tzadoq and Benayahu and then have to pause to remind the reader that Nathan was already present.

Notes to P3

3b one of my mollies: A molly is an informal term for a female mule. More formally, female mules are called mare mules.

3c he's the one I've chosen to be supreme leader over Yisra'el and Yehudah: The author uses the phrase ואתו צויתי להיות נגיד ("him I've appointed to be supreme leader"). This must have been formulaic language, perhaps originating in the ancient coronation rites in Yehudah, for the construction צוה לנגיד ("appoint as supreme leader") is used three times in Samuel, with Yahweh as the subject and either Sha'ul or Dawid as the one being appointed. See Sam P25,1, P53, and P79,1.

Note also that the author of the succession narrative uses Yisra'el here as the name for the territories of the northern tribes (or the name of the former territory of the northern kingdom), and not as the name for the territories of all the tribes. Two sentences prior to this, the author uses Yisra'el to mean all tribal territories, including Yehudah. But now he reverts to the usage of the term during the period of the monarchy. This is natural given that his story is set in the period of the monarchy, and—with a few exceptions, such as his use of the term "king of Yisra'el" directly above and the instance discussed in note 2a—he is fairly consistent throughout the succession narrative in distinguishing between between Yisra'el and Yehudah. It is worth emphasizing that the use of the name Yisra'el was quite fluid in the Persian period, when the author of the succession narrative was writing. It served as the name for Yahweh's devotees as a whole, wherever they lived; it was both the name of an ethnic group and the name of the ethnic group's founder. In a geographical sense, it designated the entire territory that Yahweh gave this ethnic group, and it was also the name of a former kingdom where the majority of this ethnic group once lived.

3d the king's personal guard: The king's personal guard may have been composed of foreigners, for the name of the guard was הכרתי והפלתי ("the Kerethites and the Pelethites"). As mentioned above in note 1m, the leader of the personal guard was Benayahu Yehoyadasson. In Samuel, the king's personal guard is mentioned in Sam P82,1, P96, and P100,8.

The personal guard is a separate group from the royal guard discussed above in note 1i.

3e Yahweh's tent: The Hebrew reads simply "the tent." This is a reference to the tent shrine inside Fort Dawid that Dawid set up as the place where Yahweh's battle chest was kept; below in P7, the tent shrine is called "Yahweh's tent," and I have used that terminology here in my translation to make the reference explicit to the reader. The tent shrine in Fort Dawid is also mentioned in Sam P79 and P81. I do not believe we should understand this tent as equivalent to the Meeting Tent known from the books of the Torah. For my thoughts on the Meeting Tent, see the introduction to my translation of Leviticus.

The Meeting Tent is mentioned in Kgs P19, where the author does in fact equate it with the tent shrine inside Fort Dawid. However, I understand the mention of the Meeting Tent in P19 to be part of a Persian period addition to Kings, made to harmonize the tent shrine in Fort Dawid with the Meeting Tent known from the books of Exodus, Leviticus, and Numbers. See note 19c below.

3f "Long live King Shelomo!"...all the noise that they made: Compare the scene here depicting the celebration following Shelomo being made king with the account of Yo'ash's coronation in P82 - P82,1. That account belongs to King's first compositional stage, and the author of the succession narrative may have borrowed details from that for his scene here in P3, as there are a number of similarities between the two.

3g I trust you bring good news: Note the author's use of irony—the reader already knows that the news is not good for Adoniyyahu.

3h our lord King Dawid has made Shelomo king: From this statement, we should understand that Dawid has established a co-regency with his son Shelomo. I think that very little of the material about Shelomo's accession in P1 - P7,2 has any real basis in history, including this co-regency. That said, however, co-regencies were not unusual in the ancient Near East. The authors of Kings do not explicitly mention any co-regencies among Yisra'el's kings, but they do speak of one in Yehudah—that of Azaryah (=Uzziyahu) and his son Yotham (see P95). Although the only co-regencies explicitly mentioned in the text of Kings are the one between Dawid and Shelomo and the one between Azaryah and Yotham, it is possible to infer instances of other co-regencies in both Yisra'el and Yehudah based on the accession dates that we find in Kings. In the appendix to this book, I provide my reconstruction of the chronologies of Yisra'el and Yehudah; in that reconstruction, I propose three co-regencies for Yisra'el's kings and five for Yehudah's kings.

3i your god: The consonantal text of both the Aleppo Codex and the Leningrad Codex reads "your god" (אלהיך). This has been corrected with a *qere* in the margin indicating that the text should be read as "God" (אלהים). The incorrect word in the consonantal text has also been vocalized with the vowels of the correct reading, as was standard practice in the *qere-ketiv* corrections.

3j the king prostrated himself on his bed: Dawid prostrates himself to Yahweh, expressing his gratitude to his god both in the physical act of prostration and also in the words that he speaks while prostrate.

3k he went straight away to the altar and grabbed its horns: This is almost certainly the altar associated with the tent shrine inside Fort Dawid, which is mentioned below in P7 (see note 7c below). Adoniyyahu takes refuge at the altar because he believes Shelomo would not dare defile the altar by having him killed there. Attaching himself physically to the altar thus allows him to negotiate with Shelomo for his life. It is interesting to note that in the earliest version of the book of Samuel, there is no mention of an altar associated with Dawid's kingship. (The material in Sam P110,1, which mentions an altar at Arawnah, is part of a late addition to the text.)

Notes to P4

4a You must keep the service due to your god Yahweh...: The view of kingship expressed by the author of the succession narrative here in Dawid's speech is interesting. I believe the author was writing early in the Persian period, and his views reflect a meshing of ideas that were developed during earlier compositional stages of Kings. In the earliest version of Kings (which I date to the 630s BCE), the Dawidic promise is unconditional, and there is a binding agreement (ברית, which may also be translated as "treaty") between Yahweh and the king. However, there is no treaty between Yahweh and the people. In the second compositional stage of Kings, which I date to the first decades of the Babylonian exile, the authors explain the destruction of Yerushalem and of Yahweh's house by reinterpreting the Dawidic promise as a conditional promise. With the composition of the earliest versions of Deuteronomy and Exodus-Numbers during the Babylonian exile and in the early Persian period, the notion of the binding agreement between Yahweh and the king was replaced with the idea of a treaty between Yahweh and his people Yisra'el—a treaty mediated by Mosheh. The author of the succession narrative was writing around this time or shortly thereafter, and so we see a merging of these ideas in his speech here in P4: the Dawidic promise is presented as a conditional promise, and the obligations that the king has to Yahweh are no longer the obligations he has as head of the cult, but rather they are the same obligations that all Yisra'elites have—that is, the obligations that are "written in Mosheh's Torah" (i.e. the book of Deuteronomy). By combining the ideas of the conditional nature of the Dawidic promise and the obligations of Mosheh's Torah, the author presents a view of kingship in which the Dawidic promise is conditioned on the king's observing the laws and commandments in Deuteronomy.

4b in order to adhere to his laws...exactly as is written in Mosheh's Torah: The author here has in mind an early version of the book of Deuteronomy, which in his day was commonly referred to as "Mosheh's Torah." (This term appears again in Kings near the end of P116.)

4c the obligations under his treaty: The author uses the word עדות ('ēdōt), which here means "treaty obligations." The term is a loan word from Akkadian adê, which came over into Aramaic as ᶜdy. The status of this term as a loan word is unfortunately not recognized by many translators, who erroneously render the word as "testimonies." On this term and its meaning "treaty obligations" or simply "treaty," see note 4d in my translation of Deuteronomy.

4d in order that Yahweh might fulfill the promise he made about me: The author here alludes to Sam P80,2, in which Dawid receives the promise from Yahweh that his son will build Yahweh a house and that Dawid's dynasty "will be firmly established for all time" and his throne "will last forever."

4e that if my sons were careful about their ways, walking before him in truth, with all their heart and with their entire being: This language does not appear in the dynastic promise in Sam P80,2. In that *parashah*, which was part of the earliest version of Samuel, the dynastic promise is unconditional. Here in Kgs P4, the author of the succession narrative qualifies the dynastic promise by adding language to make it clear that the promise is a conditional one. The author of the succession narrative is writing in the Persian period, when it was commonly understood that the Dawidic promise was conditional. (It was the authors of Kings' second stage, who wrote in the early decades of the exile, who first reinterpreted the Dawidic promise in this fashion.)

4f what he did to the two heads of Yisra'el's armies, Avner Nersson and Amasa Yethersson, murdering them and committing war crimes: The story of Yo'av's murder of Avner, which was in revenge for Avner killing Yo'av's brother Asa'el, is given in Sam P72,3. The story of Yo'av's murder of Amasa, which was in retribution for Amasa's leading role in Avshalom's rebellion, is given in Sam P100,9.

Dawid's condemnation of Yo'av here in Kgs P4 is somewhat surprising, as it is not wholly consistent with Yo'av's portrayal in the succession narrative in Samuel. In that book, although the author of the succession narrative presents Yo'av as a flawed character, he mostly portrays Yo'av in a positive light: he is instrumental in putting down the rebellions of Avshalom and Sheva Bikriysson, and he is unerringly loyal to Dawid. In my opinion, the author of the succession narrative likely chose to kill off Yo'av in Kings out of literary concerns. He makes the events of Kgs P1 more dramatic by presenting all but a few of Dawid's officials as allied with Adoniyyahu. Because he included Yo'av in this group, he is then able to achieve powerful literary effects by killing off Yo'av later in the narrative. Specifically, killing off Yo'av in P7 makes the picture of Shelomo consolidating power more compelling, and it also creates a more dramatic transition between Yo'av and Benayahu as head of the army.

4g but don't let a peaceful death in his old age be the way he enters She'ol: The Leningrad Codex has a *parashah setumah* after this clause; see L185 v.1.3. Compare with the Aleppo Codex (A72 v.1.20), which has no *parashah* break here.

The language of this clause is idiomatic, and I have departed further than usual from a literal rendering to capture the force of the Hebrew. A literal translation would be, "but don't send his grey [head] peacefully down to She'ol."

4h Barzillai the Gil'adites' descendants... they provided me with similar support when I was fleeing from your brother Avshalom: See Sam P99,5, when Barzillai brings food and supplies to Dawid and his men after their long flight, and Sam P100,1 - P100,2, when Barzillai meets Dawid at the Yarden River on his return and Dawid agrees to allow Barzillai's relative (?) Kimham to join his retinue. (It is somewhat odd that Kimham is not mentioned here in P4.)

4i Shim'iy Gerasson the Binyaminite from Bahuriym... he cursed me with a noxious curse: The story of Shim'iy's cursing Dawid appears in Sam P96,4 - P96,6. The story of Shim'iy's meeting Dawid on his return at the Yarden river appears in Sam P99,18 - P99,20; Dawid's oath to Shim'iy that he wouldn't put him to death is given in P99,20.

In Sam P99,20, Dawid appears as magnanimous, as is befitting a great king. The desire to exact revenge here in P4 is not wholly in keeping with the picture of David in the succession narrative in Samuel. As with the portrait of Yo'av discussed above in note 4f, I think it most likely that the author of the succession narrative has chosen to kill off Shim'iy for literary effect. Shim'iy belonged to Sha'ul's clan; killing off the head of the clan of Dawid's rival makes the portrait of Sholomo's consolidation of power more compelling.

4j Dawid then lay down with his ancestors and was buried in Fort Dawid: The phrase "he lay down with his ancestors" (וישכב עם אבתיו) typically implies burial in the family tomb. Here, however, the phrase is entirely formulaic and implies nothing about burial with the ancestors—Dawid's family tomb would have been in Beth-Lehem, where his father Yishai would have been buried.

Fort Dawid (עיר דוד, which is commonly mistranslated "the City of Dawid") was a citadel in Yerushalem on Mount Tziyyon. The original name of the citadel was Tziyyon Fortress (מצדת ציון), which Dawid changed to Fort Dawid after he took control of Yerushalem (see Sam P74,1). Fort Dawid was the location of the tent shrine that Dawid established for Yahweh, and after Dawid's time the fort served as the royal cemetery for the kings of Yehudah. For עיר meaning "fort, citadel," see BDB, p. 746, def. 2 and def. 3.

5a Dawid's reign over Yisra'el lasted forty years...: In this *parashah*, the author of the succession narrative imitates the regnal summaries found for the kings of Yisra'el and Yehudah in the earliest version of the book of Kings. Those summaries were based on the royal chronicles, *The Chronicles of the Kings of Yehudah* and *The Chronicles of the Kings of Yisra'el*. Those books began with Rehav'am and Yarov'am. There were no entries in them for either Dawid or Shelomo.

Notes to P5

5b his hold on it was unassailable: Literally, "his kingship was quite firmly established." The language used here is an indirect allusion to the end of Sam P80,2, where Yahweh promises Dawid that "your throne will last forever" (כסאך יהיה נכון עד־עולם). In both instances, the verb is the *niph'al* of כון ("be firm, be established").

5c —: The Leningrad Codex does not have a *parashah* break here. See L185 v.1.25.

5,1a Adoniyyahu Haggiythsson went to see Bath-Sheva Shelomosmother: Adoniyyahu goes to Beth-Sheva to ask her to act on his behalf because he is afraid of Shelomo (recall that at the end of P3, Shelomo threatens him with death if he ever finds him guilty of wrongdoing).

Notes to P5,1

On the unusual surnames Haggiythsson and Shelomosmother, see note 1p above.

5,1b "You had no problems in your journey here, I trust?"..."None at all": The exchange of pleasantries between Bath-Sheva and Adoniyyahu is fascinating, as the language here almost certainly reflects the idioms of spoken Hebrew. A literal translation of Bath-Sheva's question is "Was your coming [i.e. trip, journey] here a peaceful one?" And a literal translation of Adoniyyahu's response is "[Yes, it was] peaceful." I have translated with equivalent English idiomatic speech.

5,1c all Yisra'el expected me to become king: As Adoniyyahu was Dawid's eldest surviving son, he was first in line to the throne, and the people would naturally expect him to succeed his father. (Note that at the end of *parashah*, Shelomo explicitly states that Adoniyyahu is his oldest [surviving] brother.) For the birth order of Dawid's sons, see note 1h above.

5,1d the kingship passed out of my hands: The verb here is סבב ("turn around, go around"). The verb has an idiomatic use which means to "transfer ownership" or "change hands." The verb is also used with this sense in Num P93. See BDB, p. 685, def. 1a.

5,1e So now I'd like to make a request of you: Adoniyyahu wishes to make a request that will compensate him for losing the kingship—but he overreaches, and the request becomes his undoing.

5,1f for he won't refuse you: Adoniyyahu naively believes that Shelomo won't be insulted by the request to give the extraordinarily beautiful Aviyshag to his rival to the throne. The author of the succession narrative perhaps has put these words into Adoniyyahu's mouth in order to show him to be a man who lacks a deep understanding of human behavior and motivation—someone not fit to rule as king.

5,1g I shall speak favorably about you to the king: The author of the succession narrative has left it ambiguous as to whether Bath-Sheva understands how Shelomo is likely to react to Adoniyyahu's request. It is possible to see her as naive, and as agreeing to make the request in good faith. It is also possible to see her as shrewd and fully understanding that making this request is likely to result in Adoniyyahu's death. The ambiguity on the part of the author may be intentional. Intentional or not, the ambiguity opens the door for readers to form their own opinions about Bath-Sheva's actions. Here, for example, I like to think of Bath-Sheva as skillfully working within the strict confines of allowable female behavior to ensure that the one remaining threat to her son's kingship is eliminated. This view is consistent with the somewhat more cynical view of Bath-Sheva as having agency in the book of Samuel—that her intention in putting herself on display in the rooftop bath in Sam P84,1 was to gain the king's attention and, if things worked out, to "trade up" to a more powerful and wealthier husband (see the discussion in note 1s above). But there too, the author is ambiguous in his depiction of Bath-Sheva, and it is up to readers to form their own opinions—there is no "correct" way to understand Bath-Sheva's actions in either Samuel or Kings.

5,1h a throne had been set up for the king's mother, and she sat down to his right: Note the literary skill of the author in establishing a visual picture in the reader's mind. The ensuing conversation between the king and the queen mother is more dramatic and powerful because the words are spoken as they are sitting side by side on their thrones, in the room where the kingdom's most important business is conducted and surrounded by the trappings of their authority.

5,1i for I won't refuse you: This *parashah* provides a good example of how the author of the succession narrative employs narrative strategies designed to heighten the drama and emotional impact of the events he describes. In this *parashah*, he does this through repetition of statements expressing hope and reassurance about a request before the request is made. Adoniyyahu first expresses hope to Bath-Sheva that she won't refuse his request and she reassures him she won't (although she doesn't yet know what his request is). Then Bath-Sheva expresses the same hope to Shelomo and he reassures her likewise (although he too doesn't yet know what is being requested of him). Through this repetition the author creates an expectation in the reader that Aviyshag will be given to Adoniyyahu; because of this expectation, the scene in which Shelomo refuses the request is all the more dramatic.

5,1j and for Evyathar the Priest and Yo'av Tzeruyahsson: Recall from P1 that Evyathar and Yo'av actively supported Adoniyyahu's claim on the throne, whereas the other leaders of the army, the palace administration, and the cult of Yahweh did not.

Notes to P6

6a So may God to do me, and so may he do again: This phrase is a common introduction to an oath, similar to the phrase "as Yahweh lives." The phrase means something like, "So may God punish me repeatedly if I don't do what I have sworn to do in this oath." For an interesting variant of this phrase, see Iyzevel's oath in P51,1 and the comment in note 51,1ac.

Shelomo's response here—that Adoniyyahu's request of Aviyshag is equivalent to asking for the kingship and is a capital offense—might seem to modern-day readers an overreaction. Shelomo, however, views the request to be given a woman belonging to the king as a direct threat to his authority. In this regard, it is interesting to note that in Sam P98 (which was also written by the author of the succession narrative), Avshalom's first action upon seizing control of Yerushalem was to establish his authority as king by publicly having sexual intercourse with Dawid's concubines.

6b who gave me a dynasty, just as he promised: The word בית ("house, family") is often used to refer to the dynastic succession of a king, and I believe that is the way to understand the usage here given the reference to Yahweh's promise. This is the promise that Yahweh makes to Dawid in Sam P80,2 to give him a "dynasty" (בית) that will be "firmly established" (נכון) for all time. The language here in P6 draws directly from the language used in Sam P80,2. It is somewhat strange, however, that Shelomo refers to the dynastic promise as given to him rather than to his father. It is possible that the text originally said "who gave him a dynasty, just as he promised" and that the pronoun was changed through a scribal error. That said, the Hebrew reads quite naturally, and I am inclined to think that the phrasing in the text is original.

6c Benayahu Yehoyadasson: Benayahu was the head of Dawid's personal guard, and was famous for numerous violent exploits (see note 1m above). Shelomo uses him to carry out executions of prominent political opponents—Adoniyyahu, Yo'av, and Shim'iy—and rewards him by making him head of the army (see P7).

6,1a "Go to Anathoth, to your properties," the king said to Evyathar the Priest: In this *parashah*, Shelomo removes another threat—Evyathar, one of the two leaders of Yahweh's cult in Yerushalem, who had supported Adoniyyahu's claim to the throne. The text is somewhat ambiguous, but the most straightforward way to read the text is that Evyathar escapes death and is only punished with removal from serving as priest to Yahweh.

Notes to P6,1

6,1b you carried my lord Yahweh's battle chest in advance of my father Dawid: I believe this may be a reference to Evyathar carrying the battle chest on Dawid's military campaigns early in his kingship (although this is mentioned nowhere in Samuel). Note that in Sam P96,1 - P96,2, Tzadoq and Evyathar take the battle chest from Yerushalem and meet up with Dawid as he is fleeing from Avshalom, and then Dawid tells them to take the battle chest back to Yerushalem to the shrine inside Fort Dawid. The mention of the battle chest here in P6,1 does not fit that incident in Sam P96,1 - P96,2 and must refer to something else.

6,1c you suffered all the travails that my father suffered: This is most likely a reference to Dawid's years living as an outlaw in the desert wilderness prior to becoming king. Evyathar flees the slaughter of priests at Nov and joins Dawid in the wilderness in Sam P51,6. In Sam P51,10, we learn that Evyathar brought the *ephod* with him when he fled, and Evyathar uses the *ephod* to consult Yahweh on behalf of Dawid (see Sam P51,10 - P51,13 and P62,4).

It seems less likely to me that the "travails" here refer to Dawid's flight from Avshalom because at that time Dawid sent Evyathar back to Yerushalem, where he served as a source of intelligence for Dawid about Avshalom's plans (see Sam P99,2).

6,1d to fulfill the promise Yahweh made concerning Eliy's family in Shiloh: Sam P3 relates Yahweh's statement of doom against Eliy's family; this statement is also referenced in Sam P6. In Sam P3, Yahweh tells Eliy through a prophet that he will cut down his progeny and none will live a long life—the "entire male increase" of his family will die off and not serve at Yahweh's altar. And in P6, Yahweh tells Shmu'el that the wrongdoing of Eliy's family can never be propitiated. The author of the succession narrative has in mind the part of the promise that Eliy's family will no

NOTES AND COMMENTS

longer serve at Yahweh's altar—this is the part of the promise that is fulfilled here in Kgs P6,1.

Evyathar is the son of Ahimelek Ahituvsson (Sam P51,6). In Sam P25,4, we learn that Ikavod Phinhasson (who is Eliy's grandson) is the cousin of Ahiyah Ahituvsson. Presuming Ahiyah and Ahimelek were brothers, this would mean Evyathar's father Ahimelek was also cousin to Ikavod. In this scenario, Evyathar is a second cousin to Ikavod; this is no term in English for Evyathar's relationship to Eliy—he is simply the second cousin of Eliy's grandson.

Notes to P7

7a when the report of these events came to Yo'av: That is, the report of Adoniyyahu's execution and the banishment of Evyathar.

7b [*though he hadn't been in league with Avshalom*]: This clause reads as an addition to the text; it is the sort of comment that we often see in late compositional stages of the books of the Torah and the Former Prophets, and I assign it to the last compositional stage of Kings. Yo'av played an important role in putting down Avshalom's rebellion. He led one-third of Dawid's forces in the battle against Avshalom near Mahanayim in the Gil'ad region (Sam P99,6), he killed Avshalom when he was caught in a terebinth tree (Sam P99,8), and he convinced Dawid to come to his senses and make an appearance to his forces to ensure their loyalty (Sam P99,14 - P99,15).

7c he fled to Yahweh's tent and grabbed hold of the altar's horns: This is a reference to the tent that Dawid set up inside Fort Dawid to house Yahweh's battle chest (see note 3e above). It is notable that the statement here tells us that the tent shrine included an altar—this is the sole explicit reference to an altar associated with that tent shrine. The succession narrative is a literary creation of its author, and I don't believe it provides us with any real historically reliable information. In the case here, the author likely did not rely on any source and simply assumed that if there was a shrine in Fort Dawid, the shrine would have an altar attached to it.

7d come out!: Benayahu orders Yo'av to come out from the shrine, for he wants to avoid killing Yo'av inside the shrine, which would defile it.

7e the pointless blood-guilt that Yo'av brought upon us: This is a reference to Yo'av's murder of Avner in Sam P72,3 and his murder of Amasa in Sam P,100,9. Note especially the end of Sam P72,3, where the author portrays Dawid's thoughts on the matter: "When Dawid heard a little while later what had happened, he thought, 'I am wholly innocent—Yahweh will never hold me—or my kingship—culpable for Avner Nersson's murder. Yo'av's head is dripping with his blood, as is everyone's in his family.'"

7f [*the head of Yisra'el's army, Avner Nersson, and the head of Yehudah's army, Amasa Yethersson*]: Although it is possible to read this phrase as original to the text, I believe it is best understood as a late gloss added by an editor of Kings' sixth stage to clarify for the reader the identities of the two men whom Yo'av killed. One clue that it is a gloss is the identification of Amasa as head of Yehudah's army, which is quite strange and is inconsistent with Kgs P4, where the author of the succession narrative calls him one of the two heads of Yisra'el's armies. I believe the author of this gloss must have had in mind Sam P100,7 (which is also part of the succession narrative); in that *parashah*, David gives Amasa responsibility for mobilizing the Yehudeans to put down Sheva Bikriysson's rebellion.

7g Benayahu Yehoyada'sson went back and attacked and killed Yo'av: It's worth noting here that this implies Benayahu did defile the tent shrine in Fort Dawid, although this is not stated in the text.

7h He was buried in his house in the desert: In Sam P71,1, we learn that the tomb of Yo'av's ancestors is in Beyth-Lehem. However, it seems unlikely that the author intended us to understand that Yo'av was buried there—if that had been his intention, he would have explicitly mentioned Beyth-Lehem rather than using the phrase "in the desert."

7i he appointed Tzadoq the Priest to replace Evyathar: This is the position of chief priest to Yahweh at the tent shrine inside Fort Dawid. On Tzadoq, see note 1m above. The mention of Shelomo appointing Tzadoq as chief priest is somewhat odd. The author of the succession narrative either did not know, or has overlooked, the fact that Tzadoq was already co-chief priest with Evyathar (see Sam P101,1, which is not part of the succession narrative). Perhaps he intentionally ignored this fact in order to make the narrative more dramatic here by showing Shelomo taking specific action to replace Evyathar.

7j Build yourself a house in Yerushalem…where you shall live: Shim'iy was a Binyaminite who belonged to Sha'ul's clan and was from the town of Bahuriym. The author of the succession narrative viewed Shim'iy as the leader of Sha'ul's clan, and as such, he represented a threat to Shelomo's kingship. Shelomo seeks to remove the threat by putting Shim'iy under house arrest in Yerushalem.

7k and it will be entirely your own fault: The author uses the phrase דמך יהיה בראשך (literally, "your blood will be on your head"). The phrase often refers to the punishment for a crime involving blood-guilt (i.e. murder)—in those instances, the phrase means something like "you're guilty of murder, and will be punished accordingly." However, that is not what the phrase means here. In some instances, the phrase means simply "you will be the cause of your own death." For another example of this usage, see the speech of the spies to the prostitute Rahav in Yeriyho in Jos P4: "should anyone exit the doors of your house and go outside, it will be his own fault if he dies" (the exact wording there is דמו בראשו, "his blood will be on his head").

7,1a Akiysh Ma'akahsson King of Gath: Akiysh is a character from the book of Samuel who gives aid and refuge to Dawid when Dawid is on the run from Sha'ul; Dawid stays with him for a number of years and ultimately serves as Akiysh's personal bodyguard. See Sam P50,2 - P50,3; P57 - P59; and P61 - P62,2. Note that it seems unlikely Akiysh would still be alive at this point—he must have been a few years older than Dawid. In this instance, the author has not given much thought to chronology, and he may have chosen to use Akiysh here because he knew his readers would have been familiar with this character from the book of Samuel.

Notes to P7,1

7,1b ask for his slaves: The verb here is בקש, which is usually translated "seek." In some instances, it is used with the nuance of "ask, request" (although, with the exception of the usage here, all these instances are very late). See BDB, p. 135, def. 6.

7,1c —: The Leningrad Codex does not have a *parashah* break here. See L186 r.2.27.

7,2a the harmful things that your mind contemplated: The verb is ידע, which is usually translated "know," but that is clearly not the meaning here. The verb is sometimes used with the meaning "consider, contemplate" which fits the context a little better. I have adopted this translation, although I am not confident that the verb would be used like this in this instance. It is possible that the text is corrupt. For ידע with the meaning "consider," see BDB, p. 394, def. 1g.

Notes to P7,2

7,2b the harm...that you did to my father Dawid: This is a reference to the scene in Sam P96,4, where Shim'iy curses the king as the king is fleeing Yerushalem.

7,2c "Blessed be King Shelomo! May Dawid's throne be secure in front of Yahweh for all time!": The author doesn't indicate a speaker for this sentence, which is somewhat unusual for ancient Hebrew. It is clear, however, that the speaker must be Shim'iy. Note especially Shim'iy's wish that Dawid's throne be "secure" (נכון) for all time. The author likely intended the reader to see this as a reference to the dynastic promise given Dawid in Sam P80,2. Shim'iy expresses his understanding that Yahweh has specially selected Dawid—a noteworthy admission from the head of the clan of Sha'ul, in essence acknowledging that his family has no claim on the throne. If we believe that the author of the succession narrative wrote during the Persian period and that one of the main purposes of his composition was to critique the popular conception of Dawid and the idea of the Dawidic promise, then it is possible to read Shim'iy's reply to Shelomo as ironic—the Persian period audience reading this passage knows very well that Dawid's throne did not remain secure "for all time."

7,2d And so the kingship was secure in Shelomo's hands: Again, a reference to the dynastic promise in Sam P80,2. The statement here serves as the conclusion to the succession narrative, marking the removal of all the threats to Shelomo and Shelomo's fulfillment of Dawid's last wishes. With the deaths of Adoniyyahu, Yo'av, and Shim'iy, and the banishment of Evyathar from the priesthood, the kingship is "secure" (נכונה) in Shelomo's hands, in keeping with the language of—and in fulfillment of—the portion of the dynastic promise in Sam P80,2 regarding Dawid's successor: "When your days come to an end...I will raise up one of your sons after you—the offspring of your loins—and I will make his kingship secure" (והכינתי את־ממלכתו).

7,2e Shelomo made a marriage alliance with Phar'oh King of Egypt...: The material from here to the end of the *parashah* is not written in the style of the author of the succession narrative—rather it is written in the style of the authors of the earliest version of Kings. Moreover, the narrative here does not flow smoothly from what precedes. While this is wholly speculative, I believe it likely that this material appeared immediately after P11,1 in the earliest version of Kings, and that it was still in that position when the succession narrative was added to Kings (early in the fifth compositional stage). Some decades later, when the material about Shelomo's dream in P8-P8,1 and the story of the prostitutes in P9-P10,1 was added, I believe the editors of the fifth stage transposed the material about Shelomo's marriage alliance and the offerings in the open-air shrines from its original location to the end of P7,2.

There are numerous indications in the material about Shelomo reflecting a close relationship with Egypt and deep Egyptian influence on Shelomo's administration. Here in P7,2, the mention of Shelomo's marriage alliance with Phar'oh and the detail about Phar'oh's daughter living in Fort Dawid likely appeared in the source documents used by the authors of the Josianic study books, in particular the scroll *The Acts of Shelomo*, which is mentioned in P30,3.

7,2f However, the people continued to make sacrificial offerings in the open-air shrines...: This is the first appearance of an important theme in Kings—the problem of the people making offerings in the open-air shrines. The open-air shrines are mentioned more than thirty times in Kings by the authors of the Josianic study books, always in a negative sense. I believe that these authors used this theme as part of their strategy to convince the young king Yoshiyyahu of the requirement to centralize all cult activities in Yerushalem "in the place that Yahweh chose as his very own."

7,2g no house that was Yahweh's own had yet been built: Literally, "no house for Yahweh's name had yet been built." In this instance the use of "name" draws on the idiom "place one's name," which means to claim ownership of. If we understand this meaning here, the distinction is between the open-air shrines, which Yahweh shares with other gods, and the "house" that is Yahweh's own and that is not shared with other gods. This latter view fits well with one of the principles of Yoshiyyahu's reforms, which was to banish the cults of other gods from Yahweh's house on Mount Tziyyon, so that his house was reserved for his cult alone. See note 20c below for a more detailed discussion of the figurative use of "name" in connection with Yahweh's house; for a discussion of the open-air shrines in the cult of Yahweh, see note 8b below.

8a Shelomo loved Yahweh...: This *parashah* introduces the theme of Shelomo's great wisdom, which runs throughout the account of Shelomo's reign. The theme also appears in P9-P10,1; P11,2; P11,4; P12; P25, and P30,3. With the exception of P30,3, I view all the material about Shelomo's wisdom as late. The mention of the theme in P30,3 indicates that there was some material in the source document *The Acts of Shelomo* that mentioned Shelomo's great wisdom. However, none of the other material in Kings that is related to this theme reads as though it came from or was based on that source document. Rather, the other occurrences of the theme have strong literary elements and/or are fabulous in nature. None of this material is characteristic of a palace administrative document. The stories in P9-P10,1, P11,2, and P25 are in keeping with very late compositions about legendary figures of the past, and the occurrences of the theme in P11,4 and P12 read simply as late comments added to the text.

Notes to P8

8b he would regularly make his sacrificial offerings and burn his incense offerings in open-air shrines: That is, he didn't make offerings to Yahweh at the altar in the tent shrine inside Fort Dawid, where Yahweh's battle chest (later treaty chest) was kept.

The author uses two verbs in combination—זבח and קטר. Both verbs can have multiple shades of meaning when used in the context of the cult. The root meaning of זבח is "slaughter." It sometimes has this meaning in cultic contexts, but more often it is used as a general term for making a sacrificial offering of any kind, which is the meaning it has here. The root קטר is used as a verb only in the *pi'el* and *hiph'il* forms. In the context of the cult, both forms of the verb can either have a generic meaning—"make a burnt offering, burn an offering" (with the type of burnt offering being unspecified)—or they can mean "make an incense offering." When קטר appears in combination with זבח, as here, I believe it is best to translate זבח as the general term ("make a sacrificial offering") and קטר as meaning "make an incense offering." This combination appear numerous times in Kings, and that is the approach I have taken in each instance. That said, it would also be possible to understand the two verbs in combination in a generic sense—"slaughter and burn an offering." In that approach, the translation here would be "he would always slaughter and burn his offerings in open-air shrines."

The word that I translate as "open-air shrine" is במה (*bāmāh*). Apart from the temple in Yerushalem, nearly all shrines to Yahweh during the period of the monarchy were open-air shrines. In fact, there is no indisputable archaeological evidence of a temple to Yahweh in the northern kingdom. With the possible exception of Tel Dan (where the evidence is ambiguous), all archaeological evidence from the Iron Age related to Yahweh's cult in the north is associated with open-air cult sites. (For a discussion of the archaeological evidence and its implications, see A. Faust, "Israelite Temples: Where was Israelite Cult Not Practiced, and Why,"

Religions 2019, 10(106).) The open-air shrines (במות or *bāmōth*) typically consisted of an altar on a large elevated platform, on which also stood sacred pillars (מצבות, which functioned in some respects as images of the god) and which often included a wooden post representing the goddess Asherah. Some shrines, but not all, had permanent structures attached. These structures were not temples—they did not house an image of the god—but rather were storerooms and/or living quarters for the priests and other cult officials. For detailed discussions of the open-air shrine, see "בָּמָה *bāmāh*," *Theological Dictionary of the Old Testament*, vol. 2 (Grand Rapids, Michigan: Eerdmans, 1975), 139-145; L. Kogan and S. Tishchenko, "Lexicographic Notes on Hebrew bamah," *Ugarit Forschungen* 34 (2003), 319-352; and B. Alpert Nakhai, "What's a Bamah? How Sacred Space Functioned in Ancient Israel," *Biblical Archaeology Review*, May/June 1994, 18-29.)

8c the most prominent open-air shrine: An equally plausible translation is "the largest open-air shrine." The platforms on which the altars in the open-air shrines sat could be quite large, as could be the altars themselves. The platform discovered at Tell Dan, for example, measured 18.2 by 18.7 meters (60 feet by 61 feet); the altar that sat on the platform was 4.75 meters square (approx. 15.5 feet by 15.5 feet) and three meters (approx. 10 feet) in height. For an interesting discussion of the cult at Tell Dan, see D. Ilan and J. Greer, "A Pilgrimage to Iron Age II Tell Dan," *Advances in Ancient, Biblical, and Near Eastern Research* 1, no. 3 (Autumn 2021): 143-190.

8d (the people you chose, a vast people so populous they can be neither counted nor numbered): I understand this parenthetical comment to be original to the *parashah*, which I believe was composed in the late Persian period or early Hellenistic period. The comment integrates themes from Deuteronomy and Exodus (Yahweh choosing his people) and from Genesis (the blessing of descendants so numerous that they can't be counted) into Shelomo's speech.

8e for otherwise, how would one be able to judge this great people of yours?: That is, the people governed by Shelomo are so numerous that one would not be able to administer justice to them effectively unless Yahweh had given him an especially discerning mind.

Notes to P8,1

8,1a Shelomo woke up...: I understand this *parashah* to belong with P8, and I view both *parashot* together as a literary composition from the late Persian period or early Hellenistic period. Here in P8,1, note in particular the unusual phrase "the Lord's treaty chest" (ארון ברית אדני). The concept of the treaty chest is not original to the Josianic study books and is an invention of the Persian period authors who composed Deuteronomy. But the authors of the early versions of Deuteronomy, Exodus-Numbers, and Joshua always use the phrase "Yahweh's treaty chest." The use of "Lord" in place of "Yahweh" is an indication that this *parashah* likely dates to the late Persian period or Hellenistic period, when authors were less comfortable writing the name Yahweh.

8,1b following which he offered up whole offerings and prepared welfare offerings: The author, who is writing in the Persian period or Hellenistic period, implies that Shelomo here breaks from his usual practice of making offerings in open-air shrines and in this instance makes these offerings on the altar in front of the tent shrine inside Fort Dawid, where Yahweh's battle chest (later treaty chest) was located.

Notes to P9

9a Now at that time, two prostitutes...: The famous story of Shelomo's judgement of the dispute between the two prostitutes begins here in P9 and runs through P10,1. While the story may be based on an old folk legend, it is written in a highly literary style and I understand it to be a composition of the late Persian period or Hellenistic period. It can be thought of as a companion to the story in P8 - P8,1, as it illustrates how Shelomo used the "discerning mind" that Yahweh granted him to administer justice and adjudicate legal disputes. One interesting aspect of the story is that it is almost entirely in dialog form; the language is quite lively, and it is likely that the author strove to capture as accurately as possible the Hebrew of everyday speech.

9b two days after I gave birth: Literally, "on the third day of my giving birth." When relating two events to each other in time, ancient Hebrew speakers began the count on the day the first event occurred. So to say an event happened "on the third day of my giving birth" is equivalent to an English speaker stating an event happened "two days after I gave birth."

9c there isn't anyone else in the house with us: Literally, "there isn't any non-family member in the house with us." The participle of זר refers to a person outside one's clan or community. It is typically used in places where an English speaker would use the words "foreigner," "stranger," or "outsider." Here in P9, the prostitute uses the term to designate an unrelated person staying in the house as either a guest or a lodger.

10a —: The Leningrad Codex does not have a *parashah* break here; see L187 r.1.13.   Note to P10

10,2a King Shelomo was king over all of Yisra'el: I believe the earliest version   Note to P10,2
of Kings began with this *parashah*. Originally, the book of Kings was unconnected to Samuel. Like many scholars, I place the earliest composition of Kings in the reign of Yoshiyyahu. As discussed in my introductory note, I speculate that the composition of the earliest versions of Judges, Samuel, and Kings was associated with the education of Yoshiyyahu, who assumed the throne at the age of nine. Thus I refer to the earliest versions of these three books as "the Josianic study books." The books likely were composed in a piecemeal process over the course of the king's education; in this scenario, each book would have served a separate purpose in the "curriculum" designed for the king. Thus, there were stories offering exemplars in military leadership (Judges), stories about the Yoshiyyahu's great ancestor, Dawid, the founder of the Dawidic dynasty and of Yahweh's cult in Yerushalem (Samuel), and lessons regarding the importance of the king following Yahweh and pleasing him in matters of the cult (Kings). The authors of the king's curriculum—likely officials in the palace (some of whom must have been from northern families)—used their influence with the young boy to promote an ambitious political and religious agenda, which included bringing the former territories of the kingdom of Yisra'el under the king's control and the centralization of Yahweh's cult in Yerushalem.

The material in P10,2 - P10,23 plus the first part of P10,24 is a cohesive unit; I believe the authors of the Josianic study books reproduced this material largely verbatim from their primary source document for Shelomo, the scroll called *The Acts of Shelomo*.

Here in P10,2, in the very first sentence of the earliest version of Kings, the authors use the phrase "all of Yisra'el." It is unclear how we should understand this language. Was the phrase in the source document, or does it represent an editorial comment of the authors of the Josianic study books? If it appeared in the source document *The Acts of Shelomo*—and if that document was a genuine record from Shelomo's administration—then this raises the question as to whether Shelomo ruled both Yisra'el and Yehudah, or whether he ruled Yisra'el only. And if it is possible that he ruled only Yisra'el, then that further begs the questions as to whether he was in fact the son of Dawid or whether there was ever a united kingdom of Yisra'el and Yehudah. Such questions take us deep into speculative territory and so probably are not worth spending much time on. I will just make two points here. First, the material in Kings about Shelomo that I have identified as from the source document is not inconsistent with the idea that Shelomo may have been a king of Yisra'el only. For example, none of the twelve tax districts in P10,12 - P10,24 appear to have been located in Yehudah. (In fact, Yitzhak Lee-Sak has proposed the authors of Kings based the Solomonic districts on actual tax districts of the kingdom of Yisra'el in the early eighth century BCE; see "The Solomonic Districts and the Nimshide Dynasty Administrative System in the Southern Levant," *Religions* 2023, 14(5), 598.) Second, while the traditions connecting Shelomo with construction projects in Yerushalem are especially strong, it is possible that during his reign Yerushalem belonged to the tribal territory of Binyamin and so at the time was part of Yisra'el, not Yehudah. There is no doubt that Shelomo was a genuine historical figure; but given the ambiguous and uncertain evidence about him, there likely will always be questions about whether he ruled both Yisra'el and Yehudah and about whether he was a son of the Yehudean king and founder of Yahweh's cult in Yerushalem, Dawid.

With respect to Shelomo's lineage, it is interesting to note that he is never referred to with the surname Dawidsson—this is quite unusual, as in the royal chronicles used as sources by the authors of Kings, it was standard practice to refer to a king with a surname based on his patronym. We would expect that *The Acts of Shelomo* would have referred to Shelomo in this fashion. Thus the fact that the authors of Kings never refer to Shelomo by his patronym does make one wonder if they did not do so because his patronym was not Dawidsson. In fact, in the account Shelomo's reign, he is never given a surname—he is always called Shelomo or King Shelomo. Only in P116 and P118—in passages by authors of Kings' second and fifth stages—is Shelomo given a surname, and that surname is King of Yisra'el.

If we choose to view the phrase "all of Yisra'el" as a comment by the authors of the Josianic study books and not as language borrowed from the source document *The Acts of Shelomo*, then this has implications for how we understand these authors' intentions in writing their book. If they were writing to educate the young king Yoshiyyahu, then they may have decided to begin their book with the phrase "king over all of Yisra'el" as a way to support their agenda of unifying Yisra'el and Yehudah under the rule of King Yoshiyyahu. In the source documents used by these authors, the term Yisra'el always refers to the territory of the northern kingdom alone, never the territory of both kingdoms combined. In fact, I believe the authors of the Josianic study books were the first individuals to use the term Yisra'el to refer to the territories of both Yisra'el and Yehudah (see note 19a below for a discussion of their expansive use of the term Yisra'el). In literature pre-dating these authors, when the term Yisra'el was used in a geographical sense, the reference was either to the northern kingdom or to the collective tribal territories of Ephrayim, Binyamin, Menashsheh, and Yissakar. (See Sam P70, which defines Yisra'el in this fashion, although it uses Yizre'el in place of Yissakar and western Menashsheh, and it uses Gil'ad and the Ashurites [note: Ashurites is likely an error for Geshurites] in place of eastern Menashsheh.)

Note to P10,3	**10,3a These were his chief officials:** The list of officials in P10,3 - P10,11 and the list of tax commissioners in P10,13 - P10,24 are very likely based on *The Acts of Shelomo*, a copy of which was presumably in the palace archives in Yerushalem.
Note to P10,4	**10,4a —:** The Leningrad Codex does not have a *parashah* break here; see L187 r.1.23.
Notes to P10,5	**10,5a Yehoshaphat Ahiyludsson: chief recorder:** Yehoshaphat Ahiyludsson also served as recorder under Dawid. See Sam P82,1 and Sam P101,1.
	10,5b —: The Leningrad Codex does not have a *parashah* break here; see L187 r.1.24.

10,6a —: The Leningrad Codex does not have a *parashah* break here; see L187 r.1.25. — Note to P10,6

10,7a Tzadoq and Evyathar: priests: Note the inconsistency here with P1 and P6,1 (both which are part of the succession narrative). In P6,1, Evyathar supports Adoniyyahu's claim on the kingship, and in P6,1, one of Shelomo's first acts as king is to banish Evyathar from the kingship. As discussed above, I view the material in P1 - P7,2 as a literary creation by the author of the succession narrative, which was composed and added to Kings early in the book's fifth compositional stage (late sixth or early fifth century BCE). The list of officials in P10,3 - P10,11 is without a doubt more historically accurate. — Note to P10,7

Recall that both Tzadoq and Evyathar were the chief priests under Dawid (see notes 1l and 1m above). Both would have been attached to the tent shrine inside Fort Dawid where Yahweh's battle chest was kept.

Note that in P10,3, we are told that Tzadoq's son Azaryahu was chief priest under Shelomo. In my translation, I have treated P10,7 as original to the earliest version of Kings, but given that Azaryahu was already listed as chief priest, it is possible that the inclusion of Tzadoq and Evyathar in the list of Shelomo's officials is in fact a late addition to the text.

10,8a the tax commissioners: The term that I translate as "tax commissioner" is נציב. The literal sense of the term is something like "one who is stood up" (i.e. appointed); it is usually translated as "prefect." Tax farming was the standard system utilized by kings and rulers in the ancient Near East for raising revenue to run their states. The material here in Kings provides a fascinating picture of tax farming in the kingdom of Yisra'el, and—in my opinion—it is very likely that the names of the individuals and the districts they "farmed" are historically accurate. — Notes to P10,8

10,8b —: The Leningrad Codex does not have a *parashah* break here; see L187 r.1.27.

10,9a [*confidante to the king*]: I understand this phrase to be variant reading that has been preserved by the editors of the final stage of Kings. — Notes to P10,9

10,9b —: The Leningrad Codex does not have a *parashah* break here; see L187 r.2.1.

10,10a Ahiyshar: palace chamberlain: The phrases על הבית ("over the house") and אשר על הבית ("[one] who is over the house") were the terms for the job title of the palace chamberlain—the man who managed the day-to-day affairs of the palace. In modern-day terms, the palace chamberlain had a role similar to that of a chief operating officer or the chief of staff of the executive officer of a government or large corporation. The term אשר על הבית is the usual term for the role of chamberlain, but the less common term על הבית is the one that is used here. — Notes to P10,10

10,10b —: The Leningrad Codex does not have a *parashah* break here; see L187 r.2.2. It is interesting to note that initially there was no *parashah* break here in the Aleppo Codex either, but the scribe of the consonantal text, Shelomo ben Buya'a, then changed his mind. We know this because ben Buya'a filled in the line about Ahiyshar the chamberlain with a doodle so that there was no blank space at the end of the line (see A74 r.2.25). A scribe would only do this if there were no new *parashah* beginning on the following line. Initially then, ben Buya'a did not plan to start a new *parashah* on the following line. However, he must have reconsidered—perhaps after discussing with Aharon ben Asher (who added vocalization and the *masorah* to the Aleppo Codex) or after consulting additional manuscripts—because he did choose to indent the next line of the manuscript (A74 r.2.26), indicating a new *parashah setumah*.

Note to P10,11	**10,11a Adoniyram Avda'sson: head of the labor gangs:** This officer is also mentioned in P12. I believe he is the same individual as the person named Adoram in P31, who oversaw Rehav'am's labor gangs and who was stoned to death by the Yisra'elites. (There is also an Adoram who oversaw Dawid's labor gangs who is mentioned in Sam P101,1, although that *parashah* is a late addition to Samuel, and the authors of the Josianic study books would not have known it.) The authors of the Josianic study books almost certainly viewed the Adoniyram here in P10,11 and P12 and the Adoram in P31 as the same individual.
Note to P10,12	**10,12a Shelomo had twelve tax commissioners over the whole of Yisra'el:** The list that follows provides the names of twelve tax commissioners and the regions that they "farmed." I believe that from this list we can get a relatively accurate picture of the true extent of the area ruled by Shelomo. The following tribal areas are mentioned: Yissakar, Naphtaliy and Asher in the north, the Ephrayim hill country and Binyamin in the center; towns associated with the territory of Dan in the west; towns associated with the northern and western parts of the territory of Menashsheh; and, east of the Yarden river, the Gil'ad region (inhabited by Menashshehites and Gil'adites) and the Bashan region. (Note that in Shelomo's time, the Gil'adites were considered a "tribe;" these clans seem to have later been absorbed into Menashsheh.) As discussed above in note 10,2a, the list of tax districts can be understood to imply that Shelomo ruled the northern territories only—that is, Yisra'el—and that he did not have dominion over Yehudah.
Note to P10,14	**10,14a in Maqatz and in Sha'alviym, and Beyth Shemesh; Eylon, Beyth Hanan:** Sha'alviym, Beyth Shemesh and Eylon are all listed in Jos P43 as located in the tribal territory of Dan, directly west of Ephrayim. Maqatz and Beyth Hanan are mentioned only here in the Tanakh; they must have been near the other towns in Dan listed here, although their exact locations are unknown.
Note to P10,15	**10,15a Arubboth...Sokoh...the Hepher region:** Sokoh is listed as one of the towns in the low country in the western part of Yehudah in Jos P31,1; there is a second Sokoh listed in Jos P31,6 which is located in the mountainous eastern part of Yehudah. However, there is no reason to think that either of these two towns is the Sokoh here in P10,15. The town of Arubboth and the Hepher region are unknown, but presumably they are near Sokoh, wherever that may have been.
Note to P10,16	**10,16a Dor Heights:** Dor Heights (or Dor) is mentioned several times in Joshua. The mentions in Jos P22 and Jos P34 make it clear that the town is near the Mediterranean coast in the territory of Menashsheh and is relatively close to the towns of Ta'nak and Megiddo (which are part of a different tax district).
Notes to P10,17	**10,17a Ba'ana Ahiyludsson: Ta'nak and Megiddo, plus all of Beyth She'an:** This tax district lies in the tribal territory of Menashsheh and covers the heart of the Yizre'el Valley. The tax commissioner Ba'ana Ahiyludsson belonged to the same family as Yehoshaphat Ahiyludsson, who is mentioned in P10,5 as the recorder for Shelomo's palace administration.
	10,17b the region from Beyth She'an to Dancing Meadow to just beyond Yoqme'am: I understand Yoqme'am to be an error for Yoqne'am. The region described cuts across the heart of the Yizre'el Valley. Beyth She'an is located close to the Yarden River at the southern edge of the valley. The tax region runs northwest from Beyth She'an through the Yizre'el Valley (where Ta'nak and Megiddo are located) all the way up to Yoqne'am, which is north of the valley and just south of the Mount Karmel area near the Mediterranean coast.

10,18a Ya'iyr Menashshehsson's hamlets...the Argov district: This tax district consists of parts of the Gil'ad and Bashan regions east of the Yarden River. Note that Ya'iyr Menashshehsson's settlements are also mentioned in Num P87, Deut P1,4, and Jos P27,1.

Notes to P10,18

10,18b [*sixty large towns with walls and with gates secured by bronze bars*]: The material I have placed in brackets reads as a comment added in Kings' sixth stage. The author of the comment knows of the passage in Deut P1,4 that states the Argov district contains sixty towns fortified with walls and barred gates, and he helpfully adds that information for the reader here.

10,19a Mahanayim and vicinity: Mahanayim was the largest town in the Gil'ad region. It was the town Dawid fled to during Avshalom's rebellion, and it was the royal seat of the kingdom of Yisra'el under Ish-Ba'al Sha'ulsson before he was murdered (see Sam P70).

Notes to P10,19

10,19b —: The Leningrad Codex does not have a *parashah* break here. See L187 r.3.3.

10,20a —: The Leningrad Codex does not have a *parashah* break here. See L187 r.3.5.

Note to P10,20

10,24a an additional tax commissioner who collected taxes in that territory: Gever Uriysson represents a thirteenth tax commissioner. He almost certainly was the father of Geversson, who is listed in P10,18 as the tax commissioner for Ramoth Gil'ad. The region of Gil'ad was large and populous, and it makes sense that the commissioner responsible for that region might have enlisted another family member (in this case, his father) to help manage the work in such a large territory.

Notes to P10,24

10,24b Yehudah and Yisra'el were large in population... for Shelomo for his entire life: This passage reads as a late addition to the text, likely made in the late Persian period or Hellenistic period as part of what I call Kings' fifth compositional stage. The author embellishes Shelomo's legend with additional details of his greatness and power, which he likely drew from the folk stories of his own day about Shelomo.

The imagery of Yehudah and Yisra'el being large in population and "as numerous as the sand on the seashore" recalls Yahweh's promise in Gen P21 to Avraham to make his descendants "as numerous as the grains of sand on the seashore" and a similar promise to Ya'aqov in Gen P28 ("I shall...give you so many descendants that they can't be counted—like the sand on the shore of the sea"). I believe that the author of the addition here in P10,24 based his language on these passages in Genesis, and he expected his readers to pick up on the allusion.

10,24c the Perath River: The Hebrew reads simply "the River." The Perath River (what we today call the Euphrates) was often referred to as "the River" in ancient Hebrew. I have translated with the river's actual name to avoid confusing the reader.

10,24d [*including the Philishtines' country*]: This phrase is a gloss from the book's final compositional stage. The author was clarifying that Shelomo's empire included the Philishtines' country along the Mediterranean coast.

11a The food consumed at Shelomo's court each day...: I view the first sentence of this *parashah* as part of the earliest version of Kings. The amounts of food listed are reasonable if we assume this food supported not only palace staff but also royal officials based outside Yerushalem and the king's close allies and friends throughout his kingdom (this in fact is suggested by the conclusion of P11,1). If the opening sentence of P11 is original to Kings, then the numbers in it likely came from the source document *The Acts of Shelomo*.

Notes to P11

11b *kor*: A *kor* was equivalent to 220 liters. For a good overview of the biblical weights and measures and their modern equivalents, see the article on "Weights and Measures" at the Jewish Virtual Library website.

11c fatted cattle...grass-fed cattle: The distinction here is likely between cattle fatted in stalls before slaughter and cattle that remain in the pasture before slaughter.

The amount of food consumed by Shelomo's royal administration each day is quite large. Ninety *kor* of grain is equivalent to nearly 20,000 liters, or 12,000 kilograms. Assuming the meat yielded from cattle and sheep was half of the yield today, thirty head of cattle would produce approximately 5,000 kilograms of beef and 100 sheep would produce approximately 1,500 kilograms of mutton. One kilogram of grain provides 3,400 calories, one kilogram of beef provides 2,500 calories, and one kilogram of mutton 1,500 calories. If we assume the average person in Shelomo's time consumed 2,500 calories daily, the amounts of grain and meat given here in P11 would feed more than 22,000 people. These numbers are clearly fantastic if they represent the food consumed at the palace in Yerushalem; however, they seem reasonable if—as is suggested by the conclusion to P11,1—they represent the food that the tax commissioners supplied to royal officials based outside Yerushalem and to the king's close allies and friends living throughout the kingdom.

11d fatted *barburim*: It is unclear what animals the word *barburim* refers to. Traditionally, it has been assumed to be a kind of bird (such as a goose). However, the word occurs in a list of ruminants—rams, gazelles, and roebucks—and for that reason, I believe the word denotes a species of ruminant, likely a species of antelope or gazelle.

11e For he had dominion...: I view the material from here to the end of the *parashah* as an addition made by authors of Kings' fifth stage. This first sentence of the addition reads as a comment reminding the reader that Shelomo ruled a large area (and thus would have had no difficulty obtaining the amounts of food listed in the previous sentence). The second sentence of the addition, which states that Yehudah and Yisra'el lived peacefully in Shelomo's days, may represent a separate addition made during the fifth compositional stage.

11f the entire region of Beyond-the-River: The author uses the term עבר הנהר ("Beyond-the-River"), which was name of the region southwest of the Perath river— roughly the southern half of modern day Syria plus. The term was sometimes used expansively to include the Levant as well. The term Beyond-the-River appears frequently in Akkadian cuneiform documents and in Hebrew and Aramaic documents.

11g from Tiphsah to Azzah: The phrase identifies the northernmost and southernmost extremities of Beyond-the-River. The mention of Azzah as the southernmost extremity indicates that the author here uses the term Beyond-the-River expansively to include Kena'an.

11h [*that is, over all the kings in the Beyond-the-River region*]: An editor of the sixth compositional stage likely added this comment to clarify that Shelomo didn't directly rule the entire region of Beyond-the-River, but rather was suzerain to the kings of that region.

11i he had peaceful relations with his neighbors on all sides: The Hebrew phrasing is a little unusual—a literal rendering is "he had peace from all his neighbors around him" (ושלום היה לו מכל-עבריו מסביב).

11j each person enjoying the fruit of his own land: The author uses a Hebrew idiom. Literally, "each man under his grapevine and under his fig tree."

11k from Dan in the north to Be'er Sheva in the south: I have added the phrases "in the north" and "in the south" to make clear to the reader how the author intends his language to be understood. Dan was at the northernmost extremity of the tribal territories and Be'er Sheva at the southernmost extremity. The phrase "from Dan to Be'er Sheva" was a common way to indicate the entirety of the Yisra'elite tribal territories within Kena'an. Note the similar construction ("from Tiphsah to Azzah") used to qualify Beyond-the-River earlier in this *parashah*.

11,1a Shelomo had forty thousand stalls [*horses*] for his chariotry and twelve thousand chariot horses: I view this *parashah* as belonging to Kings' first stage. As with P11, the source of the numbers here in P11,1 likely was *The Acts of Shelomo*.

Notes to P11,1

The term that I translate as "chariot horses" is פרשים. The word פרש has two meanings: (1) a horse used in warfare (most often, but not exclusively, a horse that pulls a chariot), and (2) a cavalryman or warrior on horseback. The earliest evidence of true cavalry in the ancient Near East is from the reign of the Assyrian king Ashurnasirpal II (883-859 BCE). Prior to that, horses were used in war only to pull chariots and carts. Thus, in Shelomo's day, the term could only refer to a chariot horse or a cart horse, and I have translated here accordingly. On the history of horses in warfare see J. Ellis, *Cavalry: The history of mounted warfare*, New York: Putnam's Sons, 1978; the discussion of horses in early warfare can be found on pp. 7-21.

Note that a later editor has added a gloss indicating that "stalls" should be understood to mean "horses." This editor may have been confused by the text because he understood פרשים to mean "cavalry" (its usual meaning in his day); he consequently attempted to clarify the confusing text by indicating that "stalls" should be understood to mean "horses." One final note: the parallel text in P27,1 states that Shelomo had fourteen hundred chariots rather than forty thousand. This is a much more sensible number and may represent the original reading here in P11,1. Depictions of chariots on ivories from Late Bronze Age Megiddo show chariots being pulled by two horses. Assuming Shelomo's chariots were also pulled by two horses, the ratio implied by the passage in P27,1—maintaining between eight and nine horses to support each chariot—seems a reasonable one. The passage in P27,1 also offers some support for viewing "horses" (סוסים) in P11,1 as a late gloss on "stalls."

11,1b These tax commissioners supplied King Shelomo...: This sentence follows naturally from the end of the list of tax commissioners in P10,24, and it may have appeared that way in the source document, *The Acts of Shelomo*. If that is the case, that implies the authors of the first stage took the first sentence of P11 and the first sentence of P11,1 from a different section of their source document and inserted them before the end of P11,1 to provide context on the amounts of food supplied by the tax commissioners.

If we take the view that the first sentence of P11 and all of P11,1 are from *The Acts of Shelomo*, then we should presume the amounts of food listed at the beginning of P11 represent the amounts that the tax commissioners supplied to Shelomo and "all those who sat at the king's table."

11,1c all those who sat at the king's table: This phrase describes all those who regularly receive food rations from the king. It is important to note that this would include friends and allies of the king who live throughout the kingdom, not just those living in Yerushalem. It likely also includes royal officials who live in the provinces and perform government functions there. The phrasing at the end of this *parashah*, which mentions barley and straw and bringing supplies to various locales, suggests that "those who sat at the king's table" may also have included officials and soldiers based in military outposts. If we assume the information here in P11,1 has some basis in reality, then we should conclude that the amounts of food listed in P11 likely did not include any supplemental grain given to Shelomo's 12,000 chariot horses.

Notes to P11,2

11,2a God endowed Shelomo with extraordinary amounts of wisdom...: I view this *parashah* as a late expansion, added as part of Kings' fifth compositional stage. The addition here may be by the same authors who added the story of Yahweh appearing to Shelomo in a dream in P8, for once the dream was added, these same authors would then want to show the fulfillment of the promise that Yahweh made to Shelomo in his dream.

11,2b all the men of the eastern lands: The eastern lands represent Mesopotamia, which to the authors of Kings was an ancient civilization and the source of both culture and wisdom, similar to Egypt. Although the phrase כל־בני קדם could possibly be understood as "all the men of ancient times," all other occurrences of the term בני־קדם clearly mean "men of the east." For that reason it is best to read "men of the east" here as well.

11,2c He discoursed on the trees... and he discoursed on all the animals: Ancient proverbs and wisdom sayings commonly made observations about trees and animals and then from these observations drew lessons about how humans should live their lives. The book of Proverbs is full of such observations, and the books of the Torah and Former Prophets sometimes quote proverbs and sayings of this nature. See, for example, Yotham's speech in Jud P29,1, which is a lengthy parable involving trees, and which concludes with a proverb about the thornbush and the mighty cedars of Levanon.

Note to P11,3

11,3a Hiyram had been a close friend to Dawid his entire life: The only reference to Hiyram in Samuel is in P75, when he sends a delegation to Dawid along with cedar wood and carpenters and stonemasons and then has a palace built for Dawid.

Notes to P11,4

11,4a a house that would belong to his god Yahweh: Literally, "a house for his god Yahweh's name." On the figurative use of "name" to express ownership, see note 20c below.

11,4b the constant warfare with those surrounding him: The author alludes to the events described in the book of Samuel: as king, Dawid fights Sha'ul's family in Sam P71,1 and P72; he fights the Philistines in Sam P76 - P78 and P82; he fights Mo'av, Tzovah, and Aram in Sam P82; and he subjugates Edom in Sam P82,1. I view Kgs P11,4 as part of the earliest version of Kings. As such, the version of Samuel known by the author of this *parashah* would not have included the succession narrative. In the parts of the succession narrative belonging to Samuel, David fights two additional wars with his neighbors: in Sam P83 - P83,1, he fights the Ammonites and their allies (Aram Tzovah, Aram Beth-Rehov, Ma'akah, and Iysh-Tov); and, in his final war with a neighbor, he and his forces fight the Ammonites alone (Sam P84, P84,2 and P86).

11,4c just as Yahweh promised my father Dawid...he's the one who will build the house that will be my very own.": The author here loosely quotes Sam P80,2: "I will raise up one of your sons after you—the offspring of your loins—and I will make his kingship secure. He is the one who will build a house that will be my very own."

11,4d "Blessed be Yahweh...because he gave Dawid a wise son to rule over such a populous nation!": I view this sentence as an addition to the text made by an author of the fifth compositional stage. The authors of the fifth stage added much material to Kings regarding the theme of Shelomo's great wisdom, and here they have put words into Hiyram's mouth to remind the reader of Yahweh's gift of wisdom to Shelomo and of the large population that Shelomo rules. Both these themes were introduced by the authors of the fifth stage with the addition of P8, but they are completely out of place here in P11,4—they have nothing to do with the surrounding narrative. The language about a "populous" nation may be an allusion to Genesis, one of the most important themes of which is Yahweh's promise to give Abraham, Isaac, and Jacob descendants "as numerous as the stars in the sky, as numerous as the grains of sand on the seashore" (see, for example, Gen P21).

11,4e Hiyrom: The author writes Hiyram's name as "Hiyrom," which is not an error but simply an alternate spelling.

11,4f twenty thousand *kor* of wheat...and twenty *kor* of freshly-pressed oil: A *kor* was equivalent to 220 liters (see note 11b above). Shelomo's annual payment to Hiyram was equivalent to 4.4 milllion liters of wheat (roughly equal to 2.6 million kilograms) and 4,400 liters of olive oil. Twenty *kor* of olive oil is immaterial in comparison to the wheat, and I think it quite likely that the word for "thousand" (אלף) has fallen out of the text. If this were the case, the amount of olive oil included in Shelomo's annual payment to Hiyram would have been 4.4 million liters and not 4,400 liters.

12a [*Now as Yahweh had given Shelomo wisdom, just as he had promised him,*]: The mention of Yahweh's gift of wisdom here is completely incongruous with what follows, and for that reason I view this clause as a late addition to the text made by the authors of the fifth compositional stage. It is unclear to me what prompted this addition, as it doesn't enhance the narrative of P12 in any way.

Notes to P12

12b Adoniyram supervised the labor gangs: This is the same Adoniyram mentioned in P10,11. See note 10,11a. In my translation, I have treated this sentence as part of Kings' first stage; however, it is possible that this sentence is a comment by the authors of the sixth stage reminding readers that Adoniyram would have been involved in this work.

12,1a Shelomo employed seventy thousand men...: The material in P12 and here in P12,1 describes a vast work project: thirty thousand forced laborers assigned to Levanon (ten thousand deployed at a time) helping with cutting down trees, eighty thousand men in the mountains of Ephrayim and/or Yehudah quarrying stone, and seventy thousand men carrying materials to Yerushalem. The latter two groups were managed by 3,300 overseers, who in turn were supervised by the head tax commissioners in Shelomo's twelve tax districts. The numbers are clearly exaggerated—such a sizable work force would not be needed to construct the relatively small structure that was Yahweh's "house," nor the larger palace complex that we are told Shelomo built for himself. Even though the numbers do not reflect historical reality, there is no reason to think that this material was not part of the earliest version of Kings. The authors of the Josianic study books had just as much incentive to exaggerate numbers as the authors who worked on the books of the Former Prophets and the Torah in later centuries.

Notes to P12,1

12,1b —: The Leningrad Codex does not have a *parashah* break here. See L188 r.1.20-21.

12,2a and the Gevalites: The text here, which reads והגבלים, is probably in error. BDB, p. 148, suggests "and they edged them" (ויגבלם), which is the reading of the Septuagint and which is likely correct. If this reading were adopted, the text would be translated as, "Shelomo's construction workers and Hiyram's construction workers finished them and edged them, and then they fixed the timber and the stones...."

Notes to P12,2

NOTES AND COMMENTS

12,2b finished the stones: The verb is פסל, which is typically translated "hew, hew into shape." Context indicates that the use of the verb here must refer to the finish work done on the stones at the construction site, for the stones were hewn into a standard size when quarried.

12,2c they fixed the timber and the stones in place so that the house could be built: I understand the fixing of the timber and the stones to refer to the building of the foundation only, as this is the topic of this *parashah*.

Notes to P13

13a [*In the four hundred and eightieth year after the Yisra'elites left Egypt*]: I view this clause as a late addition by the editors of Kings' sixth compositional stage. The addition reflects the growing antiquarian interest among individuals within Yahweh's cult during the Persian period, which included a desire to establish a uniform chronology in which to place the great events of the past. In the instance here, the editors of Kings' sixth stage wish to relate the construction of Yahweh's house in Yerushalem—perhaps the most important event in the book of Kings for them—to the exodus, the event that marked the beginning of Yahweh's relationship with his people. It is noteworthy, in my opinion, that this addition to P13 is the only instance we see of such a chronological system in the Tanakh, suggesting that this particular system of dating events in relation to the exodus was never adopted in a meaningful way.

It should be noted that the authors of the Josianic study books date events only in relation to royal chronology. The dating of the construction of Yahweh's house to the fourth year of Shelomo's reign is almost certainly part of the earliest version of Kings. The authors of the Josianic study books have based this first sentence of P13 on the summary statement about the construction of Yahweh's house which I believe appeared in *The Acts of Shelomo* and which they inserted verbatim in P15 (see note 15q below).

13b the month of Ziw [*that is, the second month*]: Ziw is a Phoenician month name; other Phoenician month names are also used in the *parashah*. An editor of the sixth stage has glossed this as the "second month," which corresponds to a period between April and May. In my composition history, I view the sixth stage as contemporaneous with the other five stages of Kings, although I believe most of the editorial activity of the sixth stage was quite late. The gloss here in P13 is an example of an edit from the sixth stage that might be very early—possibly even part of the earliest version of Kings.

13c sixty cubits in length, twenty cubits in width, and thirty cubits high: In the measurement system used in ancient Yisra'el and Yehudah, there was both a "long" cubit and a "short" cubit. Although there is some uncertainty about the precise length, scholars estimate that the long cubit measured 0.521 meters and the short cubit 0.446 meters. If we assume that the author of this *parashah* expressed his measures in terms of the long cubit, then we can infer the dimensions of Yahweh's house as indicated here in P13 were 31 meters in length, a little over 10 meters in width, and 15½ meters high. In terms of English measures, this equates to 102½ feet long, a little over 34 feet wide, and 51¼ feet high. For a good discussion of the measurement systems used by the authors of the Tanakh, see the article "Weights & Measures" at the Jewish Virtual Library website.

13d the house's great hall: The term that I translate as "great hall" is היכל (*hēkāl*). This term is a loan word from Akkadian *ekallu*, which itself is a loan word from Sumerian *é.gal* ("large house").

13e side chambers were made on all sides: The text reads סביב ("on all sides"), but in fact the author clearly intended the reader to understand that the side chambers were on three sides—the north and south façades (the long sides of the house) and the west façade (the back side of the house). The eastern façade (the front of the house) had a large porch attached to it and a grand entrance; thus, there would have been no place for side chambers on the front of the house.

13f the lower corniche: The three cornices function as roofs to the three levels of side chambers. The cornices are attached to Yahweh's house, and the side chambers are free-standing structures that abut the house, but they are not attached to it.

13g neither hammers, nor saws, nor any sort of iron tool were heard in the house: This statement seems inconsistent with the comment in P12,2 that the construction workers "finished" (פסל) the stones on site. See note 12,2b above. I attribute the inconsistency here to the authors' lack of concern for strict narrative logic; I do not see any sign of a different literary layer.

13h the middle side chambers: The text is almost certainly in error. The description of the building makes perfect sense if the word for middle (תיכנה) is replaced with the word for lower (תחתנה). This would result in a text that read "the door to the lower side chambers." It is easy to see how a scribe might have inadvertently made such an error.

14a The following oracle was Yahweh was given to Shelomo...: I view this *parashah* as an addition and assign it to the second compositional stage. There are two indications that it is an addition. First, it disrupts the narrative describing the construction of Yahweh's house. Second, it radically reinterprets the Dawidic promise. In the earliest version of Samuel and Kings, the Dawidic promise is unconditional: the Dawidic dynasty will last forever, and Yahweh will "dwell" in his house in Yerushalem alongside the king. Here in P14, Yahweh's promise to Dawid is very different. It is now a promise that Yahweh will live among the Yisra'elites and never abandon them as long as the king remains loyal to Yahweh and (as leader of the cult) follows Yahweh's laws and commandments.

Notes to P14

14b **: The Leningrad Codex has a *parashah setumah* here. See L188 r.3.19.

15a Shelomo built the house and completed it...: I view the entire account of the construction of Yahweh's house in P15 (which ends with the construction of the inner courtyard) to represent a series of additions by the authors of the fifth compositional stage. Apart from the original addition of P15, there are three subsequent additions to this *parashah*—see notes 15f, 15j, and 15m below. Note that P13 (which is part of the Josianic study books) concludes with a statement that "construction on the house was complete." The account in P15 repeats some of the details of the construction in P13 and adds many new details about the interior decoration. I view the account of the construction of the Levanon Forest House in the second half of P15 to be original to the Josianic study books.

Notes to P15

15b the great hall in front: It is possible the text is corrupt. The Septuagint reads "the great hall in front of the cella," which suggests a Hebrew text that had the word דביר after לפני.

15c to plasce Yahweh's treaty chest there: For the authors of the Josianic study books, the term is always ארון יהוה, which is best translated as "Yahweh's battle chest." Later authors took the old idea of Yahweh's battle chest and transformed it into a chest for storing Yahweh's treaty with the Yisra'elites (that is, the book of Deuteronomy)—

hence the name "Yahweh's treaty chest" (ארון ברית יהוה). I briefly discuss this proposal in my work on Numbers (see p. 196 of the digital edition of that book).

The special interest that the authors of the first half of P15 have in the treaty chest indicates that the account of the construction of Yahweh's house here in P15 cannot have been composed by the authors of the Josianic study books.

The authors of this passage use an unusual spelling of the infinitive of the verb נתן ("give, place, set"). I have reflected this in translation with an archaic spelling of the verb "place." The same unusual spelling of this verb also appears in P49,3, where it is corrected by the Masoretes with a *qere* in the margin. See note 49,3h below. It is interesting that the Masoretes did not correct the spelling here in P15 with a *qere*.

15d *sagur*-gold: This possibly refers to braided gold or patterned gold. The word *sagur* (the *qal* passive participle of סגר) means "closed up" or "joined." The term is used to describe the scales of a crocodile in Job 41.7, which offers some support for understanding the gold as being "braided," for braided metal to some extent resembles scales of a reptile.

15e the cedar altar: This is almost certainly an incense altar located in front of the cella, on which offerings of incense were made. In the book of Leviticus, which I believe reflects ancient cult rule books from one or more open-air shrines to Yahweh from the northern kingdom, there are numerous rites involving the offering of incense on the altar inside the Meeting Tent. This cedar altar in Yahweh's house in Yerushalem must have played a similar role in the rites in Yahweh's cult on Mount Tziyyon.

15f Shelomo overlaid the house on the inside...the cella's altar he overlaid entirely with gold: I understand these two sentences to be an addition to the text (but still part of the editorial work on the fifth stage). This addition likely dates to late in the Persian period or to the Hellenistic period, when the text of Kings was embellished in numerous places with details about the great wealth of Shelomo and the magnificence of the temple.

15g the cella's altar: This is the cedar altar mentioned above. The altar is not inside the cella, but is located just outside it in the back of the great hall.

15h each of its wings measured five cubits: Note that the author's description implies that the four wings of the sphinxes extend twenty cubits—the full width of the cella—leaving no room for the sphinxes' bodies. This error on the part of the author indicates he is describing something he has never seen in person—a fact which supports a late date for this part of the *parashah*.

15i the inner structure: The author uses the phrase הבית הפנימי ("the inner structure") as a synonym for the cella (הדביר).

15j On all the house's walls...and the date palms: The text here—the entire four-sentence paragraph in my translation—reads as an addition to the text from late in the fifth compositional stage (i.e. the late Persian period or the Hellenistic period). The purpose here was to embellish the magnificence of Yahweh's house. Note how the description of his house in this paragraph is at odds with the description of the house at the beginning of the *parashah*. In that description, there is only gold in the area of the great hall in front of the cella, and the walls of the great hall are carved with gourds and flower garlands. There are no carvings of winged sphinxes or date palms mentioned in the earlier description of Yahweh's house.

15k the inner room and the outer room: The author uses the terms "inner room" (הפנימי) and "outer room" (החיצון) as synonyms for the cella and the great hall.

15l with the wall joist serving as a fifth door post: The meaning of the Hebrew is obscure, and it is not entirely clear what the author is describing. The word איל is a term for a support beam and is usually translated as "pilaster," which is a vertical support. I understand the word here to refer to a horizontal, not a vertical support, and thus translate as "joist." I believe the author is describing a horizontal beam running the length of the outer wall of the cella; the top of the two doors is just below this beam, so that the beam functions as a fifth "door post" for the two doors, each of which has two vertical door posts. A literal translation of the Hebrew in my understanding is "the joist [with respect to] door posts a fifth [one]."

15m He did the same thing... exactly over the engraving: I understand this entire sentence to be a late addition to the text, made as part of the work belonging to a late edition within Kings' fifth stage. This addition may have been made by the same individual who made the addition discussed above in note 15j, as both additions describe similar decorative carvings.

15n door frames of wild olive wood square in shape: The Hebrew is somewhat obscure, but I believe the meaning is clear. Literally, "door frames of wild olive wood from a square [shape]."

15o each door consisting of two folding panelqs: The Hebrew text contains a misspelling—in the description of one of the doors, the author or a later scribe copying the text mistakenly wrote קלעים ("curtains") instead of צלעים ("panels"). I have reproduced the spelling error by inserting the letter "q" into the word "panel."

15p Next he built the inner courtyard...: In the earliest edition of Kings, this sentence likely followed directly from the end of P13.

15q In the fourth year of Shelomo's reign, in the month of Ziw... the month of Bul... its construction taking seven years: These two sentences, which I believe are a verbatim insertion from *The Acts of Shelomo*, are the conclusion of the account of the construction of Yahweh's house as it appeared in the version of Kings belonging to the Josianic study books. They follow naturally from the end of P13. I view the material from here to the end of this *parashah*, which describes the construction of Shelomo's palace, the Levanon Forest House, to be original to the Josianic study books.

Ziw and Bul are Phoenician month names. Ziw was mentioned in P13 and glossed there by an editor of the sixth stage (see note 13b above). The same editor here glossed the name Bul as the eighth month of the year, which corresponded to a period between October and November.

15r Levanon Forest House: The description of Shelomo's palace bears many similarities to ancient Egyptian palaces, and it seems certain that the design of the building (assuming the account in this *parashah* reflects a true memory of the palace) was influenced by Egyptian practice. The text describes a complex of three structures: the Levanon Forest House (consisting of two pillared halls, which likely were the location for the activities of the government bureaucracy), a porch of columns serving as a grand entry to the Levanon Forest House, and a porch that served as the location for judicial activities (the Judgment Porch). Shelomo's personal quarters occupied a rear court inside the larger Judgement Porch. Separate from the palace complex, Shelomo also built a grand living quarters for Phar'oh's daughter that was similar to his personal quarters. The marriage alliance with Phar'oh, presuming this reflects a real historical fact, provides support for the view that the palace design reflects the influence of Egypt, the wealthier and more powerful neighbor to the south.

The term אולם ("porch") in Hebrew does not necessarily imply a structure without a roof or without walls. Rather, the term seems to have been used to denote any structure with some component that was completely open to the elements—that is, it may have lacked a roof and/or it may have lacked one or more walls. In the case of the Judgement Porch, we should imagine the Judgement Porch as having a roof and as having two or three walls.

A team led by the French egyptologist Franck Monnier has created an impressive three-dimensional reconstruction of the palace of Amenhotep III; the reconstruction can be viewed at The Pharaonic Palace 3D project website. The reconstruction can help the reader visualize details such as the pillared halls in the Levanon Forest House, the rows of windows in the pillared halls, and a throne room (the functional equivalent of the Judgement Porch).

15s it was supported by four rows of cedar pillars, with cedar beams on top of the pillars: The pillars—at least twenty-five cubits in height—must have been the trunks of large cedar trees from the Levanon mountains; hence the palace's name: "the Levanon Forest House." Based on the comment below about the columns being arranged in rows of fifteen, we should understand there to have been sixty pillars total in the palace. The long rows of pillars must have given the palace the appearance of a forest. I understand the cedar beams to connect the tops of all the columns in a single row; in architectural terms, the cedar beams functioned as the architrave that supported the roof.

15t it was paneled with cedar on the ceiling—panels laid over the ribbing that sat atop the pillars: The Hebrew is difficult, both because it is elliptical and because it represents technical terms used in architecture. Literally, "it was paneled with cedar above, on ribs that were atop the pillars." I understand the ribs as running horizontally from a row of columns to the adjacent wall and providing the support for the ceiling panels. The architecture described here is imitative of Egyptian palaces and temples. For readers wishing to visualize the construction of the Levanon Forest House, I would recommend exploring the reconstruction of the palace of Amenhotep III at The Pharaonic Palace 3D project website referenced above in note 15r. Interested readers may also want to visit the University of Memphis website devoted to The Karnak Great Hypostyle Hall project, which has nice visualizations of many of the same architectural features.

15u (forty-five, or fifteen per row): The description of the Levanon Forest House is confusing, and it is difficult to form a clear picture of the building. The text here implies there were three rows of pillars, but the preceding clause states there were four rows of pillars. Assuming the text is not in error, I believe the author is describing a structure of two long halls, each one hundred cubits in length and separated by a large courtyard ("the Great Court," which is described later in the *parashah*). One of the exterior rows of pillars was completely walled while the other three rows had windows and doors set in them. Such a structure would have three rows of pillars that were nearly identical in appearance (the two middle rows that abutted the Great Court and one of the exterior rows), and one row that was entirely different in appearance because it was fully walled.

15v three rows of cased windows, aperture facing aperture three times: I understand this to describe the rows of windows at the top of the pillars on each of the two long halls, with the windows on each row of pillars being set in identical places. Note there are three rows of windows because the fourth row of pillars (the exterior side of one of the long halls) is fully walled.

The phrase מחזה אל מחזה שלש פעמים ("aperture facing aperture three times") is somewhat awkward in Hebrew. Based on the parallel phrase in the following clause, the noun מול ("front") may have fallen out of the text in the description of the windows.

15w aperture directly facing aperture three times: I understand this to describe the doorways that were framed along each row of pillars, with three rows of pillars containing perhaps five or six doorways set in identical places in the rows. (The fourth row of pillars was completely walled and had no doors or windows.)

15x further east were more columns and an *av*: I understand this clause to describe a walkway lined by columns that served as the grand entrance to the palace complex. The word *av* (עב) is an architectural term of unknown meaning. Possibly it refers to an arched(?) roof for the columns lining the walkway. Numerous examples of grand walkways lined with columns are known from Egypt. The Amun temple at Luxor, for example, contained a processional colonnade that linked the Sun Court and the Great Court.

15y He constructed the throne porch: This is not the porch described in the previous paragraph. Rather, I understand it to be a separate structure, adjacent to the Levanon Forest House.

15z from the floor to the floor: The text may be corrupt. BDB, p. 903, suggests "from the floor to the rafters" (reading הקורות in place of הקרקע) on the basis of the Syriac and the Vulgate.

15aa his personal quarters... were of similar design: That is, they were paneled in cedar "from the floor to the rafters." Shelomo's personal quarters likely were a series of apartments that surrounded an inner courtyard on three or four sides. This courtyard was "on the inside" (that is, behind) the Judgement Porch. It is unclear from the author's description how these buildings are attached to one another and how they related to the Levanon Forest House.

15ab finely chiseled: The root גרר means "to drag." The Hebrew reads מגררות במגרה—that is, "dragged with a dragging tool." Traditionally, this has been understood as a description of stones being cut with a saw. However, it seems more likely to me that the author is describing the process of finishing the stones, in which both their interior faces and exterior faces would be smoothed or polished by fine chiseling. The stones were of "standard quarried size," so there would have been no need for workers on site to cut them to size.

15ac the Great Court: I speculate that the Great Court was a large courtyard in the Levanon Forest House and that the two pillared halls ran along it on opposite sides.

15ad Great Court: There is a small error in the text, with the definite article missing from the term for "court" (חצר). I have reflected this error in my translation.

15ae the house's porch: It is unclear whether this phrase refers to the porch on Yahweh's house or the large porch (50 cubits by 30 cubits) in the Levanon Forest House. I have a slight preference for the latter.

Notes to P16

16a He possessed the wisdom, skill, and knowledge to make all sorts of things in bronze: The language here is strikingly similar to the language in Exodus P59 that describes the expertise of Betzal'el Uriysson Hursson, who fashioned the Meeting Tent and the items for Yahweh's cult, following the instructions that Yahweh gave to Mosheh at Mount Siynai. The text in Kings reads: "He was filled with the wisdom, the skill, and the knowledge to make all sorts of things in bronze" (וימלא את־החכמה ואת־התבונה ואת־הדעת לעשות כל־מלאכה בנחשת). And the text in Exodus reads: "Inspiration from God filled him with wisdom, skill, and knowledge, and with all sorts of expertise in order to design the plans to be used, to work with gold, silver, and bronze..." (וימלא אתו רוח אלהים בחכמה בתבונה ובדעת ובכל־מלאכה ולחשב מחשבת לעשות בזהב ובכסף ובנחשת).

I view the material about the making of the equipment for Yahweh's house in P16 - P17,1 and the first two-thirds of P17,2 as a late addition to Kings, and I believe that the language used to describe Hiyram here in P16 was modeled on the language in Exodus P59. My understanding—which is wholly speculative—is that the material in Exodus about the construction of the Meeting Tent and the fashioning of the items used in Yahweh's cult was the product of a collaboration between the priesthoods in Samaria and in Yehud, and was composed in the late fifth or early fourth century BCE. Once this material was added to Exodus, it seems likely to me that there would have been an interest among the priesthood in Yehud in composing similar material in Kings about the making of the cult items for use in Yahweh's house. I do not believe the authors of the Josianic study books, who were writing to educate the king about his role, would have thought it necessary to compose the detailed descriptions of the items used in Yahweh's cult. (They do mention the cult equipment at the end of P17,2, but the descriptions there are quite brief.) These authors' concerns about the cult were focused primarily on the need for the king to "please Yahweh" in cult matters, which in their view required the exclusive worship of Yahweh and the centralization of Yahweh's cult in Yerushalem. Apart from the "house" where Yahweh resided (which is part of the Dawidic promise), the equipment used in the cult was not especially relevant to their purposes in writing their work—hence they devote just a couple sentences to the equipment at the end of P17,2.

16b each was eighteen cubits in height and twelve cubits in circumference: Literally, "the height of the first one was eighteen cubits, and the circumference of the second one was twelve cubits." Rather than give the dimensions of the first pillar and then repeat that for the second pillar (as is often done in Hebrew), the author expresses the same idea more economically, by assigning one dimension to one pillar and the other dimension to the other pillar.

It is interesting to note that in the Aleppo Codex, the word for "the height of" (קומה) extends out into the left margin. The scribe ben Buya'a must have accidentally omitted this word in writing this leaf and then added it in the margin when he noticed it was missing during proofreading (see A76 r.3.15).

16c lattice-work and twisted cordage: The lattice-work is the bottom cubit of the capital; the top four cubits are the flower bulb with petals; the seven twisted cords hang down from the capital like streamers. For a depiction of pillars with a similar design and decoration, see the reconstruction of the pillars beside Amenhotep III's throne at The Pharaonic Palace 3D project website. For various features of Egyptian columns, a convenient (but non-scholarly) reference guide is the article "Columns of ancient Egypt" at the Tour Egypt website (/www.touregypt.net). See also examples of capitals found on Egyptian columns in the Wikipedia article "Column."

16d He made the pillars... The statement here that Hiyram made the pillars is nonsensical, as the description of their making appears earlier in the *parashah*. The entire sentence appears to be severely corrupt. It is likely, in my view, that several words have fallen out of the text—originally, I believe the first clause may have read something like "He made the ornamentation for the capitals that were on top of the two pillars" (ויעש את־מלאכת הכתרת אשר על־שני העמדים).

16e on top of the: The phrase העמודים ("the pillars") appears to have fallen from the text after the phrase על ראש ("on top of"). I have reflected this in my translation by omitting a noun after the phrase "on top of the."

16f The capitals atop the two pillars also were ornamented above...: This sentence reads as a variant to the second sentence preceding, which also describes the pomegranate ornamentation. The text of this sentence may be corrupt, as the mention of the second capital at the end of the sentence is nonsensical.

16g the porch of the great hall: That is, the porch in front of the entrance to Yahweh's house. The construction of the porch is described in P13.

16h Next he made the Sea of cast metal: This object was a basin for holding water; it was named "the Sea" because of its large capacity. The role that the Sea played in Yahweh's cult is not stated by the author of this *parashah*. In my opinion, it was most likely a water storage tank. Cleaning the blood from the sacrificial offerings and cleaning the equipment used in the cult rites would have consumed a significant amount of water on a daily basis. If there were no well within the grounds of Yahweh's house, then a large storage tank of water would have been needed to serve as a source of water. I suspect this was the true function of the Sea. In 2 Chr 4.6, we are told that "the Sea was for the priests to wash in;" however, the author of that passage may simply be guessing, as he was writing in the fourth century BCE, some two hundred years after the destruction of the Sea by the Babylonians.

16i It was circular in shape and had a diameter of ten cubits. It was five cubits in height and its circumference was thirty cubits: The shape is a near perfect half sphere. Presumably the author had in mind that the Sea was perfectly circular, but the ratio of the circumference to the diameter is slightly less than *pi* (3.0 instead of 3.14).

16j There were knobs below its rim... ten cubits in circumference: We should not imagine the knobs to be directly below the rim. The statement that they were "ten cubits in circumference" indicates that they must have been roughly midway between the rim and the base of the Sea, at a place where the Sea's diameter was a little over three cubits.

16k Standing atop twelve head of cattle: The description of the Sea is written in an abbreviated style with incomplete sentences and forms that would be considered "ungrammatical" in formal prose. I have translated in the style in which such a passage might be written in English, but I have retained some of the ungrammatical features where it felt relatively natural in English to do so. The sentence here is a good example of that, where the sentence begins with a participle with no explicit indication in the Hebrew of the noun that the participle modifies.

16l a flower blossom rim on a cup: I understand the author to be using a term for a common type of rim on a cup. I presume the "flower blossom rim" was one that curled outward, but there is no way to be certain.

16m Its capacity was two thousand *bath*: The *bath* was a unit of volume. It likely represented the volume of a standard-sized storage jar. Scholars estimate the *bath* as equivalent to approximately 22 liters. Using this estimate, we can calculate the capacity of the Sea as stated in this *parashah* to be 44,000 liters.

It is an interesting exercise to calculate the volume of the Sea from the measurements given here and to compare that with the estimated 44,000-liter capacity of the Sea. The formula for the volume of a sphere is Volume = $(4/3)*\pi r^3$. The Sea is a half sphere, so the formula for its volume would be simply $(2/3)*\pi r^3$. If we use 10 cubits as the diameter of the Sea and assume the diameter is measured on the inside of the rim, then its radius would be 5 cubits and its volume 261.8 cubic cubits. The rim of the Sea is said to be one hand-breadth. If the diameter was measured on the exterior of the rim, then the diameter would be 10 cubits minus 2 handbreadths. As there were 6 handbreadths to the cubit, the adjusted diameter of the Sea would be 9.67 cubits and its adjusted radius 4.83 cubits, resulting in a volume of 236.5 cubic cubits.

The cubit was used in two forms: a short cubit (estimated by scholars at 0.446 meters) and a long cubit (estimated by scholars at 0.521 meters). It is unclear which form of the cubit the author of this passage had in mind. If we use a diameter of 9.67 cubits for the Sea, its volume would be 21.0 cubic meters (or 21,000 liters) with the short cubit and 33.4 cubic meters (or 33,400 liters) with the long cubit. Assuming a diameter of 10 cubits, the volume of the Sea would be 23.2 cubic meters (or 23,200 liters) if the short cubit is used and 37.0 cubic meters (or 37,000 liters) if the long cubit is used.

It's worth noting that the estimate of 37,000 liters—the calculation that uses the long cubit and that assumes the diameter of the Sea represents a measurement taken on the inside of the rim—implies that the capacity of the *bath* was 18.5 liters. The figure of 18.5 liters is not far from the standard estimate of the *bath* as equivalent to 22 liters. This suggests that the source used by the author of this *parashah* had a relatively accurate measurement of the Sea's capacity.

Notes to P17

17a Here is the design of the stands...: The author's description of the ten bronze stands, which runs to the end of the *parashah*, is exceedingly difficult to follow. He writes in an elliptical style characteristic of Hebrew technical writing and he uses rare technical terms of uncertain meaning, making it hard for the modern-day reader to visualize the details of the stands' construction. My translation reflects my best guess as to the design of the stands.

17b plating: The author uses the relatively common term מסגרות, which traditionally is translated as "rims" or "borders." The root סגר means "to close, shut." Prefixing the letter *mem* to the root turns the word into a noun—thus מסגרת is "a thing that closes." I understand the term here to mean a piece of metal plating that "closes" the open space between the lateral ribs of the stands.

17c Likewise on the ribs, both above and below: hanging wreaths of lions and cattle: The Hebrew is somewhat difficult to follow, and I have ignored the Masoretic accentuation in order to make sense of the text. I understand the author to mean that small bronze figures of lions and cattle were joined together by wire or string to make a decorative wreath, and these wreaths were then hung from the upper and lower ribs that formed the frame of the stands.

17d and on their four feet they had supports: The text is nonsensical. BDB, p. 822, def. 1.c proposes that "its feet" (פעמתיו) is an error for "its corners" (פנותיו), which I believe is correct. This proposal is supported by the variant description of the stands later in the *parashah* which states that there were supports (probably rods) sticking up from the corners of the stands. See note 17i below.

17e beneath the lavers: The lavers sat on top of the stands; they are described in P17,1.

17f one-and-a-half cubits: This must be the circumference of the opening, not the diameter.

17g the plating for the openings: Each opening is set in the capital (or top section) of the stand. I understand each opening to be set in a cube-like structure rising one cubit above the stand. The square plating refers to the top surface of the capital in which the circular opening is set. The plating is "square" because the capital itself is square in form. As the lavers sat on top of the capitals, the bottom of the lavers (which are described in P17,1) would have extended down into the openings in the capitals, thus helping hold the lavers in place.

17h the four wheels below the plating: The plating referenced here is the plating between the ribs of the stand's frame.

17i Each stand had a support on each of its upper corners: These supports jutted up from the top of the stand and presumably served to support the laver that sat atop the stand. I understand the material from here to the end of the *parashah* to be a variant version of the description of the stands that the editors of the fifth compositional stage have chosen to preserve in their version of Kings. This is the simplest way to explain the inconsistencies between the description of the stands here and the description that precedes. Note that in the description here, the stands are topped with a circular construction one-half of a cubit in height; by contrast, in the preceding description, the stands are topped with a square capital that was one cubit in height and that had a circular hole. In the description here, the stands are decorated with winged sphinxes, lions, and date palms, whereas in the preceding description, the stands are decorated with lions, cattle, and winged sphinxes. Note also the different terminology in the two descriptions: the term for the ribs on the stands in the first description is השלבים (which are joining pieces that are arranged laterally), but in the second description the term used for the ribs is ידות (which are joining pieces that are arranged vertically). Similarly, in the first description the term for the plating is מסגרות, and in the second description the term is לחות.

17j Engraved on the plates [*its vertical ribs*] [*that is, on the stands' plating*]: The Hebrew here is practically incomprehensible. I believe that the ancient editors were also confused by the difficult-to-understand description of the stands and that they added two glosses here in an attempt to clarify the meaning of the text. The first gloss tells the reader that the term for plates (לחות) is a mistake and that "vertical ribs" (ידות) is the correct term. The second gloss (made by a different editor) tells the reader that the term for plates (לחות) is synonymous with the term used for the plating elsewhere in the *parashah* (מסגרות).

17,1a The capacity of each laver was forty *bath*, and each laver was four cubits: Notes to P17,1
The "four cubits" must refer to the diameter of the laver. If the laver were a perfect half sphere and the diameter were four cubits, its capacity would be around 1,800 liters. If we assume approximately 22 liters to the *bath*, a perfect half-sphere four cubits in diameter would have a capacity of 82 *bath*. From these calculations, we can deduce that the lavers would not have been a half sphere, but would have been shallow—roughly two-and-a-half cubits deep.

17,1b One laver sat atop each of the ten stands: The lavers would have been placed on the openings on the capitals described in P17 and supported by the four supports extending up from the corners of the stands.

Notes to P17,2

17,2a the lavers: The mention of lavers here is an error. Note that Hiyram made the lavers in P17,1. The summary later in the *parashah* indicates that the text here originally read "the caldrons" (הסירות) and not "the lavers" (הכירות). It is easy to see how a scribe might have made a copying error here, as the two words look and sound similar, and have a similar meaning.

17,2b serving to cover the two bulbs of the capitals on the front side of the pillars: The description implies that the bulbs were carved only on the front side of the capitals, meaning the capitals' back side was undecorated. This seems unlikely to me, as the descriptions of the lattice work and the pomegranates in P16 suggest these surrounded the capitals entirely. Given that, I think it is most likely that here in P17,2 the preposition "on the front side of" (על-פני) is an error for the prepositional phrase "on the top of" (על-ראש).

17,2c because of the extraordinary quantity of them, the weight of the bronze used was not measured: I do not follow the Masoretes' accent marks here, as the text is nonsensical in their accentuation. Retaining the Masoretic accentuation yields the following translation, "Shelomo put all these items in place due to their great abundance." The text makes perfect sense, however, if we understand the clause about the extraordinary amount of the equipment to be connected to the following clause. It's worth noting that the observation here about not measuring the weight of the bronze, which is by the authors of Kings' fifth stage, is woven into a comment by the authors of the sixth stage in P119,2 about the looting of Yahweh's house by the Babylonian army. Note that the comment in P119,2 indicates that the editors of the sixth stage understood the text here in P17,2 as I do and not as it was accented by the Masoretes.

17,2d Shelomo made all the equipment associated with Yahweh's house...: I understand the material from here to the end of the *parashah* to be original to earliest version of Kings (the one associated with the Josianic study books). Moreover, I believe that this material likely was lifted verbatim from the source document *The Acts of Shelomo*. Note that here Shelomo is the one who "makes" the equipment associated with Yahweh's house, not Hiyram. (Hiyram the bronzesmith is entirely absent in the earliest edition of Kings.) The attribution of the making of the cult equipment to Shelomo is consistent with the early authors' portrayal of Shelomo in P13 as the one who "built" Yahweh's house; it is also consistent with their views of the king as the head of Yahweh's cult.

Notes to P18

18a Once all the work that King Shelomo did on Yahweh's house was complete...: I believe that P18 is a composition by the authors of Kings' first stage and that the information here did not appear in the source document *The Acts of Shelomo*. There is no reason to think that *the Acts of Shelomo* mentioned Dawid. In that work, Shelomo is a king of Yisra'el, not Yehudah, and there is no indication that he had a connection to Dawid or the Dawidic dynasty.

18b Shelomo transferred the cult equipment belonging to his father Dawid: These must refer to the cult implements used in the rites carried out in the tent shrine inside Fort Dawid. In earliest version of Samuel (the version associated with the Josianic study books), the account of the establishment of the tent shrine inside Fort Dawid is given in Sam P79.

Notes to P19

19a The King Shelomo summoned Yisra'el's elders...: I understand this *parashah* and P20 to be from the hands of the authors of the Josianic study books. This material is among the most important pieces of this earliest version of Kings, for it celebrates the construction of a house that belongs to Yahweh and it looks forward to Yahweh's fulfillment of the (unconditional) Dawidic promise. Because of the importance of this material, it attracted numerous edits and additions from later authors.

In composing P19, I believe the authors of Kings' first stage drew on material from their source document *The Acts of Shelomo*, and they may have inserted some material verbatim. Note in particular the authors' use of the term Yisra'el's elders. If the beginning of P19 were composed by the authors of the first stage, we would expect to read "the elders of Yisra'el and Yehudah." The omission of Yehudah suggests that parts of the *parashah* are from *The Acts of Shelomo*, which spoke of Shelomo as the king of Yisra'el, but not Yehudah. In the account of Shelomo's reign in P10,2-P30,3, Yehudah is mentioned only twice—in P10,24 and P11—in places that represent material added by the authors of Kings' fifth stage.

Although the authors of the Kings' first stage typically used Yisra'el to refer only to the northern kingdom, there are several instances where they use the term more expansively. In three places—here in P19 and also in P10,2 and P13—they incorporate material from their source document *The Acts of Shelomo* that contains the term Yisra'el. In the source document, the term had a limited meaning, but in these three instances, the context suggests that the authors intended the reader to understand the term expansively. The other places where the authors of Kings' first stage use the term Yisra'el expansively is in their citations of the dynastic promise to Dawid. In these passages, the phrasing they use is "my people Yisra'el" (implying all the tribes) and "the town that Yahweh chose out of all Yisra'el's tribes." See the mentions of the dynastic promise in Kgs P20, P30,1, P113, and in Sam P80,2. This expansive use of the term Yisra'el by the authors of Kings' first stage is consistent with their desire that their pupil, the young king Yoshiyyahyu, would extend his authority over the former kingdom of Yisra'el and "reunite" the peoples of Yisra'el and Yehudah. Other passages in Kings where they use Yisra'el with an expansive meaning are the end of P21 ("all Yisra'el" and "[Yahweh's] people Yisra'el") and P39 ("the town that Yahweh chose out of all Yisra'el's tribes").

19b Yahweh's ~~battle~~ *treaty* chest: In the earliest versions of both Samuel and Kings, Yahweh's chest functions as a "battle chest" and there is no association whatsoever with the treaty between Yahweh and his people. The authors of the earliest version of the books of the Torah (Deuteronomy and Exodus-Numbers) repurposed the battle chest as a "treaty chest" in order to put the treaty at the center of the cult. In numerous places in Samuel and Kings, later authors then attached the word ברית ("treaty") to the chest in order to transform the battle chest into the treaty chest known from Exodus, Numbers, Deuteronomy, and Joshua. I have reflected this edit in my translation by striking through the word "battle" and showing the word "treaty" in italics.

I understand the two mentions of the battle chest in P19 to be part of the material composed by the authors of Kings' first stage. While there is some material in P19 from *The Acts of Shelomo*, there is nothing in Kings to indicate the battle chest appeared in that work, and consequently I believe that Shelomo originally had no connection whatsoever to the battle chest.

19c [*and the Meeting tent*]: I believe that authors working as part of what I call Kings' third compositional stage (ca. fifth century BCE) inserted the phrase "and the Meeting Tent" into the text in order to link the old material in Kings about Dawid's tent shrine with the Persian period material from Exodus and Numbers about the Meeting Tent and the cult equipment fashioned for it.

19d were making sacrifices of sheep and cattle: It is very odd that the authors here omit any mention of the altar, which was by far the most important piece of cult equipment. One wonders if the authors of the earliest version of Kings had some problem with the main altar in the Yerushalem cult during Shelomo's time.

It is noteworthy that they omit any mention of the altar in their account of the construction of Yahweh's house in P13 and in their account of the construction of the cult equipment associated with Yahweh's house at the end of P17,2. See notes 21f and 24,1b below.

19e Yahweh's ~~battle~~ *treaty* chest: See note 19b above.

19f the sphinxes' wings were extended towards the spot where the chest was: The sphinxes' wings serve to cover the chest and hide it in the deep darkness of the cella.

19g the great hall: The author wrote הקדש ("the holy place"), which was often used as an alternate name for the great hall. I have translated as "great hall" here to avoid confusing the reader.

19h [*but they could not be seen from the outside*]: This clause reads as a late comment and I assign it to Kings' sixth compositional stage. The author is clarifying that from inside the great hall, the stave ends could be seen through the two doors to the cella; however, from a position outside Yahweh's house, one could not see the stave ends through the opening of the outer doors.

19i There was nothing in the chest except the two stone tablets...after they left Egypt: I view this sentence as an addition made in Kings' third compositional stage, the authors of which made numerous additions to Kings in order to harmonize it with the books of the Torah. Note that here in P19, the copy of Deuteronomy, which Mosheh placed in the chest in Deut P30, is not mentioned. This is intentional on the part of the authors. They cannot mention it here, as it has to be "discovered" in P116 to set in motion the reforms of Yoshiyyahu. (The account of the discovery of "the Torah scroll" during the reign of Yoshiyyahu was composed by the authors of the Kings' third stage, not the authors of the Josianic study books nor the authors of Kings' second stage; see the notes to P116 and the discussion of P116 in my account of Kings' composition history.)

19j a And when the priests emerged from the great hall, a smoke cloud filled Yahweh's house...: The concluding sentence of this *parashah* provides a good example of the difficulties of reconstructing Kings' composition history. It is possible to understand the sentence as original to the Josianic study books or as addition from the Persian or Hellenistic period that was made in order to ensure the manifestation of Yahweh's presence in his house on Mount Tziyyon was consistent with the manifestation of his presence in the Meeting Tent in the wilderness. The language used here in Kings is reminiscent of the language in Exodus P70 when Yahweh's radiant splendor filled the Meeting Tent after Mosheh finished setting up Yahweh's shrine. In my composition history of Kings, I have for treated the sentence here in P19 as an addition, and I believe the authors modeled their language on the language in Exod P70—they wished to draw a parallel between Yahweh's radiant splendor filling his house after Shelomo furnished it with all its equipment and Yahweh's radiant splendor filling the Meeting Tent/shrine after Mosheh had furnished it with all its equipment (see Exod P69,1 - P69,8). Note the similarities between the two texts:

והענן מלא את־בית יהוה ולא־יכלו הכהנים לעמד לשרת מפני הענן כי־מלא כבוד־יהוה את־בית יהוה (Kgs P19)

וכבוד יהוה מלא את־המשכן ולא־יכל משה לבוא אל־אהל מועד כי־שכן עליו הענן וכבוד יהוה מלא את־המשכן (Exod P70)

Notes to P20

20a As Yahweh intended to live in a storm cloud, I have now built a mountain house for you: In this sentence, the authors of this *parashah* have borrowed terminology from the cult at Mount Tziyyon, as is appropriate given that these *parashot* are about the formal establishment of the cult on Mount Tziyyon. Yahweh is associated with a storm cloud (ערפל) in Ps 18 and Ps 97. In Isaiah 63, the speaker asks him to look down from "your beautiful and holy mountain house" (זבול קדשך ותפארתך). The material in Isa 63 is late, but it reflects language from the cult at Mount Tziyyon, as does much of the book of Isaiah.

20b 'From the time I brought my people… to be responsible for my people Yisra'el.': I view this entire quote from Yahweh to be a later addition to the text from the third compositional stage. The promise quoted here is never made to Dawid in the book of Samuel. Moreover, the "promise" quoted here addresses Dawid in the third person rather than the second person, which provides further support for the view that this quote is a later addition to the text. The only promises that Yahweh made to Dawid were that his dynasty would last forever and that his son would build Yahweh's house. And in fact, this latter promise is quoted in the next paragraph, which in the earliest version of Kings would have followed directly from the phrase "and who installed him [as king]" (ובידו מלא). See note 20e below.

As many scholars have noted, the evidence of the fragments of Kings from Qumran (4Q54, fragment 7) and of the parallel passage in 2 Chronicles 6.5f indicates that a sentence has fallen out of Yahweh's speech here. (In my composition history, this sentence is part of the addition to this *parashah*.) The earlier version of Yahweh's statement (which was added as part of Kings' third stage) read, " 'From the time I brought my people Yisra'el out of Egypt, I didn't choose a town from any of Yisra'el's tribes where a house might be built that would be my very own, nor did I choose a man to serve as supreme leader responsible for my people. Then I chose Yerushalem as the town I would claim as my own, and I chose Dawid to be responsible for my people Yisra'el.' "

20c that would be my very own: Literally, "for my name." It is a mistake to understand "name" here in its literal sense. The phrasing is related to the phrasing found elsewhere in Kings—"to place [one's] name" (לשום שם) on a thing or in a place, which is an idiom expressing a claim of ownership. A variant of this idiom appears numerous times in Deuteronomy—לשכן שמו שם. This phrase is often mistranslated "to cause his name to dwell there," but in fact the phrase is borrowed from the Akkadian idiom *šuma šakanu* ("to place [one's] name"). In Akkadian, the idiom is commonly associated with monuments or stelae inscribed with a king's name that the king has erected on a building or in a territory in order to claim as belonging to him. The American scholar Sandra Richter has written extensively on these Hebrew and Akkadian idioms and the implications for the so-called "name theology," which is based on a misunderstanding of the idioms. She provides a good discussion of the issues in her recent article "Does YHWH's Name Dwell in the Temple?" at the website www.thetorah.com.

While I believe that it is best to understand the phrase "for my name" in Kings as related to the idiom "to place [one's] name," there is one alternative interpretation that is also plausible. The word שֵׁם ("name") often has the figurative meaning of "fame, reputation," and it is possible to understand that as the meaning here in P20. (English has a similar figurative use of the word "name"—"to make a name for oneself" is to become famous or become prominent because of one's accomplishments.) In this interpretation, "to build a house for my name" would mean something like "to build a house for my fame/reputation"—that is, a house where Yahweh would receive honor in the form of offerings from his devotees.

NOTES AND COMMENTS

20d it was my father Dawid's deepest wish: Literally, "it was with my father Dawid's heart." The word לבב ("heart") has been almost wholly erased from the Aleppo Codex here—see A77 v.2.4. This page of the Aleppo Codex is otherwise in almost pristine condition, which makes one wonder if the erasure may have been intentional.

20e Yahweh said to my father Dawid...your son...is the one who will build the house that will belong to me: Shelomo here specifically alludes to Yahweh's promise to Dawid (the so-called Dawidic promise) in Sam P80,2. Note the alternative translation: "is the one who will build the house for honoring me."

I believe that in the earliest version of Kings, the statement beginning "Because it's been your deepest wish..." followed directly from the above clause "...and who installed him as king, saying to him." As discussed in note 20b, I understand the intervening material as an addition by the authors of Kings' third stage.

20f Moreover, I made a place there for the chest that holds Yahweh's treaty...out of Egypt: I view this sentence as an addition made by the authors of Kings' third stage, who were active throughout the Persian period and who introduced into Kings ideas and themes from the early versions of the books of the Torah. In the addition here, the author expresses the view that the cella of Yahweh's house was built specifically to house the document recording the treaty between Yahweh and his people that was agreed to at Mount Siynai. I believe the author has in mind the two treaty tablets that Yahweh gave to Mosheh. If the author was thinking of the book of Deuteronomy here, he likely would have written "the scroll of Mosheh's Torah." See note 19i above.

Notes to P20,1

20,1a Shelomo stood before Yahweh's altar...be confirmed!: I view the material specified here—the first third of P20,1—as an addition by the authors of the second stage of Kings. In the preceding *parashah* (part of the original version of Kings), Shelomo alludes to the unconditional Dawidic promise. For the authors of the second stage, the destruction of Yahweh's house and the removal of the Dawidic king from the throne proved that the promise could not have been an unconditional one. Consequently, in many places in Kings, they made additions clarifying that the Dawidic promise was in fact conditional. This is the reason for their addition here—to "correct" the statement that Shelomo makes in P20.

20,1b honor the binding agreement with and show lovingkindness toward your servants who walk before you with all their heart: The servants here are the kings in Yerushalem (that is, the Dawidic kings who ruled Yehudah). I believe this language was originally part of Judean royal ideology. Sometime in the Persian period, the authors of what I call Deuteronomy's third stage borrowed this language and applied it to Yahweh's relationship with his people. Thus, we see identical language near the end of Deut P6,4 and at the beginning of Deut P7.

20,1c uphold for your servant, my father Dawid, the other part of your promise to him...: The Dawidic promise has two elements: the first element is the promise that Dawid's son will build a house that will be Yahweh's own in Yerushalem; the second element is that Yahweh will ensure the Dawidic dynasty remains on the throne for eternity. The author of this *parashah* here introduces the second part of the promise, which he then qualifies by making it conditional on Dawid's descendants being careful "to walk before" Yahweh just as Dawid himself did.

20,1d But can God truly live on earth...: I view the material from here through the first half of P21 as an addition by the authors of Kings' fifth stage. The material functions as a meditation on the nature of the relationship between Yahweh and his people in the situation where a minority of his people live in the land and the majority in the diaspora. With respect to those in the land, the prayer asks Yahweh to ease the people's suffering and hardship when they make their pleas to him. With respect to those in the diaspora, the prayer explores the idea of the power of repentance expressed through prayer that is directed toward the (far-off) place that Yahweh chose for his house. There are numerous indications that this material does not belong to the earliest version of Kings. Most significantly, Shelomo's prayer and blessing has numerous touchpoints with the Persian-period additions to Deuteronomy, and the prayer alludes in multiple places to the conditions of life in the diaspora.

This lengthy expansion of Shelomo's prayer is the most important material added by the authors of Kings' fifth stage. It is important to point out that it appears to have been written over a long period of time. It reads not as a single addition, but as multiple additions made over the course of the Persian period. There are multiple perspectives expressed in the material, and there are numerous places where it does not cohere or flow smoothly—all of which suggest multiple authors had a hand in the composition of this prayer. The prayer is certainly not the work of a single individual working at a single point in time, as is commonly assumed by some scholars who argue for the traditional idea of a Deuteronomistic History.

20,1e May you give your attention, O Yahweh...give heed to them and forgive us: This lengthy sentence captures well how the authors of the authors of Kings' fifth stage come to terms with the fact that a majority of Yahweh's people live in the diaspora, which requires them to broaden their understanding of the function of Yahweh's house and—more importantly—of Yahweh's own nature. Yahweh's house is not the place where he dwells (indeed, no place can contain him), but rather it is merely the place where he has chosen "to place his name"—that is, the place he has chosen to claim as belonging to him alone. Even though he allowed his house to be destroyed, the place where it stood still has special power, because he is especially attentive to that place, and if one directs one's prayers toward that place, Yahweh will hear those prayers and give heed to them. The picture of Yahweh has begun to evolve away from the purely transactional god who acts solely within the terms of the treaty with his people, bestowing blessings or effecting curses on his people because they have or have not upheld their obligations under the treaty. The picture of Yahweh has now incorporated an element of magnanimity—he is a god who will forgive his people and answer their prayers simply because they pray to him in sincerity and direct their prayers toward the place that is special to him.

20,1f the place that you said would be yours alone: Literally, "the place where you said your name would be." On this translation, see note 20c above. Note also the alternative translation: "the place where you said you would be honored."

20,1g "And should your people Yisra'el suffer defeat...: The Leningrad Codex has a *parashah setumah* before this sentence. See L190 v.2.23.

Note again in the conclusion to this *parashah* the evolution of thought in the authors of Kings' fifth stage as compared to the authors of the Josianic study books, and note also the focus on the condition of life in the diaspora. Yahweh is a compassionate god who will forgive those who have wronged him when they "come back to him" and seek his compassion—and, moreover, he will return them to the land that he gave their ancestors.

20,1h lauding your great name: The author uses the verb phrase והודו את־שמך. This phrase has a strong association with the cult on Mount Tziyyon—the phrase and variations on it occur eight times in Psalms. In this context, שמך ("your name") carries connotations of "fame, reputation, renown," which I have reflected in translation with the addition of the adjective "great."

Note to P20,2   **20,2a lauding your great name:** See note 20,1h directly above.

Notes to P20,3   **20,3a in order that all the world's peoples might know of your name:** Here too "name" has connotations of "fame, reputation, renown." However, I have translated as "name" in this instance because the world's peoples must know the name of this god in order to give reverence to him.

20,3b this house which I built belongs to you: Literally, "your name is proclaimed over the house that I built." The author uses a variant of the phrase נקרא שם על ("name [of the owner] is proclaimed over [the thing owned]"), which is an idiom expressing ownership. See BDB, p. 896, def. 2d (4) of the *niph'al* and the citations there; see also BDB, p. 1027, col. 2, def. 2a and p. 1028, def. 3.

20,3c as your very own: Literally, "for your name." For this translation, see note 20c above. Note also, the statement discussed in note 20,3b directly above that the house Shelomo built "belongs to" Yahweh. As discussed in note 20c, the alternate translation "for honoring you" is also plausible.

20,3d Should they do wrong to you... listening to them whenever they call out to you: It's worth noting the extraordinary length of this periodic sentence—in translation, it contains thirty-four verbs. The authors of the later stages of Deuteronomy (which I date to the mid- and late Persian period) are especially fond of long periodic sentences. The author of this *parashah* has clearly been influenced by Deuteronomy: in addition to the similar prose style, he borrows specific language and imagery from Deuteronomy near the end of the *parashah* (see notes 20,3g and 20,3h below).

20,3e as your very own: Alternatively, one may translate "for honoring you."

20,3f making their captors have compassion on them: The phrasing used by the author—נתן רחמים לפני—may be idiomatic, for the identical construction also appears in Gen P37: "I pray that El Shaddai make that man have compassion on you."

20,3g for they are your people... from the flames of an iron furnace: The author here specifically borrows language from Deut P2, which belongs to the Persian-period additions to Deuteronomy. The relevant passage in Deut P2 reads: "he [i.e. Yahweh] has taken you for himself, bringing you out of the iron smelter [כור הברזל]—out of Egypt—so that you might become the people assigned to him, just as you are today."

20,3h out of all the peoples in the world, you selected them for yourself as your very own possession, just as you said you would through your servant Mosheh: The author's statement "just as you said you would through your servant Mosheh" indicates that he has a specific passage in Deuteronomy or Exodus in mind. There are no places in Exodus that refer to Yahweh taking his people as his possession, but there are three in Deuteronomy: Deut P2, Deut P10, and Deut P23,2. The author's allusion here appears to draw from both Deut P2 and Deut P23,2. Note in Deut P2: "For your god Yahweh assigned them [i.e. other gods] to all the peoples on earth, whereas he has taken you for himself." And in Deut P23,2: "today Yahweh has solemnly declared that you shall be his special people and prized possession, just as he promised you... placing you above all other nations...."

Notes to P21   **21a he rose from his kneeling position in front of Yahweh's altar:** Note the inconsistency in the text: the beginning of P20,1 states that Shelomo was standing when he delivered the prayer in P20,1 - P20,3, and now in P21 we are told he had been kneeling. This inconsistency, in my view, reflects different authors. The first third of P20,1 represents an expansion by the authors of Kings' second stage (see note 20,1a above), whereas the first half of P21 is part of the series of additions made to

Shelomo's prayer by the authors of Kings' fifth stage (see note 20,1d above). Here in P21, the authors of the fifth stage were a bit sloppy and overlooked the statement in P20,1 (from Kings' second stage) that Shelomo delivered the prayer from a standing position.

21b who has given safety and security to his people Yisra'el, just as he promised: Whenever the authors of the Tanakh write phrases such as "just as he [i.e. Yahweh] promised" (כאשר דבר), they almost always have in mind a specific passage from their version of the books of the Torah. It is usually possible to determine which passage the author has in mind because his allusion quotes exact language and terms from the source passage. In this instance, the author's use of the term מנוחה (which typically means "resting place," but here in P21 means something closer to "safety and security") indicates that he is alluding to a passage from Deut P12,5. That passage reads as follows: "For at present you have not yet arrived at the resting place [מנוחה] and the property that your god Yahweh is going to give you. When you cross over the Yarden and reside in the land that your god Yahweh is going to give you as your property, he will give you respite from all your enemies in the surrounding regions, so that you may live safe and secure."

21c Yahweh is the supreme god—there is none besides him: The author here may be quoting the conclusion to Deut P3 (a Persian period addition to Deuteronomy), where the identical phrasing appears.

21d At this time, the king along with all of Yisra'el...: I view the material from here to the end of the *parashah*, excluding the final sentence, as part of the earliest version of Kings.

21e the welfare offering which he made to Yahweh—twenty-two thousand head of cattle and one hundred and twenty thousand sheep: I believe the clause specifying the number of animals slaughtered is an addition from Kings' fifth stage. The numbers are clearly fantastical, and the author hasn't given serious thought to how such a welfare offering could have been carried out. For example, it would have taken weeks to slaughter this number of animals. Welfare offerings are associated with occasions of great celebration—in a welfare offering, the celebrants receive the meat portions and the fat is offered to Yahweh. In this instance, it is unclear how the fat of more than one hundred and forty thousand animals could have been collected and transported to the court in front of Yahweh's house, where it would then have been burned in offering to Yahweh.

21f the bronze altar that was in front of Yahweh: This is the large altar in front of Yahweh's house. This is the first mention of the altar in the original version of Kings (the mention of the altar at the beginning of P20,1 is part of material added by the authors of the second compositional stage—see note 20,1a above). It is very odd that the construction of this altar is not mentioned in the account of Hiyram's fashioning the bronze equipment for Yahweh's house in P16 - P17,2. It is hard to believe that the single most important item in the cult was omitted from the account of fashioning of the cult equipment in the earliest version of Kings; and if the altar's construction was in the original account, it is hard to believe such an important item would have fallen out of the text through a scribal error. See my comments in note 19d above and note 24,1b below.

21g a huge congregation extending from Hamath's Gateway in the north to the Egypt Wadi in the south: This clause reads as an addition by the authors of the fifth stage. It was common in ancient Hebrew to express the concept of entirely through the juxtaposition of opposites. Hamath's Gateway and the Egypt Wadi are the northernmost and southernmost limits of the territory traditionally inhabited by the Yisra'elite tribes, and the author here uses these terms as a way of saying the entirety of the land inhabited by the Yisra'elites.

There are several other examples in Kings of the juxtaposition of opposites to express the idea of totality. See, for example, notes 38i, 94a, 106i, and 116t below.

21h On the eighth day: The author here means the day after the second set of seven days—that is, on the fifteenth day.

21i all the good things that Yahweh had done for his servant Dawid and for his people Yisra'el: This is an allusion to the fulfillment of the Dawidic promise in Sam P80,2, in which Yahweh tells Dawid that he will raise up a son after him who will build a house that will be Yahweh's own and that in return he will make Dawid's dynasty and kingdom secure for all time.

21j Now it so happened that...: I view the final sentence of this *parashah* as an addition by the authors of the second stage, who inserted it here to introduce P22, the first two-thirds of which is a composition from their hands.

Notes to P22

22a [*Yahweh showed himself to Shelomo a second time, similar to when he appeared to him in Giv'on.*]: I understand the first sentence of P22 to be an addition by the authors of the fifth stage, who remind the reader of Shelomo's dream in P8, which is a composition by their hand. The language of the addition—"similar to when he appeared to him in Giv'on"—implies that they wanted the reader to understand Yahweh's appearance here as also occurring in a dream. The authors may have added this sentence in P22 because they were uncomfortable with the original account in which Yahweh spoke directly to Shelomo without any mediation. However, if that is the reason for their addition here, it is odd that they didn't make a similar change in P29, where Yahweh also speaks directly to Shelomo.

22b "I have heard your prayer and your plea...: I view the majority of Yahweh's speech to Shelomo in this *parashah* as belonging to Kings' second compositional stage. The specific phrasing here in P22 refers to Shelomo's prayer in the first third of P20,1. It does not refer to material in the last two-thirds of P20,1, nor to the material in P20,2 -P20,3—all that material belongs to Kings' fifth compositional stage.

The authors of Kings' second stage understood the Dawidic promise as a conditional promise, and the material they added to P22 is their primary expression of its conditional nature. To wit, if Dawid's descendants observe Yahweh's commandments and laws regarding the king's management of the cult, their place on the throne of Yisra'el (the combined kingdoms of north and south) will be secure forever; but if Dawid's descendants give service to gods other than Yahweh, he will exile his people (the king's subjects) from their land. Note that in the material in this *parashah* belonging to the second compositional stage, there is no treaty between Yahweh and his people. The authors of the second stage, who were writing during the exile, still viewed Yahweh's relationship to his people through the lens of Judean royal ideology. Yahweh's relationship with his people is mediated through the king, and his actions toward his people are conditional on the king's own loyalty to him. Note also that Yahweh gives his laws and commandments to the king, not to the people, and that there is no mention of Mosheh as the giver of these laws and commandments.

The authors of the third stage of Kings, who were writing in the Persian period and who were writing to harmonize Kings with the early versions of the books of the Torah, completely overturn this framework: they remove the king from the picture so that the people have a direct relationship with Yahweh consistent with the portrayal in Deuteronomy and Exodus-Numbers. They replace Yahweh's conditional promise to the king with a treaty between Yahweh and his people—it is now the people, not the king, who are required to follow Yahweh's laws and commandments. These laws and commandments are no longer simply cult rules for the king, but have developed more broadly into the Torah for all of Yahweh's people.

With respect to this *parashah* (P22), the authors of the third stage left the original material untouched, but added new material at the end which expresses the idea that it was the people who forsook Yahweh (the king is irrelevant) and they are the cause of Yahweh's rejecting his house and allowing it to turn into ruin heaps. It is also worth noting that this material borrows language from Deuteronomy (something never seen in the material in Kings' first and second stages) and makes mention of the exodus from Egypt (another theme absent from Kings' first and second stages).

22c marking it as my own for all time: Literally, "to place my name there for all time." As discussed above in note 20c, the phrase "place one's name" commonly appears in Akkadian royal inscriptions, where it refers to the king inscribing his name on a building or memorial stele to mark that it belongs to him. This is how the phrase "to place my name there" (לשום את־שמי שם and its variant לשכן את־שמי שם) should be understood—they refer to inscribing the name "Yahweh" on his "house" on Mount Tziyyon to mark it as his. For a good discussion of this phrase and its relation to the Akkadian usage, see Sandra Richter's article "Does YHWH's Name Dwell in the Temple?" cited above in note 20c.

22d if you walk before me…in keeping with my promise regarding your father Dawid that none of his descendants would be removed from Yisra'el's throne: This is an allusion to a conditional version of the Dawidic promise that is not found in the Tanakh. This conditional version of the Dawidic promise is also referred to in P4 (part of the succession narrative) and in P20,1. See note 4e above.

22e if you go and give service to different gods and worship them: The phrasing is almost identical to language found in Jud P9, a *parashah* which I view as composed by the authors of the Josianic study books. The phrasing consists entirely of common terms, however, and the authors of Kings' second stage likely composed this passage without intending any allusion to Judges.

22f I shall wipe Yisra'el off the face of the land I have given them: The authors of the second stage here give their opinion on the cause of the destruction of the kingdoms of Yisra'el and Yehudah and their peoples: Yahweh wiped them "off the face of the land" because Shelomo and the Dawidic kings who followed him turned away from Yahweh. The judgement is due to the kings' actions, not the people's actions.

22g and at the same time I shall reject the house that I consecrated as my own…: I understand the material from here to the end of the *parashah* to be an addition by the authors of Kings' third stage. Note that for the authors of the second stage, Yahweh's devotion to his house is unconditional; they have Yahweh state at the beginning of the *parashah* that he has placed his name there (i.e. marked it as his own) for all time, and that his eyes and heart will be there always. The authors of the third stage, who are writing in the Persian period when a "new" house for Yahweh has been built in Yerushalem, have had much more time to come to terms with the destruction of Yahweh's "original" house, and so they understand that Yahweh's commitment to his original house must have been conditional.

22h a proverbial insult and a taunt: The author has borrowed this phrasing from the treaty curses in Deut P26. This provides some support for seeing this material as belonging to a Persian period addition, as the authors of Kings' first and second stages never allude to Deuteronomy.

22i this house shall be high: The text must be corrupt. The adjective עליון ("high") is nonsensical in this context. Possibly the text originally read עיין ("ruin heaps"), as it is easy to see how a scribe might mistakenly have written עליון for that.

22j it must be because they forsook their god Yahweh: Note that the king's actions, which were what mattered at the beginning of the *parashah*, are irrelevant to the authors of the material here—that is, the authors of the third stage. For the authors of the third stage, who no longer see the king as mediating the relationship between Yahweh and his people, it is the people's actions that lead to the destruction of the land and the ruin of Yahweh's house.

Note to P23

23a At the end of the twenty years...: In my proposed composition history, I treat this *parashah* as part of the earliest version of Kings. However, it is equally plausible to view it as a late addition, made as part of the work on Kings' fifth compositional stage, when several stories about Shelomo with folk-like elements were added to Kings.

Notes to P24

24a Hiyram sent the king one hundred and twenty *kikkar* of gold: The reader should understand Hiyram as being Shelomo's vassal; the 120 *kikkar* of gold represent a payment of tribute. A *kikkar* was three thousand sheqels; at a little more than 11 grams to the sheqel, 120 *kikkar* is equivalent to more than four thousand kilograms, or nearly nine thousand pounds. For a convenient discussion of weights and measures used by the authors of the Tanakh, see the article Weights and Measures at the Jewish Virtual Library website.

I believe that the material in the first two-thirds of this *parashah* comes from the main source document that the authors of the Josianic study books used for their account of Shelomo's reign—the scroll known as *The Acts of Shelomo*, which is mentioned in P30,3. The material in P24 that I believe is derived from that source offers support for the idea that Shelomo's kingdom was oriented primarily to the northern tribal territories. The tribal territory of Yehudah was poor and sparsely populated, and nearly all the kingdom's resources and wealth were located in the north. In that sense, we can consider Shelomo to be a northern king. His royal city, Yerushalem, was located at the southern end of his kingdom, in the tribal territory of Binyamin. Note that all the locations mentioned in this *parashah* are in the north: Hatzor, Megiddo, the Levanon mountains, Gezer (on the Ephrayim border), Beyth Horon (in Ephrayim), Ba'alath (in Dan), and Tadmor (in the Aramean desert northeast of Kena'an).

24b Here is the record of the forced labor that King Shelomo conscripted: Oddly, there is no record of the forced labor given in this *parashah*. I think it likely that the *parashah* originally included such a record, informing the reader of how many men Shelomo conscripted and from where, and that this information was removed from the text by the editors responsible for adding the material at the end of this *parashah* discussed below in note 24f. The only material from the record of forced labor that these editors retained in the text appears to be the first sentence of P24,1. I speculate that the original record of forced labor indicated that Shelomo primarily conscripted Yisra'elites, and these editors found such a statement offensive. Thus, they deleted the material and replaced it with the material at the end of the *parashah* about the native peoples of Kena'an serving as forced labor and the Yisra'elites serving as officials in the royal government and the army.

24c Phar'oh King of Egypt...captured Gezer: The author views Gezer as an old Kena'anite town that was not part of Shelomo's kingdom until Phar'oh gifted it to his daughter when he and Shelomo made a marriage alliance. Note the inconsistency here with the understanding of the occupation of the land in the book of Joshua: the king of Gezer is listed in Jos P24,7 as one of the kings whom Yehoshua subdued. The material here in Kings is part of the book's earliest edition (630s BCE); the reference to Gezer in Joshua is part of that book's first compositional stage, which I place in the early Persian period (late sixth century BCE).

24d in the land of: The name of the region where the town of Tamar ("Palm") was located has clearly fallen out of the text here.

24e forts for his war horses: The role of the war horses was to pull chariots and to pull supply wagons. There were no cavalry in Shelomo's time. See note 11,1a above. Akthough there were separate forts for storage of chariots and maintenance of the war horses, presumably many of the chariot horses were kept in forts where the chariots were stored.

24f All the remaining descendants of the Amorites...: I understand the text from here to the end of the *parashah* to be a Persian-period addition from Kings' fifth compositional stage, made by the same authors who introduced into the books of Joshua and Judges the theme of the conscription of the native peoples who escaped the ban devotion. The native Kena'anite peoples serving as "slave labor" are mentioned in Jos P33 and P34; in Judges, they are mentioned in P5, P5,2, and P5,4. See note 33d of my translation to Joshua and note 5,2a in my translation of Judges.

The tradition about the invasion and occupation of the Kena'an is absent from the Josianic study books. The earliest versions of Judges, Samuel, and Kings make no reference to this tradition, and the stories in these books are at odds with the complete elimination of the native peoples of Kena'an that is the subject of the first half of the book of Joshua.

24g the ban devotion: On the ban devotion and its role in the occupation of Kena'an, see the discussion in the introduction to my translation of Joshua.

24h as they remain in the present day: The Persian period authors of this addition want the reader to think that their addition is original to the text; thus they add a fake comment about the native peoples still serving as forced labor "in the present day."

24i for they served as his soldiers...and the captains of his chariotry and cavalry: Compare with Sam P16,2, which the author of this passage here in Kings may have had in mind. The use of פרשים here with the meaning "cavalry" offers support for a late date of this section of P24, for cavalry did not exist in Shelomo's time (see note 11,1a above).

24,1a three times each year Shelomo would offer up whole offerings and welfare offerings: There is no reason to think that these offering rites have any relation to the three annual festivals—the Festival of Unleavened Bread, the Festival of Weeks, and the Festival of Huts—mentioned in Deuteronomy (Deut P17). Rather, I believe the text here is referring to specific cultic rites that the king was obligated to perform in honor of Yahweh. There is no indication of a larger festival involving additional people beyond the king and the people closest to him (his family members and senior officials in the cult and palace administration).

Notes to P24,1

24,1b the altar that he built to Yahweh: Recall that there is no account in Kings of the altar that Shelomo built for Yahweh's house. The omission of the single-most important piece of equipment in the cult in the account of the construction of the Yahweh's house is very odd. Its absence cannot have been an oversight, but must have been purposeful. There must have been something objectionable about the altar that Shelomo built that led the authors of the Josianic study books (or later authors) to omit any mention of it in the narrative about the construction of Yahweh's house. The only other mention of the altar built by Shelomo for Yahweh's house in the early material in Kings is in P21, where it is said to be a bronze altar. In P103, we are told that Ahaz built a new altar based on the design of the main altar in Dammeseq and that he moved the original bronze altar to a new location, where he used it for haruspicy.

24,1c he would make incense offerings at the companion altar that was in front of Yahweh: The Hebrew is elliptical and the precise meaning of the term אִתּוֹ ("with it" or "with him") is not entirely clear. I understand את in this instance to function not as a preposition meaning "with", but as a substantive meaning "one with" (i.e. companion). Thus, a literal translation would be "he would make incense offerings at its companion, which is in front of Yahweh." The pronoun "its" here refers back to the bronze altar outside Yahweh's house. I understand the altar that is "in front of Yahweh" to refer to the cedar altar in the great hall, which served as an incense altar. In the earliest version of Kings, there is no account of the construction of either the bronze altar outside Yahweh's house or the incense altar inside his house. The passage here in P24,1 is the first mention of the incense altar in the early material in Kings, and as discussed above, the language used in referring to it is obscure. In P15, there are two brief mentions of the incense altar, but both are part of an addition from the fifth compositional stage. (This altar is discussed in notes 15e and 15g above.)

Because the incense altar is positioned in front of the cella, it is said to be "in front of Yahweh." This phrasing—describing something placed in front of the cella as "in front of Yahweh"—represents specific cult terminology. The phrase "in front of Yahweh" occurs more than sixty times times in Leviticus, where it can mean either "in front of the Meeting Tent" or "in front of the Meeting Tent's inner sanctum." Likewise, in Kings, the phrase means either "in front of Yahweh's house" or "in front of the cella." Here I think it is clear it must have the latter meaning.

24,1d and so he would fulfill his annual obligations at Yahweh's house: It is possible to read the Hebrew here as straightforward or as elliptical. BDB, p. 1022, follows the straightforward reading and understands the text to mean "he finished building Yahweh's house." However, this reading seems nonsensical to me for two reasons. First, the work on Yahweh's house has already been completed. Second, and more significant, the verb here is the perfect with *waw* consecutive and indicates a habitual action. For this reason, I prefer to understand the text here as elliptical. Context suggests that the habitual action described by שלם should be related in some way to the habitual actions of offering up whole offerings and making incense offerings. The *pi'el* of שלם is often used in the context of fulfilling a vow (נדר) or other cult obligation, and I believe that is how the term should be understood here. The text is confusing because of the elliptical style—the author has omitted the direct object of the verb (i.e. the annual cult obligations Shelomo has as king).

24,1e In addition, King Shelomo built a fleet of ships...: The passage here in P24,1 describing Shelomo's trading ships and the related passage in P27 have a number of similarities to the account of King Yehoshaphat's naval activities in P60. It is unclear if the authors of Kings' first stage based the accounts of Shelomo's merchant navy in P24,1 and P27 on material in their source book *The Acts of Shelomo*, or whether they invented these details for Shelomo on the basis of P60. That said, I lean to the latter view.

24,1f four hundred and twenty *kikkar* of gold: A *kikkar* was equivalent to three thousand sheqels. Four hundred and twenty *kikkar* of gold was equivalent to over 14,000 kilograms, or more than 31,000 pounds.

25a Now when the Queen of Sheva heard the report...: I understand this entire *parashah* to be an addition from the late Persian period or Hellenistic period. The story of the Queen of Sheva's visit to Shelomo reads as a literary composition that draws from oral traditions about Shelomo's great wisdom and wealth. Scholars believe the region of Sheva was located in the southwestern part of the Arabian peninsula.

Notes to P25

The Hebrew in the first sentence of the *parashah* is elliptical and somewhat awkward. A literal translation of the phrase that I represent as "the report about what Shelomo did to honor Yahweh" is "the report of Shelomo with respect to Yahweh's name." This of course is a reference to his construction of Yahweh's house. On the figurative use of "name" with respect to Yahweh, see note 20c above.

25b the house that he had built: The phrase is ambiguous—it may refer either to the royal palace or to Yahweh's house. Given the mention at the beginning of the *parashah* of "what Shelomo did to honor Yahweh," I think it is most likely that the authors here had in mind Yahweh's house, but there is no way to be certain.

25c (not to mention the whole offerings he would offer up at Yahweh's house): This clause reads as a very late comment added to the text to insert a measure of piety into the story.

25d [*because of Yahweh's eternal love for Yisra'el*]: Another comment added by the editors of Kings' sixth stage; here the commenter wishes to "correct" the theology of the *parashah* by stating that Yahweh's actions toward Shelomo were done out of his love for his people. For the author of this comment (as well as the author of this *parashah*), the Dawidic promise has little or nothing to do Yahweh's decision to place the great and wise Shelomo on the throne.

25e so that you might render justice and vindicate those in the right: The author uses an idiomatic phrase, עשה משפט וצדקה. The phrase is used in Sam P82,1 to describe Dawid's effectiveness as king, but the phrase is used there with a slightly different sense than the way it is used here in Kings. In Sam P82,1, I translated as "he continually acted with fairness and justice toward his people."

25f She gave the king one hundred and twenty *kikkar* of gold: Recall that in P24 Hiyram gave Shelomo 120 *kikkar* of gold. The authors of P25 likely borrowed the figure here from what they read in P24.

25g [*In addition, Hiyram's fleet... down to the present day.*]: I understand the two sentences that I have placed within brackets to be late additions to the text. However, with the exception of the final clause of the second sentence, it is also very reasonable to view this material as original to the Josianic study books and as continuing from the end of P23,1. I have a preference for seeing the material as an addition because it would be unusual for later authors to insert a block of new material (in this case, the story of the Queen of Sheva) around a section of older material. It would be more typical for later authors to add the block directly before or after the older material rather than to break the older material apart.

25h *mpingo wood*: It is unclear what type of wood אלמנים (sometimes spelled אלגמים) refers to. Based on the facts that the wood must be native to the region around

Ophiyr (the southern Arabian peninsula), is precious, and is used in the construction of musical instruments, I think it most likely that this is wood from the mpingo tree (*dalbergia melanoxylon*), which is native to dry regions of Africa, including Eritrea, which is directly west of the southern Arabian peninsula. On this tree, see the article "*Dalbergia melanoxylon*" in Wikipedia.

25i *balusters for Yahweh's house and the royal palace*: The author uses the term מסעד, which is traditionally translated as "support." I believe the term most likely refers to some sort of decorative architectural feature. I have translated as "balusters," but this is just a guess.

25j *apart from what was given her out of the king's own generosity*: The author here uses idiomatic phrasing—כיד המלך ("according to the king's hand"). The idiom occurs here and twice in the book of Esther—Est 1.7 and 2.18. The word יד ("hand") is often used with the meaning of "power, ability" and that is its use in this idiom. In all three occurrences of the idiom, there is a connotation of generosity—it goes without saying that if a king gives "according to his ability," his gift will be very generous.

25k *made ready and returned*: For the construction פנה ("turn") followed by a verb of motion with the meaning "make ready and go," see note 1d in my translation of Deuteronomy.

25l **: The Leningrad Codex has a *parashah setumah* here. See L192 v.1.18.

Notes to P26

26a *six hundred and sixty-six kikkar*: This is equivalent to roughly 22,500 kilograms, or nearly 50,000 pounds. The number is clearly fantastical. Although the authors of the Josianic study books might have included such fantastical numbers in their work—or that such numbers might have been in their source document *The Acts of Shelomo*—it seems more probable to me that the text here is from the hand of a Persian period or Hellenistic period author.

26b *the country's satraps*: The author uses the term פחות ("satraps") as the designation of provincial governors. The term is a loan word from Akkadian and was used as a designation for high officials and provincial governors in the Assyrian and Persian empires. The use of the term here offers support for a late date for this first sentence of P26, for in the Josianic study books, the government officials responsible for different regions of Shelomo's kingdom are called נצבים (which I translate as "tax commissioners," but which is often translated as "prefects").

26c *King Shelomo made two hundred body shields...and three hundred warrior's shields*: The body shields were plated with the equivalent of a little less than seven kilograms, or roughly fifteen pounds. One *maneh* was equivalent to fifty *sheqels*, or a little more than 550 grams. Each warrior's shield, then, would have been plated with the equivalent 1.7 kilograms.

The last two sentences of this *parashah* may be original to the Josianic study books.

Notes to P27

27a *The king made a large ivory throne...*: This *parashah* illustrates the difficulties of assigning material confidently to one or another of the proposed compositional stages. The *parashah* paints a picture of fabulous wealth that would be in keeping with the late stories that grew up around legendary figures of the distant past. If one understands the *parashah* in this way, a composition date in the late Persian period or in the Hellenistic period would make the most sense. However, this material is also perfectly understandable as part of the Josianic study books, particularly if one accepts the proposal that these books were written to serve in the education of the boy-king Yoshiyyahu. In this scenario, the *parashah* reads as something its authors composed to entertain their young pupil—a composition not necessarily based on any source documents, but simply elaborating on the themes of Shelomo's wealth, fame, and wisdom. In my proposed composition history, I assign all but the end of this *parashah* to the Josianic study books, but it would certainly be reasonable to assign the entire *parashah* to a later date, particularly if one had different views about the circumstances surrounding the original composition of Kings.

Although much material relating to Shelomo's wealth and wisdom was added as part of the work in the fifth compositional stage, these themes were already present in the earliest version of Kings. References to Shelomo's great wealth in material from Kings' first stage can be found in P24,1 (wealth procured by trading ships), here in P27, and also in P27,1.

27b *muphaz*-gold: This phrase indicates gold that has been processed in some way. However, it is unclear what sort of processing is meant. The parallel passage describing Shelomo's throne in 2 Chron 9.17 uses the phrase זהב טהור ("pure gold"), indicating the authors of Chronicles understood the processing to involve cleansing, refining, or purifying.

27c *sagur*-gold: This may refer to braided or patterned gold; see note 15d above.

27d Tarshiysh-ships: Tarshiysh was the site of a major trading port located somewhere in the western Mediterranean. "Tarshiysh-ship" was the term for a large ocean-going trading ship. The material here in P27 about Shelomo's trading ships should be viewed together with P24,1; see note 24,1e above.

27e *qophiym* and *tukkiyyiym*: These terms are obscure, and it is unclear what they mean. Traditionally, they have been translated as "monkeys" and "peacocks," but this seems extremely doubtful to me. Context suggests they refer to some precious metal or good and not live animals.

27f King Shelomo was greater than any of the world's kings with respect to wealth and wisdom...: I view the material from here to the end of the *parashah* as an addition by the authors of Kings' fifth compositional stage. These authors added much material relating to Shelomo's wealth and wisdom, and the addition here serves as a sort of summary statement of these themes. The use of the term אלהים ("God") instead of Yahweh offers support for a late date of the material here, for the early material in Kings rarely uses "God" when referring to Yahweh.

27g in fulfillment of their annual obligation: Translation of the phrase דבר־שנה בשנה. The phrase is somewhat obscure, but it must almost certainly mean "annual obligation, annual due," based on the related phrase דבר־יום ביומו, which is relatively common and which means "daily quota, daily task." The annual obligation is specifically the annual tribute that vassals owe their suzerain.

Note that the author of this passage (which is a late addition to Kings) is somewhat confused: he first implies that people came of their own freewill to hear Shelomo's wisdom, but then he follows this up with the statement that they brought gifts "in fulfillment of their annual obligation." Such inconsistency in the narrative is characteristic of late authors who often borrowed language and phrases from older material that isn't quite appropriate for the new context and who felt obligated to include multiple themes important to them, regardless of how well these themes fit with one another.

Note to P27,1

27,1a fourteen hundred chariots and twelve thousand chariot horses On these numbers and the translation "chariot horses," see my comment in note 11,1a above. The number of chariots in the related passage in P11,1 is corrupt. Note also the mention of forts for chariotry and war horses in P24.

27,1b when importing on behalf of Aram's kings or any of the Hethites' kings: I understand the text to mean that part of the business of Shelomo's trading "company" was to serve as middlemen for various kings to the north and northeast and to earn a profit by procuring for them chariots and horses from Egypt.

Notes to P28

28a women from the nations regarding which...after other gods.": I understand this clause to be a comment added in a later compositional stage. The author here is alluding to Deut P6,4: "You mustn't make any marriage alliances with them—don't give your daughters to their sons, nor take their daughters for your sons. For if they turn your sons away from me...." I understand that *parashah* in Deuteronomy to have been composed in the book's second compositional stage (the mid-Persian period). The comment here may have been added by the authors of Kings' third stage, who added many comments to Kings harmoizing it with the books of the Torah, or it may have been added by the authors of the sixth compositional stage. I have a preference for the former view.

28b [*Yet these were who Shelomo was attached to and loved.*]: I understand this sentence to be a comment added by the editors of Kings' sixth stage.

28c (and his wives did in fact pervert his heart): I understand this clause to be a late comment to the text. I have assigned it to the authors of the third stage, as it is related to the comment added by these same authors discussed in note 28a above. That said, however, it would be equally plausible to treat the comment here as an addition by the editors of the sixth stage.

28d Ashtoreth Goddess of Tziydonians: I understand אלהי צידנים as a surname and thus translate as "Goddess of Tziydonians." The goddess Ashtoreth was worshipped throughout the ancient Near East as both a goddess of love and a goddess of war, and there were many local versions of her. The version that Shelomo revered was the one associated with the city of Tziydon. She was especially venerated in ancient Phoenicia, which included the city of Tziydon. A good brief overview of the extra-biblical evidence for the veneration of Ashtoreth in Phoenicia is given in H.-P. Muller, "עשתרת '*štrt*" in the *Theological Dictionary of the Old Testament*, vol. 11, pp. 428f; the same article provides a full discussion of Ashtoreth in the Bible in pp. 429-434.

28e the Ammonites' abominable god Milkom: The author writes "Milkom Abomination of Ammonites," which is a play on the god's full name, Milkom God of Ammonites. I have not translated the phrasing as a surname in order to capture the pejorative sense of the author's language.

In both the Bible and in archaeological evidence, the god Milkom is associated with the region of Ammon (northwestern modern-day Jordan). Based on this evidence, most scholars view him as the national god of the Ammonites. A convenient overview of Milkom can be found in E. Puech, "Milcom," in K. van der Toorn, B. Becking, and P. van der Horst, eds., *Dictionary of Deities and Demons in the Bible*, 2nd edition (Leiden: Brill, 1999), 575f; the Wikipedia article "Milcom" is also well done and worth consulting.

28f Shelomo did what was displeasing to Yahweh: This is the first appearance of one of the leading themes of Kings: that the various kings of Yisra'el and Yehudah support the cults of gods other than Yahweh, actions which are "displeasing" to him.

The phrase that the author uses—עשה הרע בעיני יהוה (literally, "he did that which was bad in Yahweh's eyes")—is idiomatic. The phrase "to do bad in the eyes of someone" means "to displease" or "to do what displeases" a person. Hebrew has a parallel idiom "to do good [טוב or ישׁר] in the eyes of someone," which means to "to please" or "to do what pleases" a person. In the idiom indicating displeasure, the word רע ("bad, displeasing, injurious, evil") almost always appears with the definite article, and it sometimes also has the mark of the direct object (את) attached. There is no difference in meaning, as far as I can tell, when the mark of the direct object is used and when it isn't used.

This phrase "do what is displeasing to Yahweh" is very important in the Josianic study books. It is used some thirty times in material from Kings' first compositional stage, always as a way that the authors express their judgement of a king's merit. It is also used eight times in material from the earliest version of Judges, always in connection with the Yisra'elites' forsaking Yahweh for the gods of the surrounding peoples. In Judges, I translated the phrase as "did what Yahweh considered the worst thing." However, the usage of the phrase in Kings is applied to a wider range of actions (some of which are not necessarily "the worst thing"), and I have adjusted my translation to reflect this looser usage in Kings. As I discuss in my introductory note, I believe the authors of the earliest version of Kings sought to teach their pupil King Yoshiyyahu the importance of the king's pleasing Yahweh in his role as head of the cult, and the consequences of the king's displeasing Yahweh. In support of this effort, they composed Kings as a "study book" for the young king, structuring the book around the accounts of the reigns of the kings of Yisra'el and Yehudah known from the royal chronicles and then adding their own editorial commentary about whether each king "pleased" or "displeased" Yahweh.

Scholars have traditionally treated the phrase "do what is displeasing to Yahweh" as evidence that Kings was written by individuals who were part of a "Deuteronomistic" school or who were deeply influenced by Deuteronomy. I think this is incorrect, and that it was the authors of Deuteronomy who adopted this phrasing from the authors of Kings. The phrase "do what is displeasing to Yahweh" is used four times in Deuteronomy—at the beginning of P3, in the account of Mosheh's supplication of Yahweh in P10, in the law in P17,4, and at the end of Mosheh's speech in P30. In Deut P17,4 the phrase is applied to an individual who violates the terms of Yahweh's treaty with the Yisra'elites. In the other three usages in Deuteronomy, the phrase is used in connection with the Yisra'elites as a whole, similar to the use in Judges. However, these three occurrences are all much later than the usage in Kings and Judges: Deut P30 is from Deuteronomy's second compositional stage (early to mid-fifth century BCE) and Deut P3 and P10 are from Deuteronomy's third and fourth compositional stages (mid- to late Persian period).

28g he didn't exclusively carry out rites for Yahweh: The author uses unusual terminology—מלא אחרי ("to fill after"). The phrase appears several times in connection with Kalev Yephunnehsson, where it always means "follow exclusively, follow wholly after" (see Num P54 and Jos P29). Here, however, it is used in connection with a king, and the king is the sponsor of Yahweh's cult. I understand the use here to be in the context of Shelomo's support of Yahweh's cult, and I have translated to make that explicit. It's worth noting that the *pi'el* of מלא has a strong association with cult terminology—for example, the phrase מלא יד ("fill the hand of") means "to consecrate as a priest."

Notes to P28,1

28,1a At that time, Shelomo built...: I view this entire *parashah* as a late addition from Kings' fifth stage. It repeats themes already given in P28—Shelomo's worship of gods other than Yahweh and Yahweh's displeasure/anger with Shelomo. The authors of P28,1 know of other traditions about Shelomo's support of the cults of gods other than Yahweh, and they incorporated this material here to create a more complete account of Shelomo's reign. Many additions to the books of the Torah and the Former Prophets that were made late in the Persian period were motivated by a desire to create a more complete or comprehensive record in what were by then authoritative texts. I believe this was the motivation for a number of the additions in Kings' fifth stage, including the one here.

28,1b Mo'av's abomination, Kemosh: The author's phrasing plays on Kemosh's surname, which was God of Mo'av. See note 28e above. Kemosh was a martial god who was revered as the national god of Mo'av; there is little evidence for worship of Kemosh outside the territory of Mo'av, which was located directly to the east of the Dead Sea. The Wikipedia article on Kemosh is quite good; see also H.-P. Muller, "Chemosh," in K. van der Toorn, B. Becking, and P. van der Horst, eds., *Dictionary of Deities and Demons in the Bible*, 2nd edition (Leiden: Brill, 1999), 186-189.

28,1c He did likewise for all his foreign wives: That is, he built open-air shrines where his foreign wives could make offerings to their gods.

28,1d the Ammonites' abomination Molek: The author's phrasing here plays on Molek's surname, which was God of Ammonites.

There is some disagreement among scholars as to whether the term *molek* was the name of a god or the name for the rite of offering one's child to a god. And for those who believe Molek was a god's name, there is some disagreement as to whether Molek was identical to Milkom (who is mentioned in P28), or whether they were distinct gods. For what it's worth, I think that the references to Molek in the Tanakh are unequivocal that Molek was the name of a god, and that one of the ways this god was venerated was through the sacrifice of one's child (almost certainly in connection with some extraordinary vow). Furthermore, I view Molek as distinct from Milkom. The passage here in Kings associates Molek with the Ammonites, but there is much evidence he was venerated elsewhere, including the ancient kingdoms of Yisra'el and Yehudah. The Wikipedia article on Molek provides an excellent discussion of Molek; there is also a very good discussion in G. Heider, "Molech," in K. van der Toorn, B. Becking, and P. van der Horst, eds., *Dictionary of Deities and Demons in the Bible*, 2nd edition (Leiden: Brill, 1999), 581-585.

28,1e who had twice shown himself to him: In the earliest versions of Kings, Yahweh speaks to Shelomo, but he never appears to him. The authors of the fifth stage introduced two instances of Yahweh appearing to Shelomo—they composed the story of Shelomo's dream in P8 and they recast Yahweh's speech to Shelomo in P22 as a visual manifestation by adding the first sentence of that *parashah*, which references the appearance in P8. Here in P28,1, the authors of the fifth stage remind the reader of Yahweh's showing himself to Shelomo in P8 and P22.

28,1f he had warned him about this matter so that he wouldn't follow the ways of other gods: This is an allusion to the warning that Yahweh gave to Shelomo in P22: "if you and your descendants turn away from me...I shall wipe Yisra'el off the face of the land...and at the same time I shall reject the house that I consecrated for my name." Note how the warning in P22, which belongs to Kings' second stage and which was written to serve as an explanation of the Babylonian exile, doesn't fit the context here in P28,1 (from Kings' fifth stage), where the author's focus is the set-up for the dissolution of the united kingdom. Such inconsistencies and tensions in the text are to be expected when the text itself is the product of many authors writing, adding, editing, and revising over a period of centuries.

29a "Because of this thing associated with you...: This *parashah* is critical to the narrative arc of the earliest version of Kings that I associate with the education of King Yoshiyyahu. It explains why there are two kingdoms, Yisra'el and Yehudah, and it establishes a rationale for Yoshiyyahu's claim on the lands of the former northern kingdom as lands that rightfully belong to the Dawidic king as ordained by Yahweh.

It's worth noting that the speech here in P29 is the only instance in the earliest version of Kings in which Yahweh addresses Shelomo. It's also worth noting that the speech is unmediated—that is, Yahweh speaks directly to Shelomo.

29b the binding agreement with me: This is an allusion to Yahweh's unconditional binding agreement (ברית) with Dawid and his descendants that the Dawidic dynasty shall last for all time. This was a core part of Judean royal ideology. The unconditional "binding agreement" between Yahweh and his king in Yerushalem appears in Ps 89 in verses 4 and 35. The binding agreement between Yahweh and his king also appears in Ps 132.12; there it is part of a late addition to the psalm and it is expressed as a conditional agreement, not an unconditional one. For further thoughts on this topic, see the discussion of Judian royal ideology in my introductory note to this book.

29c the place I've chosen as my very own: I have added the phrase "as my very own" (which reflects the phrase לשמי), as this is implied in the Hebrew. On this phrasing, see note 20c above.

29d —: The Leningrad Codex does not have a *parashah* break here. See L193 r.2.10.

29,1a Yahweh raised up an adversary for Shelomo—Hadad the Edomite...: I view this *parashah* as an addition by the authors of the fifth stage. It is not at all integrated into the base narrative of Shelomo's reign, and I view it as another example of late authors incorporating traditions they believed to be ancient in order to complete a work they viewed as authoritative.

A further complication is that the material in this *parashah* doesn't hang together very well. For example, in the story of Hadad the Edomite, there is no mention of what he did that was adversarial or threatening to Shelomo. Perhaps some material has fallen out of the text that provided an account of his actions against Shelomo or perhaps, as I suggest in my essay on Kings' composition history, the *parashah* was started but never completed by its author. Similarly, the material about Rezon Elyada'sson (which I view as a separate addition to the *parashah*) is disjointed and some material may have fallen out of the text there as well.

29,1b Now when Dawid was with Edom...: The text is clearly corrupt. Either a verb—perhaps נלחם ("doing battle")—has fallen out of the text or the infinitive בהיות ("when [Dawid] was") is an error for בהכות ("when [Dawid] defeated"). The story of Yo'av's slaughter of the Edomite males is not preserved in Samuel. The only mention of conflict between Dawid and Edom in the book of Samuel is in P82,1, which states that Dawid established garrisons in Edom and that "all of Edom became his vassals." However, the previous sentence in Sam P82,1 states that Dawid defeated Aram in the Salt Valley, and it is likely that the text originally said "Edom" and not "Aram" (the two words look very similar in Hebrew). It is this version of Samuel that the author of Kgs P29,1 knows. Note that in 1 Chr 18.12f (which is parallel to Sam P82,1), Dawid defeats Edom, not Aram, in the Salt Valley. In that passage, Yo'av's brother General Avshai slaughters eighteen thousand Edomites in battle, which is perhaps an alternate version of Yo'av's slaughter mentioned here in Kgs P29,1.

Notes to P29

Notes to P29,1

29,1c Adad: This is a variant spelling of Hadad.

29,1d He gave them shelter...they be supplied...gave them some land: Where I have translated as "them" and "they," the Hebrew reads "him" and "he." This sentence is a good example of how one must depart from a literal rendering of the text to create a functionally equivalent translation. Hadad was a member of the royal family of Edom, and the men with him were his subordinates. It was natural for the ancient author to express the idea in the sentence as a transaction between Phar'oh and the representative of Edom's royal family. The ancient reader would have understood that by giving Hadad food and shelter and land, the men accompanying him would be taken care of through the gift to Hadad. Modern-day English usage, however, requires one to acknowledge the men accompanying Hadad—neglecting to mention them here would make the narrative feel disjointed.

29,1e he gave him a wife—the sister of his own wife: There is some minor tension in the text. If Hadad was a young boy at the time, as mentioned earlier in the *parashah*, he would have been too young to marry and the queen's sister likely would have been a decade or more older than him. This tension disappears if we treat the comment about Hadad being a young boy as an addition by the editors of the sixth stage.

29,1f arranged for him to be broughd up: The Hebrew reads ותגמלהו ("she weaned him"), which I believe is a mistake for ותגדלהו ("she reared him"). I have reflected what is essentially a spelling error in the text with the translation "broughd" in place of "brought."

29,1g God raised up an adversary to him—Rezon Elyada'sson...: The Hebrew is very disjointed and awkward, which I have reflected in translation. The pronoun "him" refers to Shelomo. The material about Rezon reads as secondary and later than the material about Hadad. Note the use here of "God," whereas the material about Hadad uses "Yahweh." I treat both additions as belonging to Kings' fifth stage.

29,1h King of Tzovah: Tzovah was the Hebrew name for the city known in English as Aleppo.

29,1i he was the leader of a bandit gang when Dawid killed them: This story is not preserved in Samuel. The Hebrew is a little confusing, but the reader should infer that Dawid killed some, but not all, of the bandit gang. Presumably the author of this *parashah* intended for the reader to understand that it was Rezon and the survivors of the bandit gang who went to Dammeseq and ruled there.

29,1j in addition to the harm associated with Hadad: This clause reads very awkwardly in Hebrew, and it may be an addition from the final compositional stage, inserted by an editor who was bothered by the lack of a statement regarding Hadad's opposition to Shelomo.

Notes to P30

30a Yarov'am Nevatsson was an Ephrathite...: This *parashah* introduces the character of Yarov'am, who is a central figure and the primary "bad guy" in the earliest version of Kings. He is the first king of Yisra'el after the dissolution of the "united kingdom" under Shelomo, and the authors of the Josianic study books place the blame for the fall of the northern kingdom on him. In their view, he wronged Yahweh by creating cult statues depicting Yahweh in the form of a gold bull calf and installing them in Yahweh's shrines in Beyth-El and Dan—a wrong that was perpetuated by all the succeeding kings of the northern kingdom.

The account of the split of Shelomo's kingdom into Yisra'el and Yehudah, which is part of the earliest version of Kings, appears in P30-P31,1 (excluding P30,3, which is the summary statement of Shelomo's reign that appeared in the earliest version of Kings). The narrative in these *parashot* is somewhat disjointed. I believe the disjointed nature of these *parashot* is due to the composition process of the authors of Kings' first stage, in which they combined material about Yarov'am from their source document, *The Chronicles of the Kings of Yisra'el*, with material that they freely composed. The material about Yarov'am from the source document is P30, P30,2, the first two sentences of P30,4, the first two sentences of P31, and the first sentence of of P31,1. The material that the authors of Kings' first stage composed, which had a very different understanding of events than the source document, is P30,1, all of P30,4 but the first two sentences, the final sentence of P31, and the second sentence of P31,1. (I view the last sentence of P31,1 and all of P32 as an addition by the authors of Kings' fourth stage and thus not relevant for the discussion here; see note 31,1d below.) Adding to the disjointed nature of the narrative in its current form is that the story of the Yisra'elites' rejection of Rehav'am in P30,4 originally did not mention Yarov'am, and he was clumsily inserted into that story by later editors (see note 30,4b below).

The Chronicles of the Kings of Yisra'el began with Yarov'am's reign, and I believed it included a short account of how he came to succeed Shelomo as king of Yisra'el. We can see the broad outlines of that account in the material that the authors of Kings' first stage chose to incorporate into their work. At stated above, these parts are P30 (how Yarov'am came to Shelomo's attention and the responsibilities Shelomo gave him), P30,2 (Yarov'am's flight to Egypt, almost certainly after his insurrection against Shelomo failed), the first two sentences of P30,4 (Rehav'am's trip to Shekem to be installed as king while Yarov'am remains in Egypt), the first two sentences of P31 (the Yisra'elites' rebellion against Rehav'am), and the first sentence of P31,1 (the Yisra'elites' selection of Yarov'am as their king). The authors of Kings' first stage omit a significant amount of material that must have been in the source document, including the details of Yarov'am's insurrection and its failure. They almost certainly omitted this information because it did not fit well with the themes that they developed in P30,1 regarding why Yahweh selected Yarov'am and in P30,4, which presented Yisra'el's rebellion as a rebellion against the Dawidic king. It is worth emphasizing that the theme that these authors had to establish—that Yisra'el broke away from Yehudah and from Dawidic rule—was not present in their source, *The Chronicles of the Kings of Yisra'el*. Their source for Shelomo's succession was written from the perspective of the kingdom of Yisra'el. Thus, the source would have presented Yarov'am as the legitimate king chosen by the people of Yisra'el, and it would have portrayed Yehudah as the disloyal region; moreover, it would not have viewed the Dawidic king as special in any way.

30b his mother, who was a widow, was named Tzeru'ah: The citation of the name of Yarov'am's mother is surprising. Whereas the royal chronicles of Yehudah used by the authors of Kings always recorded the name of the king's mother, this information was almost certainly not recorded in the royal chronicles of Yisra'el, for—with the exception of Yarov'am—the authors of Kings never cite the mother's name in their accounts of the kings of Yisra'el.

30c one of Shelomo's officials: The Hebrew appears to be corrupt. The pronoun הוא ("he") must have fallen out of the text. If the pronoun is restored, the text would read "He was one of Shelomo's officials."

30d he gave him responsibility for all forced labor in the nation of Yoseph: The nation of Yoseph was a subunit of the kingdom of Yisra'el that consisted of the tribal territories of Ephrayim and Menashsheh. Yarov'am was an Ephrathite—that is, he was from Ephrayim. Assuming that there is a historical basis for the information in the *parashah* (I believe the material in it is from *The Chronicles of the Kings of Yisra'el*), Yarov'am's tribal background likely factored into the decision to give him responsibility for the forced labor in the nation of Yoseph.

Notes to P30,1

30,1a the prophet Ahiyyah the Shiylonite: Yarov'am is a very important figure for the authors of Kings' first stage, and they employ prophetic figures at three different places in the material about Yarov'am to develop themes important to them, as well as to move the narrative forward. Here in P30,1, the authors use Ahiyyah the Shiylonite to explain that Yahweh selected Yarov'am to be king of Yisra'el and that, just as Yahweh made a dynastic promise to Dawid, so he also made a dynastic promise to Yarov'am (although the promise to Yarov'am was conditional on his doing what was "pleasing" to Yahweh). Next, in P33—which is the most important material involving a prophet in the earliest version of Kings—an anonymous holy man delivers an oracle foretelling Yoshiyyahu's birth and his destruction of the cult in Beyth-El. Lastly, in P38, Ahiyyah the Shiylonite delivers an oracle foretelling the destruction of Yarov'am's dynastic line. It should be stressed that in all three instances, the prophetic speeches read as compositions of the authors of Kings' first stage that reflect their own views and that are not based on any tradition. There is only one other instance in which a prophet appears as a character in the earliest version of Kings. In P60,3 Eliyyahu delivers an oracle telling Ahazyah King of Yisra'el that he will die; however, in this instance, the text seems to preserve an actual oracle of Eliyyahu that was in a source used by the authors of Kings' first stage or that the authors knew from oral tradition. It should also be noted that at the end of P44,1 and again at the end of P45 the authors of Kings' first stage mention an oracle that Yehu Hananiysson the Prophet pronounced against Ba'sha King of Yisra'el; however, they simply allude to this oracle—Yehu the prophet does not appear as a character. (His appearance in the first half of P44,1 is an addition by the authors of Kings' fourth stage—see notes 44,1a and 44,1e below.)

Finally, it's worth pointing out that prophets play a major role in later additions to Kings (specifically the fourth compositional stage), but the role of prophets in that material is entirely different than their role in the material from the first stage.

30,1b He was wearing a new tunic: The subject of the sentence is ambiguous—it may refer to either Yarov'am or Ahiyyah. That said, I believe the author intended the reader to understand Ahiyyah is wearing the tunic, as the action that follows in the narrative is slightly more understandable if Ahiyyah is the one wearing the new tunic.

30,1c Only one tribe will be his: There is a missing tribe in the author's account—Yahweh gives ten tribes to Yarov'am and lets Shelomo keep only one tribe. As Shim'on's territory was carved out of Yehudah's territory (see Jos P38), I presume that the author here has combined Yehudah and Shim'on into a single tribe (the tribe kept by Shelomo). The missing tribe must be the tribe of Lewiy, which possesses no territory of its own.

Recall that there are thirteen tribes: Asher, Zevulun, Naphtaliy, Yissakar, Menashsheh, Ephrayim, Binyamin, Dan, Yehudah, Shim'on, Re'uven, Gad, and Lewiy. In northern traditions (as reflected in Genesis, which I view as a Samarian composition), Ephrayim and Menashsheh are combined into a single tribe represented by the nation of Yoseph. But in the view of the author of Kgs P30,1, who is writing as part of the Josianic study books, Ephrayim and Menashsheh are distinct tribes, and it is Yehudah and Shim'on that are combined into a single tribe represented by Yehudah.

30,1d Because they've abandoned me...like his father Dawid did: These two sentences more closely reflect the concerns of the authors of Kings third stage than the authors of the Josianic study books, and for that reason I have assigned them to the work of the former. Note how these sentences, the subject of which is "they" (i.e. the people), disrupt the narrative; the sentences immediately before and after are focused on Shelomo, not the people, and flow naturally: "Only one tribe will be his..." followed by "I won't take the entire kingdom from him...." The addition here may have been prompted by the corruption of the text discussed below in note 30,1f.

30,1e Ashtoreth Goddess of Tziydonians, Kemosh God of Mo'av, and Milkom God of the Ammonites: Note the author's use of the gods' actual surnames here rather than pejorative phrasing in P28 and P28,1. On these gods, see notes 28d, 28e, and 28,1b above. It's also worth noting that here the author includes mention of Kemosh, although that god is not included among the gods venerated by Shelomo in P28. (Kemosh appears in P28,1, but that *parashah* is an addition by the authors of the fifth stage and would not have been known to the authors of the Josianic study books.)

30,1f They haven't followed in my ways...by doing what pleases me like his father Dawid did: The text is corrupt. Originally, it must have read "He hasn't followed" (ולא הלך) instead of "They haven't followed" (ולא הלכו). The clause about "my laws and my precepts" reads as a comment by the editors of the sixth stage.

30,1g so that there might always be a lamp belonging to my servant Dawid that is present with me: That is, so that there might always be a descendant of Dawid who rules Yehudah and who serves as the head of Yahweh's cult in Yerushalem. The lamp imagery is applied to Dawid and his descendants once in Samuel and three times in Kings. In Sam P102, the term "lamp of Yisra'el" refers specifically to Dawid as the living king. In all three instances in Kings—here in P30,1, in P41, and in P75—the term "lamp" refers specifically to Dawid's descendants who sit on the throne of Yehudah. The lamp imagery also appears near the end of Psalm 132, where the lamp appears to be a physical object inside Yahweh's house (see the discussion of this psalm in my introductory note above).

It is important to note that the lamp imagery here in P30,1 implies the unconditional Dawidic promise—the Dawidic king will always be present in Yerushalem, the town that Yahweh has chosen as his own. The presence of the unconditional Dawidic promise offers strong support for viewing this *parashah* as belonging to the earliest version of Kings.

30,1h the town that I've chosen to claim as my very own: Literally, "the town where I've chosen to place my name." On the use of the formulation "place my name" to indicate a claim on ownership, see note 20c above.

30,1i although not for all time: Note how the authors of the Josianic study books here subtly refer to the vision for a united kingdom under Yoshiyyahu: Yahweh will make Dawid's line "suffer" by taking away ten tribes from its dominion—but "not for all time." That is, at some time in the future, the Dawidic line will again have dominion over all the Yisra'elites' tribes.

30,2a Shelomo attempted to have Yarov'am killed...: This *parashah* reads as a verbatim insertion from *The Chronicles of the Kings of Yisra'el*. It is odd that the authors of the Josianic study books incorporated the material here but did not include an account of Yarov'am's offense against Shelomo. This offense almost certainly was Yarov'am's insurrection mentioned in P30, which must have failed. As discussed in note 30a above, I believe that *The Chronicles of the Kings of Yisra'el* began with

Notes to P30,2

an account of Yarov'am's rise to prominence and that it included details about the insurrection he led against Shelomo.

30,2b —: The Leningrad Codex does not have a *parashah* break here. See L193 v.3.3.

Notes to P30,3

30,3a The rest of Shelomo's acts—including everything he did and his great wisdom—are recorded in the book *The Acts of Shelomo*: I view *The Acts of Shelomo* as the major source of the information about Shelomo used by the authors of the earliest version of Kings. I believe this was the source for nearly all the information given in P10,3 - P10,24 and P24 - P24,1. It addition, it was possibly the source of the information appearing in P11; P11,1; P15; P17,2; P19; P23; P26; and P27,1. It is noteworthy that the citation here suggests that *The Acts of Shelomo* contained material about Shelomo's wisdom. If we accept that the book was a genuine royal chronicle, then the theme of Shelomo's wisdom must have originated in his lifetime. The stories about Shelomo's wisdom in Kings, however, all appear to date to the Persian period. See the discussion in my treatment of Kings' composition history at the end of this book.

30,3b Shelomo reigned in Yerushalem...Rehav'am succeeded him as king: The last three sentences of this *parashah* follow a formula that we see with the kings of Yehudah and that likely were based on the formulaic sentences used in the one of the main source documents for Kings, the book *The Chronicles of the Kings of Yehudah*. It is worth noting that this book is not mentioned as a source for either Dawid or Shelomo. That is to say, neither Dawid nor Shelomo seem to have been included in the book that served as the official records of the kingdom of Yehudah.

30,3c Shelomo reigned in Yerushalem over all Yisra'el for a period of forty years: As stated above, I believe the concluding three sentences of P30,3 are not from the *The Acts of Shelomo*, but were composed by the authors of the Josianic study books. Note that the authors here use the phrase "all Yisra'el," which I believe in this instance they understood to be inclusive of Yehudah. The clearest indications that the authors of the Josianic study books sometimes understood "Yisra'el" to be inclusive of Yehudah are the occurrences in P30,1 ("the town that I've chosen for myself out of all Yisra'el's tribes") and P39 ("the town that Yahweh chose out of all Yisra'el's tribes"). By contrast, when the term "Yisra'el" or the phrase "all Yisra'el" appear in the source document for Shelomo's reign, *The Acts of Shelomo*, they can always be understood as excluding Yehudah. Note especially P10,2 (discussed above in note 10,2a) and P19 ("Yisra'el's elders" and "all the Yisra'elites").

30,3d he was buried in his ancestral fortress Fort Dawid: As we will see in the accounts of the other kings of Yehudah, Fort Dawid (עיר דוד or "the Fortress of Dawid") must have served as the royal burial ground for Yehudah. Most scholars believe that Fort Dawid was located on a hill in Yerushalem known as the Ophel ("the mound"). The Ophel has been intensively excavated, but no royal tombs have been found there. The account of Dawid's capture of Yerushalem in Sam P74,1 states that when Dawid captured the town's citadel, which was called Fort Tziyyon (מצדת ציון), he renamed it Fort Dawid.

The word עיר, which typically has the meaning "city, town," may originally have meant "fortress, fortified place," and there are many places in the Tanakh where it retains this meaning—most commonly in the name Fort Dawid.

Notes to P30,4

30,4a Rehav'am travelled to Shekem, for all Yisra'el had gone to Shekem to install him as king: I view the first two sentences of this *parashah* as a verbatim insertion from the source document, *The Chronicles of the Kings of Yisra'el*. The remainder of the *parashah*, which is the account of the Yisra'elites' rejection of Rehav'am and the dissolution of the "united kingdom," reads as a literary composition by the authors of the Josianic study books.

I believe the phrase "all Yisra'el" here appeared in *The Chronicles of the Kings of Yisra'el*, where it designated the entire territory occupied by the northern tribes, including the territories east of the Yarden River. (As I suggest in note 10,2a above, it likely had that meaning as well in *The Acts of Shelomo*.) The authors of the Josianic study books, however, seem to have understood the phrase in their source documents as referring to the combined territory of the two kingdoms, and that is how they use the term in the material that they themselves composed about the period prior to the divided monarchy.

The mention of Shekem here is extraordinary. It indicates that the authors of *The Chronicles of the Kings of Yisra'el* viewed Shekem, not Yerushalem, as the royal seat of Shelomo. It is unclear whether they presented Shekem as the royal seat due to their own bias in favor of the north and their wish to deny legitimacy to Yerushalem, or whether in fact Shekem really was the royal seat for Shelomo and Yerushalem a secondary capital for him.

30,4b He was summoned by messenger, and then Yarov'am and the full assembly of Yisra'el went to speak to Rehav'am: Along with many scholars, I believe that in the earliest version of Kings, Yarov'am was not present at the people's audience with Rehav'am. I believe the editors' of Kings' sixth stage inserted him into P30,4 in two places. In the sentence here, they added the language "He was summoned by messenger, and then Yarov'am and" (וישלחו ויקראו־לו... ירבעם ו); then toward the end of the *parashah*, they added the phrase "Yarov'am and" (see note 30,4e below). In P30, which is a verbatim insertion from the source document, we are told that Yarov'am led an insurrection against the king. This king was without a doubt Shelomo. The editors of Kings' sixth stage, however, must have identified the king against whom Yarov'am led an insurrection as Rehav'am, and it was this understanding that led them to insert Yarov'am into P30,4.

The verb "went" in the consonantal text is written as the third person plural (ויבאו), but the *qere* in the margin corrects this to the third person singular (ויבא). (See A81 r.3.10 and L193 v.3.18.) I have translated the *ketiv* here; if I were to translate the sentence with the *qere*, I would translate slightly differently, to make clear the verb applies only to Yarov'am: "Yarov'am went, along with the full assembly of Yisra'el."

30,4c Go away for two days: Literally, "Go away for three days." In ancient Hebrew, unlike modern English, when referring to future time, the speaker counts the present day as the "first day." Thus, to "go away for three days" to an ancient Hebrew speaker is equivalent to a modern English speaker saying to "go away for two days."

30,4d "My little pinky is fatter than my father's prick...: Rehav'am's childhood buddies propose an especially vulgar and obnoxious response. The Hebrew is not quite as vulgar as what I have translated; where I have "prick," the Hebrew reads "loins" (מתנים). A functionally equivalent English translation, however, requires a vulgarity. The force of the Hebrew would be completely lost if one translated with a euphemism here.

In composing this scene, the authors of this story wished to draw a strong contrast between the older advisors of Shelomo, whose counsel is informed by their long life experience, and the young men advising Rehav'am, who are rash and overconfident and lack the wisdom that comes with life experience. One wonders if the authors of the Josianic study books, who likely were men in their forties and fifties and sixties, are making a subtle point here about the value of their own advice to Yoshiyyahu versus the advice he was receiving from other palace factions.

30,4e Yarov'am and: I believe these words were added by the editors of Kings' sixth stage in order to give Yarov'am a role in Yisra'el's rebellion against Rehav'am. See note 30,4b above.

30,4f cam back: There is a small spelling error here in the Aleppo Codex, which reads ויבו instead of ויבוא. I have reflected the spelling error in translation, which otherwise would read "came back." See A81 v.1.19. There is no *qere* in the margin showing the correct spelling, perhaps because the misspelled word would be pronounced identically to the correctly spelled word. It is interesting to note that the misspelling also appears in the Leningrad Codex, but the scribe Shmu'el ben Ya'aqov has written a *qere* in the margin with the correct spelling. See L194 r.1.25.

30,4g "My father yoked you with hard labor....: Note that the authors do not repeat the obnoxious comment by which Rehav'am asserts his virility. It is unclear whether they intended the reader to understand that he repeated this phrase, or whether they intended the reader to understand that he showed the judgement to ignore that piece of his buddies' advice.

30,4h We have no territory with Dawid! Nor any property with Yishaysson!: The authors here quote a famous saying. The saying also appears in Sam P100,6, which is the beginning of the account of Sheva Bikriysson's rebellion against Dawid. The parallel structure of the saying—two sentences in which the second sentence repeats the information of the first sentence in more forceful terms—is commonly seen in songs, proverbs, and folk sayings. In the version of the saying in Samuel, the second sentence includes the phrase לנו ("we have"); this phrase is omitted in the version here in Kings. The phrase is not strictly necessary, as it can be understood as carrying over from the first sentence. To understand the second sentence, the reader must be aware that Yishaysson is a synonym for Dawid—recall that Dawid was the son of Yishay and here he is referred to by his surname, Yishaysson. The terms "Dawid" and "Yishayyson" here are poetic ways of referring to the territory ruled by Dawid.

30,4i the Yisra'elites who were living in Yehudah's towns: It is unclear what the authors mean by this phrase. It is possibly an oblique reference to all the people of Yehudah (who would be Yisra'elites because Yehudah was one of the tribes of Yisra'el), or—more likely in my opinion—it is a reference to the people belonging to the ten northern tribes who were living in Yehudah.

Notes to P31

31a King Rehav'am sent Adoram Boss of the Labor Gangs to confront the Yisra'elites....: I believe the first two sentences of this *parashah* are a verbatim insertion from *The Chronicles of the Kings of Yisra'el*, which began with an account of how Yarov'am succeeded Shelomo as king of Yisra'el. See note 30a above. The source document must have included a sentence or two regarding the dispute the Yisra'elites had with Rehav'am, which prompted him to send Adoram to confront them. However, the authors of the Josianic study books omitted that material and in its place they composed the story of Rehav'am's audience with the Yisra'elites in P30,4.

The phrase אשר על-המס is a job title ("overseer of the labor gangs") that is here used as a surname. On this individual named Adoram, see note 10,11a above.

31b And so Yisra'el rebelled against the Dawidic dynasty, as is the case today: I view this sentence as an editorial comment by the authors of the Josianic study books. The clause "as is the case today," which reads almost as an afterthought by the author, offers support for the proposal that the earliest version of Kings was written when the kingdom of Yehudah was still independent. The authors of the Josianic study books present the dissolution of the "united kingdom" under Shelomo as a rebellion of Yisra'el against the Dawidic king. Their hope was that when King Yoshiyyahu grew to manhood, he would bring the former territory of Yisra'el back under the rule of the Dawidic king and in so doing reunite Yahweh's people.

31,1a When the people of Yisra'el heard that Yarov'am had returned...: I believe the first two sentences of this *parashah* are a verbatim insertion from *The Chronicles of the Kings of Yisra'el*. I understand the statement that Yehudah alone remained under Dawidic rule as an editorial comment by the authors of the Josianic study books, and I view the last sentence of the *parashah* to be an addition from Kings' fourth stage (see note 31,1d below).

Notes to P31,1

Note the apparent inconsistency in the narrative: in P30,4 Yarov'am was present at Rehav'am's meeting with the Yisra'elites at Shekem, whereas the statement here in P31,1 implies he was absent. As discussed in notes 30a and 30,4b above, later editors inserted Yarov'am into the narrative in P30,4 at Shekem. In the earliest edition of Kings, Yarov'am was not present at the Yisra'elites' meeting with Rehav'am in P30,4, and thus there was no inconsistency between P30,4 and P31,1 in that edition.

31,1b the assembly at Shekem: I have added "at Shekem" in translation, as it is most natural in the conventions of English prose to remind the reader in this situation that the location of the action hasn't changed.

31,1c No one remained under Dawidic rule except the tribe of Yehudah alone: The author here combines Yehudah and Shim'on into a single tribe under the name Yehudah. See note 30,1c above.

31,1d Once Rehav'am arrived in Yerushalem...: In the consonantal text, the verb "arrived" is written as the third person plural form. The vocalization in the text and the *qere* in the margin correct this to the third person singular. See A81 v.3.4 and L194 r.3.8.

The material from here through the end of P32 describes Rehav'am's plans to go to war with Yisra'el, followed by his decision to abandon those plans after receiving an oracle from Shema'yah the Holy Man. This material provides an excellent illustration of the difficulties of developing a clear understanding of the composition history of Kings. In the framework that I have developed for Kings, there are three possible ways to understand the composition of this material (the last sentence of P31 plus all of P32). One may view it as material from *The Chronicles of the Kings of Yisra'el* that the authors of Kings' first stage have incorporated into their work; one may view it as a literary composition of the authors of Kings' first stage not based on any source document; or one may view it as an addition by the authors of Kings' fourth stage, who knew of a famous oracle attributed to Shema'yah the Holy Man and who composed a scenario in which Rehav'am seeks to go to war against Yisra'el in order to create an appropriate place to insert the oracle into Kings. Of these three options, I have a preference for the last option. I think the first option—that this material is an insertion from *The Chronicles of the Kings of Yisra'el*—is unlikely because that work doesn't otherwise mention any oracles of Yahweh in its accounts of the early kings of Yisra'el; moreover, the material in question is written from the perspective of Yehudah and not Yisra'el. I view the second option—that this material is a literary composition of the authors of Kings' first stage—as unlikely because Rehav'am's involvement of Binyamin in his plans is inconsistent with the statement by these authors in P30,1 and in the previous sentence in P31,1 that only one tribe would belong to the Dawidic king.

31,1e as well as the tribe of Binyamin: Note the inconsistency in the text. The previous sentence—an editorial comment by the authors of the Josianic study books—stated that only Yehudah remained under Dawidic rule, and here Binyamin (or parts of Binyamin) are allied with the Dawidic king. The inconsistency is indicative of a change of authorship. As discussed in note 31,1d directly above, I view the last sentence of P31,1 and all of P32 as an addition by the authors of Kings' fourth stage.

Notes to P32

32a Shema'yah the Holy Man received the following oracle...: The author uses "the Holy Man" (איש האלהים) as a surname for Shema'yah; occupational surnames were quite common in ancient Hebrew, just as they are quite common in English. The authors of Kings often use איש האלהים ("holy man") as a synonym for נביא ("prophet"). This is the first occurrence of the term "holy man" (literally "man of God" or "divine man") in Kings. The term occurs frequently in connection to Eliysha, where it is associated with his ability to work miracles.

32b the people who remain: I understand this as a reference to the Yisra'elites who were living in towns in Yehudah and who are mentioned at the end of P30,4. It is interesting to note that the authors of Kings' fourth stage here refer back to material by authors of the first stage.

32c what has happened is my doing: I have departed further than usual from a literal rendering to express the idea in natural English. Literally, "for this thing happened because of me."

Notes to P32,1

32,1a Penu'el: Penu'el is a relatively common place name. There is no reason to believe the Penu'el mentioned here is necessarily the town east of the Yarden that is mentioned in Judges P24 and in Gen P28 (where it is called Peniy'el).

32,1b As things are now: Translation of the particle עתה ("now" and various related nuances). For the use of the word to describe a present state ("as things are"), see BDB, p. 774, def. 1d.

32,1c For if the people go make welfare offerings at Yahweh's house in Yerushalem: Yarov'am here may be alluding to the custom of families of the northern tribes making an annual welfare offering to Yahweh, which apparently could be a multi-day celebration. See the story of Elqanah and his family travelling to Shiloh for such an offering in Sam P1.

32,1d The ones that brought you up out of Egypt!: I believe that this phrase is an addition from either the third or the sixth compositional stage, and that originally Yarov'am's words were simply "Here are your gods, Yisra'el!" A later editor borrowed the phrase "The ones that brought you up out of Egypt" from Exodus P51,1 and inserted it here, thus connecting Yarov'am's speech with Aharon's speech to the Yisra'elites at the foot of Mount Siynai.

While it is certainly possible to understand the phrase "the ones that brought you up out of Egypt" as belonging to the earliest version of Kings, against this view is that it would be the only instance in Kings in which the authors of the Josianic study books make reference to the exodus tradition.

32,1e He installed one of them in Beyth-El, and the other he placed in Dan: The two shrines are in the far south and the far north of the kingdom of Yisra'el. It is worth noting that although the cults in Beyth-El and Dan had royal support, they differed from the cult in Yerushalem in that they were not associated with the seat of kingship. Beyth-El was a full day's journey south from Shekem, and Dan was a journey of four to five days north.

32,1f He also established open-air shrines: The authors of Kings use two different but related terms to refer to the open-air shrines dedicated to Yahweh: במות (literally "elevated places") and בית במות / בתי הבמות ("house[s] of [the] elevated places"). The author of P32,1 uses the latter term here. The use of the term בית במות does not necessarily imply that there was a physical structure attached to the shrine. The shrines to Yahweh in both Yisra'el and Yehudah typically were open-air shrines consisting of an altar on an elevated platform without any other permanent structure. (No permanent structure was needed because there was no image of the deity that needed a "house;" the deity instead was represented by a sacred pillar.) Some shrines, however, may have had permanent structures that were used for storage of equipment used in offering rites or that served as priests' living quarters. See note 8b above for more details on the open-air shrines.

32,1g he designated people everywhere as priests: Literally, "he designated priests from the ends of the people." The phrase מקצה ("from the end of") was often used to designate totality, which is the use here. That is, "the ends of the people" is equivalent to "people everywhere." On this use of קצה, see BDB, p. 892, def. 3.

32,1h [*none of whom were Lewites*]: The author of this clause must have been writing when the Lewites had an exclusive claim on the priesthood, which I believe was not the case until the Persian period. Thus I understand this phrase to be a later addition to the text.

32,1i a festival on the fifteenth day of the eighth month, similar to the festival in Yehudah: It is unclear what festival the author is referring to here. There is no festival on this date mentioned elsewhere in the Tanakh. It is likely that this was some sort of harvest festival, as the first month of the ancient Hebrew calendar was in the spring.

32,1j making a great number of welfare offerings: The verb זבח, which is usually translated as "sacrifice," very often has the specific meaning of "make a welfare offering." The verb form is the *pi'el*, which here indicates repetitive action and which I represent by the phrase "a great number of." Unlike other types of offerings, where all or nearly all of the meat of the animal is reserved for Yahweh and his priests, the meat from welfare offerings was consumed by the offerer and his or her family, friends, and guests. Welfare offerings thus are associated with occasions of celebration, such as the fulfillment of a vow, or—as here—a large festival.

32,1k On the fifteenth day of the eighth month...: The final two sentences of this *parashah* read as a variant version of the previous two sentences. Possibly the editors of the sixth compositional stage had scrolls of Kings which contained these different endings to the *parashah*, and they chose to preserve both versions.

32,1l in a month that he had invented: This phrase is nonsensical. It is almost certain, in my opinion, that the text is corrupt and that it originally read בחג ("in a festival") instead of בחדש ("in a month").

32,1m apart from: In the consonantal text, the term מלבד ("apart from") is written here. The vocalization of the word and the *qere* in the margin correct this to מלבו ("from his heart"), which I understand as an idiom for "on his own initiative." See A82 r.2.2 and L194 v.2.2.

Notes to P33

33a One day out of the blue, a holy many from Yehudah showed up...: This *parashah* plays an important role in the earliest version of Kings, for it states that Yoshiyyahu has been selected by Yahweh to destroy the abhorrent Yahwistic cult in the territory of the former northern kingdom. If one accepts the proposal that the earliest versions of Samuel and Kings were written to educate the young king Yoshiyyahu and to indoctrinate him into the authors' views about the proper conduct of Yahweh's cult, then the rationale for authors' composition of this *parashah*—which I assign to Kings' first stage—is perfectly clear.

A note on the translation: I have departed further than usual from a literal rendering of the text in order to capture the force of particle והנה ("look here"), which is often used to indicate that an event is unexpected or surprising. A literal rendering of the opening sentence would be "Consider this: a holy man went from Yehudah at Yahweh's command to Beyth-el."

33b the following sign shall be given: The phrase נתן מופת can mean either "give a sign" or "perform a miracle." (For the latter sense, see Ex P10.) The former sense fits the context best here. I understand the subject of the verb to be indefinite and thus translate in the passive voice. It is possible to understand the sentence to mean that Yoshiyyahu will perform a miracle, but I do not believe that was what the authors of the *parashah* intended here.

33c he stretched out his hand from atop the altar: The Hebrew is awkwardly expressed, and I believe there is an error in the text. The construction שלח יד מעל ("to stretch out one's hand from upon") is nonsensical. The text, however, would make perfect sense if the preposition read על ("upon, against") instead of מעל ("from upon"). At some point during the book's transmission history, a scribe must have written the incorrect preposition, and the error was not caught during editing. It's worth noting that the following sentence has the construction proposed here—שלח על, which appears in the clause "the hand that he had stretched out against it shriveled up."

The account of the king's shriveled hand is somewhat reminiscent of the scene in Exodus P4,1, where Yahweh turns Mosheh's hand "leprous" before returning it to normal in order to remove Mosheh's doubts about his power. I do not believe, however that the authors of the Josianic study books knew of that scene in Exodus, as the earliest version of Exodus was composed roughly a century after they wrote their work.

33d [*That's when the altar split into pieces ... in Yahweh's oracle.*]: I understand this sentence to be a late comment inserted by an editor during the book's final compositional stage. The editor may have been bothered by the fact that the account of Yoshiyyahu's destruction of Yahweh's cult at Beyth-El makes no mention of the miraculous self-destruction of the altar. Rather, in the account in P116, Yoshiyyahu (i.e. the men carrying out work under his orders) simply tears down the altar. Thus, in order to make the oracle come true, the editor has the miraculous self-destruction of the altar take place after the holy man delivered his oracle.

33e so that I get my hand back... it was normal again: I have translated these phrases into natural English. Literally, "so that my hand returns to me" and "it was as before."

33f half of everything you owned: The noun בית ("house") is often used with the sense of "personal possessions, personal property," and that is the meaning here. On this nuance of the word, see BDB, p. 110, def. 6.

33g For that's what I was ordered... go back the way I came: This sentence is somewhat incongruous with the preceding narrative; I believe it may be an addition by the authors of P34-P35, who would have inserted this sentence to set up their story in the following two *parashot*.

Notes to P34

34a Now there was an old prophet...: I view this *parashah* and the one that follows (P35) as a late addition belonging to the prophetic expansions made by the authors of Kings' fourth stage. In my opinion, the story here in P34 - P35 was composed to serve as a commentary on the nature of prophecy. The main point that the authors wish their readers to understand is that it is not possible for one to discern a true oracle from a false oracle (even if one were a holy man); a secondary lesson of their story is perhaps that one must never disobey Yahweh's instructions, even when a prophet states that Yahweh has given new instructions superseding the previous ones.

For another story from Kings' fourth stage commenting on the nature of prophecy and involving Yahweh making prophets lie, see P59 - P59,1.

34b Once they had recounted all this: Strangely, the author of this *parashah* has shifted from a single son to multiple sons. While it is common to find inconsistencies in Hebrew narrative, the inconsistency here is very unusual, and it is surprising that the author or a later editor didn't remove the inconsistency by changing the initial mention of a son from the singular to the plural.

34c a terebinth tree: The terebinth tree has a strong association with the northern cult to Yahweh. See for example, Gen P16 and P29 and Judges P29,1. (See also Jos P55, where אלה is vocalized as "oak" but which should almost certainly be vocalized as terebinth.)

34d **: Both the Aleppo Codex and the Leningrad Codex have a *parashah petuhah* here. See A82 v.1.28 and L195 r.1.23. This is a good example of the somewhat rare use of the *parashah petuhah* to mark an ellipsis.

Notes to P35

35a An oracle from Yahweh came to the prophet who had brought him back: In Kings, the terms "holy man" and "prophet" are often used synonymously (see note 32a above). Because of this, the author here qualifies "the prophet" with the phrase "who had brought him back" so that there is no confusion about which man is meant. Note also in the next sentence the author for the same reason qualifies "the holy man" with the phrase "who had come from Yehudah."

35b your remains won't join your ancestors in their grave: Literally, "your corpse won't enter [or "won't go to"] your ancestors' grave." In ancient Yisra'el and Yehudah, and elsewhere in the ancient Near East, men aspired to die a peaceful death and to be buried with their ancestors. Such a death was viewed as a sign that the man had won his god's favor, for it meant that his descendants would regularly honor his memory when they performed rites for their dead ancestors. The old man's speech to the holy man doesn't use the strong condemnatory language that is typical of oracles, but given the social importance of being remembered by one's descendants, ancient readers likely perceived the oracle's content as something that the holy man would take as a personal affront.

35c on his journey back, a lion encountered him on the road: The authors' use of details in P35 suggest that they took a perverse delight in portraying the consequences of the prophet's disobeying Yahweh. Thus the body is "sprawled" in the road, and a vivid picture is given of the lion and the donkey remaining at the scene, standing by the body.

35d [*Just like Yahweh's oracle that he had spoken to the holy man.*]: I view this statement as an addition by the editors of the sixth stage, who remind the reader that at the beginning of this *parashah*, the old prophet pronounced an oracle telling the holy man he wouldn't be buried with his ancestors (i.e. he would die an unnatural death).

35e laid it on the donkey: That is, laid it on the donkey that the holy man had ridden from Beyth-El. Recall that this donkey belonged to the old prophet. In addition to taking the holy man's body back to Beyth-El to give it a proper burial, he is also recovering the donkey he had given the holy man.

35f what he proclaimed at Yahweh's command...against all the open-air shrines: Recall that in P33, the holy man proclaimed that Yoshiyyahu would slaughter the open-air shrines' priests on the altar in Beyth-El.

35g Shomeron: The author uses the word Shomeron here because at the time of his writing (sometime during the Persian period), that was the name of the province which encompassed the southern half of the former territory of the kingdom of Yisra'el. (Note that the town of Shomeron didn't exist in Yarov'am's day, when the story in P34 - P35 is set. It was built more than a century later by Omri.)

Notes to P36

36a so that they could serve as priests in the open-air shrines: The Hebrew is elliptical and somewhat difficult. Literally, "so that there might be priests of open-air shrines."

36b It was this action that turned into the great error of Yarov'am's royal line: To the authors of the earliest version of Kings, Yarov'am commits two great errors: the installation of the cult statues of Yahweh in the form of bull calves in the shrines in Beyth-El and Dan, and the consecration of anyone, regardless of qualification, to serve as priests in the open-air shrines in the northern kingdom. The latter error leads to the destruction of Yarov'am's royal line. But for the authors of the earliest version of Kings, it is Yarov'am's causing the people to follow his own errors (i.e., to venerate the gold bull calves) that results in the downfall of the northern kingdom. See the end of P104, where these authors give their opinion on the fall of the kingdom of Yisra'el: "For Yisra'el broke away from Dawid's family and made Yarov'am Nevatsson king, and Yarov'am drave Yisra'el away from Yahweh and caused them to commit a very great wrong. The Yisra'elites followed all the errors which Yarov'am committed, not abandoning them until Yahweh removed Yisra'el from his presence."

Notes to P37

37a Now around that time Yarov'am's son Aviyyah fell ill...: This *parashah* and the following one (P38) recount the story of the visit of Yarov'am's wife to the prophet Ahiyyah, who pronounces doom on Yarov'am and his family. While it is possible to view the story as belonging to the prophetic expansions of the fourth compositional stage, there are no themes and no language that clearly support a late date. Consequently, I assign this story to the earliest edition of Kings, where it plays an important role: it establishes Yahweh's rejection of Yarov'am and explicitly attributes the fall of the northern kingdom to Yarov'am's wrongdoing.

37b No one must know thine identity: This is a functionally equivalent translation of the Hebrew, which literally reads, "They mustn't know that thou art Yarov'amswife." In this statement, the term "Yarov'amswife" functions as a surname. Yarov'am is not saying "no one must know you're my wife." Rather, he is saying "no one must know who you are."

The author writes the archaic form of the second person feminine singular pronoun אתי ("thou"). Aharon ben Asher added a *qere* in the margin of the Aleppo Codex correcting the archaic form of the pronoun with the regular form את ("you"), which I show in the margin of my translation. Likewise, Shmu'el ben Ya'aqov wrote the same *qere* in the margin of the Leningrad Codex. See A83 r.1.10 and L195 v.1.3.

37c Ahiyyahu was unable to see, for his eyes had frozen due to his old age: Ahiyyahu has cataracts in his eyes. Note that nearly identical language is used by the author of Sam P8 to describe Eliy, who was the head priest in Shiloh: ועלי בן־תשעים ושמנה שנה ועיניו קמה ולא יכול לראות. The author of this passage in Kings would have known of the passage in Samuel, and he would have expected the reader to pick up on the subtle allusion to Eliy, who, like Ahiyyahu, lived in Shiloh.

37d **: The Leningrad Codex has a *parashah setumah* here. See L195 v.1.13.

38a she was making like she was a foreigner: The account of Yarov'am's wife coming to see Ahiyyahu has a humorous element that is perfectly understandable if this was a story written for a young boy. If we assume the story was written for the young king, it is interesting to observe how the authors of the *parashah* mix humor with more serious instruction regarding the importance of following Yahweh's commandments and doing the "correct things" like Yoshiyyahu's great ancestor, Dawid.

Notes to P38

38b I've been given a difficult message for you: Literally, "I've been sent to you with a difficult message." The author employs a construction common to prophetic literature—שלח אל ("to send [a person] to [another person or a group]"). The construction is typically used in situations where Yahweh "sends" a prophet to deliver an oracle of doom or warning. The language is thus appropriate here even though Ahiyyah wasn't physically "sent" anywhere and delivers Yahweh's oracle from his own home. Because the verb "send" is jarring in English in this instance, a functionally equivalent translation requires a different verb—hence my translation "given."

38c you didn't behave like my servant Dawid...doing only what was pleasing to me: For the authors of the Josianic study books, Dawid was the perfect king, the one most pleasing to Yahweh, and the standard against which all other kings are judged. This is a key theme of the earliest edition of Kings, which promotes the Dawidic ideal in support of Yoshiyyahu's kingship.

The language in this sentence is highly formulaic. The phrase "doing what was pleasing to Yahweh"—like the related phrase "doing what was displeasing to Yahweh"—should be understood to refer specifically to cult matters. For the authors of the Josianic study books, Dawid's actions with respect to the cult were wholly pleasing to Yahweh and without fault. (As discussed in note 1a, I view the succession narrative, which is found in Sam P82,2 - P101 and Kgs P1 - P7,2, to be a Persian period composition. In the earliest versions of Samuel and Kings, Dawid as king is without fault.)

38d worse than anyone who preceded you: The language here is highly formulaic, and the author doesn't have in mind the specific kings who preceded Yarov'am—that is, Sha'ul, Iysh Bosheth Sha'ulsson, Dawid, and Shelomo.

38e making for yourself different gods and statues of gods: The language here is entirely formulaic. There is no indication that Yarov'am performed service to any god but Yahweh.

38f throwing me behind your back—: The Lenigrad Codex has a *parashah setumah* after this clause. See L195 v.2.8-9.

38g therefore I'm going to bring misfortune to Yarov'am's line: Note the shift in address: Yahweh's oracle begins by addressing Yarov'am in the second person and now shifts to the third person. Ancient Hebrew was not always consistent in its use of pronouns. Here, however, I believe the shift in address reflects the fact that the oracle is a wholly literary composition. The authors were more concerned to express a key theme of their work—Yahweh's rejection of Yarov'am and his destruction of Yarov'am's family and of the kingdom of Yisra'el—and less concerned to represent "real life" speech.

38h pissing himself against a wall: For this phrase, see note 53h in my translation of Samuel.

38i every last one: The author uses the idiomatic phrase עצור ועזוב (literally, "one locked up and one set free"). The idiom is an expression of totality. Ancient Hebrew (like modern English) often juxtaposed opposites—young and old, rich and poor—as a way to express comprehensiveness or entirety. In the context here, the phrase is used in reference to "every last one" of Yarov'am's descendants.

The idiom עצור ועזוב occurs only five times in the Tanakh—once in Deuteronomy (the Song of Mosheh in Deut P31), and four times in Kings (here, P56, P77, and P94). The uses in Deut P31 and Kgs P94 are nearly identical, and I translate both as "free and unfree." The context of the idiom here and in Kgs P56 and Kgs P77 is a little different, and in all three of these places, the most appropriate translation is "every last one." I provide additional comments on this idiom in note 31v of my translation of Deuteronomy.

38j I shall incinerate the remains of: Translation of ובערתי אחרי. The parallelism with the following clause ("someone burning manure until it's completely gone") indicates that אחרי here must function as a substantive and not a preposition. On the plural construct form אחרי as a substantive, see BDB, top of p. 30, def. 1.

38k he alone of Yarov'am's family will go to the grave: A sign that one has been favored by one's god. See note 35b above.

38l Yahweh will raise up for himself a king over Yisra'el who will cut down Yarov'am's family: This king is Ba'sha. See P43, which is the account of Ba'sha's reign and the fulfillment of the oracle that Ahiyyah relates to Yarov'am's wife.

The account of Ba'sha's reign in P43 specifically alludes to Ahiyyah's oracle here in P38. It is possible to view the story of the visit of Yarov'am's wife to Ahiyyah in P37 - P38 as a Persian period addition to the text belonging to the prophetic expansions of the fourth stage and composed specifically to provide context and color for that oracle. (In fact, the story of Navoth's vineyard provides a close parallel to this: there is a reference to an old oracle about Navoth in the earliest edition of Kings, and a lengthy story about Navoth was later added as part of the prophetic expansions of Kings.) That said, I view the story in P37 - P38 as part of the earliest edition of Kings, as the themes in this story are consistent with the themes of the Josianic study books, and there are no themes that obviously belong to the Persian period.

38m all at once: The Hebrew is זה היום ("that's the day"). When the particle זה ("this, here") is prefixed to expressions of time, it adds a sense of immediacy or emphasis. See BDB, p. 261, def. 4i. In the usage here, the phrasing implies that the action will happen "all at once" or "right away."

38n What more is there to say?: The Hebrew is difficult, and the exact meaning of the author's phrasing is not clear. Literally, "What also now?" I have used context to inform my translation.

38o Yahweh will strike down Yisra'el...: The statement that Yahweh will strike down Yisra'el sits oddly with the remainder of Ahiyyah's speech, which is otherwise solely concerned with pronouncing doom on Yarov'am's family. Although it is tempting to read this statement as a later addition, I have chosen to treat it as belonging to

Kings' first stage for two reasons. First, if it was an addition from Kings' third stage or later, the authors would have placed the blame for Yisra'el's exile on the Yisra'elites' violation of their treaty with Yahweh (in fact, in the lengthy addition in the first three-fourths of P104, the authors of the third stage do exactly that). Instead, the authors here place the blame entirely on Yarov'am, which fits best with the concerns of the authors of Kings' first stage. (Note that the authors of the second stage show no interest in the reason for the fall of the northern kingdom.) Second, there is no other place in Kings prior to the material in the last one-fourth of P104 where the authors of the first stage state their view that the fall of the northern kingdom was due to the errors of Yarov'am. One can easily see how the authors of the first stage might have wanted to introduce this theme into their account of Yarov'am's reign, especially as it provides context for the actions of the kings who succeeded him and who "perpetuated" his errors. It is unfortunate, however, that the authors have introduced the theme here in a very clumsy way, as if they realized only after they had composed the *parashah* that it would be a good idea to make this theme part of their account of Yarov'am's reign.

Note that for the authors of the Josianic study books, the destruction of the northern kingdom is attributed to two things: Yarov'am's wrongful acts and the wrongful acts that he caused the people of Yisra'el to commit. That said, the language used at the end of the oracle indicates that the authors of the Josianic study books viewed Yaro'am as bearing more of the blame: בגלל חטאת ירבעם אשר חטא ואשר החטיא את ישראל—"on account of Yarov'am's wrongs—those which he committed and those which he caused Yisra'el to commit."

38p to the east of the Perath River: The Hebrew reads מעבר לנהר, a literal translation of which is "beyond the River." In ancient Hebrew, the name for the Euphrates River was "the Perath;" however, it was often referred to as "the Great River" or simply "the River." There is some potential for confusion here because the term עבר הנהר ("Beyond-the-River") was the name for the region southwest of the Euphrates River. But this was not what the author intended the reader to understand—he wrote מעבר לנהר, which cannot be understood as a proper name. Note there is an identical construction in Isa 18.1: מעבר לנהרי־כוש ("beyond the rivers of Kush").

38q [*because they made Asherahs for themselves, thus enraging Yahweh*]: This sentence reads as a comment added by the editors of Kings' final compositional stage.

38r Yarov'am's wife left immediately and went to Thirtzah: The text implies that Yarov'am's home is in Thirtzah. There is some tension here with P32,1, where we are told that Yarov'am lived in Shekem. One way to resolve the tension is to assume that Shekem was the royal seat and Thirtzah was Yarov'am's ancestral town. However, it is also possible that the authors had conflicting sources, in which case the tension can't be resolved. Complicating matters, Thirtzah does serve as the royal seat for the kings of Yisra'el following Yarov'am (see P44,1, for example); this perhaps offers support for the view that the authors of the account of Yarov'am's reign had conflicting sources.

It should be noted that the site of Thirtzah is unknown; on the basis of the town's mention in P46, it seems most likely that it was located in the tribal territory of Ephrayim (see note 46b below). Some scholars have speculated that the town must have been somewhere close to Shekem, but this speculation is solely motivated by the desire to resolve the tension in the text here in P38. There is a Thirtzah mentioned in Jos P24,30; however, that Thirtzah may have been a different town than the Thirtzah mentioned here in P38 and that served as the royal seat for later kings.

38s The rest of Yarov'am's acts...are recorded in the book *The Chronicles of the Kings of Yisra'el*: This is the first mention of the major source document for the kings of Yisra'el that was consulted by the authors of the earliest edition of Kings. The book is cited as a source for all the kings of Yisra'el from Yarov'am down to Peqah Remalyahusson, the second to last king of Yisra'el, in P100. The accounts of all the kings of Yisra'el for which this source is cited contain formulaic material that was likely lifted verbatim from the source document; this material typically appears at the beginning and at the end of the account of each king's reign. The first example of this formulaic language for the kings of Yisra'el appears here in P38: the authors tell us how long Yarov'am reigned (twenty-two years), whether or not he died a peaceful death (see note 38u below), and who succeeded him on the throne (his son Nadav).

38t the wars he fought: The authors tell us that the account of Yarov'am's reign in the source document *The Chronicles of the Kings of Yisra'el* included information about the wars he fought. These must have been his wars with Rehav'am and Yehudah, as P40 states that "there was perpetual war" between Rehav'am and Yarov'am. Note the inconsistency with P32: information in P38 and P40, which are based on the ancient source documents, indicates there was war between Rehav'am and Yarov'am, whereas P32, which is part of an addition from Kings' fourth stage, suggests that Rehav'am did not attack Yisra'el after the break-up of Shelomo's kingdom.

38u he lay down in death with his ancestors: This clause is from the source document, *The Chronicles of the Kings of Yisra'el*, and implies that Yarov'am died a peaceful death. Note the inconsistency with Ahiyyah's oracle, which is a literary creation of the authors of the Josianic study books, and which states that Yarov'am's son is the only one in his family who will be buried in a grave.

Notes to P39

39a Rehav'am Shelomosson ruled as king in Yehudah...: The account of Rehav'am's reign is given in P39 - P40. At the end of P40, the authors of the Josianic study books imply that they consulted the book *The Chronicles of the Kings of Yehudah* as a source for Rehav'am's reign. This book is cited for all the kings of Yehudah from Rehav'am down to Yehoyaqiym (Yoshiyyahu's son) in P117,1. The accounts of all the kings of Yehudah for which this source is cited contain formulaic material at the beginning and the end of the account which was likely lifted verbatim from the source document. The first example of this formulaic language appears here in P39: the authors tell us Rehav'am's age when he became king (forty-one years), the town he ruled from (Yerushalem), and the name of his mother (Na'amah the Ammonite). This information for all the kings of Yehudah appears at the beginning of the accounts of their reigns.

39b the town that Yahweh chose out of all Yisra'el's tribes to claim as his own: This clause reads as a comment by the editors of the sixth compositional stage. The authors of the Josianic study books never make such edits to the material about the beginning and end of each king's reign that they reproduce from their source documents. It is unclear to me what prompted the addition of this comment in this particular place. It is interesting to note that a reference to the theme of "the town that Yahweh chose" does not appear again in Kings until the account of the reign of Yoshiyyahu in P116, in material that was composed by the authors of the second stage.

The phrase that I translate "to claim as his own" is לשום את־שמו שם ("to place his name there"). On this phrase and its translation, see note 20c above.

39c Yehudah did what was displeasing to Yahweh...: It is important to note that the Septuagint here reads "Rehav'am" instead of Yehudah. I believe the Septuagint reading must reflect the original text. There are two reasons to believe this. First, the authors of Kings' first stage never use the phrase "did what was displeasing to

Yahweh" in reference to the people—they only use it in reference to the king. Second, in the current text of the Hebrew, Rehav'am is the only king who does not receive a summary judgement. (The summary judgements always state that the king "pleased" or "displeased" Yahweh; there are only one or two exceptions to this, such as P41, where the authors judge Aviyyam by stating "his heart was not wholly with his god Yahweh.") It is inconceivable that the original authors of Kings would have omitted a judgement for Rehav'am. For these reasons, it is preferable to view the Septuagint reading here as original.

Complicating matters, the material that follows this clause shows many signs of lateness. I suspect that the sentence originally read "Rehav'am did what was displeasing to Yahweh, provoking him more than anything that his ancestors did through the wrongs that they committed." After Rehav'am was corrupted to Yehudah, the wording of the sentence was "corrected" to read "Yehudah did what was displeasing to Yahweh, provoking him more than anything their ancestors did in the wrongs that they committed." Once the sentence had that form, later editors expanded the comment about Yehudah's wrong by adding the final two sentences of the *parashah*, which draw on a mishmash of language and themes known from Deuteronomy and Joshua.

In Kings, the phrase "did what was displeasing to Yahweh" is almost always used in reference to the king. The phrase is characteristic of the versions of Judges and Kings that were part of the Josianic study books. In Judges, this phrase is always applied to the people as a whole (the Yisra'elites). In Kings, the phrase appears thirty-one times—27 times in reference to individual kings, once in reference to Yisra'el (P104) and three times in reference to Yehudah (once here and twice in P113,1). The instance of the phrase in P104 and one instance in P113,1 are clearly from the hand of the authors of the third stage. The other instance in P113,1 is from the authors of the second stage, and the reference here is due to a scribal error. All of the 27 other instances of this phrase in Kings apply to individual kings and are from the authors of the Josianic study books.

39d Moreover... they built for themselves open-air shrines with sacred pillars and Asherah poles: With the use of the particle גם ("also, too, moreover"), the authors point out that the Yehudah is doing the same thing that Yisra'el did under Yarov'am—both built open-air shrines where they made offerings to Yahweh and to his consort Asherah. Yahweh's cult in the north was dominated by the open-air shrines—these were the primary sites of veneration for the people. The evidence of Kings suggests that the situation in the south may not have been very different. The people likely venerated Yahweh mainly in the open-air shrines. The cult on Mount Tziyyon was primarily a cult for the king and his family and government officials. The Israeli scholar Avraham Faust has written extensively on the paucity of archaeological evidence of temples in the territories of Yisra'el and Yehudah during the monarchic period. See for example, "Israelite Temples," *op. cit*, and "The Archaeology of the Israelite Cult: Questioning the Consensus," *Bulletin of the American Schools of Oriental Research* 360 (2010), pp. 23-35.

39e There was also *qedesh*-prostitution practiced in the land: This sentence reads as original to Kings' first stage; the surrounding material was added by the editors of the sixth stage when they made the "correction" discussed above in note 39c. On *qedesh*-prostitution, see note 42c below.

39f the things the people did... that Yahweh cleared away from the Yisra'elites: This clause reads as a comment added by the editors of Kings' sixth stage, who use formulaic langauge found in Numbers, Deuteronomy, Joshua, and Persian-period additions to Judges.

Notes to P40

40a In the fifth year of Rehav'am's reign...: The information in this *parashah* about Shiyshaq's invasion and plundering of Yahweh's house and the palace is almost certainly from the main source document that the authors of the Josianic study books used in their account of the reigns of the kings of Yehudah—*The Chronicles of the Kings of Yehudah*. Note the chronological information here, which must have been a feature of the source document.

40b In fact, he carried off everything in them...: The repetition of the verb "carried off" is unusual, and in my opinion represents a seam in the text. I understand this sentence about the gold shields made by Shelomo and the following two sentences about their replacement with bronze shields to be literary creations of the authors of the Josianic study books. There is no reason to think these three sentences were based on a source document. (For the account of the gold shields made by Shelomo composed by the authors of the Josianic study books, see P26.)

40c the royal guard who protected the entry to the royal palace: The name for the royal guard was "the Runners" (הרצים). See note 1i above for a discussion of this group and their specific role.

40d Fort Dawid: Fort Dawid (עיר דוד) served as the royal cemetery for the kings of Yehudah. On this fort, see note 30,3d above.

40e [*His mother's name was Na'amah the Ammonite.*]: This sentence is clearly an addition, which repeats the sentence given at the beginning of the P39. It is unclear to me what prompted the addition of this sentence to P40.

Notes to P41

41a In the eighteenth year of King Yarov'am Nevatsson's reign: This clause is the first appearance of the chronological "synchronisms" that the authors of Kings' first stage use to date the reigns of the individual kings of Yisra'el and Yehudah. There is some scholarly debate as to whether these synchronisms appeared in the royal chronicles used as source documents by the authors of Kings or whether the authors of Kings devised the synchronisms on their own. The presence of synchronisms in some Assyrian and Babylonian Chronicles is often cited in support of the idea that the synchronisms in Kings might be original to the royal chronicles of Yisra'el and Yehudah. The mere existence of such parallels, however, does not prove that the synchronisms were necessarily in the royal chronicles used by the authors of Kings. Over the course of my work on this book, I have gone back and forth on this issue, but I am now of the opinion that the synchronisms likely were in the source documents. My primary reason for believing this is that some of the synchronisms are easier to explain if they were part of the source documents than if they were created by the authors of Kings' first stage (see my comments in note 107a below).

41b his mother's name was Ma'akah Aviyshalomsdaughter: The name Aviyshalom is a variant of Avshalom, and one wonders if Ma'akah might actually have been the daughter of Dawid's son Avshalom. If this were the case (and this is mere speculation), it would mean that she was married to her half-cousin Rehav'am, who was the son of Shelomo. Marriage between cousins (or half-cousins) was relatively common in the ancient Near East, including among royal families. It's worth recalling here that in the book of Genesis, Avraham, Ya'aqov, and Yitzhaq each married their first cousins.

It is also worth noting here that Samuel and Kings preserve conflicting traditions about Avshalom's children. Sam P92,3 states that Avshalom had four children—three sons and a daughter named Tamar. This is at odds with Sam P99,8, which states that Avshalom had no sons. We can only speculate as to why the traditions conflict. It is conceivable that there might have been a daughter named Ma'akah, and that in the oral traditions behind the stories in Samuel, the prominence of Tamar and her connection to Avshalom led to the displacement of the name Ma'akah in favor of Tamar. But this is simply speculation, and the truth about these people and their family relationships is lost to us.

41c he continued all the erroneous practices... his heart was not wholly with his god Yahweh: The language is vague and it is unclear what Aviyyam's "erroneous practices" were. The authors state that he continued the practices of his father Rehav'am, but that doesn't clarify matters, as the account of Rehav'am's reign has suffered in transmission (see note 39c above). I believe it most likely that the authors intended the reader to understand that Aviyyam gave service to Yahweh but did not faithfully carry out the rules of the cult as required of the king. The authors of Kings' first stage applied the phrase "to do what was displeasing to Yahweh" to two types of actions: extreme violations of cult rules (such as Yarov'am fashioning images of Yahweh) and giving service to other gods (such as Shelomo's support for the cults of his wives' gods). Neither of these actions apply to Aviyyam; he was thus neither "pleasing" nor wholly "displeasing" to Yahweh.

41d (For it was on acount of Dawid... the affair regarding Uriyyah the Hethite.): The passage in parentheses reads as an addition to the text. Because it alludes to the events of the succession narrative, which I view as a composition of Kings' fifth stage, I have assigned the addition here to the fifth stage. The addition was clearly prompted by the statement in the preceding sentence that Dawid's heart was "wholly with" Yahweh, which the authors of the fifth stage felt necessary to qualify by reminding the reader of Dawid's moral failing in ordering Uriyyah's death.

41e Yahweh placed a lamp for him in Yerushalem: The lamp (or beacon) imagery in Kings appears three times: here, P30,1, and P75. In P30,1 (from Kings' first stage), the lamp represents Dawid's descendants—that is, the Dawidic line. This too seems to be the meaning of the lamp here in the addition to P41. The lamp imagery in P75 (also from Kings' first stage) also signifies Dawid's descendants. (It is interesting to note that P75 specifically mentions the "promise" of a lamp; the "promise" language is an allusion to Psalm 132, where the lamp refers not to Dawid's descendants but rather to a physical object inside Yahweh's house.) Finally, it's worth noting that in Sam P102, which is a Persian period addition to Samuel, Dawid himself is the "lamp of Yisra'el." The term in the late passage in Samuel has a quite different meaning than its meaning in Kings—in Sam P102, it refers to Dawid's eminence and authority over his people.

41f except in the affair regarding Uriyyah the Hethite: This comment is an allusion to the story of Dawid and Bath-Sheva in Sam P84,1 - P84,3 (Uriyyah was Bath-Sheva's husband, who was killed on orders from Dawid). The story of Dawid and Bath-Sheva is part of the succession narrative, which I view as a Persian period composition.

41g During Rehav'am's reign, there was perpetual war between him and Yarov'am: The mention of Rehav'am is nonsensical, and the entire sentence is a repeat of a sentence in P38. It is possible that the entire sentence was accidentally transcribed here, or—what I think more likely—that at some point in Kings' transmission history, a scribe inadvertently copied Rehav'am instead of Aviyyam.

41h There was war between Aviyyam and Yarov'am: There are two ways to understand the text here: Either (1) this sentence is original to the *parashah* and the preceding sentence about war between Rehav'am and Yarov'am was introduced through a copyist's error, or (2) the preceding sentence about Rehav'am and Yarov'am originally mentioned Aviyyam instead of Rehav'am, and this sentence was added in a later compositional stage to correct the text after Rehav'am erroneously replaced Aviyyam in the preceding sentence. I have a slight preference for the second option.

Notes to P42

42a his mother's name was Ma'akah Aviyshalomsdaughter: Asa was the son of Aviyyam and Ma'akah. In the account of Aviyyam's reign in P41, the authors state that Ma'akah was Aviyyam's mother—thus, as Asa was the son of Aviyyam and Ma'akah, Aviyyam must have married his mother. Later in the *parashah*, the authors again state explicitly that Ma'akah was Asa's mother, so there can be no question about the fact that Aviyyam married his mother. It is very strange that later authors of Kings didn't add a comment condemning the abhorrent incestuous relationship between Aviyyam and Ma'akah. While incestuous marriages among royal families are known from ancient Egypt, there is no indication of this practice in ancient Yisra'el and Yehudah, apart from the marriage of Aviyyam and Ma'akah. It goes without saying that incestuous relations were strongly condemned in the laws of the Torah—see Lev P36,1 - P36,11 for laws prohibiting sexual relations with family members and Lev P36,2 for the law prohibiting sexual relations with one's father and mother.

42b like his ancestor Dawid: Only three kings are likened to Dawid in the book of Kings: Asa in this *parashah*, Hizqiyyahu in P106, and Yoshiyyahu in P115. The passages likening Asa and Hizqiyyahu to Dawid belong to the earliest version of Kings, or what I call the Josianic study books; the passage likening Yoshiyyahu to Dawid belongs to Kings' second stage. I believe the authors of the Josianic study books held up Asa and Hizqiyyahu as examples of ideal Dawidic kings for their student Yoshiyyahu to imitate. In particular, both Asa and Hizqiyyahu instituted significant reforms to Yahweh's cult that were exemplars for the reforms that Yoshiyyahu's teachers hoped he would carry out. Asa eradicated *qedesh*-prostitution from Yehudah, removed all the statues of the "worthless gods" that previous kings had made, and destroyed the "horrid thing" dedicated to the Asherah (likely a wooden post representing the goddess). Hizqiyyahu abolished the open-air shrines in Yehudah where the people made offerings to Yahweh, destroyed the sacred pillars and the Asherah post used in Yahweh's cult, and chopped up the bronze image of the snake-god that Mosheh had made. For additional thoughts on how I believe the earliest version of Kings was used in Yoshiyyahu's education, see note 106a below.

42c *qedesh*-prostitution: It is interesting to note that the mention of *qedesh*-prostitution occurs in association with abhorrent cult practices (statues of worthless gods, and the horrid thing for Asherah). The consensus among scholars today is that *qedesh*-prostitution has nothing to do with the cult, but the appearance of the term here in P42 in a clear cultic context does make one wonder if maybe the scholarly consensus in this instance is incorrect. Elsewhere in Kings, *qedesh*-prostitution is mentioned in P39 and P60. There is a good short discussion of the occurrences of the terms *qadesh* and *qedesha* and their ambiguity in "קדשׁ *qdš*" in G. Botterweck, H. Ringgren and H.-J. Fabry (eds.), *Theological Dictionary of the Old Testament* Vol. XII (Grand Rapids: Eerdmans, 2003), pp. 542f. For a recent article arguing against cult prostitution in Yisra'el and Yehudah, see J. DeGrado, "The *qdesha* in Hosea 4:14: Putting the (Myth of the) Sacred Prostitute to Bed," *Vetus Testamentum* 68 (2018), pp. 1-33.

42d the statues of the worthless gods that his ancestors had made: His ancestors were Aviyyam, Rehav'am, Shelomo, and Dawid. With respect to statues made by the ancestors, P39 mentions the establishment of open-air shrines with Asherah poles during the reign of Rehav'am and P41 states that Aviyyam "continued all the erroneous practices" of his ancestors. For Shelomo's support of the cults of other gods, see P28 and P28,1 (although neither *parashah* mentions statues of gods). The authors of P42, which is part of Kings' first stage, must have had P28, P28,1 and P41 in mind in the allusion here. However, they would not have known of the passage in P39, which is part of an addition from Kings' fifth stage (see note 39c above).

42e she made a horrid thing for the Asherah: This is almost certainly a wooden post representing the goddess. It likely was placed somewhere on the grounds of Yahweh's house, as Yahweh and Asherah were often associated in Yahweh's cult in Yerushalem during the era of the monarchy.

42f the open-air shrines weren't removed: The open-air shrines were cult sites devoted to Yahweh (which he sometimes shared with other gods). Thus, in the authors' view, it is possible for Asa's heart "to be wholly with Yahweh" even though he didn't remove the shrines and centralize the cult. The authors of the earliest edition of Kings repeatedly state their disapproval of the open-air shrines. The centralization of the cult at Yahweh's house on Mount Tziyyon was a key pillar of the reform program they promoted with their pupil King Yoshiyyahu.

42g —: The Leningrad Codex does not have a *parashah* break here. See L196 r.3.21.

42,1a He restored the cult equipment that had belonged to his grandfather and the cult equipment used in Yahweh's house: The author here uses the term אב ("father") to refer specifically to the king's grandfather, Rehav'am; on this rare use of אב, see BDB, p. 3, def. 4(a). Recall that in P40 (the account of Rehav'am's reign) everything in the storerooms of Yahweh's house and in the palace storerooms was plundered by Shiyshak King of Egypt. Asa thus rebuilds the stocks of wealth stored in the palace and on the grounds of Yahweh's house, including the equipment used in the cult, which was fashioned of gold and silver.

Notes to P42,1

It should be noted here that in the accounts in Kings, one important function of Yahweh's house is as the king's treasury. In the daily operations of Yahweh's house, individuals make offerings and pay poll taxes. Gold and silver accumulate from the poll taxes, and to a lesser extent, from the sale of animals to be used as offerings; the funds collected from these activities are then kept in the storerooms of Yahweh's house. The storerooms of Yahweh's house are one of the primary sources of funds available to the king in managing the affairs of the kingdom, and they are a primary source of funds for the tribute owed to the suzerain. See, for example, Ahaz's payment of tribute in P102 and Hezekiah's payment of tribute in P108.

42,1b There was perpetual war between Asa and Ba'sha King of Yisra'el during the time that both reigned: In P44, the authors state that Ba'sha became king in the third year of Asa's reign and that he ruled for twenty-four years. As Asa ruled for forty-one years, the statement here implies there was war between Yisra'el and Yehudah for all twenty-four years of Ba'sha's reign. Note that the sentence here is repeated below in P43, which is the account of Nadav Yarov'amsson's reign and of his assassination by Ba'sha. I view the repetition of the sentence in P43 as an addition from Kings' sixth stage. See note 43g below.

42,1c HaRamah: I understand HaRamah to be the name of a strategically located fort or citadel. The name means "the Height." Ba'sha likely located the fort on Yehudah's territory, but in a place easily accessible from Yisra'el.

42,1d making any military maneuvers: The author uses an idiomatic construction, יצא ובא ("one going out and one coming in"). In a military context, the idiom is used in reference to carrying out military missions or campaigns. The idiom, for example, is used in Sam P41,2 to describe Dawid's military missions that he performed as a young man when still in Sha'ul's service.

42,1e all the silver and gold that remained in the storehouses...: This must be the gold and silver with which Asa had restocked the storerooms in the palace and on the grounds of Yahweh's house.

42,1f Iyyon, Dan, and Avel Beyth-Ma'akah…everything in the territory of Naphtaliy: These sites are all in the far northern parts of the kingdom of Yisra'el. The Kinroth district is the area called Galilee by English speakers. It is interesting to note that the town of Dan is said to be part of Naphtaliy. In later tradition, the area around the town of Dan was considered to be its own tribal territory, independent of Naphtaliy. (In earlier tradition, the tribal territory of Dan was just to the west of Ephrayim and south of Menashsheh.)

42,1g King Asa built Geva in Binyamin: It's worth noting that the king of Yehudah here takes control of part of Binyamin—territory that properly belonged to the northern kingdom. The tribal territory of Binyamin belonged to Yisra'el but bordered Yehudah and was just a short distance from Yerushalem, the power center of Yehudah. Thus, it is not surprising that the territory was fiercely contested, with control of parts of it shifting back and forth between the two kingdoms over the centuries.

42,1h (except it doesn't mention that he suffered from a foot disease when he was old): This appears to be a comment from the authors of the Josianic study books, who knew of a tradition about Asa's foot disease that had been omitted from their primary source about the kings of Yehudah, *The Chronicles of the Kings of Yehudah*. The fact that they mentioned this detail gives us some insight into how they viewed their work. They viewed their work as one that would be read alongside their two main source documents, the chronicles of the kings of Yisra'el and Yehudah, and in addition to "reinterpreting" those two documents in light of the fall of the northern kingdom, they occasionally also included information they knew from oral tradition or other written sources. It is unclear why they added the mention of Asa's foot disease here—possibly this was such a well-known fact about him that they thought it should be included it even though it did not appear in their source document.

It is important to note that the authors of the Josianic study books assume that their student has access to both chronicles, copies of which would have been kept in the royal palace. This indicates, in my opinion, that their work was intended for an individual or individuals living and/or working in the palace. As I argued in my translation of Judges, the composition of their work makes the most sense if it was intended to serve in the education of the young king, Yoshiyyahu, who would have been a teenager in the 630s BCE. (See footnote 23 of the introduction to my translation of Judges.) With regard to the copy of *The Chronicles of the Kings of Yisra'el*, presumably refugees from the northern kingdom brought that document with them to Yehudah after the Assyrian conquest of Shomeron.

Notes to P43

43a perpetuating the error which his father caused Yisra'el to commit: The "error" of Yarov'am that he caused Yisra'el to commit and that Nadav perpetuated was to support the cults of Yahweh in Dan and Bethel, which venerated gold statues of Yahweh in the form of a bull calf.

43b Gibbethon of the Philishtines: Gibbethon ("Mound" or "Ridge") must have been a relatively common place name. Thus the author specifies that this Gibbethon is the one that was controlled by the Philishtines. In the allotment of territory to the Danites in Jos P43, the town of Gibbethon is listed. The Danites' territory bordered the Philishtines, and the Gibbethon mentioned here in Kings P43 is almost certainly the Gibbethon mentioned in Jos P43.

43c any living soul: For the translation of כל־נשמה as "any living soul," see notes 4h, 21,1c, and 23,1b in my translation of Joshua.

43d as foretold by the oracle that Yahweh delivered through his servant Ahiyyah the Shiylonite: For this oracle, see P38. The allusion to the oracle here in P43, which definitely belongs to the earliest version of Kings, provides some support for treating the story in P37-P38 as original to Kings and not as part of the prophetic expansions of the fourth stage.

43e the errors that Yarov'am committed...: There are two sets of errors that Yarov'am commits—fashioning two cult statues of Yahweh in the form of gold bull calves (P34) and designating people "from all over" as priests (P36). See note 36b above. In addition, Yarov'am "caused" Yisra'el to commit errors—specifically, by installing statues of bull calves in Dan and Beyth-El, he caused the people of Yisra'el to venerate images of Yahweh.

43f his outrageous actions: His outrageous actions are identical to "the errors" he committed: fashioning statues of the bull calves and installing them in Yahweh's cults in Dan and Beyth-El, and appointing people "from all over" as priests to Yahweh.

43g There was perpetual war between Asa and Ba'sha King of Yisra'el during the time that both reigned: This sentence is a repetition of a sentence in P42,1. I view the sentence here in P43 as an addition made by the editors of Kings' sixth stage, who must have meant it to apply to the account of Ba'sha's reign. However, the addition was clumsy: the sentence appears in a summary of Nadav's reign, when it properly belongs in the account of the reign of Ba'sha, who succeeded Nadav. See also note 42,1b above.

44a Ba'sha Ahiyyahsson ruled as king over Yisra'el in Thirtzah for twenty-four years: The Hebrew likely reflects the formulaic language of the source document, *The Chronicles of the Kings of Yisra'el*. Both royal chronicles were living documents composed over very long periods—some two centuries in the case of *The Chronicles of the Kings of Yisra'el* and a little over three centuries in the case of *The Chronicles of the Kings of Yehudah*. Given that, it is not surprising that the formulaic language in each document is not always consistent. With respect to *The Chronicles of the Kings of Yisra'el*, the standard formula introducing a king was "PERSONAL NAME ruled as king over Yisra'el in TOWN NAME for NUMBER years." This formula appears in P44, P45, P46 (in abbreviated form), P86, P87, P94, P96, P98, P99, P100, and P103. There are two variants to this. In P43, the introductory formula is "PERSONAL NAME became king of Yisra'el...and he ruled Yisra'el for NUMBER years." The other variant appears in P49 and P60,1: "PERSONAL NAME became king of Yisra'el. PERSONAL NAME ruled over Yisra'el in TOWN NAME for NUMBER years."

Note to P44

On the town of Thirtzah, see note 38r above.

44,1a On account of the fact that even though: Yehu's oracle has a number of parallels with the oracle about Yarov'am delivered by Ahiyyah the Shiylonite to Yarov'am's wife in P38. Note the identical phrasing, "On account of the fact that even though" and "made you supreme leader over my people Yisra'el," and note the identical punishments in death. I understand the oracle here at the beginning of P44,1 to be a later addition to the text. The conclusion to this *parashah* only makes sense if the version of Kings belonging to the Josianic study books lacked the oracle here at the beginning of this *parashah*. See note 44,1e below.

Notes to P44,1

44,1b I'm going to send a conflagration to chase after: Translation of הנני מבעיר אחרי. The author bases his phrasing on language from P38, but he did not recognize the use of אחרי there as a substantive; instead, he uses a formulation in which אחרי functions as a preposition, which is its typical use. See note 38j above.

44,1c I'll make your family just like Yarov'am Nevatsson's family...: See the doom pronounced on Yarov'am's family in P38.

NOTES AND COMMENTS

44,1d Ba'sha lay down in death with his ancestors and was buried in Thirtzah: That is, Ba'sha died a peaceful death. The peaceful death and burial is completely at odds with the preceding oracle, and offers additional support for the proposal that the preceding oracle is a later addition to the text.

44,1e In addition, Yahweh delivered an oracle through Yehu Haniniysson the Prophet about Ba'sha and his family...: The conclusion of this *parashah* is original to the Josianic study books' version of Kings. I believe that version of Kings did not have a record of Yehu's actual oracle. The oracle that we have at the beginning of the *parashah* I believe is a later addition to the text, likely from the authors of the fourth compositional stage of Kings, who used the oracle in P38 as their model for composing this oracle.

The conclusion to the *parashah* is another example of the authors of the Josianic study books adding material that had been omitted from their primary source documents. (See note 42,1h above for the earlier example.) In the instance here in P44,1, they make mention of an oracle of Yehu condemning Ba'sha to a fate like Yarov'am's, but they likely did not know the exact wording of the oracle. To enliven what would otherwise be an uninteresting passage, they add their own commentary to the oracle ("because of all the things he did that displeased Yahweh, enraging him with the cult objects that he made for other gods").

44,1f enraging him with the cult objects that he made for other gods: Translation of להכעיסו במעשה ידיו; literally, "to enrage him with work of his hands [i.e. thing fashioned by his hands]." The author here uses a stock phrase that refers specifically to cult objects that offend Yahweh. The phrase is usually used in reference to statues of gods other than Yahweh (see the citations for this phrase given in BDB, p. 795, col. 2, def. 1.a.(2)), and that is what the author intended here in P44,1.

Notes to P45

45a ruled as king over Yisra'el in Thirtzah for two years: On the specific phrasing used here, see note 44a above. On Thirtzah, see note 38r above.

45b Artza the Chamberlain's house: The phrase אשר על־הבית ("the one who is over the house") is a job title for the individual responsible for managing the daily operations of the royal palace—the palace chamberlain. Artza was Elah's palace chamberlain, and here the phrase is used as Artza's surname.

45c (this includes his kinsmen and his associates): Note that the term for "his associates" here is written רעהו. This is the normal form for the singular with attached suffix ("his associate"), but the form is sometimes used to represent the plural with attached suffix. That is, the text is probably not in error. On the unusual form of the plural with attached suffix used here, see GKC § 91 *k*.

45d Zimriy exterminated Ba'sha's entire family, as foretold by the oracle that Yahweh delivered about Ba'sha through Yehu the Prophet: Note the implausibility—if not impossibility—of Zimriy exterminating everyone in Ba'sha's family. As we learn in P46, Zimriy ruled for only seven days, and during that entire time he was dealing with the threat on his life from Omriy. It seems almost impossible to believe that Zimriy would have had the time and resources to hunt down and kill all Ba'sha's family members. Nonetheless, the author tells us he did so, because for the author Yahweh's oracles must come true.

The oracle cited here in P45 is mentioned twice in P44,1. See the discussion above in notes 44,1a and 44,1e. The author of P45 specifically alludes to the second mention of the oracle, discussed in notes 44,1e and 44,1f.

45e provoking Yahweh God of Yisra'el with their useless gods: This is an allusion to the language used at the end of P44,1: "enraging him with the cult objects he made for other gods."

46a Yisra'el's forces were in position to attack Gibbethon of the Philishtines: The town of Gibbethon must have been hotly contested territory between the Philishtines and Yisra'el. In P43, Nadav fought the Philishtines at Gibbethon, and here in P46—twenty-six years after the events of P43—Yisra'el is again engaged in combat against the Philishtines at Gibbethon.

Notes to P46

46b withdrew from Gibbethon and besieged Thirtzah: Given that Zimriy ruled for only seven days, we can deduce from the language here that Thirtzah must have been located no more than a two- or three-day march from Gibbethon of the Philisthines. If Gibbethon was located in the tribal territory of Dan (see note 43b), Thirtzah must have been somewhere to the east, in Ephrayim, or to the north, in Menashsheh. The former is more likely given Thirtzah's association with Yarov'am, who was from Ephrayim.

46c following in the footsteps of Yarov'am and perpetuating the error that he committed: It's worth noting the highly formulaic nature of the language here. Zimriy was king for only seven days—not enough time to provide any meaningful support to the cults in Beyth-el and Dan.

46d are recorded: The phrase that I translate as "are recorded" is הלא הם כתובים ("aren't they written?"). In the Aleppo Codex, Shelomo ben Buya'a originally ended the last line of a page with the first two words of this phrase, הלא הם; however, he then erased the הם and began a new page with it. However, he did not fill in the erasure with a doodle. See A84 v.3.28. Because of the blank space at the end of the line, it is possible to interpret this as a *parashah* break, although I think it is clear that ben Buya'a did not intend for the reader to see a new *parashah* here. I have represented this oddity with a blank space after "instigated" in the final sentence of the *parashah*.

47a Tivniy Giynathsson: There is no real information provided about Tivniy, such as the length of his reign or the location of his royal seat. I believe this is likely because there was only a highly abbreviated account of his reign in the main source document for the northern kingdom, *The Chronicles of the Kings of Yisra'el*. The entirety of P47, excluding the gloss in the first sentence, reads as though it was lifted verbatim from the source document, and this material may be the only information the document contained about Tivniy. In my reconstruction of the regnal dates of the kings of Yisra'el and Yehudah in the appendix, I propose that Tivniy ruled Yisra'el from 884 to 882 BCE—these must have been years of civil war between his forces and Omriy's, with Omriy only gaining the throne after Tivniy died.

Notes to P47

47b prevailed over: Note the very unusual use of the mark of the direct object את with the verb חזק. We expect the preposition מן or על or אל.

48a In the thirty-first year of the reign of Asa King of Yehudah, Omriy ruled as king over Yisra'el...: This brief *parashah* is the account of the reign of Omriy, who ruled Yisra'el from 882-871 BCE (see the appendix to this book for my reconstruction of the regnal dates for the kings of Yisra'el and Yehudah). The authors of the Josianic study books know very little about Omriy's accomplishments, apart from the fact that he founded Shomeron, the capital of the northern kingdom. We know, however, that Omriy must have been a very important king—perhaps the most important king of the northern kingdom—as Assyrian inscriptions from the ninth and eighth centuries BCE frequently refer to the kingdom of Yisra'el as *bīt humri* ("house of Omriy" or

Notes to P48

"nation of Omriy"). For a brief discussion, see S. Hasegawa's article "House of Omri" at the Bible Odyssey website.

48b two *kikkar* of silver: One *kikkar* was equivalent to three thousand sheqels. In modern terms, one *kikkar* would be equivalent to 33.6 kilograms or approximately 68 pounds.

48c Shomeron, after the name of the hill's previous owner, Shemer: The derivation of the name Shomeron is uncertain. BDB, p. 1037, speculates that the name means "belonging to the clan Shemer," although the suffix ן ("ōn") never is used to indicate possession. Complicating matters is that Shomeron is the Masoretic vocalization of the name. It is likely that the name was originally vocalized as "Shamrayin." In cuneiform documents, the town is called "Samerina," and in the Septuagint the name is most often vocalized as "Samareia."

48d committing greater errors than any of his predecessors: This is a formulaic phrase that is here used somewhat thoughtlessly. In the theology of the authors of the Josianic study books, it is Yarov'am (who is one of Omriy's predecessors) who committed the greatest errors of Yisra'el's kings.

48e He followed exactly in the footsteps of Yarov'am...: This sentence is composed entirely of formulaic phrases. The error that Yarov'am "caused Yisra'el to commit" was the participation in the cults at Dan and Beyth-El, where the statues of Yahweh in the form of a bull calf were installed. The formulaic clause about provoking Yahweh's rage with "useless gods" is nonsensical in this context and I view it as an addition by the editors of Kings' sixth stage. They have borrowed the phrase about "provoking Yahweh with their useless gods" from P45, where it is used in reference to Ba'sha and Elah. To the authors of the Josianic study books, Yarov'am's crime was not worship of other gods, but rather making images of Yahweh and incorporating them into the practice of the cult.

Notes to P49

49a in the thirty-eighth year of the reign of Asa King of Yehudah: Ah'av must have had a co-regency with his father Omriy. Note from P48 that Omriy became king in Asa's thirty-first year and his rule lasted twelve years. Ah'av became king in Asa's thirty-eighth year, so the first five years of his reign must have been in a co-regency with his father.

49b more so than any of his predecessors: See note 48d above.

49c [*that is, the Ba'al's temple which he built in Shomeron*]: This clause reads as a comment added by the editors of Kings' sixth stage, who inform that reader that the phrase "an altar to the Ba'al" specifically means the Ba'al's temple that Ah'av built in Shomeron. This particular comment is interesting, as it is an example of a sixth-stage edit that might be by the authors of the Josianic study books, who here would be commenting on somewhat ambiguous language that they inserted verbatim from their source document. For another example of a sixth-stage comment that was likely by the authors of the Josianic study books, see P47 where "the people" (part of a verbatim insertion from the source document) is glossed as "Yisra'el."

49d Ah'av made an Asherah post: Asherah was a consort to both the Ba'al and to Yahweh. It seems mostly likely that the Asherah post that Ah'av made would have been installed on the grounds of the Ba'al's temple. There does not appear to have been a shrine to Yahweh in Shomeron. The nearest shrine to Yahweh likely was either in Shekem, roughly twelve kilometers to the southeast of Shomeron, or in the old royal seat of Thirtzah.

49e (In his time Hiy'el the Beyth-elite rebuilt Yeriyho...the oracle that Yahweh delivered through Yehoshua Nunsson.): This sentence reads as a later addition to the text and is an allusion to the curse on Yeriyho given in Jos P13. I believe the sentence here was most likely added in the late Persian period or Hellenistic period, as additions that insert bits and pieces of old traditions is one of the key features of the editorial work on the books of the Torah and the Former Prophets in those years. It is interesting to note that the curse on Yeriyho in the book of Joshua, which I view as a product of the early Persian period, does not present the curse as an oracle of Yahweh. Rather, it is simply a curse uttered by Yehoshua Nunsson against the town. In later tradition—towards the end of the Persian period and during the Hellenistic period, when the books of the Torah and the Prophets began to be studied as holy writings—Yehoshua's curse must have been understood as a statement that was somehow inspired by Yahweh.

49,1a Eliyyahu the Tishbite: This *parashah* is the first appearance of Eliyyahu the Tishbite, who must have been the most prominent prophet of the northern kingdom. The book of Kings contains numerous stories about him, beginning here and continuing through P62. It is very odd, given Eliyyahu's importance and the amount of material about him in Kings, that there is no introduction of him as a character in the narrative. The lack of introduction may be due to the fact that this *parashah*, along with nearly all the material about Eliyyahu, was not part of the earliest version of Kings, but was added to the text as part of the prophetic expansions (Kings' fourth compositional stage) made sometime during the Persian period and early Hellenistic period.

Notes to P49,1

The material in Kings about Eliyyahu added as part of Kings' fourth stage is as follows: an oracle about drought delivered to Ah'av (P49,1); a brief story about Eliyyahu living at a wadi and being brought food by ravens during the drought (P49,2); a story about Eliyyahu's miraculous provision of food to a widow and her family (P49,3); a story about Eliyyahu's resuscitation of the son of the same widow (P50); a scene in which Eliyyahu encounters Ovadyahu the palace chamberlain (P51); the story of Eliyyahu's contest with the prophets of the Ba'al (first half of P51,1); a scene about Eliyyahu and Ah'av traveling separately to Yizre'el as a tremendous rainstorm ends the drought (middle of P51,1); the story of Eliyyahu's flight into the desert and his experience of a theophany at Mount Horev (last part of P51,1); the story of Eliyyahu meeting Eliysha, who becomes his deputy (P51,2); the story of Navoth's vineyard (P55 - P58); the story of Eliyyah and the battalion commanders (P60,2); and the story of Eliyyahu being taken up to the skies as Eliysha looks on (P62).

This large body of material has a very complex composition history, not least because some of the stories about Eliyyahu and about the famous holy man Eliysha influenced each other, with each man taking on characteristics of the other. I offer some thoughts on the evolution and composition history of the Eliyyahu stories in notes 51,2a and 60,2a below.

49,1b [*from the residents of Gil'ad*]: This phrase is a gloss that has been corrupted during the transmission process. The phrase מתשבי גלעד ("from the residents of Gil'ad") originally must have read מתשבה גלעד ("from the Tishbeh in Gil'ad"). When referring to towns with common names, it was customary for ancient Hebrew authors to follow the town name with the region where the town was located, and that is likely what is going on here. It is easy to see how מתשבה might have been corrupted to מתשבי under the influence of the adjacent word התשבי ("the Tishbite").

For another example of authors adding a parenthetical comment to specify the location of a town that had a common name, see note 49,3b below.

49,3a Then a message from Yahweh came to him as follows...: This *parashah* is the story of Eliyyahu and the widow, and his miraculous provision of food to her. The

Notes to P49,3

stories about Eliyyahu present him as both a prophet to Yahweh and a miracle-worker. Most scholars believe that the traditions about Eliyyahu originally portrayed him solely as a prophet and not a miracle worker. The stories about Eliyyahu as a miracle worker have numerous parallels with the traditions about Eliysha, and I follow the many scholars who have argued that the authors of the Eliyyahu stories in Kings composed the miracle-working stories about him by borrowing material and themes from the old miracle-working traditions about Eliysha.

This *parashah* (P49,3) is the first example of the presentation of Eliyyahu as a miracle-worker that is based on material about Eliysha. Note that the Elijah story here has several the parallels with the Eliysha story in P66; most prominently, both stories concern the prophet's miraculous provision of food to a widow who is in dire circumstances. In the story in P66, the folk elements are quite strong and Yahweh is completely absent. The authors of P49,3 have changed the setting of the story in P66 to fit the drought narrative introduced in P49,1. In addition, they have made the story theologically acceptable by presenting Eliyyahu's miracle as Yahweh's doing.

49,3b Tzarephath (the one in Tziydon's territory): Tzarephath (which in Hebrew means something like "Smithville") must have been a relatively common name for a town. The author here adds a parenthetical comment to let the reader know that this is the Tzarephath that is part of the Tziydonians' territory. This way of referring to towns—the name of the town followed by its location to specify to the reader which of the towns with this name is the intended one—is commonly used by the authors of the Tanakh. Elsewhere in Kings, for example, the authors refer to "Gibbethon of the Philistines" (P43 and P46) and "Be'er Sheva in Yehudah" (P51,1). In Judges, note the phrases "Beyth Lehem in Yehudah" in Jud P64 and "Giv'ah in Binyamin" in Jud P66. Beyth Lehem and Giv'ah were common town names, and in referring to them, it was sometimes necessary to specify which town with that name one was speaking of.

49,3c When he arrived at the entrance to the town, he noticed a widow there collecting kindling: The scene is set at Tzarephath's main town gate: Eliyyahu has arrived at the gate and notices a widow collecting kindling outside the town wall.

49,3d "Please put a little water in this jug for me to drink": The verb that I translate as "put" is לקח. This verb has a very wide range of meanings, including "procure, get," which is how it is used here. A literal translation of the Hebrew is, "Please get a little water in this jug for me so that I may drink." The usage of לקח to mean "procure, get" in this specific context is quite unusual. It is usual to see the verb נתן ("give") in the specific context of one person asking another for food or drink (e.g. "please give me"). I believe the unusual use of לקח here may be characteristic of informal Hebrew speech spoken during the Persian period, when this story was composed. The stories of Eliyyahu and Eliysha exhibit many unusual features of grammar and vocabulary. The grammar and vocabulary of the Eliysha stories may reflect the dialect of the old traditions about Eliysha, which are associated with the area just north of the Dead Sea. By contrast, the stories about Eliyyahu are entirely literary compositions, and their grammar and vocabulary must reflect the Hebrew spoken and written at the time of the authors.

I don't comment on all the instances of unusual vocabulary and grammar in the Eliyyahu and Eliysha stories. However, I do comment on the more interesting instances, and when I believe the Hebrew used reflects colloquial speech, I translate into colloquial English.

49,3e to get him some water... "Please get out a bit of food...: Both of the verbs here are לקח, and reflect the usage discussed in the preceding note. In both these instances, it would be more usual for an author to write נתן ("give") and not לקח.

49,3f I'm going to go and make something to eat for myself and my son before we die: Recall from P49,1 that Yahweh has created famine conditions in the territory of Yisra'el. Tzarephath is part of the territory of Tziydon, which lay immediately north of Yisra'el. The author of this story presumably expects the reader to understand that the famine conditions extended to Tziydon. The woman's comment indicates that she and her son are starving and she has given up hope that they will survive.

49,3g For thus says Yahweh God of Yisra'el: The Leningrad Codex has a *parashah setumah* before this clause. See L197 v.3.18.

49,3h until the day Yahweh allowes: The Masoretic text here has an unusual form of the verb נתן ("give, let, allow"); the infinitive is written as תתן rather than the standard תת. It is unclear whether the spelling is an error or whether it represents a dialectical variant or archaic form. Both the Aleppo Codex and the Leningrad Codex correct the unusual form to the standard form with a *qere* in the margin. This variant form of the infinitive also appears in P15, where the Masoretes do not correct it. Here in P49,3, I have translated with an archaic spelling of "allow."

50a After these events, the son of the woman who owned the house fell ill: This *parashah* is the second story about Eliyyahu as a miracle worker. On the dependence of the Eliyyahu miracle-worker stories on the Eliysha traditions, see note 49,3a above. The story in P50 has a number of close parallels with the story of Eliysha's miraculous revival of a boy in P67, and I believe the story in P50 was modeled on the story in P67. Note the significant parallels in the narratives: in both stories, the son of a woman who has a close relationship with the prophet falls mortally ill; the boy is taken up to a room on the roof of the woman's house where the prophet stays and is laid down on the prophet's bed; and the prophet lies down on top of the boy multiple times and revives him.

Although both P50 and P49,3 present Eliyyahu as a miracle-worker, it is possible to read the story in P50 as added to Kings well after P49,3. In this regard, it is interesting to note that the first sentence of P51 follows naturally from the conclusion to P49,3. As I discuss in my presentation of the compositional history of Kings, I view each compositional stage as taking place over a long period of time, with additions and expansions being made in an iterative fashion in multiple "editions" of the book.

50b mister holy man: In the earliest stories about Eliyyahu, he is always called a prophet, and never a holy man. Eliysha was most commonly called a holy man, and the term is closely connected to his ability to perform miracles independent of any help from Yahweh. As discussed in the preceding note, the story in P50 is based on the story about Eliysha in P67. As a result, the authors of the story apply the term "holy man" to Eliyyahu. See the discussion in note 60,2e below.

50c You only came here to find fault with me: While the meaning of the Hebrew is clear, the exact nuance of the phrasing, which may be idiomatic, is uncertain. The *hiph'il* of the verb זכר means "to make mention of [a thing to someone], to make [someone] remember [a thing]." The noun עון most often means "wrongdoing" or "guilt." Thus the woman is accusing Eliyyahu of "making mention of [or making me remember] my wrongdoing." I understand the language here as idiomatic and I have translated with an equivalent idiomatic expression in English that is appropriate for the context. An alternative, but slightly less plausible, translation is "You only came here to make me feel guilty."

50d Now I really do know that you're a holy man!: The ending of the story is very strange: Eliyyahu performed a miracle for the woman in P49,3, so she already knows that he is a "holy man" and that the oracles he speaks from Yahweh are true. Thus there is no reason for her to make this statement here in P50. I believe that the story's authors may have concluded their story in this fashion as a way to give the story a theological point. The parallel story about Eliysha in P67 makes no theological point whatsoever. When the authors of the Eliyyahu material chose to create the story in P50 on the basis of P67, they perhaps felt it necessary to give the story a theological justification, even if the justification they provide is odd because of the narrative that preceded.

With regard to the term "holy man" (איש אלהים), it is worth pointing out that in the material from Kings' first stage, holy man is often used synonymously with the term for prophet (נביא). However, in the Eliyyahu and Eliysha stories—which I view as Persian period additions made as part of Kings' fourth stage—the term holy man is closely connected to the role of both men as miracle workers. This connotation is absent in the use of the term in the other compositional stages of Kings.

Notes to P51

51a in the third year of the drought: The Hebrew reads simply, "in the third year." This may refer to either the third year of the drought or the third year of Ah'av's reign. Because drought is a key theme that drives the narrative in the Eliyyahu stories, I have chosen to emphasize this theme by associating the "third year" language with the drought rather than Ah'av's reign. In support of the interpretation here, note also that in P49,1 we are told that the drought will last for "years." In the earliest edition of the fourth stage, before the Eliysha stories had been added and before the material about Eliyyahu as a miracle-worker had been composed, the material in P51 would have followed directly from P49,1. In that "edition" of Kings, it would have been most natural to understand the mention of the "third year" here as referring to the drought.

51b While Ovadyahu was on the road, he by chance happened to see Eliyyahu, who coincidentally was coming his way: Literally, "It so happened while Ovadyahu was on the road [that all of a sudden] there was Eliyyahu [coming] to meet him." The Hebrew particle הנה (literally, "to here") had a very wide range of uses in ancient Hebrew. It was often used to express the surprise someone feels at noticing some specific thing or event that is unexpected. This is how the particle is used here, and to capture the specific nuance in English in this situation requires many more words than is typical when translating this particle. In my translation, the force of הנה is represented by "he by chance happened to see... coincidentally."

With regard to Eliyyahu "coming his way," recall that at the beginning of the *parashah* Yahweh told Eliyyahu to make an appearance to Ah'av—he is on the road heading to Shomeron when he meets up with Ovadyahu.

51c Is that really you?: Ovadyahu can't believe he has met up with Eliyyahu. Eliyyahu has been in hiding for the entirety of the drought (presumably between two and three years), and as we learn in the following sentences, Ah'av has been looking everywhere for Eliyyahu for quite some time.

51d "What have I done wrong...: Ovadyahu here launches a lengthy complaint to Eliyyahu about the risks he will face if he informs Ah'av of Eliyyahu's return. The tone of the Ovadyahu's speech is highly colloquial and I believe the author must have been trying to capture Hebrew as it was spoken in daily life. I have translated with a relatively informal and colloquial English. The author is making a deliberate effort to display his literary skill in the speech; he wishes both to entertain his audience with it and to make them appreciate his ability to create a scene that is vivid and true to life. Speeches such as this one that demonstrate the author's skill and that entertain and impress the reader are important features of ancient Hebrew narrative art. They are especially common in Genesis and Samuel, which are the two most literary books in the Torah and Former Prophets.

51e a wind from Yahweh's going to carry you off to who knows where: The language used by the author is highly colloquial. I have used the English colloquialism "to who knows where" to represent the colloquial Hebrew phrase "to I don't know where." The wind imagery used by Ovadyahu is interesting, as it is reminiscent of Eliyyahu's disappearance in P62. The author of P51 would have known of that famous story, and he intentionally alludes to it here in the words that he puts into Ovadyahu's mouth.

51,1a As Yahweh of Armies, before whom I stand lives...: The name Yahweh of Armies (יהוה צבאות) is an abbreviated form of "Yahweh God of Armies." Like "God of Yisra'el" or "[God] of Shomeron," the phrase "[God] of Armies" is one of Yahweh's surnames. This surname of Yahweh may originally have been associated with Yahweh's identity as a god of war, but in later literature the surname is associated with Yahweh's identity as the supreme god and god of the stars. The surname "[God] of Armies" is strongly associated with the temple in Yerushalem (where the chief object of veneration was Yahweh's battle chest), and I do not believe it was common in the northern kingdom. The use of the surname here in P51,1 indicates that the author was familiar with the cult in Yerushalem, and is consistent with a Persian period date for the Eliyyahu material. If the material were part of the Josianic study books, I think it very unlikely that this surname would be associated with a northern prophet. See note 2,1c above for additional comments on Yahweh's surnames.

Notes to P51,1

This *parashah* (P51,1) consists of three stories and, from a theological perspective, represents the most important material within the stories about Eliyyahu and Eliysha. The first story in the *parashah* recounts a contest between Eliyyahu and the Ba'al's prophets about whether Yahweh or the Ba'al is the supreme god. This is followed by a brief and somewhat confused story about a great rainstorm that ends the drought as Eliyyahu and Ah'av separately make their way to Yizre'el. The third story tells of Eliyyahu's flight into the southern desert to escape Iyzevel, and of his subsequent journey to Mount Horev, where he experiences a theophany and speaks directly to Yahweh. Because of the importance of the material in this *parashah*, it is not surprising that—as discussed in the notes below—it shows evidence of expansions and additions by multiple authors.

51,1b the biggest trouble-maker in Yisra'el: "Trouble-maker" is from the verb עכר. The participle form (used here) refers to someone who is a trouble-maker, agitator, or provocateur. The Hebrew has a negative connotation that is not far from the American expression "pain in the ass," except that there is some vulgarity in the American expression that is not present in the Hebrew.

51,1c who take their meals at Iyzevel's table: The phrase "eat at the table of" is idiomatic; it means simply that a person received a regular allowance of food from a superior. It should not be understood to mean that the person took all of his or her meals at the superior's table. It's worth noting that the four hundred prophets of the Asherah don't appear again in this *parashah*. The Asherah and her prophets have no role in the contest to decide who is the greatest god, and the passage about Eliyyahu's slaughter of the Ba'al's priests makes no mention of the prophets of the Asherah. Because the Asherah and her prophets are not integral to the story, it is possible to view the mention of them as a later addition to the text. Narrative logic and consistency, however, were not as important to ancient Hebrew authors as they are to modern-day readers, and for that reason I do not see a compelling reason to treat the comment about the Asherah and her prophets as an addition.

51,1d hopping over two branches: That is, worshipping and giving service to both Yahweh and the Ba'al.

51,1e they were continually hopping up and down on the altar that had been built there: BDB, p. 820, somewhat strangely proposes that the verb פסח has a secondary meaning of "limp," and it cites this passage in support. However, the core meaning of the verb is "pass over, spring over," and I believe that is clearly the meaning here. BDB gives the meaning "limp" for three occurrences of the verb (two in this *parashah* and one in Sam P73,1). The two instances here in Kings are best understood as "hop, jump up, jump over," in my opinion. With respect to Sam P73,1, the *niph'al* form of the verb is best understood as a term for walking with a crippled gait—in English, we say "limp," but in Hebrew the crippled gait is described as a sort of "hopping" (if one has only one good leg, one's movement looks something like a hop).

The phrase המזבח אשר עשה is ambiguous. The subject of the verb can be understood as definite, in which case the phrase means "the altar that he had made." However, there is no proper antecedent—if the subject were definite, we would expect the third-person plural "they" in reference to the Ba'al's prophets. Alternatively, the subject can be understood as indefinite, in which case the phrase literally would mean "that one had made." Ancient Hebrew commonly used the third person singular verb with an indefinite subject to express the passive voice. I believe that context requires this meaning here, and I have translated accordingly.

I view the story of the contest between Eliyyahu and the Ba'al's prophets as a literary creation of the Persian period. It is unclear to what extent the author may have drawn on oral tradition about the places and events he describes. For example, I speculate below in note 51,1j that "the altar that had been built" might be based on a historical memory of an open-air shrine to the Ba'al on Mount Karmel.

51,1f Call out in a really loud voice! He's a god after all: That is, he lives high up in the sky—so far away that he can't hear you. You must call much louder than you've been doing in order to get his attention.

51,1g he might be daydreaming. Or maybe he's running an errand or went on a trip: The Hebrew is highly colloquial. How a native speaker would have perceived the exact nuances of the phrasing is uncertain, although we know that the language must have come across as mocking and derisive.

51,1h cut themselves (as was their custom): There are several references in the books of the Torah and the Prophets to the practice of cutting oneself or tattooing oneself, but this practice is always in relation to mourning for the dead—it was not done in connection with the regular presentation of offerings to Yahweh or any other god.

The practice of cutting oneself as an act of mourning is condemned in Deut P13,3 and in Lev P40; however, the references in Jeremiah do not speak of the practice in negative terms and seem to suggest that cutting oneself was a standard mourning practice (see Jer 16.6, 41.6, and 47.5).

51,1i the presentation of the grain offering: The author of this first story in P51,1 depicts the grain offering as a normal component of whole offerings. The Ba'al's priests as well as Eliyyahu present a grain offering to their god after arranging the whole offering on the altar. We should imagine that the grain offering was placed on top of the whole offering. It should be noted that in the rules for whole offerings in Leviticus, the whole offering is never supplemented with a grain offering. That said, because Leviticus is comprised largely of ancient cult rule books that are written in an abbreviated and elliptical style, it is possible that whole offerings may sometimes have been supplemented with a grain offering placed on top of them and that this practice simply wasn't mentioned in the rule books preserved in Leviticus. In this regard, it is interesting that in the rules for welfare offerings, the offerer does have the option of presenting a grain offering on top of the welfare offering (see Lev P18). On my proposal that Leviticus preserves a number of ancient cult rule books, see the introduction to my translation of Leviticus and the accompanying notes and comments.

51,1j He worked to repair Yahweh's ruined altar: The mentioned of a ruined altar suggests that the author believed that there once had been an open-air shrine to Yahweh on top of Mount Karmel that was destroyed. If there is some historical truth to the tradition about Iyzevel's attack on Yahweh's cult in the kingdom of Yisra'el as mentioned in P51, we can speculate that if there ever was an open-air shrine to Yahweh on Mount Karmel, it may have been destroyed as part of that attack, and that an open-air shrine to the Ba'al was then built nearby to replace it.

51,1k [*whose ancestor received an oracle from Yahweh saying that his name would be Yisra'el*]: I understand this to be a comment added as part of the work of the sixth compositional stage. The author of this comment wishes to remind the reader of the account in Gen P30 about how Ya'aqov received the name Yisra'el. In Genesis, there are two accounts of Ya'aqov receiving the name Yisra'el: in the story of his wrestling with the mysterious god in Gen P28 and in a theophany in P30. The author of this comment is clearly referring to Gen P30 and not P28. In my opinion, the material in Gen P30 clearly dates to the Persian period, and the comment here could only have been added sometime in a late compositional stage of Kings.

51,1l about the size of a two-*se'ah* container for seeds: I believe the author is implying that the width of the trench is roughly equal to the diameter of a two-*se'ah* container, which must have been a standard jar size. A *se'ah* was a liquid and a dry measure equivalent to one-third of an *eyphah*. In modern terms, one *se'ah* is equivalent to roughly 7.3 liters; thus a two-*se'ah* container would have held a little less than 15 liters.

In the United States, a standard container is a five-gallon bucket, which holds around 19 liters, or roughly two-and-a-half *se'ah*. The five-gallon bucket is around 30 centimeters (or 12 inches) in diameter, and it is reasonable to suppose that the diameter of a two-*se'ah* container was roughly similar. On the size of the *se'ah*, see the article "Weights & Measures" at the Jewish Virtual Library.

51,1m the whole offering: That is, the pieces of the butchered bull that have been arranged on the wood on the altar. Eliyyahu refers to the pieces as a "whole offering" (עלה) because he intends for the fire from Yahweh to consume the pieces entirely, just as the animal parts placed on the altar as a whole offering are entirely consumed by fire.

51,1n And so they did: I have added this sentence, which does not appear in the Hebrew. In ancient Hebrew narrative, authors often omitted details or events when they would be obvious to the reader. English, by contrast, typically places a greater importance on narrative logic. An English author would feel obligated to state here that Eliyyahu's command was carried out, whereas an ancient Hebrew author would not necessarily feel the need to do that. In this situation, a functionally equivalent translation requires the translator to add the sentence, in keeping with the practices of English narrative. A good example elsewhere in the Tanakh of an author omitting the narration of events is in the plague narrative in Exodus (P10,1 - P16), where for several plagues the author simply reports Yahweh's command to Mosheh regarding what to say to Phar'oh, but then doesn't provide an account of Mosheh delivering

Yahweh's speech to Phar'oh, as that action is easily deduced by the reader. (It is interesting to note that in the Samaritan Torah, however, the authors have added these accounts, indicating that by the Hellenistic period, the omission of events in the narrative sequencing was thought to be problematic.)

51,1o god of Avraham, Yitzhaq, and Yisra'el: The mention of the patriarchs suggests a late date for this story—sometime in the Persian period, after the Samarian book of Genesis had been become part of the cult library in Yerushalem and had been attached to the book of Exodus through the composition of the Joseph narrative.

51,1p let it be known today that you are god in Yisra'el: That is, in this contest between you and the Ba'al, let it be known that you—not the Ba'al—are the god that Yisra'el should revere.

51,1q through your commands: The consonantal text in the Aleppo codex reads ובדבריך ("through your commands"), but the word is vocalized as the singular "through your command." Oddly, there is no *qere* in the margin noting the correction to the consonantal text. See A86 v.2.8. The Leningrad Codex does have a *qere* in the margin here—see L198 v.3.25. To reflect the absence of the *qere* in the Aleppo Codex, I have translated the consonantal text rather than what is vocalized.

51,1r it was you who made their hearts turn backwards: Note the unusual theology, which is completely at odds with the versions of Kings associated with the first and second compositional stages. The author of this passage implies that Yahweh forced his people to be unfaithful to him. The theology here reflects an understanding of Yahweh that did not develop until the Persian period: there is no other god but him, and he is omnipotent—all things happen because of him. The presence of this theology here in the Eliyyahu material provides strong support for viewing the stories about him as Persian period compositions.

51,1s it consumed the whole offering and the wood, as well as the stones and the dirt: The author presumably does not mention the grain offering here because once it is placed on top of the whole offering, it would be considered part of the whole offering.

The mention of "the stones and the dirt" is a reference to the altar to Yahweh that Eliyyahu had repaired. (The "dirt" is the packed earth between the stones that helps give the altar its shape.) Presumably the fire must destroy the altar because the author (and his audience) are aware that there was no altar to Yahweh on Mount Karmel.

51,1t while vaporizing the water that was in the trench: Literally, "while licking up the water that was in the trench."

51,1u they threw themselves flat on their faces: The verb that I translate as "threw themselves flat" is the *qal* of נפל. The basic meaning of the *qal* of this verb is intransitive—"to fall, fall down." However, when an individual is the subject of the verb, it sometimes has a reflexive meaning—"to throw oneself down." I have commented on this nuance of the verb in a number of places in my other translations. See, for example, note 53i in my translation of Samuel.

51,1v "Yahweh is the supreme god!": The people acknowledge that Yahweh has won the contest with the Ba'al.

51,1w Eliyyahu took them down to the Wadi Qiyshon and slaughtered them there: Note the unrealistic nature of the narrative, something often seen in stories of legendary figures such as Eliyyahu. It is absurd to suppose that one man could kill all four hundred and fifty of the Ba'al's prophets.

The Wadi Qiyshon was a wadi in the western part of the Yizre'el Valley near Megiddo. The wadi is mentioned in the narrative account of the Yisra'elites' batttle with Yaviyn King of Hatzor's army in Jud P15 and in the lyric account of that battle in the Song of Devorah in Jud P16. The wadi flows into the Mediterranean very close to Mount Karmel, where the story here in Kgs P51,1 is set.

51,1x Go now and have some food and drink… Ah'av went to have some food and drink: The Hebrew is ambiguous. It is unclear if the verb עלה here means "go to your tent/lodging here in Karmel" or "go back to Shomeron." The verb is very often used in the context of making a journey over some distance, which would support the latter reading. That said, it can be used to refer to journeys of a shorter distance, and that fits the narrative logic best in this passage. For that reason I have a slight preference for understanding Eliyyahu to mean that Ah'av should go back to his tent/lodging, and I have translated as such.

51,1y Go tell Ah'av to harness his chariot and proceed to: The phrase "to Yizre'el" (יזרעאלה) must have fallen out of the text. The verb here is from the root ירד ("go down, descend"), and typically is used to describe traveling from a higher elevation to a lower elevation or to describe traveling from the north toward the south. The former usage fits the situation here, if we presume Ah'av had remained in his lodging near Karmel and was now being asked to proceed to the town of Yizre'el. It's worth noting that the Hebrew here is a little awkward: we expect the command to be prefixed with a phrase such as "Eliyyahu said to his attendant," but the author has somewhat unusually not provided an indication of speaker or audience. This is one of several places in this *parashah* where the author has employed a more elliptical style than is customarily seen in ancient Hebrew prose, and the effect is somewhat confusing to the reader—even to very experienced readers of Hebrew.

51,1z And tell him the rain's not going to slow him down: The Hebrew is ambiguous. The message that Eliyyahu tells his attendant to give to Ah'av is presented in direct discourse, and it is unclear where the order ends. In my translation, I have assumed the message to Ah'av includes the sentence here, which serves to reassure him that he won't be delayed by the rain on his travels to Yizre'el. However, it is also possible to read the message to Ah'av as ending with "proceed to [Yizre'el]" (רד). In that case, the sentence here—ולא יעצרכה הגשם—would represent speech that Eliyyahu addressed to his attendant, and the appropriate translation would be "The rain's not going to slow you down." While both readings of the Hebrew are plausible, the Hebrew reads slightly more naturally if this sentence is understood as part of the message to Ah'av.

51,1aa Ah'av mounted his chariot and proceeded to Yizre'el: Presumably, Ah'av was present at the contest between Eliyyahu and the prophets, and he returned to his tent/lodgings nearby after the contest was over (see note 51,1x above). That said, the author never informs us of Ah'av's whereabouts—this is not something that would have occurred to him to do, as the rules and practices for ancient Hebrew narrative are very different than the rules and practices of modern-day narrative—and it is possible the author intended us to understand that Ah'av had returned to Shomeron. Note that the author here omits any mention of Eliyyahu's attendant delivering the message to Ah'av. Given the elliptical narrative style of much ancient Hebrew prose, we don't necessarily expect to read here that the attendant delivered the message; however, the number of such narrative gaps in this *parashah* is unusually large.

51,1ab He tied his belt tight and took off at a run...: I understand Eliyyahu to be the subject of this sentence. The action here is strange, and it is unclear to me what the author intended by having Eliyyahu run to Yizre'el, presumably to meet Ah'av again. At the end of the sentence, the author employs an idiomatic prepositional phrase עד־באכה (literally, "until your going") which has the meaning "as far as, all the way to." The infinitive form of בוא ("go, go in, arrive") with the second-person pronominal suffix כה is used on its own several times in Genesis as a preposition meaning "as far as, in the direction of." The usage of the verb form here in Kings is related to those in Genesis.

51,1ac So may the gods do, and so may they do again...: This phrase serves as the introduction to an oath, similar to a phrase such as "As Yahweh lives." Iyzevel uses a variant form of a common oath that is used numerous times in Samuel and Kings. The usual form reads "So may God do to me." Iyzevel has altered this to "So may the gods do." It is unclear if Iyzevel intentionally omitted the phrase "to me" (לי) or if the phrase has fallen from the text due to a scribal error. Elsewhere in Kings, the oath appears in P6, P52, and P71.

51,1ad just like one of them: That is, like one of the prophets of the Ba'al whom Eliyyahu slaughtered.

51,1ae When he saw the messenger: As is common in ancient Hebrew narrative, the prose is elliptical and the reader must supply the missing information based on context. The Hebrew here reads simply "[When] he saw." I have added the phrase "the messenger," which I believe is closest to the author's intent. Alternatively, one could supply the phrase "the message," (that is, "when he saw the message"). However, it would not be natural for the author to use the verb ראה ("see"') if that was the intended meaning—the expected verb would instead be שמע ("hear").

51,1af All of a sudden, a divine envoy was touching him: I believe the material from here to the end of the *parashah*, which is the famous account of Yahweh's theophany to Eliyyahu on Mount Horev, is secondary to the text. The earliest version of the Eliyyahu stories, which I attribute to the fourth compositional stage of Kings and date to sometime in the Persian period, did not include this story. The story of the theophany at Horev was added in a later edition of the fourth compositional stage, perhaps in the early or mid-fourth century BCE. The rationale for adding this material likely was to present Eliyyahu as a (near-)equal to Mosheh. The theophany here in P51,1 is clearly related to Yahweh's theophany to Mosheh in Exod P56. Although it is difficult to be certain about the direction of dependence, I have a preference for viewing the material here in Kgs P51,1 as dependent on the theophany in Exod P55 - P56.

Note that the story of the theophany was itself expanded with a small addition, which I discuss in note 51,1ai below.

51,1ag you have a big journey ahead of you: Literally, "the journey is too much for you" or "the journey is bigger than you are." The author uses colloquial Hebrew here, and I have translated with an equivalent colloquial phrase in English.

51,1ah Horev, the mountain of God: Alternatively, one may translate "the divine mountain Horev."

51,1ai Suddenly, a message from Yahweh came to him... stand on the mountain in front of Yahweh.": I understand this passage of dialog (five sentences in my translation) to be an addition to the text from one of the final editions of the fourth compositional stage very late in the Persian period. I believe it preserves a variant of the theophany, but the addition is quite muddled, as though only part of the variant version of the theophany were inserted. Once this passage is removed, the text that remains—the original version of the theophany—reads very smoothly.

51,1aj Yahweh God of Armies: The epithet "God of Armies" is one of Yahweh's surnames; it is closely associated with the cult on Mount Tsiyyon. The surname never appears in the books of the Torah; in the Former Prophets, it only appears in this *parashah* in Kings and in Samuel at the end of P74. See the discussion of the shortened version of this name, Yahweh of Armies, in note 51,1a above.

51,1ak the Yisra'elites have abandoned your treaty with them: The concept of a treaty between Yahweh and the Yisra'elites is absent in the editions of Kings from the book's first and second compositional stages. The concept first appears in the earliest versions of Exodus-Numbers and Joshua (which I date to the early Persian period) and in the contemporaneous expansions of Deuteronomy. The presence of this concept here is consistent with a Persian period date for the original theophany scene and its variant, both of which I view as additions to this *parashah*.

51,1al Go outside and stand on the mountain in front of Yahweh: This statement is an explicit allusion to Yahweh's order to Mosheh in Exodus P55 to stand on an outcrop on Mount Siynai.

51,1am All of a sudden, Yahweh was passing right by...: In the original version of the theophany (which itself was added to P51,1), this sentence followed directly from the statement above that Eliyyahu came to a cave "where he spent the night." See note 51,1ai above for my thoughts on the intervening material.

Compare the theophany to Eliyyahu that follows with Yahweh's theophany to Mosheh in Exodus P54 - P56. The two are clearly related to one another. As I state above in note 51,1af, it seems more likely to me that the theophany here in Kings is dependent on the theophany in Exodus.

51,2a "Go, make your way back through the desert...: Yahweh's speech here seems disconnected from the theophany. As discussed above, I believe the theophany is a later addition to the text. I believe that originally Yahweh's speech to Eliyyahu occurred at the lone broom-shrub about a day's journey from Be'er Sheva, and followed directly from the statement in P51,1 that Eliyyahu lay down and fell asleep.

This *parashah* introduces the character of Eliysha who serves as Eliyyahu's deputy and successor. The material about Eliyyahu and Eliysha is quite complex. The stories about the two prophets show signs of being added in stages, but it is unclear whether the earliest addition included stories about both men or only about Eliyyahu. I have a slight preference for the latter option. In this view, the initial additions about Eliyyahu included P49,1 (an oracle delivered to Ah'av), P51 - P51,1 (Eliyyahu's encounters with Ovadyahu and Ah'av, the contest between Eliyyahu and the Ba'al's prophets, the arrival of rain and the journey of Eliyyahu and Ah'av to Yizre'el, and Eliyyahu's flight to the broom-shrub) and P55 - P58 (the story of Navoth's vineyard). Sometime later in the fourth compositional stage, the authors of Kings decided to add a body of stories about the holy man Eliysha, which they did by introducing him as the deputy and successor to Eliyyahu (the second half of P51,2 and P62). The Eliysha stories then would have inspired the expansions to the Eliyyahu material in P49,2 - P50 (the two stories about Eliyyahu and the widow from Tzarephath), where Eliyyahu takes on the aspect of a miracle worker, similar to Eliysha. This in turn might have led to the expansion in P60,2 (the story of Eliyyahu and the battalion captains), which contains many fantastic elements. Independently of the additions to the Eliyyahu stories that were influenced by the Eliysha traditions, the material about Eliyyahu was further

Notes to P51,2

expanded at the end of P51,1 with the addition of the story of the theophany at Mount Horev.

Parallel to the Eliyyahu stories, I believe that the Eliysha stories were added in multiple stages. See notes 68a and 69a below for my thoughts on the evolution of the Eliysha stories.

51,2b Dancing Meadow: This village is also mentioned in Jud P24. The reference in Judges indicates it is near (likely to the east of) the Yarden River, near Acacia Town (where Yehoshua leads the Yisra'elites into Kena'an) and Yeriyho.

51,2c all those whose knees didn't kneel…all those whose mouths didn't kiss: The author here employs metonymy (using one word or phrase in place of another with which it is closely associated) for literary effect. The Hebrew literally reads, "every pair of knees that didn't kneel…every mouth that didn't kiss." While metonymy is relatively common in English, I have not translated as such here, as doing so creates an awkward effect that is not present in the Hebrew.

51,2d Eliyyahu departed from there and found Eliysha Shaphatsson: The author's geographical reference would be awkward if he understood Eliyyahu to be on Mount Horev, however his text as written is perfectly natural if he understood Eliyyahu to be at the lone broom-tree, which is one-day's journey from Be'er Sheva.

Note also that the actions in the text are not consistent with Yahweh's orders to Eliyyahu. He doesn't anoint Eliysha, nor does he go to Dammeseq to anoint Haza'el, nor does he anoint Yehu Nimshiysson. I believe that Yahweh's command to Eliyyahu at the beginning of this *parashah* is a later addition to the text, and that the *parashah* originally began with the sentence here about Eliyyahu departing and finding Eliysha. Furthermore, I believe that the addition was made because the authors of the fourth stage intended to compose stories in which Eliyyahu carried out these actions (that is, anointing Elisha, Haza'el and Yehu). However, they later abandoned these plans and instead composed stories about Haze'el and Yehu for Elisha. With regard to the ideas proposed here, see my discussion of the fourth stage addition to P51,2 in the composition history following the notes and comments.

On the complex compositional history of the Eliyyahu and Eliysha stories, see note 51,2a above and notes 60,2a, 68a, and 69a below.

51,2e he was plowing twelve acres of land: Literally, "he was plowing twelve pairs." Here the term צמד ("pair, couple") is used as a measure of land. The root צמד means "bind, join" and by association was used to refer to a pair of working animals—horses, donkeys, or cattle. By extension, the term was also used to refer to the amount of land that a pair of oxen could plow in a single day. It just so happens that a pair of oxen in a single day can plow roughly what is an English acre. On plowing with oxen, see the article "Small Farming with Oxen" at the website /https://grit.com, which is devoted to "rural American know-how."

The author's mention of Eliysha plowing twelve acres and "working the twelfth acre" perhaps betrays an ignorance of farming. It typically takes one or two people a full day to plow an acre with a pair of oxen. If the author was aware of this fact, I believe he would likely have written his text differently—perhaps something like "Eliyyahu departed from there and found Eliysha Shaphatsson when he was plowing an acre of land. As he was finishing his work, Eliyyahu went over to him…"

51,2f because of what I've done for you: The Hebrew is nonsensical. It is possible the text is corrupt.

51,2g he took his two oxen and slaughtered them: The details about Eliysha slaughtering his valuable and well-trained oxen are unrealistic. It would be most natural for him to give the animals to family members, as presumably the twelve acres he was plowing would remain in the family. I am unclear as to the author's intent in including these unrealistic details in his account.

Note also the inconsistency in the narrative: Eliysha asks Eliyyahu permission to kiss his parents good-bye, but instead of doing that he slaughters his oxen and puts on a feast in the village.

51,2h After he cooked them [*the meat*] in a cattle pot, he gave the portions to the people in his village: In the traditions preserved in Kings about Eliysha, the preparation of meals for large groups of people and the provision of food during famine are important elements in several stories. The mention of Eliysha's feeding his fellow villagers here in P51,2 is the first appearance of the theme of feeding large groups; other examples appear in P68 and P68,1. The theme regarding provision of food during famine is present in the story in P71 - P73, and the story in P73,1 - P73,2. Note also P66, where Eliysha provides food to a destitute widow and her family.

52a Now Hadadsson King of Aram had marshaled his entire army...: This *parashah* introduces the story found in P52 - P54, which is set in the time of Yisra'el's wars with Aram. The story is a late addition to the text, and it is unrelated to the Eliyyahu and Eliysha stories. Once the material about Eliyyahu and Eliysha was added to Kings, that material inspired the composition and addition of other stories involving the prophets such as the one here. These stories always have a theological point relevant to the author's time, but they also were intended to enrich and enliven the book. I assign the story in P52 - P54 and nearly all of the other stories in Kings involving the prophets to the book's fourth compositional stage. The material in Kings' fourth stage shows evidence of a long and complex composition history. The story here in P52 - P54, for example, is related to P54,1, which was added as a comment on the unsatisfying conclusion to P54.

Notes to P52

Although the story in P52 - P54 contains some folk elements, I believe it is purely a literary composition. The author's main purpose was to make a theological point about Yahweh (see note 52h below), but he also sought to entertain through lively dialog, the addition of unusual details, and the occasional use of humor.

52b You realize, don't you, that this jerk simply wants to humiliate me: I have departed further than usual from a literal rendering to capture the force of the Hebrew. Literally, "Please know and see that this man is seeking [my] harm." The particle נא ("please") softens the tone of the statement, which I capture with the phrase "don't you." The demonstrative זה ("this man") is very often used with a pejorative or derogatory sense; I believe that is how Ah'av uses it here, and thus translate "jerk." (On this use of the demonstrative elsewhere in Kings, see notes 59,1c, 59,1e, 69d, 71h, and 109e below.) Finally, context suggests that the "harm" Hadadsson specifically seeks to inflict on Ah'av in his second request is humiliation.

52c so may the gods do to me, and so may they do again: This is a very common oath form, and it is used numerous times in Samuel and Kings. See note 51,1ac above. See also BDB, p. 415, def. 1 of the *hiph'il*.

52d if even handfuls of Shomeron's dirt suffice: The meaning of this phrase is uncertain. I believe the meaning of Hadadsson's oath is something to the effect of "I'll be damned if my troops are satisfied with anything less than the complete destruction of Shomeron." That is to say, even after his troops raze Shomeron to the ground and there is nothing left but dirt, they still won't be satisfied and will seek to inflict further harm on the place.

52e a man dressing before battle ought not make boasts like someone removing his gear afterwards: Ah'av here quotes a proverb; however, I have not translated with the terseness of a proverb, as doing so would fail to capture the force of Ah'av's response.

52f Set your battle lines... they set their battle lines: The Hebrew is elliptical and the meaning is uncertain. The verb here is שׂוּם ("put, place, set"), which I believe is used in a technical military sense with the meaning "set [the battle line]," with the direct object "battle line" (מערכה) being implicit. There is no reason to think that the text here is corrupt, as BDB, p. 964, def. 4a suggests.

52g Do you see this vast army?: The prophet is pointing out to the king the battle lines of the Aramean forces, which have now been set.

52h then you shall know that I am Yahweh: Recall that Ah'av is a devotee of the Ba'al. The point of the story in P52-P54 is to show Ah'av's unworthiness: Yahweh proves to him that he is greater than other gods, yet Ah'av remains disloyal. The phrase "know that I am Yahweh" has special significance in the book Exodus, where it is typically used in connection with a demonstration of Yahweh's great power. See the usages Exod P6,1, P9, P10,1, P11,2, P15, P23, P24. The phrase is sometimes addressed to Phar'oh and the Egyptians, and sometimes to the Yisra'elites. When it is addressed to the Yisra'elites, the phrase serves as a proof-point that Yahweh deserves to be worshipped and revered by the Yisra'elites as their god. The author of this *parashah* in Kings uses the phrase in an identical fashion, and I believe that his use of the phrase derives from his familiarity with the phrase in Exodus.

52i cavalry: The Hebrew term here is פרשׁים. On this term, see note 11,1a above. The story in P52-P54 is set in the mid-ninth century BCE, right around the time cavalry was first developed by the army of Ashshur. It seems doubtful that Aram would have adopted the use of cavalry so quickly after its initial development. The author of the story, however, is writing in the Persian period, and he would have been unaware that Aram did not yet possess cavalry in the period he is writing about.

52j **: The Leningrad Codex has a *parashah setumah* here. See L.200 r.2.9-10.

Notes to P54

54a Apheq: There are four towns named Apheq that are mentioned in the Tanakh (see BDB, pp. 67f): one near the Yizre'el Valley (Jos P24,18 and Sam P61), one in the territory of Asher (Jos P41 and Jud P5,3), one north of the territory of Yisra'el in land controlled by the Tzidonians (Jos P25), and one near Mitzpah in the territory of Binyamin (Sam P8). Given that the battle is meant to be "in the plains," the author likely had in mind the Apheq that is near the Yizre'el Valley.

54b a distance roughly equal to two strips of goats: It is unclear how we should imagine "a strip" of goats. Possibly a "strip" refers to the distance a flock of goats would spread out when grazing a line of brush—perhaps a distance of one hundred meters or so for a single "strip." But this is simply a guess, and there is no way to know for certain what the text means. Some scholars think the text here might be corrupt, although it does not seem so to me.

54c On account of the fact that Aram claimed Yahweh is a mountain god: The holy man alludes to the king of Aram's discussion with his officers in P53. This allusion only makes sense if we understand the story in P53-P54 as a wholly literary composition without any basis in history. If the story had a basis in history, then the holy man's oracle would have been incomprehensible to the king of Yisra'el, as he would not have had any knowledge of the discussion between the king of Aram and his officers. But taken as a literary composition, the story reads perfectly naturally and the reader may not even notice the gap in narrative logic here.

54d I shall deliver this entire vast army...you all will know that I am Yahweh!: The holy man's oracle here is almost identical to the anonymous prophet's oracle to Ah'av in P52.

54e to Apheq [*that is, to the town*]: Apheq seems to have been both a town and the region around the town. A later editor has added a gloss here informing the reader that the town, and not the region, is meant. A possible reference to Apheq as a region and not a town appears in Sam P61. As discussed above in note 54a, the town in question here was likely located near the Yizre'el Valley.

54f deep in the bowels of the town: The Leningrad Codex has a *parashah setumah* after this phrase. See L200 r.3.20-21.

54g put sackcloth around our waists and cords on our heads: These are traditional actions of mourning and contrition. In a military context, they represent a statement of submission, similar to the modern-day actions of waving the white flag and putting up one's arms.

54h They seized upon the king's answer: The Hebrew is somewhat difficult, but I do not believe the text is corrupt. Literally, "They snatched that which was from him." The definite article ה in the phrase הממנו functions as the mark of the relative clause. This use of the definite article is characteristic of late Hebrew and supports a date in the late Persian period for the story in P52-P54.

54i and had him step up onto his chariot...made a treaty with him and sent him off: The narrative logic seems to break down at the end of this *parashah*. It is the defeated king (Hadadsson) who invites victorious king (the king of Yisra'el) into his chariot, and it is the defeated king who offers to make a treaty and who sends the victorious king away. The verb used here—the *pi'el* of שלח ("send away")—almost always describes an action that a person in a superior position does to a person in an inferior position.

54j you may establish streets for yourself in Dammeseq: That is, your representatives may occupy a small section of Dammeseq and conduct business as merchants and traders. Essentially, they will have royal authorization to conduct trade between Aram and Yisra'el—undoubtedly a very profitable enterprise for them. The term "streets" (חוצות) refers specifically to a neighborhood or small commercial district. See BDB, p. 300, def. 2a.

54,1a "As Yahweh has directed...: This *parashah* is an addition to the story about the war between Aram and Yisra'el in P52-P54, which itself was an addition to Kings made in the Persian period. I believe the author of P54,1 composed this *parashah* because he took exception to the conclusion of P54, in which the king of Yisra'el shows compassion to Hadadsson. See the discussion of this *parashah* in note 54,1e below.

Notes to P54,1

54,1b when you leave here, a lion's going to kill you: The fate of the prophet's companion is reminiscent of the fate of the holy man in P35 who was killed by a lion because he didn't obey Yahweh. The story of that holy man's death is also a Persian period addition to Kings, and it is not inconceivable that the individual who composed that addition was also the author of the story here in P54,1.

54,1c a *kikkar* of silver: A *kikkar* was three thousand sheqels, equivalent to more than 33 kilograms (see note 24a above). This is an enormous amount of silver beyond the reach of anyone but a king and the wealthiest landowners and merchants.

54,1d a Well, it appears you got what you deserved: The sense of the Hebrew is obscure. The king replies with what I believe must have been a common saying. A literal meaning of the Hebrew is something like, "So you have decided your own case" or "you've decided your own case correctly." That is, based on the facts you just told me, the outcome [i.e. the injuries you suffered because you weren't able to pay the *kikkar* of silver] seems just. I have translated with what I believe is an equivalent English expression.

54,1e on account of the fact that you let go free… your people instead of his people: The prophet pronounces an oracle of doom on the anonymous king of Yisra'el and his people. The term *ḥerem* may be applied to either people or things. When applied to things, it refers to an item that is "banned" from common use and "devoted" to Yahweh's cult, where it may either be destroyed or become the property of the priests. When applied to people, *ḥerem* refers specifically to the extermination of persons who have offended Yahweh or are hostile to him. The term is frequently found in military contexts: in the books of the Torah and in Joshua, it is applied to the Yisra'elites' opponents, and in Samuel and Kings it is applied to the opponents of the kingdom of Yisra'el. It also appears in Isaiah, where it is once applied to Edom and once to Yahweh's people Yisra'el. For additional discussion of the concept of the ban devotion, see my comments in the introduction to my translation of Joshua.

The author of the story in P54,1 writes in the style of old folk tales and so makes all of his characters anonymous. However, we should view the story as a literary work written as a comment on the conclusion to P54. When the prophet in P54,1 refers to the "man" whom the king set free, the author intends the reader to identify the man as Hadadsson King of Aram, whom the king of Yisra'el freed in P54. The point of the prophet's oracle is that because the king let go free a man who should have been exterminated as part of the ban devotion, Yahweh will therefore make the king of Yisra'el and the people of Yisra'el subject to the ban devotion instead. The message here in P54,1 recalls the story in Jos P13,1 - P13,2, in which Yahweh inflicts defeat on the Yisra'elites at Ay as punishment for Akan Karmiysson's violation of the ban devotion proclaimed on Yerihyo.

54,1f sullen and upset: The phrasing is quite unusual. The author of P54,1, which is one of the latest additions to Kings' fourth stage, may have borrowed this language from P55, which is an earlier addition from the fourth stage.

Notes to P55

55a After these events…: This *parashah* and the three that follow (P56 - P58) recount the story of Navoth's vineyard. This story belongs to the cycle of stories about Eliyyahu, which I believe were added to Kings during the second half of the Persian period. At the time this story was added to Kings, it likely followed directly after Iyzevel's message to Eliyyahu in P51,1. It is also possible that it followed directly from P51,2 (the account of Eliysha Shaphatsson's joining Eliyyahu's service), but I think this is less likely. See note 51,2a above.

The story of Navoth's vineyard exemplifies the difficulties and uncertainties of constructing a composition history of Kings. In my composition history, I have felt the most reasonable way to understand the stories about Eliyyahu is as Persian period additions. My decision was driven especially by what I viewed as the presence of late concepts and themes in these stories. The story of Navoth's vineyard, however, is not clearly dependent on any late ideas or themes and it would be possible to treat this story as the only extended material about Eliyyahu that belongs to the earliest version of Kings. The only signs of lateness in P55 are the phrase "King of Shomeron" (see note 55c below) and the substitution of "bless" for "curse" to avoid the phrase "curse God" (see note 55j below), and it is possible to explain both of these away if one wishes to view the *parashah* as early. In my view, the most compelling reason for viewing the story of Navoth's vineyard as a late composition is that the details in it are completely at odds with the statement about his death in P77, which belongs to the earliest version of Kings. In the reference to his murder in P77, there are three—and possibly four—key differences with the story in P55 - P58: (1) in P77, Navoth is murdered on his farm, whereas in P55, he is executed in a public stoning; (2) in P77, Navoth's children are killed alongside him, whereas in P55, only Navoth is killed; (3) it P77, it is Ahav who is responsible for Navoth's murder, but in P55, it is Iyzevel; and (4) the statement in P77 can be understood to imply that Ahav carried out the murders himself with the assistance of teams of men on horseback, whereas in P55 the citizens of Yizre'el (including its leading citizens) carried out the stoning. With respect to the reference to Navoth's murder in P77, see note 77s below.

55b Navoth the Yizre'elite... Yizre'el: This is the town of Yizre'el, not the valley of that name. The town Yizre'el was located in the tribal territory of Yissakar, in the Yizre'el Valley on the northwest spur of Mount Gilboa. The town's location was some 30 kilometers northeast of Shomeron, which was in the Ephrayim mountains.

Many scholars have argued that the mention of Ah'av's palace in Yizre'el indicates that the town served as an important administrative center and a "second capital" alongside Shomeron during the reign of Ah'av. However, given the Persian period date for this *parashah*, it is unclear to me whether any of the information in it preserves an accurate historical memory.

55c King of Shomeron: Note the surname King of Shomeron instead of the expected King of Yisra'el. The kingdom of Yisra'el was sometimes referred to by the name of its capital, Shomeron, as here. Moreover, after the territory of the former kingdom of Yisra'el became a province of the Assyrian empire, the province was called Shomeron. This was also its name when it was a province of the Persian empire. The use of the surname King of Shomeron would be less unusual if we view P55 - P58 as a Persian period composition—that is to say, the presence of the surname makes it less likely that this story belongs to the earliest version of Kings.

55d Ah'av went home: That is, he went back to the palace in Shomeron, not the palace in Yizre'el. We know he must have returned to Shomeron because later in the *parashah* the author's language implies that Ah'av's wife Iyzevel is not in Yizre'el when she sends the letters to Yizre'el's elders.

55e Why don't you feel like eating anything?: There is no interrogative particle here in the Hebrew, but the force of the interrogative particle from the previous clause carries over. An equally plausible functionally equivalent translation that treats this as a statement rather than a question would be "You don't have any appetite" or "You're not eating anything at all."

55f For now, you should just concern yourself...: The author of this story is a masterful writer of dialog. The interaction between Ah'av and Iyzevel is exceptionally vivid—it comes across as true to life and skillfully captures the familiar dynamic between husband and wife. In the Hebrew, Iyzevel emphasizes what Ah'av should do and what in turn she herself will do to help him by using the personal pronouns "you" (אתה) and "I" (אני) in combination with the imperfect form of the verb. To capture the nuance of the Hebrew, I have had to depart further than usual from a literal rendering.

55g sent them: The Hebrew consonantal text reads ותשלח הספרים ("she sent the letters"). Oddly, the Masoretes placed a *qere* in the margin to remove the definite article so that the text reads ותשלח ספרים ("she sent some letters"). The resulting text is grammatically incorrect, as the definite article should be used here according to normal Hebrew practice. See A88 v.2.17 and L201 r.1.3.

55h in his town [*that is, who lived with Navoth*]: The phrase הישבים את נבות ("those who lived with Navoth") may be understood either as a variant reading of "in his town" that has been preserved by a later editor or as a gloss made to clarify that "his town" means the town where Navoth lived. I have a slight preference for the former.

55i two scoundrels: Literally, "two worthless men." The author uses the term בליעל ("worthless"). I believe that when used in a legal context, the term may have had the specific connotation of "false witness," although I have not translated as such here. In particular, see Pvb 19.28: "A false witness [עד בליעל] casts scorn on justice—guilty men by their testimony gulp down trouble." That is, by lying in their testimony, guilty men show disrespect to justice; but in the end, they simply bring [more] trouble on themselves through their lies.

55j 'blessing': The author writes "blessing" as a euphemism for "cursing" (קלל). He specifically uses the euphemism to avoid writing the phrase "curse God." This attitude is characteristic of late literature, and offers some support for the view that the story of Navoth's vineyard was added to Kings in the Persian period.

55k [*that is, the elders and the nobles who lived in his town*]: Another instance of language that may be understood as either a variant reading or a gloss on the preceding phrase, likely by the same editor who preserved the variant (or added the gloss) discussed in note 55h above. The phrase that precedes this editorial intervention is אנשי העיר, which literally means "the men of the town." This phrase often has the specific nuance of "the leading men of town," and—if we understand the bracketed text here as a gloss—then the author of the gloss wished to indicate that the phrase has that meaning here. See note 24m to my translation of Judges for another example of the phrase being used with this nuance.

55l [*that is, exactly as was written in the letters she sent them*]: A third instance of a passage that may be understood as either a gloss or a variant, likely added by the same individual responsible for the two other instances discussed above. If one understands the text here to be a gloss, then it is likely that the author of the gloss wished to explain to the reader the meaning of the verbal phrase שלחה אליהם ("she sent to them"), which is somewhat elliptical. That said, my own view is that all three instances most likely represent variant readings, and not glosses.

55m and had Navoth sit at the head of the people: The verb here (והשיבו) is the perfect with the *waw* consecutive, although we expect the imperfect with the *waw* consecutive (וישיבו). The text does not appear to be in error, however. There are numerous places in Kings where this phenomenon appears, none of which seem to be corrupt. This use of the perfect with the *waw* consecutive as a narrative tense may be due to the influence of Aramaic. See the discussion in GKC § 112 *pp-tt* and the examples cited there. I have translated as though the text is grammatically correct, as this usage of the perfect with the *waw* consecutive happens too often for the occurrence here to be treated as a grammatical error. The author's use of the perfect with the *waw* consecutive here in P55 offer some additional support for viewing this *parashah* as a Persian period composition.

55n They sent a message to Iyzevel: Note the inconsistency in the text. Iyzevel wrote the letters in Ah'av's name and sealed them with his seal. Thus the town's elders should have sent their message to Ah'av. The detail about Iyzevel writing the letters as though they were from Ah'av apparently slipped the author's mind, and consequently he has the town's elders send their message to Iyzevel.

55o Ah'av made ready to go down: The verb ירד ("descend, go down") is used here because Ah'av's journey will take him from Shomeron (in the mountains at an elevation of 440 meters above sea level) down to Yizre'el, less than 100 meters above sea level.

The author uses the construction ויקם ("he stood") followed by the infinitive. This construction has the meaning "make ready" to do the verb in the infinitive. On this construction, see note 14d in my translation of Joshua. Another use of this construction appears in Kgs P73, and is highlighted in note 73b below.

55p **: The Leningrad Codex has a *parashah setumah* here. See L201 r.2.8-9.

56a who in Shomeron: The Hebrew is clearly corrupt. The singular masculine participle form of ישב ("sit") appears to have fallen out of the text. Originally the text must have read "who sits [i.e. is enthroned] in Shomeron." The phrase "who sits in PLACE NAME" is a common expression used to indicate the seat of the king's royal government. The construction is used especially with the kings Siyhon and Og in Numbers (P72) and Deuteronomy (P1; P1,4; and P4).

Notes to P56

56b This is what you must say to him... Then say this to him: There are two consecutive oracles given here. I believe that the first oracle belongs to the original version of P56. Nothing in this *parashah* following this first oracle flows naturally from the narrative or reads as original to the text. The text that follows this first oracle is a mishmash of statements borrowed from elsewhere in Kings that only partially make sense for the Ah'av narrative. I believe that the best explanation for what we currently see in P56 is that all the original material in the *parashah* following the first oracle fell out of the text at some point—several decades or more after the original composition—and that editors working very late in the fourth (or in the sixth) compositional stage "repaired" the *parashah* by patching together a series of statements that appear elsewhere in Kings and that they have applied to Ah'av.

Originally, the *parashah* must have included a scene in which Eliyyahu delivers the first oracle to Ah'av. Note how the *parashah* does not currently include such a scene. Note also how the first oracle does not include an action promising death and destruction to Ah'av and his family. The original version of the first oracle would have certainly included such a statement, and it is this statement that Ah'av is reacting to in P57.

The second oracle here is part of the "repair work" on the *parashah*. The editors making the repair here may cite an actual oracle (or a variant of that oracle) spoken by the historical Eliyyahu. That oracle was originally directed at Iyzevel, but the editors of the repair to P56 have applied it to Ah'av as they need to replace the missing piece of the first oracle promising death and destruction to Ah'av and his family. The original "historical" oracle that is quoted here is also quoted in variant form later in this *parashah* and also in P78 (see the discussion in note 78g below).

56c Did you really commit murder just to seize some property?: Note that in the narrative in P55, Ah'av is not culpable—rather his wife Iyzevel is the guilty one. The oracle here may be an actual oracle of the historical Eliyyahu in reference to the crime against Navoth. There appears to be a reference to the original crime of Ah'av in P77, where Yehu quotes an oracle of Yahweh indicating that Navoth and his children were murdered in his vineyard. If Yehu's quote of the oracle in P77 alludes to an actual historical event, then we must conclude that the authors of the material in P55 - P58 have freely adapted the traditions about Ah'av and Navoth and shifted the blame primarily to Iyzevel.

56d Thus says Yahweh...where dogs will also lap up your blood: As discussed above in note 56b, I believe that this second oracle is not original to the text, but was added as part of the late repair work on this *parashah*. This oracle must have originally been addressed to Iyzevel, and the editors repairing P56 have applied this oracle to Ah'av. Note that this oracle fits Iyzevel's fate in P78.

56e why are you here?: Literally, "have you found me?" I have departed further than usual from a literal rendering of the text to capture the force of the Hebrew. The verb מצא ("find") is often used with the meaning "chance upon, meet unexpectedly." Here Ah'av is expressing surprise and irritation at seeing Eliyyahu, who is always causing him problems. The idea behind Ah'av's statement is something to the effect of "did you really just find me?"—in everyday English the idea is something like "how did you get here?" or "why are you here?"

56f you sold yourself to do what is displeasing to Yahweh: The phrase is nonsensical in this context and is characteristic of the mishmash of borrowed material added to this *parashah* in the repair of the text that was lost (see note 56b above). The authors of the repair have borrowed the phrasing here from P105 (from Kings' third stage), where it is used in reference to the Yisra'elites' apostasy and where it makes perfect sense in its context: "the [i.e. the Yisra'elites] enslaved themselves to doing things that displeased Yahweh, thereby provoking his rage."

56g 'And now I'm going to brin disaster on you...how you provoked me and made Yisra'el err in its ways.': This passage should be understood as the direct speech of Yahweh; it represents an oracle of Yahweh that Eliyyahu delivers to Ah'av. Unusually, there is no phrase introducing the oracle. We expect to read something like, "Therefore, thus says Yahweh" (על־כן כה אמר יהוה). The introductory phrase may be missing because the editors repairing P56 simply omitted it, or it may be that they included the phrase in their repair and it subsequently fell out of the text due to a scribal error.

56h I'm going to brin disaster: Both the Aleppo Codex and Leningrad Codex have an error in the spelling of the participle in the consonantal text, writing מבי instead of the correct form מביא. The Leningrad Codex has a *qere* in the margin correcting the error, but in the Aleppo Codex Aharon ben Asher neglected to place a *qere* here with the correct reading. See A89 r.1.12 and L201 r.2.24. There are two other instances in Kings where ben Asher omits a *qere* with a form of the verb בוא that lacks an *aleph*; see note 30,4f above and note 58a below.

56i I shall cut down Ah'av's last remaining descendant...wherever they are in Yisra'el!: The language here, which is idiomatic, is borrowed from P36 (from Kings' first stage), where it appears in Ahiyyah the Prophet's condemnation of Yarov'am. On the phrases used here and their translation, see notes 38h and 38i.

56j (In addition, this is what Yahweh says about Iyzevel...on Yizre'el's ramparts.'): The oracle about Iyzevel likely represents an actual historical oracle that the editors of the sixth compositional stage have added as a supplement to the repaired condemnation of Ah'av. This is a variant of the oracle discussed in note 78g below and of the second oracle discussed in note 56b above.

56k Anyone in Ah'av's family... will be eaten by the birds!: Note that the authors of this speech have borrowed the exact language of the condemnations of Yarov'am (P38, from the first stage) and of Ba'sha (P44,1, from an earlier edition of the fourth stage) and applied it to Ah'av, in keeping with the earlier statement to make Ah'av's family "just like Yarov'am Nevatsson's, and like Ba'sha Ahiyyahsson's."

56l (Indeed, there's never been the like of Ah'av... the Amorites whom Yahweh drove away from the Yisra'elites.): I view the conclusion to this *parashah* as an editorial comment added by the authors of the sixth compositional stage. Note especially the reference to Yahweh's driving away the Amorites, a theme that is entirely absent from the original material involving Eliyyahu and Eliysha.

56m **: The Leningrad Codex has a *parashah setumah* here. See L201 r.3.16-17.

57a **: The Leningrad Codex has a *parashah setumah* here. See L201 r.3.21.

Note to P57

58a I'm won't brin disaster: Both the Aleppo Codex and Leningrad Codex have an error in the spelling of imperfect verb form in the consonantal text, writing אבי instead of the correct form אביא. The Leningrad Codex has a *qere* in the margin correcting the error, but in the Aleppo Codex Aharon ben Asher neglected to place a *qere* here with the correct reading. See A89 r.2.14 and L201 r.3.25. It is interesting to note that there is a nearly identical spelling error in P56, which is corrected in the Leningrad Codex with a *qere*, but which is not corrected in the Aleppo Codex. See note 56h above.

Notes to P58

58b instead, I'll bring disaster on his family during his son's reign: The story of Navoth's vineyard originally ended with this sentence and was followed directly by the formulaic statement at the end of P59,1 summarizing Ah'av's reign. The conclusion to the story provides the authors' solution to the problem they perceived in the version of Kings as it existed in their day. In that version, Ah'av dies a peaceful death (see the end of P59,1) and Yahweh's oracle condemning him to die in Navoth's vineyard as punishment for Navoth's murder is instead applied to Ah'av's son Yehoram (see P77). To explain this discrepancy, the authors of the story in P55 - P58 conclude their story with a scene in which Yahweh states he will delay carrying out his punishment until the reign of Ah'av's son.

58c Conditions remained peaceful for three years...: The Hebrew is elliptical. Literally, "They lived for three years." The author has omitted the word לבטח ("at peace"), which the reader must supply from context—the phrase ישב לבטח ("live securely") is a common idiom in Biblical Hebrew, and I believe this is what the author intended the reader to understand here. The subject of the verb is indefinite. In using the phrase "three years," the author almost certainly was referring back to the end of P54, when Hadadsson and Ah'av agree to a peace treaty.

I understand the last sentence of this *parashah* to belong to the prophetic material that was appended to the Eliyyahu stories late in Kings' fourth compositional stage. The sentence here introduces the story in P59 - P59,1; it is possible that the author of P59 - P59,1 (and its introduction here in P58) was the same individual who wrote the story in P52 - P54, which also concerns Yisra'el's conflict with Aram.

58d there was no: In the Aleppo Codex, Aharon ben Asher has very strangely placed a *dagesh* in the *yodh* of the particle אין ("there isn't"). I have no explanation for the presence of the dagesh, but merely point it out. Note that the *dagesh* is absent in the Leningrad Codex. See A89 r.2.17 and L201 r.3.27.

Notes to P59

59a It so happened...: I understand the story in P59-P59,1 as purely a literary creation of its author, who uses his composition to argue theological points important to him regarding the nature of prophecy. Note that the author of the story makes the king of Yisra'el anonymous, likely because he wished the reader to focus on the theological points he was making, and not on the character of the notorious Ah'av. In crafting his story, the author appears to have taken details about the death of Yehoram Ah'avsson and applied them to Yehoram's father Ah'av.[2]

I believe the story in P59-P59,1 was added late in the fourth compositional stage, several decades after most of the additions about Eliyyahu and Eliysha, and certainly after the story of Navoth's vineyard in P55-P58. Note that the author of the story in P59-P59,1 has changed the circumstances of Ah'av's death so that he now dies a violent death, as predicted in Yahweh's oracle in P56 and in what was the original oracle about Ah'av in P77. I do not believe the portrayal of Ah'av's death as a violent one was necessarily intentional or a well thought-out decision on the part of the author—rather Ah'av's violent death is simply a by-product of the author's choice to borrow details about Yehoram's death for his story. This, however, created inconsistencies with the earlier narrative about Ah'av in P58 (which states Yahweh wouldn't bring disaster during Ah'av's reign) and at the end of P59,1 (which states that Ah'av died a peaceful death).

The story in P59-P59,1 contains a fascinating depiction of prophecy. Although the author of the story was writing long after prophecy had ceased, his comments give us some insight into how the prophets of old were understood by individuals in Yahweh's cult during the Persian period. Three points stand out. First, the author implies that prophets of one god sometimes gave oracles in the name of another god (see note 59d directly below). Second, he viewed prophets' delivery of their oracles as highly performative in nature: one prophet in his story dons iron horns and imitates a bull when delivering his oracle, while a second prophet recounts in vivid detail his vision of Yahweh sending a divine being to trick the king's prophets. Finally, the prophets deliver oracles in ways that are intended to provoke and offend—and in fact, one prophet's oracle in P59,1 prompts a second prophet to assault him.

59b Will you go with me into battle at Ramoth Gil'ad?...my cavalry alongside your cavalry: The author of the story presents Yehudah's alliance with Yisra'el as a voluntary one, but he is writing centuries after the period in which the story is set. During that period, Yehudah was a vassal state of Yisra'el, and to the extent that Yehudah ever did join Yisra'el in battle against Aram, it would have been under coercion. Note here also the author's mention of cavalry. The earliest evidence of cavalry is from the kingdom of Ashshur in the mid-ninth century BCE. At the time this story is set (also mid-ninth century), it is likely that neither Yisra'el nor Yehudah would have yet established a true cavalry—a fact of which the story's author would have been unaware. See notes 11,1a and 52i above.

---

2   Specifically, he has borrowed the detail about Yehoram being mortally wounded in his chariot during a battle with Aram, which he may have known from oral tradition. Note that the authors of Kings' first stage have changed the circumstances of Yehoram's death for their own literary purposes; in their account in P77, it is Yehu who kills Yehoram in his chariot. However, evidence from the Tel Dan inscription suggests that in fact it was Haza'el who killed Yehoram King of Yisra'el and Ahazyahu King of Yehudah. For the reconstruction of the inscription proposing that these two kings were killed by Haza'el, see A. Biran and J. Naveh, "The Tel Dan Inscription: A New Fragment," *Israel Exploration Journal* 45 (1995), pp. 1-18.

59c Midpoint of the book: As a means to help safeguard the integrity of the text, the Masoretes marked the exact midpoint of each book in the Tanakh with a marginal note stating חצי הספר ("halfway point of the scroll"); these notes were typically adorned with a simple geometrical design. For Kings, the midpoint of the book is the sentence beginning "So the king of Yisra'el gathered the prophets." I have reproduced the note for Kings here along with the geometrical design found in the Aleppo Codex. See A.89 r.3.7 and L201 v.1.15 for these notes and the designs adorning them.

59d lord Adonay: The term אדני (traditionally translated "my lord") was often used as an epithet of Yahweh. In many instances, the term functions as a divine name in its own right, in much the same way "El" and "El Shaddai" function as the names of gods with which Yahweh is identified. I believe אדני here serves as a divine name, and thus I translate as "lord Adonay" rather than the traditional rendering "my lord." There is quite a large scholarly literature on how best to understand the term *'adōnay* when used as a divine name; I follow those scholars who see the suffix *-ay* as a "nominal afformative" that emphasizes the root meaning of the word. For a detailed discussion of the issues, see O. Eissfeldt, "אָדוֹן *'adhón*," in G. Botterweck and H. Ringgren (eds.), *Theological Dictionary of the Old Testament*, Vol. 1 (Grand Rapids: William Eerdmans, 1974), pp. 59-72.

It's worth noting the oddness of the narrative in this *parashah*: these are not prophets of Yahweh (as we know from Yehoshaphat's question that follows this oracle), yet the prophets state that Adonay (i.e. Yahweh) will give the king of Yisra'el victory in his fight for Ramoth Gil'ad. The fact that he mentions there are four hundred prophets suggests that he intends the reader to understand that these are prophets to the Ba'al (recall that there are four hundred prophets of the Ba'al in the story in P51,1) and that they are giving oracles in Yahweh's name. It is especially odd that in response to Yehoshaphat's original request to consult an oracle from Yahweh, the king of Yisra'el chose to consult the prophets to the Ba'al instead of Yahweh's prophet Miykayehu. One final comment: it is interesting that one of the Ba'a'ls prophets has a Yahwistic name—Tzidqiyyah Kena'anahsson, who gives an oracle from Yahweh that the king of Yisra'el will "gore Aram again and again."

59e Isn't there any prophet of Yahweh still here from whom we can seek an oracle: The reader should understand Yehoshaphat's statement to mean that he didn't trust the oracle of the four hundred prophets whom the king of Yisra'el gathered together. Although they delivered an oracle in Yahweh's name, they were not true prophets of Yahweh.

59f but I despise him... he never prophesies good things about me: I believe the author intended this passage to be humorous. The depiction of the prophets in P59 and P59,1 contains a number of humorous elements, which I point out in the notes below.

59g sitting on their own special chairs... in the threshing area in front of Shomeron's town gate: It is not clear whether the threshing area was inside or outside the town gate, as just inside all town gates was a large plaza (רחוב) where business and trade was conducted. That said, I have a preference for understanding the kings as sitting outside the town gate, as the plaza would not have been large enough for four hundred prophets plus the two kings and their attendants.

59h all the prophets were chanting similarly: The scene depicted here—Tzidqiyyah running around holding iron horns to his head and the other prophets egging him on—is farcical, and I believe the author intended his readers to see it that way. There was a strong element of performance art in the behavior of the prophets during the times of the monarchy—behavior that many people undoubtedly found absurd and mocked, as the author of this *parashah* is doing here.

59i your oracles ought to be like one of theirs—say something agreeable: The author likely intended the scene between the messenger and Miykayehu to be humorous.

The consonantal text of both the Aleppo Codex and the Leningrad Codex reads דבריך ("your oracles" in the context here), but then correct this by vocalizing the word as the singular ("your oracle"). The Leningrad Codex has a *qere* in the margin with the correct consonants, but somewhat unusually, Aharon ben Asher has neglected to write a *qere* in the margin here. See A89 v.1.15 and L201 v.2.21. See notes 56h and 58a for other examples of ben Asher omitting a *qere*. My translation reflects the consonantal text.

59j "Go and prevail!... Yahweh's going to deliver it into the king's hands: Miykayehu repeats the "agreeable" words the prophets had chanted to the king of Yisra'el. However, the reader should understand Miykayehu's tone here to be one of sarcasm and contempt, as is clear from the king of Yisra'el's response to him in the following sentence. The author likely intended the interaction between Miykayehu and the king to be humorous.

59k "I now see all Yisra'el scattering to the mountains...: Miykayehu is in a trance, and he is reporting the vision that he sees while entranced. There are many indications in the Tanakh that prophets in both Yisra'el and Yehudah entered a trance-like state in order to receive oracles from Yahweh, and they often experienced these oracles as visions.

59l Didn't I tell you...that he wouldn't prophesy something good about me: The king of Yisra'el's comment to Yehoshaphat is another instance of humor.

59m —: The Leningrad Codex does not have a *parashah* break here. See L201 v.3.14.

Notes to P59,1

59,1a I see Yahweh sitting on his throne, with the entire army of the sky standing next to him: The author likely intended the reader to understand that Mikykayehu is in a trance. See note 59k above. Miykayehu's vision of Yahweh seems to have been influenced by the special name of Yahweh that was associated with the cult on Mount Tziyyon: "Yahweh [God] of Armies" (יהוה צבאות). The word צבא means both "army" and "star;" thus the phrase צבא השמים ("army of the sky") can be understood as a reference to the stars.

Miykayehu reports his vision with verbs in the past tense. In my translation, I have rendered the verbs in the present tense, as the present tense is more natural in English when reporting an event as it occurs.

59,1b Who will trick Ah'av: This is the sole mention of Ah'av in the story in P59-P59,1. Everywhere else in this story, the king of Yisra'el is anonymous. As discussed above in note 59a, in crafting this story, the author borrowed details about Yehoram Ah'avson's's death and applied them to the king of Yisra'el (the mostly anonymous Ah'av).

59,1c When the hell: The author uses the phrase אי־זה—literally "where this." The particle זה ("this") was often used in Hebrew speech in a pejorative sense, to express strong negative emotion or disapproval, or to denigrate. That is clearly the use here, and I have reflected the force of the Hebrew phrasing by translating with a functionally equivalent English phrase.

59,1d It's when you had a vision of how in the future you'd run off in a panic and go hide in a closet: Miykayehu's retort is obnoxious and insulting to Tzidqiyyahu, but the author also intends the reader to find it humorous. In my translation I have departed a little further than usual from the Hebrew in order to capture the humor in Miykayehu's response.

59,1e this bastard: The author writes simply זה—literally "this [man]." This is another example of the pejorative use of the demonstrative particle. See note 59,1c above.

59,1f all them people here: The text is awkward and is very likely corrupt. The Hebrew reads כלם ("all of them"); it is possible that the letter *kaph* has fallen out of the text. Adding that to the text produces כלכם ("all of you"), which is a more natural reading: "all you people here." It also seems likely to me that Miykayehu added some further condemnation of the king of Yisra'el following the command to "listen up" and that this additional condemnation has fallen out of the text.

59,1g Now the king of Aram had given orders...: The orders not to engage anyone except the king of Yisra'el apply only to the chariotry. We should assume that all the infantry of Aram are engaged in general combat.

59,1h The chiefs of the charioty then realized that he wasn't the king of Yisra'el: It is not clear how they recognized Yehoshaphat wasn't the king of Yisra'el; possibly the author intended the reader to understand that when Yehoshaphat gave the loud cry, the chiefs of the charioty recognized the accent as Yehudite and not Yisra'elite.

59,1i on the seam of his armor between the breastplate and the shoulder flaps: Literally, "between the attachments and the breastplate." It is uncertain what the author is describing, and my translation represents my best guess as to his intent.

59,1j the battle continued throughout the day: The author uses somewhat unusual phrasing—ותעלה המלחמה (literally, "the battle went up"). The verb עלה ("go up") can mean "to extend" in a geographical sense (see BDB, p. 749, def. 9 of the *qal*), and here context requires that it mean "to extend" in a chronological sense.

59,1k the dogs lapped up his blood, just as Yahweh's oracle foretold: It is doubtful that the author had a specific oracle in mind in this statement. I think it more likely he added the comment "just as Yahweh's oracle foretold" to make the the concluding scene of his story more dramatic. Note that there is no oracle about Ah'av that fits these circumstances. The second oracle in P56 (which is part of the material added in the "repair" of that *parashah*) states that the dogs will lap up Ah'av's blood where they lapped up Navoth's blood—that is, in Yizre'el, not Shomeron. (Moreover, as I suggest in note 56b above, that oracle was originally about Iyzevel.) And the original oracle about Ah'av, which appears in P77, states simply that Yahweh "will pay back" Ah'av on the plot of land where Navoth was killed (that is, on Navoth's farm).

The imagery in this scene has a nice literary quality to it: the juxtaposition of the prostitutes bathing while the dogs lap up the blood in the rinse water as it drips from the king's chariot nearby is quite striking.

59,1l The rest of Ah'av's acts...: The last two sentences of the *parashah* are part of the earliest edition of Kings. Originally, they followed directly from material in P49. In the earliest version of Kings, the account of Ah'av's reign was very short—just the first seven sentences of P49 and the last two of P59,1.

59,1m the ivory house that he built: Ivory was a highly valued luxury good in the ancient Near East. Royalty and many of the wealthiest members of society prized furniture with elaborate ivory inlays and they often used ivory inlays to decorate architectural features in their houses. The prophet Amos refers to the "ivory houses" of Yisra'el in an oracle condemning Yisra'el in Am 3.15, and in the first oracle in Am 6, he mentions "those who lie upon ivory beds."

The site of Shomeron was excavated in the early twentieth century by the British archaeologist Kathleen Kenyon. In the excavations, some 12,000 ivory fragments were found, nearly all of which decorated furniture or interior architectural features of buildings. Only a small number of the ivory pieces were published in the final excavation report in 1938. Claudia Suter of the University of Basel is currently working on a comprehensive catalog of the Samarian ivories. She has published several papers on the ivories which are available on her webpage at academia.edu.

59,1n Ah'av lay down in death with his ancestors: This formula is used in *The Chronicles of the Kings of Yisra'el* and in *The Chronicles of the Kings of Yehudah* in connection with kings who died a peaceful death. The statement here is an indication that in fact Ah'av died a peaceful death, and the prophetic story about Yehoshaphat and the king of Yisra'el in P59 - P59,1 has no connection to the historical Ah'av.

Notes to P60

60a Yehoshaphat made a peace agreement with the king of Yisra'el: This sentence likely appeared in the source document, *The Chronicles of the Kings of Yehudah*. It is somewhat unusual that it does not specify which king of Yisra'el the peace agreement was with. Yehoshaphat's reign overlapped with three kings of Yisra'el—Ah'av, Ahazyahu, and Yoram; assuming the statement about a peace agreement is historically accurate, his peace agreement would have been with one of those three kings. Recall that prior to Ah'av there was "perpetual war" between the kings of Yisra'el and Yehudah. See P40, P41, P42,1, and P43.

60b The remainder of the *qedesh*-prostitutes... but Yehoshaphat wouldn't give his consent.): The paragraph represented here I believe is a later addition to the text, as it interrupts the formula about Yehoshaphat's death. This material was likely added by the authors of Kings' second compositional stage, and they may have lifted it directly from their source *The Chronicles of the Kings of Yehudah*. It is worth noting that the text here suggests the source document contained material about *qedesh*-prostitutes during the time of Yehoshaphat's father Asa. And in fact, the account of Asa's reign in P42 - P42,1 does mention that he abolished the *qedesh*-prostitutes. The mention of the *qedesh*-prostitutes in P42 suggests that they were in some way connected to Yahweh's cult, although many scholars today argue this association of prostitution with Yahweh's cult is incorrect. See note 42c above.

60c Yehoshaphat mare Tarshiysh-ships for voyaging to Ophiyr... but Yehoshaphat wouldn't give his consent.): The material in P60 about Yehoshaphat's trading ships has numerous details in common with the material in P24,1 and P27 about Shelomo's trading ships. It seems likely to me that the material about Yehoshaphat's trading ships reflects actual historical events, and that the authors of the Shelomo material in P24,1 and P27 borrowed from the material about Yehoshaphat in the *The Chronicles of the Kings of Yehudah*. That is to say, the comments about Shelomo's trading operations likely have no basis in history and were an invention of the authors of the Josianic study books. (On the term "Tarshiysh-ship," see note 27d above.)

60d (At the time Ahazyahu Ah'avsson had proposed to Yehoshaphat...: The Hebrew is somewhat ambiguous. There is no distinction between the perfect and pluperfect tenses in Hebrew verb forms, and the sentence reads naturally in either understanding of the verb tense. I have translated with the pluperfect and treat the sentence as a comment by the author providing additional context about the failed trading mission—that Yehoshaphat refused the offer to make this mission a joint venture with Yisra'el (which possessed experienced naval officers). It is also possible, although less likely in my opinion, to understand the verb in the perfect and continuing the narrative. In this understanding, the translation would read, "Ahazyahu Ah'avsson then proposed to Yehoshaphat"—that is, he proposed a joint venture with Yehoshaphat after the failure of Yehoshaphat's original plan.

60,1a Yarov'am Nevatsson who caused Yisra'el to do wrong: A reference to the efforts of Yarov'am to expand and support the cult of Yahweh in the northern kingdom in ways that the authors of the Josianic study books believe are abhorrent to Yahweh (see P32,1 and P36 for these authors' account of Yarov'am's actions). The actions that "caused Yisra'el to do wrong" include installing statues of Yahweh in the form of a bull calf in the shrines in Beyth-El and Dan, establishing shrines to Yahweh on the hill tops and designating "people from all over" as priests. The authors of the Josianic study books viewed anyone who made an offering at the shrines in Beyth-El or Dan, or who made an offering in one of the open-air shrines, as "doing wrong;" thus, by promoting and supporting these cult sites, Yarov'am "caused Yisra'el to do wrong."

Notes to P60,1

60,1b He gave service to the Ba'al... similar to all the things his father had done: Yahweh is the national god of Yisra'el, but Ahazyahu chooses to give service to the Ba'al in preference to Yahweh. Recall that Ahazyahu's father Ah'av was also a devotee of the Ba'al (see P49).

60,1c Lord Horse Fly: I understand זבוב (the name for a kind of flying insect) to be a divine name. The construction בעל זבוב (Lord Horse Fly) is similar to other terms that prefix a divine name with "lord," such as בעל גד (Lord Gad) and בעל המון (Lord Hamon). Lord Horse Fly is the local god of the Philisthine town Eqron, hence his surname is God of Eqron.

60,2a "Go at once to meet the king of Shomeron's messengers...: The story in P60,2 - 60,3 is part of the cycle of stories about Eliyyahu and reads as a very late addition to the text. As discussed above in note 51,2a, I view the stories about Eliyyahu and Eliysha as being added in a piecemeal fashion over a period of a century or more. The earliest stories added were likely those about Eliyyahu in P49,1 and P51,1, followed later by P55 - P58. At a later time, the first material about Eliysha was added. The material about Eliysha in turn led to the creation of new stories about Eliyyahu in which Eliyyahu took on supernatural powers similar to those of Eliysha; these stories are found in P49,3 and P50. The story here in P60,2 likely post-dates the stories in P49,3 and P50, and represents the latest material about Eliyyahu, where the ideas of him as a holy man with supernatural powers find their fullest expression.

Notes to P60,2

There are numerous indications of a late date for the story in P60,2—note in particular the use of the term "King of Shomeron" and the fantastical element of the divine fire coming down from the sky and obliterating two of the three battalions sent to Eliyyahu. The story disrupts the Josianic study books' account of the death of Ahazyahu—it seems likely to me that when the story in P60,2 - 60,3 was added, a sentence or two about Ahazyahu's death was removed. It was quite rare for later authors and editors to delete material from the work they expanded, but there is good reason to think that it did happen on occasion. The text here provides a good example of that. One indication that the original text has been disrupted is the confusing and disjointed nature of the transitions between P60,3 and P61 and between P61 and P61,1, where *parashot* appear in places they are normally not seen. See notes 60,3a and 60,3b below.

60,2b Therefore, thus says Yahweh: 'You won't get down from the bed you climbed into...: Note the tension in the text due to the change of address. The previous sentence of Yahweh's oracle is addressed to the king of Shomeron's messengers, but this sentence is addressed to the king of Shomeron himself (Ahazyahu). In my opinion, this tension is an indication of an editorial intervention. I believe that the earliest version of Kings included a short passage in which Yahweh commands Eliyyah the Tishbite to go to Ahazyahu and deliver an oracle condemning him to death. This passage has been replaced by the story in P60,2. The original version of the oracle in the lost passage is reproduced in P60,3 (all but the first sentence of which is from Kings' first stage). The authors of the story here in P60,2 altered the scene in which Yahweh (or his envoy) tells Eliyyah to deliver the oracle in order to fit their story. Specifically, they changed the original oracle so that Eliyyah addresses the king's messengers rather than the king himself.

60,2c The king then dispatched a battalion captain and his battalion of fifty men: This sentence illustrates one of the oddities of Hebrew pronoun usage that creates difficulties for the translator. The verb here is the *qal* of שׁלח ("send") conjugated as the third person masculine singular. The subject of the verb may be understood in two ways: (1) the king is the subject, which is a natural way to understand the verb given that the king was the subject of the verb in the previous sentence; or (2) the subject is indefinite, which the author has used to represent the passive voice (ancient Hebrew prose authors very often used the active verb with an indefinite subject in contexts where English uses the passive). Both options are equally plausible. Complicating matters, ancient Hebrew prose authors frequently did not specify the subject of their verbs when it is clear from context who or what the subject is, and the author of the story in P60,2 - P60,3 has an especially strong tendency to do this. Taking all this into account, I have a slight preference for understanding the king as the subject here, and I have translated as such. The one downside of this approach is that it does smooth over the awkwardness in the Hebrew, which is not captured by my translation.

60,2d The captain went up: The Hebrew reads simply "he went up." This sentence is a good example of an instance of the author of this story not specifying the subject of his verbs when it is expected. See note 60,2c directly above.

60,2e Holy man: In the earliest stories about Eliyyahu (P49,1, P51 - P51,1 and P55 - P58), he is never called a holy man (איש האלהים). In P49,1 and P55 - P58, although he is called only by his gentilic ("the Tishbite"), he acts strictly as a prophet, receiving and delivering oracles from Yahweh. In P51,1, he also acts as a prophet and—equally important—specifically refers to himself as a prophet (נביא) to Yahweh. As discussed above in notes 51,2a and note 60,2a, in the later stories about him, he took on aspects of Eliysha, who was commonly called "holy man." Thus we see here in P60,2, which I believe is the latest story about Eliyyahu, he is always called holy man and never called prophet.

60,2f So another battalion caption and his battalion of fifty men were dispatched: See note 60,2c above. Here I have chosen to translate with the passive rather than to supply the subject of the verb in order to capture some of the awkwardness of the Hebrew. It is possible, however, that the author intended the verb to be understood as active, with the king as the subject.

60,2g answered and said to him: The Hebrew is nonsensical, and there is likely an error in the text. I believe the text originally read "went up and said to him"—this requires the change of only a single letter, from ויען ("he answered") to ויעל ("he went up"). It is easy to see how a scribe might have made this error under the influence of the following sentence, which contains the verbal construction "answered and said."

60,2h Eliyyah said in reply to them: We expect to read "Eliyyah said in reply to him." Hebrew is much more flexible than English in its use of pronouns, and it is not unusual for authors to shift use of pronouns in ways that an English-speaker would find illogical. In the text here, however, I believe the shift in pronouns may be the result of a later scribal error. Because the accounts of Eliyyahu's audience with each of the battalion captains are repetitive and formulaic, it seems likely to me that the text here originally read "Eliyyah said in reply to him" (ויען אליה וידבר אליו).

60,2i So a third battalion caption and his battalion of fifty men were dispatched: See note 60,2f above.

60,3a And so he died... Yehoram became king in his place ...: The account of Ahazyahu's death, which begins here at the end of P60,3 and continues in two very brief *parashot*, P61 and P61,1, is quite jumbled. In the accounts of the deaths of other kings of Yisra'el and Yehudah, the statement regarding the king's successor typically occurs after the statement that a full account of the king's reign can be found in the kingdom's royal chronicles. In the account of Ahazyahu's death, however, the statement about the successor occurs here at the end of P60,3 and in P61, before the reference to the source document, which is given in P61,1. The jumbled character of the account is somewhat explicable, however, if one accepts the proposal that the authors of the story about Eliyyahu in P60,2 - P60,3 have rewritten the account of Ahazyahu's death to accommodate their story. See notes 60,2a and 60,2b above.

Notes to P60,3

60,3b **: While *parashot petuhot* occasionally are used to mark an ellipsis, there is no logical reason for an ellipsis here between P60,3 and P61. The presence of a *parashah petuhah* here adds to the jumbled character of the account of Ahazyahu's death, and offers some support for the proposal that the original version of the account was altered in a later compositional stage. See notes 60,2a, 60,2b, and 60,3a above.

61a in the second year of the reign of Yehoram Yehoshaphatsson: There is an inconsistency in the chronology of Yehoram Ah'avsson's reign that is challenging to resolve. In fact, the chronology of his reign provides a good example of the extreme difficulties of making sense of the various chronological references in Kings in a satisfactory way. Here in P61, Yehoram Ah'avsson succeeds his brother Ahazyahu on the throne of Yisra'el in the second year of Yehoram Yehoshaphatsson. However, in P64, we are told that Yehoram Ah'avsson became king in the eighteenth year of Yehoshaphat. This inconsistency can be resolved if we understand that Yehoshaphat in the latter years of his reign placed his son Yehoram on the throne and the two then ruled as "co-regents," with the co-regency being established in Yehoshaphat's seventeenth year. However, this doesn't completely solve our problem: the proposal for a co-regency beginning in Yehoshaphat's seventeeth year creates an inconsistency with the chronology at the beginning of P75, which alludes to the co-regency and states that Yehoram Yehoshaphatsson became king of Yehudah in the fifth year of Yoram Ah'avsson's reign. This would mean that the co-regency of Yehoshaphat and his son began in the twenty-third year of Yehoshaphat's reign, not the seventeenth year. In the chronology that I propose in the appendix to this book, a co-regency between Yehoram and Yehoshaphat beginning in Yehoshaphat's twenty-third year best fits the requirements of fitting the chronology of Yisra'el and Yehudah to events

Notes to P61

firmly dated from Mesopotamian inscriptions.

In my proposed chronology in the appendix, I treat the synchronisms in P64 and P75 as correct and the synchronism here in P61 as incorrect. With respect to this error, it's worth noting that the original account of Ahazyahu's death and Yehoram's assumption of the throne was heavily revised when the material about Eliyyahu was added (see the notes above to P60,2 and P60,3). It is most likely, in my opinion, that the erroneous synchronism crept into the text when the material about Ahazyahu was rewritten.

61b —: The Leningrad Codex does not have a *parashah* break here. See L203 r.1.26.

Notes to P62

62a Eliyyahu and Eliysha had left Gilgal on a journey: The travels of Eliyyahu and Eliysha in this *parashah* are somewhat confusing. Four sites are mentioned: Gilgal, Beyth-El, Yeriyho, and the Yarden River. It is most natural to assume that the Gilgal where the men start is the prominent cult site which is just west of the Yarden River and very close to Yeriyho. In this reading, after leaving Gilgal, they travel west into the Ephrayim hill country to Beyth-El, the most important cult site in the northern kingdom. From Beyth-El, they reverse their course and head back in the direction they started and arrive at Yeriyho, which is only a few kilometers from Gilgal. From Yeriyho they cross the Yarden River, at which point a fiery chariot appears and a whirlwind takes Eliyyahu up into the sky. The rationale for the roundabout trip is unclear; possibly, the author of the story simply wished to include Beyth-El because of its importance, even though including it made the route of the journey nonsensical.

It is possible that the author had in mind a different Gilgal. Deut P12,5 mentions a site called Gilgal that is near Shekem. If this was the Gilgal intended by the author, then the route of the journey would be much more logical, as the entire journey would be in a southeastern direction. While this reading produces a more logical journey, I do not think that this is what the author intended. If he had intended the reader to identify this Gilgal with the site near Shekem, he most likely would have written "Gilgal in Menashsheh" (הגלגל אשר למנשה).

62b Please stay here: That is, please stay in Gilgal.

62c Eliyyahu...struck the water...whereupon the water split into two: Note the implicit comparison of Eliyyahu to Mosheh and, to a lesser extent, Yehoshua. See Exod P25 and Jos P6.

62d I wish that a double portion of your power might be given to me: In the following sentence, Eliyyahu replies that Eliysha's wish will be granted if Eliysha sees him being taken away, which Eliysha does. This interaction establishes the foundation for the many miracles of Eliysha, which are more numerous than those of Eliyyahu. As discussed above, Eliyyahu was not originally a miracle-worker. The stories about him as a miracle worker are based on the stories about Eliysha; by portraying Eliyyahu as possessing powers similar to Eliysha, the authors of Kings' fourth stage make Eliysha a more worthy successor of Eliyyahu. That is to say, if Eliyyahu were not a miracle worker, one might question why Eliysha possessed supernatural powers when his master and mentor did not.

62e Eliyyahu shot up into the sky in a whirlwind: The whirlwind that the author had in mind is likely what we today call a dust devil (or sand devil), which is relatively common in modern-day Israel. The dust devil is a wind vortex of low to intermediate strength, and is significantly weaker than a tornado. There is a nice photo of a dust devil near Hebron in the article "Like the pillar of a cloud – about tornados, dust devils, and water and land spouts in Israel" at the Israel Meteorological Service website.

62f Yisra'el's chariotry and cavalry!: Eliysha's cry is somewhat cryptic. It is unclear what he means by likening Eliyyahu to Yisra'el's military forces. The phrase also appears in P88, where Yo'ash King of Yisra'el applies it to Eliysha, who is on his deathbed. The phrase does make some sense in P88, as the traditions about Eliysha show him serving in military contexts and contributing to Yisra'el's military success (see especially the story in P70). It seems likely to me that the phrase originally was part of the Eliysha traditions, and the authors of Kings' fourth stage applied it to Eliyyahu as part of their broader effort to connect Eliysha to Eliyyahu, which involved the figure of Eliyyahu taking on numerous characteristics that were original to Eliysha and vice versa.

62g he did grab hold of his clothes, tearing them into two pieces: The detail about Eliysha grabbing Eliyyahu's clothes and tearing them in two is strange, as the pieces are not mentioned again. The torn clothing is separate from the cloak, which fell off Eliyyahu and which seems to possess some magical power.

62h Where is Eliyyahu's god Yahweh? Where is he?: The Hebrew is somewhat ambiguous. The author uses the phrase אף־הוא ("even he"), which may refer to either Eliyyahu or to Yahweh. I have a slight preference for the latter option, and I understand the phrase as serving to repeat the question for emphasis, which is reflected in my translation. If we view the phrase as referring to Eliyyahu, then an appropriate translation would be, "Where is Yahweh, the god of our very own Eliyyahu?"

62i He struck the water again, and it split into two: This is the first miracle of Eliysha and it repeats the miracle performed by Eliyyahu earlier in the *parashah*.

The following represents the full list of Eliysha's miracles and supernatural powers: parting the waters of the Yarden (P62), curing the waters of Yeriyho (P62,1), causing the death of forty-two boys through a curse (P63), causing a jar to have an inexhaustible supply of olive oil (P66), pronouncing a barren woman fertile (P67), resurrecting a dead boy (P67), curing Na'aman of leprosy (P69), seeing Gehaziy visit Na'aman (P69,1), inflicting leprosy on Gehaziy (P69,1), causing an ax-head to float (P69,1), seeing the location of the Aramean army (P70), making his servant see Yahweh's hidden army (P70), blinding the forces of Aram (P70), foreseeing the arrival of his intended assassin (P71), and foretelling the death of the king's deputy (P72). The prediction of Yisra'el's victory over Aram in P88 may also be seen as stemming from Eliysha's supernatural powers. In addition, it is possible to view Eliysha's fixing the bitter-tasting stew in P68 and his feeding one hundred men with twenty loaves of bread in P68,1 as miracles, although I do not understand either story in that way. It is especially interesting that in many of the miracles performed by Eliysha, Yahweh is entirely absent or has minimal involvement—this likely reflects the folk background of these stories, which portrayed Eliysha as a miracle worker and not a prophet.

Apart from the identical miracles of dividing the Yarden River, in the two other instances where Eliyyahu and Eliysha perform similar miracles, Eliysha's miracles are more impressive. Eliysha's miracle in P66 can be viewed as "twice as powerful" as Eliyyahu's miracle in P49,3—Eliyyahu produces enough food for the family to eat "for several days," whereas Eliysha produces enough oil for the widow to pay off her oppressive debts and to support herself and her sons thereafter. Likewise, Eliysha's resurrection of the boy in P67 seems "twice as powerful" as Eliyyahu's miracle in P50—the boy dies in P67, whereas he is only near death in P50.

62j they pressed him to the point of embarrassment: The author uses a common Hebrew idiom here—"to the point of embarrassment" (עד בוש). For another example of this idiom, see the story of Ehud in Jud P12.

62k —: The Leningrad Codex does not have a *parashah* break here. See L203 v.1.24.

Note to P62,1

62,1a Yeriyho's leading townsmen: I have added the reference to Yeriyho, which is required by the usual practices of English prose composition. Ancient Hebrew prose writers, by contrast, often did not feel the need to inform the reader of the geographical setting if it could easily be inferred from context, as is the case here. The phrase that I translate "leading townsmen" in Hebrew reads simply "the men of the town" (אנשי העיר). This phrase has a range of meanings, one of which is "the leading men of the town," and the reader must use context to determine which meaning is intended by the author. For further discussion of this phrase, see note 24m in my translation of Judges.

Notes to P63

63a As he ascended the road: Yeriyho lies nearly nine hundred feet below sea level, whereas Beyth-El, which is approximately 15 miles to the west, has an elevation of over 2,500 feet above sea level. Much of the elevation gain is in the first miles, and the road Eliysha would have been traveling on must have been relatively steep.

63b some little boys came out from town: That is, they came from Yeriyho. The phrase נערים קטנים ("little boys") most likely describes boys somewhere in the age range of six to ten. In the next sentence the author describes them as ילדים ("children"), which would also fit that age range.

63c From there he proceeded to Mount Karmel...he returned to Shomeron: The narrative seems confused—it is unclear whether the author intended the phrase "from there" to be understood as from Beyth-El or from the place near Yeriyho where the bears attacked the children. If it is the latter, then no explanation is given for why the trip to Beyth-El was abandoned. Moreover, the author gives no rationale for why Eliysha went to Mount Karmel. Finally, the author states that Eliysha "returned" to Shomeron, but up to this point in the narrative, he has never been to Shomeron.

Notes to P64

64a Yehoram Ah'avsson became king over Yisra'el...: In the earliest edition of Kings, this *parashah* followed directly from P61,1. On the chronology of Yehoram Ah'avsson's reign, see note 61a above.

64b although not to the extent of his father and mother: I have expressed the idea of the Hebrew in natural English. Literally, "although not like his father nor like his mother."

64c he persisted in the errors of Yarov'am Nevatsson: That is, he maintained royal support for the cults in Beyth-El and Dan.

64d **: The Leningrad Codex has a *parashah setumah* here. See L203 v.3.4.

Notes to P65

65a Meysha King of Mo'av was a breeder of sheep...: This *parashah* (P65) and the following *parashah* (P65,1) tell the story of the war between Mo'av and the allied forces of Yisra'el, Yehudah, and Edom. This story belongs to the Eliysha material and was added to Kings as part of the work in the book's fourth compositional stage. While the broad outline of the story may reflect the memory of actual historical events, the story was added to Kings three to four centuries after the events it describes and it is doubtful that many of the details are historically trustworthy (see note 65b directly below). In fact, I believe that P65-P65,1 represents a very late story composed in order to represent Eliysha as a "prophet" and not just a holy man. When the authors of the fourth stage added the Eliysha material, they did much work to connect Eliysha to Eliyyahu in order to make him appear as a natural successor. This involved composing stories that showed Eliyyahu as a miracle-working holy man and other stories that showed Eliysha as a prophet of Yahweh in the traditional mold.

Meysha King of Mo'av who appears here in P65 is the Meysha of the famous Mesha Stele (also called the Moabite Stone). Although most scholars believe this inscription is genuine, I think the arguments for it being a forgery are compelling. See A. Yehuda, "The Story of a Forgery and the Mēša Inscription," *The Jewish Quarterly Review*, vol. 35, no. 2 (1944), pp. 139-164 and D. Ventura, "The Mesha Stele: A Reappraisal of a Forgery," Figshare (2021).

Meysha is called a נקד (*nōqēd*), which I have translated as "a breeder of sheep." In Arabic, the word *naqada* denotes a small sheep with abundant wool.

65b When Ah'av died... In response King Yehoram left Shomeron and embarked on a military campaign: Note that the author of this story is either unaware of or chooses to ignore the reign of Ahazyahu—in the story here, Yehoram rather than Ahazyahu succeeds Ah'av. The author of this story is writing at a time far removed from the events he describes, and he may not have felt a need to include historical details that were inconvenient for his narrative. Although the author may have drawn some elements of his story from oral tradition, the story reads as a wholly literary creation by the author, whose primary purpose was to show Eliysha as a prophet. To that end, the author has borrowed a number of elements from the story of the kings of Yisra'el and Yehudah fighting Aram in P59 - P59,1. See note 65c directly below.

The translation "embarked on a military campaign" reflects the idiomatic use of the verb יצא ("go out, leave"), which often appears in military contexts with the meaning "depart on a military campaign." Related to this usage is the phrase יצא ובא ("one going out and one coming in"), which often means to perform military missions or to complete a military campaign. See, for example, Sam P41,2.

65c I'll be your partner in full... my cavalry alongside your cavalry: The story of Yehoram's and Yehoshaphat's campaign against Mo'av in P65 - P65,1 has numerous parallels with the story of the alliance between the anonymous king of Yisra'el and Yehoshaphat and their battle against Aram in P59 - P59,1. For example, Yehoshaphat's response here—"I'll be your partner in full—my troops will fight alongside your troops, and my cavalry alongside your cavalry"—is identical to the answer Yehoshaphat gives to the king of Yisra'el's invitation to join him in battle against Aram in P59. Then, at the beginning of P65,1, Yehoshaphat asks whether there is a prophet of Yahweh present from whom they can seek an oracle—a nearly identical question to the one he asks in P59. The two stories have two other noteworthy parallels: both contain numerous elements of humor (see notes above on P59 and P59,1 and the notes below to P65,1), and both show an interest in how the prophet accesses the divine realm in order to receive an oracle from Yahweh (see note 65,1e below).

While it is possible to find plausible arguments that P59 - P59,1 is dependent on P65 - P65,1, my own view is that the author of P65 - P65,1 modeled parts of his story on P59 - P59,1. The language that the two stories have in common seems more original to P59 - P59,1. As discussed above in note 65a, I believe that the authors of Kings' fourth stage composed the story in P65 - P65,1 to show Eliysha as a traditional prophet to Yahweh in order to strengthen the connection between him and Eliyyahu. In composing this story, they borrowed numerous elements from P59 - P59,1, as that story provided them a good example of how traditional prophets to Yahweh served in military contexts.

65d marching in this roundabout direction: Edom lies directly south of Mo'av. The author is describing a campaign that goes around the south end of the Salt Sea, and then heads north through Edom to Mo'av. The region of Mo'av was directly east of the Salt Sea. The path taken is "roundabout" because a road just to the north of the Salt Sea would be a more direct route for the kings of Yisra'el and Yehudah.

65e But there was no water to be had for the army, nor any for the animals that were following them: The animals following them are the horses and asses in service of the army, and goats and sheep and cattle used for food. The situation here is somewhat reminiscent of the situation in Num P71, in which Mosheh and the Yisra'elites "go around the land of Edom" and become discouraged because there is no food or water; this is just before the Yisra'elites go to battle against Siyhon in Num P72 and conquer his territory (which included all of Mo'av). That there are three points of connection with Numbers—the roundabout journey, the lack of water, and the battle against Mo'av—make me inclined to think that the author of P65 - P65,1 may have also drawn from his knowledge of the wilderness stories in Numbers when composing the story here.

65f "Ugh," groaned the king of Yisra'el: The author intended the scene to be humorous. I have translated in such a way as to draw out the humor in English.

65g —: The Leningrad Codex does not have a *parashah* break here. See L203 v.3.25-26.

Notes to P65,1

65,1a One from whom we can seek an oracle from Yahweh: As we will see later in the *parashah*, the request of Yahweh was specifically about where the kings might find water for their armies and livestock.

65,1b the guy who was Eliyyahu's handwasher: The officer's demeaning reference to Eliysha is meant to be humorous.

65,1c Go consult your father's prophets, or your mother's prophets: Yehoram's father and mother are Ah'av and Iyzevel. With this comment, the author of the story is alluding to Ah'av's and Iyzevel's support of the prophets to the Ba'al, as presented in P51 and P51,1. The comment here in P65,1 thus offers further support for seeing this story as later than the Eliyyahu stories, and as dependent on P59 - P59,1.

65,1d "No, dammit!" insisted the king of Yisra'el: The negative particle אל ("not") when used absolutely, as here, often expresses strong opposition to an idea proposed by the other speaker. On this usage, see the citations in BDB, p. 39, def. a. (*b*) (*beta*) Functionally equivalent expressions in English would be expressions such as "no, dammit!" or "absolutely not!" or "no way!"

65,1e So then, get me a musician: Eliysha needs to hear music (possibly a special type of music) in order to bring on the trance-like state that enables him to hear Yahweh's words and/or see the vision that Yahweh shows him. It is interesting that the author of this story portrays the delivery of the oracle to Eliysha as "Yahweh's hand" coming down onto Eliysha. Compare this to the various means by which oracles of Yahweh are delivered in P59 -P59,1: the oracle is something that "Yahweh tells [the prophet] to say"; the prophet "sees" a scene of future events and reports what he sees; and Yahweh's "wind" (or spirit) enters the prophet and speaks to him.

The depiction of the experience of prophecy here in P65,1 bears some similarity to Sha'ul's experience in Sam P19 - P19,1. In that story "Yahweh's spirit" rushes onto Sha'ul when he meets up with a band of prophets who are chanting in a trance to the accompaniment of music from flutes, tambourines, lutes, and lyres. The author of P65,1 certainly would have been aware of this story in Samuel, and that story may have influenced his decision to have Eliysha request a musician to play music for him so that he might enter a prophetic trance.

65,1f You won't see any wind... yet this wadi is going to be full of water: Eliysha's response makes clear that the oracle requested of Yahweh was only about where the kings might find water; it was not about whether they would defeat Mo'av.

65,1g And Yahweh considers this but a trifle: That is, the miraculous production of water in the desert so that the troops and their animals may drink is a trifle to Yahweh. Eliysha's statement here sets up his main point that follows, which is that Yahweh will deliver Mo'av into the three kings' hands.

65,1h troops from all the men of fighting age: The author uses what appears to be idiomatic language—מכל חגר חגרה ומעלה (literally, "some of all those who [can] put on a [warrior's] belt and older"). I have derived the meaning from context. Compare the somewhat similar terminology used in the military census of the tribes in Num P1,1 - P12 to describe men of fighting age: מבן עשרים שנה ומעלה כל יצא צבא ("those twenty years of age or older, all those available to march out to battle").

65,1i "That's blood," they concluded...to the spoils, Mo'av!": The verb אמר is used with a very wide range of nuances in Hebrew. The base meaning is "say," but if the recipient of the speech is not specified (e.g. "X said to Y"), the word very often means "think." In some situations, as here, the word seems to take on both meanings. The two statements—that the red color in the distance must be blood and that the kings' armies turned on one another—read as mental observations not necessarily spoken aloud, but the last statement encouraging a dash to collect spoils is clearly meant to be understood as spoken. I have tried to capture some of the ambiguity of the verb use here by translating אמר as "concluded," which in English is used for both thoughts and speech.

65,1j Yisra'el leapt up and attacked Mo'av: The author is somewhat lazy in his description of the battle, omitting mention of Yehudah and Edom. In addition, he has used a common verbal construction in an ambiguous manner. Typically, the phrase ויקם followed by another verb in the *waw*-consecutive has the meaning "do [a thing] at once." However, in descriptions of battles the verb קום is often associated with an ambush force that "leaps up" to attack (see, for example, this usage in Jos P14 and Jos P15). My translation reflects the association of קום with ambush; although this is less logical than the alternative ("attacked at once"), it is more vivid and I believe it more closely reflects the author's intent, who in several places in this *parashah* is careless in his use of language.

65,1k They depeated them by it, defeating Mo'av: The Hebrew is nonsensical, and the text is clearly corrupt. The corruption has been partially corrected with a *qere* in the margin, but I believe the corruption goes deeper than just the one verb.

65,1l At the same time, they despoiled their land: In order to produce a smooth English translation, I have added the phrase "they despoiled their land." The passage reads naturally in Hebrew, but to read naturally in English, the passage requires some transition between the statement of defeat and the description of the actions taken to despoil the land.

65,1m This resulted in a tremendous rage against Yisra'el: That is, the king's offering of his son was successful, inciting Mo'av's god Kemosh to great rage and leading him to drive Yisra'el away. Note the sloppiness of the author here: he neglects to mention Yehudah and Edom, but presumably Kemosh drove them away as well. The author's overlooking small details like this is a clear indication that the story is a literary composition and is not based on any genuine recollection of historical events.

Notes to P66

66a One of the prophets' wives cried to Eliysha for help…: The story in this *parashah* served as the model for the story in P49,3. I view the story here as older, and the story in P49,3 as a literary composition intended to show that Eliyyahu had miraculous powers similar to Eliysha's.

I believe that in the original traditions about Eliysha, he was not a prophet but rather a miracle-worker (a "holy man" or איש אלהים). The story in P66 reflects that very clearly—note that there is no oracle of Yahweh that Eliysha delivers, and in fact, his connection to Yahweh plays no real role in the story.

66b youe: The story in P66 contains four instances of an alternative spelling of the second person singular feminine suffix, כי, rather than the standard spelling ך. In each instance, the Masoretes have corrected the spelling in the margin with a *qere*. The spelling likely preserves a dialectical difference from standard Hebrew—either the dialect of the author of P66, or—if the author relied on a written source for this story—the dialect of the author's source document. It is noteworthy that the story in P67 also contains instances of this alternative spelling, indicating both stories were composed by the same individual, or that both stories were part of a single source document.

66c stopping only when each is full: I have departed further from a literal rendering than usual to produce a functionally equivalent translation. More literally, "moving the full one aside"—that is, moving each jar to the side once it is full in order to start filling another jar.

66d peour: There is a misspelling of the feminine singular participle of the *hiph'il* form of the verb יצק, which I represent in translation and which the Masoretes have corrected with a *qere*. It is unclear whether this misspelling is true error or whether it represents another example of a dialectical difference, similar to that discussed above in note 66b.

66e all the jars were full… And then the oil stopped: Eliysha has twice the power of Eliyyahu, and so his miracles are more powerful. In P49,3, Eliyyahu's miracle provides food for a widow and her family and Eliyyahu for "several days" only. By contrast, here in P66, Eliysha's miracle produces so much oil that the proceeds from its sale enable the widow to repay her debt and provide an abundance of funds for her and her sons to live on thereafter.

Notes to P67

67a One day Eliysha happened to pass through Shunem…: The story in this *parashah* served as the model for the story in P50, which tells of Eliyyahu's revival of a widow's young boy, who was near death (but does not seem to have been dead). It's worth noting that the story here in P67 presents Eliysha's miracle as more powerful than Eliyyahu's—Eliyyahu revived a boy who was at death's door (he was "barely breathing"), whereas Eliysha revives a boy who has been dead for close to half a day. (We know the boy has been dead for this long because once he dies, his mother travels from Shunem to Mount Karmel to fetch Eliysha. The round trip distance is roughly forty kilometers, suggesting her travel time would have been six to eight hours.)

On the town of Shunem, which was located in the tribal territory of Yissakar, see note 1e above.

67b "Call the Shunammite woman up here…: The scene that follows is odd because Eliysha chooses to speak to the Shunammite woman through Geyhaziy rather than speaking to her directly, even though she is standing right in front of him. It is unclear to me what the author intended to portray by having Eliysha interact indirectly with the woman. There are a number of other instances in the Eliysha stories where

Eliysha speaks through Geyhaziy even though the individual being addressed is in Eliysha's presence. Possibly the author wishes to convey the idea that, as a holy man with special powers, there is some risk to individuals if he interacts with them directly—recall that in P63, for example, Eliysha's utterance of a curse in response to being mocked results in the mauling of forty-two boys. Perhaps the author intended the reader to understand that by speaking through Geyhaziy, Eliysha reduced the risk that others face in speaking to him.

67c Is there something you'd possibly like us to speak with the king about on your behalf: The Hebrew is colloquial. More literally, "Is there possibly something to speak to the king [about] on your behalf?" The Hebrew particle יש ("there is") is often used in contexts where an English speaker would say a thing was "possible," just as the particle אין ("there isn't") is often used in situations where an English speaker would say a thing was impossible.

67d "Then what can we do for her?": Ancient Hebrew prose authors were typically quite sparing of information if they believed the information wasn't critical to the reader in understanding the story. This sentence provides a nice illustration of this. The natural way to understand this sentence is as a continuation of the preceding dialog, with the Shunammite woman still present in the room. However, two sentences later, Eliysha tells Geyhaziy to call the Shunammite woman up to his room, indicating that the question about what Eliysha might do for her represents a new scene and not a continuation of the preceding conversation.

The scene that begins here with Eliysha's question is reminiscent of Yahweh's visit to Avraham in Gen P19, when he announces that Sarah will have a son the following spring. Note that in both stories, the woman has no children, her husband is old, a visitor announces that the woman will have a son in the spring, the woman hears the news while standing in a doorway/entrance, and she reacts to the visitor with disbelief. While it is possible that there is no connection between the two stories and that the authors of both stories simply employed standard tropes known to them from folk tales, I think it more likely that the author of the Eliysha story knew of the story in Gen P19 and modeled the interaction here on that story. This is also suggested by similarities in vocabulary between the two stories—in particular, the rare particle אבל ("indeed, in fact, actually"), which appears in both.

67e her husband is quite old: Gehaziy is saying that the Shunammite woman can no longer become pregant because of her husband's age—a clear reference to age-related erectile dysfunction.

67f "Nine months from now in the spring...: The Hebrew phrase that I translate as "nine months from now" is למועד הזה. A literal rendering would be "at this appointed time." The word מועד ("appointed time, appointed place, meeting") carries a wide range of nuances and is often difficult to translate. In this instance, the author uses the word as a way to refer to the human gestation period, which is fixed (or "appointed") at nine months; therefore the most appropriate translation here is "nine months from now."

It's noteworthy that in this passage, Eliysha speaks directly to the Shunammite woman rather than using Geyhaziy as his intermediary.

67g "Please send me one of the servant boys...: What is said and left unsaid in the narrative here strikes a modern-day reader as completely illogical. However, there is no problem in the story—rather, this is simply a reflection of the differences between the modern-day reader's expectations and the strategies employed in ancient Hebrew narrative art. For example, the Shunammite woman speaks directly to her husband, yet she is still at home and he is far away, out in the fields (if she were in the fields, she wouldn't need to ask her husband to send her a servant and a jenny). Moreover, it seems bizarre to the modern reader that the Shunammite woman doesn't tell her husband that their boy has died. But neither of these two examples would have been a problem for the author of our story—like other authors of his day, one of his primary concerns was to create a narrative that readers found especially dramatic or that provoked a strong emotional response from them. For other examples of this narrative strategy in Kings, see notes 2,1a and 5,1i above and notes 73c and 78,11 below.

67h It's not the new moon or the Shabbath: The new moon and the Shabbath were special days in Yahweh's cult. Originally the Shabbath was a full moon festival (the day the moon "stopped" waxing and began waning), and that seems to be what the woman's husband is referring to here. On the Shabbath as a full moon festival, see the article by J. Wright, "Shabbat of the Full Moon" at www.thetorah.com.

67i going to Mount Karmel to see the holy man: Note the connection to Eliyyahu, who has a strong association with Mount Karmel. In the folk traditions about Eliysha, he is a holy man active in the region around Yeriyho and Gilgal near the Yarden River—he has no connection whatsoever to Mount Karmel. The author of the story in P67 has placed Eliysha on Mount Karmel as a way to connect him more closely to Eliyyahu. As discussed above in several notes, the Eliyyahu stories and Eliysha stories influenced each other in many places, resulting in each man taking on characteristics of the other.

67j She told him things were fine...: Again, note how the actions and dialog in this scene come across as bizarre to the modern-day reader, which is simply a reflection of the differences between modern-day expectations of narrative and the techniques of ancient Hebrew narrative art. To wit, she tells Geyhaziy things are "fine," but of course they are not; even more strangely, she doesn't tell Eliysha that the boy has died, leaving Eliysha to muse that "she's in distress about something" and that Yahweh has hidden it from him. Note also that in this scene Eliysha never directly addresses the woman (see note 67b above).

67k Put my staff on the boy's face: Presumably the author intended the reader to understand that Eliysha's staff has magical powers. Eliysha's words here indicate that after hearing the Shunammite's lament ("Did I ask my lord for a son?"), he understands that something is very wrong with the boy, although he still hasn't been told that the boy has died.

67l there were no sounds, nor any signs of life: After the phrase ואין קול ("there were no sounds"), the remaining part of the line in the Aleppo Codex is erased. The text has the appearance of a *parashah petuhah*, but I think it is best to treat this as a simple erasure and I do not show a *parashah* break here. It's worth noting that the Leningrad Codex does not have a *parashah* break here. For the erasure in the Aleppo Codex, see A92 v.3.23. In the Leningrad Codex, this clause is in L205 r.1.4.

In the Aleppo Codex, the *lamedh* on the following line is written the way that ben Buya'a wrote the letter when there was a line of text above. Where there is no line of text above, he writes the top of the letter nearly vertical, and it is elongated. When there is text above, the top of the letter is angled slightly to the left and is slightly shorter (although even at that length, it still encroaches into the line above). So there was some text there that was erased during proofreading, but oddly, ben Buya'a did not go back and fill the blank part of the line with doodles. Compare the *lamedh* here to the *lamedhs* in A93 r.2.6, which are written below the blank space of a *parashah setumah*—they are not angled, but are close to vertical.

How can one explain the erasure here in the Aleppo Codex? I believe that ben Buya'a most likely wrote the erroneous phrase ואין קול ואין ענה ואין קשב under the influence of the identical language that appears in the story of Eliyyahu's contest with the Ba'al's prophets, where the phrase describes the lack of a response from the Ba'al to the invocations of his prophets. In proofreading—or perhaps when P67 was being vocalized—he and ben Asher must have caught the extraneous ואין ענה and erased it.

To complicate matters, the specific language used by the story's author—"there were no sounds, nor any signs of life" (ואין קול ואין קשב)—was very likely based on the phrase in P51,1, the full version of which ben Buya'a seems to have accidentally written here before correcting it by erasing the extraneous words. There are many touchpoints between the stories of Eliyyahu and Eliysha, and there are numerous instances in which the Eliysha stories and the Eliyyahu stories appear to have influenced each other. See notes 51,2a and 60,2a above for additional discussion of the complicated relationship between the Eliyyahu and Eliysha stories.

67m Eliysha arrived and went inside the house...: The scene describing Eliysha's revival of the boy has numerous parallels with Eliyyahu's revival of the widow's boy in P50, and I believe that the scene here in P67 served as the model for that in P50. Note that in both stories, the boy is lying on the holy man's bed in a room on the roof, and in both stories, the holy man lays himself down on top of the boy multiple times. It is also quite interesting to note one major difference in the stories: Yahweh is almost completely absent in the Eliysha story (Eliysha prays to him, but no actions are attributed to Yahweh), and the story seems to function primarily as a proof of Eliysha's great powers. By contrast, Eliyyahu invokes Yahweh to make the boy's life-force reenter his body, and the story concludes with the widow's observation that the boy's revival is proof the oracles of Yahweh that Eliyyahu speaks must be true.

67n there the boy was, laid out on his bed: That is, Eliysha's bed. Recall that before leaving to find Eliysha, the Shunnamite woman took her boy up to the roof chamber and laid him down on Eliysha's bed.

67o and puttered around for a bit: The phrase that the author uses—אחת הנה ואחת הנה ("once to here and once to there")—is an idiom. The same idiom appears near the end of P54,1 with the verb עשה, where I translate "your servant continued going about his business" (ויהי עבדך עשה הנה והנה). Another possible interpretation of the meaning of the Hebrew here in P67—although less likely, in my opinion—is that the author intended the reader to understand that Eliysha is going back up to and down from the room on the roof. If one was to understand that to be the meaning of the idiom, the appropriate translation of the phrase would be "went back up and down again." The full sentence would then read, "He went back down into the house, went back up and down again, and then he went back up."

68a Now it happened that after Eliysha returned to Gilgal...: This *parashah* and the one that follows record two tales about Eliysha serving food to the band of prophets in Gilgal. They are both noteworthy in that there is nothing particularly miraculous about the events in them. In this *parashah*, Eliysha demonstrates his skills as a cook and fixes a terrible-tasting stew by adding some barley flour, presumably to soften the bitter taste of the wild gourds. In P68,1, he shares a small amount of food with one hundred of the prophets, yet they do not consume all the food. But there is nothing in the text to indicate anything miraculous has occurred or that the food has magically "multiplied," unlike the stories of the widow and the oil in P49,3 and P66 (both of which are related).

Notes to P68

It is interesting to note that the author here states that Eliysha "returned" to Gilgal. The only previous mention of him being in Gilgal is in P62: Eliyyahu and Eliysha depart from there before Eliyyahu is taken up into the sky in a whirlwind. The narrative introduction in P68 follows naturally from P63, and I believe that the intervening stories about Eliysha—P65 - P65,1 and P66 and P67—were likely added later in the fourth compositional stage than the stories in P62, P62,1, P63, P68, P68,1, and the latter part of P69,1, all of which take place in Gilgal or its vicinity.

The Eliysha stories in their current state exhibit quite a bit of rewriting and revising, making any reconstruction of their evolution highly speculative. With that caveat in mind, I would suggest the following broad composition history: I believe the second half of P51,2 (the story of Eliysha's joining up with Eliyyahu), P62 (the story of Eliyyahu being taken up in a whirlwind), and the stories set in Gilgal were the earliest material added about Eliysha. Perhaps at the same time or a little later, the stories in P66 and P67—where Eliysha acts as a miracle-worker and not a prophet—were added. Later in the fourth compositional stage, the authors composed stories that portrayed Eliysha more as a traditional prophet (though he retained his powers as a miracle worker) and that connected him to the base narrative of Kings; these stories included the first half of P51,2, P65 - P65,1, P74, the first half of P77, and P88. I would place next the two Eliysha stories that are the most sophisticated from a literary and theological perspective—the story of Na'aman in P69 and the story of the famine in P71 - P73. The final group of stories, in my opinion, are those that read as late expansions and that seem to have been composed primarily to entertain. These are the story of Gehaziy's leprosy (P69,1), the story of Eliysha striking the army of Aram temporarily blind (P70), and the story of the skeleton in Eliysha's tomb (P89).

68b and loaded them onto his tunic: Literally, "the fullness of his garment"—that is, "a tunic-full." The image is of the prophet picking up the bottom hem of his tunic so that it was even with his waist, filling the loose cloth with gourds, and then securing the load by holding the cloth in which the gourds had been loaded against his stomach or chest.

68c Get some barley meal: There is nothing at all miraculous about what Eliysha has done. He has merely fixed a dish that was too bitter to eat by adding an ingredient that will absorb the bitterness of the gourds and so make the dish edible. It is unclear why this story was included in the Eliysha material added to Kings. It is possible that it may have been part of a connected group of stories known from a source document or from oral tradition. As discussed above in note 68a, the stories in P62, P62,1, P63, P68, and P68,1 all take place in or near Gilgal and have a natural coherence. To this group of stories, I would also add the story at the end of P69,1, which is about Eliysha's magical recovery of an ax head that has fallen into the river.

Notes to P68,1   **68,1a said the holy man to his attendant:** The Hebrew reads simply "he said." Although the Hebrew is more elliptical than usual, it is clear from the sentences that follow that the speaker must be the holy man and that he is addressing his personal attendant/deputy (משרת). The term משרת, which appears in the following sentence, specifically designates Eliysha's deputy. This is an important role: note that Yehoshua was the משרת to Mosheh, and Eliysha served as משרת to Eliyyahu.

68,1b For thus says Yahweh, 'Eat and there'll be leftovers.': The purpose of the story in P68,1 is as ambiguous as that of the preceding story in P68. Yahweh is completely absent in P68, and in P68,1 he is present but to no real effect. That is to say, Yahweh's oracle addresses a completely inconsequential problem—that a man's gift of bread may not suffice for a complete meal for one hundred of Eliysha's followers. Note also, the fact that there are leftovers is not necessarily a miracle—it could be that the bread wasn't very tasty, or that the men were filled with other food that they were eating.

68,1c there'll be leftovers: The author uses the *hiph'il* of יתר ("to cause to remain, to leave over") idiomatically; here it has a meaning equivalent to the English phrase "leftovers." The idiom also appears at the end of Exodus P59, where I translate as "with some left over."

69a Na'aman, who was the head of the king of Aram's army...: This *parashah* relates the story of Eliysha's curing the great Aramean general Na'aman of his skin condition. As discussed below in note 69f, the story explores the nature of prophecy and it addresses the implications of Yahweh being a universal god rather than just the god of the Yisra'elites. The story is written in a sophisticated style and its author displays a deep understanding of human behavior and psychology. Along with the story of the siege of Shomeron in P71 - P73 (which may be by the same author), this story represents the most outstanding literary material in the Eliyyahu-Eliysha cycle.

In this story, Eliysha is called both a prophet and a holy man. Most of the stories in which Eliysha is a holy man have their basis in folk tradition; the story here is purely a literary composition. The portrayal of Eliysha as a prophet is a late development in the Eliyyahu-Eliysha cycle. Over the course of the work on Kings' fourth stage, the authors added stories in which the two men took on characteristics of the other—stories about Eliyyahu as a miracle-working holy man were composed to make him similar to Eliysha, and conversely, stories about Eliysha as a prophet to Yahweh were composed to make him similar to Eliyyahu. Examples of late stories about Eliyyahu as a miracle worker are P49,3 and P50 (both of which are modeled on the stories about Eliysha in P66 and P67) and P60,2 (a very late literary composition). Examples of late stories about Eliysha as a prophet are P65 - P65,1 (a literary composition that draws on the story in P59 - P59,1 and on the traditions about the wilderness wandering in Num P71 - P72), the story here in P69, the story in P70, and the story in P71 - P73. The stories about Eliysha as a prophet are especially interesting in that he retains his abilities as a miracle-worker in them (and even gains new supernatural powers—see note 70e below), and these abilities play an integral role in their plots. For my speculations on the chronology of the composition of the Eliysha stories, see note 68a above.

69b through him Yahweh had given Aram great military success: Note the depiction here of Yahweh as a universal god. One of the key themes of the story in P69 is that Yahweh is the sole god on earth, and that all peoples should worship him. The presence of this theme offers strong support for a late date for this *parashah*—the late Persian period, in my opinion.

69c ten *kikkar* of silver, six thousand sheqels of gold: Na'aman takes along an enormous sum of money. Ten *kikkar* of silver is equivalent to thirty thousand sheqels. In terms of modern-day measures, Na'aman took more than 330 kilograms (or nearly 750 pounds) of silver and a little over 65 kilograms (or almost 150 pounds) of gold. An average donkey or mule will carry 75 kilograms (roughly twenty percent of its body weight). It's doubtful the author of this story gave much thought to Na'aman's entourage, but he would have needed a caravan of five or six donkeys just to carry the silver and gold on his journey to Yisra'el.

Notes to P69

69d if you just think about it, you'll realize: I have translated into colloquial English. Literally "please know and realize." The author doesn't specify whom the king is speaking to. The same idiomatic expression—דע־נא וראו—appears in P52 in a statement by Ah'av, where I translate "you realize, don't you."

69e this jerk's asking me to rid some guy of his skin disease: The king of Yisra'el's tone is extremely disrespectful to the king of Aram. It would be most natural for him to refer to the king by title—"Am I God Almighty... that the king of Aram is asking me...." Instead, the king of Yisra'el refers to the king with only the demonstrative pronoun זה ("this"). The demonstrative pronoun was very frequently used by ancient Hebrew speakers when they wished to disparage or demean a person, and that is the usage here. I have commented on this use of the demonstrative pronoun frequently in my other translations. See, for example, notes 9q and 24f in my translation of Judges.

There are many elements of humor in the story of Eliysha and Na'aman in P69, and I believe that the king's massive overreaction to this politely worded letter is meant to be humorous. Note how his reaction—he tears his clothing (an act usually reserved for more upsetting situations) and he equates curing a skin condition to some miraculous event that only a god has the power to do—is completely out of proportion to the request being made. The author likely intended the reader to see the king of Yisra'el as a bumbling fool.

The beginning of this *parashah* provides a good example of how Hebrew narrative art prioritizes dramatic impact over consistency and logic. Note how the author has had to manipulate his narrative in order to create the humorous scene in which the king of Yisra'el reacts to the letter he received: at the beginning of the story, the little girl explicitly mentioned that "the prophet who's in Shomeron" could cure her lord; the author purposely has the king of Aram omit from his letter that his request is to arrange an audience with the prophet, as otherwise the king of Yisra'el's humorous reaction to the letter would not be possible.

69f Then he'll see that there really is a prophet in Yisra'el: Note that Eliysha doesn't say "god," which is the term we expect to see, but instead says "prophet." It is possible that the text originally said "god," for this would be consistent with Na'aman's reaction later in the *parashah* after he is cured of his skin disease, when he declares, "Now I realize there are no gods anywhere on earth except in Yisra'el." My personal opinion is that the text originally did say "god" and that the word was replaced by "prophet" due to a simple scribal error. There is no obvious reason why someone would have intentionally made this edit.

The story about Na'aman has two themes. First, it reads as an exploration of (and critique on) the nature of prophecy. In the scene that follows, Na'aman's behavior toward Eliysha reflects the common understanding of prophecy, and the author uses humor to mock that understanding and to show the reader that it is incorrect. Second, the story explores the implications of Yahweh being a universal god, rather than just the god of the Yisra'elites—that is, if Yahweh is the sole god on earth, what does that mean for non-Yisra'elites?

69g Eliysha sent a messenger out to him with this message: Eliysha uses an intermediary rather than speak to Na'aman directly. He also used an intermediary in many of his interactions with the Shunammite woman in P67 (see note 67b above).

69h "I really expected he would come out...: Note the humor in Na'aman's speech, which is intentional on the part of the author. The author is mocking the common understanding of prophecy, which in his day has taken on aspects previously associated with the "holy man" (איש־האלהים). Na'aman thus wants to see a performance appropriate for a prophet who also works miracles; in his view, this requires some sort of public spectacle with the prophet in the role of a performance artist. Instead, Na'aman is not allowed to see Eliysha, but only receives a message from an anonymous messenger, which he finds insulting. And then he is further insulted that the only instruction he is given is to bathe in the river seven times. There is nothing "magic" in the instruction—he doesn't need a prophet to tell him to go bathe in the river. And anyway, what's so special about the Yarden River? It's not even as good as the rivers back home in Dammeseq.

69i the Avanah and the Parpar [*Dammeseq's rivers*]: The Leningrad Codex has a *qere* in the margin correcting "Avanah" to "Amanah." The margin of the Aleppo Codex at this place in the text is damaged, but it does not appear to have had a *qere* here. See L205 v.1.19 and A93 v.1.4. I understand the phrase "Dammeseq's rivers" to be a gloss added by an editor in the sixth compositional stage to inform the reader of the location of the two rivers, the Amanah and the Parpar. It is noteworthy that this is one of only four glosses in the entire body of material about Eliysha (one of the other glosses is in P51,2 and the other two appear in P77). In all other material in Kings, glosses and comments are much more common.

69j He turned around and left: The wording of the Hebrew (ויפן וילך—"he turned around and went on his way") implies that Na'aman has decided to start his journey back home.

69k there are no gods anywhere on earth except in Yisra'el: The monotheistic viewpoint expressed in this statement is a clear indication of a Persian-period date for this *parashah*, as I suggest above in note 69b.

69l let your servant be given two mule-loads of dirt: Na'aman uses what was undoubtedly a common expression in the author's time, but its meaning is unclear. Two mule-loads of dirt would be roughly one hundred and fifty kilograms (or 330 pounds); see note 69c above. The Israeli scholar Nadav Na'aman interprets this as a request to take dirt from Yisra'el to make an altar to Yahweh back in Aram, an interesting but not wholly convincing proposal. See N. Na'aman, "An Altar for YHWH in the Land of Aram (2 Kings 5:17)," *Journal of Ancient Near Eastern Religions* 18 (2018), 133-144.

69m welfare offering: The author writes זבח, which is the abbreviated form of זבח שלמים. The abbreviated form is especially common when the term is used in conjunction with "whole offering," as here. The use of זבח as an abbreviated term for "welfare offering" is briefly discussed in BDB, p. 257, def. 5.

69n my lord: That is, the king of Aram. The king of Aram is also referred to as Na'aman's "lord" at the beginning of the *parashah*.

69o Rimmon: The name of a god worshipped in Aram. The god's name appears as an element of the personal name Tavrimmon in P42,1 above.

69p because he had put his trust in me...: The Hebrew from here to the end of Na'aman's address to Eliysha is awkwardly expressed and somewhat difficult to understand. The author uses an idiom "lean on the hand of," which means "put one's trust in." I believe Na'aman is saying that because he was with the king when the king was worshipping at Rimmon's temple and because the king held him in a position of trust, he felt obligated to worship alongside the king. He asks to be forgiven for participating in the worship of Rimmon. The idiom here is also used in P72 and P73. See the discussion below in note 72c.

Notes to P69,1

69,1a "Look here," thought Eliysha the Holy Man's attendant Gehaziy...: The first two-thirds of this *parashah* relates the story of Eliysha's condemnation of Gehaziy for his greed. Although the story in P69,1 continues the narrative of P69, it is not as sophisticated as the story it follows, and I believe it was likely written by a different individual than the author of P69.

69,1b what he brought as a gift: I have added the phrase "as a gift" in translation, to make explicit the connection with Na'aman's request to Eliysha earlier to accept a "gift" (ברכה) from him for healing his skin condition. In purely transactional terms, the gift of course is simply a payment for the services rendered. Gehaziy's greed has got the better of him—he saw how much gold and silver Na'aman brought, and he sees in Eliysha's refusal to accept anything from Na'aman an opportunity to get some of the money for himself.

69,1c My lord sent me with a message...: Gehaziy is lying.

69,1d he would like you to give them a *kikkar* of silver: Gehaziy's request is absurd. A *kikkar* of silver is an enormous sum of money—three thousand sheqels (equivalent to more than 33 kilograms or nearly 74 pounds)—and it is not what someone might give to help out two young men whom one has just met. The author clearly chose such a large sum to highlight Gehaziy's greed, which is central to the story. However, the author otherwise ignores the implications of such a large amount of money for his narrative; at a minimum, the reader expects Na'aman to question why so much money is needed for two young men visiting Eliysha.

69,1e Be so kind as to accept two *kikkar* of silver: It is possible to understand Na'aman's offer here as a subtle strategem to entrap Gehaziy in his crime. By insisting he take two *kikkar*, the gift is almost impossible to hide from Eliysha due to its size and weight—67 kilograms, or nearly 150 pounds. I am uncertain whether the author intended the reader to perceive Na'aman as acting purposefully in this way, although it is certainly a possibility.

69,1f pressing him with some insitsence: The verb is misspelled in the Hebrew—the author wrote ויפרץ בו ("he broke him") instead of ויפצר בו ("he pressed him"). I have reflected the misspelling in translation with "insitsence" instead of "insistence."

69,1g I didn't like it: Literally, "My heart didn't go." The meaning of this phrase, which may be an idiom, is unclear. Context suggests a meaning like "I wasn't in agreement with [what happened]." Assuming that meaning is correct, a functionally equivalent translation would be "I didn't like it when I saw a man turning from his chariot to greet you," which I have reflected in my translation. Alternatively, the text may be corrupt. In any case, the words that follow this phrase suggest that Eliysha the Holy Man, who has magical powers, has somehow "seen" Gehaziy's meeting with Na'aman even though he was miles away.

69,1h And so he left him: The Hebrew is ambiguous. It may be understood as implying that Gehaziy left Eliysha's service, or it may be understood simply as Gehaziy leaving Eliysha's presence at that time (but still in his position as Eliysha's attendant).

69,1i stricken with a disease that made his skin white as snow: The Leningrad Codex has a *parashah setumah* after this phrase. See L.206 r.1.5. The Leningrad Codex here is much preferable to the Aleppo Codex, as the text that follows begins a new story.

69,1j the place where we're living with you: This phrase is almost certainly a reference to the town of Gilgal near the Yarden River, as this is where Eliysha and the prophets are living in the story in P68.

69,1k they began cutting wood into planks: Literally, "they divided wood." BDB, p. 160, oddly thinks the verb here must mean "cut down." But the root גזר normally has the meaning "divide," and that meaning fits the context here very well.

69,1l the head of his ax dropped into the water: Somewhat unusually, the subject of the sentence ("the head of his ax") is prefixed with the mark of the direct object את. This is often seen when the verb of the sentence is in the passive. Here, however, the verb (נפל, "to fall") is in the *qal* and is intransitive. This may be an example where the author was influenced by his use of the same verb in the previous clause, where it occurs in the *hiph'il* and has a transitive meaning (literally, "cause to fall"). Because in the previous sentence the verb carried a transitive meaning, and because there is just a subtle difference between the intransitive and passive ("fell" vs. "was dropped"), the author may have subconsciously treated the verb as passive and so used the mark of the direct object with the subject.

The ax-head would have been made of iron. In fact, the word for ax-head in ancient Hebrew is the same as the word for iron (ברזל).

69,1m God knows where it went!: The Hebrew is difficult, but it appears to be an idiom. Literally, "It is requested." The verb שאל ("ask, request") is often used in situations where one "asks" a god for an oracle in order to address some problem that one has, and I believe that is the function of the idiom here. In using this idiom, the man in effect is saying, "we would need to request an oracle from Yahweh in order to know where the ax-head went." I have translated with a functionally equivalent English idiom.

69,1n causing the ax-head to float up: The holy man performs another miracle. This story at the end of P69,1 belongs with the other "holy man" stories about Eliysha; these stories, which have no discernible theological point, have their basis in folk tradition. When the authors of Kings' fourth stage decided to incorporate the legendary figure of Eliysha the Holy Man into their book, they included several of the old "holy man" stories that they made only minor changes to. In addition to the story at the end of P69,1, the other old folk stories about Eliysha are P62,1, P63, P66, P67, P68, and P68,1. In these old stories, Eliysha is a miracle-working holy man only. He is not a prophet to Yahweh, and he never has any interactions with the king. The stories about Eliysha where he functions as a prophet and interacts with the king are all literary creations; they were composed to create parallels with Eliyyahu and to demonstrate that Eliysha was a true successor to him. On the composition history of the Eliysha stories, see notes 68a and 69a above.

Notes to P70

70a waging war in Yisra'el: The Hebrew is ambiguous. The construction נלחם ב may mean either "wage war in" or "wage war against." Either meaning works well here; I have opted for the former as the sentences immediately following imply that the king of Aram and his army are in territory under the control of Yisra'el's king. Note also, the final sentence of the *parashah* supports my translation choice here, as it is explicitly concerned with the presence of Aram's raiding parties in Yisra'el.

70b where Aram is capming: The Hebrew reads נחתים ("descending"), which is nonsensical in the context. I believe the text originally read חנים ("is camping") and that at some point in the transmission history, a scribe accidentally transposed the *nun* and the *ḥeth* and added a *taw*. It is easy to see how a scribe might have made this mistake under the influence of the word תחנתי ("my encampment") in the previous sentence. In my translation, I have represented the error by transposing the "m" and the "p" in the word "camping." BDB, p. 639, proposes the text originally read נחבים ("hiding"); however, I think this less likely than חנים ("camping"), as the previous sentence specifically mentions the Aramean encampment and there is no obvious explanation for the scribal error proposed by BDB.

70c and not just one or two messages: The Hebrew is elliptical and awkward, and the meaning is uncertain. Literally, "not one [time] and not two [times]." I understand this to mean that the king sent multiple messages to the town near the Aramean army's camp. It is possible, but less likely in my opinion, that the author is referring to Eliysha sending multiple warnings to the king. If that were the case, the appropriate functionally equivalent translation would be, "and it wasn't just one or two warnings."

70d The king of Aram became enraged: Literally, "the king of Aram's heart raged against itself." The verb סער is in the *niph'al*, which very often connotes reflexive action. The reflexive is used here because there is no specific object that the king directs his anger toward.

70e Eliysha the Prophet...can tell the king of Yisra'el things you say in the privacy of your bedroom: One of Eliysha's special powers, which is presented to the reader as an independent ability not requiring assistance from Yahweh, is the ability to see and hear people who are far away. This power is not present in the old folk stories about Eliysha—rather, it is present only in the stories about him that read as pure literary compositions. Thus in P69,1, Eliysha "sees" Gehaziy accept silver and clothing from Na'aman even though he is miles away. Later, in P71, Eliysha "sees" that the king has sent an executioner to kill him. This is a power that Eliyyahu did not possess, and the authors of the Eliysha material may have granted Eliysha this power in their stories as a way of further demonstrating that he had twice the power of Eliyyahu (see P62).

70f Dothan: Dothan was a town to the north of Shomeron that is also mentioned in Gen P34 as the place where Yoseph's brothers have gone to graze their father's flocks. Scholars have identified the town with the site of Tel Dotân, which is roughly twenty kilometers north of the site of Shomeron (modern-day Tel Sebastia).

70g the holy man's attendant: The authors of the Eliysha stories use two terms for Eliysha's personal attendant: in this sentence, he is Eliysha's משרת ("one who tends to, serves," which I usually translate as attendant) and in the following sentence, he is called Eliysha's נער ("servant"). The terms are used synonymously here, but typically משרת connotes a role that combines aspects of a "deputy" and an "attendant." See note 68,1a above.

70h What are we going to do now?: The Hebrew is elliptical and likely represents a common expression. I have translated with a functionally equivalent English expression. A literal translation of the Hebrew is, "How will we do [anything]?" That is, "How can we do anything that would be effective against this huge army?"

70i those with us are stronger than those with them: The Hebrew is strangely phrased. Eliysha is alluding somewhat cryptically to Yahweh and his divine army as being stronger than Aram's gods. For the use of רב ("many, much") with the meaning "strong," see BDB, p. 913, def. 2.b.

70j while the hills were full of horses and chariots, there were flames all around Eliysha: I break up the text here differently than other commentators, who follow the Masoretic accents and read "the hills were full of horses and fiery chariots surrounding Eliysha." I find the traditional reading of this sentence to be completely nonsensical. Eliysha's servant has already seen Aram's army in the surrounding hills, so there is no need for Yahweh to "open" his eyes to see them again. Moreover, why would Yahweh give supernatural (presumably invincible) chariotry to Aram? The passage makes much more sense if Yahweh opens the servant's eyes to see that it is Eliysha who is surrounded by fire and who has been made invincible.

70k Don't kill them: Eliysha tells the king he must show compassion to his captives. Compare Eliysha's advice here to the story in P54, where the king of Yisra'el has compassion on Hadadsson King of Aram after defeating his army at Apheq.

71a After these events, Hadadsson King of Aram... besieged Shomeron: Note the inconsistency in the narrative. At the end of P70, we are told that "Aram's raiding parties never again entered Yisra'el's territory," and now in P71, Hadadsson King of Aram is laying siege to Shomeron. I believe the best explanation for this inconsistency is that the stories about Eliysha were added in a piecemeal fashion over a number of years and decades, and later authors did not always take care to ensure that their material was fully consistent with the stories that had been added by earlier authors. In the instance here, I believe the inconsistency is due to the fact that—as I suggest in note 69a above—the story in P70 was added after the story in P71 - P73. For another example of an inconsistency in the Eliysha material that is best explained as due to stories being added at different times, see note 73,1d below. Finally, note also the inconsistency here with material that is unrelated to the Eliysha stories but that also belongs to Kings' fourth stage and is roughly contemporaneous with the Eliysha stories: at the end of P54, the king of Yisra'el and Hadadsson agree to a peace treaty.

Notes to P71

The story in P71 - P73 is one of the two outstanding pieces of literature in the cycle of stories about Eliyyahu and Eliysha. I think it is possible that the author of this story was also the author of the other outstanding piece, the story of Na'aman's skin disease in P69 (but see note 71h below for an argument against common authorship of the two stories). The story in P71 - P73 contains two scenes especially notable for their vivid detail and dramatic action: the opening scene of the hapless king unable to help his starving subjects and the scene in P73 of the four lepers entering the abandoned Aramean camp. In writing the story, the author likely started with material from a story about a drought-induced famine, adapted that material for a siege setting, and then composed scenes that illustrated the conditions during and after the siege in the most dramatic way he could imagine. See note 72a below for the idea that in composing the story here the author has adapted material from a story about a drought.

71b donkey's heads: A donkey's head normally has no value as food; the brains are edible and little else. Eighty sheqels is a very large sum of silver, likely equivalent to several months of a day laborer's wages.

71c a fourth of a *qav* of dove shit: A *qav* is a dry measure that scholars believe was equal to approximately 1.2 liters. One fourth of a *qav* thus would be roughly equivalent to 300 ml. The term חרי ("shit") was deemed offensive by the Masoretes, and they have added a *qere* in the margin that informs the reader the word חרי ("shit") should be read as דב ("droppings"). The *qere* in the Aleppo Codex is very difficult to see, as it is on the far left margin, which has been damaged by mold (see A94 r.3.21). It's worth noting that in the only other instance in which the term חרי appears, the Masoretes also supply a *qere* with a less offensive term: in Kgs P110, חריהם ("their shit") is corrected to צואתם ("their feces"). See note 109i below. (The *qere* also appears in the parallel passage in Isa 36.12.)

71d "This other woman said to me...: The dispute between the two women has some similarities with the dispute between the two prostitutes in P9. The author may have wanted the reader to think of that story when reading the dispute here. The famine has made conditions in Shomeron so hopeless that there is no point in the king's trying to settle the dispute—both women's children are dead. If the author did have the story in P9 in mind, then we can be confident that this story in P71 - P73 is quite late—perhaps dating to the very end of the Persian period—as the story in P9 is itself very late.

In composing this scene, the author must also have had in mind the passage in Deut P26 (the treaty curses) in which siege conditions become so dire that parents resort to eating their children: "In the siege and in the dire conditions that your enemies inflict on you, you shall consume your very own offspring" and—even more vividly—"The most soft-hearted woman among you... shall turn churlish... against any children whom she bears—for lacking any sort of food, she shall eat them [i.e. her children] in secret, in the siege and in the dire conditions that your enemies inflict on you in your towns!" The author almost certainly would have expected his audience to recall the passage in Deuteronomy when reading this scene in Kgs P71.

71e he had sackcloth on his loins: I understand בשר in this clause to refer specifically to the loins, and not the flesh on the body, as is usually understood. Parallel passages indicate that sackcloth is typically worn over the מתנים, which is the usual term for loins. But בשר is often used as a euphemism for the genitals or loins (see BDB, p. 143, def. 3).

The king was wearing sackcloth under his clothes presumably as a sign of penitence during the famine. Once he tore his clothing, the sackcloth underneath became visible to the townspeople.

71f So may God do to me... if... Eliysha Shaphatsson's head is still attached to his body: It is unclear in the narrative why the king blames Eliysha for the troubled situation that Shomeron is in (the siege and the famine). The king uses a very common oath—"so may God do to me, and so may he do again." On this oath, see notes 6a and 51,1ac above.

71g A man had been dispatched on the king's orders: The Hebrew is elliptical, but the meaning is clear; I have translated into functionally equivalent English. I understand the subject of the verb שלח to be indefinite. As I have commented frequently in my translations, ancient Hebrew writers often used the *qal* form of a verb with an indefinite subject to express the passive, which is how I understand the verb here. The phrase מלפניו ("from his presence") means specifically "from the king's presence," which I have represented by the equivalent phrase in English, "on the king's orders."

71h Do you realize that goddamn murderer has sent somebody...: Another example of Eliysha's special power of seeing events from far away. See the discussion above in note 70e.

The phrase that I translate as "that goddamn mass murderer" is בן־המרצח הזה (literally, "this son of the mass murderer"). The demonstrative pronoun זה ("this") was often used in Hebrew to express derision or opprobrium. In these instances, a functionally equivalent English translation is typically a mild expletive such as "goddamn." I have commented frequently on this usage of the demonstrative pronoun in my other translations, and that is clearly how it is being used here. The noun בן

("son") is frequently prefixed to a noun to designate a class of individual or a person who is characterized by a certain trait. Here the construction is used in a way that adds to the disparaging tone of Eliysha's speech.

I understand the phrase "that goddamn mass murderer" to be the subject of the verb and to be a reference to the king. It is possible to understand the phrase as the object of the verb—that is, "he sent that goddamn mass murderer." However, it is more natural to read the phrase as the subject because of the presence of the demonstrative particle זה. That said, if one wished to take the phrase as the object of the verb, it would be best to understand the subject of the verb to be indefinite and translate in the passive voice: "that goddamn mass murderer's been sent."

The antagonism between the king and Eliysha in this story is very strange and is out of keeping with the other stories about Eliysha, where he has friendly relations with the king and is his close advisor. I have no explanation for this. In P69, Eliysha and the king have close relations, so perhaps the story in P69 and the story here are not by the same author.

71i his lord's henchmen: The adjective רגלי ("on foot") is often used in plural form as a noun meaning "footmen" or "foot soldiers." I understand רגלים here to be used in that way, as that is the most natural way to read the Hebrew given the context. I have translated as "henchmen" to reflect the tone of Eliysha's speech, which is quite disparaging toward the king. Surprisingly, BDB, p. 920, seems to understand רגלי (the plural construct) here as meaning "feet," for it does not include this passage in its citations for רגלים as "footmen."

71j I certainly can't wait: Literally, "how can I wait?" See BDB, p. 553, def. 2a.(*b*), for the adverbial use of the interrogative particle מה ("what") to mean "how [can]," which then shades into the meaning "[can] not." This usage of the particle מה is unusual, and it may be an example of the author's local dialect of Hebrew.

It is unclear why Eliysha blames Yahweh for the trouble he's in, and why he says he can't wait for Yahweh (presumably to save or protect him).

71k **: The Leningrad Codex has a *parashah setumah* here. See L206 v.2.19-20.

72a Hear Yahweh's oracle!: Note the narrative inconsistency: the executioner sent to kill Eliysha has vanished from the scene. There are a number of possible explanations for this inconsistency. One explanation is that the author introduced the executioner in P71 to create a scene of great drama. Once he accomplished his purpose there, he saw no reason to continue with that scene, and so he moves on to a new scene needed to drive his narrative forward. He sees no reason to ensure consistency between the two scenes, as—unlike modern narrative practice—consistency was not a requirement of ancient Hebrew narrative art.

Alternatively, it is possible to understand the narrative inconsistency as being temporal. In this interpretation, this *parashah* represents an entirely separate scene at an unspecified location; temporally it would have been before P71, and the author has inserted it here to prepare the reader for the story in P73.

A third explanation—and the one that I think to be most likely—is that the author borrowed material from a different story and inserted it as P72. In this scenario, one may imagine that in composing the story in P71 - P73, the author would have started with the material in P72, which was part of an old story that takes place during a drought; he then would have repurposed the material he borrowed by composing P71 and P73, which are a story about a siege. One benefit of this explanation is that the narrative inconsistencies discussed above in this note and below in notes 73j and 73k can be understood as due to the author's decision to borrow material from a drought story for his story about a siege.

Notes to P72

72b Shomeron's market: Literally, "Shomeron's [main] gate." Walled towns in ancient Yisra'el and Yehudah were constructed with an open plaza inside the town in the area adjacent to each of its town gates. These plazas (רחוב in Hebrew) were the equivalent of the public square or town common, and were where much commerce was conducted, including buying and selling food. (On the role of these plazas, see my comments in note 64q in my translation of Judges.) There is no word for "market" in ancient Hebrew; in its place, ancient Hebrew speakers would use either רחוב, or as here, שער ("gate"). In those situations, the correct functionally equivalent translation is "market."

72c A deputy of the king—the one he trusted most: The author uses two idiomatic constructions that are missed by many translators, in part because they are combined in a way that is not "grammatically correct." The first idiomatic construction takes the form "NOUN which belongs to NOUN." Here in P72, the phrase used is השליש אשר למלך (literally, "the deputy who is the king's"). This phrase means "one of the king's deputies." There is no natural way in Hebrew to refer to a particular individual who belongs to a larger group, and this construction is the most common way to do so. The second idiomatic construction is the phrase נשען על יד (literally, "lean oneself on [another's] hand"). This idiom means "to put one's trust in" or "to rely on" and here it is used to characterize the king's deputy. The author has combined these two phrases in a way that violates grammatical norms, likely because to express the concept following those norms would be quite wordy and awkward: השליש אשר למלך ואשר המלך נשען על ידו ("one of the king's deputies in whom the king places his trust"). The idiom for "placing one's trust in" is also used in P69; see note 69p above.

72d You think Yahweh's going to make sluices in the sky?: The deputy's response does not make sense in the context of a siege, but it does make sense in the context of a general famine due to lack of rain. As discussed above in note 72a, it is possible that the author may have borrowed the oracle and the deputy's response from a different story about a drought and left the deputy's words unchanged.

72e you won't eat any of what's sold there: The Hebrew is elliptical—"you won't eat any from there." That is, you won't eat any of the food that is sold there in the plaza adjacent to the town gate. The elliptical verbal construction is perhaps the author's attempt to represent informal everyday speech.

72f **: The Leningrad Codex has a *parashah setumah* here. See L206 v.3.4.

Notes to P73

73a and were talking with one another...: It is common in literary Hebrew to represent group speech as a series of statements without obvious change in speaker, but each statement to be understood by the reader as spoken by a different member of the group. It was most common to represent group speech through four separate statements, but sometimes there were more and sometimes fewer. Here there are four lepers and four statements. I have commented on this literary technique frequently in my other translations. See, for example note 34p in my translation of Genesis.

The Hebrew dialog is interesting because it is written in a colloquial style, and gives us a glimpse of the spoken Hebrew known to the author. I have translated into the style of colloquial English. The speaker of the first statement, for example, uses the particle מה ("what, how") in a very informal way. The exact nuance of the particle is to emphasize the pointlessness and/or futility of the current circumstances. In English this can be accomplished with the adverb "just," as I have done in my translation. But other possible translations are comments like "What's the point of us sitting here until we die?" or "Why should we just sit here until we die?"

73b they made ready to go: On the use of the construction קום followed by the infinitive to mean "make ready to do a thing," see note 55o above and note 14d in my translation of Joshua.

73c leaving behind... their horses, and their donkeys: Note the unrealistic actions on the part of the Arameans—if they were fleeing, those who had horses or donkeys would certainly have ridden them rather than going on foot. The lack of realism is due to the nature of Hebrew narrative art: the biblical authors prioritized drama and emotional impact over logical consistency, and thus they often introduce elements that make their scenes more dramatic, even when those elements are illogical or inconsistent with human behavior. The entry of the lepers into the camp is certainly more vivid and dramatic with the presence of the animals than it would be if they were absent.

73d they started talking with one another: What follows is another example of group speech. Here it is quite natural to represent this in English as only two separate statements. However, I have elected to show the speech as four statements, both because I believe an ancient Hebrew reader would have perceived more than two statements here and because there are four lepers present in this scene. On the literary technique of group speech, see note 73a above.

73e they told them: Note the shift from singular to plural. The antecedent to "them" is "the guard at the town gate" in the previous sentence. Ancient Hebrew narrative was much less rigid than English regarding consistency in person and number, and it is common to see shifts between singular and plural and between second person and third person in the books of the Torah and Former Prophets. When translating, I often ignore the inconsistency, because the functionally equivalent translation in English should be one in which consistency is maintained. In this instance, however, the shift between singular and plural is quite jarring in the Hebrew, and so I have reproduced the inconsistency in the translation. Note that in the narrative that follows, the shift to the plural is maintained—there are multiple guards rather than a single guard. Given how jarring the inconsistency is here, it seems likely to me that the previous sentence is corrupt and originally read "So they went and called out to the guards at the town gate."

73f They're thinking that we'll come out...: There was no specific word for "think" in ancient Hebrew; in its place, Hebrew speakers often used the verb אמר ("say"). The sentence here provides a really nice example of this usage. The text following the infinitive לאמר ("thinking" in this instance) is in direct discourse. I have translated as indirect discourse, as indirect discourse is much more natural in English in this particular instance.

73g May I suggest fetching: The use of the particle נא ("please") softens the tone of the sentence and makes it more polite. An equivalent English expression in this instance is "may I suggest." The subject of the verb here is indefinite and can be understood as "let some men fetch" or as a circumlocution for the passive "let five horses be fetched."

73h two chariots with horses were fetched: In depictions in the Megiddo ivories (from the Late Bronze Age), chariots are pulled by two horses; however, in reliefs from Iron Age Mesopotamia, three horses per chariot is most common (although there are chariots shown with two horses). It is unclear to me whether the author of P73 assumed two horses or three horses per chariot. Either way, however, five horses is not the right number for two chariots. It is somewhat odd that the author brings chariots into the picture rather than staying with the original proposal of five horses.

Minor inconsistencies such as we see here are typical of Hebrew narrative, and they were often introduced by authors to add variety to their stories and so make them more interesting to the reader. Because Hebrew narrative tended to be very sparing in its use of detail and description, authors needed to find other strategies to make their stories interesting and vivid.

73i in the their panic: The Masoretic consonantal text reads בההפזם, which is an error for בחפזם. As is usual with corrections, the word in the consonantal text is vocalized for the correct reading. The Leningrad Codex has a *qere* in the margin with the correct reading. In the Aleppo Codex, Aharon ben Asher vocalized the consonantal text with the correct reading; however, he omitted the *qere*. I have translated the consonantal text to represent the omission of the *qere*. See A95 r.1.20 and L207 r.2.11.

73j when the king came down to execute him: Note the inconsistency in the narrative. In P71, the king sends an executioner to Eliysha, but does not go himself. As I have commented several times above and frequently in my other translations, this sort of narrative inconsistency is common in ancient Hebrew prose. Writers often sought to maximize the emotional or dramatic impact in their narrative, even when it meant violating narrative logic and introducing inconsistencies into the storyline. Alternatively, if we accept the proposal above that the author borrowed the material in P72 from an old story about a drought, then it is possible that the statement about the king coming down to execute Eliysha may be a case of the author inadvertently alluding to a detail from his "source" story.

73k just as the holy man had said to the king: Note the inconsistency in the narrative: in P72, Eliysha did not deliver his oracle to the king. There are a number of ways that one may explain this inconsistency, but I think the most likely explanation is that the detail about an oracle being delivered to the king is from the author's "source" story and that the author has inadvertently alluded to that, having forgotten that in his own story the oracle was not delivered to the king. See note 72a and note 73j directly above.

73l Shomeron's market: See note 72b above.

Notes to P73,1

73,1a "Leave at once—youe and your family...: See P67 for the story of Eliysha reviving the son of the woman he is addressing here. In P67, the woman's husband is old, and the reader should presume that the husband has died by the time of the events in P73,1.

Note also the *qere-ketiv* correcting the archaic (or dialectical) spelling of the feminine singular form of "you," which I have represented in translation. As discussed above in note 66b, the author of the stories in P66 and P67 (the latter of which is about the woman who appears here in P73,1) consistently used an old variant spelling of the second person feminine pronoun and suffix, and in each instance the Masoretes corrected the variant spelling with a *qere* in the margin.

73,1b her personal property: The word בית, which is typically translated as "house," has a wide range of meanings, including "family" and "possessions, personal property." At the beginning of the *parashah*, בית is used in the sense of "family," and here and in the following *parashah* (P73,2), it is used with the sense of "personal property." In this use, the term denotes movable property—livestock, equipment and tools, household furnishings, etc. The woman left all or nearly all of her personal property behind when she left the country, and she now seeks the king's help in recovering it.

73,1c her family farm: The story in P67 states that the woman is prominent—that is, she is very wealthy. The setting for one of the scenes in P67 is the harvest on the farm owned by the woman and her husband. The harvest was most likely of barley or wheat, but there is no way to be certain. Given the woman's wealth, we should assume that the farmland her family owned was extensive.

The word שׂדה has a wide range of meanings depending on context. It often means "countryside," but it is also used to denote a "field"—both cultivated fields and uncultivated fields. Here in P73,1, the word is clearly being used to denote cultivated fields, and I translate as "family farm."

73,1d the holy man's attendant Gehaziy: Note the inconsistency in the narrative. Gehaziy is still in Eliysha's service in this *parashah*, whereas the story of Na'aman in P69,1 seems to imply that Gehaziy left Eliysha's service. The most likely explanation of this inconsistency is that the Eliysha stories were added to Kings in a piecemeal fashion over some period of years or decades, and later authors were not always careful to make sure what they added was fully consistent with the other stories about Eliysha. For another example of an inconsistency likely created in such a way, see note 71a above.

73,1e —: The Leningrad Codex does not have a *parashah* break here. See L207 r.3.22.

73,2a including all the production from her family farm: Note the complete lack of narrative logic—the woman's recovery of the farm's production in her absence is wholly unrealistic. If the woman and her family abandoned the farm, who cultivated it in the seven years they were gone? And how much food could the farm have produced given the poor growing conditions during this seven-year famine? Finally, how would it be possible to determine how much food the farm had produced during those seven years? As discussed in numerous notes elsewhere, ancient Hebrew authors often ignored narrative logic to achieve dramatic impact, and this is certainly the case here: the woman's return home is all the more dramatic because the king makes a special point of restoring the "lost" income from her farm.

Note to P73,2

74a Eliysha arrived in Dammeseq: This *parashah* recounts the story of Hadadsson's request that Eliysha seek an oracle from Yahweh regarding his illness. In the story, Eliysha receives a vision from Yahweh that Haza'el, who was one of Hadadsson's officials, will become king of Aram and will cause great harm to Yisra'el.

It is noteworthy that in P51,2, Yahweh tells Eliyyahu to go to Dammeseq to anoint Haza'el as king of Aram. But there is no account in Kings of Eliyyahu carrying out this command. The story in P74 seems related to the material in P51,2, but it does not serve as the fulfillment of Yahweh's command to Eliyyahu, as Eliysha only informs Haza'el that he will be king—he does not anoint him.

Notes to P74

74b Hazah'el: Note that the author of this *parashah* sometimes spells the name Haza'el as Hazah'el. The latter spelling reflects the final letter of the verbal root חזה ("to see, perceive"); the letter is silent when in the final position of a word, which gave rise to the abbreviated (and more common) spelling Haza'el.

74c an enormous load... carried by forty camels: Note the fantastic elements here. As I discuss in several notes above, the figure of Eliysha was originally a holy man and not a prophet. The stories about him as a holy man are based on old folk traditions, whereas the stories about him as a prophet are literary compositions that date to the mid- and late Persian period. The story in P74 belongs to this latter group. Because of the large body of folk legends about Eliysha as a holy man, the stories about Eliysha as a prophet occasionally incorporate elements that are characteristic of folk legends, as we see here with the fantastic quantity of gifts that Haza'el takes to Eliysha. Note also the reference to camels, which suggests a Persian period date for this story. Camels were not used as beasts of burden in the Levant in the period in which this story is set (the ninth century BCE).

74d your dear friend Hadadsson: Literally, "your son Hadadsson." The term בן ("son") is often used as a term of endearment in Hebrew, and that is the use here. In English, the word "son" is often used in a similar fashion.

74e tell him he definitely won't live... Yahweh's shown me that he'll definitely die: There is a very interesting *qere-ketiv* here. The written text reads אמר לא חיה תחיה ("say, 'You definitely won't live' "). In the *qere*, this is corrected to אמר לו חיה תחיה ("say to him, 'You'll definitely live' "). It is not clear to me which is the superior reading, as there are problems with both. The uncorrected text is awkward because we expect the preposition "to him" (לו) after the verb אמר, and in fact, the *qere* fixes this problem by replacing the particle לא ("not") with the expected preposition. The corrected text, however, is problematic because it implies that Eliysha tells Haza'el to lie to Hadadsson: "Tell him he'll definitely live. [Although] Yahweh's shown me he'll definitely die." I suspect that the text originally read אמר לו לא חיה תחיה ("say to him, 'You definitely won't live") and that the preposition לו fell from the text due to a scribal error. Given the problematic nature of the text here, I think it is a mistake to read the text with the *qere* and then attempt to derive some theological insight from the fact that Eliysha tells Haza'el to lie.

74f he fixed his face in a frozen position: That is, Eliysha enters a trance in order to access the vision that Yahweh will show him. The prophetic stories from Kings' fourth compositional stage provide numerous interesting details about the nature of prophecy in ancient Yisra'el and Yehudah. These stories were written in the Persian period, but they likely preserve some genuine memories of the prophetic experience. The stories demonstrate that there were a number of different ways that prophets accessed the divine realm in order to receive Yahweh's spoken words (an oracle) or to receive a vision of the future that Yahweh has revealed to the prophet. The language used in Kings for visions that the prophets receive suggests that the prophet often would enter some sort of trance in order to access the vision. At other times, the prophet undertakes dramatic actions or engages in performative speech that is "inspired" by wind from Yahweh or that is prompted by Yahweh's "hand" touching the prophet. The story in P59-P59,1 contains a fascinating depiction of the prophetic experience, as does the story in P65-P65,1.

74g so long that it made one uncomfortable to look at him: The author uses a common Hebrew idiom עד בוש (literally, "to the point of embarrassment"). The idiom also appears at the end of Kgs P62 (the story of Eliyyahu being taken up into the skies) and in the story of Ehud's murder of Eglon King of Mo'av in Jud P12.

74h slaughter their young men, run their babies through, and slice open their pregnant women: Nearly identical language appears in Hos 14.1. The author of P74 may have used this language in an intentional allusion to Hosea, where the imagery appears in an oracle predicting disaster on Shomeron for rebelling against its god Yahweh.

Notes to P75

75a In the fifth year of the reign of Yoram Ah'avsson King of Yisra'el and Yehoshaphat King of Yehudah: The phrase "and Yehoshaphat King of Yehudah" is jarring in the Hebrew. It is possible that the phrase was added by a later editor, although I treat it as original in my translation. Along with many scholars, I think it most likely that the author of P75 mentions Yehoshaphat here as a way of indicating his son Yehoram ruled as co-regent with him. We are told in in P60 that Yehoshaphat ruled for twenty-five years, and in P64 we learn that Yoram Ah'avsson assumed the kingship of Yisra'el in Yehoshaphat's eighteenth year. Thus, if Yehoram Yehoshaphatsson became king in Yoram Ah'avsson's fifth year, that would indicate he became co-regent with his father Yehoshaphat in Yehoshaphat's twenty-third year.

The introductory statement about Yehoram's reign is unusual in that it does not tell us the name of his mother. For all other kings of Yehudah after Rehav'am, the formula used in the introduction to the king's reign includes the name of his mother. Because Yehoram's reign began as a co-regency with his father, it is possible that the account of his reign in the source document *The Chronicle of the Kings of Yehudah* omitted the information about his mother. Alternatively, this information may have simply fallen out of the text due to a copying error.

75b He followed in the footsteps of the kings of Yisra'el... for Aha'v's daughter became his wife: The author implies that Yehoram supported the cult of the Ba'al under the influence of his wife Athalyahu, who was Ah'av's daughter. The marriage alliance between the kings of Yisra'el and Yehudah is noteworthy, as it indicates the close political relationship between the two kingdoms at this time (mid-ninth century BCE). Yehudah was clearly the junior partner in this relationship, and as numerous scholars have argued, was effectively a vassal to Yisra'el.

75c he was married to Ah'av's daughter: Yehoram's wife, as we learn in P76, was the infamous Athalyahu. She installs herself as queen of Yehudah (see P81) after her son Ahazyahu is killed by Yehu (see P77).

75d But Yahweh wasn't willing to destroy Yehudah on account of his servant Dawid...: This sentence is an editorial comment by the authors of the Josianic study books. Note the emphasis on the unconditional promise to Dawid, the complete absence of any treaty between Yahweh and his people, and the authors' indication that Yehudah was a living political entity at the time this sentence was written. This sentence could only have been written by the authors of the Josianic study books, and it offers strong support for the proposal (made by many scholars) that there was an early version of Kings composed in the seventh century BCE that knew nothing of the destruction of Yehudah and of Yahweh's house.

This passage is noteworthy in being one of the few instances where the authors of the Josianic study books explicitly refer to the unconditional Dawidic promise, which I believe was a key motivation of their work and of the political program that they wanted Yoshiyyahu to implement. The other explicit reference by these authors to the unconditional promise to Dawid appears in the prophet Ahiyyah the Shiylonite's speech to Yarov'am in P30,1.

75e in keeping with his promise to him to give him a lamp [*for his descendants*] that would last forever: The language used here—כאשר אמר לו ("just as he said to him")—typically indicates the author is alluding to a specific speech or oracle found elsewhere in the Tanakh. There is no promise given to Dawid that uses the lamp imagery in the book of Samuel or Kings. The author here in P75 is almost certainly alluding to Psalm 132.17: "There [i.e. on Tziyyon] I shall make a horn grow for Dawid—there I have set up a lamp for my anointed one." In the eyes of the author of P75, the "horn" and the "lamp" are Dawid's descendants, who shall rule as king and uphold the binding agreement (ברית) between Yahweh and Yehudah's king. I understand the phrase [*for his descendants*] to be a gloss on the term "lamp" that was added by an author of the sixth compositional stage. For further discussion of the lamp imagery, see notes 30,1g and 41e above.

For the sake of comparison, in Samuel, the unconditional promise to Dawid appears in P80,2. The language reads: "I will raise up one of your sons after you... he is the one who will build a house for my name, in return for which I will make secure his kingdom's throne for all time... Your dynasty and your kingdom will be firmly established for all time..." Compare also the other key expression of the unconditional promise in Ps 89, which I quote at length in my introductory note to this book.

The "lamp" imagery in Ps 132 originally referred to a physical object in Yahweh's house; however, by the time the authors of the Josianic study books were writing, the "lamp" imagery was understood to be a reference to Dawid's descendants. It is easy to imagine a scene in the young king Yoshiyyahu's education in which his tutors teach him about Yahweh's unconditional promise to his great ancestor Dawid and explain to him the binding agreement between Yahweh and the Dawidic king—and most especially help him see that he himself is now the "lamp" put in place by Yahweh.

75f when they had surrouwnded him along with the leaders of his chariotry: The Hebrew is a little awkward, but I believe the meaning is clear. There is a defective spelling of the participle (הסביב instead of the expected הסבב); I have represented the spelling error in my translation. In addition, one object of the participle is somewhat unusually attached to the preposition אל ("to") while the other object of the participle receives the mark of the direct object, as expected. Although somewhat awkward, the Hebrew does not read unnaturally, and I have translated with a slightly awkward but natural equivalent in English.

75g resulting in Edom's forces fleeing: The Hebrew is ambiguous—whose forces are fleeing is not specified. Context suggests that we should understand it is Edom's forces who fled, and I have supplied "Edom's" in translation.

75h (And Edom has remained in rebellion against Yehudah's rule down to the present day.): Another editorial comment from the authors of the Josianic study books. The presence of this parenthetical remark suggests that at least some of the parenthetical comments appearing in Kings are original to the text, even if most were added at a relatively late stage in the compositional process.

75i Livnah: This town has not been identified with a modern location, but references elsewhere in Tanakh suggest it was located in the southwestern part of Yehudah. It is mentioned a number of times elsewhere in Kings as well as in Joshua, Isaiah, Jeremiah, and Chronicles.

Notes to P76

76a Athalyahu Omriysdaughter, the daughter of Yisra'el's king: Athalyahu was the granddaughter of Omriy and the daughter of Ah'av. It is interesting to note that her surname is not based on her father's name. Rather, it was based on the name of her grandfather Omriy. Based on evidence from the historical record, Omriy appears to have been the most prominent king of Yisra'el, as Assyrian inscriptions sometimes refer to the kingdom of Yisra'el as *bīt humri*, or "the nation [or house] of Omriy." See note 48a above.

76b He followed in the footsteps of Ah'av's family: Yehudah was likely a vassal to Yisra'el during this period (the mid-ninth century BCE). Ahazyahu's actions with respect to the military, taxation, and the cult would have been greatly influenced, if not directed, by Yoram King of Yisra'el and his officials.

76c he was Ah'av's maternal grandson: Ahazyahu was the son of Ah'av's daughter Athalyah. The phrase used here to describe Ahazyahu's relationship to Ah'av's family is חתן בית־אחאב. The term חתן designates a male who is related by marriage to another person or another person's family. In Hebrew custom, Ahazyahu's family is that of his father. Thus his family name is Yehoramsson. Ahazyahu is related to

Ah'av's family through Yehoram's marriage to Athalyah. Thus, in Hebrew social custom, he is described as a "grandson-in-law" to Ah'av and he does not belong to Ah'av's family. The closest equivalent concept in English is "maternal grandson," which is how I have chosen to translate the Hebrew here.

76d He went with Yoram Ah'avsson to fight against Haza'el King of Aram: To follow and understand Ahazyahu's actions, it is helpful to keep in mind that he is Yoram Ah'avsson's nephew and that Yehudah at this time is effectively a vassal of Yisra'el. Ahazyahu is little more than a puppet king and is at Yoram's beck and call. The royal family of Yisra'el, the Omrides, were the real power in Yehudah and they undoubtedly worked through Athalyah to maintain a firm grip on the palace administration in Yerushalem. (Ah'av was Omriy's son, so בית־אחאב is simply the term that the author of P76 uses to refer to the Omrides in place of בית־עמרי.)

76e Ramah: Ramah ("Height") is an alternative name for the town Ramoth ("Heights"). The Ramoth here in P76 is the Ramoth in the region of Gil'ad. Because there were many towns called Ramoth, it was common when referring to the town to specify which Ramoth was meant. Thus we read here in P76 of Ramoth Gil'ad. Other Ramoths/Ramahs mentioned in the Tanakh are Ramoth Negev (the Ramoth in the southern desert) in Sam P63,2 and Ramath Lehiy ("Jawbone Height") in Jud P55.

76f Now around the time that Ahazyahu...had gone to see Yoram...because he was wounded...: This *parashah* ends in an incomplete sentence with an ellipsis. I believe that in the earliest version of Kings, this was a complete sentence. The second half of the original sentence can be found midway through P77 in the sentence beginning, "Yehu Yehoshaphatsson conspired against Yoram." The intervening material is an addition by the authors of the Eliysha stories. See note 77a directly below.

77a Eliysha the Prophet summoned one of the prophets...: I understand the first half of this *parashah* to be an addition by the authors of the Eliysha stories. They composed this material to represent the fulfillment of the command given to Eliyyahu at the beginning of P51,2 to anoint Yehu as king of Yisra'el. The material in the first half of P77 was likely composed by the same authors of P74, as P74 represents the (partial) fulfillment of one the other two commands given to Eliyyahu in P51,2. See note 74a above.

Notes to P77

Note that in P77, Eliysha's surname is "The Prophet" and not "The Holy Man." As discussed above, the stories about Eliysha in which he appears as a prophet have no basis in folk tradition and are wholly literary compositions. The fact that Eliysha fulfills a commandment given to Eliyyahu suggests that the stories about Eliysha as a prophet were composed after the authors of Kings' fourth stage decided to expand the initial additions about Eliyyahu by adding a large body of tradition about Eliysha and making Eliysha the successor of Eliyyahu. On the complex composition history of the Eliyyahu and Eliysha stories and their relationship, see note 51,2a above.

77b [*the young man is the prophet*]: I understand the text in italics to be a comment added by an editor from the Persian period or Hellenistic period. The editor must have thought the reader might be confused as the young man is only called a prophet at the beginning of the *parashah* and not again. It is interesting to note that the editorial comment here is one of only four comments or glosses in the large body of material about Eliysha. One other comment is discussed in the note directly below, a third comment appears in P69 (see note 69i above), and a fourth comment is found in P51,2.

77c the murder of my servants the prophets [*and the murder of all Yahweh's servants*] by Iyzevel: I understand the text in italics to be a comment added by an editor from the Persian period or Hellenistic period. See P51 for the reference to Iyzevel's murder of the prophets. There is no mention of her murder of other "servants of Yahweh" apart from the prophets, so it is unclear to me why the reference to the murder of "all Yahweh's servants" was added by a later editor.

77d I shall cut down Ah'av's last remaining descendant...wherever they are in Yisra'el: Note that the young prophet's oracle here duplicates much of Eliyyahu's oracle in P56, in which he condemns Ah'av's family to destruction. As discussed above in note 56b, I believe the original version of P56 was severely corrupted, with all the material after the first oracle in that *parashah* lost. Later editors of the fourth stage repaired P56 by using material from elsewhere in Kings to recreate a new version of the lost oracle that condemned Ah'av's family to destruction. It is this "repaired" version of P56 that the authors of P77 quote, indicating that they were writing very late in the fourth stage, after the repair of P56. In quoting the oracle in P56 condemning Ah'av's family, the authors of the first half of P77 prepare the reader for the oracle's fulfillment, which begins in the second half of P77 when Yehu kills Yehoram and culminates with the murders of Ah'av's remaining descendants in P78,1.

It is interesting to note that the second half of P77 belongs to Kings' first stage and that material quotes a famous oracle of the historical Eliyyahu (see note 77s below). One of the reasons that the authors of the fourth stage may have composed the first half of P77 was to make clear that the events later in P77 and in P78,1 are the fulfillment of the oracle in P56.

77e there won't be anything left of her to bury: The Hebrew here is ואין קבר. The particle אין ("there is not") is often used in contexts where an English speaker would say a thing is "impossible," and that is the nuance here. A literal translation of the phrase is "there isn't a person burying [her]"—that is, it won't be possible for someone to bury her. I have translated with a functionally equivalent phrase in English that captures the force of the Hebrew.

77f Yehu went out to rejoin his lord's officers: The scene that follows is meant to be humorous. It is especially fascinating to see the humor in the dialog, as this provides us a window into how ancient Hebrew speakers jested with one another. The presence of humor in the first half of P77 supports the proposal that this material is an addition to Kings. The material in Kings that I assign to the earliest version of Kings (which was part of the Josianic study books) is almost completely lacking in humor, whereas there are many humorous elements in the Eliysha stories. The authors of the Josianic study books did employ humor in their versions of both Judges and Samuel—in fact, I believe that a major function of both books was to entertain the young king as well as educate him—but humor is almost entirely absent from their version of Kings. In large part, this may have been due to the nature of their primary sources in Kings, which were the official chronicles of the kingdoms of Yisra'el and Yehudah and which recorded the events of each king's reign in matter-of-fact prose.

77g Okay, here's what he said to me: The phrase כזאת וכזאת (which is used here) and the related phrase כזה וכזה are idiomatic. A literal translation of both is "like this and like this." The first phrase appears five times in the Tanakh—Jos P13,2, Sam P99,2 (twice), Kgs P65, and here—and the second phrase three times—Jud P62, Sam P84,3, and Kgs P34. In all but one instance the idiom is used in connection with a verb of speaking, and in those instances, the way the idiom is used implies that the speaker provides a "detailed" or "exact" account of a prior event to his or her audience.

77h Each man quickly took his coat... jesting "Yehu rules as king!": The officers in the scene are clearly joking around and having fun with the idea of the crazy prophet proclaiming Yehu as king over Yisra'el. The author intended this scene to be humorous, and I have reflected that in my translation.

77i at Yehu's feet: The men lay their cloaks down in front of Yehu in a mock mark of respect for the would-be king. The author writes תחתיו (literally, "under him"); when used in reference to individuals, the preposition often has the meaning "the place in which one stands." See BDB, p. 1065, def. 2a. That is clearly how the preposition is used here, and I have translated with a functionally equivalent idiom in English.

77j Yehu Yehoshaphatsson Nimshiysson conspired against Yoram: In the earliest version of Kings, this sentence continued directly from the end of P76. See note 76f above. Before the addition of the first half of P77, I believe the original sentence read: "Now around the time that Ahazyahu Yehoramsson King of Yehudah had gone to see Yoram Ah'avsson in Yizre'el because he was wounded, Yehu Yehoshaphatsson Nimshiysson conspired against Yoram."

77k (Recall that... in his battle with Haza'el King of Aram.): This long parenthetical comment was either added by the authors who composed the first half of P77 or it was added by authors of the final compositional stage of Kings. I have a preference for the former option, although both are plausible. Once the authors of Kings' fourth stage added the first half of P77, they must have been concerned that readers would lose track of the preceding narrative that they had interrupted. To address this, I believe they added this long parenthetical comment, which reminds the reader of the events in P76. The language in their addition repeats verbatim some of the language near the end of P76.

77l don't let anyone leave town, lest he make a run for it and tak news of my plans to Yizre'el: That is, "don't let anyone leave Ramoth Gil'ad." I believe this sentence is part of the addition by the authors of Kings' fourth stage. The audience that Yehu addresses is the army officers with Yehu at the beginning of the *parashah*. Recall from the beginning of the *parashah* that Yehu and his officers are in Ramoth Gil'ad, which was the site of the battle between Yoram King of Yisra'el and Haza'el King of Aram.

The Hebrew here is somewhat difficult because the author uses the word פליט ("escapee, fugitive, refugee") in an unusual way: it refers not to someone escaping battle, but rather to someone who opposes Yehu and who escapes from the town under Yehu's control. Literally, "A fugitive mustn't leave town to go inform [officials] in Yizre'el [of my plans]." I have tried to capture the sense of פליט here with the translation "make a run for it."

Note also that the verb "inform" (להגיד) is misspelled in the written text, and there is a *qere* in the margin providing the correct spelling. I reflect the error by translating as "tak news."

77m (At the time, Ahazyahu... had gone to see Yoram.): I believe this parenthetical comment was added by the authors of Kings' fourth stage, to remind the reader of the events in P76, which had been interrupted by the addition of the first half of P77. See note 77k above.

77n the fortress: This is the large military fort in the town of Yizre'el that guarded access to the Yizre'el Valley. See note 55b above. For Yizre'el's role as a military site, see the article by N. Franklin, "Jezreel: A Military City and the Location of Jehu's Coup," at the website /https://www.thetorah.com.

77o I see 's patrol: The word "Yehu" has fallen out of the text. Originally it must have read "I see Yehu's patrol." My translation reflects the error in the text, in which the word שפעה is in construct, but is not followed by a noun. I conjecture that the word שפעה (literally, "wave") was sometimes used as a technical military term for a small unit of soliders, equivalent in size to a squad (6 to 12) or a patrol (12 to 24) in the modern-day army. Given Yehu's position as head of the army, the watchman would be familiar with him, and presumably his patrol would be recognizable by its uniforms and the decorations on its chariots.

77p Get out of my way!: A literal translation of Yehu's language is "Turn behind me" or, more colloquially, "get behind me." I believe the language here is idiomatic and is equivalent to the English phrase "get out of my way."

77q the property belonging to Navoth the Yizre'elite: This is the first mention of Navoth in the material belonging to Kings' first compositional stage (the version that I associate with the Josianic study books); the material about Navoth in P55-P58 is an addition from the fourth compositional stage of Kings.

77r your mother Iyzevel is whoring around and carrying on her incessant hocus-pocus: As the queen mother, Iyzevel would have retained a great deal of power. Recall that she killed Yahweh's prophets and was an enthusiastic supporter and promoter of the cult of the Ba'al (see the references to her in P51 and P51,1). It is her support for the Ba'al's cult that Yehu refers to here with his derogatory language.

77s the teams of riders following his father Ah'av and how Yahweh delivered that oracle against him…: A literal rendering of רכבים צמדים (which I translate as "the teams of riders") is "those riding in teams." The allusion to the teams of riders and the oracle that follows is original to the earliest version of Kings. Note that the material here (including the oracle) is at odds with the account about Navoth in P55-P56. Here a reference is made to the murders of Navoth's children, but in P55, only Navoth is murdered. And the allusion to "the teams of riders" is mysterious, as these individuals are nowhere to be seen in P55. I believe they most likely were the henchmen who accompanied Ah'av and helped him carry out the murder of Nadav and his children. The authors of the Josianic study books here are referring to a famous story about Ah'av that their readers would be familiar with, but they have not included that story in their composition. The oracle quoted here condemning Ah'av is not attributed to any prophet, but I strongly suspect that this oracle should be attributed to Eliyyahu given that the authors of P78,1 and P78,2 refer to another oracle of Eliyyahu in which he condemns Ah'av and his family. See notes 78,1h and 78,2g below.

77t hit him in the chariot when he's at Gur's Pass: Presumably the geography of Gur's Pass made it a favorable position for archers, perhaps because the road there was difficult and a chariot had to proceed slowly.

77u He fled as far as Megiddo and died there: I believe the authors of Kings' first stage have altered the circumstances of the deaths of Yehoram and Ahazyahu in order to elevate the status of Yehu and present him as an agent of Yahweh. Both kings appear to be mentioned in the Tel Dan inscription, which scholars believe to be a ninth-century BCE stele commemorating the great deeds of Haza'el King of Aram. A widely accepted reconstruction of this inscription suggests that in fact Haza'el killed both kings, not Yehu. (For this reconstruction, see the article by A. Biran and J. Naveh cited above in the footnote to note 59a). Some scholars explain the discrepancy between the biblical account and the evidence of the Tel Dan inscription by proposing that Yehu was allied with Haza'el and/or acting on Haza'el's orders. See, for example,

W. Schniedewind, "Tel Dan Stela: New Light on Aramaic and Jehu's Revolt," *Bulletin of the American Schools of Oriental Research*, No. 302 (1996), pp. 75-90. It seems to me, however, that their primary motivation in proposing this is a discomfort with the idea that the authors of the core narrative of Kings (who many scholars view as "historians") might fabricate details in their stories and not present a true account of events. As I argue in the introduction to this book, I believe that the authors of Kings should not be viewed as historians or writers of historiography. Moreover, a close reading of Kings indicates that all of its authors—including the authors of the first stage, who were responsible for the book's base narrative—very frequently fabricated details in their stories in support of their own literary goals.

78a In the eleventh year... Ahazyah ruled as king over Yehudah: This sentence is a near duplicate of the introduction to Ahazyahu's reign in P76, and its presence here immediately after the account of Ahazyahu's death is very strange. It is possible that originally the first sentence of P78 introduced Yehu's reign, as there is currently no place in the text where his reign is introduced. If the beginning of P78 did introduce Yehu's reign, it is conceivable that the sychronism was with his predecessor Yoram rather than Ahazyahu, with the sentence reading something like "In the eleventh year of Yoram Ah'avsson, Yehu ruled as king over Yisra'el."

Notes to P78

If the original introduction to P78 was lost, it likely was due to a scribal error: a scribe could have been confused by the anomalous synchronism which dated the beginning of Yehu's rule in relation to his predecessor rather than in relation to the king of Yehudah. In this scenario, to fix what he thought was an error, the scribe would have replaced the statement that "Yehu ruled as king over Yisra'el" (מלך יהוא על-ישראל) with the statement that "Ahazyah ruled as king over Yehudah" (מלך אחזה על-יהודה). One other oddity of this passage is that the chronology is slightly different from the chronology in P76: here Ahazyah assumes the throne in the eleventh year of Yoram Ah'avsson, and in P76 he assumes the throne in Yoram's twelfth year.

78b Yehu proceeded on to Yizre'el. When Iyzevel heard he was coming: That is, Yehu proceeded on to the town of Yizre'el, which was located on a ridge at the southeastern end of the Yizre'el Valley. On this town, see note 55b above.

Recall that Iyzevel is King Yoram's mother; as queen mother she still has much power and influence. Thus, after killing Ahazyah, Yehu proceeds to Yizre'el to dispose of Yoram's mother.

78c prettied up her face and hair, and then stood by the window and looked out: Literally, "prettied up her head and looked down through the window." In English, it is more natural in this context to say "face and hair" than "head," which I have reflected in my translation. Similarly, the lack of a transition between Iyzevel's applying her make-up and then looking out the window is jarring in English (though not in Hebrew). It is more natural in English to state that she moved to the window after prettying herself up, which I also have reflected in my translation.

78d Did things work out for Zimriy when he killed his lord?: An allusion to the abortive seven-day reign of Zimriy over Yisra'el. See the account in P45 - P46.

78e For she is the daughter of a king after all: Iyzevel was the daughter of Ethba'al, the king of the Tziydonians. See P49.

78f Yahweh's oracle, which he spoke through his servant Eliyyahu the Tishbite: This is one of only five mentions of Eliyyahu in the earliest version of Kings; the others occur in P60,2, P60,3, P78,1 and P78,2. The two references to Eliyyahu in P78,1 and P78,2 allude to an oracle that he delivered in condemnation of Ah'av and his family—an oracle that may have once been preserved in P56 but is now lost (see note

56b above and note 78,1j below). His appearance in P60,2 and P60,3 is to deliver an oracle to Ahazyahu Ah'avsson. It's worth noting that Eliyyahu is not called a prophet in any of the five mentions of him in the earliest version of Kings. He is given the surname "the Tishbite" in P60,2, and he is called Yahweh's "servant" in P78,1.

78g In a section of Yizre'el, the dogs will eat Iyzevel's body: The oracle quoted here is a variant of the oracle that Eliyyahu delivers about Iyzevel near the end of P56. The oracle in P56 states simply, "The dogs will eat Iyzevel on Yizre'el's ramparts." Although the material in P78 is original to the Josianic study books, and although the material in P56 was added some two centuries later, the oracle in P56 appears to be the original version. The oracle about Iyzevel's death in Yizre'el in P78 seems to have attracted language from the original version of the oracle about Navoth's death in Yizre'el, which appears in P77—specifically the language about the "plot of land" (חלק).

78h [*And 'Iyzevel's corpse wil be like manure...shall never be uttered.'*]: This text represents a second oracle about Iyzevel, separate from the one about the dogs eating her body. The oracle does not fit the context nearly as well as the preceding oracle, and it seems unlikely to me that this oracle is original to the *parashah*. The best way to understand this oracle, in my opinion, is as a comment added by the editors of the sixth stage. The editors must have known of a second oracle about Iyzevel's death and included that oracle here out of a desire to "complete" the account of her death.

78i —: The Leningrad Codex has a *parashah petuhah* here. See L208 v.3.24-25.

Notes to P78,1

78,1a Now Ah'av had seventy sons in Shomeron...: The story of the murder of Ah'av's seventy sons has a number of similarities to Aviymelek's murder of Yeruba'al's seventy sons in Jud P29. I believe the author of the Aviymelek story in Judges, which I date to the Persian period, may have drawn from parts of the account here in P78,1 in crafting his story.

Ancient Hebrew authors often used seventy to signify a large number in general, and that is how it is used here. We should not presume that the author means Ah'av had exactly seventy sons. This use of the number seventy in ancient Hebrew is similar to how English speakers use the term "dozens of" to refer to a large number of a thing when the precise number is unknown. In fact, it would be reasonable to translate the first sentence of P78,1 as "Now Ah'av had dozens of sons in Shomeron."

78,1b the leaders of Yizre'el [*that is, the elders*]: It is unclear if the leaders of Yizre'el here are meant to denote the leaders of the military town Yizre'el or the region Yizre'el (for Yizre'el as the name of a region see Sam P70). A later editor has added a gloss interpreting the phrase to mean the elders, but that does not really clarify the matter. I have a preference for understanding the phrase here as referring to the elders of the region (or administrative district) Yizre'el, as the town itself was little more than a military headquarters of the kingdom of Yisra'el. Regardless of how the phrase is understood, it is somewhat odd that the leaders/elders are gathered in Shomeron rather than at home in Yizre'el. Possibly the author wished the reader to understand that they fled to Shomeron because they feared for their lives after Yehu murdered Yoram. Another possibility is simply that the text is corrupt: the text would make much more sense if it read "the leaders of Yisra'el" (שׂרי ישׂראל) instead of "leaders of Yizre'el" (שׂרי יזרעאל)—the two phrases sound nearly identical and differ by just two letters.

78,1c those who remained loyal to Ah'av: That is, those loyal to Ah'av's family. Recall that Ah'av died previously (see P59,1) and that he was succeeded first by his son Ahazyahu Ah'avsson (see P60,1) and then by a second son Yehoram Ah'avsson (see the end of P60,3 and P64), both of whom are now dead.

The presence of the *qal* participle האמנים is a bit unusual; based on context, I believe it must have the sense of "those who supported" (i.e. were loyal to) Ah'av, although this would be the only such use of the verb. The *qal* form of the verb typically has the meaning "care for or provide support to [a person who is a dependent]," but that meaning is nonsensical here.

78,1d when they heard the letters: I have added this phrase in translation, which does not appear in the Hebrew.

78,1e come to me here in Yizre'el sometime tomorrow: The author uses the idiom כעת מחר ("like a time tomorrow"). In spoken language, the idiom clearly means "at [or around] this time tomorrow." However, the idiom also appears in letters, as here. In letters, the idiom cannot mean "at this time tomorrow," as the recipient of the letter doesn't know at what time the letter was dictated or written. Thus, when the idiom appears in letter, it is best translated simply as "tomorrow" or "sometime tomorrow." An example of the idiom in spoken language appears in the oracle at the beginning of P72, which is then repeated near the end of P73. Examples of the idiom in letters appear in Iyzevel's message to Eliyyahu in P51,1 and in Hadadsson's second letter near the beginning of P52. Other examples of the spoken idiom appear in Ex P13,1, Jos P23, Sam P18,1, and Sam P47,3.

Yizre'el was roughly fifty kilometers from Shomeron—a very long day's journey—and it would not be possible for the elders to arrive "at this time tomorrow." Arriving "sometime tomorrow" would be possible only if they departed very early in the morning.

78,1f men who had been their childhood mentors: The author adds this detail to heighten the pathos of the scene. As I have frequently commented in my other translations, it was common for ancient Hebrew authors to heighten the drama of their narrative by introducing details or use expressions that play on the reader's emotions. The language here is an excellent example of this technique.

78,1g sent them to Yehu in Yizre'el: Literally, "sent to Yehu in Yizre'el." I have added "them" (i.e. the heads) as the object of the verb to make clear to the reader what I believe was the author's intent. The omission of the object of a verb was common in ancient Hebrew, especially if the speaker/writer believed that the object of a verb would have been obvious to his audience. In this instance, it is possible that the object of the verb is "the messenger" (who appears in the next clause to deliver the news to Yehu that the deed has been done). However, it is slightly more natural to understand the object of the verb here as the heads, which I have reflected in my translation.

78,1h in front of the town gate: That is, in the plaza inside the town adjacent to the town gate. The author does not mean outside the town gate. The plaza was where most public business in town was conducted, and it would make most sense for Yehu to place the heads there as a statement to all those present in the town (which would include the delegation from Shomeron). For more on town plazas in the walled towns of ancient Yisra'el and Yehudah, see note 64q in my translation of Judges.

78,1i You all bear no responsibility for this crime: Literally, "You all are innocent [of wrongdoing]." The author uses specific legal terminology; he writes צדיקים, which in a legal context may either mean "those who are in the right" (i.e. those who win a lawsuit) or "those who are acquitted/innocent of a criminal accusation." BDB, p. 843, def. 2, recognizes the usage here in this passage.

78,1j Yahweh's oracle which he spoke in condemnation of Ah'av's family: I assign the material in P78,1 to the earliest version of Kings. The oracle alluded to here cannot be the oracle quoted near the end of P77, for that oracle makes no mention of Ah'av's family. Moreover, I believe that the oracle alluded to here in P78,1 was never part of the earliest version of Kings, although it must have been sufficiently well-known that the authors of the first stage did not think it was necessary to quote it.

I suspect that the oracle alluded to may have been part of the original version of P56; although that *parashah* was added by the authors of the fourth stage, the authors may have had access to this old oracle by Eliyyahu and incorporated into their composition. If this was the case, however, that oracle is no longer in Kings. As I propose above in note 56b, the original version of the second half of P56 is lost and what we have is a clumsy "restoration" based on language found in oracles elsewhere in Kings. See also the discussion of this oracle in note 77d above.

Finally, it's worth noting that the mention of Eliyyahu here is one of only five mentions of him in the earliest version of Kings. See note 78f above.

78,1k all his important allies—those involved with him and his priests: The author's phrasing is unusual—he writes כל-גדליו (literally, "all his important ones"), which I translate as "all his important allies." This is followed by the clause ומידעיו וכהניו ("those involved with him and his priests"). I understand that clause as original to the text, but it is equally plausible to read it as a later gloss on the unusual phrase preceding it.

I presume that in referring to the king's "allies," the author intended this to include all the individuals mentioned at the beginning of the *parashah*—the leaders of Yizre'el, the elders, and those who remained loyal to Ah'av (האמנים אחאב); this would also include the palace chamberlain and the town mayor, who are mentioned subsequently.

The priests are also mentioned here as the king's allies. Recall that Ah'av was a devotee of the Ba'al. The reference thus must be to the priests of the Ba'al, not the priests of Yahweh.

78,1l We've come to see if the king's children and the queen mother's children are safe: I understand גבירה ("queen") here to refer to Iyzevel and so translate as "queen mother." Ahazyahu's kinsmen have heard the news of Yehu's killing of Ahazyahu, Yehoram, and Iyzevel, and they would have been aware of the threat to Ah'av's family posed by Yehu. Note that Ahazyahu's kinsmen distinguish between the children of the queen mother and the children of her son King Yehoram.

Recall from P75 that Ahazyahu's mother Athalyah is the daughter of Ah'av. As mentioned above in note 75b, Yehudah at the time was a vassal state to Yisra'el, and Athalyah was likely the real power in Yehudah, not her husband (King Yehoram) nor her son (King Ahazyahu). It would be natural for her to send a delegation to Shomeron to check on the safety of her brothers and sisters given that Yehu had just killed Iyzevel (her father's wife and possibly her mother) and Yehoram King of Yisra'el (her full or half-brother), as well as her son Ahazyahu. The delegation is described as "Ahazyahu's kinsmen" because he was king and head of the royal family, even if Athalyah held the real power.

The response of Ahazyahu's kinsmen suggests that they did not recognize the man they were speaking to as Yehu. This small detail is another example of the author adding an element of pathos to his story to create greater emotional impact.

78,1m Not a single one of them was spared: I have a slight preference for understanding the subject of the verb as indefinite, and I thus translate in the passive voice. It is equally plausible, however, to understand Yehu as the subject of the verb, in which case the translation would be, "He didn't spare a single one of them."

78,2a Yehonadav Rekavsson: Unusually, the author of this *parashah* gives the reader no introduction to Yehonadav—he assumes the reader knows who this person is. He must have been a historical figure well-known in ancient Yisra'el and Yehudah, but no other record of him has come down to us apart from the mention here. The lack of information about Yehonadav adds to the difficulty of understanding this brief *parashah*. It is obvious that he is an ally of Yehu, but the exact nature of their relationship is unclear. In my composition history, I have assigned this *parashah* to Kings' first stage, but it is also possible that the *parashah* is an addition from a later compositional stage. The *parashah* is not essential to the narrative of Kings, and it is noteworthy that there is no other material in Kings that is dependent on it.

Notes to P78,2

78,2b who was coming to meet him: The Hebrew is awkward and somewhat ambiguous. It is possible to understand the phrase לקראתו to modify Yehonadav, which is how I have translated, or to understand it as the object of the verb מצא ("find, happen upon"). In the latter case, a functionally equivalent translation would be "happened upon Yehonadav Rekavsson, meeting him."

78,2c Does it please you when you and I agree on things?: The Hebrew here is very difficult. The author uses idiomatic and highly colloquial phrasing, and I am not certain my reading is correct. I understand the adjective ישר ("straight, right, pleasing") to function as a substantive. I understand the phrase לבבי עם-לבבך ("my heart is with your heart") to be idiomatic, similar to the English phrase "you and I are of the same mind." A literal translation of Yehu's question is, "Is there pleasure with your heart when my heart is with your heart?" I understand Yehu's comment about him and Yehonadav "agreeing on things" to be a reference to their agreeing that Ah'av's family must be wiped out.

78,2d Well if so, then give me your hand: No change of speaker is indicated in the Hebrew, which is very unusual. The lack of indication of a change of speaker contributes to the awkwardness of the passage and makes one wonder whether the text here may be corrupt.

78,2e raising it up to Yehu in the chariot: The Hebrew verb phrase ויעלהו אליו ("he raised it to him") is elliptical and ambiguous. I understand Yehonadav to be the subject of the verb and his hand to be the direct object. It is also possible to understand Yehu as the subject of the verb, which would describe a scene in which Yehu grabs Yehonadav's outstretched hand and pulls it toward himself in preparation for helping Yehonadav get in the chariot. A third possibility is that Yehu is the subject of the verb and Yehonodav is the direct object—"he [Yehu] lifted him [Yehonadav] up to himself into the chariot." This last possibility seems least likely to me, as the second sentence following states that "they [i.e. Yehu and the chariot driver] got him [Yehonadav] into the chariot."

78,2f they pulled him into the chariot: The plural subject of the verb ("they") suggests that there is a chariot driver with Yehu. Three men in the chariot would be a tight fit.

Notes to P79

78,2g just as Yahweh foretold in the oracle that he spoke to Eliyyahu: This oracle is the same oracle mentioned above in P78,1. This oracle was not part of the earliest version of Kings, but it may have been added to a (now lost) part of P56. See the discussion in notes 56b and 78,1j above.

79a Ah'av gave service to the Ba'al: That is, the king supported the Ba'al's cult and participated in its rites and festivals. The verb עבד ("serve") in the context of the cult always implies participation in rites in honor of the god, especially offering rites associated with the care and feeding of the god. Note also that the author of this *parashah* uses the term עבדי הבעל ("those who give service to the Ba'al") a number of times. This term refers to the commoners in Yisra'el who participated in his cult; I translate in it once as "those who participated in the Ba'al's cult" and other times as "the Ba'al's devotees."

79b a great welfare offering: Yehu uses the word זבח, which is usually translated as "sacrifice." However, זבח alone is frequently used as an abbreviation of זבח שלמים, which is the term for a "welfare offering." This is how Yehu's audience would have understood his use of the word here. That said, it's worth noting the base meaning of זבח is simply "slaughter," and the author may have intentionally used the word here because of this ambiguity. Yehu himself is thinking of a "great slaughter," but he knows his audience will understand him to mean "a great welfare offering."

79c (Now Yehu did this as a trick...the Ba'al's cult.): Although it is possible to view this sentence as a late addition to the text, I have a preference for viewing it as original to the *parashah*, which is part of the earliest version of Kings. If it were an addition, the presence of the phrase ויאמר יהוא ("Yehu said") in the following sentence would be inexplicable, as the sentence would have been part of Yehu's preceding speech.

79d and the summonses went out: Literally, "and they summoned [them]." The Hebrew here is elliptical and somewhat awkward, which I have reflected in translation. I have a slight preference for understanding the subject of the verb here as indefinite. Alternatively, one may translate "and they were summoned."

79e the grounds of the Ba'al's temple: The word בית ("house") here is used expansively to designate the entire temple grounds; it does not mean only the building where the Ba'al's image is kept.

79f Yehonadav Rekavsson: It is unclear why the author mentions Yehonadav; he is a mysterious character and plays no role whatsoever in the narrative. I treat the mention of him here as original to the text, but if P78,2 (where he is introduced) is viewed as a late addition, then his presence here should also be seen as an addition.

79g the welfare offerings and the whole offerings: The author uses the phrase זבחים ועלות. This is a common phrase that means "welfare offerings and whole offerings." The use of זבחים in this phrase is as an abbreviation of זבחי שלמים ("welfare offerings"). The use of the abbreviation here provides some support for my understanding of Yehu's earlier use of זבח as an abbreviation for welfare offering, as discussed above in note 79b.

79h the men I'm making you responsible for: The author uses what must be an idiomatic construction—הביא על יד ("to bring [something or someone] onto the hand [of another person]") There is a related idiom, נתן על יד ("to put [a person or a thing] upon the hand [of another person]"), which means to entrust something or someone to another's care. On this latter idiom, see note 37ap of my translation of Genesis.

79i it will be one's own life instead of his: The Hebrew is awkward and it is likely that an error has crept into the text. The standard phrase is נפשך תחת נפשו ("your life instead of his"), which differs from the text here by just a single letter. Elsewhere in Kings, the standard phrase appears near the end of P54,1.

79j Once they had finished preparing the whole offering: That is, once they had finished slaughtering the animal, butchering it, and arranging its pieces on the altar. When a whole offering and a welfare offering are both being presented, the whole offering—which is a gift to the god (in this case, the Ba'al)—is always performed first. Only then is the welfare offering performed, the meat from which is shared among all those invited in a celebratory feast. See, for example, Num P29,6 - P41, which enumerates the offerings given by each of the twelve tribes at the dedication of the altar used by the Yisra'elites during their wilderness wanderings. In each set of offerings, the order of animal sacrifices is first the whole offering, then the error offering, and then the welfare offering.

79k the royal guard and the army captains: I understand these men to be the same as the eighty men whom Yehu stationed outside the temple grounds. That said, it is certainly possible to see them as a different group, for it is a somewhat odd that the author didn't specify earlier that the eighty men consisted of the royal guard and the army captains.

79l the citadel: The word here is עיר, which usually means "town, city." The word may originally have meant "fort, citadel," and there are many places in the Tanakh where it still has this meaning, including here and in the name Fort Dawid (which is often mistranslated as the City of Dawid). See BDB, p. 746, defs. 2 and 3, for some citations where the word is used in reference to a fortress or fortified place.

79m brought out the sacred pillars belonging to the Ba'al's temple: These pillars were in storage in the citadel; presumably they were smaller than the primary pillar on the temple grounds that the royal guard and army captains knocked down. The pillars mentioned here perhaps were used only in certain rites or festivals, and so were typically kept in storage. It was common for temples to have fortified structures on their grounds that also served as storage areas. For another example of a fort on temple grounds, see Jud P32 and my comments in note 32b of my translation of Judges.

79n and burned down the citadel: Literally, "and set it on fire." Hebrew can be quite inconsistent in its use of pronouns, and it is not uncommon to see singular pronouns referring to plural objects, and *vice versa*. Thus, it is unclear if the feminine singular pronoun here refers to the sacred pillars or to the citadel, as both these nouns are feminine. Because the sacred pillars more likely would have been made of stone than wood (and therefore would have been difficult to destroy by burning), I have a slight preference for understanding the pronoun here to refer to the citadel.

79o [*that is, the gold bull calves which were in Beyth-El and in Dan*]: I understand this to be a gloss added by the editors of the sixth compositional stage. The authors of the earliest version of Kings typically avoid explicit mention of the bull calves by using the circumlocution "the errors of Yarov'am Nevatsson."

79p **: The Leningrad Codex has a *parashah setumah* here. See L209 v.2.9-10.

Notes to P80

80a "On account of the fact that you've excelled... four generations of your descendants will occupy Yisra'el's throne: I believe this sentence is original to the earliest version of Kings. The four descendants of Yehu who succeeded him on the throne were Yeho'ahaz Yehusson (P86), Yeho'ash Yeho'ahazsson (P87), Yarov'am Yo'ashsson (P94), and Zekaryahu Yarov'amsson (P96), who was assassinated by Shallum Yaveshsson.

80b (Yehu, however, didn't take care... by which he made Yisra'el go wrong.): It is possible to understand this sentence as belonging to the earliest version of Kings, or as a late addition made by either the authors of Kings' third stage or the editors of the sixth stage. In the first option, one would understand תורה (*tōrāh*) here as Yahweh's "instructions"—that is, the rules for managing his cult. This is the meaning of the term in early literature preserved in the Tanakh; *tōrāh* has this meaning in several places in Hosea, in Ps 89 (an early exemplar of Judean royal ideology), and in the ancient cult rule books preserved in Leviticus. If one views this sentence instead as a late addition, one would understand it to be simply a comment by late editors for whom the Torah was the frame of reference for all things, and who felt it necessary to point out that even though Yehu "pleased" Yahweh, he did not abide by Yahweh's Torah.

My personal preference is to understand this sentence as a late addition, and I have reflected this in my translation. In favor of this view is that the term *tōrāh* appears only ten times in Kings, and all instances apart from this one clearly belong to late compositional stages. In addition, the authors of the first stage mention at the end of P79 that Yehu "didn't abandon" Yarov'am errors; thus, there would be no need for them to repeat this point two sentences later. In my proposed composition history, I have assigned this sentence to the sixth stage rather than the third, as I believe the addition is more in keeping with the motivations of the editors of the sixth stage. In this instance, their motivation was simply to clarify that Yehu was still a "bad" king even if he did please Yahweh in eradicating the Ba'al's cult.

80c [*the region of the Gadites, the Re'uvenites, and the Menashshehites... the Bashan region in the north*]: I understand this clause to be an addition by the authors of the third stage, who in many places added comments that harmonized Kings with the books of the Torah and Joshua. The language used is formulaic; similar language appears in Numbers, Deuteronomy, and Joshua. The language here is closest to phrasing in Deut P1,4 and Jos P25, and likely was based on one of those *parashot*.

80d The rest of Yehu's acts—everything that he did and all his valorous deeds...: The famous black obelisk of Shalmaneser III has a depiction of Yehu prostrating himself and paying tribute (see figure 1 below). This is the only contemporary depiction of a king of either Yisra'el or Yehudah that has come down to us. The account of Yehu's reign in Kings makes no mention of Yehu being a vassal to the king of Ashshur. However, it seems quite likely that the account of his reign in the book *The Chronicles of the Kings of Yisra'el* would have mentioned his paying tribute to the king of Ashshur. The book of Kings' accounts of the reigns of other kings often mention their tribute to Aram and Ashshur, so we know that these must have been mentioned in the official chronicles of both kingdoms. The authors of the Josianic study books may have omitted mention of Yehu's position as vassal because they wished to portray him as favored by Yahweh.

Especially interesting is that the inscription on the obelisk names Yehu as "son of Humri"—that is Omriy. In Kings, however, Yehu is not a descendant of Omriy, but rather he exterminates Omriy's descendants by killing Ah'av's entire family. It is certainly possible that Yehu was a direct descendant of Omriy and belonged to a branch of the family that was a rival to Ah'av's line. However, I think it more likely

"I received the tribute of Iaua [=Yehu] son of Humri [=Omriy]: silver, gold, a golden bowl, a golden vase with pointed bottom, golden tumblers, golden buckets, tin, a staff for a king, spears."
Figure 1: Image of Yehu Omriysson paying tribute to Shalmaneser. Black obelisk of Shalmaneser III (British Museum number 11885), second register from top.
Public domain image available at: /https://commons.wikimedia.org/wiki/File: Black_Obelisk_Yehu_in_front_of_Shalmaneser_III.jpg

that the author of the inscription was mistaken. He may have been misinformed or, more likely, he may simply have assumed that Yehu belonged to the royal line by which Yisra'el was known in the ancient Near East—Yisra'el is referred to as "the house of Omriy" (*Bit-Humri*) in a number of inscriptions from Ashshur.

81a When Ahazyahu's mother Athalyah and saw that her son had died: Recall from P76 that Athalyah was a northerner and was the daughter of Ah'av and Iyzevel. See notes 75c and 76a above. During the reigns of her husband Yoram and her son Ahazyahu, Yehudah was effectively a vassal state of Yisra'el and Athalyah almost certainly was the person who held the real power in Yehudah during those years (see also the discussion in note 78,1l above). With Yehu having killed all of Ah'av's remaining family in both Shomeron and in Yehudah (see the end of P78,1 for the elimination of Ah'av's family members in Yehudah), the kinship network that served as the basis of Athalyah's power was destroyed. If the events described in P77 and P78,1 are historically accurate (which they may not be, as we know the authors of these *parashot* changed or fabricated a number of key details), then this would be the context for her actions in P81. In this scenario, one should presume she was much hated by the royal family of Dawid and by most if not all of the leading families in Yehudah, who would have viewed her as an outsider and resented the control by Yisra'el wielded through her. Given the events described in P82, it would be reasonable to suppose that she never had the support of the leadership of either the cult or the royal guard. If one accepts that the events in P81-P82,2 have a firm basis in history, then a likely scenario would be that the execution of the king's sons was carried out by officers belonging to Athalyah's personal guard, and that the plan was successful only because Athalyah acted so quickly after Ahazyahu's death, before those who opposed her could get organized.

Alternatively, we may view the material in P81-P82,2 as a literary creation of the authors of Kings' first stage. In fact, I find this preferable to the idea that this material

Notes to P81

NOTES AND COMMENTS

has a firm basis in history. See note 81c below.

In the first sentence of this *parashah*, there is an error in the consonantal text that I represent in translation. The text has a superfluous "and" (the letter *waw*) attached to the verb "saw." The Masoretes have corrected this with a *qere* in the margin. See A97 v.2.23 and L209 v.3.9.

81b taking him and his wet nurse when they were in the dormitory: It is unclear who slept in the dormitory. Possibly it was a nursery where the king's newborn children stayed with their wet nurses.

81c while Athalyah ruled the country as queen: Note that the authors of Kings' first stage do not provide an introduction to Athalyah's reign as they do with the other rulers of Yisra'el and Yehudah. The only rulers who have no introduction to their reign are Athalyah and Yehu (and Tivniy, if one wishes to include him in the list of kings of Yisra'el).

The material from Kings' first stage about Athalyah, like the material about Yehu, is full of literary elements that do not appear to be based on any source documents. Given that, I think that we have to question how much the account of Athalyah's reign and the account of the accession of Yeho'ash have a basis in history. I think it is reasonable to view the story of Athalyah's murder of her grandsons and of Yeho'ash's escape as a literary creation of the authors of Kings' first stage. They may have wished to make Yeho'ash more prominent in their narrative because they believed their pupil Yoshiyyahu would "identify" with him and view him as a model due to the young age at which both became king. Thus, it is certainly conceivable that Athalyah did not slaughter her own grandchildren and that she instead ruled as queen until Yeho'ash was old enough to assume the kingship under the guidance of a regent.

Notes to P82

82a Yehoyada: It is odd that the author provides no surname for Yehoyada. We expect to read "Yehoyada the Priest," and it is possible that the surname has fallen out of the text due to a scribal error.

82b the officers of the militarie [*those of the Karian guard and the royal guard*]: There is some confusion in the text of P82 - P82,2 regarding the phrase שרי המאות (literally, "chiefs of the hundreds"), which I translate as "officers of the military." I believe the phrase is best understood as a generic term for senior military officers, as is indicated by the gloss in P82,1 "those who oversaw the army" (פקדי החיל). The confusion stems from the fact that the term is consistently misspelled in P82 and P82,1 and from the fact that the author uses it in P82 to refer specifically to a subset of military officers responsible for keeping the watches at the palace and at Yahweh's house. A later editor was apparently confused by the author's use of the term in this way, and so he added the gloss "those of the Karian guard and the royal guard" to specify that it was those military officers who were meant. The term "the Karian guard" (הכרי) is an abbreviated form of the guard's full name, which was "the Kerethite and Pelethite guard" (הכרתי והפלתי). This guard, which elsewhere in my translation I call "the personal guard," shared responsibility with the royal guard for protecting the king. On these two guards and their names, see notes 1i and 3d above.

While the phrase שרי המאות is a generic term for senior military officers, in its original sense it referred to the commanders of one of the fighting units in the army of Yehudah—the "hundreds," which would be roughly equivalent to a company within a modern-day army. On the organization of the military into armies (צבאות), battalions (אלפים), companies (מאות), platoons (חמשים), and squads (עשרות), see note 1f of my translation of Numbers.

82c A third of you will come in on the Shabbath...: The passage beginning here and describing the actions of the three groups of the guards is awkward in Hebrew and very difficult to follow. The prose is technical in nature, and ancient Hebrew technical writing is often elliptical and difficult to understand. In my translation, I have supplied additional terms and rearranged clauses in order to express the language of the Hebrew text in functionally equivalent English, as English technical writing is not necessarily elliptical to the same degree as Hebrew.

82d The rest of you will be on the palace watch when the guard changes at that time: I have moved this clause to the beginning of the sentence to facilitate understanding; in the Hebrew, the clause appears at the end of the sentence, after the statements about the location of the other two-thirds of the guards. I have also supplied additional language to make clear what is going on. A literal translation of the entire sentence is: "One third [of you] will be at the Sur Gate and one third at the gate behind the Royal Guards [Gate]—you will be keeping the palace watch at the changing of the guard."

82e when the guard changes at that time: The Hebrew is obscure, but context helps us understand the meaning. I understand the word מסח to mean "changing [of the guard]." The root of the word is נסח, which means "pull away, tear away, remove." The meaning proposed here fits the context well and is consistent with the core meaning of the root; it is unclear to me why BDB, p. 650 and p. 587, makes no attempt to discern the word's meaning and proposes instead that the text is in error. I have added the phrase "at that time" to help the reader understand the sequence of actions that the author is describing: on the Shabbath, one-third of the officers will come to the palace to replace the two-thirds who are on watch there; the two-thirds who depart the palace will then go to Yahweh's house to assume watch guarding the king's son, who will be installed as king by Yehoyada.

82f the Sur Gate...the gate behind the Royal Guards Gate: The Hebrew is somewhat confusing because the author uses elliptical language. I understand there to be three gates mentioned here, not two, and I understand all three of these gates to be palace gates that were guarded as part of the regular palace watch. The phrase that I translate as "behind the Royal Guards Gate" is אחר הרצים—literally "behind the Royal Guards." I believe that in this instance "the Royal Guards" is an abbreviated form of the Royal Guards Gate (שער הרצים), which is mentioned in P82,2, where it appears in the name of a road, the "Royal Guards Gate Road." That road leads to the palace and indicates that the Royal Guards Gate must be one of the palace gates.

BDB, p. 694, understands Sur Gate to be a gate at Yahweh's house, which I believe is incorrect. It is clear from a close reading of the Hebrew, in my opinion, that this is a palace gate.

82g the spears and shields that had belonged to King Dawid: These items are not mentioned elsewhere in Samuel or Kings, and presence of this detail here is very strange. If P18 has any basis in reality, one might presume that the spears and shields belonging to King Dawid were included with the cult items that Shelomo transferred from Fort Dawid to the storerooms in Yahweh's house (see P18 above). It is entirely unclear why Yehoyada would need to give the guards any weapons, as they would be carrying their own weapons as part of their normal duty on the watch, unless it was the practice not to carry weapons inside the grounds of Yahweh's house.

82h The royal guard took their stations: Note the change of scene. The action here is clearly on the Shabbath, after the changing of the guard, whereas the setting of the previous sentence seems to be in the days prior to the Shabbath, when preparations are being made. After describing the plans in detail earlier in the *parashah*, our author has not thought it necessary to describe the actual execution of those plans. This narrative technique—the omission of information that can be derived from context and that would be repetitive to describe, even if such omission creates a "gap" in the narrative—is fairly common in ancient Hebrew prose. The best example of this is the plague narrative in Exodus, which famously omits descriptions of Mosheh's relaying Yahweh's threats to Phar'oh. See note 51,1n above.

The author does not mention the Karian guard here, perhaps because the Karian guard was the group that assumed the palace watch.

82i thus surrounding the king: Note the inconsistency in the narrative: the boy Yo'ash has not yet made an appearance, nor has he yet been crowned king.

82j the ar-bands: The Masoretic text reads "the treaty" (העדות) here, which is nonsensical and clearly in error. This language also appears in the parallel passage in 2 Chr 23.11. BDB proposes that the text originally read הצעדות (arm-bands) based on the passage in Sam P66 (=2 Sam 1.10), which I think is almost certainly correct. My translation ignores the Masoretic vocalization and reads the consonants as a misspelling for "arm-bands." I have reproduced the misspelling in translation.

Notes to P82,1

82,1a all the commotion [*the people*]: A more literal rendering of the Hebrew is "the sound of those running about [*the people*]." A later editor has added a comment telling the reader that those who are running about in the streets are "the people." The editor has added the comment because the Hebrew is ambiguous—הרצין can be understood either as the name of the royal guard ("the Runners") or as a participle "those running [about]." My translation follows the later editor's suggestion.

It's worth noting that the term for "those running about" is written with the Aramaic form of the plural, which ends in ין- instead of ים- as in Hebrew. The unusual plural form adds to the difficulty of the text and may have been a factor in the later editor choosing to gloss this term.

82,1b the cult trumpeters: The Hebrew reads simply החצצרות ("clarions, horns"), with the author using the term for the instrument in place of the term for the player of the instrument. English has a similar practice, where musicians are sometimes referred to by the name of the instrument they play—e.g. the violins or the cellos rather than the violinists or the cellists. However, in this instance, a literal translation yields very awkward English, and a functionally equivalent translation requires one to translate with a term for a musician rather than the instrument played by the musician.

82,1c "Conspiracy!": The Leningrad Codex has a *parashah setumah* after Athalyah's second cry of conspiracy. See L210 r.2.13-14.

82,1d Horse Parade Road: On this road, see note 116w below.

Notes to P82,2

82,2a [*and the people, to become Yahweh's people*]: This clause is clearly not original to the earliest edition of Kings, which emphasizes the treaty (or binding agreement) between Yahweh and the Dawidic king, and which does not recognize a treaty between Yahweh and the people under the Dawidic king. The idea of a treaty between Yahweh and his people first appears in the last decades of the Babylonian exile and the early Persian period, in the book of Deuteronomy and in the books of Exodus-Numbers and Joshua. The clause here may have been added by the authors of Kings' third stage, or it may have been added as part of the editorial work during the Persian and Hellenistic periods that I refer to as Kings' sixth compositional stage. In my proposed composition history, I have assigned this clause to the sixth stage.

82,2b the Ba'al's temple: Recall that Athalyah's father Ah'av was a devotee of the Ba'al (see P49). Given her family background, Athalyah likely venerated both Yahweh and the Ba'al, and she would have provided royal support to the cults of both gods during her reign. Moreover, as the real power behind the throne during the reigns of her husband and son, she certainly would have ensured that the cult of the Ba'al in Yerushalem received royal support during their reigns. This is the context for the statement in P75 that Yehoram did "exactly as Ah'av's family did"—that is, he venerated the Ba'al and provided royal support to his cult in keeping with the expectations of his wife's family.

82,2c Yehoyada the Priest set up a new system of oversight for Yahweh's house: This sentence doesn't flow naturally in the sequence of events in the narrative and leaves the reader expecting more information about what this "system of oversight" (פקדת) entailed; the author, however, says nothing more on this topic and instead narrates the procession of the young king to the palace to take his seat on the throne. I disagree with BDB, p. 824, which understands פקדת here as "overseers." The term typically means "oversight" and that meaning fits perfectly well here.

82,2d Royal Guards Gate Road: This road is one of two roads that lead from Yahweh's house to the royal palace. The other road was Horse Parade Road, which is mentioned above in P82,1.

82,3a Yeho'ash was seven years old when he became king: This sentence is part of the standard formula used to introduce the kings of Yehudah; however, it is out of place. It typically appears as the second sentence of the account of the king's reign. Perhaps the authors of Kings' first stage reordered the formula for Yeho'ash in order to highlight the fact that he was a young boy when he became king (similar to their pupil Yoshiyyahu).

Note to P82,3

83a In the seventh year of Yehu's reign, Yeho'ash became king: The beginning of the account of Yeho'ash's reign is odd in that it omits the surnames of the kings and it omits the name of the kingdom that Yeho'ash ruled. If the authors had used their usual formula, they would have written "In the seventh year of the reign of Yehu Nimshiysson King of Yisra'el, Yeho'ash Ahazyahusson ruled as king of Yehudah." It is unclear to me why they authors chose to abbreviate their usual formula—possibly they did so because they felt Yeho'ash's reign had already been sufficiently introduced in P81 - P82,2.

Notes to P83

83b Yeho'ash did what was pleasing to Yahweh: In the material from Kings' first stage, Yeho'ash is one of six kings of Yehudah who did what was pleasing to Yahweh. The other kings were Asa, Amatzyahu (Yeho'ash's son), Azaryah (Yeho'ash's grandson), Yotham (Yeho'ash's great-grandson) and Hizqiyyahu. While the authors of the earliest version of Kings would have held up all these kings as examples for their student Yoshiyyahu, they especially would have wanted him to imitate Asa and Hizqiyyahu, who are the only kings that these authors liken to Dawid. Both of these kings made significant reforms to Yahweh's cult, just as the authors of the earliest version of Kings hoped their student would do.

83c things that Yehoyada the Priest directed him to do: It is interesting to note that Yehoyada serves as regent to Yeho'ash. Presumably his mother Tzivyah was either a minor wife to Ahazyahu or she had died (perhaps being an ancillary victim of the slaughter described in P81). With the mother not around to serve as regent, and with all males of royal descent having been killed, it was perhaps natural that the role of regent would fall on the chief priest in Yahweh's cult.

NOTES AND COMMENTS

83d tax contributions in silver: More literally, "silver that is contributed." This is an idiomatic usage of the *qal* participle of עבר. See BDB, p. 717, def. 4e. This refers to an obligatory payment (that is, a tax), distinct from a freely given contribution.

83e each priest ought to recruit one of his customers: The word that I translate as "customer" is מכר, from the root נכר ("regard, recognize"). The word appears only twice—once here in Kgs P83 and once more in Kgs P84. BDB, p. 648, proposes "acquaintance, friend." However, the word is used in P84 to refer to individuals who engage the priests to present their offerings to Yahweh—that is, the priests' "customers." As I discuss below in notes 84c and 84i, priests who presented an individual's guilt offering or error offering received the meat from the offering as payment for their service. These payments were the primary means of the priests' support. I believe the priests must also have supplied the animals for these offerings—this would ensure that the animal was unblemished and met the requirements of the offering. The offerer would thus purchase the animal being offered from the priests rather than bring his or her own animal. The money from the sales of the animals provided an additional source of profit for the priests' maintenance, and it is this money that is mentioned twice in P84.

Notes to P84

84a Now, as it happened...: A close reading of this *parashah* suggests that there must have been a dispute between Yeho'ash and the priesthood regarding the repair of Yahweh's house. The chief priest Yehoyada seems to have been allied with Yeho'ash in the dispute. The exact nature of the dispute is not clear from the text. The fact that the money for the repairs is collected in a secure chest unavailable to the priests suggests that the dispute may have centered around how to pay for the repairs: Yeho'ash possibly wanted to use income that normally would have gone to the priesthood as the source of funds for the repairs, and the priests must have objected to the loss of their regular income. One can imagine the priests objecting that Yeho'ash should pay for the repairs out of his own income, which would have been considerable, rather than funding the repairs out of the priests' income.

84b What possible reason do you have for not repairing: The author here uses the particle אין ("there is not"), which is often used in situations where an English speaker would say a thing was "impossible." An alternative translation here would be "Why is it impossible for you to repair the problems in Yahweh's house?" Through use of the particle אין, Yeho'ash expresses his extreme frustration with the priests, a tone which I have reproduced in translation.

84c From now on, don't take any of your customers' money for yourselves: The comment at the end of this *parashah* is a clue that the reference here is to the priests supplying (for a fee) the live animals to be presented as error offerings and guilt offerings, the meat of which was always part of their maintenance. Apparently already by the time of Yeho'ash it was the practice for priests to supply the live animal to the offerer for these two types of offerings. See notes 83e above and 84i below.

84d the priests had agreed among themselves not to take money from the people, so as not to repair the house's structural problems: I understand this to mean that the priests had agreed to accept only payment in kind rather than silver for the animals to be presented as error offerings and guilt offerings. This would have been a way to protect their income, as any silver they received (which in the past they had used for their own maintenance) would have been confiscated by Yeho'ash.

84e the high priest: That is, Yehoyada.

84f anyone who would come out to assist in the repair of the house: The Hebrew is somewhat awkwardly expressed. Literally, "anyone who would come out on account of the house with respect to [its] being strong." That is, with respect to its being structurally sound. The verb חזק ("to be firm, strong") is vocalized as the *qal* infinitive construct; the *qal* form of this verb is typically intransitive, but here it seems to be used with a transitive meaning—"to make strong, strengthen, repair." Elsewhere in this *parashah*, the same verb is vocalized in the *pi'el* form, where it does have a transitive meaning.

84g the workmen overseeing the work: The authors of this *parashah* use the term workmen (עשי המלאכה) in two ways: to refer to those overseeing the repair work and to refer to those carrying out the repair work. In the instance here, context suggests that the reference is to those overseeing the work. I have added the phrase "overseeing the work," which is not in the Hebrew, to make the authors' meaning clear to the reader.

84h They didn't demand strict accountability from the men who were entrusted with the money to pay the workmen: The author uses the *pi'el* form of חשב, which here means "to hold [someone] strictly accountable [for a thing]." The *pi'el* form of this verb has the related meanings of "give close consideration to" and "count carefully." BDB, p. 363, oddly understands the meaning here to be "count," which I think is nonsensical.

The phrase that I translate "who were entrusted with" is the idiom נתן על־יד (literally, "place upon the hand"), which is discussed above in note 79h. The idiom specifically means "entrust to, make responsible for." This idiom also appears earlier in the *parashah*.

84i (Money from guilt offerings... for the priests' maintenance.): In my translation of Leviticus, I argued that the core of Leviticus consists of a number of ancient rule books regarding the proper conduct of offerings to Yahweh. There are rule books both for the offerers and what they should do, and rule books for priests and what they should do. The rules for the role of priests in error offerings and guilt offerings are found in Lev P16 and P17. The meat of both types of offerings belongs to the priest who officiates the offering. Note in Lev P16: "The priest who presents the error offering may eat it." And in Lev P17, we read: "The guilt offering is identical to the error offering—there is one set of rules for them," and "Its [i.e. the guilt offering's] meat belongs to the priest who makes propitiation with it." The parenthetical comment here in Kgs P84, which I attribute to the editors of Kings' sixth stage, indicates that in addition to the meat, the money associated with these offerings (i.e. the money received from the sale of the animal) was also reserved for the priests' maintenance.

85a His officials instigated a coup against him, and they killed Yo'ash in the citadel: It is noteworthy that even though Yo'ash "pleased Yahweh," the authors of King's first stage nonetheless report that he died a violent death. For the kings favored by Yahweh, it is more typical for the authors of Kings to withhold information that suggests the king might have done something wrong or lost favor in any way with his god. Thus, for example, the authors of Kings' second stage omit an account of Yoshiyyahu's death in P116 (the account of his death was added by the authors of the fifth stage); the authors of the first stage omit a mention of Yehu's paying tribute to Shalmaneser (see note 80d above); and the authors of the first stage omit to mention that Hizqiyyahu desecrated Yahweh's house in order to pay tribute to Sanheriyv (the account of his desecration of Yahweh's house in P108 is from the Kings' second stage).

Notes to P85

85b a ladder: The word סֻלָּא is obscure and the meaning is uncertain. It is from the root סלל, which means "to lift up." I translate as "ladder" on the basis of the related word סֻלָּם, which is used in Gen P27,3 to describe the "ladder" with divine beings going up and down it in Ya'aqov's dream. The reading "ladder" here is also consistent with the location where Yeho'ash was murdered—ladders were commonly used in citadels and forts.

Notes to P86

86a he maintained the support for the errors of Yarov'am Nevatssson: That is, Yeho'ahaz continued the royal support of Yahweh's cults at Beyth-El and Dan, which venerated statues of Yahweh in the form of a bull calf. The language here likely also implies that he continued support of the local priests in the open-air shrines, which the authors of the Josianic study books also viewed as one of the "errors" of Yarov'am.

86b But Yeho'ahaz beseeched Yahweh...in Shomeron: I view this entire paragraph as a later addition to the text. We know it cannot have been part of the earliest edition of Kings as it states that the Yisra'elites "didn't abandon the errors of Yarov'am's family," and this formulation is at odds with the views of the authors of the Josianic study books. For them, it is always kings who are compared to Yarov'am, never the people.

It is important to note that the author of this addition was influenced by the book of Judges and he applies the cyclical structure of Judges to Yeho'ahaz's reign: to wit, the people are delivered into the hands of a foreign oppressor, the king cries out to Yahweh, Yahweh has compassion on his people's suffering and sends them a liberator (מושיע, the term used in Judges) who frees them from their oppressor. I believe the addition was prompted by the language in the preceding sentence that Yahweh "put them [i.e. Yisra'el] into the hand of" Haza'el and his son Hadadsson. The construction "put into the hand of" (נתן ביד) is frequently used in Judges, and the author of the addition here seems to have responded to that language by adding a passage modeled on the action in Judges. The addition itself is incongruous with the surrounding narrative and, frankly, is somewhat nonsensical. While it borrows the cyclical framework of Judges, it does not strictly fit that framework: unlike Judges, the Yisra'elites here do not abandon their errors after being "liberated."

Although it is possible that this material could have been added as early as the second compositional stage (the exilic expansion of Kings), the characteristics of the addition—its drawing on themes of old authoritative texts and its use of anonymous characters—are more typical of editorial activity in the late Persian period and Hellenistic period. Becasue this addition doesn't fit neatly with the concerns of any of the compositional stages that I propose, I treat it as a "miscellaneous" addition and for convenience I have grouped it with the material from the fifth stage.

86c the king of Aram was oppressing them...Yahweh gave Yisra'el a liberator: The terms used here—"oppress" (לחץ) and "liberator" (מושיע)—are common to Judges and are clearly borrowed from that book. It is interesting that the liberator here is anonymous. It is possible that the author of the addition did not have any specific individual in mind as the liberator. However, it seems most likely to me that he viewed Yeho'ahaz's son Yeho'ash as the liberator. Note that in P90 (which is an addition that I attribute to the authors of Kings' fourth stage), Yeho'ash restores towns to Yisra'el that were taken by Haza'el. The author of the addition to P86 may have been inspired by the story in P88, in which Eliysha foretells that Yeho'ash will defeat Aram three times.

It is also possible that the author of this addition viewed the liberator as Yarov'am Yo'ashsson, although I think this is slightly less likely than his father Yeho'ash. Note that the account of Yarov'am's reign in P94 shares themes with Judges—specifically the theme of Yisra'el's suffering, Yahweh having compassion on Yisra'el, and then Yahweh saving Yisra'el through a great individual. Most notably, the author of P94 states that Yahweh "saved" (הושיע, a common term in Judges) Yisra'el through Yarov'am. Moreover, Yarov'am restored a significant amount of territory to Yisra'el that had been taken by Aram (see note 94a below).

86d the Yisra'elites remained in their homes as previously: That is, because they were freed from Aram's control, they no longer faced the threat of being forcibly resettled to a new land.

86e in fact, they actively supported them: The Hebrew is awkward. Literally, "in it he walked." The pronoun "it" refers to the errors of Yarov'am, and the subject of the verb "walked" is Yisra'el. The phrase הלך ב ("walk in") is often used idiomatically to denote the manner in which a person habitually lives, and that is the usage here.

86f the cult of the Asherah persisted in Shomeron: Literally, "[the statue of] the Asherah remained standing in Shomeron." It's noteworthy that the references here are consistent with the inscriptions found at Kuntillet Ajrud, which speak of "Yahweh [God] of Shomeron and his Asherah." The inscriptions depict Yahweh and Asherah as a bull and a cow, and the images of Yahweh at Beyth-El and Dan (that is, "the wrongs of Yarov'am") were bull calves. On the name Yahweh of Shomeron, see note 2,1c above. The Israeli scholars Nadav Na'aman and Nurit Lissovsky have proposed that the site of Kuntillet Ajrud was a cult site devoted to Asherah and was likely founded by a northern king; see N. Na'aman and N. Lissovsky, "Kuntillet 'Ajrud, Sacred Trees and the Asherah," *Tel Aviv* 35 (2008), pp. 186-208.

87a rather he continued supporting them: That is to say, Yeho'ash—like his father Yeho'ahaz—continued the royal support of Yahweh's cults at Beyth-El and Dan, which venerated statues of Yahweh in the form of a bull calf. See note 86a above.

87b The rest of Yo'ash's acts...: The material from here to the end of the *parashah* is a near duplicate of the material at the end of P92. I believe that both passages are original to the earliest edition of Kings. See note 92f below for my proposed explanation of the duplication.

87c Yarov'am occupied the throne: This is the first time the reader is introduced to this Yarov'am (he is Yo'ash's son), yet the text does not provide any additional identifying information about him, which is at odds with the usual practice. I believe originally the text read "His son Yarov'am occupied the throne," and the phrase for his son (בנו) fell out of the text due to a scribal error. Note that the parallel passage in P92 reads "his son Yarov'am."

87d Yo'ash was buried in Shomeron with the kings of Yisra'el: This statement implies that the kings of Yisra'el were buried together, even though many of them were not related by blood. It's interesting to note that several royal graves have been found in the excavations at Sebastia (=Shomeron). See N. Franklin, "The Tombs of the Kings of Israel: Two Recently Identified 9th-Century Tombs from Omride Samaria," *Zeitschrift des Deutschen Palälastina-Vereins* 119 (2003), 1-11.

88a "Master! Master!" he lamented. "Yisra'el's chariotry and cavalry!": Yo'ash's lament over Eliysha when Eliysha is on his death-bed is identical to Eliysha's lament over Eliyyahu when Eliyyahu is being taken up in a whirlwind (see P62). The language fits the context better here than it does in P62, and it likely is original to this *parashah* (see note 62e above). If so, the authors of P62 would have added it there to reinforce the connection between Eliyyahu and Eliysha. As discussed in several notes above (51,2a, 60,2a, 62i and 65a), the authors of Kings' fourth stage created numerous parallels between Eliysha and Eliyyahu after adding the Eliysha stories to Kings.

88b Eliysha put his hands over the king's: Note the incongruity in the narrative: if Eliysha has fallen mortally ill, it seems doubtful he would have the energy to stand beside or behind the king and place his hands on the bow that the king is holding. The *parashah* is wholly a literary creation, and the author chooses details that heighten the drama of his story, even if those details might be nonsensical.

88c "Open the east window...Now shoot!": Eliysha has the king shoot the arrow to the east, in the direction of Yisra'el's enemy, Aram.

88d **: The Leningrad Codex has a *parashah setumah* here. See L211 r.3.22.

Notes to P89

89a (it was the beginning of the year): The Hebrew is obscure and grammatically inconsistent if we follow the Masoretic vocalization. However, if we ignore the Masoretic vocalization, it is possible to understand בא as an infinitive, yielding the meaning, "arriving of a year"—that is, the beginning of the year, which I have reflected in my translation.

89b it came to life and stood on its feet: The man's body came to life, not Eliysha's skeleton. In the author's view, Eliysha's magical powers were so great that they were present in his skeleton after his death and had an efficacy that was not dependent on Yahweh in any way.

Notes to P90

90a Haza'el King of Aram oppressed Yisra'el...: I view this entire *parashah* as a late addition to the text. In my composition history, I have assigned it to Kings' fourth stage, and I believe it was composed to show the fulfillment of Eliysha's promise to Yo'ash in P88 that he would defeat Aram three times. The *parashah* cannot be part of the earliest edition of Kings, for if it were, this material would have appeared in P87, which is that edition's account of Yeho'ash Yeho'ahazsson's reign.

90b But Yahweh had mercy on them...binding agreement with Avraham, Yitzhaq, and Ya'aqov...until now: This sentence provides support for my proposal to treat P90 as a late addition to the text, made late in the book's fourth compositional stage toward the end of the Persian period. The concepts in the sentence are typical of the theology of the Persian and Hellenistic periods, and are not found anywhere in the early layers of Kings. The mention of Avraham, Yitzhaq, and Ya'aqov is especially jarring. The only other mention of Avraham and Yitzhaq in Kings is in the account of Eliyyahu's contest with the priests of the Ba'al in P51,1, a story that I date to the Persian period. The patriarch Ya'aqov is mentioned three times elsewhere in Kings: once under the name Yisra'el in P51,1 alongside Avraham and Yitzhaq; once in a Persian period or Hellenistic era comment added to P51,1; and once in a Persian period addition to P105.

90c the towns that Haza'el had taken from his father Yeho'ahaz in their war: I have supplied Haza'el's name in translation. The text reads simply "the towns that he had taken." Although this *parashah* is late, the mention of Yisra'elite territory taken by Haza'el recalls real historical events. In the account of Yehu's reign in P80 (from Kings' first stage), the authors state that Yahweh "began to carve up Yisra'el's territory" and that Haza'el attacked "in every part of Yisra'el's territory." Note also that in P86, we are told that Yisra'el was a vassal of Haza'el and of his son Hadadsson for Yeho'ahaz's entire reign.

Notes to P91

91a Yeho'addayn: The Leningrad Codex and other Masoretic manuscripts have a *qere* here correcting the spelling of the name of Amatzahu's mother to Yeho'addan.

The Aleppo Codex vocalizes the consonantal text to reflect that correction like the other Masoretic manuscripts, but it lacks the *qere* in the margin. See A99 v.1.6 and L211 v.1.26. My translation reflects the consonantal text only.

91b [*not, however, like his ancestor Dawid*]: I understand this to be a comment added by editors from the sixth compositional stage. Note the parallel passage in P95 about Amatzyahu's son Azaryah, where this phrase is absent.

91c (However, he didn't put to death... for his own crime."): I understand this passage to be an addition to the text. I assign it to the authors of Kings' third compositional stage, who added a number of comments harmonizing Kings with the books of the Torah and Joshua. However, it is equally plausible to view it as a much later addition from the sixth compositional stage.

91d the book *The Torah of Mosheh*: This is the name the biblical authors gave to an early version of what we know today as Deuteronomy. The law that is quoted from this book in the following sentence is from Deut P21,28, and confirms that *The Torah of Mosheh* must be the name for an early version of Deuteronomy. The authors of Kings' third stage mention *The Torah of Mosheh* again in P116, in a passage where they praise King Yoshiyyahu for his obedience to "Mosheh's Torah" (see note 116ap below).

91e "Parents mustn't be put to death... for his own crime.": This sentence is taken nearly verbatim from Deut P21,28.

91f Cliffville... Yoqthe'el: This site has traditionally been identified as Petra in modern-day Jordan. The meaning of the name Yoqthe'el is uncertain, as there is no evidence in ancient Hebrew for a verbal root קות or קתה.

92a A brierbush in the Levanon sent a message to a cedar in the Levanon...: The Levanon brierbush and Levanon cedar must have often appeared together as the subject of proverbs that contrasted the small and weak with the large and strong. See, for example, Yotham's fable in Jud P29,1, and the comments in note 29,1e in my translation of Judges. The language in Yeho'ash's response to Amatzyahu is quite interesting, as it is an example of what male bluster and bragadoccio (or "trash-talking") sounded like in ancient Hebrew.

Notes to P92

The point of this little story is that the brierbush is wildly presumptuous in thinking itself the equal of the mighty cedar. In reality, the brierbush is so insignificant that it can be killed when it is merely stepped on by a wild animal that is passing by. Similarly, Amatzyah is presumptious in thinking himself the equal of the mighty Yeho'ash.

92b Go on thinking you're a big shot: Literally, "hold yourself in high regard." The tone of the Hebrew is highly insulting, and a functionally equivalent translation should reflect that.

92c stir up trouble for yourself: The Hebrew phrasing—התגרה ברעה—is idiomatic and the exact meaning is unclear. Literally, "stir up oneself against a bad thing [i.e. to your misfortune]." Possible functionally equivalent Engish idioms are "stir up trouble for yourself" and "bring trouble on yourself." It's worth noting that the same verbal construction (התגרה ב) appears in Deut P1,1, P1,2, and P1,3. There the phrasing clearly means "initiate a military attack against another." (In my translation of Deuteronomy, I misunderstood the idiom and translated as "provoke," which misrepresents the exact nuance intended by the author.)

92d was routed by: The author uses an idiomatic construction, the *niph'al* of נגף followed by the preposition לפני. On the meaning of this phrase as "was defeated by" with the preposition expressing agency, see note 14k in my translation of Joshua and note 55b in my translation of Numbers.

92e a distance of four hundred cubits: This is equivalent to roughly two hundred meters.

92f The rest of Yeho'ash's acts... Yarov'am became king in his place: This passage is out of place—it occurs in the middle of the account of Amatzyahu's reign—and it repeats information given in P87. I believe that all or nearly all of the material in P92 originally appeared in the account of Yeho'ash Yeho'ahazsson's reign in P87, and that this material draws from *The Chronicles of the Kings of Yisra'el*. When the authors of the Josianic study books wrote their account of Amatzyahu's reign, they must have decided to move the story of the battle between Amatzyahu and Yeho'ash from P87 to here. When they copied over the material from P87, they must have accidentally also copied the conclusion of that *parashah* ("The rest of Yeho'ash's acts... Yarov'am became king in his place").

The material in P92 gives us some insight into the composition method of the authors of the earliest edition of Kings. It is especially interesting that they appear to have decided to repurpose material from *The Chronicles of the Kings of Yisra'el* for their account of the reign of one of the kings of Yehudah. It is also interesting that they were somewhat sloppy in their work and didn't catch during the editorial process that they had copied over the conclusion to Yeho'ash's reign from P87, thus disrupting the narrative about Amatzyahu's reign.

Notes to P93

93a A conspiracy was perpetrated against him...: The account of Amatzyahu's murder is odd and leaves many unanswered questions. Unlike other accounts of coups in Kings, this account doesn't name the perpetrators, nor does it state that they were caught and put to death in punishment. See, for example, the account of Yo'ash King of Yehudah's murder (P85), followed by Amatzyahu's execution of his father Yo'ash's assassins (P91).

93b The people of Yehudah took: This phrase represents the last words on what is now leaf 99 of the Aleppo Codex. The three leaves following this have been lost. The text of Kings in the Aleppo Codex resumes in P108; see note 108a below.

The material in Kings that is missing from the Aleppo Codex covers just under three leaves in the Leningrad Codex, beginning with L212 r.1.20 and ending with L215 r.1.4.

93c He rebuilt Eylath...: The location of this sentence is strange. It reports details about Azaryah's accomplishments, and thus it would be more appropriate as part of the account of Azaryah's reign in P95. It is unclear to me why the authors of Kings' first stage placed this sentence in P93; possibly the sentence may have appeared in the source document, *The Chronicles of the Kings of Yehudah*, in the events listed under Amatzyahu's reign rather than with the events listed for Azaryah's reign.

Notes to P94

94a He restored Yisra'el's territory from Hamath's Gateway in the north to the Desert Sea in the south: The author suggests Yarov'am restored all of the territory lost to Aram, including the territory east of the Yarden River. We know that Yarov'am must have recovered the territory to the east because in P100, the author tells us that Tiglath Pil'eser captured this territory from Yisra'el and exiled its inhabitants to Ashshur.

Hamath's Gateway was considered the northernmost point of the territory controlled by the kingdom of Yisra'el. The Desert Sea, which was more commonly called the Salt Sea in the Tanakh and which is known as the Dead Sea in English, here serves as the southernmost point of the territory controlled by the kingdom of Yisra'el.

Ancient Hebrew authors commonly expressed totality or comprehensiveness by combining two opposites in a single phrase; this is common in English as well—"rich and poor" or "great and small." The phrase here in P94 uses geographic opposites—the northernmost and southernmost points of Yisra'el's territory—to express geographic totality. Note the similar phrasing in P21, which I discuss in note 21g above.

94b Yonah Amittaysson the Prophet: This individual is the subject of the book of Jonah, a composition of the mid- or late Persian period.

94c For Yahweh had seen that...he saved them through Yarov'am Yo'ashsson: These two sentences are quite incongruous with the surrounding narrative. At the beginning of the *parashah*, the authors tell us that Yarov'am is one of the kings who did what was "displeasing to Yahweh." But in the passage here, Yarov'am is presented as the one whom Yahweh chose to save Yisra'el (from some unspecified threat) and relieve its suffering. It is most likely, in my opinion, that the two sentences about Yarov'am as "liberator" were in the authors' main source document, *The Chronicles of the Kings of Yisra'el*. The sentences quoted here almost certainly draw from the specific language in Yonah the Prophet's oracle about the restoration of Yisra'el's territory under Yarov'am. This, I believe, is the best explanation for the tension between the authors' condemnation of Yarov'am at the beginning of the *parashah* and the presentation of him here as Yisra'el's liberator.

94d Yisra'el's suffering was growing especially wretched, there being no one anywhere at all who could help Yisra'el: The Hebrew is somewhat difficult, but there is no reason to think the text is corrupt. The phrase ואפס עצור ואפס עזוב employs a common idiom (עצור ועזוב, "one restrained and one let loose") that is used to express totality. On this idiom, see comment 31v in my translation of Deuteronomy. See also note 38i above for a discussion of this phrase.

94e Yahweh had no intention of obliterating Literally, "Yahweh didn't say [he would] erase." The author uses an idiomatic grammatical construction—a verb of speech ("say" or "speak") followed by the infinitive. Ancient Hebrew authors used this grammatical construction to express the concept of "intent." Depending on context, the construction is sometimes best translated as "promise" and other times as "intend." There is a similar idiomatic construction in English, where a phrase such as "he said he would do" is equivalent to "he intended [or intends] to do" or "he promised to do." The construction is briefly discussed in BDB, p. 56, def. 3 and p. 181, def. 6.

94f the town of Hamath in Yisra'el that had been under Yehudah's control: This Hamath is not the same Hamath mentioned earlier in the *parashah*. This Hamath likely was in the territory of Binyamin, and was a small and relatively insignificant town. The passage here is the only mention of this Hamath in the Tanakh. The other Hamath was a major town in the far north of Yisra'el's territory, and is mentioned frequently in the Tanakh.

94g [*that is, with the kings of Yisra'el*]: The comment here is very interesting. The author has added it to correct the preceding formulaic statement that Yarov'am "lay down in death with his ancestors." The formula typically implies burial in a family tomb; here the author of the comment clarifies that in this instance, Yarov'am was buried with the other kings of Yisra'el and not in his family tomb. It is possible, in my opinion, that the formulaic statement may have been in the main source for the kings of Yisra'el, *The Chronicles of the Kings of Yisra'el*, and that the statement was reproduced verbatim in Kings. It is also possible that the comment here may belong to the earliest edition of Kings—that is, it is possible that the authors of that edition felt the need to add the comment in order to correct any possible misunderstanding their student King Yoshiyyahu might have had regarding the meaning of the phrasing copied over from the source document. (For another example of a comment that may have been added by the authors of Kings' first stage to clarify language they found in their source document, see the beginning of P47.)

Notes to P95　　**95a In the twenty-seventh year of the reign of Yarov'am King of Yisra'el, Azaryah Amatzyahsson ruled:** The synchronism given here is incorrect. Based on my reconstruction of the chronology of the kings of Yisra'el and Yehudah in the appendix to this book, I believe that Azaryah became king in Yarov'am's fourth year and that the text of P95 originally had the correct synchronism. I hypothesize that the erroneous synchronism here in P95 was introduced into the text by a well-meaning editor who "corrected" this and two other synchronisms on the basis of a corruption of a synchronism given at the end of P100. See the discussion in notes 100a, 100d, 101a, and 102a below.

95b Prince Yotham... assumed responsibility for adjudicating the citizenry's legal disputes: This was one of the principal responsibilities of the king in ancient Yisra'el and Yehudah, and in the surrounding ancient Near Eastern kingdoms. This is why the ideal king is one who possesses great wisdom, for it is his wisdom that enables him to weigh opposing arguments fairly and to render just decisions. In P15, we are told that in Yerushalem, the king would decide cases at the Judgement Porch, so we should imagine Yotham performing his judicial duties there.

Notes to P96　　**96a Zekaryahu Yarov'amsson ruled as king over Yisra'el in Shomeron for six months:** The final years of the kingdom of Yisra'el were a period of great instability, characterized by short reigns, assassinations, and invasions by the Assyrians. Zekaryahu rules for six months and is assassinated by Shallum Yaveshsson. Shallum rules for one month and is assassinated by Menahem Gadiysson. Menahem rules for ten years, during which time Yisra'el is invaded by the Assyrians and made a vassal to Phul King of Ashshur. Menahem is succeeded by his son Peqahyah who reigns for two years before being assassinated by Peqah Remalyahusson. During Peqah's reign, Yisra'el is again invaded by the Assyrians and reduced to a rump state with many people exiled to Ashshur. Shortly thereafter, Peqah is assassinated by Hoshea Elahsson. Hoshea ruled for nine years and presided over the demise of the northern kingdom. Shalman'eser invaded Yisra'el and made the kingdom a vassal state; then after Hoshea failed to pay tribute, Shalmaneser imprisoned Hoshea, besieged Shomeron and ultimately made the remaining territory of Yisra'el a province of Ashshur.

The political situation in Yehudah was quite a bit more stable. Yehudah maintained close ties to Egypt, and suffered less from the Assyrians as the kingdom was geographically less accessible than Yisra'el.

96b just as his ancestors had done: The language is formulaic, and I doubt the authors intended the reader to see this phrase as a specific reference to the four generations of Zekaryahu's family who preceded him on the throne. In that regard, it's worth noting that Yehu (Zekaryahu's great-great-grandfather) is the only king of Yisra'el that the authors of Kings' first stage judge as "pleasing" Yahweh (see P80).

96c *en plein jour*: The author writes קבלעם, which appears to be an idiom from Aramaic. The literal meaning of the phrase is "in front of [the] people" and functionally equivalent terms in English are "in public" and "in broad daylight." To reflect the use of a foreign idiom, I have translated with a common French phrase. Some Septuagint manuscripts here suggest an underlying Hebrew text that read "in Yivle'am" (ביבלעם),

which many scholars believe is the original reading. While that is certainly possible, I do not believe the presence of an Aramaic idiom is particularly unusual, and I see no reason to emend the text here. Note that other accounts of assassinations also add specific details about the site of the event—see, for example, the accounts in P45 ("at his chamberlain Artza's house"), P85 ("as he was coming down a ladder"), and P99 ("in the citadel of the royal palace").

96d the oracle that Yahweh delivered to Yehu: This oracle is given at the beginning of P80. The author quotes the oracle verbatim; however, I have represented the oracle as indirect discourse, as that is more natural in English.

96e And that's exactly what happened: The four generations of Yehu's descendants were Yeho'ahaz Yehusson, Yeho'ash Yeho'ahazsson, Yarov'am Yo'ashsson, and Zekaryahu Yarov'amsson.

97a Uziyyah King of Yehudah: Uziyyah is a variant of the name Azaryah. The text here may be confusing to the reader because the previous mentions of this king in P95 and P96 used the names Azaryah and Azaryahu.

Notes to P97

97b Thirtzah: Recall that Thirtzah was the old royal seat of the kingdom of Yisra'el. It is mentioned as the royal seat of Ba'sha (P44), who moved the seat of government there from Shekem after assassinating Nadav Yarov'amsson. Thirtzah also served as the royal seat under Elah (P45) and Zimriy (P46) and for the first half of the reign of Omriy (P48). Omriy built Shomeron and moved the royal seat there, where it remained until the end of the northern kingdom as an independent political entity in 722 BCE. On the location of Thirtzah, see note 38r above.

97c After that, Menahem...: The Leningrad Codex has a *parashah setumah* before this sentence. See L212 v.1.25. This part of the Aleppo Codex is lost; however, the notes recording the *parashot* of the Aleppo Codex made by Joshua Kimhi indicate that there was no *parashah* break here. See Y. Ofer, "The Aleppo Codex and the Bible of R. Shalom Shachna Yellin," in M. Bar-Asher (ed.), *Rabbi Mordechai Breuer Festschrift: Collected Papers in Jewish studies* (Jerusalem, 1992), 1:295-353; see in particular p. 320 and p. 332, note 1 for this part of Kings.

97d Tiphsah: Tiphsah also appears in P11, where it is mentioned as a town in the Beyond-the-River region (roughly equivalent to the southern and western regions of modern-day Syria). We have no information on the reason for Menahem's hostility toward Tiphsah.

97e When he didn't succeed in opening the town: The Hebrew is elliptical and somewhat difficult, as the author has omitted the object of the verb. The text reads simply, "he didn't open [it]." I have supplied the object according to context. The verb פתח is often used with the object עיר ("town"), which is how I understand the sentence here. See, for example, Jer 13.19 and Is 22.22. See also the end of Jos P14.

97f he slaughtered all the pregnant women in its territory by slicing open their bellies: This especially heinous act was carried out in large part to terrify one's foes, putting them on notice that they would suffer a similar fate if they did not submit. This act of terror is mentioned a number of times in the Tanakh. Elsewhere in Kings, it is mentioned in P74. It also appears in an oracle against Shomeron in Hos 14.1 and in an oracle against the Ammonites in Amos 1.13.

I have rendered the phrase כל־ההרותיה ("all its pregnant women") as "all the pregnant women in its territory" to make clear that the pregnant women in the town of Tiphsah wouldn't have been slaughtered given that Menahem was unable to

	breach its defenses.
Notes to P98	**98a one thousand *kikkar* of silver:** There were three thousand sheqels in a *kikkar*. Menahem paid Phul one thousand *kikkar* of silver, or three million sheqels. A sheqel was equivalent to approximately 11.2 grams; thus, three million sheqels of silver is equivalent to 33,600 kilograms.

98b imposed a tax of silver on Yisra'el: The Hebrew phrase הוציא על ("bring out [a thing] upon") appears to be idiomatic, and the exact meaning is unclear. The phrasing here may mean "imposed [a tax of] silver on Yisra'el" or it may mean "brought out silver in proportion to Yisra'el." Although I have a preference for the former option, both meanings fit the context. See BDB, p. 425, def. 4g.

98c fifty sheqels of silver per soldier: Menahem paid Phul three million sheqels of silver. Calculating fifty sheqels per soldier implies that Menahem's armed forces numbered sixty thousand men—a relatively small army that would be severely outmatched by the Assyrian forces. |
| Note to P99 | **99a Argov and 'the Lion':** The Hebrew is ambiguous, but the most natural way to read the sentence is that Peqah killed these two individuals at the same time that he assassinated Peqahyah. Presumably these two men were allies of the king or high officials in the king's administration. Unusually, the author provides no additional information about them, such as what town they were from, which tribe they belonged to, their patronym, or their occupation. These individuals may have appeared in the author's source document without other identifying information, and the author knew nothing else about them. |
| Notes to P100 | **100a Peqah Remalyahusson ruled as king over Yisra'el in Shomeron for twenty years:** The consensus among scholars who have studied the chronologies of the kingdoms of Yisra'el and Yehudah is that Peqah's reign was much shorter than twenty years. Most scholarly reconstructions of the chronology of Yisra'el suggest Peqah ruled for just two or three years; in my proposed reconstruction in the appendix to this book, I give Peqah a reign of roughly four years, from 735 to 731 BCE.

    I believe that the earliest version of the book of Kings must have had the correct length of Peqah's reign, which likely was four years. This is the length of Peqah's reign that the authors of Kings' first stage would have found in their source document, *The Chronicles of the Kings of Yisra'el*. I hypothesize that the synchronism given near the end of this *parashah* (P100) for Hoshea's assassination of Peqah was corrupted, and that a later editor then "corrected" the length of Peqah's reign at the beginning of this *parashah* to twenty years based on the corrupt synchronism.

    The account of Hoshea's reign in P103 contains the correct synchronism for him, which is that he assumed the throne in the twelfth year of Ahaz King of Yehudah. The text there reads בשנת שתים עשרה לאחז מלך יהודה. I believe that the original reading of the synchronism at the end of P100 given for Hoshea's assassination of Peqah was almost identical: בשנת שתים עשרה לאחז בן־יותם ("in the twelfth year of Ahaz ben-Yotham"). While it may seem unlikely, it is conceivable that this wording was corrupted through a scribal error to read "in the twentieth year of Yotham ben-Uzziyah" (בשנת עשרים ליותם בן־עזיה). This would require just three small changes to the text, each of which might have resulted from a fatigued scribe losing his concentration: omitting the word שתים ("two") in a sort of haplography with "year" (שנת), mis-seeing "ten" (עשרה) as "twenty" (עשרים), and writing the name of Ahaz's father Yotham ben-Uzziyah in a mental error when he read the name Ahaz ben-Yotham. Once the text was corrupted in this fashion, later editors "corrected" the length of Peqah's reign at the beginning of P100 to be twenty years. (Their calculation was based on the fact that Peqah became |

king in the last year of Azaryah's reign and their belief that he died in the twentieth year of the reign of Azaryah's successor.)

100b Iyyon, Avel at Beyth Ma'akah, Yanoah, Qedesh, Hatzor, the Gil'ad region, and the Circle region: These sites represent the entire region of the kingdom of Yisra'el east of the Yarden River plus the northern part of the kingdom's territory that was immediately to the west of the Yarden. These areas bordered Ashshur's territory, so it is not surprising that they were the areas seized by Tiglath Pil'eser.

100c [*that is, the entire territory of Naphtaliy*]: This phrase is a gloss added by an editor of the sixth compositional stage, informing the reader that the Circle region is identical to the tribal territory of Naphtaliy.

100d the twentieth year of Yotham Uziyyahsson's reign: Recall that Uziyyah is a variant of the name Azaryah; see note 97a above. The synchronism with Yotham's reign given here is incorrect. I believe that the text is corrupt and originally read "in the twelfth year of Ahaz Yothamsson's reign." See the discussion above in note 100a for my reasoning and hypothesis for how this corruption may have happened.

101a In the second year of the reign of Peqah... Yotham Uziyyahusson ruled as king of Yehudah: This is one of the few places in Kings where the synchronism given cannot be correct. I believe the error here was introduced by the same editor who "corrected" the synchronism given for Hoshea's assassination of Peqah discussed above in note 100a. In the chronology in the appendix to this book, I suggest that the correct synchronism for Yotham is the thirty-first year of Yarov'am Yo'ashsson. This is likely the synchronism that appeared in the earliest version of Kings.

Notes to P101

101b The rest of Yotham's acts which he accomplished: The formula summarizing Yotham's reign is slightly different than the formula used for the other kings of Yehudah. It is likely that the phrase וכל ("and all") has fallen out of the text, which originally would have read "The rest of Yotham's acts and all that he did."

101c (In those times, Yahweh started sending... raids on Yehudah.): The sentence highlighted here is somewhat strange, as it implies that Yahweh caused harm to Yotham and Yehudah even though Yotham "did what was pleasing to Yahweh." In my composition history, I have assigned this sentence to Kings' first stage. However, it is also reasonable to view it as an addition by the authors of the second stage, who still had access to *The Chronicles of the Kings of Yehudah*, which must have been the source for the information of the raids on Yehudah. If this statement is from the authors of Kings' first stage, then it is revealing of how they approached their work: while they seem to have felt obligated to include the most important events of a king's reign (such as raids by foreign kings), they downplay events that are counter to their main theme. Here an event that shows Yotham must not have "pleased Yahweh" is mentioned only as an aside, and then the authors continue on with their narrative as though the event has no implications for their judgement of Yotham as a good king.

101d Yottam: I have reproduced the Leningrad Codex's vocalization of Yotham's name, in which the letter *taw* has erroneously been written with a *daghesh*. See L213 r.2.5.

102a In the seventeenth year of the reign of Peqah Remalyahusson: The synchronism given here is incorrect. I believe this is yet another instance of a "correction" to the synchronisms made by the editor who "corrected" the length of Peqah's reign to twenty years in P100 based on the corruption of the synchronism for Peqah's assassination given at the end of that *parashah*. See the discussion above in note

Notes to P102

100a. I hypothesize that based on the corruption of the synchronism in P100, this editor made three "corrections" to the synchronisms in Kings: the one for Yotham in P101, the one for Ahaz here in P102, and the one for Azaryahu in P95. I believe that the correct synchronism—and the one that likely appeared in the earliest version of Kings—is the fourth year of Menahem.

102b [*similar to the abominable practices...from the Yisra'elites*]: This clause is clearly a comment added by a later editor. I have assigned it to the authors of Kings' third stage, who peppered Kings with comments that referenced the books of the Torah and the book of Joshua. (The comment here alludes to the settlement of the land in the book of Joshua.) However, it is also plausible that the comment was added much later, by an editor of the sixth compositional stage sometime in the late Persian period or the Hellenistic period.

102c [*and also on the hills and underneath every leafy tree*]: I understand this as an editorial comment added by the editors of Kings' sixth stage. This comment clarifies that the reader should understand the open-air shrines (במות, a term that does not appear in the books of the Torah or in Joshua) as equivalent to the places where the native peoples of Kena'an worshipped their gods, as mentioned in Deut P12,5: "all the places where the nations whom you are dispossessing gave service to their gods—whether on lofty mountains, or on the hills, or underneath any leafy tree." I believe that the authors of the comment here in P102 were also responsible for the addition to P39, which I discuss in note 39c above, and which also equates the open-air shrines with the sites of worship found "on top of every high hill and beneath every leafy tree."

Note that the open-air shrines are also equated with the places of worship on the hills and under the leafy trees in P104; P104 is part of Kings' third stage, the earliest parts of which I date to late exilic and early Persian period, and which is the original place that this equation was made.

102d Eyloth: Eyloth is an alternative vocalization of Eylath. The town was located at the site of modern-day Eilat on the Gulf of Aqaba. It served as an important port, for it provided access to trade with the eastern coast of northern Africa and the western and southern coasts of the Arabian peninsula. The town is mentioned in P29,1 as the base for Shelomo's fleet of merchant ships.

102e [*It was then Arameans arrived...down to the present day.*]: The Masoretes added a *qere* in the margin correcting "Arameans" to "Edomites." I view the parenthetical comment about the Arameans and Eylath as an addition by the editors of Kings' sixth compositional stage.

102f Ahaz sent a delegation...: The Leningrad Codex has a *parashah petuhah* before this sentence; see L213 r.3.5-6. This passage appears in one of the three leaves of Kings that are missing from the Aleppo Codex. Our source for the *parashot* in the missing leaves of the Aleppo Codex is the notes on the Aleppo Codex's *parashot* taken by Joshua Kimhi. Because he did not mark a *parashah* here in his notes, I do not show a *parashah* break in my translation. Note that Codex Cairensis also lacks a *parashah* here (C262 3.12). See Ofer, op. cit, p. 332 note 1.

102g your servant and subject: Literally, "your servant and your son." The use of the word בן ("son") here is unusual. The word אב ("father") is sometimes used with the meaning "master," and I understand the use of "son" here in parallel with that—as a son is to his father, so a subject is to his master.

102h whatever silver and gold he could find in Yahweh's house and in the palace storerooms: Literally, "the silver and gold that was found at Yahweh's house and in the palace storerooms." The *niph'al* form of מצא here has the sense of "happen to be present, chance to be present." That is to say, silver and gold would regularly come in and go out of the treasuries of the palace and of Yahweh's house, and whatever amount happened to be there at the time is what was collected and sent. I have tried to reflect the nuance of the verbal form with a functionally equivalent translation in English.

Silver and gold were accumulated in Yahweh's house from the collection of poll taxes, from free-will offerings, and possibly also from the sale of animals to individuals who had an obligation to make an offering to Yahweh (these funds belonged primarily to the priests, but they may have had to give a share to "the house"—see notes 83e and 84c above). Silver and gold accumulated in the palace storerooms from the work of the king's tax commissioners. The funds that would normally go to support the operation of the cult and the royal administration now had to be used to pay tribute, resulting in the impoverishment of the kingdom. I believe that it is this dynamic that led to the centralization of the cult under Hizqiyyahu and then later under Yoshiyyahu. Both kings needed a more efficient way to collect taxes to maintain the palace coffers which had been depleted by the tribute paid to their overlords.

102i When the king arrived from Dammeseq...: The passage from here to the end of the *parashah* provides a fascinating picture of the king's involvement in the cult of Yahweh on Mount Tziyyon. The king clearly functions as head of the cult and the high priest is subordinate to him in all matters of the cult. Thus, the king personally carries out rites for presenting offerings to Yahweh just as a priest would do, he replaces altars and gives them new functions, he modifies and reorganizes the equipment used in the cult, and he even practices divination through the inspection of the entrails of animals offered to Yahweh.

102j poured out a drink offering: Drink offerings were a practice in the cult on Mount Tziyyon, but do not seem to have been part of the rites in the cult to Yahweh in the northern kingdom. See my comments on this topic in note 47e in my translation of Leviticus and also my discussion of Num P56 - P57,2 in the appendix to my translation of Leviticus.

102k the old bronze altar: The bronze altar is the original altar outside Yahweh's house where whole offerings (עלות), grain offerings (מנחות), drink offerings (נסכים), welfare offerings (זבחי שלמים), error offerings (חטאות), and guilt offerings (אשמים) were made. Oddly, its construction is never described; it is mentioned in P21 in material from Kings' fifth stage as the altar that is "in front of Yahweh" (i.e. in front of Yahweh's house). I have added the adjectives "old" and "new" in translating the passage here in P102 to help the reader understand which altar is which.

102l where it sat between the new altar and Yahweh's house: The old altar was directly east of Yahweh's house, and it would have been on the western side of the new altar before it was moved to the north so that there would be nothing between the new altar and Yahweh's house.

102m Splash the blood from any whole offerings and any welfare offerings on it: The term for welfare offering is זבח שלמים, but it is often abbreviated as זבח, especially when it is used in conjunction with the term for whole offering (עלה). The abbreviated form is used here. The blood of animal offerings was never to be consumed; after the blood was drained from the animal, it was always disposed of by splashing against the altar. For splashing the blood of a whole offering against the altar, see Lev P1, P1,1, P21 and P21,1, and for splashing the blood of a welfare offering against the altar, see Lev P3, P4, P5, P18, P21,1 and P35. See Lev P17 for splashing the blood of a guilt offering against the altar.

102n I'll use the bronze altar for haruspicy: Literally, "the bronze altar will be for me to make inspections." I presume the king is inspecting entrails of slaughtered animals. Perhaps these animals were slaughtered specifically for haruspicy, or perhaps he inspected the entrails of the animals slaughtered as offerings to Yahweh. The entire animal was burned on the altar in a whole offering, but in welfare offerings only the kidneys, fat parts, and some ligaments were burned on the altar (see Lev P3 - P5 for the rules for welfare offerings). Thus, apart from the kidneys, the internal organs and intestines of a welfare offering would be available to be used for haruspicy. One can imagine a scenario where Ahaz would present a welfare offering to Yahweh on the big altar, and then use some of the entrails of that offering for haruspicy on the bronze altar.

102o the rims...the bronze stands...the lavers: For a detailed description of these items, see P17 and P17,1 above.

102p the Metal Sea...the bronze cattle: For a detailed description of these items, see the end of P16 above.

102q the Shabbath *miysak*: The exact meaning of מיסך (*mīsāk*)—or מוסך (*mūsāk*) if we follow the *qere* given by the Masoretes in the margin—is uncertain. The word comes from the root סכך, which means to "to screen, cover," so possibly it referred to some sort of covered structure, such as a gazebo.

102r he surrounded with walls in Yahweh's house, so that the king of Ashshur wouldn't see them: The Hebrew is obscure, and the meaning is uncertain. I have translated according to context. The *hiph'il* of סבב is sometimes used to mean "surround [with a wall], encompass" (see BDB, p. 686, def. 2b and 2c of the *hiph'il*) and that is how I understand the usage here. A literal rendering of the phrase that I translate as "so that the king of Ashshur wouldn't see them" is "away from the king of Ashshur."

It is interesting to note that once Ahaz has become a vassal of Ashshur, he must worry about being taken advantage of—thus, he must hide the valuables in Yahweh's house so they aren't discovered by the king of Ashshur, whom he fears might covet them.

Notes to P103

103a In the twelfth year of the reign of Ahaz King of Yehudah, Hoshea Elahsson ruled over Yisra'el: There are two synchronisms that are given for Hoshea: one here in P103, which I believe is correct, and one at the end of P100, which I believe is incorrect and was corrupted through a scribal error. See the discussion in note 100a above.

103b accused Hoshea of treachery: The verbal construction is idiomatic: מצא ב ("to find [a thing] in [or against] [a person]"), which is used in situations when one person discovers a wrong that another person has committed, or when one person finds another person blameworthy in some way. See BDB, p. 593, def. 2b. The idiom is used four times in Samuel: Sam P23, P61, P62,1, and P62,2. I translated the idiom quite softly in Samuel because there is nothing (מאמה) blameworthy that is found. Here in Kings, the force of the idiom is much stronger, because "treachery" (קשר) is found. Hence the translation is more forceful ("accuse").

103c in Helah, in Havor on the Gozan River, and in towns in Maday: The location of Helah is unknown. I understand Havor to be a town located on the Gozan River. Gozan is also the name of a region mentioned in P109 as one of the "nations" conquered by the king of Ashshur. Maday is the Hebrew name for Persia, which at the time was controlled by Ashshur.

BDB, p. 289, understands Havor to be the name of the principal river in the region of Gozan; this understanding, however, requires one to view the text of 1 Chr 5.26 to be corrupt, as that text mentions Havor and נהר גוזן ("the Gozan River" or "Gozan's river") as two entirely distinct locations.

104a And so it happened that the Yisra'elites wronged their god Yahweh...: This *parashah* serves as a summary of the wrongdoing committed by the people of the northern kingdom, thus causing Yahweh to reject them and ultimately bringing about their exile from Yahweh's "presence." The *parashah* is full of language and concepts characteristic of the authors of Deuteronomy, and proponents of the idea of a Deuteronomistic History view this *parashah* as one of the central compositions of the principal authors of that work, alongside the farewell speech of Yehoshua Nunsson (Jos P53), the historical apostasy/punishment/repentance/rescue scheme in Judges (Jud P9), the farewell speech of Shmu'el (Sam P23 - P24,1), and Shelomo's prayer at the dedication of Yahweh's house (Kgs P20 - P23). As I discuss in the introductory note, along with a number of other scholars, I have abandoned the idea of the so-called Deuteronomistic History. In my case, this decision arose from my translation work on Judges and Kings, which made it apparent to me that the concept of a Deuteronomisic History provided a wholly inadequate explanation of these books' composition history.

Notes to P104

As discussed throughout this book, in place of an edition of Kings that was composed by the authors of the "Deuteronomistic History," I see three compositional stages: (1) the original edition of Kings, composed as one of three "study books" for the education of the young king Yoshiyyahu; (2) a revision of that work in the early decades of the exile that explained the destruction of Yerushalem and of Yahweh's house in terms of a conditional (not unconditional) promise to Dawid; and (3) a series of (mostly small) additions to Kings made primarily in the fifth and fourth centuries BCE by authors associated with Yahweh's cult on Mount Tziyyon. The additions made by the authors of this third stage were largely in the form of editorial comments that introduced into Kings ideas and concepts from the books of the Torah and the book of Joshua—most especially, the idea of a treaty between Yahweh and his people (which replaced the older idea, now discredited, of a treaty between Yahweh and the Dawidic king). In my view, the authors of Kings' third compositional stage composed only one lengthy piece in Kings: the passage here in P104 providing their interpretation of the destruction of Yisra'el in light of the idea of Yahweh's treaty with his people.

It is especially interesting to note that Mosheh is entirely absent from this *parashah*. Given the importance of Mosheh to the authors of Kings' third stage, we would expect to see mention of him in this *parashah*, particularly since the *parashah* refers to the exodus from Egypt, to Yahweh's "commandments and laws" and "the Torah which he commanded to their ancestors," and to "the treaty that he made with their ancestors." The exodus, the Torah, and Yahweh's treaty with the Yisra'elites all are closely associated with Mosheh, so his absence from this *parashah* is quite surprising. I view the work of the authors of Kings' third stage as taking shape over a period of two centuries or more, during which the authors reworked and revised the older editions of Kings in keeping with the evolution of cult leaders' views about the destruction of Yahweh's house and the loss of the land. It seems most likely, in my opinion, that their work on this *parashah* was done relatively early in that process, before the cult leaders' ideas about the role of Mosheh were fully formed.

104b the nations that Yahweh had driven from the Yisra'elites' path: This language is characteristic of Deuteronomy. It first appears in the second compositional stage of Deuteronomy, when the book was significantly expanded in tandem with the composition of the earliest versions of Exodus-Numbers and Joshua. I date all this work to the late sixth century and early fifth century BCE. It should be noted that this language was also used very frequently by later authors in their expansions of Deuteronomy, Joshua, and Judges. The passage here is one of several places in this *parashah* where language typical of the early versions of the books of Torah and Joshua appear, and for that reason I assign the first three-fourths of this *parashah* to Kings' third compositional stage. Early passages where this language appears are Deut P12,3, Deut 18,5 and Jos P53.

104c military outposts: A literal rendering of the phrase I translate as "military outpost" is "watchmen's tower."

104d on every lofty hill and under every leafy tree: This phrase is a specific allusion to Deut P12,5 (a passage from the earliest version of Deuteronomy). The author would have expected his audience to recognize the allusion.

104e they made burnt offerings: The verb here—the *pi'el* of קטר—is used as a generic term for any kind of offering that is burned on an altar. The verb may also mean "make an incense offering," but context suggests that is not the meaning here. See note 8b above for further discussion of this verb.

104f Yahweh warned Yisra'el and Yehudah: The presence of Yehudah here fits better with the themes of the authors of Kings' third stage than the Josianic study books, and adds support for viewing the material in the first three-fourths of this *parashah* as belonging to Kings' third compositional stage.

104g all his prophet [*every seer*]: The text is clearly corrupt. I think it likely that the letter *yodh* has dropped out of the text; if so, the text would have originally read "all his prophets." The phrase "every seer" reads as a gloss on "all his prophets," but the reason for the gloss is unclear to me. The text as written reads "all his prophet;" there is a *qere* in the margin correcting "his prophet" to "the prophets of." See L214 r.1.3.

104h the treaty he made with their ancestors: This concept is absent from Kings' first and second compositional stages, which knew only of a treaty (or "binding agreement") between Yahweh and the Dawidic king. The presence of the treaty between Yahweh and his people here offers strong support for treating this portion of the *parashah* (P104) as a composition by the authors of Kings' third stage.

104i the treaty terms which he invoked against them: In using the word for "treaty terms" (Hebrew עדות), the author specifically had in mind the treaty curses that customarily appeared at the conclusion of treaties, and which imposed curses on those who did not uphold the terms of the treaty. (For עדות meaning "treaty terms, treaty obligations," see note 4d of my translation of Deuteronomy.) Thus, we should understand that the author here is alluding to the treaty curses in Deuteronomy, which appear in Deut P26 in the present-day version of the book. As with the allusion to Deut P12,5 discussed in note 104d above, the author would have certainly expected his audience to understand he was referring to Deuteronomy's treaty curses here.

104j Yahweh had grown furious with Yisra'el...: I understand the text from here to the end of the *parashah* to be part of the earliest version of Kings. Originally, it followed directly from the end of P103. Note how the apportionment of the blame in this paragraph differs from the apportionment of the blame in the previous three paragraphs. Here the crime revolves around the Dawidic kingship and the actions of the non-Dawidic king—the people's crime was choosing as king someone not descended from Dawid, and the non-Dawidic king in turn made the Yisra'elites commit "a very great wrong" (their veneration of the bull calves). References to the latter crime in particular are found throughout the material that I associate with the earliest version of Kings.

By contrast, the first three paragraphs of P104 are full of themes related to ideas found in the books of the Torah and in Joshua and that are absent from Kings' first two compositional stages. In this material, the people are entirely to blame and the king plays no role whatsoever in the breach between Yahweh and the people—an idea that is wholly consistent with material found in Exodus, Numbers, Deuteronomy, and Joshua and that is alien to the early material in Kings. The crime in the first three paragraphs of P104 is the people's violation of Yahweh's commandments, of his Torah, and of their obligations to him under their treaty (ברית) with him. These paragraphs are also full of language characteristic of the books of the Torah and Joshua, including the reference to the exodus, the allusion to Yahweh "driving" other nations "from the Yisra'elites' path," and the accusation that the people "followed the customs [or practices]" of the "nations around them."

104k [*But Yehudah didn't observe... the practices that Yisra'el carried out.*]: This sentence is clearly an addition to the text, made by the authors of either the third or the sixth compositional stage. The addition may have been prompted by the presence of Yehudah earlier in the *parashah* (see note 104f above).

104l delivering them into the hands of people who terrorized them: The author's phrasing—ויתנם ביד שסים (translated here as "delivering them into the hands of people who terrorized them")—draws on Jud P9, where this language appears twice: ויתנם ביד שסים (which I translated as "he delivered them up into the hands of bandits") and מיד שסיהם (translated as "from those terrorizing them"). In my translation of Judges, I argued that P9 was composed by the authors of the Josianic History (a term which I have now abandoned and replaced with the Josianic "study books"). The connection here with Judges offers some support for my proposal that the conclusion of Kings P104 was part of the Josianic study books, one of which was the earliest version of Kings.

105a The king of Ashshur brought people from Bavel...: Many scholars view this *parashah* as a late Persian period or Hellenistic period addition to Kings. However, I view a large portion of it (the first two-thirds plus the last three sentences) as original to the earliest edition of Kings. The *parashah* explains why Yahweh is still worshipped in the Assyrian province of Shomeron, even though the land is no longer occupied by Yisra'elites, but by people from the countries to the east. It is necessary for the authors of the Josianic study books to offer this explanation, for otherwise Yoshiyyahu's actions in destroying Yahweh's cult in the province of Shomeron are inexplicable. The cult must still exist for him to destroy it, and the cult's practices must be in violation of Yahweh's cult rules (that is, his *tōrāh*) in order that its destruction be justified. For these reasons, the authors of the Josianic study books must include an account of why the cult to Yahweh still exists there. The authors of the Josianic study books were opposed to worship of Yahweh in the open-air shrines rather than "in the place that he chose for himself." And even more offensive was that in these same shrines the people worshipped other gods alongside Yahweh. Note that the authors of the Josianic study books explicitly mention the practice of "doing service" to Yahweh and to other gods in the same shrines later in the *parashah*.

Notes to P105

105b the towns of Shomeron: The author here uses Shomeron as the name of the province in the Assyrian empire that formerly represented the heart of the kingdom of Yisra'el. The term Shomeron has this meaning throughout P105—it is not used as a town name in this *parashah*.

105c they didn't acknowledge Yahweh: The verb is ירא, which is traditionally translated as "fear." In the context of the cult, the exact nuance of the verb can be difficult to capture succinctly in translation. The verb means "to acknowledge, honor, give reverence to, give respect to." The implication is both that one acknowledges the god as a true god and that one acknowledges the god as powerful by regularly making offerings to him—including thanking him when he grants you success and asking him to absolve you of your guilt when you offend him in some way. The author of this *parashah* uses this verb numerous times in this fashion. I have varied my translation throughout this *parashah* to capture the range of meanings, sometimes translating as "acknowledge," sometimes as "give honor to," and sometimes as "revere."

105d as it wasn't possible that any of them could know: The particle אין ("there is not") was often used in ancient Hebrew in situations where a native English speaker would say a thing was "not possible." I have reflected this in my translation here. I have frequently commented on this use of אין and on the similar use of the particle יש in my other translations. For other examples in Kings, see notes 67c and 77e above.

105e took up residence in Beyth-El: There were many places named Beyth-El. The Beyth-El mentioned here is most likely the Beyth-El that served as the principal site of Yahweh's cult in the north during the era of the monarchy, as this was the site favored by the kings of Yisra'el. However, there is some possibility that this may be a different Beyth-El. It is interesting to note, for example, that the principal cult to Yahweh in the province of Shomeron during the Persian period was located on Mount Gerizim, and that Samaritan tradition equates Mount Gerizim with the Beyth-El where Yahweh appeared to Ya'aqov (see the beginning of Gen P27,3).

105f he began teaching them how they should acknowledge Yahweh: I speculate that the actions referred to here—a priest to Yahweh (or several priests to Yahweh) returning to Shomeron to teach the newly settled peoples from the east about the local god—are connected to the original composition of the book of Genesis. I understand the earliest version of the book to have been composed in the late eighth and early seventh centuries BCE to educate the new inhabitants of the region about the region's god and about their own connection to that god. The stories in Genesis make clear that this god Yahweh has a special relationship to Aram, having chosen a family from that region as his own people and giving them land in Kena'an. To give further reassurance to the new inhabitants of Shomeron about this local god named Yahweh who demands that they acknowledge him, the authors of Genesis suggest that Yahweh is a god they already know. In the stories in Genesis, the authors explicitly equate Yahweh with the god Bethel, who was one of the local gods of Aram and who would have been familiar to many of the region's new settlers. The clearest expression of this is near the end of Genesis P27,3, when Ya'aqov recounts to Rahel and Le'ah a divine being's appearance to him in a dream that he had about sheep and goats; in his dream, the divine being states "I am the god Beyth-El, where you consecrated a sacred pillar with a smear-offering to me when you made a vow to me there." The identity of Yahweh and the god Bethel continued well into the Persian period, and is especially well attested in the evidence from Elephantine. On this topic, see T. Holm, "Bethel and Yahō: A Tale of Two Gods in Egypt," *Journal of Ancient Near Eastern Religions* 23 (2023), pp. 25-55.

105g the open-air shrines: The author uses the term בית הבמות for "open-air shrines" rather than the more usual הבמות. On these two terms, which are synonymous, see note 32,1f above.

105h Shomeronians: That is, the people of the Assyrian province of Shomeron. See note 105b above.

105i They appointed shrine priests for themselves in every place they lived, and the priests made offerings for them in the shrines: These are priests to Yahweh chosen from the newly settled peoples from the east, and they are reinstituting Yahweh's cult in the local shrines alongside the cults to the gods of their own native lands. It is interesting to note that the language used here is nearly identical to the language describing Yarov'am's appointment of shrine priests "from all over" in P32,1 and P36—two passages that I also assign to the authors of the Josianic study books. Compare ויעשו להם מקצותם כהני במות ("they appointed shrine priests for themselves in every place they lived") here in P105 with ויעש מקצות העם כהני במות ("he continued designating people from all over as priests of the open-air shrines") in P36 and ויעש כהנים מקצות העם ("he designated people everywhere as priests") in P32,1.

105j similar to the customs of the peoples that had been exiled from there: That is, similar to the Yisra'elites, who gave service to Yahweh and to other gods such as the Ba'al, and who moreover did this in the same open-air shrines.

105k (Even in the present day... rescue you from your enemies' clutches."): The entire paragraph that I have placed within parentheses reads as a Persian period addition to the text. I have assigned it to Kings' third compositional stage because of its numerous connections to the books of the Torah. I believe this passage must have been added relatively early in the third stage because Mosheh is entirely absent. On Mosheh's integration into Kings at a relatively late point in the third stage, see note 104a above.

105l none of them give honor to Yahweh: Note that this statement is inconsistent with the statements above and below that the new settlers did acknowledge and give honor to Yahweh. The inconsistency here provides support for viewing the text that I have placed in parenthesis as a late addition to the text.

105m commanding them as follows, "You mustn't acknowledge other gods... from your enemies' clutches.": Often when biblical authors allude to a commandment by Yahweh and include the phrase "as follows," they then directly quote a passage from another biblical book. In the instance here, however, the speech that follows is not a direct quote. Instead the author has composed this speech with stock language and imagery borrowed from the paraenetic sections of Deuteronomy. In that book, for example, language about Yahweh taking Yisra'el out of Egypt "with his mighty strength and outstretched arm" appears six times; the warning not to "forget the treaty" with Yahweh appears twice; warnings about and prohibitions against "acknowledging [or serving or some similar verb] other gods" appear twelve times (thirteen if the first commandment is included); and the promise of "rescue from enemies" as a reward for honoring Yahweh appears once.

105n So they didn't really pay heed... as is still the case today: That is, although the new settlers in Shomeron revered Yahweh, they didn't pay heed to the teaching of Yahweh's priests regarding the requirement to give service to Yahweh alone and to no other gods. I understand this final paragraph of the *parashah* to be original to the earliest edition of Kings.

Notes to P106

106a similar to all that his ancestor Dawid had done... After him, there hasn't been another like him: Hizqiyyahu is one of only three kings in the book of Kings who are said to be like Dawid. The other kings are Asa (see P42) and Yoshiyyahu (see P115). Because of the positive portrayal of Hizqiyyahu, a number of scholars believe that the earliest version of Kings was composed during Hizqiyyahu's reign, in support of his cult reforms. These scholars see three major early "editions" of Kings (and of the books they call the Deuteronomistic History)—the original version composed under Hizqiyyahu, a revised version composed during Yoshiyyahu's reign in support of his cult reforms, and a second revision during the Babylonian exile that these scholars associate with the final form of the so-called Deuteronomistic History. Many of these scholars also identify extensive additions to Kings made during the Persian period, most especially the stories about Eliyyahu and Eliysha, but they do not characterize this material as "Deuteronomistic."

I do not find the arguments for an early edition of Kings (plus Samuel and perhaps Judges) composed during Hizqiyyahu's reign to be compelling. In my view, the account of Hizqiyyahu's reign in the earliest material in Kings is quite brief—just P106 and the end of P112. Moreover, the narrative of his cult reforms in P106 is a single sentence that is almost entirely formulaic, as though the author had no personal knowledge of the events of Hizqiyyahu's reign. There are very few "real" facts about Hizqiyyahu's reign in the original account of his reign: only that he destroyed the bronze snake, that he rebelled against the king of Ashshur and that he defeated the Philishtines—facts that the authors of this *parashah* would have read in the source document *The Chronicles of the Kings of Yehudah*. With the account of Hizqiyyahu's reign being entirely formulaic except for these three small facts, it is impossible, in my view, to think that there was an early version of Kings composed in support of Hizqiyyahu's reforms. If there had been, surely the account of Hizqiyyahu's reign would have been much more extensive and more detailed.

As I discuss in my introductory note, I understand the earliest version of Kings to have been composed as part of the education of the young king Yoshiyyahu. I believe Kings was one of three "study books" that were composed for the king, the others being Samuel and Judges. In this scenario, the authors of the Josianic study books held up Asa and Hizqiyyahu (the two kings said to be like Dawid) to their student as the model kings to imitate. With respect to Hizqiyyahu, his reforms of the cult were actions "similar to all that his ancestor Dawid had done;" moreover, because Hizqiyyahu "held fast to Yahweh," Yahweh was "with him" and gave him success in "whatever he ventured to do" (which included rebelling against the king of Ashshur). These are all behaviors that the authors of the Josianic study books hoped to inculcate into their young pupil.

Viewing the earliest version of Kings as a study book for the young king helps us understand the need of the authors to pass judgement on every single king as either doing what was "pleasing" to Yahweh, or doing what was "displeasing" to him. There is no reason for this language in a work written in support of Hizqiyyahu's reforms; the language has a clear rationale, however, if the work was composed as a study book for the young Yoshiyyahu, with examples of kings whose actions should be imitated and kings whose actions should be avoided. We see the same thing in Judges and Samuel—stories about great heroes and kings of the past who offer lessons about how to lead and how not to lead.

106b he removed the open-air shrines: It hardly bears repeating that there is no record in the book of Samuel of Dawid doing any of the cult reforms listed here as Hizqiyyahu's accomplishments. I believe the rationale for Hizqiyyahu's efforts to centralize the cult in Yerushalem was simply a mechanism to increase the tax revenues for his administration (the cult was a major source of the palace's revenue).

The coffers of the palace and temple must have been severely depleted during the reign of Hizqiyyahu's father Ahaz. Yehudah was a vassal of Ashshur for much of Ahaz's reign, and Ahaz gave over nearly all of Yehudah's wealth to Ashshur to buy protection, as is explicitly stated in P102: "Ahaz took whatever silver and gold he could find in Yahweh's house and in the palace storerooms and sent it to the king of Ashshur as a bribe."

There is no reason to think that Hizqiyyahu's cult reforms were mentioned in the source document *The Chronicles of the Kings of Yehudah*. Apart from the statement about his destruction of the bronze snake made by Mosheh (which may have been in the source document), the language about his reforms is entirely formulaic. It is interesting to note the mention of Mosheh in this *parashah*, which is the only time he appears in material that I assign to the Josianic study books (including the earliest versions of Judges and Samuel). It is fascinating that in this very early tradition about Mosheh, he is associated not with Yahweh but with worship of a foreign snake-god—a practice that was abhorrent to the authors of the Josianic study books and that they would have viewed as abhorrent to Yahweh.

106c he smashed the sacred pillars: The sacred pillars served as representations of Yahweh and for this reason they were highly objectionable to the authors of the Josianic study books. It is interesting that the sacred pillars seem to have played a role within the cult on Mount Tziyyon—a practice that must have been adopted from Yahweh's cult in the open-air shrines. The sacred pillars were an especially important feature of Yahweh's cult as practiced in the open-air shrines, where they would have served as physical representations of the god and would have been the object before which devotees present their offerings. Elsewhere in Kings, see P39 and P116 for the connection of sacred pillars to the open-air shrines to Yahweh. And of course, sacred pillars representing Yahweh feature prominently in Genesis—see Gen 27,3 and P30. Finally, it's worth noting that sacred pillars were also a feature of the cult to the Ba'al (see Kgs P64 and P79).

106d [*For up until that time... offerings to it. They called it 'Bronzey.'*]: I understand these two sentences to be a late addition to the text. The fact that the term "Yisra'elites" is used to describe the people of Yehudah indicates the addition is very late, and I have assigned it to Kings' sixth compositional stage.

106e After him, there hasn't been another like him among all Yehudah's kings: In my view, this sentence makes most sense if we understand the earliest version of Kings to have been composed for the education of the young king Yoshiyyahu as part of the collection of works that I call the Josianic study books. In that work, Hizqiyyahu was held up as the model of an ideal king of the Dawidic line—someone for Yoshiyyahu to imitate. At the time the Josianic study books were written (early in Yoshiyyahu's reign), the only kings who were "after" Hizqiyyahu were Menashsheh and Amon.

106f [*including those who were before him*]: An obvious addition to the text. It is unclear to me what prompted the addition or when it was made. It seems most likely to me that the addition belongs to the sixth compositional stage.

106g [*that is, those which Yahweh had given Mosheh*]: This phrase is clearly an addition to the text; I believe that it most likely was added by the authors of Kings' third stage, who inserted references to Mosheh in numerous places in Kings. In the Josianic study books' version of Kings, Mosheh is only mentioned once—the reference is here in P106, where Mosheh is said to be the maker of a bronze image of a snake-god that Hizqiyyahu destroyed as part of his reforms of Yahweh's cult in Yehudah (see note 106b above). Moreover, in the Josianic study books, Yahweh's commandments are given through the prophets. It is they, not Mosheh, who pass on Yahweh's commandments.

106h he rebelled against the king of Ashshur and didn't pay tribute to him: I speculate that the reason Hizqiyyahu didn't pay tribute was because he actually lacked the means to do so; the palace coffers likely had been severely depleted under Ahaz (see P102 and note 106b above). Even with the increased revenues brought about by cult centralization, the king apparently still had insufficient funds to meet the financial obligations imposed on him by the king of Ashshur.

106i from the smallest military outposts to the largest fortified towns: In ancient Hebrew, it was common to express totality with a phrase combining two opposite things—"young and old," "rich and poor," etc. That is the function of the phrase used here. I have made the contrast more explicit in translation by adding the adjectives "smallest" and "largest" and by stating that the conquest was of "the entirety" of Azzah's territory. Note that the phrasing used here also appears in P104; see note 104c above.

Notes to P107

107a In the fourth year of King Hizqiyyahyu's reign....: This entire *parashah* (apart from the final sentence) repeats information given in P103. I believe that the most likely explanation is that Josianic study books' main source for the kings of Yehudah—*The Chronicles of the Kings of Yehudah*—included information about the subjection of the sister kingdom Yisra'el, and that the authors of the Josianic study books have reproduced that information here in P107. Likewise, in my view, the authors of the Josianic study books based the account given in P103 on their main source document for the kings of Yisra'el—*The Chronicles of the Kings of Yisra'el*.

It is interesting to note the chronological synchronism at the beginning of the *parashah* equating Hizqiyyahu's fourth year with Hoshea's seventh year, and then a second synchronism in the following sentence. The presence of both synchronisms is quite odd and, in my opinion, is best explained as having been present in the source for this *parashah* (*The Chronicles of the Kings of Yehudah*). There would have been no reason for the authors of this *parashah* to provide this synchronism on their own, and we know that the authors of the Josianic study books frequently incorporated material verbatim from their main two source documents for Kings. This *parashah* thus provides strong evidence for the proposal that the synchronisms that we see in Kings were a feature of the source documents themselves.

107b He captured it: Literally, "they captured it." The subject of the verb should be understood as indefinite, and thus the sense of the Hebrew is the passive voice—"it was captured." The passive would be awkward in this context in English, although it is not awkward in Hebrew. A functionally equivalent translation in this instance thus calls for the active voice, which is more natural in English.

107c in Helah, in Havor on the Gozan River, and in the towns of Maday: On these locations, see note 103c above.

107d [Because they didn't obey their god Yahweh... anything that Mosheh Yahwehsservant had commanded.]: This passage is a clear addition from the authors of Kings' third compositional stage, who peppered Kings with additions and comments alluding to the books of the Torah and the book of Joshua. Note the mention of Yahweh's treaty with the Yisra'elites and the use of the surname Yahwehsservant, both of which appear in the books of the Torah and Joshua and are absent from material associated with the Josianic study books.

108a In the fourteenth year of Hizqiyyah's reign...: It is likely, in my opinion, that nearly this entire *parashah* is a verbatim quote from the book *The Chronicles of the Kings of Yehudah*. I believe that the authors of the Josianic study books omitted this information from their work because it reflected negatively on Hizqiyyahu, who they wished to be a role model for young King Yoshiyyahu. I speculate that the material in this *parashah* was then inserted into Kings by the authors of Kings' second stage, who still had access to the old royal chronicles and who had no special need to elevate the status of Hizqiyyahu in their work.

This *parashah* states that Sanheriyv's campaign against Yehudah occurred in the fourteenth year of Hizqiyyah's reign. I believe that originally this read the twenty-eighth year of Hizqiyyah's reign and that an editor of Kings' sixth stage—who knew Hizqiyyah ruled for twenty-nine years—"corrected" the date to the fourteenth year on the basis of the story in P111,1, in which Yesha'yahu informs the mortally ill Hizqiyyah that Yahweh will "add fifteen years" to his life. For more on this idea, see the discussion of the chronology of Hizqiyyah's reign in the appendix to this book.

This phrase "of Hizqiyyah's reign" represents the first words on what is now leaf 100 of the Aleppo Codex The three leaves between P93 and here have been lost from the Aleppo Codex.

108b Sanheriyv King of Ashshur embarked on a campaign against all of Yehudah's fortified towns: Sanheriyv's campaign against Yehudah was part of a broader campaign in 701 BCE against rebellious kingdoms in the Levant. His actions against Yehudah were almost certainly undertaken as punishment for Hizqiyyahu's rebellion and failure to pay tribute, as mentioned near the end of P106.

The site of Nineveh (spelled Niyneweh in this translation), where Sanheriyv based his administration, was excavated in the 1840s. The highlight of the excavations was the discovery of Sanheriyv's palace, which was lined with stone reliefs depicting events of his reign. Among the reliefs was a series telling the story of his siege of the town of Lakiysh (these are now in the British Museum). A. H. Layard, who led the excavations at Nineveh, published illustrations of many of the reliefs in a book devoted to the monuments of Nineveh. Figure 2 below, which is a picture of Sanheriyv's siege of Lakiysh, is from Layard's book.

108c three hundred *kikkar* of silver and thirty *kikkar* of gold: These are enormous amounts of silver and gold. One *kikkar* was equivalent to 3,000 sheqels; one sheqel was equivalent to a little over 11 grams in today's metric system. Thus one *kikkar* was the equivalent of approximately 33.5 kilograms (or 74 pounds in the English system). In today's terms, Hizqiyyah's tribute to Sanheriyv would have amounted to 10,000 kilograms (or 22,000 pounds) of silver and 1,000 kilograms (or 2,200 pounds) of gold. Hizqiyyah had no hope of paying such sums given that his father Ahaz had bankrupted the treasuries of Yahweh's house and the palace in buying the protection of the king of Ashshur.

A cuneiform document known as *The Annals of Sennacherib* includes a contemporary account of Sanheriyv's third campaign in the Levant, which includes his war against Hizqiyyahu and Yehudah; the document is often called the Taylor Prism (after its discoverer). Several versions of the annals are known from archaeology. The version nearest in time to the events it describes—written just a few months after the campaign—is known as the Rassam Cylinder. In that document, Sanheriyv claims that Hizqiyyahu's tribute was 30 *kikkar* of gold (in agreement with the account in Kings) and 800 *kikkar* of silver (compared to 300 *kikkar* in Kings). The Rassam Cylinder adds that Hizqiyyahu's tribute included his daughters, his concubines, his palace singers, numerous luxury items—furniture inlaid with ivory, precious stones and rare wood, and purple-dyed cloth and garments—along with metal utensils, chariots, and

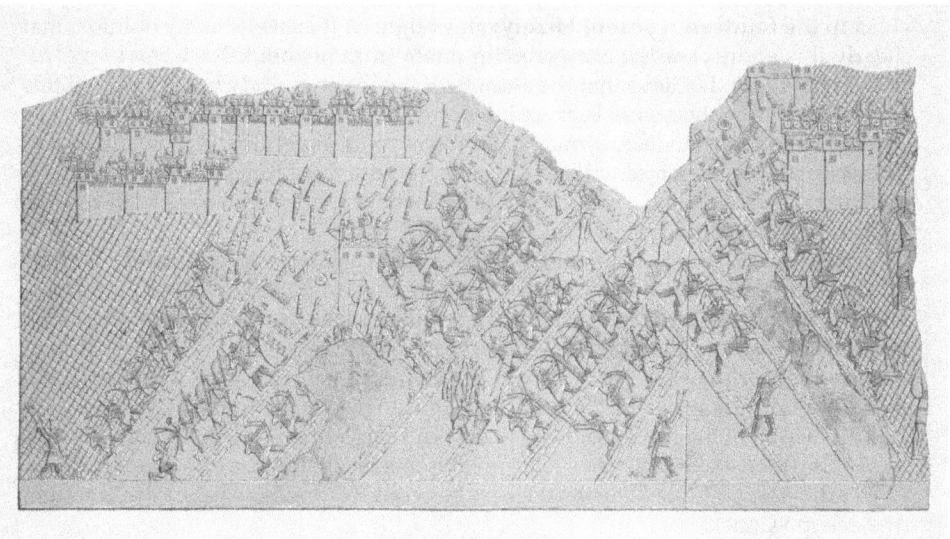

Figure 2: The siege of the city of Lachish by Sennacherib, from A. H. Layard, A Second Series of the Monuments of Nineveh (London: John Murray, 1853), plate 24. Public domain image available at:
`/https://digitalcollections.nypl.org/items/510d47dc-4720-a`
`3d9-e040-e00a18064a99/book?parent=724cf9c0-c6e6-012f-c238-58d385a`
`7bc34#page/23/mode/2up`

weaponry. While there may be some exaggeration regarding Hizqiyahhu's tribute in the Rassam cylinder, it does present a much more vivid picture than we see in Kings of how Sanheriyv's victory utterly bankrupted and humiliated Hizqiyyahu. For a good recent analysis of Sanheriyv's third campaign, see M. Cogan, "Cross-examining the Assyrian Witnesses to Sennacherib's Third Campaign: Assessing the Limits of Historical Reconstruction," in I. Kalimi and S. Richardson (eds.), *Sennacherib at the Gates of Jerusalem: Story, History, and Historiography* (Leiden: Brill, 2014), pp. 51-74.

108d all the silver that was found: Note that there is no mention of gold, most likely because the storerooms contained no gold. This is why Hizqiyyah "chopped up" the doors to the great hall of Yahweh's house—to scrounge together some gold to send Sanheriyv, even if it was nowhere near thirty *kikkar*.

108e Hizqiyyah chopped up the doors to the great hall of Yahweh's house: This action is a clear sign that the tribute imposed by Sanheriyv completely bankrupted the palace administration. Desperate to find additional funds to meet the onerous tribute, Hizqiyyah chops up the doors to Yahweh's house to remove the gold plating from them. On the gold plating of these doors, see P15.

The "great hall" (היכל) refers to the main room in Yahweh's house in front of the cella. The doors to the great hall served as the grand entry to the house. For a description of the great hall and its doors, see P15.

108f [*and the door pillars that Hizqiyyah King of Yehudah had plated with gold*]: This clause reads as a late comment added by an editor of Kings' sixth stage. I have added the phrase "with gold." The description of the doors in P15 mentions they were plated with gold, so it reasonable to assume that the editor who added this comment intended the reader to understand that Hizqiyyah used gold as the plating for the door pillars. It should be noted that the editor's comment is likely of no real historical value: given that Hizqiyyah's father Ahaz had taken all the gold and silver from the storerooms of Yahweh's house and the palace to pay as a bribe to Tiglath Peleser (see P102), and it seems doubtful that Hizqiyyah would have had enough gold at his disposal to plate the door pillars to the great hall of Yahweh's house.

109a The king of Ashshur sent...: The material from P109 through P112 (excluding the last two sentences of P112) consists of three stories about Hizqiyyahu that involve the great prophet Yesha'yahu (more familiar to English speakers as the prophet Isaiah). The subject of the first story, which is found in P109 - P110,2, is Sanheriyv King of Ashshur's threats against Hizqiyyahu, who had rebelled against Sanheriyv and allied himself with Egypt. The second story, which appears in P111 - P111,1, takes place when Hizqiyyahu has fallen mortally ill; the story concerns his interactions with Yesha'yahu when he is ill and in the immediate aftermath of his being cured by Yesha'yahu. The topic of the third story, which covers nearly all of P112, is an oracle that Yesha'yahu delivers to Hizqiyyahu predicting the Babylonian exile.

Notes to P109

These three stories appear in nearly identical form in the book of Isaiah: the first story in Isa 36 - 37, the second in Isa 38, and the third in Isa 39. In my proposed composition history, I have assigned these stories to Kings' fourth compositional stage, and I view all three stories as Persian period compositions. I believe the stories were originally composed as additions to the various prophetic stories incorporated as part of Kings' fourth stage, and they were written in order to balance the stories of the great northern prophets Eliyyahu and Eliysha with stories about the greatest southern prophet. The addition of this material gave Hizqiyyahu much more prominence than he had in the earlier versions of Kings as it existed in the Josianic study books, in the editions associated with the second and third compositional stages, and in the editions of the early fourth compositional stage.

With respect to the three stories, I view P109 - P110,2 as the earliest story and place it sometime in the mid-Persian period. This story may have been based on official correspondence from Hizqiyyahu's reign that had been preserved in Yahweh's cult due to its association with Yesha'yahu. In the decades that followed, as the figure of Yesha'yahu took on greater prominence within Yahweh's cult, this story then attracted two separate expansions—the story in P111 - P111,1 and the story in P112, both of which are purely literary compositions and which illustrate the prophet's greatness and special connection to Yahweh.

109b his general darmay, a chef descadron, and a minister detat: The text here has Hebraicizations of Aramaic/Akkadian terms for two types of officer in the Assyrian army and one type of high Assyrian government official. I have translated with lightly anglicized versions of similar French terms to replicate the experience of reading these titles in the Hebrew. The term תרתן (tartān) is the Hebraicization of turtānu, which was the title for a senior military commander of an entire region or province; the term רב־סריס (rab sārīs) is the Hebraicization of rab ša rēši, which was the title of a commander of a group of soldiers; and רב־שקה (rab šāqē) is the Hebraicization of rab šāqî, which was the title of a senior government official serving in a non-military capacity. For these terms in Akkadian, see the following citations in *The Assyrian Dictionary of the Oriental Institute of the University of Chicago*: T (vol. 18), pp. 489f; Š part 2 (vol. 17), pp. 30ff; and R (vol. 16), pp. 289f.

109c which is located on Fuller's Field Road: This phrase modifies the location of the conduit, not the location of the Upper Pool. The term for road here is מסלה, which describes a major roadway that has been built up and is regularly maintained by the royal authorities. It is the ancient version of a highway.

109d who have you put your trust in that you've rebelled against me?: Note that the historical background of the story in P109 - P110,2 is Hizqiyyahu's rebellion against the king of Ashshur described in P106.

109e you're hoping that Egypt—that pitiful crushed reed—will keep you standing upright: I have taken some liberties with the translation to capture the insulting tone of the Hebrew. More literally, "you've put your trust in the staff of that [pitiful] crushed reed." Note that the demonstrative pronoun זה often has a strongly pejorative force, as it does here; this is often best captured in English by a mild expletive, although in this instance I have chosen to represent it with the adjective "pitiful" rather than a profane term. I have commented on this use of the demonstrative pronoun in several places above and numerous times in my other translations. For other examples in Kings, see notes 52b, 59,1c, 59,1e, 69d, and 71h above.

109f And if you tell me…: In the message that Sanheriyv's senior official (the "minister detat") delivers, he first relays words spoken in the king of Ashshur's voice and then he switches and speaks in his own voice. I understand the sentence here to be spoken in the minister detat's own voice, as he refers to Hizqiyyahu in the third person. Towards the end of his message, he appears to switch back to speaking in the king's voice.

109g telling Yehudah and Yerushalem that they must worship in front of that altar in Yerushalem: It is interesting to note that the Persian period authors of this story view Hizqiyyahu's removal of the open-air shrines as cult centralization. It is also worth noting that they do not mention any connection to the book of Deuteronomy.

109h Now do you think that my marching up against this place isn't Yahweh's doing?: The speaker (the "minister detat") now switches back to the voice of the king of Ashshur. In this part of the speech the king of Ashshur implies that Yahweh has ordered him to attack Yehudah as punishment for Hizqiyyahu's destroying the open-air shrines to Yahweh. He argues to Hizqiyyahu that Yahweh in fact objects to his cult reforms (which, as I argue above, were undertaken purely for financial reasons).

109i who will soon be eating their own shit and drinking their own piss: A reference to the famine conditions brought about by the siege of Yerushalem. Note the *qeres* in the margin of the Masoretic text "correcting" the obscene language with terms that can be read aloud without offending anyone.

109j escape to me: That is, escape the dire conditions in Yerushalem and switch your loyalty from Hizqiyyahu to me. (The change in loyalty is implied by the demand to enter a peace treaty.) For the use of יצא ("go out, come out") to mean "escape," see BDB, p. 423, def. 1.d of the *qal*.

109k take you to a land like yours: That is, the king of Ashshur informs the people that if they make a peace treaty with him, he will spare their lives and send them into exile in a favorable land.

109l For they should have saved Shomeron from me: This statement only makes sense if one understands Hamath, Arpad, Sepharwayim, Hena, and Iwwa to have been allied with Hoshea King of Yisra'el in his rebellion against Ashshur. Hamath and Arpad were towns in the northern part of what is modern-day Syria, and it is possible that Sepharwayim, Hena, and Iwwa were towns located in the same region. In this understanding, the king of Ashshur is saying, "if the gods of those countries were strong, they collectively should have been able to save Shomeron."

Against this understanding is that P103 states Hoshea allied himself with Egypt and it mentions no other allied nations. It is especially interesting to note that some Septuagint manuscripts here read "Where are the gods of the nation of Shomeron? For they should have saved Shomeron from me!" This reading solves the problem of the apparent inconsistency regarding Hoshea's alliance, and, in my opinion, it likely represents the original text of Kings. In this scenario, the confusion in the present text is simply due to the phrase "Where are the gods of the nation of Shomeron?" falling out of the text due to a scribal error.

109m each having ripped his clothes to show his distress: The Hebrew reads, "with ripped clothes." In ancient Yisra'el and Yehudah, it was common to tear one's clothing as a way to demonstrate publicly one's own deep distress or mourning. This action is mentioned dozens of times in the Tanakh, and it is challenging to translate into natural English while being faithful to the meaning of the Hebrew.

109n Yesha'yahu the Prophet Amotzsson: Note the use of the dual surnames for Yesha'yahu. While we often see dual surnames, such as a patronym plus an occupational name, it is much more common for the patronym to precede the occupational name. Here the occupational name precedes the patronym—a construction that reads awkwardly in Hebrew as well as in translation.

109o "Here's Hizqiyyahu's message...the faithful ones who are still here.": This passage is the message from Hizqiyyahu that his officials deliver to Yesha'yahu; it contains language and terms that do not fit the context very well, and I view the entire passage as an addition made very late in the fourth compositional stage.

109p fetuses are now crowning, but there's no strength to give birth: I believe that this sentence may be a well-known folk saying that the author of the addition has put in Hizqiyyahu's mouth, but the saying doesn't fit the context of the story. If this is a famous saying, its meaning is not entirely obvious. Possibly the intent is something along the lines of "Even when the end is in sight, disaster can strike."

109q the faithful ones who are still here: The phrasing—השארית הנמצה (literally, "the [faithful] remnant that is found [here]")—is strange and doesn't fit the context very well. The scene at the beginning of the *parashah* implies that Yerushalem is under siege, but there is no indication of citizens fleeing or being taken captive. Thus, the language about a "remnant" doesn't really fit the situation in the story. If this passage were part of the earliest version of the story, we might expect to read "raise up a prayer on behalf of the inhabitants of Yerushalem" rather than "raise up a prayer on behalf of the faithful ones who are still here." The term "[faithful] remnant" (שארית) is often seen in late prophetic literature, and its presence offers some support for the proposal that this specific passage is a late addition to the story (which is itself a Persian period composition).

109r King Hizqiyyahu's officials went to see Yesha'yahu: The narrative seems confused because in the preceding sentences the officials deliver Hizqiyyahu's message to Yesha'yahu. However, if we view the preceding sentences as an addition, as I suggest in note 109o above, then the Hebrew reads relatively smoothly. Removing that addition, I would translate as follows: "He sent Elyaqim the Chamberlain, Shevna the Secretary, and the elders of the priests—all of whom had covered themselves in sackcloth—to Yesha'yahu the Prophet Amotzsson. When King Hizqiyyahu's officials arrived to see Yesha'yahu, he said to them, 'Here's what you should say to your lord....'"

109s the king of Ashshur's lackeys: Note the disrespectful attitude toward Ashshur in Yesha'yahu's oracle. Rather than refer to the delegation sent by the king of Ashshur with the standard phrase "the officers of the king of Ashshur" (עבדי מלך־אשור), he disparages them by calling them the king's "lackeys" (נערים).

109t Don't let your god...deceive you when he tells you Yerushalem won't be delivered into the king of Ashshur's hands: In other words, the king of Ashshur promises to return and take care of his unfinished business.

109u spread them out in front of Yahweh: That is, he spread them out in the great hall directly in front of the cella, where Yahweh is somehow present. The use of the verb פרש ("spread out") indicates the letters were written on papyrus or leather and needed to be unrolled in order to be read.

Notes to P110

110a Hizqiyyahu prayed in front of Yahweh...: The image painted by the author is quite striking: Hizqiyyahu is inside Yahweh's house, standing in front of the cella where Yahweh is present; Sanheriyv's letters lie at his feet, spread out for Yahweh to read, while Hizqiyyahu addresses Yahweh, praying to him in a dramatic fashion with his arms outspread.

110b Yahweh God of Yisra'el, Who Sits Astride the Winged Sphinxes: Hizqiyyahu addresses Yahweh by invoking the name of his battle chest. In Sam P79, we are told that the battle chest is called by the name written in it, which is "Yahweh of Armies, Who Sits Astride the Winged Sphinxes." Hizqiyyahu has substituted the surname "God of Yisra'el" for "[God] of Armies," but his invocation of the battle chest's name here is indisputable. It is appropriate that Hizqiyyahu invokes the battle chest in his prayer, as the chest represents Yahweh in his aspect as war god, and Hizqiyyahu's prayer is a request for Yahweh to save Hizqiyyahu and his subjects from Sanheriyv and his army.

110c You alone are God for all the world's kingdoms: The idea that Yahweh is the sole god for the entire world is characteristic of the Persian period, not the era of the monarchy, and offers some support for the view that the material in P109-P112 is a late composition. As discussed above in note 109a, in my proposed composition history I have assigned this material to Kings' fourth compositional stage.

110d Bend your ears...Open your eyes...Hear Sanheriyv's words: Hizqiyyahu is beseeching Yahweh to read the letters which he has spread out in front of the cella, where Yahweh is somehow present. The fact that Hizqiyyahu asks Yahweh also to "hear" Sanheriyv's words may imply that Hizqiyyahu also reads the letters aloud to Yahweh.

110e they weren't gods—rather, they were the handiwork of humans...you alone, Yahweh, are God: The monotheistic language here suggests a Persian period date for this *parashah*, and supports the proposal that the material about Hizqiyyahu in P109-P112 is a late addition to Kings. See note 110c above.

110f and so they were destroyed: Literally, "and so they [the kings of Ashshur] destroyed them [the gods of the nations they laid waste to]." I have translated in the passive voice here, as the active verb is awkward in English due to the duplication of the third person plural pronouns.

Notes to P110,1

110,1a Here is what Yahweh said about him...: Yesha'yahu's message to Hizqiyyahu contains a lengthy and somewhat confusing report of what Yahweh has said about Sanheriyv. Yahweh's speech has four parts: a short oracle about the "Tziyyon's lovely daughter," a lengthy and highly literary speech comparing the king of Ashshur's accomplishments with Yahweh's, a pair of oracles mentioning a "faithful remnant" and a second pair of oracles about Yahweh protecting Yerushalem. The first two parts are indeed "about" Sanheriyv and I view them as original to the story in P109 - P110,2. The other two parts, as I discuss below, are not exactly "about" Sanheriyv and I view them as later additions.

110,1b 'Tziyyon's lovely daughter snubs you... behind your back!': I believe that the author, who is writing in the Persian period, here quotes a genuine oracle of Yesha'yahu that had been preserved in the oracle collections associated with the prophet.

"Tziyyon's lovely daughter" and "Yerushalem's girl" (literally, "Yerushalem's daughter") are poetic terms for the inhabitants of Yerushalem or for Yerushalem itself. On the phrase בתולת בת־ציון, where two words in construct are understood as being in apposition ("the lovely girl, Tziyyon's daughter" and not "the lovely girl of Tziyyon's daughter"), see GKC §130 e.

110,1c the Holy One of Yisra'el: An epithet of Yahweh that likely goes back to the second millennium BCE. If the epithet does pre-date the monarchy, the term Yisra'el originally would have been understood to refer to the regions of Ephrayim, Menashsheh, and Binyamin. (Note that in Sam P70 "Yisra'el" is defined as Ephrayim, Binyamin and three regions that later were consolidated under the name Menashsheh—Yizre'el, the Gil'ad region, and the territory of the otherwise unknown "Ashurites.") In the Persian period, however, the epithet would have been understood as the "the Holy One of [the people] Yisra'el."

110,1d the Holy One of Yisra'el...the Lord: Somewhat unusually, in this oracle, Yahweh refers to himself in the third person by using epithets commonly applied to him.

110,1e boasting that you climbed high into the mountains...that you dried up all Egypt's watercourses with just the soles of your feet: The language in this passage is characteristic of the language found in royal Assyrian inscriptions, and it is possible that the author is quoting an actual inscription or other document here. As suggested in note 109a above, although the author of P109 - P110,1 was writing in the Persian period, he likely had access to genuine documents from Hizqiyyahu's reign that he used as sources for his composition.

110,1f Didn't you hear...what I did in ancient times, the thing I devised?: The most natural way to read the consonantal text is as I have translated. I have ignored the Masoretic accents. A functionally equivalent translation that follows the Masoretic accents would be "Didn't you hear...what I did? It was in ancient times, and I devised it." The meaning of the text is somewhat cryptic, as it is unclear what event Yahweh is referring to in his speech. Possibly it is an allusion to his destruction of Sedom and Emorrah, which the authors of the Tanakh liked to cite as an example of Yahweh's awesome destructive power. See, for instance, Am 4.11 and Is 13.19.

110,1g When I brought it about: The particle עתה (translated here as "when") is formed by adding the *he*-locative suffix to the word for "time" (עת). The core meaning of the particle is thus "at the time." The particle almost always refers to the present or the immediate future and should be translated as "now." However, in a small number of instances, I believe it refers to the past, and that is how I understand it here—literally, "At the time, I brought it about, and it resulted in fortified cities crashing...." The particle may also refer to the past in Hos 10.3 ("For at the time, they were saying...").

110,1h a nose band around your snout and a bridle bit in your mouth: The author describes placing a bridle on a horse. I understand the words חח and מתג to refer to parts of the bridle. The word חח has a range of meanings, including "hook," "ring," and "restraint." Here it is used to describe the part of a horse bridle that is placed over the snout. I do not believe the author uses the word in reference to a ring in the animal's nose, although it is certainly possible to understand the text in that way. For a seventh century BCE depiction of a bridle that clearly shows both a nose band and bridle bit, see figure 3 below.

Figure 3: Detail of a lion-hunting scene of Ashurbanipal, seventh century BCE, from the North Palace at Nineveh, Iraq. Alabaster bas relief. Public domain image available at Wikimedia Commons:
`/https://commons.wikimedia.org/wiki/File:Assyrian_horse.jpg`

110,1i And here's the sign by which you'll know that it's happening…: The material from here to the end of the *parashah* is incongruous with the preceding text. The language about the restoration of "survivors" and a "remnant" is characteristic of late prophetic literature. I believe this material represents an addition to the text made late in the Persian period or in the Hellenistic period, but it is unclear to me what prompted this addition. The language about the land lying fallow and relying only on volunteer plants for food is somewhat reminiscent of the material about the Shabbath year in Lev P51 and the ram's horn year in Lev P51,1, both of which date to the second half of the Persian period.

110,1j 'the first year volunteer plants will be eaten… bear fruit above it.': The author quotes what must have been a well-known oracle. I view the oracle as a late Persian period literary composition, but the author applies it to Sanheriyv's siege of Yerushalem. In its current context, the oracle should be understood to mean that after a period with little food (i.e. the period of the siege and its immediate aftermath), conditions will return to normal and the people of Yehudah will once again prosper.

110,1k For, 'a steadfast remnant shall come forth from Yerushalem—yes, a faithful band of survivors emerge from Mount Tziyyon!': The author quotes a second oracle, which also must have been well-known. Like the first oracle, I believe this oracle is a late Persian period literary composition that the author has applied to Sanheriyv's siege of Yerushalem. In its current context, the oracle simply promises that the siege shall be lifted and the inhabitants of Yerushalem will survive.

110,2a Therefore, thus says Yahweh... for the sake of my servant Dawid: I view the paragraph indicated here as an addition to the story in P109-P110,2. It was added before the addition at the end of P110,1 discussed above in note 110,1i. This addition in P110,2 consists of two (likely genuine) oracles that the author has applied to Sanheriyv's siege of Yerushalem. There are a number of indications that this material is an addition. Note the shift in speech: the oracles are addressed to the king of Ashshur, whereas directly before this, Yesha'yahu is delivering a message to Hizqiyyahu about the king of Ashshur. Note also the oracles in P110,2 are unnecessary to the narrative—the original conclusion of Yahweh's speech in P110,1 fits the narrative much better and suffices to explain the events that follow. If one accepts that this material at the beginning of P110,2 is an addition, it is easy to see how a later editor may have wished to add it to the story, as the oracles fit the context of Sanheriyv's siege quite well.

Notes to P110,2

110,2b 'This town won't be entered... This town won't be entered: I believe this passage represents a genuine oracle that was preserved in an oracle collection of Yesha'yahu. The Hebrew is ambiguous, as it is possible to read the oracle as either being about the king of Ashshur or as being addressed to the king of Ashshur. That said, I am confident that the latter reading (that it is addressed to the king of Ashshur) is the correct one, as it yields an oracle that is cryptic and elliptical, both of which are characteristic of prophetic speech during the monarchic period. In this reading, all the verbs—which are active—have indefinite subjects and so are understood in the passive voice. We can ascertain that the verbs likely would have been perceived as passive, as there is no stated subject in the oracle. If Yesha'yahu had intended his oracle to be understood in the active voice, he would have said "The king Ashshur will not enter this town..." rather than "One will not enter this town...."

The oracle is less interesting—and is less characteristic of prophetic speech—if we read it not as being addressed to the king of Ashshur, but as being about him. In that reading, the king of Ashshur is understood as the subject of all seven verbs in the oracle. The translation for this approach would be: "He won't enter this town. He won't fire arrows into it, nor confront it with shields, nor throw up siegeworks against it. The road he arrives by is the road he'll return on. He won't enter this town."

110,2c I will shield this town and rescue it, for my own sake as well as for the sake of my servant Dawid: This statement represents a second oracle that must have been well known. (This oracle is also quoted in P111,1 in the story about Hizqiyyahu's illness.) In this *parashah*, the oracle serves to provide commentary on the oracle immediately preceding it. It is unclear to me if the citation of the oracle here is a comment on the text added by a later editor, or if it was added at the same time as the oracle preceding it. In any case, it seems likely to me that both oracles quoted in P110,2 are genuine oracles of Yesha'yahu.

110,2d That very night... lying on the ground, dead corpses: I understand these two sentences as a very late addition to the text, made in one of the "final" editions of the fourth stage. The fantastical numbers are characteristic of very late additions.

110,2e So Sanheriyv decamped and left: In the earliest version of P109 - P110,2, this sentence followed directly from Yahweh's statement in P110,1 that "I shall lead you back the way you came." Note that in the earliest version of this story, Sanheriyv specifically left in response to the report he heard in P109 about Tirhaqah King of Kush embarking on a military campaign against him. The text is somewhat confusing to the reader because of the large amount of intervening material (some of which is original to the story and some of which represents later additions), but the report about Tirhaqah is in fact the context for understanding the passage here.

110,2f Adrammelek and Sar'etzer attacked him and stabbed him to death: Note the fulfillment of Yesha'yahu's oracle given to Hizqiyyahu in P109: Sanheriyv heard a report that caused him to return to his country, where he died a violent death.

Notes to P111

111a Around that time...: This *parashah* and P111,1 tell the story of Hizqiyyahu's recovery from a mortal illness. I view this story as a literary creation of the Persian period. It was composed later than the story in P109 - P110,2 and added to Kings later. The story presents Yesha'yahu as a miracle-worker and may have been composed explicitly for the purpose of showing that the great southern prophet Yesha'yahu was the equal of the great miracle-working prophets of the north, Eliyyahu and Eliysha.

The author begins his story with the common phrase בימים ההם ("in those days"). The phrase usually connotes a broad time frame. The author of this story did not necessarily have in mind the period when Sanheriyv was threatening Yerushalem. To confuse matters somewhat, a later editor made a small addition which did serve to connect the story here in P111 - P111,1 to the period of the siege. See note 111,1c below.

111b I have lived my entire life in your presence with honesty and integrity, doing things that were pleasing to you: In late literature, the phrase "living one's life in Yahweh's presence" simply means living one's life as a devout observer of the laws and precepts of Yahweh's Torah. As I view the story in P111 - P111,1 to be a late composition, I believe that is how this language should be understood here.

In early literature, however, the phrase "live one's life in Yahweh's presence" should be understood to refer to the cult. Note, for example, the oracle in Sam P3 regarding Eli and his family, who were priests to Yahweh in the shrine at Shiloh: "I once said to you that your family and your relatives would live in my presence for all time." In this context "live in my presence" means "serve at the altar" and/or "serve in front of the cella."

Notes to P111,1

111,1a the middle town: Note the *qere* here that corrects an error in the consonantal text, which reads "town" in place of "courtyard." The middle courtyard refers to a courtyard in the royal palace. The author of this *parashah*, who is writing during the Persian period, would never have seen the royal palace in Yerushalem (the Levanon Forest House described in P15). He certainly did not have any real understanding of its architectural features, and one should not presume that the "middle courtyard" was a feature of the actual historical palace.

111,1b you should go up to Yahweh's house: That is, once you're cured, you should go to Yahweh's house and make a thanksgiving offering to him.

111,1c and I shall save you... for the sake of my servant Dawid: I understand this passage to be an addition to the story made by the editors of Kings' sixth stage, who wished to connect this story back to the preceding story—possibly they understood the phrase beginning P111 "around that time" to mean this story was set at the same time as the story in P109 - P110,2.

111,1d I'm going to shield this town, for my own sake as well as for the sake of my servant Dawid: The author quotes the same oracle quoted above in P110,2. The version in P110,2 has an additional verb clause ("and rescue it"), but otherwise the two oracles are identical. Note the royal ideology here: Yahweh will save Yerushalem not only for his sake (it's the town he's chosen for himself), but also for the sake of the dynastic line of Dawid. While I view the stories about Hizqiyyahu in their current form as literary compositions of the Persian period, I believe they do preserve some genuine oracles of Yesha'yahu, including the one here referring to the Dawidic monarchy.

111,1e Get a fig-cake... Hizqiyyahu recovered: These two sentences read as a later addition to the text, made by an editor who was bothered that the story omitted an account of Hizqiyyahu's recovery. Note how the sentences interrupt the narrative and how the remainder of the *parashah* implies that Hizqiyyahu has not yet been cured. It's worth noting that these two sentences do not appear in the parallel passage in Isa 38.

111,1f It's too easy for a shadow to move across ten steps... That's not a sign: Hizqiyyahu tells Yesha'yahu that a sign must be a real miracle, not a natural phenomenon; Yesha'yahu then calls out to Yahweh, and Hizqiyyahu is granted a "real" sign. It is probably not reading too much into this short passage to see it as a comment by the author of the *parashah* about the nature of prophecy and the signs associated with prophecy, which was a topic of some interest in the second half of the Persian period, long after the days of the prophets had passed.

It is interesting to compare this *parashah* with the parallel passage in Isaiah 38.1-8. In the parallel passage, there is no discussion between Hizqiyyahu and Yesha'yahu about "proof" of a cure, and there is no mention of the natural phenomenon of shadows leaving the steps. Instead, in Isaiah, Yesha'yahu's oracle promises a miracle (the shadow moving backward), and the miracle serves as proof that Yahweh will save Yerushalem, not that he will cure Hizqiyyahu. The ending of the version of this story in Isaiah seems to be later than the ending of the version in Kings: once the setting of the story was connected to the siege of Yerushalem by the edit discussed above in note 111,1c, the author of the Isaiah version of the story appears to have revised the ending to reflect the siege setting.

Notes to P112

112a Berodak... sent letters and a gift to Hizqiyyahu, for he had heard that Hizqiyyahu was ill: Note how the setting of P112 is at odds with the oracle in P111,1, which implies that Hizqiyyahu fell ill during the siege of Yerushalem by the king of Ashshur. It seems highly improbable that Berodak would have sent an emissary to Hizqiyyahu with a gift in the midst of the siege. If one views the statement in P111,1 about Yahweh saving Yerushalem as a later addition, as I propose above in note 111,1c, then the narrative inconsistency here is explicable.

112b he showed the envoys his entire treasure-house: Recall from P108 that the palace storerooms were completely emptied in order to pay tribute to Sanheriyv; thus, there should have been nothing for Hizqiyyahu to show Berodak Bal'adan's envoys. The inconsistency here in P112 is due to the fact that P112 is part of a late Persian period addition to Kings. One of the reasons for adding this material was to demonstrate that the exile to Bavel and the plunder of Yerushalem and of Yahweh's house by Bavel's army was foretold in an oracle by the great prophet Yesha'yahu.

112c everything that your ancestors accumulated down to the present day will be carried off to Bavel: But everything accumulated by the prior kings of Yehudah has already been given away as tribute to the Assyrians. Regarding the inconsistency here, see note 112b directly above.

112d Yahweh's oracle that you spoke to me is a good one...: The picture of Hizqiyyahu in P112 (and to a lesser extent in P111 - P111,1) is very unflattering. He is depicted as being concerned about his own welfare more than the welfare of his people. Here in P112, it doesn't bother him that the kingdom of Yehudah will be destroyed by Bavel so long as there will be peace in his own lifetime. Such a depiction would be impossible for the authors of the Josianic study books. For these authors, he was a model for the young king Yoshiyyahu to imitate. Thus, the unflattering picture of Hizqiyyahu here provides further support for viewing P112 as a Persian period addition.

112e Isn't it, so long as: The author uses the phrase הלא אם, which combines the interrogative particle הלא ("is it not?," implying a positive answer) and the conditional particle אם ("if")—literally "is it not if." The phrase appears two other times in the Tanakh: once in Gen P9,1 (the story of Qayin and Hevel) and once in Isa 28.25. In both instances, the phrase introduces a protasis of the form "isn't it true that if" and is followed by an apodosis. Here in Kgs P112, however, the particle הלא appears to function on its own as the apodosis ("isn't it true [that the oracle you spoke is a good one]?") with the particle אם introducing the protasis ("if [or "so long as"] there'll be peace and security in my lifetime").

112f The rest of Hizqiyyahu's acts... Menashsheh became king in his place: The final two sentences of the *parashah* are clearly original to the Josianic study books' version of Kings. It's perhaps worth reminding the reader that the authors of the Josianic study books were selective in what events they included in their newly composed book of Kings. The authors were writing to educate the young king Yoshiyyahu and they typically summarized or omitted material where they did not see a lesson for the king. Thus the accounts of the end of the reigns of the kings often mention important events that they have left out of their history, as we see here in the conclusion to P112.

Notes to P113

113a Menashsheh was twelve years old when he became king...: The account of Menashsheh's reign appears in P113 - P113,1. In the material about him in the earliest edition of Kings (the version associated with the Josianic study books), the authors present him as an especially bad king—they state that he "went to great lengths to do things that displeased Yahweh" (הרבה לעשות הרע בעיני יהוה) and they catalog the many actions he undertook within Yahweh's cult that were deeply offensive. For these authors, one of the most important aspects of the cult reforms they hoped Yoshiyyahu would implement was to eradicate the cults of the Asherah and the Ba'al and the stars from the grounds of Yahweh's house. These authors' account of Menashsheh's reign is relatively short—just the first half of P113 (excluding the additions that I show in brackets and parentheses) and the end of P113,1.

After the failure of Yoshiyyahu's political program to extend his authority to the territory of the former kingdom of Yisra'el, and after the subsequent destruction of Yerushalem and of Yahweh's house, the authors of Kings' second stage sought an explanation for Yahweh's rejection of "the place that he claimed as his own" [more literally, "the place where he set his name"]. Because they still operated within the worldview of divine kingship as expressed in Judean royal ideology, they explained these events in terms of the actions of the king. As Menashsheh was the king who within living memory displeased Yahweh the most, the authors of Kings' second stage settled on Menashsheh's actions as the cause of the destruction of Yerushalem and of Yahweh's house. The authors of the second stage thus significantly expanded the account of Menashsheh's reign, adding the end of P113 and the first half of P113,1. Because the authors of the second stage made Menashsheh such a prominent figure in Kings, it is not surprising that the account of his reign attracted a significant number of comments and additions by later authors who worked on Kings' third and sixth stages.

113b He did things that were displeasing to Yahweh: This clause introduces a long catalog of Menashsheh's actions that were displeasing to Yahweh. The material about Menashsheh in P113 attracted a number of additions and comments from the authors of the second compositional stage (the authors of the exilic revisions of Kings), from the authors of the third compositional stage (who connected Kings to the books of the Torah and Joshua by inserting numerous allusions to those books) and from the editors of Kings' sixth compositional stage. Menashsheh's reign is especially important to the authors of the second stage, for they view his crimes as the reason for Yahweh's decision to reject Yehudah and Yerushalem (the place he chose as his own). They state this explicitly in their addition in the second half of P113 and the first half of P113,1, which contains an oracle from Yahweh delivered through anonymous prophets.

113c [*similar to the abominable practices of the nations that Yahweh drove out of the Yisra'elites' path*]: This clause is clearly an addition to the text, as it interrupts the usual formula which states that a king did things that were displeasing to Yahweh and then immediately follows that statement with specific examples of displeasing actions. For some examples of this formula, see P43, P44, P48, P49, P60,1, P86, and P98. It is unclear to me when this addition was made; it is possible that it was made by the authors of Kings' third stage, although I think it slightly more likely it was added as a comment by the authors of the sixth compositional stage.

113d he rebuilt the open-air shrines that his father Hizqiyyahu had destroyed: I believe Menashsheh's reversal of Hizqiyyahu's reforms is an accurate reflection of historical events. My personal view is that Hizqiyyahu removed the open-air shrines in order to increase the taxes collected by the cult at Mount Tziyyon, which Hizqiyyahu had full control over. The issue was an urgent one for him, as he would have been desperate to find funds to pay the tribute that he owed to the king of Ashshur. When Menashsheh came of age (he was only twelve when he assumed the throne), he and his advisors must have viewed the continued subjection of Yehudah to Ashshur as proof that Yahweh was punishing Yehudah because he was displeased that Hizqiyyahu had destroyed the open-air shrines and reduced the ability of the people to make regular offerings to their god. By reinstituting the open-air shrines, Menashsheh must have hoped to win back Yahweh's favor.

113e (just as Ah'av King of Yisra'el did): I view this clause as original to the Josianic study books, although it is equally plausible to understand it as an addition by the editors of the sixth compositional stage. It is also possible to understand the clause as a comment made by the authors of the second stage, who viewed Ah'av as the paradigmatic "bad king" of Yisra'el because of his support of the cult of the Ba'al (see note 113,1a below).

113f [*He was always building altars in Yahweh's house... claim as my very own."*]: This sentence disrupts the flow of the narrative and I understand it to be a comment added to the text by the editors of the sixth compositional stage. The editor is reminding the reader that Menashsheh's building altars on the grounds of Yahweh's house—multiple altars to the Ba'al and multiple altars to the stars of the sky are included in the catalog of Menashsheh's crimes—was especially egregious because he built them in the place that Yahweh said he would claim as his own.

113g *Yerushalem is the place that I shall claim as my very own*: Literally, "In Yerushalem I shall place my name." On my translation here, see note 20c above.

113h [*He would regularly make his son pass through fire... consulting ghosts and spirits*]: This language is taken almost verbatim from Deut P18,5, which condemns a series of "abominations" practiced by the nations that Yahweh drove out of Kena'an. I understand this sentence to be an addition to the text, made by the editors of the sixth compositional stage to show that Menashsheh practiced the abominations listed in Deut P18,5. As with the addition discussed in note 113f above, one clue that the text here is an addition is the use of the perfect consecutive verb forms, which are at odds with the imperfect consecutive verb forms in the underlying narrative.

It is not certain exactly what is involved in "making one's son [or daughter] pass through fire" (העביר את־בנו [את־בתו] באש). The phrase occurs several times in the Tanakh, and sometimes takes the form "make one's son pass through fire for Molek." In addition to the occurrence here (by the authors of the sixth stage), the phrase appears in P102 (a very late addition by the editors of the sixth stage), P104 (in material added by authors of the third stage), Deut P18,5 (part of the earliest version of Deuteronomy), Lev P36,12 (in an addition from the late Persian period or Hellenistic period), Ez 20.31, Ez 23.37, and Jer 32.35. Many scholars understand the phrase to mean burning one's child on an altar as a whole offering to the god Molek. However, in each instance, the phrase may also be understood to refer to the practice of walking, running, or jumping through a fire on the altar in honor of the god Molek. While there is strong and unambiguous evidence that the people of ancient Carthage sacrificed their own children as offerings to Molek, that in no way forces us to conclude that the language in the Tanakh must refer to the same practice. It is possible that it does, but it is equally possible that it does not. Moreover, the mentions of this practice in the Tanakh occur in material separated by several centuries from the events they describe, several of the mentions are secondary to the text, and the various authors may have had different understandings about what the practice involved.

113i *He placed the statue of the Asherah that he had made in Yahweh's house*: There is a great deal of evidence that in the monarchic era at many of the cult sites devoted to Yahweh, the goddess Asherah served as Yahweh's consort. Menashsheh's actions thus were consistent with common practices of his day. Presumably, he believed that giving Asherah her proper place of honor within Yahweh's cult on Mount Tziyyon would help win back Yahweh's favor, which had been lost through what he must have viewed as the misguided reforms of his father Hizqiyyahu. It is interesting to speculate where he placed this statue of Asherah—the most logical place would have been in the cella, next to the winged sphinxes and the battle chest that was the special locus of Yahweh's "presence."

113j *This house and Yerushalem... are the places I shall claim as my own for all time*: Literally, "In this house and in Yerushalem... I shall put my name for all time." On this translation, see note 20c above.

113k [*I shall no longer make Yisra'el wander...the nations that Yahweh obliterated from the Yisra'elites' path.*]: This material, which severely disrupts the narrative, is very clearly an addition by the authors of the third compositional stage. The addition here alludes to the wandering in the wilderness, Mosheh and the Torah given through him, and Yahweh's removal of nations from the Yisra'elites' path (the latter being events in Numbers and Joshua). For the authors of this addition, "the Torah that my servant Mosheh commanded them" is a reference to the book of Deuteronomy. At the time they were writing, the term Torah had not yet come to be associated also with Genesis, Exodus, Leviticus, and Numbers.

113l Because Menashsheh King of Yehudah has done these abominable things...: I view the material from here to the end of the *parashah* plus the first half of P113,1 to be an addition by the authors of Kings' second stage. Here they provide their explanation for the destruction of Yerushalem and Yahweh's rejection of "the place that he chose as his own": it was the crimes of Menashsheh that provoked Yahweh's anger. They repeat this accusation against Menashsheh in additions in P116 and P117,1. See notes 116aq and 117,1e below. This material cannot be from the authors of the Josianic study books because their work is a work of hope—they are looking to join the territories of the former kingdom of Yisra'el with Yehudah in order to reestablish the glorious kingdom ruled by the dynastic founder Dawid.

113m he caused Yehudah to err: The authors of Kings' second stage here borrow language from the Josianic study books, and thus create an explicit parallel between Yarov'am and Menashsheh: just as Yarov'am "caused Yisra'el to err" (החטיא), which ultimately led to Yahweh's rejection of Yisra'el, so Menashsheh "caused Yehudah to err," leading to Yahweh's rejection of Yehudah.

113n —: The Leningrad Codex has a *parashah petuhah* here. See L217 r.3.9-10.

113,1a therefore, thus says Yahweh God of Yisra'el...: Yahweh's speech in this *parashah* is clearly the work of the authors of Kings' second stage. The speech plays an important role in their work, for it marks Yahweh's rejection of Yerushalem and Yehudah. In this speech, the authors state their views of the cause of the exile of the people of Yehudah and the destruction of Yerushalem: these are due to the crimes of Menashsheh.

Perhaps unsurprisingly, the authors of the speech compare the destruction of Yerushalem to the destruction of Shomeron. But it is interesting that they imply that Ah'av was the blameworthy king rather than Yarov'am (this is almost certainly because Ah'av was a devotee of the Ba'al, whereas Yarov'am was a devotee of Yahweh). The authors of the Josianic study books consistently hold up Yarov'am as the model "bad king." Ah'av's presence here in P113,1 is thus a clear indication that the speech is not a composition of the authors of the Josianic study books.

113,1b plumb line...plumb bob: In construction and carpentry, a plumb is used to create a vertical reference line for the purposes of measurement; it consists of a line to which is attached a weight called a "bob." This is clearly what the author has in mind here. BDB, p. 1054, proposes instead that משקלת ("weight") does not denote a plumb bob, but that it is a tool for creating a horizontal reference, or what in English is called a "spirit level." I believe BDB in this instance is incorrect; there is no reason to depart from the natural sense of the Hebrew.

Notes to P113,1

113,1c [*it is wiped and then flipped over*]: This clause reads as a comment added by the editors of the sixth compositional stage, who must have thought readers might wrongly understand the simile in a positive manner. By specifying that a dish is flipped over after it is wiped clean, they make clear to the reader that the simile implies the destruction of Yerushalem.

113,1d [*Because they did what was displeasing to me...Egypt down to the present day*]: This sentence reads as a comment added by the authors of the third compositional stage. Note both the allusion to the exodus and the attempt to extend the blame to the people as a whole. (For the authors of the first and second stages, it is the king who bears the blame, not the people.) Note also that the "they" here clearly refers not to the people of Yehudah but to Yahweh's people as a whole. This is another indication that the sentence is from the authors of Kings' third stage and not the second stage.

113,1e In addition, Menashsheh killed a great many innocent people...to do what was displeasing to Yahweh: I view this sentence as an addition by the authors of the second stage (although it is also plausible to understand this as an addition from the sixth stage). The sentence repeats the observation from the end of P113 that Menashsheh caused Yehudah to err, which I view as an addition from the second stage (see note 113m above).

It bears repeating that the statement that Yehudah has displeased Yahweh is at odds with the views of the authors of the Josianic study books. For them, Yehudah remains in Yahweh's favor as the place he has reserved for Dawid's line (see P30,1) and as the location of Yerushalem, the town that he has chosen as his own. Those authors held out hope that Yoshiyyahu would follow in the footsteps of Dawid (and Asa and Hizqiyyahu), reforming the cult and winning Yahweh's favor, and ultimately expanding his dominion to include the territories of the former kingdom of Yisra'el.

113,1f He was buried in a garden in his palace: It is noteworthy that Menashsheh was not buried in Fort Dawid, which served as the royal cemetery for the Dawidic kings. The last king of Yehudah said to be buried in Fort Dawid was Hizqiyyahu's father Ahaz (see P102). It is interesting to speculate about the state of the royal cemetery after Ahaz's time. Given that Hizqiyyahu desecrated Yahweh's house by stripping it of its gold in order to pay tribute to Ashshur (see P108), it would certainly be reasonable to think that Hizqiyyahu also might have desecrated the cemetery by plundering the grave goods there in order to include them with his tribute to Sanheriyv.

Notes to P114

114a Amon was twenty-two years old when he became king: Recall from P113 that Menashsheh ruled for fifty-five years. Thus Amon was born in the thirty-second or thirty-third year of Menashsheh's reign, when Menashsheh was around forty-five years of age. Given how old Menashsheh was when Amon was born, Amon almost certainly was not his first-born son. It seems likely there would have been several sons ahead of him in line for the throne, and one can only wonder how it was that Amon assumed the kingship ahead of his older brothers. One can ask the same question for Menashsheh: his father Hizqiyyahu died at age fifty-four, and Menashsheh was just twelve when he assumed the throne. Thus it is almost impossible to believe that Menashsheh was Hizqiyyahu's oldest living son when Hizqiyyahu died.

114b He was buried in his grave in Uzza's Garden: Recall from P113,1 that Amon's father Menashsheh was buried in Uzza's Garden, which seems to have replaced Fort Dawid as the royal cemetery (see note 113,1f above).

114c his son Yoshiyyahu ruled as king in his place: I believe that this *parashah* represents the original end of the earliest version of Kings. As discussed in my introductory note, I believe that the book of Kings, as well as Judges and Samuel, was originally composed for the education of the young king Yoshiyyahu in the years shortly after he assumed the throne. Judges likely was composed first, and the stories in it were intended both to entertain the young king and to provide lessons in what it means to be an effective (and an ineffective) leader. Samuel likely was composed a few years after Judges, when the king had reached his teenage years and had the capacity to comprehend more complex material and themes. Like the stories in Judges, many of the stories in Samuel were meant to entertain the king; but the stories also offer important lessons in leadership, and—more importantly—the material in Samuel introduces the idea of Yahweh's binding agreement (ברית) with the Dawidic king, and the idea of the Dawidic king as the head of all the Yisra'elite tribes, both those in the north and those in the south. Of the three works that comprise what I call the Josianic study books, Kings was likely composed last. It provided Yoshiyyahu with an account of the kings of Yisra'el and Yehudah and of those kings' relationship with Yahweh. Because the book was written specifically to educate Yoshiyyahu, it naturally would have ended with his assumption to the throne.

115a Yoshiyyahu was eight years old when he became king...: The authors of Kings' second stage were responsible for the base narrative of Kings from P115 through the end of the book, which covers the reigns of Yoshiyyahu and his successors. While I believe there were multiple "editions" within the second stage, the earliest edition of the second stage was likely written in the 580s BCE, after the destruction of Yerushalem and of Yahweh's house. If the book of Kings was used in the education of Yoshiyyahu's sons, the version used likely would have been the original version of the book that was composed for Yoshiyyahu's own education.

Notes to P115

115b Yediydah Adayahsdaughter of Batzeqath: As the queen mother, Yediydah likely was quite powerful in the early years of her young son's reign. Yediydah herself, however, was likely very young. She bore Yoshiyyahu to Amon when Amon was just sixteen. If Yediydah were the same age as her husband, she would have been only twenty-four when her son became king. As I discuss above in my introductory note to Kings, I believe that Yediydah came under the influence of palace officials whose families had come to Yehudah after the fall of Yisra'el and allowed them to assist with, if not lead, the education of her son. This group may have been ardent proponents of the idea of the exclusive worship of Yahweh and they likely strongly opposed the practices of Yahweh's cult at Beyth-El. Both of these ideas served as central tenets of Yoshiyyahu's program of religious reforms.

116a In the eighteenth year of King Yoshiyyahyu's reign...: This *parashah*, which is one of the most important in the book of Kings, is the account of Yoshiyyahu's reforms of Yahweh's cult in Yehudah and his attack on the Yahweh's cult in Beyth-El and elsewhere in the province of Shomeron. The authors of the *parashah* promote the idea that "the Torah of Mosheh" (their name for the book of Deuteronomy) was the basis for his reforms. They write that this document, which was the record of a treaty between Yahweh and his people, was discovered during construction work on Yahweh's house. When the document was brought to the attention of Yoshiyyahu, he recognized at once that Yahweh must be furious with Yehudah over the failure of previous generations to fulfill their treaty obligations to Yahweh. Yoshiyyahu publicly agrees to the treaty and commits the people to following its obligations, and he then embarks on a radical and violent reform of Yahweh's cult. He removes the cults of other gods from Yahweh's house and destroys their cult objects, he defiles the open-air shrines everywhere in Yehudah so that no offerings can be made to any

Notes to P116

gods in them, he destroys all altars to Yahweh and to other gods except Yahweh's altar in front of his house, and he "puts an end to" (which can be understood either as "kills" or simply as "removes royal support for") all priests associated with the open-air shrines. Yoshiyyahu next turns his attention to the province of Shomeon—he destroys the shrine to Yahweh in Beyth-El and defiles its altar, and he forces the abandonment of the open-air shrines in the province by slaughtering their priests and defiling their altars. The authors of the *parashah* tell us that Yoshiyyahu also instituted the observance of passover (which had not previously been observed during the monarchy) and he eradicated the practice of consulting ghosts and spirits of the dead.

Perhaps the most obvious question for readers to ask about this *parashah* is to what extent its account of Yoshiyyahu's reforms is an accurate reflection of real historical events. Because most scholars believe that the earliest version of Kings (or a revision of Kings) was composed during Yoshiyyahu's reign, they tend to view the account of his reforms as, by and large, historically accurate. Indeed, prior to writing this book, I too held this view. My views, however, changed dramatically over the course of writing this book. In the composition history that I have proposed, the earliest version of Kings ends with the reign of Amon (P114) and the account of Yoshiyyahu's reign in P116 consists entirely of material from Kings' second, third, fourth, fifth, and sixth stages—a composition period spanning more than three centuries. As I discuss in note 116b directly below, there is strong evidence that much of P116 is a literary creation of its authors and does not reflect real events. The material that I assign to the second compositional stage, which would have been written roughly half a century after Yoshiyyahu's reforms, likely has some basis in history, and this material is concerned with only two things: Yoshiyyahu's removal of the cults of other gods from the precincts of Yahweh's house and his attack on the cult of Yahweh in Beyth-El and elsewhere in Shomeron. (Complicating matters is that much—but not all—of the material about Yoshiyyahu's attack on the cult of Yahweh in Beyth-El and the towns of Shomeron, as I suggest below in notes 116ab, 116ae, 116ag, and 116ai, appears to be a literary creation not based on real events). All the other material in the *parashah* about Yoshiyyahu's reforms—the discovery of "Mosheh's Torah," the ratification of the treaty with Yahweh, and the institution of the observance of passover—was composed more than a century after Yoshiyyahu's reign and there is no reason to believe that any of this material has any basis in history.

As I hope will be clear from the comments below, this *parashah* has an exceptionally complicated composition history. Because of the significance of the material in it, it attracted many additions and comments over the course of Kings' composition history. As stated above, in my view, none of the material in the *parashah* dates to Kings' first compositional stage. Indeed, nothing in this *parashah* reads as something that would be written by authors who composed a work explicitly to support Yoshiyyahu's reforms, as is often argued by scholars. The *parashah* is wholly backward looking, as befits Kings' second through sixth stages—note, for example, the comment that Yahweh's anger has been "sparked" against Yehudah and "it won't be extinguished." I believe that the bulk of the *parashah* stems from Kings' second and third stages. It is not always clear which material belongs to the second stage and which to the third stage. The main distinction is that the material from the second stage describes Yoshiyyahu's destruction of idolatrous cult practices, and the material from the third stage reframes this destruction around the discovery of the Torah scroll. The authors of the third stage also added material introducing the treaty between Yahweh and the people and the celebration of the passover. Finally, it is worth noting that I believe the authors of the second and third stages omitted an account of Yoshiyyahu's problematic death. The material about his death at the end of the *parashah* was added by authors of the fifth stage, who were writing so long after these events that the manner of his death no longer threatened the idea of his greatness.

116b They should give i to the workmen hired to oversee the work on Yahweh's house...: The language here borrows heavily from P84. The description of the repairs on Yahweh's house in P84 is more detailed, and the phrasing reads naturally there, whereas the description here in P116 omits a number of details that make the phrasing confusing unless one is familiar with P84. A good example of the slightly unnatural phrasing is "the workmen hired to oversee the work on Yahweh's house" (עשׂי המלאכה המפקדים בית יהוה). This is directly borrowed from P84. The phrasing reads naturally in P84, but here it is odd, as the mention of "hiring" (or appointing) overseers of work has no context, for we haven't yet been informed that Yahweh's house was in need of repair. Similarly, the authors have also borrowed from P84 the detail of the silver being collected by the door-keepers of Yahweh's house. Here in P116, this detail lacks context, and it is wholly unclear to the reader why the door-keepers are collecting silver. By contrast, in P84, the rationale for this is entirely clear—it is to stop the priests from withholding silver from Yeho'ash, who wishes to use the funds for repairing Yahweh's house. A final example is the sentence about not counting the silver entrusted to the overseers, which is based on a sentence in P84 about the honesty of the men overseeing the work. The sentence reads naturally in P84, whereas here in P116 it is almost incomprehensible due to the lack of additional context. The point of the sentence is that when the overseers were given money to pay the workers, the amount given to each overseer wasn't counted, as the overseers were honest men.

In my view, the borrowing of language from P84 suggests that the repairs to Yahweh's house under Yoshiyyahu is a literary invention of the authors of Kings' third compositional stage, who were writing more than a century after Yoshiyyahu's reign. They needed an occasion to describe the "discovery" of the Torah scroll of Mosheh, and so fabricated an account on the basis of the story of the renovation of Yahweh's house in P84. While I believe that there was a reform of Yahweh's cult that included centralization of the cult in Yerushalem during Yoshiyyahu's reign, I do not believe that we can reconstruct the specific history of how the reform was initiated, and I do not believe that the reform was in any way connected to the book of Deuteronomy. The account of Yoshiyyahu's reforms here in P116 is full of literary elements that indicate it cannot be understood as an accurate history of the events it describes.

In the Masoretic manuscripts, the final letter of the verb phrase ("they should give it") has fallen out of the text; there is a *qere* in the margin that corrects this error, which I show in the translation. In addition, on the following line there is a *qere* in the margin correcting the phrase "in the house" to "[on] the house." I do not show this *qere* in the translation. See A102 v.1.2-3 and L217 v.2.24,26.

116c the Torah scroll: The term "Torah scroll" refers to an early version of Deuteronomy known to the authors of Kings' third stage, who I believe were writing in the first half of the Persian period and who were responsible for all the material in this *parashah* regarding the discovery of the Torah scroll, the ratification of the treaty with Yahweh, and the celebration of passover. It is noteworthy that the author assumes the reader knows what the term "Torah scroll" means—this is the first time the term appears in the book of Kings, and the author doesn't qualify the term in any way. This is a clear indication, in my opinion, that the author of this passage is writing long after the (fictional) events described, at a time when Deuteronomy had become an important book in the library in Yahweh's cult on Mount Tziyyon and was well known to the priests associated with the cult there (who in that period would have been the primary, if not the only, readers of Kings).

Over the course of writing this book, I have changed my views on the date of Deuteronomy. I previously viewed it as composed during Yoshiyyahu's reign in the 630s or 620s BCE, but I now see it as a composition of the late exilic or early Persian period. I believe that Yoshiyyahu did engage in a dramatic reformation of the cult of Yahweh in Yehudah; however, I do not believe that his reforms were inspired by an early version of Deuteronomy.

116d they had dumped out the silver found in Yahweh's house: The author's verb choice here is very unusual and the Hebrew reads awkwardly. I believe the awkwardness in the text is due to the author basing his account on the renovation and repair of Yahweh's house in P84, but omitting the key detail from that *parashah* that the silver was collected in a chest. There is no mention of a chest here in P116, but the verb "dumped out" (from the root נתך, "pour out") is the appropriate verb if the silver is in a chest, which would be emptied by "dumping out" or "pouring out" its contents. Instead of mentioning the chest, the author uses the phrase "the silver found in [Yahweh's] house" (את־הכסף הנמצא בבית), which is a phrase that appears in P84 in connection to the counting of the silver.

116e Yahweh's anger that now burns against us... on account of the fact that our ancestors didn't heed the words contained in this scroll: This language alludes to a version of Deuteronomy as it existed in the fifth century BCE. It would never have occurred to the authors of the Josianic study books to write a sentence such as this—they hope to reestablish the old "united" kingdom as it was under Dawid and their outlook is still a very hopeful one. Nor could this sentence have been written by the authors of Kings' second stage; for them, Yahweh's anger at Yerushalem and Yehudah was due solely to the actions of Menashsheh.

Note how the author's language implies that his audience is familiar with the contents of Deuteronomy. This is another indication that he is writing long after the (fictional) events he is describing; see note 116c above.

116f District Two: The name of a neighborhood in Yerushalem.

116g Say this to the man who sent you to me... And to the king of Yehudah... here is what you should say to him: Huldah delivers two oracles of Yahweh: one to "the man who sent you to me" and the other to "the king of Yehudah." The formulation is strange because both individuals are Yoshiyyahu, an oddity that is indicative of an editorial seam. I view both oracles as part of the material from Kings' third stage. I believe the first oracle belongs to the original expansion of P116 by the authors of the third stage, and that the second oracle was added in a later part of the third stage. The second oracle specifically addresses the problem of Yoshiyyahu's violent death, which must have been well known. The authors of the second and third stages omit all mention of his death, and the latter group must have felt some obligation to reassure readers that Yahweh favored Yoshiyyahu, which they did through the addition of the second oracle. See the discussion of this oracle in note 116j below.

116h Know that I'm going to bring disaster to this place...: This speech of Yahweh could only have been written by the authors of the third compositional stage of Kings, who viewed historical events through the lens of Yahweh's treaty with his people as expressed in the books of the Torah—it is completely at odds with the views of the authors of the Josianic study books and the authors of Kings' second stage. See note 116e above.

116i with all the statues they made of those gods: Somewhat more literally, "with all the things they fashioned by hand" (בכל מעשה ידיהם). The reference here is specifically to the divine images produced under the cult reforms of Menashsheh, which included a statue of the Asherah placed inside Yahweh's house and numerous images associated with the cult of the Ba'al and the cult of the stars of the sky. The cults of all these gods enjoyed royal sponsorship during the reigns of Menashsheh and his son Amon (see P113 and P114).

116j 'Thus says Yahweh God of Yisra'el: 'In regards to the things that you have heard...: As discussed above in note 116g, I view this lengthy oracle addressed to Yoshiyyahu as an addition made late in the third stage, well after the oracle preceding it (which is from an earlier edition of Kings' third stage). This second oracle is quite interesting, as it represents the attempt by the authors of Kings' third stage to uphold the view of Yoshiyyahu as a great king, despite the subsequent downfall of Yehudah. Thus they paint a picture in which Yahweh has compassion on Yoshiyyahu and grants him a peaceful death. It was especially important that a king die a peaceful death, as this was proof of the favor he had won from the principal god of the people he ruled. In this instance, the authors of the third stage ignore the violent death that Yoshiyyahu suffered because it mars the picture of him as a great king favored by Yahweh. (The account of Yoshiyyahu's death at the end of P116 is an addition to the text from Kings' fifth stage; see note 116at below.)

116k that they would become an object of horror and a curse: Huldah indirectly quotes from the treaty curses in Deut P26: "you shall become an appalling example, a proverbial insult, and a taunt" (A1 r.3.8-9). This clause may be an addition by the editors of the sixth compositional stage of Kings, although I have treated it as original to the oracle here, which was part of the material added to this *parashah* by authors working on a late edition of the third stage.

116l in your graves: The plural "graves" is very strange and is almost certainly an error for "grave."

116m he read out to them everything contained in the treaty scroll...the entire people became subject to the treaty: I understand this scene as a literary invention of the authors of Kings' third compositional stage. I do not believe it describes a real historical event. In the Josianic study books (and in Yoshiyyahu's time), there was no "treaty" between Yahweh and the people. Rather, the treaty (or binding agreement) was between Yahweh and the Dawidic king. It is only with the initial composition of Deuteronomy and Exodus-Numbers—toward the end of the Babylonian exile and early in the Persian period—that the idea of a treaty between Yahweh and his people is developed, as there was no longer a king with whom Yahweh could have a treaty.

Note that the term "treaty scroll" is simply another name for an early version of the book of Deuteronomy, which also was called the Torah scroll. This is the first time the term "treaty scroll" appears in the book of Kings, yet the author does not explain the term or qualify it in any way. He assumes his audience is familiar with the term—a clear indication that, as I suggest in notes 116c and 116e above, he is writing long after the (entirely fictional) events he is describing.

116n The king stood beside the pillar: The passage about Yeho'ash's assumption of the throne in P82,1 indicates that for important rites or other business that the king conducted in Yahweh's house, he always assumed a position "beside the pillar." It is unclear which of the two pillars—Bo'az or Yakiyn—the king stood beside. On these two pillars, see P16.

116o his treaty's obligations: For עדות as "treaty obligations," see note 4d of my translation of Deuteronomy. In the books of the Torah, the word עדות always means "treaty obligations" or "treaty;" never in the books of the Torah does it mean "testimony." With the use of this term here, the author is making a specific allusion to the passage in Deut P4, where this term appears in the heading that introduces the people's treaty obligations.

116p The king ordered Hilqiyyahu…then he disposed of their ashes in Beyth-El: I believe these two sentences, which describe Yoshiyyahu's removal of the cults of the Ba'al, the Asherah, and the stars of the sky from Yahweh's house, mark the end of the material at the beginning of P116 that belongs to Kings' third stage. Note that this material largely duplicates the original description of Yoshiyyahu's removal of these cults, which begins a couple sentences later in the *parashah* and belongs to Kings' second stage (see note 116r below).

116q he disposed of their ashes in Beyth-El: I understand Beyth-El here to be the shrine dedicated to Yahweh in the territory of Binyamin where the chief object of veneration was a gold statue of Yahweh in the form of a bull calf. The mention of Beyth-El at this point in the narrative is somewhat surprising, as it is disconnected to the account of Yoshiyyahu's destruction of that cult site later in this *parashah*. Carrying the ashes to Yahweh's shrine at Beyth-El and disposing of them there is presumably a means of desecrating the place. It is possible the clause mentioning Beyth-El here is an addition to the text, made in a later revision of the third stage or made by the editors of the sixth stage.

The verb form here is not the perfect with *waw* consecutive, but rather the perfect with *waw* copulative. The perfect with *waw* copulative is the narrative tense in Aramaic, and it is used in several places in this *parashah*, likely due to the influence of Aramaic. Some of the instances of the perfect with *waw* copulative are treated by scholars as due to copyist errors. In my opinion, however, the Hebrew in the instances here in P116 reads naturally, and the variation in the verb forms give the passages something of a literary quality. I see no reason to think that the verb forms here are in error. There is a good discussion of the perfect with *waw* copulative in GKC § 112 *pp-uu*, although I believe GKC is too quick to assume some of the passages it cites are corrupt.

Six instances of the perfect with *waw* copulative appear in P116. With the exception of the one here, all of them are in material that I assign to the second stage. I believe these verb forms were in language that was lifted directly from the source document used by the authors of the second stage, *The Chronicles of the Kings of Yehudah*. The perfect with *waw* copulative here—the first instance of the form in P116—is from Kings' third stage, and I believe the authors must have chosen it in imitation of the verb forms they saw in the material from the second stage describing Yoshiyyahu's cult reforms.

116r He put an end to the *komer*-priests…: There is a clear editorial seam here. The material in P116 prior to this belongs to Kings' third stage; the material here and following it belongs to Kings' second stage. As discussed above in note 116p, the editorial seam is indicated by the repetition of the Ba'al, the Asherah, and the stars of the sky. The *komer*-priests likely were priests associated with open-air shrines, but how they differed from "regular" priests (כהנים) is unclear.

Originally this sentence would have followed directly from the end of P115. It is interesting to note that in the account of Yoshiyyahu's reign from the second stage (P115 plus parts of P116, including the material here), the presentation of his cult reforms has a format identical to the presentation of the cult reforms of Asa in P42 and Hizqiyyahu in P106. In all three accounts, there is a statement that the king "pleased Yahweh" and was like "his ancestor Dawid," and then this statement is immediately followed by a list of the cult reforms that the king made. The authors of the second stage clearly structured their account of Yoshiyyahu's reign in imitation of the accounts of Asa's and Hizqiyyahu's reigns, which belong to Kings' first stage.

Finally, note that verb form here ("He put an end to the *komer*-priests") is the perfect with *waw* copulative, which is discussed in note 116q directly above.

116s where women wove household shrines for the Asherah: Small household shrines holding an image of a god or goddess were typically constructed of wood or clay, not cloth. The Septuagint and the Old Latin here have other words in place of household shrines, and many scholars consequently view the text here as corrupt. If the text is not corrupt, we should presume that women did not weave the shrines, but rather wove decorative cloth coverings for the wooden or clay shrines. For a good discussion of the small household shrines (including numerous illustrations of examples found in excavations), see S. Schroer, "The Iconography of the Shrine Models of Khirbet Qeiyafa," in S. Schroer and S. Münger (eds.), *Khirbet Qeiyafa in the Shephelah: Papers Presented at a Colloquium of the Swiss Society for Ancient Near Eastern Studies Held at the University of Bern, September 6, 2014* (Orbis Biblicus et Orientalis 282), Fribourg and Göttingen, 2017, pp. 137-158.

116t from Geva to Be'er Sheva: Geva is on Yehudah's northern border and Be'er Sheva on the southern border. As I discuss above in note 21f above, it was common in Hebrew to express totality or comprehensiveness by joining two things that were opposite. Thus, when expressing the concept of everywhere, a speaker or writer would often mention locations at two extremities.

116u He knocked down: Another example of the perfect with *waw* copulative; see note 116q above.

116v [*However, the shrine priests... among their kinsmen.*]: This sentence disrupts the narrative, and I understand it to be a late addition to the text made by the editors of the sixth compositional stage.

116w He put an end to the horses... dedicated to the sun god Shemesh, so that they would no longer enter the grounds of Yahweh's house: This practice may provide us with the background to understand the road named Horse Parade Road, which is mentioned at the end of P82,1, and which goes from the palace to the grounds of Yahweh's house.

116x Nathan-Melek the Royal Official's room: This room may have been where a small shrine to Shemesh was located.

116y scattered their ashes: A fourth example of the perfect with the *waw* copulative in this *parashah*; see note 116q above.

116z He smashed: A fifth example of the perfect with the *waw* copulative in this *parashah*; see note 116q above.

116aa filled their sites with human remains: By filling the shrines that Shelomo had established with human remains, Yoshiyyahu defiles the sites and makes them impure so that they cannot be used again.

116ab In addition, the altar that was located in Beyth-El... (who had proclaimed these things specifically): This paragraph is the account of Yoshiyyahu's destruction of Yahweh's cult in Beyth-El. Although it is plausible to view the entire account of the attack on the cult in Beyth-El as a literary fabrication, I think it more likely that parts of it do reflect real historical events. Specifically, I believe that the authors of Kings' second stage based the first two sentences of the paragraph on their source document, *The Chronicles of the Kings of Yehudah*, and that these sentences do have a basis in history. By contrast, I view the second two sentences in the paragraph as a literary composition by the authors of the second stage, written to show that the oracle in P33 about Yoshiyyahu defiling Yahweh's altar in Beyth-El (which was part of the Josianic study books) was fulfilled. It is interesting to note that there is no mention of the gold calf at Beyth-El—it seems likely to me that this image of Yahweh was looted by the army of Ashshur when they defeated Yisra'el in 722 BCE. It is also noteworthy that the second sentence of the paragraph (which is based on the authors' source document) indicates that the Asherah, who was Yahweh's consort, played an important role in Yahweh's cult at Beyth-El.

116ac the shrine platform: The term במה specifically designates an elevated platform, made of wood or stone, that served as the central structure of an open-air shrine dedicated to a god. On top of the platform sat an altar, and all offerings to the god and other rites were carried out on this platform. Because the platform is the locus of all the activity in the open-air shrine, the term במה over time came to designate the shrine itself. In most cases in Kings, the appropriate translation of במה is "shrine" or "open-air shrine;" but in some cases—as here—the reference is clearly to the platform. For more on the term במה, see note 8b above.

116ad he incinerated its Asherah post: A sixth example of the perfect with the *waw* copulative in this *parashah*; see note 116q above. The presence of the verb form in this sentence offers support for viewing the sentence as based on the source document and not as a literary composition by the authors of the second stage.

In the Aleppo Codex, Aharon ben Asher vocalized אשרה with a *daghesh* in the *he*, yielding the reading "its Asherah [post]." In the Leningrad Codex, Shmu'el ben Buya'a omitted the *daghesh*, resulting in a somewhat awkward reading: "he incinerated Asherah." The Aleppo Codex here is clearly superior. See A103 r.3.7 and L218 v.2.16.

116ae Next, having noticed the graves ... who had proclaimed these things specifically): I view these two sentences as a literary composition by the authors of Kings' second stage, who added this material to demonstrate the fulfillment of the oracle in P33. This is not material based on the source document, *The Chronicles of the Kings of Yehudah*. Note the tension in the text here, which is a clear sign of an editorial seam: in the previous sentence (which I believe was based on the source document) we are told that Yoshiyyahu demolished the altar, but in this sentence the altar is intact and functional.

116af This was in fulfillment of the oracle of Yahweh that the holy man had proclaimed: The oracle in P33 states that Yoshiyyahu will burn human remains on the altar in Beyth-El.

116ag What's this grave marker I'm looking at... the prophet who had come from Shomeron: I view the material indicated here as an addition by the authors of Kings' fourth stage. When they added the story in P34 - P35 about the old prophet living in Beyth-El and the holy man from Yehudah, they also added this short passage in P116 referring back to that story.

116ah the prophet who had come from Shomeron: This is the old prophet living in Beyth-El who is the subject of the story in P34 - P35. The phrase "who had come from Shomeron" (אשר־בא משמרון) is confusing, as the old prophet lived in Beyth-El, not Shomeron. Although Shomeron was sometimes used to refer to the northern kingdom instead of the name Yisra'el, here Shomeron almost certainly refers to the town. If the author had intended Shomeron as the name of the kingdom, he would have written "who was from Shomeron" (אשר משמרון) instead of "who had come from Shomeron." In fact, I suspect that "who was from Shomeron" was the original reading here and that the verb בא crept into the text due to an error by a scribe, who perhaps was inadvertently influenced by language in the preceding paragraph, which qualifies the holy man with the phrase "who came from Yehudah" (אשר־בא מיהודה).

116ai In addition, at this time... Then he returned to Yerushalem.: I view this paragraph as a literary composition by the authors of the second stage; there is no reason to think it describes real events, as it can be understood as describing Yoshiyyahu's "fulfillment" of the oracle in P33. It is unclear to me if this paragraph was part of the original composition of P116 by the authors of the second stage, or if it was added as part of a later "edition" of the second stage. If it was added as part of a later edition, it would have been added to supplement the earlier material from the second stage about the destruction of Yahweh's cult in Beyth-El. The likely rationale of this supplement was to clarify that Yoshiyyahu did in fact burn the bones of the priests of the open-air shrines on illegitimate altars. In this scenario, the authors of the supplement would have been bothered by the fact that in the earlier material about Yoshiyyahu's destruction of the cult in Beyth-El, he didn't technically fulfill the oracle in P33: the bones he burned on the altar in Beyth-El were human remains from a local graveyard, not the remains of the priests of the open-air shrines. By adding the material about the destruction of Yahweh's cult throughout Shomeron, the authors of the late second stage thus correct the oversight of the earlier authors and ensure that the oracle in P33 is fulfilled in all details.

116aj Yoshiyyahu forced the abandonment of the open-air shrines: The author here uses the term בתי הבמות ("the structures of the open-air shrines"), which is simply an alternate term for "open-air shrines." The term can be confusing because there were structures attached to some open-air shrines. On the two terms for the open-air shrines, see note 32,1f above.

Note the verb הסיר, which I translate as "forced the abandonment of." One of the major themes running throughout the material from Kings' first stage is the condemnation of making offerings to Yahweh in the open-air shrines. In five places, the authors of Kings' first stage qualify the acts of kings of Yehudah who "did what was pleasing to Yahweh" by noting that "the open-air shrines weren't abandoned" during their reigns (see P60, P83, P91, P95, and P101). In each of these statements, the authors use the *qal* form of the verb סור ("turn aside") with the unusual sense of "abandon." Here in P116, the verb choice of the authors of Kings' second stage has clearly been influenced by those statements: they use the *hiph'il* form of the same verb. The usual meaning of the *hiph'il* of the verb is "remove," which would be appropriate for the translation in the context here. However, I have instead translated as "cause to be abandoned" in order to preserve the connection to the unusual usage of the verb in the previous statements about the open-air shrines.

116ak Observe the passover... in keeping with what is written in this treaty scroll: The "treaty scroll" is an early version of the book of Deuteronomy. In the current version of Deuteronomy, the rules for observing passover are given in Deut P16. Note the shift in literary layers here: the previous paragraph was composed as part of Kings' second stage, and this paragraph and the two following paragraphs—which mention the treaty scroll, the stipulations of the Torah, and Mosheh—clearly belong to Kings' third stage.

116al the days of the champions who championed Yisra'el: The reference to the period prior to the monarchy and the use of the specific term "champion" (שפט) suggests that the authors of Kings' third stage, who composed this part of the *parashah*, knew an early version of the book of Judges. If we accept the view that the authors of Kings' third stage were attached to Yahweh's cult in Yerushalem, then it would follow that the cult library in Yerushalem at that time (the first half of the fifth century BCE) included a copy of the book of Judges.

116am Not until the eighteenth year of the reign of King Yoshiyyahu was this passover rite observed: If Yoshiyyahu assumed the throne in 641 BCE, the eighteenth year of his reign would have been 624 BCE.

116an the practice of consulting ghosts and spirits of the dead...*teraphim* and divine figurines—all the destestable objects that were commonly seen in Yehudah and Yerushalem: I understand the author here to mean that Yoshiyyahu sought out and destroyed physical objects related to divination and necromancy. In a passage at the end of Lev P39, the terms אוב ("ghost, necromancer") and ידעני ("spirit, conjurer") clearly refer to tools to consult ghosts and spirits—the terms in that passage should not be understood to refer to the ghosts themselves, nor to the people who consult the ghosts. Likewise, I believe that the author of the passage here in Kgs P116 had in mind physical objects used in consulting the dead. *Teraphim* were doll-like figurines that were used to obtain oracles from the gods, including Yahweh. The phrase "all the detestable objects that were commonly seen in Yehudah and Yerushalem" may be understood as a late gloss, although I have a slight preference for treating it as original to this passage (which is part of an addition from the third stage) and I have represented it as such in translation.

116ao the stipulations of the Torah that were recorded in the document that Hilqiyyahu the Priest found: The stipulations banning the practice of divination, soothsaying, consulting ghosts, etc. are given in Deut P18,5. The author here is alluding specifically to that *parashah* in Deuteronomy.

116ap Never before was there a king like him...: In this paragraph, the authors of Kings' third stage provide their assessment of Yoshiyyahu and of the destruction of Yehudah. In their view, Yoshiyyahu was the greatest king—greater even than Dawid, because of Yoshiyyahu's adherence to Mosheh's Torah.

116aq However, Yahweh didn't relent...reject the house that I said I would be my very own: These two sentences are a key passage for the authors of Kings' second stage: here they express in the clearest terms the reason for the destruction of Yerushalem and the destruction of Yahweh's house. These sentences cannot be from the hand of the authors of Kings' third stage, as there is no mention of Yahweh's treaty with the Yisra'elites, nor any mention of the Yisra'elites' failure to uphold the treaty obligations.

It is especially interesting to note that for the authors of the Josianic study books, it was Yarov'am whose actions provoked Yahweh to anger. But those authors held out hope that Yoshiyyahu would reverse Yarov'am's crimes and restore Yisra'el to Dawidic rule (see the end of P30,1, where they state that the suffering of Dawid's line caused by the breach with Yisra'el will not be "for all time"). The authors of Kings' second stage, who wrote after the destruction of Yehudah, understood that the Dawidic promise was not unconditional, but was conditional on the king's loyalty to Yahweh. They thus explain the destruction of Yehudah as due to Menashsheh and his cult reforms—actions so offensive to Yahweh that not even Yoshiyyahu's reversal of those reforms could save Yehudah.

116ar the house that I said would be my very own: On this translation, see note 20c above.

116as The rest of Yoshiyyahu's acts... the book *The Chronicles of the Kings of Yehudah*: This sentence concludes the original account of Yoshiyyahu's reign, which is from Kings' second stage. Note that in this material, there is no account of Yoshiyyahu's death. This is almost certainly because he died a violent death. It was common belief in the ancient Near East that the manner of one's death reflected one's favor or disfavor with one's god. A king could only die by violence if he had fallen out of favor with his god and the god wished to punish him. Because Yoshiyyahu's manner of death "disproved" his greatness and Yahweh's approval of him, the authors of Kings' second stage purposely omitted any account of his death. The account of Yoshiyyahu's death at the end of this *parashah* was added much later, likely as part of the work on the fifth compositional stage, by authors who were far removed in time from Yoshiyyahu and whose belief system wasn't threatened by the manner of Yoshiyyahu's death.

116at During his reign, Phar'oh Neko of Egypt...: I understand the material from here to the end of the *parashah* to be an addition from the fifth compositional stage; see note 116as directly above. The account of Yoshiyyahu's death here in Kings is cryptic and short on detail: it says simply that King Yoshiyyahu went to meet Phar'oh Neko who was on a campaign against the king of Ashshur, and that when the king saw Yoshiyyahu, he had him killed. The authors give no reason for Phar'oh's anger at him. There is a more detailed account of Yoshiyyahu's death in the book of Chronicles (2 Chr 35.20-25). In that account, Yoshiyyahu challenges Phar'oh and Phar'oh's army as they are passing through the province of Shomeron on their way to Karkemish to fight the king of Ashshur, and Phar'oh's archers kill Yoshiyyahu in battle. Unfortunately, the account in Chronicles is mostly a literary creation of the authors (they model their account on the death of Ah'av in Kgs P59,1) and thus is of little help in understanding the true circumstances of the king's death. I believe the most likely scenario for Yoshiyyahu's death is the one proposed by the Israeli scholar Dan'el Kahn. Kahn suggests—convincingly, in my opinion—that Yoshiyyahu was a vassal to the Egyptian king Psammeticus I and then became vassal to Neko upon Psammeticus' death. Yoshiyyahu must have misjudged the new Egyptian king's character, and he likely either withheld tribute or short-changed the king what he owed. (That he lacked the funds to pay may have also factored into his decision.) In response, Neko summoned Yoshiyyahu to meet him as he was passing by Megiddo on the way to Aram to engage the king of Ashshur, and it was there Neko made an example of him and had him executed him for failure to pay his tribute. See D. Kahn, "Why Did Necho II Kill Josiah?" in J. Myrnářová, P. Onderka, and P. Pavúk (eds.), *There and Back Again – the Crossroads II: Proceedings of an International Conference Held in Prague, September 15-18, 2014* (Prague: Charles University in Prague, 2015), pp. 511-528.

If one accepts Kahn's proposal that Yoshiyyahu was executed for failure to pay tribute, it is interesting to speculate on the reasons behind Yoshiyyahu's decision not to pay. It couldn't only have been that he lacked the resources, as he simply could have imposed a tax on his subjects, just as his son Yehoyaqiym did shortly after Yoshiyyahu's death (see P117). One wonders to what extent Yoshiyyahu's decision may have been influenced by his faith in the Dawidic promise and by his belief that if he "pleased" Yahweh by purifying his cult, Yahweh would grant him "success in whatever he ventured to do" (see P106 for this phrase). Indeed, that Yahweh rewards kings who please him was the central lesson he would have learned as a young boy in studying and reading the stories in the book of Kings—a book that I believe was composed explicitly for his education.

It is conceivable that the authors of Kings' third stage may have included a sentence about Yoshiyyahu's peaceful death, for in the material they added to P116, they include an oracle explicitly stating that because of Yoshiyyahu's humility, he would join his ancestors peacefully in the grave. If so, it likely read, "Yoshiyyahu lay down in death with his ancestors, and his son Yeho'ahaz became king in his place" (וישכב יאשיהו עם־אבתיו וימלך יהואחז בנו תחתיו). If there was such a sentence, it would have been removed by the authors of the fifth stage when they added the account of Yoshiyyahu's actual death, which was a violent one.

Notes to P117

117a He did what was displeasing to Yahweh, similar to all that his ancestors had done: The authors of Kings' second stage adopt the format employed by the authors of the first stage in which each king is judged as either "pleasing" or "displeasing" to Yahweh. However, they employ this format for Yeho'ahaz in a clumsy way, as if they didn't appreciate the nuances of how their predecessors used it. For example, the authors of the first stage typically follow their judgement with specific actions that the king did which are the basis for their judgement. The authors of the second stage provide no such follow-on statement for Yeho'ahaz (although they did provide such a follow-on statement for Yoshiyyahu—see note 116r above). Note also the phrasing "similar to all that his ancestors had done"—the phrasing, which is never used by the authors of the first stage, is entirely formulaic and is meaningless in the context here. "All his ancestors" are specifically the Dawidic kings, and a number of them in the eyes of the authors of both the first and second stages did in fact "please" Yahweh, including Yeho'ahaz's father Yoshiyyahu.

117b Phar'oh Neko imprisoned him in Rivlah in the district of Hamath: One can only speculate why Phar'oh imprisoned Yeho'ahaz, but it seems most likely to me that he did so because Yeho'ahaz refused (or was unable) to pay the tribute that he owed to Phar'oh. This scenario would be consistent with the proposal that Phar'oh killed Yoshiyyahu because Yoshiyyahu refused (or was unable) to pay the tribute he owed.

In the early Iron Age, Hamath emerged as a small independent kingdom located in what is now western Syria. It was in regular conflict with Ashshur, and by the end of the eighth century BCE it had been conquered and reorganized as an administrative district of Ashshur. In 609 BCE, when the events of P117 occurred, Phar'oh Neko was campaigning in the northern Levant helping the rapidly collapsing empire of Ashshur defend itself against the army of Nabopolassar King of Bavel. Hamath at the time was still under the control of Ashshur, so it was to there that Neko had his officers bring Yeho'ahaz for an audience.

117c a levy on the country of one hundred *kikkar* of silver and one *kikkar* of gold: The amount of tribute here is just a fraction of the tribute imposed by Sanheriyv on Hizqiyyahu in P108 (300 *kikkar* of silver and 30 *kikkar* of gold). The tribute is small because Yehudah was effectively bankrupted by Ashshur—there is simply little wealth remaining in the kingdom.

117d Phar'oh Neko then made Elyaqiym Yoshiyyahusson king, and he changed his name to Yehoyaqiym: Note that the account of Yeho'ahaz's reign and his replacement by Yehoyaqiym does not contain a statement referring the reader to the source document *The Chronicles of the Kings of Yehudah*. It is likely, in my opinion, that the staff in the royal palace didn't maintain a record of Yeho'ahaz's reign in the source document because of the brevity of his reign.

Note also that Elyaqiym was Yeho'ahaz's older brother. Yeho'ahaz was twenty-three when the people made him king, and he ruled for only three months. When

Phar'oh deposed Yeho'ahaz, he made Elyaqiym king, who at the time was twenty-five. The comment at the end of P116 that "the country's citizens" made Yeho'ahaz king may imply that the royal succession was violated. It is tempting to speculate that Elyaqiym was that natural heir to the throne and that he made a deal with Phar'oh that he would deliver on the tribute demands if his brother was deposed and he were made king. The two brothers had different mothers, and it is possible that Yeho'ahaz assumed throne instead of his older brother because his mother (Hemutal Yirmayahusdaughter) had higher status within the royal family than Elyaqiym's mother (Zeviydah Pedayahsdaughter).

The statement about Elyaqiym's name change is ambiguous. The sentence can be understood to mean that Neko changed Elyaqiym's name, or that Elyaqiym changed his own name. I have a strong preference for the latter option, but numerous scholars prefer the former. I have retained the ambiguity in my translation.

117e At that time, Yeho'ahaz was taken away—he went to Egypt, where he died: This sentence provides a good example of the difficulties of translating ancient Hebrew. Although the language is straightforward, the Hebrew is deceptive and ambiguous. At first glance, the most natural way to read the Hebrew is with Neko as the subject of the verb לקח (which here means "take away"). However, that reading is very awkward, yielding the following translation: "At that time, he [i.e. Neko] took Yeho'ahaz away—he went to Egypt, where he died." The awkwardness stems from identifying the subject of following verb "he went." One expects the subject of the verb still to be Neko, yet it is clear from the following statement that "he died there" that the subject of "he went" must be Yeho'ahaz. However, the awkwardness and difficulty in understanding disappear if we instead understand the subject of לקח ("take away") to be indefinite. In that reading, the clause "one took Yeho'ahaz away" is functionally equivalent to the passive "Yeho'ahaz was taken away" and then it is quite natural to understand Yeho'ahaz as the subject of the following two verbs.

117f he had to impose a tax on the land: There is nothing of value remaining in the coffers of the palace or in the storerooms of Yahweh's house. Thus, he had to impose a poll tax in order to accumulate the funds for the tribute that was owed. Poll taxes must have been a common means of collecting the sums needed to pay tribute—see P98, where Menahem imposes a poll tax on Yisra'el to pay the tribute owed to Phul King of Ashshur.

117g at each man's usual assessed rate: Translation of איש כערכו. The term ערך is also used with the meaning of "tax assessment, assessed value" in Lev P54. See my translation of that *parashah* and the notes there. Lev P54 provides standard assessed values for males and females for four age groups: twenty to sixty years of age, five to twenty years of age, one month to five years old, and older than sixty. It seems likely to me that a similar system may have been in place for Yehoyaqiym's levy, although the assessed rates for individuals in each age group may have been different than the rates in Lev P54.

117,1a He did what was displeasing to Yahweh, similar to all that his ancestors had done: The formula here is identical to that used for Yeho'ahaz in P117. See my comments above in note 117a.

Notes to P117,1

117,1b During his reign, Nevukadnetztzar King of Bavel invaded: Egypt's power was in severe decline by Yehoyaqiym's time (609-597 BCE), and Phar'oh was no longer in a position to protect his vassal Yehudah from the threat posed by Bavel. For the few remaining years of the monarchy, Yehudah will serve as vassal to Bavel.

117,1c marauders from Kasdiym: In Hebrew, Kasdiym (כשדים) is both the name of a region located in the southwest of modern-day Iraq and the name of the people who settled there. In traditional English translations, this word comes over as "Chaldea" and "Chaldeans." The Kasdiym were an integral part of the empire of Bavel, and the ancestry of a number of Bavel's kings—including Nabopolassar and Nevukadnetztzar—was Kasdiym. The authors of Kings and other books of the Tanakh often use "Kasdiym" interchangeably with "Bavel."

117,1d in keeping with the oracles that Yahweh had spoken through his servants the prophets: It is possible that this is an allusion to the oracles of the prophet Jeremiah (Yirmayahu), who was active from sometime in Yoshiyyahu's reign down to the 590s BCE.

117,1e it was at Yahweh's command that Yehudah suffered these attacks...on account of Menashsheh's wrongdoing: The authors of Kings' second stage, who were writing during the Babylonian exile, understood the collapse of Yehudah and the ravages it suffered as punishment for Menashsheh's crimes. The comment here in P117,1 is consistent with their earlier statements to this effect in P113 - P113,1 and P116. See notes 113l and 116aq above.

117,1f (including also the innocent blood... unwilling to forgive): This parenthetical comment may be an addition to the text made by the authors of the sixth compositional stage, reminding the reader of the previous comment about Menashsheh's killing of the innocent in P113,1. (That previous comment itself was likely an addition by the authors of Kings' second stage, as I suggest in note 113,1e above.)

117,1g *The Chronicles of the Kings of Yehudah*: The final mention of *The Chronicles of the Kings of Yehudah* in the book of Kings is here in the summary statement of Yehoyaqiym's reign. It seems likely to me that the palace staff ceased maintaining this work after the end of Yehoyaqiym's reign in 597 BCE—a reflection of the extreme turmoil of the final years of Yehudah as an independent kingdom.

117,1h the lands from Egypt Wadi to the Perath River: The Egypt Wadi is a wadi at the southwestern border of Yehudah, in modern-day Gaza. The Perath is the Hebrew name for the river that English speakers today call the Euphrates.

Notes to P118

118a Nehushta Elnathansdaughter: The mother of Yehoyakiyn (and wife of Yehoyaqiym) has an interesting name. Nehushta (נחשתא) may be a variant (feminine?) form of Nehushtan (נחשתן), which was the name of the serpent-god honored in Yahweh's cult in Yerushalem prior to Hizqiyyahu's reign, and which Hizqiyyahu eradicated from the cult (see P107). Thus Yehoyakiyn's mother's name may indicate that the god continued to be venerated in Yerushalem, even within the royal family.

118b accompanied by his mother: Yehoyakiyn is just eighteen years old and is only three months into his reign. Given his circumstances, the queen mother at this time likely held as much, if not more, power than he did. It is thus highly appropriate that she would accompany him to this critical (and fateful) audience with Nevukadnetztzar.

118c He then brought out... everything in the storerooms...: At this point in Yehudah's history, the monarchy has essentially been bankrupted by the decades of tribute paid to Ashshur, Egypt, and Bavel. By the time Yehoyakiyn assumed the throne, there can have been almost nothing of value left in the storerooms of the palace and of Yahweh's house.

118d He cut into pieces all the gold items... in the great hall of Yahweh's house, just as Yahweh had said would happen: I view this sentence as an addition by the authors of Kings' fifth stage, who showed special interest in the decorations of Yahweh's house and the cult equipment associated with it. The sentence here assumes the reader is familiar with the passage in P15 describing the gold decorations in the interior of Yahweh's house (including the great hall)—a passage that I assign to Kings' fifth stage in my composition history.

118e just as Yahweh had said would happen: This is almost certainly a reference to Yahweh's speech to Shelomo in P22, in which he tells the king that he will "reject the house that I consecrated as my own" if Shelomo and his descendants turn away from and don't keep his commandments. In that speech, Yahweh says that the house will become a ruin heap, and "all who pass by" will be astounded and wonder why Yahweh did such a thing.

118f He sent all of Yerushalem into exile: The verb form here (והגלה) is the perfect with *waw* copulative, which Hebrew authors sometimes used in place of the imperfect with *waw* consecutive to advance the narrative. This use of the perfect with *waw* copulative, which may have been borrowed from Aramaic, provides for some variation in the otherwise repetitive verbal forms in the narrative and gives the narrative an elevated literary quality. Native Hebrew speakers perhaps perceived this use of the perfect with *waw* copulative as a mark of sophistication, as they likely would have perceived the influence of Aramaic (the language of the dominant culture of the time). The effect on the reader possibly was similar to the effect on a reader of English when authors sprinkle French phrases or terms in their writing. There are several examples of this verb form in P116—see notes 116q, 116r, 116u, 116y, 116z, and 116ad.

118g he then changed his name to Tzidqiyyahu: The Hebrew is ambiguous, and it is possible to understand the subject of the verb "changed" as either Tzidqiyyahu or Nevukadnetztzar. I have a strong preferece for the former option. Note the similar situation with Elyaqiym's name change in P117, which I discuss in note 117d above.

Notes to P119

119a Tzidqiyyahu was twenty-one years old when he became king...: The material from here to the end of Kings (excluding the end of P119 and all of P120) is duplicated nearly verbatim in Jeremiah 52.1-27, 31-34. The material is clearly original to Kings, and it is not clear to me why it was added to Jeremiah. It is worth noting that the events described in the passages from this material that were omitted from Jeremiah (P120 and the end of P119), which concern the flight of most of the remaining populace of Yehudah to Egypt after the assassination of Gedalyahu, are treated in much greater detail in Jeremiah chapters 40 - 43.

119b His mother's name was Hemiytal Yirmayahusdaughter of Livnah: The author does not tell us Tzidqiyyahu's patronym. However, his mother was also the mother of Yeho'ahaz (see P117). On that basis, we know that Tzidqiyyahu was the son of Yoshiyyahu and the full brother of Yeho'ahaz. He was the half-brother of Yehoyaqiym, whose son was Yehoyakiyn. Thus Tzidqiyyahu is called Yehoyakiyn's uncle in P118.

119c similar to all that Yehoyaqiym had done: For the judgement on Tzidqiyyahu, the authors of the second stage avoid their previous formulations "similar to all that his ancestors had done" (P117 and P117,1) and "similar to all the things that his father had done" (P118). Instead the authors use a formulation that compares Tzidqiyyahu to Yehoyaqiym and that omits mention of his direct predecessor Yehoyakiyn. I believe their choice of language here may reflect the hopes that grew up around Yehoyakiyn after his release from prison in 560 BCE (see P120,1). I suggest in note 116ai above and note 119,2i below that there was more than one "edition" of Kings during what I

NOTES AND COMMENTS 327

call its second compositional stage. The material at the conclusion of Kings belongs to the final edition of the second stage; in that material, the authors express a positive view of Yehoyakiyn which may hint at hopes that he would return to Yerushalem and be restored as the Dawidic king. I suspect these same authors were responsible for the judgement we see here—they likely altered the judgement found in an earlier edition from the second stage, which would have stated that Tzidqiyyahu did what was displeasing to Yahweh, "similar to all that his ancestors had done."

Notes to P119,1

119,1a In the ninth year of his reign...: The material in this *parashah* and in the first paragraph of P119,2 is duplicated almost verbatim in Jeremiah 39.1-10. In addition, the material in P119,1 and the first three paragraphs of P119,2 are duplicated almost verbatim in Jer 52.4-27. Note that in Kgs P119,1 it is ambiguous whether the author means the ninth year of Tzidqiyyahu's reign or the ninth year of Nevukadnetztzar's reign. The former is most likely, and in fact, the text in Jer 39.1 explicitly states that it is the ninth year of Tzidqiyyahu's reign.

119,1b By the ninth day of the month: Note that the author leaves the month unspecified. The parallel passage in Jer 52.6 states that it is the fourth month. I presume that the text of Kings originally stated this was the fourth month, and that this phrase fell out of the text due to a scribal error.

119,1c all Yerushalem's soldiers by night down the gate road: The Hebrew in this clause lacks a verb and reads awkwardly. Comparison with the parallel passage in Jer 52.7 indicates that the text here in Kings is corrupt. The words present in Jeremiah but missing from Kings are יברחו ויצאו מהעיר. Adding this language back to Kings yields the translation "When the town's defenses were breached, all Yerushalem's soldiers were making their getaway—they sneaked out of town by night down the gate road that runs between the double wall next to the royal garden as the Kasdians attacked the town on all sides."

119,1d the Kasdians: The Kasdians (traditionally translated as "the Chaldeans") are the peoples inhabiting the territory of Kasdiym. The Kasdians made up a significant percentage of the army of Nevukadnetztzar, who himself was a Kasdian. The biblical authors often refer to the army of Bavel as "the Kasdians." On Kasdiym, see note 117,1c above.

119,1e Yereho: The Masoretic text here has an alternate spelling and vocalization of the town name Yeriyho (called Jericho in English). I have reflected this alternate spelling in translation.

119,1f they took him to the king of Bavel at Rivlah: Rivlah is a town in the administrative district of Hamath. (Hamath was originally an independent kingdom in the northern Levant; it was conquered by Ashshur in the eighth century BCE, after which is served as an administrative district within the empire.) The mention of Rivlah here suggests that when Nabopolassar King of Bavel gained control of the territories in the northern Levant in 609 BCE, he maintained the administrative structure put in place by Ashshur. On Hamath, see note 117b above.

119,1g they rendered judgement against him...: The verb here and the following verb are conjugated with a third-person masculine plural subject ("they"); the three subsequent verbs are all conjugated with a third-person singular masculine subject ("he"). It is possible to treat all five verbs as having an indefinite subject, which ancient Hebrew authors often used in place of the passive. Thus, the shift between plural and singular subject is not problematic. I have not rendered all the verbs as passive, but have used a mix of active and passive to produce a natural English translation that I believe best captures the force of the Hebrew.

119,2a the nineteenth year of the reign of King Nevukadnetztzar King of Bavel: Note the change in the chronological system employed by the authors. As there is no longer a king of Yehudah whose reign can be used to date events, the authors use Nevukadnetztzar's reign as the framework to date events.

Notes to P119,2

119,2b the rest of the people who were still in the town... Nevuzar'adan... sent into exile: At this point, there can have been almost no one of importance left to exile. Recall from P118 that Nevukadnetztzar exiled the king, his wives and mother, his high officials and the country's leading citizens.

119,2c ... in the vineyards and the fields): The parallel material found in Jer 39.1-10 begins with P119,1, and concludes with the sentence here. See note 119,1a above.

119,2d As for the bronze pillars... the bronze stands and the bronze Sea: The bronze equipment are the only things of value that remain on the grounds of Yahweh's house—nearly everything that was gold or silver had been given away in tribute or was plundered in 597 BCE. But now the Kasdian army breaks apart the bronze items as well and takes the bronze to Bavel. The comment about the bronze stands and the bronze Sea interrupts the flow of the sentence in Hebrew and likely is an addition to the text by the authors of Kings' fifth stage. Note that the authors omit mention of the bronze lavers, which King Ahaz removed more than a century earlier and which, if not given in tribute by Ahaz's successors, were possibly looted in Nevukadnetztzar's campaign in 597 BCE (see P118).

119,2e some of which were gold and some of which were silver: The author admits that there was very little gold and silver left—nearly all the implements used in the cult at this time were made of bronze.

119,2f [*The two pillars, the one Sea... were made entirely of bronze.*]: This lengthy comment, which I view as part of the fifth compositional stage, is clearly an addition to the text and does not belong to the original version of this *parashah*. The comment is written in the style of Hebrew technical prose, and in my translation I have departed further than usual from a literal rendering in order to reproduce the passage in the style of English technical writing.

119,2g the weight of the bronze in these items is unknown: The Hebrew is difficult and awkwardly expressed. Literally, "the bronze of all these items did not have a weight." That is, these items, which were made of bronze, were so heavy that it was not possible to ascertain their weight.

119,2h The captain of the royal guard took Serayah the Head Priest...: Note that Yerushalem in the portrayal of the author is practically uninhabited—only five cult officials remained on the grounds of Yahweh's house, and only seven people associated with the palace administration. In addition to these were sixty men found in the ruins of the town. That all these men were subsequently executed suggests that they were in hiding and/or were actively resisting Nevukadnetztzar's forces in Yerushalem.

119,2i And so Yehudah was exiled from its land: This sentence reads as the conclusion to the book, and it is tempting to suppose that the earliest exilic expansion of Kings may have ended with this sentence. It is interesting to note that in the parallel material in Jeremiah 52, there is a *parashah setumah* after this sentence in the Aleppo Codex. See A162 v.1.11. (However, there is no *parashah* break after this sentence in the Leningrad Codex; see L276 v.1.4.)

NOTES AND COMMENTS

The composition process of Kings and the other books of the Former Prophets and the Torah was quite fluid. While I and other scholars identify broad compositional stages within each of these books, the work within each compositional stage spanned a number of years or decades, so that one can think of multiple "editions" within a single compositional stage. I think this is certainly the case with the material that I have included in Kings' second stage. It is conceivable, for example, that the sentence here in P119,2, may have concluded the initial "edition" of the second stage, with another "edition" in the second stage concluding with P120, and a final "edition" in the second stage concluding with P120,1.

119,2j As for the people who remained in Yehudah...: The material from here to the end of P120 tells of the murder of Gedalyahu Ahiyqamsson Shaphansson, who was appointed overseer of Yehud by the Babylonians, and the subsequent flight of many of the remaining people of Yehud to Egypt. These events are recounted in much greater detail in Jer 40-43, the author of which may have been an eyewitness to them and/or known many of the participants. The author of this material in Kings, who may have been writing in exile in Babylon, shows no awareness of the material in Jeremiah; his account of these events is somewhat confused, suggesting he relied on second-hand or third-hand information in his composition.

119,2k he appointed Gedalyahu Ahiyqamsson Shaphansson as their overseer: After this clause, the Leningrad Codex has a *parashah petuhah*. See L220 r.2.24-25.

119,2l the leaders of the army: The reference to the leaders of the army is surprising. In P118, we are told that Nevukadnetztzar sent all of Yerushalem's leaders and soldiers into exile. Possibly a number of military leaders escaped and went into hiding (recall from P119,1 that the army "scattered" and abandoned Tzidqiyyahu when he fled Yerushalem); perhaps these military leaders came out of hiding and made a reappearance after Nevukadnetztzar returned to Bavel.

119,2m Mitzpah: The seat of government administration has moved to Mitzpah, which must have been spared most of the destruction experienced in Yerushalem. There were numerous sites named Mitzpah (the name means "Lookout"); scholars believe the Mitzpah mentioned here was a site in the old tribal territory of Binyamin, located just a few miles northwest of Yerushalem.

119,2n **: The Leningrad Codex has a *parashah setumah* here. See L220 r.3.9.

Notes to P120

120a But then in the seventh month...: The events in P119,2 take place in the fifth month of the year (which was the nineteenth year of Nevadnetztzar's reign). The events in this *parashah* were two months later. Note Gedalyahu only served as overseer for the Kasdians for two months before his murder.

This *parashah* reads as the ending of one of the editions of Kings' second stage (which represents the exilic expansions of the book). See note 119,2i above.

120b Yishma'el Nathanyahsson Eliyshamasson who was of royal descent: It is interesting to note that Yishma'el belonged to the Dawidic line. His murder of Gedalyahu may have been motivated by a (deluded) desire to revive the Dawidic monarchy with himself as the king. As mentioned above in note 119,2j, Jer 40-43 has a detailed account of the events described at the conclusion of P119,2 and in P120. In that account, Yishma'el allied himself with Ba'aliys King of the Ammonites and he apparently murdered Gedalyahu on orders from Ba'aliys. Ba'aliys perhaps saw an opportunity to take advantage of the chaotic circumstances in Yehud by encouraging Yishma'el to claim the throne, as he then could easily control Yehud through Yishma'el.

120c they feared the Kasdians: Specifically, they feared the Kasdian authorities would seek revenge for their murder of the Kasdian officials in Mitzpah, who were killed with Gedalyahu.

120d —: The Leningrad Codex has a *parashah petuhah* here. See L.220 r.3.19-20.

120,1a In the thirty-seventh year of Yehoyakiyn King of Yehudah's exile...: The thirty-seventh year of Yehoyakiyn's exile is 560 BCE. This *parashah* must have been added sometime in the following decade, and must have been the final exilic expansion of the original version of Kings. This *parashah* is duplicated verbatim in Jer 52.31-34. See note 119a above.

Notes to P120,1

The favor shown to Yehoyakiyn is at odds with the judgement passed on him in P118 ("he did things that displeased Yahweh"), which belongs to the initial exilic expansion of Kings. This inconsistency provides some support for the idea that the composition process in the second stage (like the composition of process of the other stages) was quite fluid, with the text undergoing a number of additions across several decades. In the instance here, the author of P120,1 was nearly a full generation removed in time from the authors of P118, although both sets of authors belong to the book's second compositional stage. Note also the change here in the chronological system back to the Dawidic kingship as the point of reference rather than the regnal year of the king of Bavel. I believe the shift back to the former system is best explained by a change of authorship. The author of P120,1 in particular seems to hold out some hope of the restoration of the Dawidic king—something which the authors of P119 - P120 perhaps would have viewed as ill-judged and unrealistic.

It is noteworthy how the final *parashot* of Kings, which were composed by the authors of the second stage, peter out to an unsatisfying and ambiguous end. It is odd the authors of that work didn't conclude the book with a summary statement expressing their views. This omission may in part have been due to the chronicle structure that the authors of Kings' first stage imposed on their book. The version of Kings belonging to the Josianic study books is to some extent optimistic and hopeful. But this outlook is entirely gone by the time of the authors of the book's exilic expansion, who have to explain the loss of their homeland and the destruction of Yahweh's house. Indeed, the ending of the book—which I view as part of the "final" edition of Kings' second stage—strikes the modern-day reader as quite pathetic. Despite the favoritism shown to Yehoyakiyn (who would have been fifty-five years old when he was released from prison), the authors seem to be grasping at straws: if they did believe that this small act of mercy was the prelude to the restoration of the Dawidic kingship, then they were exceptionally naive.

In the decades immediately after the authors of Kings' second stage concluded their work, I believe the earliest version of Deuteronomy was composed. This book reinterpreted the treaty between Yahweh and the Dawidic king as a treaty between Yahweh and his people, but it otherwise shared the negative outlook of the authors of the second stage. The authors of that version of Deuteronomy understood the people's predicament in exile to be a result of the treaty curses that Yahweh had invoked against them for not upholding their treaty obligations. It is not until many years later, sometime in the Persian period, that a way is found to regain optimism about Yahweh's relationship with his people, as that relationship is reinterpreted in expansions to Deuteronomy and the prophetic books—especially expansions to Jeremiah and Isaiah. Deuteronomy and Jeremiah in particular reinterpret the treaty between Yahweh and his people in a positive sense. The Persian-period authors of the expansions to Deuteronomy viewed the treaty as a permanent one; despite the invocation of the treaty curses, they argued that the blessings of the treaty are still available and will be granted to those who return to Yahweh (see Deut P28,1 - P28,3).

The authors of the Persian-period expansions to Jeremiah understand the treaty in a different way: they see the old treaty as no longer valid and argue that in its place Yahweh will make a new treaty with his people—a treaty that he will inscribe on their hearts so that observance of its terms is innate (see Jer 30-33).

120,1b the other kings who were with him: Presumably these are kings of other countries who—like Yehoyakiyn—were exiled to Bavel after the king of Bavel had conquered their lands.

120,1c And so he changed... he took...: For these two verbs, the author uses the perfect with *waw* copulative as the narrative tense, which reflects the influence of Aramaic. On this usage, see notes 116q and 118f above. Note, however, that it is possible to treat the second verb as the frequentative rather than a narrative tense, in which case the translation would be, "he regularly took his daily meals in the king's presence."

120,1d As for his maintenance... for his entire life: The final sentence of Kings reads as a gloss on (or a variant of) the preceding statement that "he took his daily meals in the king's presence." That statement is difficult to understand in Hebrew, and it is easy to see how it might have attracted a gloss or a variant version that was stated in clearer terms. In my composition history, I have assigned this final sentence of Kings to the editors of Kings' sixth stage.

120,1e Total sentences in the book: As a means to help safeguard the integrity of the text, at the end of each book of the Tanakh, the Masoretes included a short note (considered part of the *Masorah magna*) that totalled up the number of sentences for that book. I have reproduced their note for Kings here.

The composition history of Kings

When I began this project of translating the Torah and the Former Prophets, I did not intend to spend a great deal of energy thinking about the composition history of these books. Very quickly, however, I realized that to be successful in expressing the books' ideas and thoughts in a natural, modern-day English, I would need to connect on an emotional and personal level with their authors and, insofar as it is possible, understand the authors on their own terms. In translating this and other books, I have found that in order to make that emotional connection with the authors, I first had to form opinions about who they were, who their audience was, and especially what motivated them to write. What follows then is a summary of my views, developed over the course of this translation, about the circumstances behind the composition of Kings and about the motivations of its authors in writing what they did.

**

As a preliminary to examining the composition history of Kings, it is important to keep in mind that the scholarly effort to reconstruct the composition history of the books of the Torah and the Former Prophets—or any of the books of the Tanakh—is an entirely speculative endeavor. This is primarily because there are very few external controls available to us that can serve as productive anchors for the analysis. In general, for the books of the Torah and the Former Prophets, our only true external controls are the manuscripts from Qumran, the Septuagint, and ancient authors' quotations of biblical texts. The main thing that we learn from these three controls is that between the third and first centuries BCE, the books had grown into a form very close to their form today. However, these controls provide us with no information about the early evolution of these books and the shape they had prior to the third century BCE. Thus, with very few exceptions, external controls provide us with little information about when these books were first composed or about the existence of different literary layers within the books.

In addition to the small number of external controls, very often there are internal controls—that is, links or references to a book found elsewhere in the Tanakh—that scholars can use to inform their understanding of a book's composition history. These internal controls take a variety of forms, but most commonly they are vocabulary and language that two books have in common, or they are explicit references made in one book to characters and events of another book or to a specific passage in that book. For example, in my translation of Judges, I used references in the book of Samuel to the "champions" Jerubaal, Bedan, and Jephthah to inform my ideas about what stories in Judges were part of the pre-exilic version of the book.[1]

Compared with the other books of the Torah and Former Prophets, the external and internal controls for Kings are unusually robust. As for external controls, in addition to the evidence of the Septuagint and a few fragments from Qumran, there is much material in Josephus that is relevant to the composition history of Kings. And with regard to internal controls, Kings shares major portions of text with 2 Chronicles, with Isaiah 36-39, and with Jeremiah 39 and 52.[2] These external and internal controls for Kings provide useful clues to the later stages of the book's composition history. Scholars who have closely studied the evidence convincingly argue that the authors of Chronicles used a version of Kings older than the one preserved in the Masoretic text; moreover this version of Kings (or one very similar to it) is represented by the evidence from Qumran and was the version known to Josephus.[3] The general consensus among scholars is that Chronicles was composed in the second half of the fourth century BCE. If we accept this view, then the material in Chronicles—as well as the references in Josephus—gives us insight into the version of Kings in circulation in the fourth century or even the late fifth century BCE.[4]

While Chronicles is a valuable control for scholars seeking to understand Kings' composition history, the evidence from the various

---

1 See footnote 12 in my introduction to Judges.
2 The authors of 2 Chronicles incorporated verbatim many passages from Kings about the kings of Judah. The material in Is 36-39, which recounts events from Hezekiah's reign, parallels Kgs P108-P112. Two blocks of material in Jeremiah about events following the Babylonians' capture of Jerusalem are nearly identical to passages in Kings: Jer 39.1-10 reproduces Kgs P119,1 and the first part of P119,2, and Jer 52 overlaps with Kgs P119-P119,2 and P120,1.
3 Good concise discussions of the issues regarding the textual history of Kings can be found in B. Halpern and A. Lemaire (eds.), *The Books of Kings: Sources, Composition, Historiography, and Reception* (Leiden: Brill, 2010). In particular, see J. Trebolle, "Qumran Fragments of the Books of Kings," pp. 19-39, and É. Nodet, "The Text of 1-2 Kings Used by Josephus," pp. 41-66.
4 An excellent treatment of the relationship between Kings and Chronicles and the implications for composition history and textual criticism can be found in S. McKenzie, *The Chroniclers' Use of the Deuteronomistic History*, Atlanta: Scholars Press, 1985.

Greek translations (collectively referred to as the Septuagint) is less useful. Scholars date the earliest translation of Kings into Greek to the second century BCE. The study of the Greek evidence for Kings is complicated by the manuscript evidence: multiple Greek translations were made in the centuries immediately before and after the beginning of the common era. Moreover, there are major questions about the quality of the Hebrew text used by the Greek translators. There is evidence that the version of Kings consulted by the authors of Chronicles and by Josephus was an official "reference scroll" of the book[5]—a scroll that likely was kept in the temple library. There is some evidence that at least one of the Greek translations of Kings relied on a reference scroll of the book;[6] however, this evidence is so deeply entwined with the other Greek translations that it is often difficult to isolate it on its own. Thus, we must treat the evidence from the Septuagint with caution when using it to inform our ideas about the composition history of Kings.

Despite the robustness of the external and internal controls for Kings, I have found them much less useful than I had initially hoped when developing my views on the composition history of Kings. This is primarily due to three things. First, because of the fluidity of the book's compositional process, where the text was regularly added to and updated and new "editions" produced every few decades, the controls provide us only a snapshot of small parts of the text at a specific point in time. In the case of Chronicles, for example, this snapshot most likely captures the text as it existed in the latter decades of the fourth century BCE. But that tells us nothing of the many changes made to the text before this point in time. Second, in many cases, it is clear that the controls are very selective in their use of the text of Kings. For example, Chronicles does not incorporate any of the material about Elijah and Elisha, nor any material from the so-called succession narrative, nor any material about the kings of Israel. This does not imply that this material was absent from the version of Kings used by the authors of Chronicles; rather, it may have simply been the case—and indeed, this is the consensus of scholars—that

---

5   See Nodet, *op. cit.*, p. 65.
6   Scholars have identified evidence of such a Greek translation in numerous passages in the so-called Lucianic recension. See the excellent discussion of Trebolle, *op. cit.*, pp. 33-39, regarding the value of the Greek evidence. For an extended treatment of the Hebrew text underlying the Septuagint, see A. Schenker, *Älteste Textgeschichte der Königsbücher: Die hebräische Vorlage der ursprünglichen Septuaginta als älteste Textform der Königsbücher*, Orbis Biblicus et Orientalis 199, Fribourg: Academic Press Fribourg, 2004.

the authors of Chronicles chose not to utilize this material because it did not support the larger themes of their work. Third, the major internal controls for Kings—the parallel passages in Chronicles, Isaiah, and Jeremiah—were subject to later edits made to harmonize these controls with their source passages in Kings; any harmonizing edits to these texts would thus obscure changes to Kings that might have been made subsequent to the composition (or insertion) of the parallel texts in Chronicles, Isaiah, and Jeremiah.

**

As discussed in my introductory note, I identify within Kings seven literary threads: one thread reflecting the source documents used by the book's authors (which I call a "pre-compositional" stage) and six threads representing six broad compositional stages that spanned a period from the book's initial composition in the 630s BCE to the final material edits made in the second century BCE.[7] While this framework helps make sense of the messiness and the many contradictions and inconsistencies in the text, it should be emphasized that the nearly continual writing, rewriting, supplementing and revising of the book over a period of centuries means that it is not always possible to separate with confidence the changes and additions made during one stage from those made in other stages. Moreover, there is an element of arbitrariness in assigning material to one stage or another. I relied primarily on similarities in content, language and theme when grouping the material in the book into compositional stages. As a result, some of the stages that I propose overlap chronologically with each other, and I believe it is likely that some individual authors and editors contributed material to more than one of my proposed compositional stages.

With these caveats in mind, I present in detail below my views on the composition history of Kings. As stated above, these views are highly speculative—they are only one way of looking at how the book of Kings came to have the form it has today, and they are very much influenced by my own starting assumptions about the histories of ancient Israel and Judah; scholars with a different set of starting assumptions will come to a very different view of the book's history.

**

---

7   The editorial process on Kings continued well into the common era, but I do not believe that the edits after the second century BCE introduced any significant changes to the text.

The authors of Kings allude to three specific written documents as containing additional information regarding the kings in their work: *The Chronicles of the Kings of Israel*, *The Chronicles of the Kings of Judah*, and *The Acts of Solomon*. Along with many scholars, I understand these to be official administrative documents that were composed by palace officials and that were kept in the palace archives.[8] Furthermore, nearly all scholars (myself included) believe that the authors of Kings used these documents as the primary sources for their own work, and that they incorporated large sections of these documents verbatim or nearly verbatim into their accounts of the reigns of the kings of Israel and Judah.

As has often been pointed out by scholars, these three source documents have numerous similarities with royal chronicles known from elsewhere in the ancient Near East.[9] The existence of such documents suggests it was common practice for royal governments to compose and maintain "chronographic" documents such as chronicles and king lists. The chronicles are most relevant for our purposes: they recorded significant events of a king's reign, with events in successive kings' reigns being added in a sort of running list to the document containing the events of preceding kings' reigns.[10] This is exactly the form the two chronicles mentioned by the authors of Kings seem to have had.

---

8   Many scholars view *The Acts of Solomon* as a fictitious source invented by the authors of Kings in order to make their account of Solomon's reign seem more credible. In my opinion, however, many of the details about Solomon's reign read as though they were lifted from a source document, and for that reason I think the source is genuine. Numerous scholars have argued that the absence of inscriptions dating to the early Iron Age from the territories of Israel and Judah suggests that there were no scribes or record-keeping culture in the administrations of the early kings of Israel and Judah. I do not find these arguments convincing—even kings of small and relatively poor territories would have greatly valued the ability to engage in diplomacy and communicate formally with neighboring kings, and it would not have been very difficult for such a king to hire a foreign scribe into his service. Indeed, the Amarna letters provide several examples from the Late Bronze Age of petty kings in the Levant employing scribes to correspond with the Egyptian pharaoh, including an example where a single scribe provides services to multiple petty kings. For a good recent treatment of the scribes in the Amarna letters, see A. Mandell, "Canaanite Literary Culture before the Bible, a View from the Canaanite Amarna Letters," *Religions* 2025, 16(8), 970.

9   The standard treatment of the chronicles from Mesopotamia is A. K. Grayson, *Assyrian and Babylonian Chronicles*, Winona Lake: Eisenbrauns, 2000.

10 The Neo-Babylonian Chronicle Series illustrates this well. For a recent translation of these chronicles, see B. Arnold and P. Michalowski, "Achaemenid Period Historical Texts Concerning Mesopotamia" in M. Chavalas (ed.), *The Ancient Near East: Historical Sources in Translation* (Oxford: Blackwell Publishing, 2006), pp. 405-419.

Because we can be confident that the three sources cited by the authors of Kings were actual written documents and because there is such clear evidence that the authors often quoted them verbatim, I have found it useful to group them together and treat them as a "pre-compositional" stage of Kings. The primary benefit of collecting the source material together like this and viewing it on its own is that it helps the reader understand more clearly the composition techniques of the biblical authors. In particular, looking at the material in this way helps us draw a sharper line between what was original source material and what was composed by later authors and editors.

In the composition history that I propose below, the individuals who utilized these three source documents were the authors of Kings' first and second compositional stages. These writers used the source documents as the basis for their narrative of the individual kings' reigns, and then added their own commentary on each king's actions. Their practice was to mention the source they used at the end of the account of each king, where they inform the reader that additional information about the king and his accomplishments can be found in the source document.

The material that I attribute to the source documents belonging to Kings' "pre-compositional" stage is as follows:

—Fragment at end of P7,2. The details at the end of this *parashah* about Solomon's marriage alliance with Pharaoh, about Pharaoh's daughter living in Fort David, and about Solomon's building projects were likely part of the source document, *The Acts of Solomon*.

—P10,2 - P10,23 and first half of P24. These *parashot* represent a list of the chief officials in Solomon's administration (P10,2 - P10,11) and a list of the tax commissioners who oversaw the twelve tax districts of Solomon's kingdom and who provided taxes and provisions to the royal government (P10,12 - P10,23 plus the first half of P24). There is no reason to think that these two lists were fabricated; I believe they must have been part of the source document *The Acts of Solomon* and that the authors of the earliest edition of Kings began their work with these two lists, which they incorporated verbatim. It is interesting to note that the first list begins with the statement that Solomon was "king over all of Israel" and omits mention of Judah. If this statement was in the source document, which I believe it was, it lends support to the idea that there was no united kingdom under Solomon. (Jerusalem at the time would have been considered part of Benjamin, not Judah.) For more thoughts on this idea, see note 10,2a above.

—Fragment of P11. The first sentence of P11 provides information about the amounts of the food consumed at Solomon's court, and is written in the matter-of-fact style of royal chronicles. This information likely came from *The Acts of Solomon*. There is no reason to think that the authors of Kings invented this information on their own and did not have a source for it.

—P11,1. The information in this *parashah* was likely based on details found in *The Acts of Solomon*. Within the source document, the sentence about the tax commissioners in P11,1 may have originally followed from material about them in P10,12 - P10,24 discussed above. See also the discussion in note 11,1b.

—Details at the end of P11,4 and in P12 - P12,1? It is possible that some of the numeric details about Hiram's supplying Solomon with wood for his construction projects and about Solomon's labor gangs were in *The Acts of Solomon*, and that the authors of the earliest edition of Kings incorporated those details into their work.

—Details in the second half of P15. The second half of P15 begins with a statement summarizing the chronology of the construction of Yahweh's house; I believe this statement appeared in *The Acts of Solomon* (see note 15q above). Following that statement is a detailed description the construction of Solomon's palace, the Lebanon Forest House. The building likely was still standing at the time the authors of the Josianic study books were writing; consequently, much of their description may be based on their own observations. However, there are some details in the description that they could not have deduced on their own, such as time it took to build the palace; they may have found these details in *The Acts of Solomon* or in some other ancient document in the palace archives.

—End of P17,2 and core of P19. The list of equipment that Solomon made for Yahweh's house at the end of P17,2 reads as an extract from an old administrative document. I believe it likely appeared in a source document used by the authors of Kings—but perhaps a different document than *The Acts of Solomon*. The account of the transfer of the treaty chest in P19 has been heavily edited and has attracted additions from multiple compositional stages. However, I believe that some of the core details in the earliest version of this *parashah*, which was about the transfer of Yahweh's battle chest from Fort David to the house that Solomon built for Yahweh, may have been from an old document from the temple library that the authors of Kings consulted.

—Possibly the core of P23. This *parashah* is a brief account of Solomon's transfer of twenty towns in the Galilee region to Hiram King of Tyre as payment for the wood and gold that Hiram supplied to Solomon's construction projects. Royal chronicles in the ancient Near East sometimes contained brief accounts such as this, and the core of this *parashah* may have been part of *The Acts of Solomon*.

—Core of the first half of P24 and core of P24,1. The material in the first half of P24 and in P24,1 lists various construction projects of Solomon, details about his participation in Yahweh's cult, and details about his navy; this material likely was part of *The Acts of Solomon*, as it is the sort of information often found in royal chronicles from the ancient Near East.

—Core of P26 and core of P27,1. These two *parashot* contain some late embellishments, but at their core are numerous details that likely were part of *The Acts of Solomon* or other ancient documents from the palace archives; this includes information about the palace armory in P26 and information about the kingdom's chariots and chariot horses and the trading business of Solomon's royal merchants in P27,1.

—P30. I believe this *parashah* combines information drawn from two source documents. I view the sentence about Solomon's construction activities as a verbatim insertion from *The Acts of Solomon*, and I view the material about Jeroboam as verbatim insertions from *The Chronicles of the Kings of Israel*.

—P30,2. This *parashah*, which is just one sentence, reads as a verbatim insertion from *The Chronicles of the Kings of Israel*. That work began with the figure of Jeroboam, and I believe it included an account of Jeroboam's insurrection against Solomon, his flight to Egypt, and his being proclaimed king of Israel upon his return instead of Solomon's natural successor, Rehoboam.

—Detail in P30,3? This *parashah* is the summary statement of Solomon's reign. It is possible that the detail about Solomon's burial in Fort David is from *The Acts of Solomon*. However, I think it slightly more likely that Solomon was buried elsewhere (possibly Shechem, which may have been the "real" royal seat of Solomon). If that was the case, then the detail about his burial in Fort David would have been invented by the authors of the Josianic study books, who based their summary statement for Solomon's reign on a formula found in *The Chronicles of the Kings of Judah*—a formula that mentions Fort David as the burial site for all the Davidic kings prior to Hezekiah.

—Beginning of P30,4. The first two sentences of this *parashah* read as a verbatim insertion from *The Chronicles of the Kings of Israel*. This material was extracted from that source's account of how Jeroboam succeeded Solomon as king of Israel. It is especially interesting to note that this material may be understood to imply that Solomon's royal seat was Shechem, not Jerusalem. See note 30,4a above.

—Core of P31 and the beginning of P31,1. The material indicated here (the first two sentences of P31 and the first sentence of P31,1) provides details on the Israelites' rebellion against the Davidic dynasty and their selection of Jeroboam as king. It is written in the matter-of-fact style characteristic of the royal chronicles, and I understand it to be extracts from the source document for Jeroboam's reign, *The Chronicles of the Kings of Yisra'el*. This material should be viewed together with the material discussed above in P30, P30,2, and P30,4, which I believe are extracts from the same document.

—Fragments of P32,1. This *parashah* records events of Jeroboam's reign. The *parashah* consists almost entirely of tendentious material reflecting the views of the authors of the Josianic study books; however, it is likely that the details about Jeroboam's building of Shechem and Penuel were incorporated from *The Chronicles of the Kings of Israel*. In addition, it is possible that the detail about Jeroboam organizing a festival similar to the one in Judah is also from the source document.

—Details in P39 plus core of P40. This material belongs to the account of Rehoboam's reign. P39 contains the standard details—such as the king's age at accession, his mother's name, and the length of his reign—that are typically listed in the source document, *The Chronicles of the Kings of Judah*; much of the material in P40 likely was inserted nearly verbatim from that document.

—Core of P41. This *parashah*, which is the account Aviyyam's reign over Judah, is exceedingly sparse on actual historical detail. The lack of detail may in part be due to the brevity of his reign, which lasted just three years. The only details in the *parashah* that are likely from *The Chronicles of the Kings of Judah* are the length of Aviyyam's reign, his mother's name, the place of his burial, and possibly the comment about his war with Jeroboam.

—Core of P42 - P42,1. These *parashot* are the account of Asa's reign over Judah. They contain much material that appears to be from the *The Chronicles of the Kings of Judah*, including details about Asa's cult reforms and the account of his war with Israel.

—Fragment of P43. This *parashah*, which is the account of Nadav's reign over Israel, contains a number of details that could have come from *The Chronicles of the Kings of Israel*. In addition to the comments about the length of his reign and the warring between him and Asa, the matter-of-fact description of Basha's conspiracy and assassination of Nadav is very likely from the source document. Note in particular the dating of the assassination by a synchronism with the reign of the king of the neighboring kingdom, which I believe was a feature of the source documents.[11]

---

[11] For a brief discussion of the chronological synchronisms in Kings as part of the source documents, see note 107a above.

—Fragments of P44-P44,1. These *parashot* are the account of Basha's reign over Israel. Only three details—the length of his reign, the place of his burial, and the name of his successor—appear to be from the source document, *The Chronicles of the Kings of Israel*.

—Core of P45. This *parashah* is the account of Elah Bashasson's reign over Israel and the account of Zimri's conspiracy against Elah. The entry on Elah in *The Chronicles of the Kings of Israel* may have been very brief. The comment at the end of P46 suggests that the account of Zimri's conspiracy was in *The Chronicles of the Kings of Israel*, but that it was part of the record of Zimri's reign and not Elah's.

—Core of P46. The material in this *parashah* is related to the account of Zimri's conspiracy, and it likely was part of *The Chronicles of the Kings of Israel*.

—P47. This *parashah* reads as a verbatim insertion from the *The Chronicles of the Kings of Israel*. One clue that it is an insertion is the use of the generic term "the people" (העם), which in the context of the book of Kings is ambiguous but which is unambiguous in the source document. To remove the ambiguity, an editor of Kings (possibly even an editor from Kings' first stage) added the gloss "Israel."

—Core of P48. This *parashah* is the account of Omri's reign over Israel. The first four sentences of the *parashah* likely were lifted verbatim from *The Chronicles of the Kings of Israel*; these state when he became king, the length of his reign, and how long he ruled in Thirtzah; they also provide information on his establishment of a new royal seat called Samaria. The last two sentences of the *parashah* may also be verbatim insertions from the source document, stating where Omri was buried and who succeeded him.

—Beginning of P49 and end of P59,1. The lengthy account of Ahav's reign over Israel contains only three details from the source document *The Chronicles of the Kings of Israel*—the date of his accession, the length of his reign, and the seat of his government in P49, which appear in the first two sentences of the *parashah*. The end of P59,1 tells us that the source document also contained information about an ivory house that Ahav built and the names of the towns that he established, but the authors of Kings have chosen not to include these details in their book.

—Core of P60. This *parashah* is the account of Jehoshaphat's reign over Judah. It contains several sentences that may have been lifted verbatim from *The Chronicles of the Kings of Judah*: the material about the eradication of the *qedesh*-prostitutes, the claim on Edom, and the abortive trading mission to Ophir. In addition, the standard details in the formulaic introductory and concluding statements—the king's age at accession, the year of his accession, the site of his royal seat, the length of his reign, the name of his mother, his place of burial, and the name of his successor—would have appeared in the source document.

—Details in P60,1. This *parashah* is part of the account of Ahazyahu Ahavsson's reign over Israel. In addition to the information in the first sentence, details in this *parashah* that are likely from the source document include the comments about Moab's rebellion and about Ahazyahu's fatal fall from a palace window.

—Details in P64. This *parashah* is part of the account of Yehoram Ahavsson's reign. The only details in P64 that are likely from the source document, *The Chronicles of the Kings of Israel*, are the information in the first sentence and the comment about his removal of the Ba'al's sacred pillar.

—Core of P75. This *parashah* is the account of Yehoram Jehoshaphatsson's reign over Judah. The material about Edom's rebellion appears to have been lifted verbatim from the source document, *The Chronicles of the Kings of Judah*. In addition, the standard details in the formulaic introductory and concluding statements—the king's age at accession, the year of his accession, the length of his reign, the site of his royal seat, his place of burial, and the name of his successor—would have appeared in the source document. The introductory statements for the kings of Judah typically include the name of the king's mother; the account of Yehoram's reign, however, omits this information, perhaps because his reign began as a co-regency, or perhaps because the sentence simply fell out of the text due to a copying error.

—Core of P76. This *parashah* is part of the account of Ahazyahu Yehoramsson's reign over Judah. Material in this *parashah* that is likely from the source document includes the standard introductory information found in the first three sentences and the account of Ahazyahu's military alliance with Yoram Ahavsson against Hazael King of Aram.

—Core of P80. The material in the last two-thirds of this *parashah* is almost certainly based on the source document, *The Chronicles of the Kings of Israel*. This includes the information about territory in Israel seized by Hazael and the details in the final sentences of the *parashah* (the site of the king's burial, the length of his reign, and the name of his successor).

—P82,3, details in P83, and the core of P85. The record of Yehoash's reign over Judah spans P82,3 through P85. The details in P82,3 and P83 are the standard ones that appear for kings in the royal chronicles of Judah—the king's age at accession, the year of his accession, the length of his reign, the name of his mother, and the seat of his government. In P85, the material in the first two paragraphs—the account of Hazael's invasion and the emptying of the temple and palace storerooms to pay him off—reads as though it was incorporated verbatim from the source document.

—Details in P86. The account of Yehoahaz Yehusson's reign over Israel is given in P86. The details in the introductory and concluding statements—the king's age at accession, the year of his accession, the length of his reign, the site of his royal seat, his place of burial, and the name of his successor—are from the source document, *The Chronicles of the Kings of Israel*. In addition, the comment about the size of Yehoahaz's remaining army after it had been destroyed by Aram is likely from the source document as well.

—Details in P87. The account of Yehoash Yehoahazsson's reign over Israel appears in P87. The introductory and concluding sentences draw from the source document, and provide the standard details found in the royal chronicles of Israel: the year of the king's accession, the length of his reign, the site of his royal seat, the place of his burial, and the name of his successor. The *parashah* states that *The Chronicles of the Kings of Israel* also included the story of Yehoash's fight with Amatzyahu King of Judah; that story appears in P92 in the account of Amatzyahu's reign (see below).

—Core of P91-P93. These *parashot* are the account of Amatzyahu's reign over Judah. Both P91 and P93 contain many details that were incorporated from *The Chronicles of the Kings of Judah*. The introductory sentences of P91 draw from the source document as does the sentence about Amatzyahu's execution of his father's assassins and the account at the end of the *parashah* about Amatzyahu's defeat of Edom and capture of Cliffville. P92 contains the account of Amatzyahu's fight with Yehoash; this account appears to have been incorporated nearly verbatim from *The Chronicles of the Kings of Israel*. All of P93 (with the exception of the sentence citing the source document) reads as a near-verbatim insertion from that document.

—Details in P94. This *parashah* is the account of Yarovam Yoashsson's reign over Israel. The details in the introductory and concluding statements are clearly based on the source document. In addition, some of the details about Yarovam's recovery of territory from Aram may be from the source document.

—Core of P95. This *parashah* is the account of Azaryah Amatzyahsson's reign over Judah. As is usual, the details in the introductory and concluding statements would have been drawn from the source document. In addition, the sentences about Azaryah's skin disease likely were incorporated verbatim from the source document.

—Details in P96. This *parashah* is the account of Zekaryahu's reign over Israel. I believe the sentence about Zekaryahu's assassination by Shallum Yaveshsson may be a verbatim insertion from the source document. The standard details in the introductory sentence—the date of the king's accession, the site of his royal seat, and the length his reign—would have appeared in the source document.

—Details in P97. This *parashah* contains the account of Shallum's reign over Israel and some additional material about the reign of Shallum's successor, Menahem. The introductory statement to Shallum's reign contains the standard details found in the source document. In addition, the material in this *parashah* about Menahem—the account of his assassination of Shallum and his attack on Tiphsah—may be verbatim or near-verbatim insertions from the source document. (It is unclear, however, whether the sentence about the slaughter of pregnant women was also part of the source document.)

—Core of P98. This *parashah* is the account of Menahem's reign over Israel. The account of the Assyrian king's invasion in P98 appears to have been incorporated verbatim from the source document. In addition, the standard details about the king's reign in this *parashah*—the date of his accession, the length of his reign, the site of his royal seat, and the name of his successor—must also be from the source document.

—Core of P99. This parashah is the account of Peqahyah Menahemsson's reign over Israel. The standard details about the king in the introductory statement are clearly based on the source document. The sentences about Peqahyah's assassination in this *parashah* read as verbatim insertions from the source document.

—Core of P100. This *parashah* is the account of Peqah Remalyahusson's reign over Israel. Material from the source document in this *parashah* includes the standard details about the king's reign in the introductory statement, the sentence about the seizure of parts of Israel's territory by Tiglath Pileser, and a near verbatim insertion of the two sentences about Peqah's assassination.

—Details in P101. This *parashah* is the account of Yotham's reign over Judah. The *parashah* contains little real detail about his reign. In addition to the standard information about the king's reign in the introductory and concluding statements, the only other information from the source document appears to be the comment that Yotham built the upper gate to Yahweh's temple.

—Core of P102. This *parashah* is the account of Ahaz's reign over Judah. The beginning and end of the *parashah* contain the standard details about the king's reign provided by the source document. The first part of the *parashah* appears to contain a verbatim quote from the source document about the invasion of Jerusalem by the kings of Aram and Israel and the subsequent loss of Elath. It is unclear how much of the material in the latter parts of the *parashah* are from *The Chronicles of the Kings of Judah*. The sentences about Ahaz sending a delegation to Tiglath Peleser to request military help and Tiglath Peleser's attack on Damascus may be a verbatim insertion, but I think it unlikely that the following material about Ahaz's construction of a new altar in front of the temple was from the royal chronicles. This material may have been based on oral traditions preserved within the cult in Jerusalem, or—less likely, in my opinion—a written document from the temple archives.

—Details in P103? This *parashah* is the account of the reign of Hoshea Elahsson, the last king of Israel. It is unclear which details in this *parashah* are from *The Chronicles of the Kings of Israel*. This was a living document, and information about each king's reign was likely added on a regular basis, if not annually. Hoshea ruled Israel for nine years, so presumably the document would have included some information about his reign. However, given the turmoil of the final three years of Hoshea's reign, when the king was imprisoned and Samaria under siege, palace officials may have been too preoccupied to keep the document current. In any case, officials fleeing the chaos must have taken the document from the palace archives and brought it with them to Judah.

—Core of P106-P108, and details at the end of P112. These *parashot* are part of the account of Hezekiah's reign over Judah. I believe the details in P106 that are from *The Chronicles of the Kings of Judah* are as follows: the age at which Hezekiah became king, the year of his accession, the length of his reign, the seat of his government, the name of his mother, his rebellion against Assyria, and his defeat of the Philistines. I do not believe the source document contained any information about Hezekiah's cult reforms except possibly the mention of his destruction of the bronze snake—given the formulaic language used to describe his cult reforms, it seems most likely to me that this information was composed by the authors of the Josianic study books, who wished to hold up Hezekiah as a model for their pupil Josiah. The subject of P107 is the fall of the kingdom of Israel. I believe this material was originally part of the account of Hezekiah's reign in *The Chronicles of the Kings of Judah*; the authors of that work would have included it in their account of Hezekiah's reign because the event was of such significance to the kingdom of Judah. The material in P107 reads as though it is a near verbatim quote from the source document. Sennacherib's invasion of Judah is the subject of P108; much, if not all, of the material in this *parashah* also appears to be a near verbatim quote from the source document, *The Chronicles of the Kings of Judah*. The end of P112 briefly mentions one royal project—

Hezekiah's construction of infrastructure to supply Jerusalem with water—that likely was recounted in a fair amount of detail in the source document.

—Details in P113 and at the end of P113,1. These *parashot* are the account of Manasseh's reign. They have incorporated the standard details from the source document: the length of Manasseh's reign, the site of his royal seat, his age when he became king, the name of his mother, the place of his burial, and the name of his successor. In addition, the conclusion to P113,1 states that the source document included some information on his cult reforms; on that basis, I believe that at least some of the information in P113 about the reestablishment of the open-air shrines, the erection of altars in Yahweh's temple to the Baal and the stars of the sky, and the installation of the Asherah inside the temple itself, was recorded in *The Chronicles of the Kings of Judah*.

—Core of P114. This *parashah* is the account of Amon's reign. It incorporates the usual details about the king from its source document, *The Chronicles of the Kings of Judah*. In addition, it is likely that the material about Amon's assassination is a near verbatim insertion from that document.

—Details in P115, parts of the material in P116 about Josiah's cult reforms, and the conclusion to P116. The account of Josiah's reign is given in P115-P116. Material from *The Chronicles of the Kings of Judah* was incorporated at the beginning of P115, in the middle of P116 and at the end of P116. In P115, the authors provide the usual details about the king: the age at which he became king, the site of his royal seat, the length of his reign, and his mother's name. The middle of P116 contains a description of Josiah's cult reforms; some of this material appears to be based on the source document and some a later composition. The material based on the source document can often be identified by the use of the perfect with *waw* copulative as the narrative tense (see note 116q). The end of P116 is the account of Josiah's death; it is written in the matter-of-fact style that is characteristic of the royal chronicles, and for that reason I believe this material may be a verbatim or near-verbatim insertion from the source document.

—Core of P117? This *parashah* is the account Yehoahaz's brief reign. Unusually, the *parashah* makes no mention of the source document, *The Chronicles of the Kings of Judah*. Given that and given the brevity of Yehoahaz's reign, it is possible that there was no individual entry for him in the source document. However, the account of his reign contains the usual details found in the source document, and it includes a number of matter-of-fact statements that are characteristic of the royal chronicles. For that reason, I think it most likely that most of the material in P117 is based on the source document.

—Details in P117,1. This *parashah* is the account of Yehoyaqim's reign. The only material in this *parashah* that I view as being from the source document, *The Chronicles of the Kings of Judah*, are the usual details about the king in the introductory statement and in the statement about his death. Notably, the last mention of a source document in the book of Kings appears here. Presumably, Yehoyaqim's reign was the last entry in *The Chronicles of the Kings of Judah*—it was not updated with the records of the two subsequent kings, Jehoiachin and Zedekiah.

**

I believe that the earliest written version of Kings was composed during the 630s BCE as one of three "Josianic study books"—the earliest versions of Judges, Samuel, and Kings—that were used in the education of the young king Josiah.[12] It is this original version of Kings that I treat as the book's first compositional stage. As discussed in the introduction, I believe that the composition of the Josianic study books was a collaborative effort between palace officials from Judean families who were ardent believers in the Judean royal ideology and individuals from northern families that had come to Judah in the late eighth century after the Assyrian conquest of the northern kingdom.

While this admittedly is wholly speculative, I believe these northern families likely had some role in one of Yahweh's cults in the north, and they may have been closely allied with the prophet Hosea and his circle. Moreover, when they came to Judah, they likely brought ancient cult rule books with them which contained the rules for the practice of their version of Yahwism—rule books that would later influence the structure and content of the book of Deuteronomy.[13] Once settled in Judah, these families (assuming they were associated with Hosea's circle) would have been virulently opposed to the reforms to Yahweh's cult instituted by Manasseh as well as Manasseh's linking of Yahweh's cult with the cults of other gods. In the scenario that I propose, some individuals from these families must have managed to secure positions within the royal court by the mid-seventh century

---

[12] In my translation of Judges, I referred to the earliest versions of these books as the Josianic History. However, I have now adopted different terminology to refer to the earliest version of these three books, as I believe it is inaccurate to characterize these early works as a "history."

[13] On the role of cult rule books within the northern cults, see the introduction to my translation of Leviticus. Many scholars have argued for "northern" origin of Deuteronomy; see footnote 34 above in my introductory note.

BCE. Following the assassination of Amon and the installment of his eight-year-old son Josiah as king, I speculate that some of these palace officials from the north must have won influence with Josiah's regent (possibly his mother, Jedidah Adayahsdaughter), who would have been responsible for selecting the tutors for his education.

This, I believe, is the most plausible scenario explaining Josiah's abolition of the non-Yahwistic cults in Judah and the idea expressed in P33 that he was also predestined to destroy Yahweh's cult in Bethel and the province of Samaria.[14] The individuals responsible for Josiah's education—a combination of individuals from northern families connected to Yahweh's cult and palace officials who ardently believed in Judean royal ideology—composed these three study books to inculcate into the impressionable young king their own political program. The two central pillars of their program were the abolition of the cults of all gods but Yahweh in Judah and the expansion of the Davidic king's control to the lands of the former northern kingdom in order to impose an identical set of cult reforms there. To accomplish this program, they educated Josiah in the qualities of great military leaders (the book of Judges), they taught him that Yahweh had granted the Davidic king dominion over the territory of the former kingdom of Israel (the book of Samuel), and they demonstrated to him the importance of the king's pleasing Yahweh as head of the cult (the book of Kings).

This earliest version of Kings consisted of two parts: a section covering the reign of Solomon (equivalent to roughly forty *parashot petuhot* and *parashot setumot*), and a section containing accounts of the reigns of all the kings of Israel and Judah through the reign of Josiah's father, Amon (equivalent to roughly sixty *parashot petuhot* and *parashot setumot*). The authors of this version of Kings relied primarily on the three source documents discussed above—*The Chronicles of the Kings of Israel*, *The Chronicles of the Kings of Judah*, and *The Acts of Solomon*. The focus of the authors of this earliest version of the book was to instill in Josiah the importance of the king "pleasing" Yahweh and to convince him that he was chosen by Yahweh to eradicate the cult at Bethel and its offensive practices. The political program that these authors promoted with Josiah reflects a worldview shaped by traditional Judean royal ideology and, more specifically, by Yahweh's

---

14 The material in P33 was composed when Josiah was a young boy, and I believe that most (but not all) of the details in P116 about him destroying Yahweh's cult in the north were fabricated. The account of his destruction of the northern cult was composed several decades after he died in order to demonstrate the fulfillment of the prediction in P33 (see notes 116ab and 116ai above).

unconditional promise to David that his dynasty would endure for all time. While these ideas do appear in this earliest version of Kings—mentions of the Davidic promise are made in P20, P29, P30,1 and P75—the ideas remain largely in the background of the book. That is to say, because these ideas were part of "the air" in which the authors and their student lived and breathed, the authors did not feel the need to highlight them in their work in an explicit way.

The material that I attribute to this earliest version of Kings—what I call the first stage of the book's composition history—follows below. Please note, in what follows, I typically do not specify exactly where the material from the first stage in each *parashah* begins and ends. For the specific sentences and paragraphs that I assign to the first stage, the reader should consult the notes to each *parashah*. It was my practice to indicate in the notes each and every place in the text there is a change in compositional stage. The only exceptions to this are the late glosses and comments, where the change in author should be obvious because in my translation I have represented that material in brackets or (less often) parentheses.

—End of P7,2. The end of this *parashah*, which is written in the style of the authors of the first stage, tells of Solomon's marriage alliance with Egypt and his placement of his Egyptian wife in Fort David, and it notes that the people at the time were making offerings in the open-air shrines. As discussed in note 7,2e above, I believe this material originally appeared immediately after P11,1 and that it was moved to its current position by the authors of the fifth stage.

—Insertion of P10,2-P10,23 and the first sentence of P10,24. The earliest version of Kings began with the statement that Solomon was "king over all of Israel" (P10,2)—a statement that likely appeared in the source document *The Acts of Solomon*. The authors of Kings' first stage then followed this statement with the insertion of a list of Solomon's senior officials (P10,3-P10,11) and a list of his tax commissioners (P10,12-P10,23 and the first sentence of P10,24) that they found in the source document.

—First sentence of P11. The first sentence of P11 enumerates the amounts of food consumed by Solomon's court each day. In the earliest version of Kings, this sentence interrupts the material about Solomon's tax commissioners, which continues in P11,1. The authors of Kings' first stage may have chosen to insert this list of foodstuffs, which likely was based on information found in *The Acts of Solomon*, within the material about the tax commissioners because supplying food to Solomon's court was one of their primary responsibilities.

—P11,1. This material in this *parashah*, which reads as a near verbatim insertion from the source document, describes how the tax farming system worked in practice and also provides details on the number of Solomon's chariots and chariot horses.

—P11,3-P12,2. These *parashot* describe Solomon's decision to build a house for Yahweh and how he secured construction materials through an agreement with Hiram King of Tyre. The *parashot* also provide details on the initial construction of the house. The source for some of details in this material may have been *The Acts of Solomon*.

—P13. This *parashah* is a detailed description of the house that Solomon built for Yahweh. Some scholars believe the authors relied on a source document from the temple archives; however, the building was still standing at the time the authors of the first stage were writing, and it seems more likely to me that they based the material in this *parashah* on their own knowledge of the building. Indeed, there is no physical detail in this *parashah* that the authors couldn't have deduced by examining the existing structure.

—Second half of P15. This material is the account of Solomon's construction of the royal palace (the Lebanon Forest House) and a detailed description of the structures comprising it. It seems most likely to me that the authors based nearly all of their account on their personal knowledge of the palace. There are some details, such as the time it took to construct the palace, that the authors of the first stage may have found in *The Acts of Solomon*.

—Insertion of the end of P17,2. The end of P17,2, which the authors of the first stage inserted from their source document for Solomon's reign, lists the equipment that Solomon made for the interior of Yahweh's house. The authors state that this material was all made of gold. There is no reason to doubt the authors on this point. However, by the time they were writing, the temple had been stripped of all its valuables by Hezekiah in order to pay tribute to the Assyrian king Sennacherib, and the temple equipment used in the authors' day appears to have been made almost entirely of bronze.[15]

—P18-P20 plus the second half of P21. These *parashot* are among the most important in this earliest version of Kings—they are the account of the consecration of the temple (including the transfer of the battle chest and other cult equipment from Yahweh's shrine in Fort David). The consecration ceremony culminates in a speech in which Solomon invokes Yahweh's promise to David that is at the heart of Judean royal ideology (P20). This is followed by great sacrificial offerings to Yahweh

---

15 Note that P119,2 states nearly all the temple equipment looted by the Babylonian army in 586 BCE—just five decades after the authors of the first stage were writing—was made of bronze.

and a two-week festival in the temple (second half of P21). Because of the importance of these *parashot*, it is no surprise that later authors made significant edits and additions to P19 and P20, which I discuss in the notes and in my treatment of Kings' third, fifth, and sixth stages.

—P23. This *parashah* is the account of Solomon's gift of twenty towns in the Galilee region to Hiram King of Tyre as payment for supplying the cedar and gold used in the construction of the palace and temple—a gift that Hiram found exceedingly dissatisfactory. This *parashah* is likely based on an account of this event in *The Acts of Solomon*, and some material from there may have been incorporated verbatim.

—First half of P24 and all of P24,1. The material in these two *parashot* reads as a compilation of entries from the source document, *The Acts of Solomon*. The entries concern the forced labor used by Solomon, the towns that he built and his construction projects, Pharaoh's gift of the town of Gezer, the management of Solomon's work projects, the offerings he regularly made to Yahweh as head of the cult, and his naval operations. Much of this material was likely incorporated verbatim from the source document.[16]

—Second half of P26, first two-thirds of P27, and all of P27,1. Much of the material in P26 and P27,1 reads as summaries of entries from *The Acts of Solomon*. These entries describe the shields in Solomon's palace (the Lebanon Forest House), his chariotry and chariot horses, the wealth of his capital city (which was likely exaggerated in the source document), and his trading operations with Egypt. I believe that the material in the first two-thirds of P27, which describes Solomon's throne, the drinking cups and utensils in the palace, and Solomon's naval trading ventures with Hiram, was not necessarily based on any source document; for this material, the authors of Kings' first stage may have drawn from oral traditions about Solomon's great wealth, or—in the case of the naval operations—invented on their own.

—P28 and P29. These two *parashot* do not appear to be based on any source documents, although they it is possible that they reflect information preserved in oral traditions. The authors of Kings' first stage have composed these *parashot* to introduce the rationale for the division of Solomon's kingdom. Thus, they portray Solomon as turning away from Yahweh and carrying out rites for foreign gods

---

[16] The material about Solomon's naval operations may have been invented by the authors of the first stage based on information that they found in *The Chronicles of the Kings of Judah* about Jehoshaphat's navy. That material appears in Kings in P60, and I believe it was added by authors of the second compositional stage. See notes 24,1e and 60b above.

due to the influence of his many foreign wives. This sets the stage for a key turning point in the earliest version of the book—the speech in P29 when Yahweh informs Solomon that he will divide the kingdom into two.

—P30 - P30,2. These *parashot* tell the story of Jeroboam's rise to prominence within Solomon's administration and of Yahweh's selection of Jeroboam as the king of Israel. It is interesting to note that Yahweh's promise to Jeroboam is conditional, unlike the Davidic promise, which for the authors of Kings' first stage was an unconditional promise. As I discuss in the notes, P30 and P30,2 read as verbatim extracts from *The Chronicles of the Kings of Israel* whereas P30,1 is a literary composition not based on any source.

—P30,3. This *parashah* provides the conclusion to the account of Solomon's reign. I do not believe the information in it is based on any source document; rather, the authors have composed it in the style they use to sum up the reigns of the kings of Judah and Israel, which was formulated from the language found in *The Chronicles of the Kings of Judah* and *The Chronicles of the Kings of Israel*.

—P30,4 - P31 plus the first half of P31,1. In these *parashot*, the authors of Kings' first stage present their account of the Israelites' rebellion against Rehoboam and the establishment of the independent kingdom of Israel. They have incorporated material from *The Chronicles of the Kings of Yisra'el* in P31, in the first half of P31,1, and at the beginning of P30,4, while adding some commentary of their own in P31 and P31,1. All of P30,4 except the first two sentences is a literary composition of the authors of Kings' first stage, who may have written the *parashah* as a lesson to their student Josiah in the importance of the king selecting (and listening to) men of experience as his advisors.

—P32,1. This *parashah* is the account of Jeroboam's reign over Israel. It treats his construction projects (the towns of Shechem and Penuel) and—most importantly—it tells of Jeroboam's errors in overseeing Yahweh's cult. His "great error" was fashioning images of Yahweh in the form of two gold bull calves and installing one in Yahweh's shrine at Bethel and the other in his shrine at Dan. His other two errors were establishing open-air shrines for Yahweh throughout his kingdom and designating people "from all over" to serve as priests in the shrines.

—P33. This *parashah* is especially important in the earliest version of Kings—it is where the authors of the Josianic study books present Josiah as ordained by Yahweh to destroy the cult in Bethel. This *parashah* is one of the clearest examples of the strategies employed by these authors to inculcate the young king Josiah with their own views and to convince him that Yahweh had chosen him to reform the cult according to the program that they themselves had conceived.

—P36-P38. These *parashot*, which are entirely a literary creation and not based on any source document, complete the account of Jeroboam's reign. In them, the authors of the Josianic study books introduce the key theme of their work—the importance of the king's pleasing Yahweh, and the consequences that the king and his people will suffer if the king does not please him. We should imagine that this theme was crafted specifically for the education of the young king Josiah. The authors wanted the boy to view his world through this lens. In these *parashot*, the authors highlight Jeroboam's displeasing acts in managing Yahweh's cult as the cause of the fall of his own dynasty and the destruction of his kingdom Israel—a cautionary lesson for the young king Josiah expressed in the most vivid terms.

—First half of P39 plus all of P40. This material represents the account of Rehoboam's reign as it appeared in Kings' first stage. The authors have borrowed heavily from their source document and added their judgement in P39 that Rehoboam did what was displeasing to Yahweh. This was later corrupted to the statement that "Judah did what was displeasing to Yahweh." This corruption later prompted multiple edits to this *parashah* by the editors of the sixth stage. See the discussion in note 39c above.

—P41. This *parashah* is the account of Aviyyam's reign over Judah. The authors of the Josianic study books have based their account on their source document; the only material they have added is a short judgement stating that Aviyyam did not follow Yahweh in the way that David did. The authors did not see a meaningful lesson here for Josiah and so kept their own commentary brief. The mention of David in the original version of this *parashah* attracted a later comment by the authors of the fifth stage; in addition, this *parashah* contains an error in the text that was corrected by the editors of the sixth stage. (On these edits, see the notes to this *parashah* above and the discussion of the fifth and sixth stages below.)

—P42-P42,1. These *parashot* are the account of Asa's reign over Judah. The authors of the Josianic study books have borrowed heavily from their source document in their treatment of Asa's reign and they likely incorporated much material verbatim. For these authors, Asa was one of only two kings who were "like Dawid" and whom they viewed as a model for their student Josiah to imitate. (The other king whom they viewed as a model for Josiah was Hezekiah.) The material that they themselves added are the judgements of Asa's actions (which, except for leaving the open-air shrines in place, were otherwise wholly pleasing to Yahweh), the comment about Asa's foot disease, and possibly the description of his cult reforms, some details of which may not have been in the source document.

—P43. This *parashah* is the account of Nadav's reign over Israel and of Basha's assassination of Nadav. The authors of the Josianic study books incorporated some details from their source document, but their main focus was on the account of the assassination, which they portray as fulfilling the oracle in P38 that they composed against Jeroboam. The source document likely contained information about the assassination that the authors have drawn on for their account.

—P44 and second half of P44,1. This material is the account of Basha's reign over Israel. The authors of the Josianic study books have drawn some details from their source document, added a brief comment of judgement (he displeased Yahweh by following in Jeroboam's footsteps), and added a comment about an oracle of the prophet Yehu Hananisson. They did not quote the oracle itself—the oracle quoted in the first half of P44,1 is a later addition to the text (see notes 44,1a and 44,1e above).

—P45. This *parashah* is the account of Elah's reign over Israel and of Zimri's assassination of Elah. The structure of this *parashah* is similar to that of P43: the authors of the Josianic study books incorporated some details from their source document, but their main focus was on the assassination, which they portray as fulfilling Yehu the Prophet's oracle mentioned (but not quoted) at the end of P44,1. The source document likely contained information about the assassination that the authors have drawn on for their account.

—P46. This *parashah* is the account of Zimri's short-lived reign over Israel. The structure of this *parashah* is similar to that of P43 and P45: the authors of the Josianic study books incorporated some details from their source document, but their main focus was on the assassination, which they portray as the consequences of his "following in the footsteps" of Jeroboam. The source document likely contained information about the assassination that the authors have drawn on for their account.

—Insertion of P47. This *parashah* is a brief account of civil war in Israel between a faction following Tivni Ginathsson and a faction following Omri. It appears to be a verbatim or near-verbatim insertion from the source document, *The Chronicles of the Kings of Israel*. Nothing is known of Tivni apart from the reference to him in this *parashah*; in the chronology for Israel and Judah that I propose in the appendix, I assign Tivni a reign of two years.

—P48. This *parashah* is the account of Omri's reign over Israel. The authors of the Josianic study books have borrowed heavily from their source document in their treatment of Omri's reign and they likely incorporated much material verbatim. The only material that they themselves added is the judgement of Omri's actions, which followed the ways of Jeroboam and thus" displeased Yahweh."

—P49 plus the end of P59,1. This material represents the account of Ahav's reign over Israel as it appeared in Kings' first stage. This account is very brief—the authors incorporated some basic details from their source document and then added a statement about Ahav's foreign wife Jezebel plus some commentary judging Ahav for his support of the cults of the Baal and Asherah. The information about Jezebel and the support of the cults of the Baal and the Asherah were not necessarily based on the source document, but may have been known to the authors from oral tradition.

—First half of P60 plus end. This *parashah* is the account of Jehoshaphat's reign over Judah. The account in the Josianic study books is almost entirely formulaic, consisting of the standard introductory formula, a statement about whether the king pleased Yahweh, a statement about the open-air shrines to Yahweh, and the standard concluding formula. The only information that is not formulaic is the statement that Jehoshaphat made a peace agreement with the king of Israel. (I view the non-formulaic material in the second half of the *parashah* as an addition from the second compositional stage; see note 60b above.)

—P60,1, beginning of P60,2, all of P60,3 except the beginning, and all of P61-P61,1. This material represents the account of Ahazyahu Ahavsson's reign as it likely appeared in the Josianic study books. It has been interrupted by a sizable addition about Elijah the prophet. The author of the addition has rewritten the original form of Elijah's oracle at the beginning of P60,2 in order to make it conform to the story he added. However, P60,3 seems to preserve the oracle in its original form. The account of Ahazyahu's reign is noteworthy as it contains two of the five instances in the earliest version of Kings in which Elijah is mentioned (see note 78f above).[17]

—P64. This *parashah* is the account of Yehoram Ahavsson's reign over Israel. The account does not follow the usual structure used by the authors of the Josianic study books; they have truncated the account in order to accommodate the story of Yehu's slaughter of Ahav's family, which is given in the second half of P77 through P78,1.

—P75. This *parashah* is the account of Yehoram Yehoshaphatsson's reign over Judah. It incorporates material from the source document

---

17 In all five instances Elijah's role is minor. In P60,2, Elijah receives an oracle condemning Ahazyahu to death, and in P60,3 he pronounces this oracle. In P78, Yehu alludes to an oracle in which Elijah condemns Jezebel, and in P78,1 Yehu alludes to an oracle in which Elijah condemns Ahav. In P78,2, the authors of the first stage allude to the same oracle mentioned in P78,1.

regarding Edom's rebellion against Judah but is otherwise almost entirely formulaic. One noteworthy item in the account is that it is one of only two places in Kings where the authors of the Josianic study books allude to the lamp (or "beacon") given to David as part of the Davidic promise.[18]

—P76. This *parashah* is the account of Ahazyahu Yehoramsson's reign over Judah. Like the account of Yehoram Ahavsson's reign in P64, the account here does not follow the usual structure but has been truncated by the authors of the Josianic study books in order to accommodate their material about Yehu. Some of material in P76 about the alliance with Yoram Ahavsson appears to be a near verbatim insertion from the source document *The Chronicles of the Kings of Israel*.

—Second half of P77 plus all of P78-P79. These *parashot* relate the stories of Yehu's conspiracy against Yoram, his murder of Jezebel, his slaughter of Ahav's family, and his slaughter of the Baal's priests. In the Josianic study books, the second half of P77 followed naturally from the conclusion to P76, but this has been interrupted by a lengthy addition regarding the anointment of Yehu by one of the prophets associated with Elisha. The stories about Yehu are interesting because they represent one of the few places where the authors of Kings' first stage do not rely on one of their primary source documents. These stories have a strong literary bent and were written to show Yehu as the instrument chosen by Yahweh to carry out his punishment of Ahav's family. In developing this theme, the authors appear to have altered some historical events and they very likely also invented many details out of whole cloth.

—P80. This *parashah* is the account of Yehu's reign over Israel. The account is unusual because the authors of the Josianic study books do not provide the standard introductory formula stating when Yehu became king, where he ruled, and how long his reign lasted. They may have chosen not to provide this formula for Yehu because the preceding stories about Yehu show him as already acting as king. However, they still felt obligated to provide information about the length of his reign, and they do so by adding a sentence after the standard concluding formula at the end of the *parashah*.

—P81-P82,2. This material is the account of Athalyah's reign as queen of Judah and the plot to depose her and install her grandson

---

[18] The lamp given to David is a core part of the Davidic promise and first appears in Ps 132 (quoted in my introductory note). The other mention of the lamp by the authors of Kings' first stage is in P30,1. I view the mention of the lamp in P41 as part of a comment added by the authors of the fifth stage. See note 41d above for further comments about the lamp.

Yehoash as king. These *parashot* are unusual because they have a number of literary features and they do not appear to be based on the primary source documents used by the authors of the Josianic study books. While it is possible that the material in these *parashot* is based on oral tradition, I think it more likely that it represents a literary creation of the authors of Kings' first stage, who may have wished to make Yehoash more prominent in their narrative because of the similar circumstances in which he and their pupil Josiah became king, and specifically because they wanted Josiah to see Yehoash as a model for himself.[19]

—P82,3-P85. These *parashot* are the account of Yehoash Ahazyahusson's reign over Judah. Most noteworthy here is the account of the renovation of the temple (second half of P83 plus P84). This material reads a literary composition by the authors of the Josianic study books, as the prose style is very different from the material attributed to the royal chronicles. That said, however, their account of the renovation very likely was informed by oral traditions preserved within the cult. The source for the other events of Yehoash's reign was *The Chronicles of the Kings of Judah*, and from that source the authors have included the usual sorts of information about the king's reign, including his most significant military engagements, how he died, where he was buried, and who succeeded him.

—P86. This *parashah* is the account of Yehoahaz's reign over Israel. Nearly the entire account consists of formulaic judgements by the authors of the Josianic study books. The only information incorporated from the source document is the sentence about the small size of Yehoahaz's army after it was destroyed by the king of Aram and the details in the introductory and concluding comments about Yehoahaz's reign. The paragraph about Yehoahaz's beseeching Yahweh and Yahweh granting Israel a liberator is clearly a late addition to the text and was not part of the Josianic study books (see note 86b above).

—P87. This brief *parashah* is the account of Yehoash Yehoahazsson's reign over Israel. It contains only the standard information given for each king—the year of his accession, the length of his reign, the site of his royal seat, where he was buried, and the name of his successor—plus a statement of judgement (he displeased Yahweh) and a comment referring the reader to the source document for additional information. At the end of the *parashah*, the authors state that the source document

---

19   Both kings assumed that throne as a young boy after his father was murdered. With respect to Yehoash's being a "role model" for Josiah, note that the cult of the Baal was eliminated under Yehoash, and Josiah's tutors must have hoped Josiah would do the same.

contains the story of Yoash's fight with Amatzyah King of Judah; this is noteworthy, as the authors chose to make that story part of the account of Amatzyah's reign, and the source for their story was clearly the royal chronicles of Israel and not the royal chronicles of Judah.

—P91-P93. These *parashot* are the account of Amatzyahu's reign over Judah. This account is interesting because it appears to draw on both source documents—the standard information about Amatzyahu's reign comes from *The Chronicles of the Kings of Judah*, whereas the account of Amatzyahu's fight with Yehoash is written from the perspective of Israel, indicating that the authors must have incorporated that material from *The Chronicles of the Kings of Israel*. As discussed above in note 92f, I believe that the authors of the first stage initially placed the material now in P92 in the account of Yehoash's reign in P87 and that they moved this material to P92 when they composed the account of Amatzyahu's reign.

—P94. This *parashah* is the account of Yarovam Yoashsson's reign over Israel. The *parashah* follows the typical structure used for the royal accounts: it incorporates material nearly verbatim from the source documents, includes a judgement by the authors of the Josianic study books about whether the king pleased or displeased Yahweh, and refers the reader to the source document for additional information. One noteworthy feature of the account is that it alludes to an oracle of Jonah the prophet; the style in which the comment about Jonah is written suggests that the authors of the Josianic study books have incorporated this comment verbatim from the source document.

—P95. This *parashah* is the account of Azaryah's reign over Judah. Like the preceding account, this *parashah* follows the typical structure used for the royal accounts: it incorporates material nearly verbatim from the source documents, includes a judgement by the authors of the Josianic study books about whether the king pleased or displeased Yahweh, and refers the reader to the source document for additional information.

—P96-P100. These *parashot* are the accounts of the reigns of five kings of Israel: Zekaryahu Yarovamsson (P96), Shallum Yaveshsson (P97), Menahem Gadisson (P97-P98), Peqahyah Menahemsson (P99), and Peqah Remalyahusson (P100). The period when these kings ruled was a chaotic time for Israel. The kingdom suffered greatly under the increasingly oppressive hand of the kings of Assyria, who extracted heavy tribute and seized control of large portions of the kingdom. The chaos of the period is reflected in the accounts of the kings' reigns, the source of which was *The Chronicles of the Kings of Israel*. The authors of the Josianic study books mostly stick to the standard format for each king's reign, and the only non-formulaic information they provide are statements about assassinations, invasions and seizures of land, and tribute paid to the Assyrian overlords—all of which they found in the source document.

—P101. This *parashah* is the account of Yotham's reign over Judah. The account follows the standard format: it provides brief statements of judgement (Yotham pleased Yahweh; however, the open-air shrines weren't abandoned), it incorporates a mention of an event from the source document (Yotham built the upper gate to Yahweh's house), and the introductory and concluding sentences include the usual details from the source document about the king's reign.

—P102. This *parashah* is the account of Ahaz's reign over Judah. The information at the beginning of the *parashah* is based on the source document. However, the story of the construction of the big altar is likely based on oral tradition, as it is written in a style that is uncharacteristic of the material attributed to the source document, *The Chronicles of the Kings of Judah*.

—P103 and the end of P104. The account of the last king of Israel, Hoshea Elahsson, is given in P103. The details of Hoshea's treachery and Shalmaneser's invasion are likely based on oral tradition, as the authors do not cite the source document in their account. However, the comment about the exile of the Israelites may have been drawn from the royal chronicles of Judah, which included an account of the fall of Samaria (see note 107a above). The last paragraph of P104 represents a summary judgement by the authors of the Josianic study books regarding the destruction of Israel, which they attribute to Israel's rejection of the Davidic king and Jeroboam's driving Israel away from (proper worship of) Yahweh through the "errors" he committed (principally the installation of the statues of Yahweh in the form of a bull calf in the shrines in Bethel and Dan).

—First two-thirds of P105 plus end of P105. The material in this *parashah* is an account of the revival of the cult of Yahweh in the province of Samaria in the years after the fall of Israel. Many scholars view this entire *parashah* as a late addition to the text. While I believe that is a very reasonable interpretation of the text, I think it is more likely that much of the material in the *parashah* is original to the Josianic study books. I believe the authors would have wanted to include an account of how the cult of Yahweh persisted in Samaria down to Josiah's day, as one of their main reasons for writing their work was to convince Josiah of the need to destroy the cult of Yahweh as it was practiced in the north and to force the residents of Samaria to travel to

Jerusalem to make their offerings to Yahweh.[20]

—P106-P107 plus the end of P112. This material represents the account of Hezekiah's reign as it appeared in the earliest version of Kings. The authors of this work held Hezekiah up to Josiah as the model of an ideal king of the Davidic line—someone for the young king to imitate. In their account, Hezekiah is presented as a king whom Yahweh "granted success in whatever he ventured to do," including his decisions to rebel against his Assyrian overlord and to withhold tribute. These are lessons that may have made a deep impression on Josiah, for he seems to have attempted to do something similar in not paying tribute to Pharaoh Necho (see the discussion in note 116at above). Tragically for Josiah, however, Yahweh did not "grant him success" in his resistance against his Egyptian overlord: Necho had him executed, likely for the crime of withholding tribute. The material in P107 is a brief account of the fall of the kingdom of Israel, which occurred in the sixth year of Hezekiah's reign. I understand the source for this material to be the account of Hezekiah's reign in *The Chronicles of the Kings of Judah*, and I believe the authors of the Josianic study books inserted it verbatim, including the parenthetical comments that synchronized Hezekiah's reign with Hoshea's reign.[21]

—First half of P113 plus the end of P113,1. This material represents the account of Manasseh's reign as it appeared in the Josianic study books. For the authors of the Josianic study books, the only noteworthy events of Manasseh's long reign were his reforms of Yahweh's cult in Jerusalem to include the worship of other gods alongside Yahweh in the temple and on the temple grounds—actions that the authors viewed as "displeasing" to Yahweh. It is important to keep in mind that the authors of the Josianic study books were writing when the kingdom of Judah was a viable political entity and they envisioned a glorious future for the kingdom under Josiah. As such, they viewed

---

20 It is interesting to note that the authors of the Josianic study books show little interest in the shrine at Dan. This is likely because Dan was not part of the Assyrian province of Samaria, and their political ambitions for Josiah were focused solely on the province of Samaria, not the areas to the far north or the east. It is also possible that at the time they were writing, the Yahwistic shrine at Dan was no longer in operation.

21 It should be noted that the material in P108, which is about Hezekiah's reign, is from the same source document. The authors of the Josianic study books almost certainly chose not to insert this material in their account of Hezekiah's reign because it contradicted their picture of him as the ideal Davidic king whom Yahweh gave success to in everything he did. Rather, I believe the material in P108 was added by the authors of the second compositional stage (see the discussion of that stage below).

Manasseh simply as one of numerous past kings who "displeased" Yahweh; it was the authors of the second stage—who wrote after Judah fell and the temple had been destroyed—who added the material in P113 and P113,1 that placed the blame for Judah's destruction on Manasseh.

—P114. This *parashah* is the account of Amon's reign over Judah. I believe that the earliest version of Kings ended here. As I discuss in the introduction, I understand the Josianic study books as works that were composed to educate the young king Josiah; as such the version of Kings that existed for his education would not have included an account of his own reign. In my opinion, viewing the original version of Kings as ending in P114 clears up many of the problems with the account of Josiah's reign. Frankly, I do not see how it is possible to argue that the earliest version of Kings was composed in Josiah's reign while also arguing that the account of Josiah's reign was part of the earliest version of Kings. For example, there is no obvious place in P116 that could serve as an ending to a work that was composed during the reign of Josiah. More importantly, if P116 was composed during Josiah's reign, there is no way to explain why the account of the events leading up to the discovery of the Torah scroll borrows so heavily from the account of Yehoash's repair of the temple in P83 and P84. Indeed, the borrowing suggests that the account of the discovery is a complete fabrication—a fact that the book's original audience (contemporaries of Josiah in this scenario) would have been aware. Equally important, if the original version of Kings ended with P116 and if this version was composed during Josiah's reign, then who was the intended audience for this book, and what exactly were the book's authors trying to achieve? I do not see that it is possible to answer these two questions in a plausible way. If the authors wished to create a document that justified Josiah's reforms after the fact to a broad group of people, they would not have written this earliest version Kings—nor would they have written Deuteronomy. The obvious choice would have been to write some other version of Deuteronomy, one which was much more focused on proper conduct of the cult and much less concerned with rules for conducting life in society. For these reasons, I believe that the most plausible scenario for the composition of Kings is that the earliest version of the book ended with P114 and not P116.

**

During the years following the destruction of the temple in Jerusalem and the exile of most of Judah's population to Babylonia, the leaders of Yahweh's cult—and possibly also the surviving members of the

Davidic royal line—must have struggled greatly to come to terms with their situation and to explain what had happened to them. Their efforts to understand the loss of their homeland and the suffering inflicted upon them ultimately led to the composition of the books of the Torah and the creation of Judaism itself. Initially, however, they turned to the Josianic study books to understand their predicament. In the first two decades of the Babylonian exile—roughly 580 to 560 BCE—these individuals composed and added new material to the earliest version of Kings in which they developed an explanation for their situation. It is the work of these authors that I understand as the second compositional stage of Kings. It is especially noteworthy that the authors of this stage continued to view events within the frameworks of Judean royal ideology and the Davidic promise. They held fast to the idea of the centrality of the king and they had not yet replaced the concept of the binding agreement between Yahweh and the Davidic king with the idea of a treaty between Yahweh and his people—that development was not to happen for another generation, sometime during the second half of the sixth century BCE.

In order to explain the destruction of Yahweh's temple, the authors of the second stage modified their view of the Davidic promise. In traditional Judean royal ideology, the promise to David was an unconditional one—David's descendants would rule in Jerusalem, which Yahweh had chosen as his own, forever. This was the view of the authors of the Josianic study books. However, for the authors of Kings' second stage, the destruction of the temple and the loss of the monarchy seemed to dispove the Davidic promise in its original form. To salvage the Davidic promise—and to salvage the belief system upon which their own worldview was founded—the authors of Kings' second stage thus reinterpreted the promise as a conditional one. Because the idea that Yahweh rewards kings who please him and punishes kings who displease him had long been a part of the Judean royal ideology, it required only a small shift in mindset for the authors of the second stage to understand the Davidic promise as conditional on the king's exclusive loyalty to Yahweh. While a number of kings of Judah gave service to gods other than Yahweh, the authors of the second stage singled out the actions of Manasseh, who went further than any other king in integrating worship of other gods into Yahweh's cult in Jerusalem, as the cause of the destruction of Yahweh's temple and the loss of the Davidic king's sovereignty over Jerusalem.

The authors of the second stage added only a small amount of material to Kings. Their work primarily consisted of four things: (1) adding material that reinterpreted the Davidic promise as conditional on the king's loyalty to Yahweh; (2) extending the book's narrative from the reign of Amon to the release of Jehoiachin from prison and his elevation to a place of favor; (3) inserting additional material from the *Chronicles of the Kings of Judah* to fix what they viewed as incomplete accounts of the reigns of Jehoshaphat and Hezekiah; and (4) adding material that placed the blame for Judah's downfall on the actions of Manasseh. Their version of Kings, as many scholars have pointed out, ends on a note of hope. Some of the authors of the second stage still held out hope in the revival of the Davidic kingship in some form, and they likely saw in Jehoiachin's elevation a promise, however small, of the future restoration of the Davidic king.

The material that I attribute to the second compositional stage is as follows:

—P14. This *parashah* is a message from Yahweh to Solomon. The *parashah* is noteworthy because it is the first instance in which the authors of the second stage express their view that the Davidic promise is not an unconditional one; rather, it is conditional on the king following Yahweh's laws and commandments. Note that these laws and commandments are specifically the rules for managing the cult. They are not the laws and commandments associated with Moses.

—First one-third of P20,1. The authors of the second stage added the material in the first third of this *parashah* to emphasize the conditional nature of the Davidic promise. In the original version of Kings, Solomon's blessing to the Israelites gathered at the temple alludes to the unconditional Davidic promise (see P20). The authors of the second stage cannot allow such a mention to stand as is, and consequently they add new material reexpressing the promise in conditional terms.

—Final sentence of P21 plus the first two-thirds of P22. The material in P22, which is introduced by the final sentence of P21, is the record of Yahweh's speech to Solomon following Solomon's construction of the temple and the royal palace. In this speech, Yahweh repeats the Davidic promise to Solomon. It was by means of this speech that the authors of the second stage expressed in greatest detail their belief that the Davidic promise was not unconditional, but rather was conditional on the king observing Yahweh's laws and precepts. It is noteworthy that the original speech ends with the statement that if the king and his descendants don't keep Yahweh's commandments and if they give service to other gods, then Yahweh will "reject the house that he consecrated as his own." This is the explanation that the authors of the second stage offer for why Yahweh's temple was destroyed and the Davidic monarchy ruined. It should be noted here that the first sentence of P22 does not belong to the material from the second stage; rather, as discussed in note 22a above, it was added by the authors of Kings' fifth stage.

—Addition to P60. Toward the end of this *parashah*, there are several sentences about Jehoshaphat's reign that interrupt the flow of the narrative and that appear to be based on the source document *The Chronicles of the Kings of Judah*. This material mentions Jehoshaphat's eradication of *qedesh*-prostitutes, his dominion over Edom, and the failure of his naval ventures. The sentences are clearly an addition to the text, and as the authors of the second stage still had access to the source document, I have assigned this addition to them.

—Possible edit to P101. In this *parashah*, which is the account of Yotham's reign, there is a parenthetical comment that during Yotham's time the kings of Aram and Israel made raids on Judah. In my composition history, I have treated this comment as part of the earliest version of Kings; however, it is quite possible that it is instead an addition by the authors of the second stage. See note 101c above.

—Insertion of P108. This *parashah* belongs to the account of Hezekiah's reign. The *parashah* portrays Hezekiah in a negative light and is at odds with the Josianic study books' portrayal of him in P106. Unlike the authors of the Josianic study books, the authors of the second stage were not committed to the vision of Hezekiah as the exemplar for Josiah. They must have thought that the account of Hezekiah's reign in the Josianic study books was incomplete, if not flawed; to correct this, they inserted the material in P108, which appears to be a near verbatim quote from the source document, *The Chronicles of the Kings of Judah*.

—End of P113 plus first half of P113,1. The authors of the second stage added this material to the account of Manasseh's reign in order to provide their explanation for the destruction of Jerusalem and the downfall of Judah. In P113,1, they added the lengthy oracle in which Yahweh states he will bring disaster upon Jerusalem and Judah, and at the end of P113, they added the sentence that introduces this oracle, including Yahweh's statement that Manasseh's abominable actions are the reason he has decided to destroy Jerusalem and Judah.

—P115; middle part of P116 plus material near the end of P116. The authors of the second stage extended the narrative of Kings down to the time they were writing (ca. 570s to 550s BCE). The first account they added was that of Josiah's reign, which is represented by P115, the middle part of P116, and some additional material near the end of P116. I believe that their account of Josiah's reign did not include the material about the discovery of the Torah scroll, nor the material about the king reading out the treaty scroll to the people, nor the material about the passover, nor the material about the eradication of the practice of consulting ghosts and spirits of the dead. All this material presupposes Deuteronomy, which I believe did not exist at the time the authors of the second stage were writing. The material in P116 belonging to their account begins in the middle of the *parashah* with the statement that Josiah eradicated the *komer*-priests; their account continues through the statement that Josiah slaughtered the priests of Shomeron's open-air shrines and burned human remains on their altars. They then conclude their account of Josiah's reign with the comment near the end of the *parashah* that Yahweh didn't relent from his anger over Manasseh, followed by the statement referring the reader to *The Chronicles of the Kings of Judah* for additional information about Josiah's reign. It is interesting that the authors of the second stage omitted a mention of Josiah's death, the violent manner of which must have been problematic for them. Although they interpreted the destruction of Jerusalem and the temple as evidence that the Davidic promise was conditional on the king's loyalty to Yahweh, they still would have held fast to the idea that Yahweh rewards kings who please him—a belief that Josiah's death challenged.

—P117 and P117,1. These *parashot* are the accounts of the reigns of Yehoahaz and Yehoyaqim. For these two accounts, the authors of the second stage adhered strictly to the format used by the authors of Kings' first stage to introduce the reigns of the kings of Judah. They begin each account with basic information about the king—how old he was when he became king, his mother's name, how long he ruled in Jerusalem—followed by a judgement about whether the king pleased or displeased Yahweh. This is followed by information incorporated nearly verbatim from the source document, *The Chronicles of the Kings of Judah*. The account of Yehoyaqim's reign retains the standard concluding format as well, referring the reader to the source document for additional information and stating that the king "lay down in death with his ancestors" and naming his successor.

—P118-P120,1. In these *parashot*, the authors of the second stage provide accounts for the final kings of Judah and narrate the destruction of the temple and the exile of the populations of Jerusalem and Judah. The authors of the second stage conclude their narrative with information on the chaotic aftermath of the destruction of Jerusalem and an account of Jehoiachin's release from prison in Babylon and his elevation to a position of favor with the king of Babylon. It is worth noting that for the reigns of the last kings of Judah—Jehoiachin and Zedekiah—the authors do not cite *The Chronicles of the Kings of Judah* as a source. On this basis, it is reasonable to assume that this document was not maintained in the chaotic final years of Judah and that it ended with the account of Yehoyaqim's reign.

**

With the exile of the leading families of Judah to Babylon in 597 and 586 BCE, the center of Yahwism shifted from Jerusalem to Babylon. Evidence from cuneiform archives of the period reveals a community that, with respect to economic and social life, largely assimilated to its new home.[22] However, with respect to religious life, we can be confident that many families must have maintained their devotion to their ancestral god Yahweh. The segments of the community that were most devoted to their god—including the priestly families—struggled especially to understand the loss of their homeland and the destruction of the place that their god had claimed as his own. Individuals from these families ultimately sought to come to terms with these events through the act of writing. Across the first half of the sixth century BCE they created a number of literary works that explored the reasons for their predicament. These included large portions of the books of Jeremiah and Ezekiel, as well as the revision of Kings represented by the book's second compositional stage discussed above.

The edict of Cyrus in 539 BCE granting the Judean exiles the right to return to their ancestral homeland spurred a second wave of literary activity greater than the wave that preceded it. Cyrus' edict gave the communities of Yahweh's devotees a "second chance" to put things right with their god. As the intellectual leaders of these communities reflected on what this second chance meant, they again turned to the act of writing. They expressed their views on the opportunity before them through the creation of a number of literary works, including what I believe were the earliest versions of the books of Deuteronomy, Exodus-Numbers (initially a single book), and Joshua.[23]

The authors writing in the late decades of the sixth century BCE abandoned the notion of the Davidic king who had a special "binding relationship" (ברית) with Yahweh and who served as intermediary between the people and their god. With the king removed from the picture, these authors repurposed the idea of the binding relationship (or "treaty") as one between Yahweh and his people directly. In the king's absence, the obligations of the treaty with Yahweh fell on the people. These authors retrojected this treaty between Yahweh and his people far into the past—in the vision created by them, this treaty had

---

[22] There is a large body of scholarly literature on this topic. For an excellent recent study, see T. Alstola, *Judeans in Babylonia: A Study of Deportees in the Sixth and Fifth Centuries BCE*, Leiden: Brill, 2020.

[23] The other important literature composed at this time that reflected on this new opportunity was the material added to Isaiah and to the other prophetic books.

been in effect from the beginning, when Yahweh chose the Israelites as his people. However, because the people had not kept their treaty obligations and had been unfaithful to Yahweh, they lost possession of their homeland. But now with the opportunity to return home, they were given a second chance: in the view of these authors, Yahweh's treaty with his people was a permanent one, and if the people kept true to their treaty obligations, then they would maintain possession of their ancestral land after their return, and Yahweh would grant them success and prosperity.

The literary activity in the late decades of the sixth century BCE—most especially the composition of the earliest versions of the books of the Torah—provided the impetus for the additions and edits made during what I call Kings' third compositional stage. The edits and additions to Kings in this stage primarily serve a harmonizing purpose: they harmonize the older material in Kings with the new ideas about the relationship between Yahweh and his people that are expressed in the earliest versions of Exodus-Numbers, Deuteronomy, and Joshua. I believe it is a mistake to view Kings (and Samuel and Judges) as part of a single large connected work that included Deuteronomy and Joshua (and Exodus-Numbers). Rather, the books of Kings and Samuel and Judges were always separate from the earliest versions of the books of the Torah. In this third stage of the composition of Kings, which I view as spanning most of the fifth century BCE and extending well into the fourth century, various individuals associated with Yahweh's cult in Jerusalem lightly edited Samuel and Kings (and barely touched Judges) so that those books could be understood as consistent with the new ideas about the relationship between Yahweh and his people as expressed in the earliest versions of the books of the Torah.[24] It should be emphasized that the expansions to Kings during the third stage were made in a piecemeal fashion, and as such they reflect the evolution in thought within Yahweh's cult across much of the Persian period.

The material that I assign to the third compositional stage of Kings is as follows:

---

[24] It is in interesting to note that the authors of the third stage didn't edit any of the material in Kings related to Elijah, Elisha, or Isaiah (all of which I have assigned to Kings' fourth stage). Moreover, the material about Elijah in several places presupposes ideas found in Kings' third stage. For these reasons, we can be reasonably confident that most of the editorial activity associated with what I call Kings' third stage was earlier than the fourth stage, even though the two stages overlapped chronologically in a fairly significant way.

—Edits to P19. In this *parashah*, the authors of the third stage have in two places transformed Yahweh's battle chest into Yahweh's treaty chest by inserting the word "treaty" (ברית) between the term for "chest" (ארון) and Yahweh. The authors have also added the sentence near the end of the *parashah* stating that nothing was in the chest except the two stone tablets that Mosheh had put there when the treaty between Yahweh and the Israelites was ratified. Near the beginning of the *parashah* the authors of the third stage inserted a reference to the Meeting Tent in order to equate it with the tent shrine in Fort David.

—Additions to P20. The authors of the third stage made two additions to this *parashah*: near the beginning, they inserted Yahweh's statement about choosing David (see note 20b), and at the end of the *parashah* they added the sentence in which Solomon states he has made a place inside the temple for Yahweh's treaty chest.

—Last third P22. The last two (or possibly last three) sentences of this *parashah* represent an addition by the authors of the third stage. In this addition, they express the view that the actions of the people, not the king, are to blame for the exile and the destruction of the temple. (By contrast, for the authors of the second stage, who composed the earliest version of this *parashah*, it was the actions of the king that are to blame.)

—Comments to P28. The authors of the third stage have added two comments to this *parashah*. In the first sentence, they have added the final clause alluding to the commandment against marriage alliances with foreigners in Deut P6,4, and two sentences later they likely added the parenthetical comment that Solomon's wives did in fact pervert his heart.

—Addition to P30,1. The authors of the third stage have added two sentences to Ahiyyah's speech to Jeroboam. In these sentences, Ahiyyah places the blame for the division of the kingdom not on the actions of the king, but on the actions of the people, who abandoned Yahweh and began worshipping other gods. This addition may have been prompted by the corruption in the text discussed in note 30,1f.

—Edit to P32,1. The authors of the third stage inserted the phrase "the ones that brought you up out of Egypt" into Jeroboam's speech presenting the gold bull calves to the Israelites as their gods. In doing so, they connect Jeroboam's images of Yahweh with the golden calf fashioned by Aaron at Mount Sinai in Exod P51,1.

—Possible edits to P80. There are two edits to this *parashah* that I have assigned to the editors of Kings' sixth stage but which can plausibly be viewed as made by the authors of the third stage. Near the beginning of the *parashah*, there is a comment stating that Yehu did not follow Yahweh's Torah, and later in the *parashah* there is a lengthy gloss defining the region of Gilead as the territory of the Gadites, Reubenites, and Manassehites. See the discussion of this *parashah* below in my treatment of Kings' sixth stage.

—Comment to P91. In this *parashah*, the authors of the third stage added a comment about Amatzyahu's execution of his father's assassins. In their comment, they specifically cite the book of Deuteronomy and the law in Deut P21,28. It is unclear to me what motivated this addition in this particular place in Kings, as none of the other accounts of assassinations in Kings have such a comment. See note 91c above.

—Comment to P102. In this *parashah*, a later author has added a comment noting that Ahaz's fire-offering of his son was similar to the "abominable practices of the nations that Yahweh drove out from the Israelites' path." I assign this comment to the third compositional stage on the basis of the formulaic language used, which also appears in Joshua, Deuteronomy, and Numbers. However, it is equally plausible to view the comment here as belonging to the sixth compositional stage of Kings, when numerous harmonizing glosses and comments were added to the text.[25]

—All of P104 but end. In this *parashah*, the authors of the third stage provide their rationale for Yahweh's rejection of Israel. In the material from the Josianic study books at the end of the *parashah*, the authors place the blame on the actions of Jeroboam. The authors of the third stage have inserted a lengthy discussion occupying the first three-fourths of the *parashah* providing their own explanation of why Yahweh "removed Israel from his presence." It was not because of Jeroboam's actions, but rather because the Israelite people wronged Yahweh by worshipping other gods and following the customs of the native peoples of Canaan. They didn't listen to the prophets Yahweh sent to warn them and they rejected his laws and the treaty that he made with their ancestors. This *parashah* was likely added early in Kings' third stage. It is noteworthy that Moses is absent despite the mention of Yahweh's treaty with his people. Moses only appears in later additions from the third stage, after his figure had gained further in stature.

—Addition to P105. This *parashah* is the Josianic study books' account of syncretistic religious practices in the province of Samaria after the fall of the northern kingdom. To this account, the authors of the

---

[25] It is worth noting that I assign two other comments in P102 to the editors of Kings' sixth stage, and the comment here that I assign to the third stage would fit easily with those two. The comments found in P102 provide a good example of the uncertainty one often experiences in attempting to assign material to one compositional stage or another.

third stage added a sizable addition in the second half of the *parashah* stating that the religious practices of Samaria are not better in their own day—the people there still don't follow the laws and precepts of the Torah. While there was a close partnership between Yahweh's cults in Samaria and Yehud during the Persian period,[26] it was also the case that the cults of other gods continued to thrive in Samaria during this period.

—Possible comments to P106 and comment at end of P107. I believe the authors of the third stage may have added three comments to the account of Hezekiah's reign—one comment in P107 and two possible comments in P106. At the end of P107, they added the comment that the Israelites were exiled by the king of Ashur because they violated the terms of their treaty with Yahweh and didn't give heed to the commandments that Moses had given them. In P106, there are two comments that I have treated as part of the sixth stage, but which it is possible to view as made by the authors of the third stage. The first comment states that the "Israelites" (who were really the people of Judah) made incense offerings to the bronze snake prior to Hezekiah's time; the second comment informs the reader that the commandments that Hezekiah obeyed were specifically those that Yahweh gave to Moses. Because the two comments in P106 are primarily editorial in nature, I have chosen to assign them to the sixth stage.

—Additions to P113 plus comment to P113,1. The authors of the third stage made at least three edits to the account of Manasseh's reign. First, in P113, they added the last sentence of Yahweh's speech, in which he alludes to the land he gave the ancestors and the Torah that Moses had commanded them. At a later time, they added the following sentence stating that the people didn't heed Yahweh's words because Manasseh led them astray and made them do things worse than the nations that Yahweh had removed from the Israelites' path. In P113,1, the authors of the third stage added a comment at the end of Yahweh's oracle, in which they have Yahweh state that the reason he abandoned the people of Judah was because they displeased him and constantly provoked his anger from the time their ancestors left Egypt down to the present. In addition to these three edits, there are a number of other edits to the account of Manasseh's reign that I have assigned to Kings' sixth stage but which could plausibly be viewed as additions from the third stage. On these edits, see the discussion of

---

26 On this partnership and the joint composition of the books of the Torah and Joshua, see my thoughts on the composition history of these books in the introduction to my translation of Joshua.

Kings' sixth stage below.

—First part of P116, plus an addition to the latter part of P116. The account of Josiah's reign appears in P116. Josiah was an especially important figure for the authors of the third stage—Deuteronomy was the foundational text for these authors, and they associated the earliest version of Deuteronomy with Josiah's reign. It is thus not surprising that the authors of the third stage significantly expanded the account of Josiah's reign. In the first half of the *parashah*, they composed a lengthy origin story for the book of Deuteronomy, tying its "discovery" to renovation work done on the temple during Josiah's reign.[27] This origin story attributes the destruction of Judah and Jerusalem to the treaty curses in Deut P26 that Yahweh has invoked because the people did not keep their treaty obligations. The origin story also contains an account of Josiah's public reading of the treaty scroll at the temple[28] and an account of the removal of the items associated with the cults of the Baal, the Asherah, and the stars from the temple. Finally, in the origin story composed by the authors of the third stage, Yahweh promises Josiah a peaceful death because of his great humility. Towards the end of the *parashah*, the authors of the third stage added the material about the observation of the passover festival and the material about Josiah's eradication of the practice of consulting the dead, in keeping with the commandments in the earliest version of Deuteronomy. They also added the summary comment that Josiah was unique among all kings in his commitment to Yahweh and to the Torah of Moses.

**

Across the entirety of the fifth and fourth centuries BCE, I believe authors associated with Yahweh's cult in Jerusalem significantly expanded the book of Kings. One strand of work during this period, which I assign to the third compositional stage, involved harmonizing Kings with the early versions of the books of the Torah and the book of Joshua. The most significant body of work on Kings during this period, however, was the addition of a large body of material about the prophets and holy men of old—especially the two most famous such figures of the northern kingdom, Elijah and Elisha. This material

---

27 The renovation of the temple under Josiah appears to be a fabrication of the authors, as their account borrows heavily from the story of Yehoash's renovation of the temple in P84. See note 116b above.

28 I view this event as a literary invention of the authors and do not believe it represents a memory of a real historical event.

makes up what I call Kings' fourth compositional stage. While there is a broad chronological overlap in my composition history of Kings between the third and fourth stages, I view most of the work on these two stages as distinct in time, with most activity in the third stage taking place in the early and mid-fifth century BCE and most activity in the fourth stage taking place in the late fifth and early fourth centuries BCE. Complicating matters, within each compositional stage, there is evidence of multiple "editions." That is to say, we should conceive of the work on each compositional stage as an iterative process taking place over several decades, with additions that I attribute to a single stage being made in several successive steps as the leaders of Yahweh's cult on Mount Zion and the keepers of the temple library reflected upon the texts they maintained and added material to them that expressed the evolution of their own views and ideas.

Many of the stories from the fourth stage about the prophetic figures of the past are ill-suited to the themes of the older material to which they were added, and they sit oddly within the larger narrative of Kings. This is especially true for the stories about Elisha and much of the material about Elijah as well. This gives us some insight into the motivations of the authors of the fourth stage. Their additions did not necessarily stem from an interest in either supporting or opposing the underlying themes of the earlier versions of the book. Rather, their motivations seemed to be of three sorts. First, a number of their additions appear to be motivated by their own theological interests—in particular, they added material expressing the view, common to the Persian period, that Yahweh is the sole and universal god and is all-powerful. Second, several stories they added reflect an interest in the nature of prophecy and in understanding the prophet's role as an intermediary of Yahweh. And third, much of the material they added was simply due to an antiquarian interest: by inserting stories about the famous prophets and holy men of old into an important temple document such as Kings, they could ensure that the memory of these individuals was not lost to posterity.

I believe that the stories in the fourth stage were added in a number of separate "editions." In my view, the earliest additions to the fourth stage were about Elijah the prophet.[29] Sometime later in the fourth stage, the authors added a body of stories about the holy man and miracle-worker Elisha and, in order to connect the two men, they made Elisha the deputy of Elijah. Over time, the Elijah and Elisha

---

29 See notes 51,2a, 60,2a, 68a, and 69a above for my thoughts on the evolution of the material about Elijah and Elisha.

stories were expanded, with Elijah taking on miracle-working powers like Elisha and Elisha taking on prophetic characteristics like Elijah. As the body of stories about Elijah and Elisha grew, it attracted other additions about the prophets of old, including the great prophet Isaiah. At a still later period within the fourth stage, this material attracted a number of further additions as authors expanded the material about the prophets in order to make theological points important to them.

The material that I assign to the fourth compositional stage of Kings is as follows:

—Second half of P31,1 plus all of P32. The authors of the fourth stage must have known of a famous oracle of Shemayah the Holy Man in which he advised the king of Judah not to wage war against Israel. It is likely that this was a genuine oracle, although the setting for the oracle is unclear—Israel and Judah were at war with each other for much of the tenth and ninth centuries BCE, and the original oracle may not necessarily have been addressed to Rehoboam. The authors of the fourth stage must have believed that the oracle was sufficiently noteworthy to merit inclusion in Kings, and they composed the material in the second half of P31,1 in order to create an opportunity to insert the oracle into the narrative, which they did in P32.

—Addition to P33. The authors of the fourth stage likely added a sentence near the end of this *parashah* that was needed to set up the lengthy story that they added in P34-P35. See note 33g above.

—P34-P35. These two *parashot* are a supplement to the story in P33 in which a holy man delivers an oracle foretelling Josiah's birth and the destruction of Yahweh's cult in Bethel. We can only guess at the motivations of the authors who added this supplement to Kings; possibly they wished to comment on the nature of prophecy and the impossibility of determining whether someone who claims to speak in Yahweh's name truly does, as well as the consequences to a prophet who directly disobeys Yahweh's commands.

—First half of P44,1. In this *parashah*, the authors of the fourth stage have inserted an oracle in which the prophet Yehu condemns Basha, the king of Israel. The original conclusion to this *parashah* (from Kings' first stage) alludes to this oracle but does not quote it, and the authors of the fourth stage must have felt that the account of Basha's reign seemed incomplete without the actual text of the oracle. Because they did not have a record of Yehu's oracle, they composed one for him on the basis of Ahiyyah the Prophet's oracle against Jeroboam in P38. (For more on this proposal, see the discussion in the notes to P44,1.)

—P49,1-P51,2. These *parashot* contain a diverse body of material about the prophet and holy man Elijah; the stories in these *parashot* are only loosely connected with each other, and they are even more loosely connected to the larger narrative of Kings. They are by and large literary compositions that have been influenced in part by oral traditions about Elijah and—in the stories about Elijah as a miracle-worker—oral traditions about Elisha. I offer specific thoughts on the composition of this material in the notes to these *parashot*, and I will only summarize the content of the stories here. The short *parashah* P49,1 is an oracle delivered to Ahav predicting a drought in Israel. The following *parashah* P49,2 is a brief story about Elijah hiding in a remote wadi (the story doesn't say why Elijah is hiding) and being sustained by food brought to him by ravens. This is followed in P49,3 by a story about Elijah staying with a widow in the town of Tzarepath and miraculously producing food for her and her family by means of an oil jug and a flour jar that never become empty. In the third story about Elijah (P50), he miraculously revives the same widow's son, who had fallen mortally ill.[30] The group of stories in the next two *parashot*, P51 and P51,1, are presented as a continuous narrative and they represent the most important material about Elijah from a theological perspective. There were originally four interconnected stories in P51 and P51,1: a story about Elijah's chance meeting of Ahav's palace chamberlain, a story about a contest between Elijah and the Baal's prophets to prove whose god is the supreme god, a story about the arrival of rain and the end of the drought, and a story about Elijah's flight into the wilderness to escape Ahav's wife Jezebel. The following *parashah*, P51,2, is the story of Elijah's meeting of Elisha, who follows him and becomes his designated successor.

—Addition of the Mount Horev story in P51,1, plus addition of a variant ending to this story. I believe that the famous story of Elijah at Mount Horev in P51,1 was added relatively late in Kings' fourth stage, well after the other stories in P49,1 - P51,2. At a still later point in the fourth stage, a variant version of the Mount Horev story was written. In my opinion, it is likely that the earliest version of the story ended with Elijah's answer to Yahweh's question, prior to the theophany; later authors who were also working as part of the fourth compositional stage composed a variant version of the story that included the theophany. I presume that they may have intended to remove the original ending; if so, it was preserved by authors of the sixth compositional stage, so that the story in its present form contains both endings. See notes 51,1af and 51,1ai above.

---

30 For a discussion of the stories in P49,3 and P50 and their relation to the Elisha stories, see the notes to those *parashot*.

—Addition in the first half of P51,2. Yahweh's command to Elijah in the first half of P51,2 sits awkwardly in the narrative, as it is completely unrelated to the text before and after it. I view this command as an addition made after the composition of the material in the second half of the *parashah*. The material in the first half of the *parashah* promises three future events in the narrative—Elijah traveling to Damascus to anoint Hazael as king of Aram, Elijah anointing Yehu as king of Israel, and Elijah anointing Elisha as his successor. Yet none of these actions occurs in Kings.[31] I speculate that the most likely explanation for these incongruities is that the authors of the fourth stage added the first half of P51,2 because they had plans to compose stories about the actions Elijah was told to carry out. However, when they decided to broaden the depiction of Elisha to be a prophet as well as a miracle-working holy man, they abandoned their plans for the additional stories about Elijah. The stories about Elijah promised in the first half of P51,2 were instead written for Elisha (see P74 and P77). When the authors wrote these stories for Elisha, they left the first half of P51,2 unchanged, resulting in the problematic text that we have today.

—P52-P54. These *parashot* contain a story involving anonymous prophetic figures and their interactions with the king of Israel (Ahav) in Israel's wars with Aram. I view this story as a purely literary composition with no real historical value, and I believe it was added relatively late in the fourth stage—well after most of the material about Elijah and Elisha. The Persian-period authors of this story knew the traditions about Ahav as a devotee of the Ba'al. In their story, they imagine that Yahweh must have tried to convince Ahav that the god who actually gives him victory—and therefore the god he should acknowledge—is Yahweh. The story's purpose is primarily to entertain and secondarily to provide additional context around Ahav's disloyalty to Yahweh.

—P54,1. I view this *parashah* as a late fourth-stage addition to the story in P52-P54. The authors of P54,1 use the setting of the preceding story to craft a brief narrative that comments on the correct principles of war. These authors make the argument that the law of the ban devotion (see Deut P19,4), which requires Yahweh's people to kill all foreign enemies who are on Israelite soil and to show no mercy, must always be followed. I believe the authors of P54,1 composed their story in order to criticize the ending of P54, in which the king of Israel shows mercy to Hadadsson King of Aram. For the authors of P54,1, the requirement to subject one's military opponents to the ban

---

31 Elijah chooses Elisha as his successor, but doesn't anoint him.

devotion is absolute and must always be followed.[32] It is especially interesting that despite the serious subject matter, the authors present their story in a lively and entertaining way. Also noteworthy is that the Septuagint places the two stories in P52-P54,1 directly after P58. The ordering in the Septuagint is more logical and it may reflect the original organization of this material: in the Septuagint, the Elijah stories in P49,1-P51,2 and P55-P58 are grouped together, and the stories about the prophets' interactions with the king of Israel in the wars between Israel and Aram in P52-P54,1 and P59-P59,1 are grouped together.

—P55-P58. These *parashot* are the story of Ahav's seizure of Navoth's vineyard and Elijah's condemnation of Ahav for Navoth's murder. I view this story is a literary composition of the authors of the fourth stage. The events in the story do not at all fit the the description of Navoth's murder from Kings' first stage that appears in P77,[33], and consequently I presume that the details in the story in P55-P58 are entirely the creation of its authors. I believe that the main motivation of the authors in composing this story is that they were bothered by the fact that the famous oracle of Elijah pronouncing doom on Ahav (the original version of which is preserved in P77) was never fulfilled. They likely were also bothered by the scene in P77 in which the authors of King's first stage apply Elijah's famous oracle against Ahav to his son Yehoram. To explain why these things were so, the authors of the fourth stage composed the story in P55-P58 showing that because Ahav humbled himself after hearing Elijah's oracle, Yahweh delayed bringing disaster on Ahav's family until the reign of Ahav's son.

—Repair of P56. At some point during the fourth stage, the original oracle in P56 pronouncing doom on Ahav was lost from the text. As this oracle was essential to the narrative, later authors of the fourth stage attempted to repair the text by composing a new oracle on the basis of statements appearing elsewhere in Kings. On the details of this repair, see note 56b above.

—End of P58. Authors of the fourth stage who were working at a later time than the authors of the story of Navoth's vineyard in P55-P58 tacked on a sentence at the end of P58 in order to introduce the story beginning in P59. Note that the authors of P55-P58 operated under the assumption that Ah'av died a peaceful death, which is consistent with how his death was portrayed in the earliest version of Kings at the

---

32 The authors of the earliest version of Samuel seem to have had similar views about the requirement to follow the ban devotion. In Sam P31-P33,3, they portray Saul's decision not to subject Amaleq to the ban devotion as the cause of Yahweh's rejection of him as king.

33 For the differences, see note 55a above.

end of P59,1. When later authors of the fourth stage added the story in P59 - P59,1, they changed the manner of Ahav's death so that Yahweh does in fact bring doom on him.

—P59 plus all of P59,1 but end. These *parashot* are a literary composition exploring the nature of prophecy and the impossibility of ascertaining who is a true prophet—indeed, the authors of this material suggest that Yahweh is not above giving false oracles to the king's prophets in order to bring about the king's death. A second motivation in adding this story was to change the manner of Ahav's death, so that he is punished for his involvement in Navoth's death. In composing the story in P59 - P59,1, the authors borrowed many of the details of their narrative from the story of the death of Ahav's son King Yehoram, which appears in P77 and which is from Kings' first stage.

—Edit to the beginning of P60,2 plus the composition of the remainder of P60,2; beginning of P60,3. In the Josianic study books' version of Kings, the sole appearance of Elijah as a character is in the account of Ahazyahu's death (the beginning of P60,2 and all of P60,3). The authors of the Elijah stories significantly expanded the account of Ahazyahu's death by editing the beginning of P60,2 and adding all the material in the remainder of the *parashah* plus the first sentence of P60,3. The edit to the beginning of P60,2 involved inserting the word "messengers" into the text and changing a prepositional phrase from "to him" to "to them." The story they added in the remainder of P60,2 is fantastical in nature and portrays Elijah as possessing supernatural powers—a picture that is objectionable to the modern sensibility but likely was not to the ancients. The edit to P60,3 consisted of the material leading up the phrase "to the king," which originally concluded the sentence in P60,2, "And off Elijah went."

—P62 - P63. These *parashot* contain three stories: the story of Yahweh taking Elijah up into the skies and Elisha inheriting Elijah's supernatural powers (P62); the story of Elisha curing the unhealthy waters of Jericho (P62,1); and the story of Elisha cursing the little boys who mocked him (P63). The second two stories seem to have their roots in folk traditions, whereas the first story contains numerous literary elements and reads as a wholly literary composition. It is interesting to note that there are no glosses or comments to the three stories here. In fact, there are only three editorial glosses/comments in the entirety of the Elisha material—one in P69 and two in P77. By contrast, in all the other stories in the book of Kings, it is quite common to see glosses and comments made by the editors of the sixth stage.

—P65 - P74. These *parashot* contain the core of the Elisha material. There are twelve stories here: the story of King Yehoram's defeat of

Moab (P65-P65,1); the story of the poor widow and her miraculous jars of oil (P66); the story of Elisha's revival of the dead boy (P67); the story of the bad stew (P68); the story of the barley loaves (P68,1); the story of Elisha curing Naaman of leprosy (P69); the story of Elisha striking Gehaziy with leprosy (first three-fourths of P69,1); the story of the lost ax-head (last one-fourth of P69,1); the story of Elisha and Aram's army (P70); the story of the famine during the siege of Samaria (P71-P73); the story of the king's restoration of the Shunammite woman's property (P73,1-P73,2); and the story of Elisha and Hazael (P74). The four stories in P66-P68,1 have their roots in folk tradition and present Elisha as a miracle-working holy man, in keeping with the original traditions about him. By contrast, the other eight stories contain extensive literary elements and I view them as literary compositions. In several of these eight stories, Elisha is presented in the role of a prophet to Yahweh, as would be expected of the successor to the great Elijah. Of these eight stories, the most noteworthy for their literary artistry are the story of the revival of the dead boy (P67), the story of Elisha and Naaman (P69), and the story of the famine during the siege of Samaria (P71-P73).

—First half of P77. The first half of this *parashah* is the story of Yehu being anointed as king of Israel by one of Elisha's followers. It reads as a wholly literary creation and contains numerous elements of humor. Because Yehu was the only king of Israel who "pleased Yahweh" in some way, the story may have been composed out of a desire to show that Yehu's ascent to the throne—which was accomplished by assassinating his lord, Yoram Ahavsson King of Israel—was approved by Yahweh. This story is one of the few places in Kings where the material from the fourth stage interacts with the base narrative from the first stage. These interactions create some messiness in the text, as in these instances the authors had to interfere with the base narrative more than is typical. The other prime example of this dynamic is the addition of P60,2 and the intrusive edits to the surrounding narrative that were required to make that insertion (see the discussion above and the notes to that *parashah*).

—Comments to the second half of P77. The addition of the first half of P77 by the authors of the fourth stage disrupted the original narrative about Yehu's conspiracy, which was part of Kings' first stage. Because the narrative was difficult to follow after the addition, the authors of the fourth stage added two clarifying comments in the second half of P77 to remind the reader of the events of P76, which directly preceded the second half of P77 in the earliest version of Kings. The first comment reminds the reader that Yoram King of Israel had fought Hazael King of Aram in Ramoth Gilead and that Yoram returned to Jezreel to recover after being defeated by Hazael. The second comment reminds the reader that when Yehu carried out his conspiracy, Ahazyahu King of Judah had gone to Jezreel to see Yoram. (See notes 77k and 77m above.)

—P88-P89. These *parashot* contain the final two stories about Elisha; like many of the other stories about Elisha, both contain magical elements. The first story (P88) reads as a literary composition, but the second story (P89) likely has its roots in folk tradition. The subject of the first story is a game that Elisha has Yoash King of Israel play involving arrows, and the subject of the second is the magical powers of Elisha's skeleton in the grave.

—P90. The authors of the fourth stage composed this *parashah* in order to show the fulfillment of Elisha's prophecy in P88. The *parashah* is interesting because it is one of the few places in Kings that alludes explicitly to traditions from Genesis. The allusion to Genesis, in my opinion, is indicative of a Persian period date for this *parashah*, for Genesis was not accepted as authoritative by Yahweh's cult in Jerusalem until sometime in the late sixth century or early fifth century BCE.[34]

—P109-P111,1 plus all of P112 but end. The authors of the fourth stage added a large body of material about the prophet Isaiah in the *parashot* indicated here. This material consists of three stories: a story about Sennacherib's invasion of Judah (P109-P110,2), a story about Hezekiah's illness (P111-P111,1), and a story (related to the second) about Hezekiah's reception of a delegation from the King of Babylon (all of P112 but end). These three stories read as independent compositions that were inserted into Kings as part of the account of Hezekiah's reign, which in earlier versions of Kings was very brief. The material about Isaiah in Kings is very close to (but not identical with) Isaiah 36-39. Most scholars, myself included, view the version in Kings as more "original" than the version in the book of Isaiah. I hypothesize that the first story may have been an independent document about Isaiah that was circulating within Yahweh's cult, and the editors of Kings' fourth stage chose to preserve that document by inserting it into Kings. I view all three stories about Isaiah as Persian period compositions, and I believe the latter two stories were written after the first story and inserted into Kings some years or decades after the first story. See my comments in note 109a above.

---

34 For a summary of my views on Genesis and its composition, see the discussion of the composition history of the books of the Torah and Joshua on pp. xv ff. of my introduction to Joshua.

—Addition in the second half of P109. In the earliest version of P109, Hezekiah sends his officials to visit Isaiah, and Isaiah then provides them with an oracle from Yahweh to take back to the king. The officials do not deliver a message to Isaiah, but simply receive an oracle from him. Authors working very late in Kings' fourth stage must have viewed the absence of a message informing Isaiah of the reason for the visit as a problem in the narrative. To address this problem, they composed and inserted into the text the message that the officials delivered to Isaiah. See the discussion in notes 109o-r above.

—Additions to P110,1 and to P110,2. In one of the very late editions of Kings, the authors expanded the oracle in which Yahweh threatens Sennacherib by adding the material at the end of P110,1. This material provides a "sign" indicating when this threat would come true and reflects late language and concepts (see note 110,1i above). Also in one of the late editions of Kings, the authors added the fantastical material in P110,2 about Yahweh's emissary killing one hundred and eighty-five thousand Assyrian soldiers. Both of these additions, with very slight changes, were also made to the parallel material in Isaiah. It is unclear whether this material was added to both books at the same time, or was added to one book first and then added some time later to the other. In any case, it seems quite possible that the authors who added this material to Kings were the same individuals who added it to Isaiah.

—Addition to P116. To this *parashah*, the authors of the fourth stage added a brief scene in which Josiah orders those desecrating the altar in Bethel not to disturb the grave of the holy man who came from Judah. The addition was likely prompted by the mention of the holy man's oracle, which appears immediately before this addition and which is part of the material in this *parashah* from Kings' second stage.

**

I view the prophetic material that I assign to Kings' fourth compositional stage as being added to the book in a piecemeal fashion across the second half of the fifth century BCE and the entirety of the fourth century and as overlapping in part with Kings' third stage. The editorial activity on Kings during this time, however, was not limited to the harmonizing additions of the third stage and the prophetic stories of the fourth stage. Rather, in this same broad time period—the fifth and fourth centuries BCE, plus much of the third century—numerous other expansions were made to Kings. These expansions, which I have grouped together as the book's fifth compositional stage, were primarily concerned with the figure of Solomon and with Yahweh's temple in Jerusalem. In addition, I identify two other Persian-period expansions that are not related to Solomon or the temple and that don't fit neatly into any of the proposed compositional stages. Rather than create a separate "stage" for these two miscellaneous additions, I have grouped them with the expansions made in Kings' fifth stage.

While some of the authors of the material that I assign to the third and fourth stages may have also contributed to the material I assign to the fifth stage, I view these three sets of authors as mostly comprised of different individuals within Yahweh's cult. Both the authors of the fourth stage and the authors of the fifth stage have clear antiquarian interests, but the former are primarily focused on the role of the prophets, whereas the latter are mainly focused on the magnificence of the temple and the greatness of Solomon.

Finally, it is worth reiterating here that while the first two compositional stages that I propose for Kings are distinct and associated with very specific time frames, I view much of the work in the last four stages as happening concurrently. I have divided this work into individual "stages" in order to organize and make sense of the different types of editorial activity during the Persian period and Hellenistic period that I have identified in the book. Unlike Kings' first stage (and to a lesser extent second stage), most of the work representing Kings' final four stages was added in an ad hoc and piecemeal fashion, and there is no unified perspective even within material that I assign to a single stage. That is to say, additions to each of the third, fourth, fifth, and sixth stages took place over a very a long time period, and authors working "early" in one stage had different views on the topics they were writing about than the later authors of that stage who wrote about the same topics. Thus, the final four stages in my proposed composition history serve primarily to organize the Persian-period and Hellenistic-period editorial activity on Kings according to the topics of greatest interest to the authors: harmonizing Kings with the books of the Torah and Joshua for the authors of the third stage; preserving stories about the great prophets of the past and exploring the nature of prophecy for the authors of the fourth stage; highlighting the greatness of Solomon and the glory of the temple for the authors of the fifth stage; and clarifying obscure or confusing language and emphasizing important theological points in the text for the editors of the sixth stage.

The material that I assign to Kings' fifth compositional stage is as follows:

—P1-P7,1 and all of P7,2 but end. In the versions of Kings from the book's first two compositional stages, the character of David was portrayed in an entirely positive light—he was the perfect king. In these versions of Kings, the book was not connected to the early versions of Samuel, which lacked the so-called succession narrative and which made only a single brief mention of Solomon.[35] By the Persian period, however, the idea of the binding agreement between Yahweh and his king had completely lost its relevance, and the dominant theological principle of Yahwism had evolved into the idea of the treaty between Yahweh and his people. Moreover, as part of this evolution in the theology of Yahwism, David was replaced by Moses as the founder of the cult. I believe that sometime early in the Persian period the leadership within Yahweh's cult must have decided to strengthen Moses' position vis-à-vis David to limit the veneration of the king in the popular imagination. To do this, they commissioned the composition of the so-called succession narrative—a significant expansion to both Samuel and Kings that connected the two books (which originally had been independent of each other) and that portrayed David in a negative light.[36] The portion of Kings belonging to this expansion is P1-P7,2.

—Transposition of the end of P7,2. The material at the end of P7,2 regarding Solomon's marriage alliance with Pharaoh belongs to Kings' first stage. The authors of the fifth stage moved this material from its original location (which likely was after P11,1) to its current location. They likely did this at the same time that they added the material in P8-P10,1.

—P8-P10,1. One special interest among the biblical authors during the Persian period was in the great figures of the past. Over the centuries, folk tradition had created a significant body of stories about these figures, and the biblical authors active in the Persian period polished these stories with literary elements and added them to the books of the Torah and the Former Prophets. A number of the great figures of ancient times benefited from this work, most especially Abraham, Moses, David, and Solomon. This is the background for a number of the expansions about Solomon that we see in Kings. The first such expansions in are in P8-P10,1. I view the story of Yahweh's appearance to Solomon in a dream in P8-P8,1 as wholly a literary work composed to explain that Solomon's greatness was the gift of Yahweh. I also understand the famous story about Solomon's judgement of the dispute between the two prostitutes in P9-P10,1 as a literary work,

---

[35] See Sam P75,1, which lists Solomon as the fourth son born to David in Jerusalem. Sam P71,2 lists six sons born to David when he ruled in Hebron, which means that Solomon was the tenth son in the line of succession. On the succession narrative as a late addition to Samuel and Kings, see note 1a above.

[36] See note 1a above for additional thoughts on the circumstances leading to the composition of the succession narrative.

although the authors may have drawn on folk tradition for some elements of the story.

—Second half of P10,24. In the latter half of P10,24, the authors of the fifth stage have inserted two sentences portraying Solomon as a suzerain over a huge kingdom extending from the Euphrates River to Egypt. The allusion to a theme from Genesis in the first sentence is a clear indication of a Persian period date for this material; as mentioned above, I believe Genesis did not become a part of the cult library in Jerusalem until the late sixth century or early fifth century BCE.

—Additions to P11. After the first sentence of this *parashah*, the authors of the fifth stage have added a description of the great wealth and extent of Solomon's kingdom and of the peaceful living conditions enjoyed by the inhabitants of Israel and Judah.

—P11,2. The subject of this *parashah* is the great wisdom of Solomon. Signs of a relatively late date include the fantastical elements and the use of "God" in place of Yahweh.[37]

—Addition to P11,4. To this *parashah*, which tells of Hiram King of Tyre's agreement with Solomon to supply him with cedar wood for the construction of the temple, the authors of the fifth stage have reinforced the themes of Solomon's wisdom and the greatness of his kingdom by adding a sentence in which Hiram expresses admiration for Yahweh, for Solomon, and for the nation that Solomon rules.

—Addition to P12. At the beginning of this *parashah* the authors of the fifth stage added a clause alluding to Yahweh's gift of wisdom to Solomon. As discussed above in note 12a, the reason for this particular addition is unclear.

—First half of P15 plus later additions to this material. The authors of the fifth stage showed a keen interest in Yahweh's temple in Jerusalem and added much material to Kings related to the temple. The account of the temple's description in the Josianic study books' version of Kings appears in P13. The authors of the fifth stage greatly expanded that description by composing the first half of P15, which provides numerous details describing the temple's construction. The authors of a later edition of Kings from the fifth stage must have thought the description of the temple was still inadequate, and they added more material in three separate places describing the temple's magnificence; in these additions, they highlighted that the entire interior was overlaid with gold and decorated with depictions of sphinxes

---

37 While both early and late authors used the terms Yahweh and "God" (אלהים) interchangeably, most early authors have a preference for Yahweh and many late authors have a preference for "God."

and date palms and flower garlands. On these additions within the fifth stage, see notes 15f, 15j, and 15m above.

—P16 - P17,1 plus the first two-thirds of P17,2. In the earliest version of Kings, the authors gave only the briefest account of the equipment associated with the temple, which appears in the last third of P17,2. The authors of the fifth stage must have felt this description was wholly inadequate. To correct the previous authors' omissions, the authors of the fifth stage composed P16 - P17,1 and the first two-thirds of P17,2, which provide detailed descriptions of the two pillars in the temple's porch, the great metal Sea, the ten bronze stands and their lavers, and the caldrons, shovels, and bowls for the blood used within the cult.

—Addition to P19. The authors of the fifth stage added the final sentence of this *parashah* in order to make explicit that Yahweh was indeed present in his new home; in adding this sentence, they borrowed language from the portrayal of the manifestation of Yahweh's presence in the Meeting Tent in Exodus P70.[38]

—Last two-thirds of P20,1, all of P20,2 - P20,3, and the first half of P21. The material in these *parashot* represents an important group of additions made by the authors of Kings' fifth stage. The first one-third of P20,1 is an addition by the authors of the second stage, who updated Solomon's prayer to Yahweh at the dedication of the temple by emphasizing the conditional nature of the Davidic promise. The authors of the fifth stage appended a lengthy addition to this prayer; their addition extends from the remainder of P20,1 through the first half of P21. In doing so, they have recast the prayer to be about the role of the site of the temple for devotees of Yahweh living in the diaspora and for those living in Yehud, and also for foreigners who have chosen to acknowledge Yahweh. Even if people cannot present offerings to Yahweh at the temple because they live in some faraway place, if they direct their prayers toward the site of Yahweh's temple, then Yahweh will forgive their wrongdoing and will grant their pleas.[39]

—Additions to the second half of P21. There are two small additions to the second half of this *parashah* that I have assigned to the authors of the fifth stage. In the account of Shelomo's slaughtering the animals for the welfare offering at the dedication of the temple, they added a clause stating the numbers of the animals being offered—

---

38 It is also possible to understand this addition as part of the work on Kings' third stage. However, I believe it fits better with the fifth stage, as its purpose seems to be simply to embellish the specialness of the temple, which was a primary focus of these authors.

39 For additional thoughts on the important additions in these *parashot*, see my comments in notes 20,1d - 20,1g.

numbers that are fantastical, in keeping with the great importance of the event. Near the end of the *parashah*, they added a clause that interpreted "all Yisra'el" as a "huge congregation" extending over the entirety of the tribal territories—another fantastical image to reinforce the importance of the event.

—First sentence of P22. The authors of the fifth stage added the first sentence to this *parashah* to indicate Yahweh spoke directly to Solomon, and not through a prophet. They state that this was the "second" time Yahweh appeared to Solomon in reference to their addition of P8, in which Yahweh appeared to Solomon in a dream at Gibeon.

—Second half of P24. The authors of the fifth stage added the material in the second half of this *parashah*, which specifies that Solomon conscripted only non-Israelites for his forced labor. This material is dependent on themes introduced into Joshua and Judges during the Persian period, and it is likely that some of the same individuals were responsible for adding this theme to all three books. See the discussion above in note 24f.

—P25 plus a later addition to this material. The authors of the fifth stage had a special interest in the great wealth and wisdom of Solomon as known from folk traditions. Drawing from those traditions, the authors of the fifth stage composed this highly literary *parashah*, which is the famous story of Solomon and the Queen of Sheva. Then, in a later edition of Kings from the fifth stage, the editors added two sentences near the end of this *parashah* on the topic of the great amounts of gold and precious stones and rare woods that Solomon received from Hiram's trading missions to Ophir.

—First half of P26. The first sentence of this *parashah* describes the fantastical amounts of gold Solomon received each year; the theme of Solomon's great wealth and the Persian-period vocabulary suggest that this sentence was likely added by the authors of the fifth stage, which they have inserted in front of the Josianic study books' mention of gold-plated armor that Solomon made for display in his palace.

—Last one-third of P27. At the end of this *parashah*, the authors of the fifth stage added two sentences that serve as a sort of summary statement of the themes of Solomon's great fame, wealth, and wisdom, which they have woven throughout the account of his reign.

—P28,1. This *parashah* contains material about Solomon's support of the cults of foreign gods. It is not necessary to the narrative as it repeats themes given in P28. I believe the authors of the fifth stage knew of additional traditions about Solomon's disloyalty to Yahweh, and they added this material here in P28,1 in order to create a more complete account of Solomon's reign. Although the authors of the fifth stage saw Solomon as a very great king, they had no reason to question the traditions about his apostasy late in life, which they would have viewed as authoritative because they were already part of the version of Kings that they knew.

—P29,1 plus a later addition to this material. This *parashah*, which tells of two "adversaries" that Yahweh "raised up" against Solomon, is very poorly integrated into Kings and serves no essential purpose to the narrative. It alludes in several places to events in David's reign, and I believe that the material in this *parashah* about Hadad the Edomite may have been composed by the author of the so-called succession narrative in Sam P82,2-P101 and Kings P1-P7,2. It is conceivable that the author had planned a story about Solomon and his adversary Hadad, but if so, he never was given permission to develop it, resulting in a *parashah* that seems out of place and incomplete. The material at the end of the *parashah* about the second adversary, Rezon Elyadasson, reads as a separate addition, made later than the material preceding it. The material about Rezon may have been added in order to give Solomon a more imposing adversary—Rezon was the king of Aram, a powerful nation, whereas Hadad was a member of the royal family of Edom, a very small and weak state.

—Comment to P41. In this *parashah* the authors of the fifth stage added a parenthetical comment to a mention of David and his loyalty to Yahweh. The comment alludes both to the Davidic promise and to events in the so-called succession narrative. The comment must have been prompted by the statement that David's heart was "wholly with his god Yahweh," which the authors of the fifth stage felt necessary to qualify by reminding the reader of David's moral failing in causing Uriyyah's death.

—Addition to P86. The middle part of this *parashah*, in which Yehoahaz beseeches Yahweh and Yahweh in turn "sees Israel's suffering" and gives them a "liberator," is clearly an addition that draws on language from the book of Judges. This material does not fit neatly into the core material from the fifth stage about Solomon and the temple. The addition primarily serves a narrative purpose in that it fills in details about Yehoahaz's reign. In the addition, the frame of judgement is not the king, but the people. This might suggest the authors of the third stage. However, because the authors of the third stage nowhere else allude to Judges (they are concerned only with the books of the Torah and Joshua), I view this middle part of P86 as a "miscellaneous" addition and have assigned it to the fifth stage.

—End of P116. I believe that at some point in the second half of the Persian period, the authors of Kings added an account of Josiah's death at the end of P116. Because the authors of the second and third stages of Kings so greatly venerated Josiah, they omitted an account of his death, as his manner of death indicated that he in fact was not favored by Yahweh and that he must have displeased him in some way. By the second half of the Persian period, however, Josiah was a figure of the remote past and the manner of his death could no longer be thought to call into question the authority of the book of Deuteronomy. Consequently, individuals working on Kings in this period—who may still have had a copy of *The Chronicles of the Kings of Judah* in their possession—added the account of Josiah's death in order to address this omission from earlier versions of Kings. This material is a second example of a "miscellaneous" addition that does not fit neatly with the material from any of the proposed compositional stages, and for that reason I have assigned it to Kings' fifth stage.

—Additions to P118 and P119,2. The authors of the fifth stage added the sentence in P118 stating that Nebuchadnezzar chopped up all the gold furnishings made by Solomon in the temple's great hall. They also added three sentences to P119,2 commenting on the bronze cult implements made by Solomon and looted by the Babylonians.

**

The activity in what I call the sixth compositional stage of Kings largely consisted of editorial work. The individuals responsible for this body of work added dozens of glosses and comments to clarify obscure terms and passages, to resolve inconsistencies, to correct errors, and to make certain theological points more explicit. This stage spanned a very long period and overlapped heavily with what I call Kings' third, fourth, and fifth stages.[40] In addition, I believe that some of the activity in the sixth stage may have been contemporaneous with Kings' first and second stages. The material incorporated from the source documents *The Chronicles of the Kings of Israel* and *The Chronicles of the Kings of Judah* would have been difficult to understand even for the earliest authors of Kings, for this material contains many unusual terms and is written in an elliptical style. Thus, some of the glosses and comments made to the material from the source documents might be quite early—possibly even made by some of the individuals who worked on Kings' first and second stages. Apart from a small number of instances, however, I view nearly all the activity in Kings' sixth stage

---

40 Some of the authors of the sixth compositional stage likely also contributed to the fifth stage and possibly the third stage. I separate out their work on what I call the sixth stage from their work on the fifth (and third?) stages because the nature of the work that I attribute to the sixth stage is motivated by different concerns and is primarily editorial in nature.

as taking place in the fourth through the second centuries BCE. In these centuries, the books of the Torah, the Prophets, the Psalms, and some of the books of the Writings first began circulating outside the temple library in Jerusalem and began to be read and studied in the diaspora communities. It was during these years that the institution of what ultimately became the synagogue began to emerge from the religious practices of Yahweh's devotees,[41] the majority of whom lived far from the Yahwistic cult centers in the provinces of Yehud and Samaria. As study and reading of the books of the Torah and the Prophets and some of the Writings became a regular part of emergent Judaism, it seems certain that questions would have arisen about confusing matters in the text or about what appeared to be omissions in the text—and it also seems certain that these questions would have been brought back to the priestly leaders in either Jerusalem (in the case of the books of the Torah, Prophets, and Writings) or Mount Gerizim (in the case of the books of the Torah alone), and that the priestly leaders would have felt some responsibility to clear up these confusions and to address the various omissions. Obviously, the scenario I have painted here is hypothetical, but I believe that a scenario such as this best explains the circumstances surrounding the sixth compositional stage of Kings.

To Kings' sixth compositional stage, I assign nearly all the material in the book that in my translation appears as italicized text within brackets and much of the material that appears within parentheses. This material is as follows:

—Glosses to P1. The editors of the sixth stage added two glosses to this *parashah*, noting that "Adoniyyahu's brothers" means all the king's sons (i.e. not just the sons of Adoniyyahu's mother) and that "Yehudah's leading men" is a reference to the king's senior officials.

—Possible comment to P4. David's farewell speech to Solomon in P4 mentions the laws and commandments of Yahweh's treaty that are recorded in the Torah of Moses. It is possible that this clause was added by the editors of the sixth stage (see note 4b). However, if we accept that P1-P7,2 is a late addition to Kings, as I have argued, it is also possible to see the reference to Moses' Torah as original to the text.

—Comments to P7. The editors of the sixth stage added the comment clarifying that Joab had not been in league with Absalom. They

---

41 For an excellent discussion of the origins of the synagogue, see L. Levine, *The Ancient Synagogue: The First Thousand Years* (New Haven: Yale University Press, 2000), pp. 19-41. The earliest firm evidence for synagogues in the diaspora comes from Egyptian inscriptions dating to the third century BCE; on these, see Levine, *The Ancient Synagogue*, pp. 75f.

also added a gloss to clarify that the two men whom Joab killed were Abner Nersson and Amasa Yethersson.

—Variant (or correction) in P10,9. In the list of Solomon's officials, Zavud Nathansson is said to be a priest. The editors of the sixth stage have inserted a comment that he was instead a "confidante to the king." It is unclear whether this comment represents the editors' wish to preserve a variant reading known to them, or whether they are simply making a correction of what they believed was an error in the text.

—Comments to P10,17 and P10,18. In P10,17, the editors of the sixth stage added a comment about the location of Beth Shean, and in P10,18 they added a comment reminding the reader that the Argov district contained sixty fortified towns.

—Glosses to P10,24. To this *parashah* the editors added a gloss about the region of Gilead in order to remind the reader that it was formerly the land of the kings Sihon and Og; they added a second gloss noting that Solomon's domain included the entirety of the Philistines' lands.

—Comment to P11. In this *parashah*, the editors added a comment clarifying that Solomon didn't directly rule the region of Beyond-the-River, but rather his authority was over the kings within that region—that is, he was their suzerain.

—Gloss to P11,1. The language in this *parashah* is confusing. The editors of the sixth stage attempted to clarify the language by adding a gloss telling the reader that the term for "stalls" should be understood to mean "horses." Unfortunately, the editors were themselves confused by the text, and their gloss added to the difficulty of the text. See the discussion in note 11,1a above.

—Possible comment to P12. At the end of this *parashah*, there is a statement that Adoniram supervised the labor gangs working in Levanon to procure cedar and cypress for the construction of Yahweh's temple. I have treated the sentence as part of the earliest edition of Kings, but the statement sits awkwardly in the narrative, and it is possible that it is in fact a comment added by the editors of the sixth stage.

—Comment and glosses to P13. At the beginning of this *parashah*, the editors of the sixth stage have inserted a comment connecting the construction of Yahweh's temple to a comprehensive chronological framework devised within the cult during the late Persian period, which dates major events in reference to the exodus from Egypt.[42]

---

[42] Note, however, that this framework was never meaningfully implemented. See note 13a above.

In addition they added two glosses: the first informs the reader that the month of Ziw is the second month of the calendar and the second clarifies that the upper cornice ran atop all the walls of the temple, not just one wall.

—Glosses to P15. In this *parashah*, the editors of the sixth stage added two glosses, one qualifying the term "cella" as "the most holy place" and a second clarifying that the month of Bul is the eighth month.

—Comments to P16. The editors of the sixth stage added two comments to this *parashah*, noting first that the pillars were located in the temple's porch and second that there was a flower design on the top of the pillars.

—Glosses to P17. In the description of the bronze stands in this *parashah*, the editors of the sixth stage added two separate glosses at different times to help the reader understand the term for "plates," which were part of the stands' construction. See note 17j above.

—Glosses to P17,2. Near the end of this *parashah*, the editors of the sixth stage added glosses to clarify that the term "inner house" specifically refers to the temple's inner sanctum and that the mention of "the house" should be understood as referring to the great hall of the temple.

—Comments, glosses, and edits to P19. The editors of the sixth stage made a number of small additions to this *parashah*: they glossed Fort David as Zion, they specified that the month of Ethanim is the seventh month, they added a comment about the priests and Levites bringing the cult equipment to the temple, they specified that the term דביר (*debīr*) refers to the temple's inner sanctum, and they added a comment noting that the ends of the treaty chest's staves could not be seen from the outside.

—Comments to P25. The editors of the sixth stage added a comment stating that Yahweh placed Solomon on the throne out of his eternal love for Israel; they also added a comment stating that the Queen of Sheva witnessed Solomon offering up whole offerings on the temple grounds.

—Comments to P28. The editors of the sixth stage made two edits to this *parashah*: they added the reference to Phar'oh's daughter and the added a comment that Shelomo was attached to and loved women who were from nations that Yahweh forbade the Israelites to "go among."

—Comments to P29,1. This *parashah* contains two parenthetical comments about Hadad the Edomite—one stating he was a young boy when he fled to Egypt and a second stating he was in Egypt when he heard that David had died. While it is possible these comments are original to the text, it seems most likely to me that they were added by the editors of the sixth stage. In addition, at the end of the *parashah*, the editors added a very awkward comment implying that Solomon suffered harm from Hadad; they added this comment to address the lack of any specific mention in the previous material that Hadad (who was an "adversary" of Solomon) had caused him any harm.

—Comment to P30,1. The editors of the sixth stage added a reference to Yahweh's laws and precepts in a sentence about the Israelites not following Yahweh's ways.

—Edits to P30,4. The original account of the Israelites' rebellion against Rehoboam in this *parashah* omitted any mention of Jeroboam. The absence of Jeroboam from this account must have been viewed as problematic, and the authors of the sixth stage inserted Jeroboam into this *parashah* in two places to correct this problem. See the discussion in note 30,4b above.

—Edits to P32,1. The editors of the sixth stage added a comment noting that none of the priests installed by Jeroboam were Levites. They also preserved a variant version of the account of the festival held by Jeroboam at the end of the *parashah*.

—Addition to P33. In this *parashah*, the editors of the sixth stage added a sentence stating that the altar in Bethel split into pieces right after Jeroboam heard the holy man pronounce the oracle against the altar.

—Comment to P35. After the prophet from Bethel reacts to hearing the news of the holy man's death, the editors of the sixth stage added a comment reminding the reader that the holy man's death was in keeping with the oracle that Yahweh gave the prophet from Bethel at the beginning of the *parashah*.

—Comment to P38. The editors of the sixth stage added a comment to Ahiyyah's oracle in this *parashah*; the comment attributes Yahweh's anger against the Israelites to the fact that they made Asherahs (i.e. Asherah posts).

—Correction and additions to P39. Sometime during the Persian period, the statement in this *parashah* that Rehoboam displeased Yahweh was corrupted to read that Judah displeased Yahweh. That corruption prompted the editors of the sixth stage to "correct" the remainder of the corrupted sentence so that it was consistent with Judah as the subject of the sentence. As part of their work on this *parashah*, these editors also inserted a clause near the beginning of the *parashah* reminding the reader that Jerusalem was the town that Yahweh chose as his own, and they added a comment at the end of the *parashah* stating that the things the people did were just like the practices of the nations that Yahweh cleared away. For the somewhat complex compositional history of this *parashah*, see notes 39b, 39c and 39f above.

—Addition to P40. At the end of this *parashah*, the editors of the sixth stage added a sentence providing the name of Rehoboam's mother; this corrected an omission in the text, as the standard introductory formula for the kings of Judah included the name of the king's mother.

—Correction to P41. In an earlier stage of Kings, an error crept into this *parashah* when Aviyyam's name was mistakenly replaced with Rehoboam's. The editors of the sixth stage corrected this error by adding a sentence near the end of the *parashah* stating that the war was between Aviyyam and Jeroboam. See notes 41g and 41h above.

—Addition to P43. The editors of the sixth stage added a sentence at the end of this *parashah* stating that there was perpetual war between Judah's king Asa and Israel's king Basha during the time that both reigned. On the clumsiness of this addition, see note 43g above.

—Gloss to P47. The editors of the sixth stage added a gloss informing the reader that the term "the people" should be understood to mean "Israel." This gloss is an example of a "sixth stage" edit to material from a source document (*The Chronicles of the Kings of Israel* in this instance) that may have been made by an individual who contributed to Kings' first or second stage.

—Comment to P48. In this *parashah*, the editors of the sixth stage added a comment clarifying that the statement that "Omri followed in Jeroboam's footsteps and in the errors he caused Israel to commit" should be understood to mean that he provoked Yahweh's rage by encouraging Israel to worship "useless gods" (i.e. the bull calves in Bethel and Dan).

—Correction and addition to P49. The editors of the sixth stage inserted a comment stating that the mention of the Baal's altar should be understood specifically as a reference to the Baal's temple that Ahav built in the town of Samaria. At the end of the *parashah*, a different editor of the sixth stage added a sentence stating that Hiyel the Bethelite rebuilt Jericho during Ahav's reign, and that his oldest and youngest sons died in the reconstruction, in keeping with an oracle that Yahweh delivered through Joshua. (See note 49e above on this addition.)

—Gloss to P49,1. The editors of the sixth stage glossed Elijah's surname "the Tishbite" by telling readers that this was the Tishbeh located in Gilead (Tishbeh was a common town name). As discussed above in note 49,1b, the gloss was corrupted at some point in the text's transmission history so that it now reads "from the residents of Gilead" rather than "from the Tishbeh in Gilead."

—Comment to P51,1. The editors of the sixth stage responded to a mention of "the tribes of the descendants of Jacob" by adding a comment reminding the reader that the ancestor of the Jacobite tribes received an oracle from Yahweh stating that his new name would be Israel (see Gen P30).

—Gloss to P51,2. The editors of the sixth stage added a gloss informing the reader that the pronoun "them" refers to the pieces of meat that Elisha cooked for the people in his village.

—Glosses to P52. The editors of the sixth stage added two glosses toward the end of this *parashah*: they clarified that the phrase "his military forces" means "all the Israelites," and they indicated that the men marching out from town should be understood as the provincial chieftains' deputies followed by the army.

—Gloss to P54. In this *parashah*, the editors of the sixth stage clarify that the mention of Apheq is a reference to the town of that name and not the region.

—Variants to P55. To this *parashah*, the editors of the sixth stage preserved variant readings in three places: in the first, they note that for the phrase "in his town" there is a variant reading of "who lived with Navoth;" second, they note that for "the leading men of his town," there is a variant that reads "the elders and the nobles who lived in his town;" in the third instance, they note that for the phrase "just as Jezebel had sent to them" there is a variant that reads "exactly as was written in the letters she sent them."

—Comments to P56. The editors of the sixth stage added two parenthetical comments to this *parashah*. The first comment informs the reader of an oracle that Yahweh pronounced against Jezebel; the second comment is a lengthy condemnation of Ahav; in this comment, the editors tell us that Ahav was corrupted by his wife Jezebel and that he performed abhorrent rites in honor of worthless gods.

—Gloss to P69. The editors of the sixth stage added a gloss clarifying that the Avanah and the Parpar are the names of two rivers in Damascus. It is interesting to note that this is one of the only glosses in the entirety of the Elisha stories. Unlike the other sections of Kings, the editors of the sixth stage barely touched the material about Elisha.

—Gloss to P75. The editors of the sixth stage added a gloss noting that the lamp that Yahweh gave David was for David's descendants.

—Edits to P77. In the first half of this *parashah*, the editors of the sixth stage added a gloss that the "young man" refers to the prophet, and they added a comment clarifying that Yahweh will avenge the murders of all his servants killed by Jezebel (not only the murders of the prophets who were killed by her). In the second half of this *parashah*, the editors of the sixth stage added a comment noting that Gur's Pass is near Yivleam.

—Additions to P78. I believe the editors of the sixth stage added the first sentence to this *parashah* in an attempt to correct for the loss of the original beginning sentence of the *parashah*. See the discussion above in note 78a. At the end of the *parashah*, the editors commented on Jezebel's death by composing an oracle likening her corpse to manure spread on the field—a comment they likely modeled on Jer 9.21.

—Gloss to P78,1. The editors of the sixth stage added a gloss clarifying that the "leaders of Jezreel" are its elders.

—Gloss to P79. At the end of this *parashah*, the editors of the sixth stage added a gloss stating that the pronoun "them" refers to the gold bull calves in Bethel and Dan.

—Edits to P80. In this *parashah*, there are two small additions that could have been made as part of the third stage or the sixth stage of Kings. I think the latter is more likely and include them here. At the beginning of the *parashah*, Yahweh tells Yehu that he is pleased with him. Following this statement, the editors of the sixth stage added a comment reminding the reader that Yehu didn't follow Yahweh's Torah with all his heart and didn't abandon Jeroboam's errors. Later in the *parashah*, they added a gloss defining the region of Gilead as including the Bashan region to the north and extending to the Wadi Arnon in the south, and further stating that this region was the territory of the tribes of Gad, Reuben, and Manasseh. Similar language appears in several places in Numbers, Deuteronomy, and Joshua, and I assign the gloss to the sixth stage, when numerous harmonizing glosses and comments were added to the text. That said, it is also plausible to view this gloss as belonging to Kings' third compositional stage.

—Edits to P82 - P82,2. In these *parashot*, which are the account Yehoyada's installation of Yehoash as king of Judah, the editors of the sixth stage made five edits: in P82, they added a gloss specifying that "the officers of the militarie" were the Karian guard and the royal guard, and they added a comment clarifying how the royal guard was stationed in front of the temple; in P82,1, they added a comment noting that the "commotion" (הרצין) was a reference to the people, and they either glossed or a preserved a variant to the somewhat unusual term "those who oversaw the army" (פקדי החיל); and in P82,2, they inserted a correction that Yahweh's treaty was not only with the king, but also with the people. The concept of a treaty between Yahweh and his people was of central importance to Yahwism during the Persian period, and thus it is not surprising to see the authors of the sixth stage "correct" the mention of Yahweh's treaty with the king here.

—Gloss to P83. The editors of the sixth stage added a gloss to this *parashah* informing the reader that the phrase "tax contributions in silver" refers to the annual poll tax paid by the people of Judah.

—Comment to P84. At the end of this *parashah*, the editors of the sixth stage added a comment reminding the reader that income which priests received from (the sale of animals to be used for) guilt offerings and error offerings was allocated for the priests' own maintenance.

—Possible edits to P86 and P87. In the appendix to this book, I suggest that there was a co-regency between Yehu and his son Yehoahaz. I believe that an editor of the sixth stage who was unaware of this co-regency likely "corrected" the original synchronisms for Yehoahaz and Yehoash by moving their accession dates forward by nine years. For more details on this proposal, see my discussion of the chronology of the final nine kings of Israel in the appendix.

—Comment to P91. The editors of the sixth stage added a comment noting that although Amatzyahu pleased Yahweh, he did not please him like David did.

—Possible comment to P93. At the end of this *parashah*, there is a parenthetical comment stating that Azaryah was sixteen years old when he became king. I view this comment as part of Kings' first stage, but it would also be plausible to treat it as an addition by the editors of the sixth stage.

—Correction to P94. In this *parashah*, the editors of the sixth stage added a gloss noting that the term "ancestors" should be understood as a reference to the kings of Israel. This gloss is a second example of a "sixth stage" correction to material from a source document that may have been made by an individual who contributed to Kings' first or second stage (see note 94g above). The other example is the gloss to P47 discussed above.

—"Correction" to P95. The synchronism for Azaryah in this *parashah* is incorrect. I believe that the synchronism was originally correct and that a well-meaning editor of the sixth stage later changed the original synchronism because he believed it was incorrect. His "correction" was based on a corruption of the synchronism at the end of P100. See the discussion in note 100a above.

—Comment to P98. The editors of the sixth stage added a comment to this *parashah* stating that Menahem's tax of silver on Israel was calculated based on the total number of the soldiers in the army.

—Gloss to P100. The editors of the sixth stage added a gloss clarifying that the Circle region is the entire region of Naphtali.

—"Corrections" to synchronisms in P100, P101, and P102. In these *parashot*, an editor of the sixth stage "corrected" the synchronisms for Peqah king of Israel and Yotham and Ahaz kings of Judah based on the corruption of a synchronism at the end of P100. See the discussion in note 100a above.

—Comments to P102. Apart from the "correction" of the synchronism for Ahaz mentioned directly above, the editors of the sixth stage added two comments to this *parashah*. After the statement that Ahaz made offerings in the open-air shrines, they added the comment that the open-air shrines are equivalent to "on the hills and under every leafy tree," which is the phrase used to describe the Canaanites' places of worship in Deut P12,5. After the statement that the king of Aram cleared the Judeans out of Elath, the editors of the sixth stage added a comment that this was when the Edomites occupied Elath. If we understand the *ketiv* "Arameans" as original ("Edomites" is the *qere*), it is also possible—in fact, preferable—to treat this latter comment as part of Kings' first stage.

—Comments and gloss to P104. The editors of the sixth stage made three minor edits to this *parashah*. In the first half of the *parashah*, they glossed the term "all his prophets" (which was later corrupted in the text) to mean "every seer."[43] Second, near the beginning of the *parashah*, they added a comment likening the customs of the kings of Israel to the customs of the nations that Yahweh drove out of the land. Lastly, they added a comment toward the end of the *parashah* noting that Judah followed Israel's practices and didn't observe Yahweh's commandments.

—Edits to P105. The editors of the sixth stage made two edits to this *parashah*: they added a gloss informing the reader that Adrammelek and Anammelek are gods of the Sepharwites, and they added a comment reminding the reader that Yahweh changed Jacob's name to Israel (an allusion to Gen P30). It's worth noting that the editors added a similar comment in P59,1, which is discussed above.

—Comments to P106. I believe the editors of the sixth stage added the comment about the worship of the snake "Bronzey" and that they added the gloss about the "commandments" being those which Yahweh gave Moses. In addition, it is likely they added the comment clarifying that the statement about Hezekiah's uniqueness applies not only to the kings who were after him, but also to the kings who preceded him. However, it is also possible that this last comment was added by the authors of the third stage, who—as discussed above—made a number of edits to this *parashah*.

---

43 It's worth noting that the Masoretes were confused by the combination of the corruption and the gloss and added a *qere* in the margin that made the text completely nonsensical.

—Comment and edit to P108. The editors of the sixth stage added a comment stating that Hezekiah chopped up the gold-plated door pillars to the temple in addition to the temple doors themselves when he was desperately trying to collect funds to give to Sennacherib as tribute. I believe the editors altered what they viewed as an incorrect date at the beginning of the *parashah*, changing the date of Sennacherib's invasion from the twenty-eighth to the fourteenth year of Hezekiah's reign. On this proposal, see my discussion of the chronology of Hezekiah's reign in the appendix to this book.

—Additions to P111,1. The editors of the sixth stage made two additions to this *parashah*. First, they inserted into this *parashah* an addition that repeated an oracle from P110,2. The purpose of this addition was to connect the story of Hezekiah's illness in P111 - P111,1 to the story of the siege of Jerusalem in the preceding *parashot* (see note 111,1c above). Furthermore, they added two sentences about how Isaiah cured Hezekiah with a fig-cake preparation. This addition must have been made by an editor who was bothered that the original story omitted an account of Hezekiah's recovery (see note 111,1e above).

—Comments to P113 and P113,1. I believe the editors of the sixth stage made three comments to P113. It is also possible to view these as made by the authors of the third stage, but I believe they are slightly more in keeping with the activity characteristic of the sixth stage. They added the comment likening Manasseh's practices to the abominable practices of the nations that Yahweh drove away from the Israelites; they added a comment reminding the reader that Manasseh "was always building" altars on the temple grounds, which is the place Yahweh has chosen as his own; and they likely added the comment stating that Manasseh made his son pass through fire and practiced divination and consulted ghosts. In P113,1, I believe the editors of the sixth stage added the brief comment explaining how a dish is wiped clean.

—Comment(s) and gloss to P116. In this *parashah*, the editors of the sixth stage made two edits and possibly a third. They added the statement that the shrine priests never went to Yahweh's altar in Jerusalem except to eat with their kinsmen, and they added a gloss that the mention of the roof altars specifically refers to the altars located on the roof of Ahaz's Upper Chamber. It is possible that they also added the clause in Huldah's speech about Jerusalem's citizens becoming "an object of horror and a curse," although I think it is more likely that this clause is original to the speech and is not an addition. See note 116k above.

—Comment to P117,1? The editors of the sixth stage may have added the parenthetical comment in this *parashah* about Manasseh's killing of innocent citizens in Jerusalem. It is also possible this parenthetical comment is original to P117,1, which was composed by the authors of the second stage. See note 117,1f above.

—Gloss to P118. Near the end of this *parashah*, the editors of the sixth stage added a gloss stating that the skilled workers and smiths were valiant warriors.

—Glosses to P119,2. The editors of the sixth stage added four glosses to this *parashah*: they added a note stating the phrase "captain of the royal guard" refers to an officer of the king of Babylon; they clarified that the king whom the men in town defected to was the king of Babylon; they noted that "the secretary" should be understood as the army general; and they reminded the reader that "the people who remained in Judah" were those whom Nebuchadnezzar had left behind.

—Gloss (or variant) to P120,1. The final sentence of this *parashah* is best understood either as a gloss by the editors of the sixth stage, or as a variant the editors have chosen to preserve. If a gloss, they would have added it to clarify the meaning of the somewhat difficult phrasing in the preceding sentence. See note 120,1d above.

Schema for the composition history of Kings

Pre-Compositional Stage Source Documents (ca. 950 – 600 BCE)	First Stage Josianic Study Books (ca. 640 – 630 BCE)	Second Stage Exilic Expansion (ca. 580 – 550 BCE)	Third Stage Harmonization with Books of the Torah and Joshua (ca. 500 – 350 BCE)	Fourth Stage Prophetic Expansions (ca. 450 – 300 BCE)	Fifth Stage Other Expansions (ca. 500 – 200 BCE)	Sixth Stage Canonical Scripture (ca. 640 – 100 BCE)
Fragment at end of P7,2 (Acts of Shelomo)	End of P7,2				P1 – P7,1; all of P7,2 but end; transposition of end of P7,2	Glosses to P1; possible comment to P4; comments to P7
					P8 – P8,1; P9 – P10,1	
P10,2 – P10,23; first half of P10,24 (Acts of Shelomo)	Insertion of P10,2 – P10,23 and first sentence of P10,24				Second half of P10,24	Variant in P10,9; comments to P10,17 and P10,18; glosses to P10,24
Fragment of P11 (Acts of Shelomo)	First sentence of P11				Additions to P11	Comment to P11
P11,1 (Acts of Shelomo)	P11,1				P11,2	Gloss to P11,1
Details at end of P11,4 and in P12 – P12,1? (Acts of Shelomo)	P11,3 – P12,2				Addition to P11,4; addition to P12	Possible comment to P12
	P13	P14				Comment and glosses to P13
Details in second half of P15 (Acts of Shelomo)	Second half of P15				First half of P15; later additions to first half of P15	Glosses to P15
					P16 – P17,1; first two-thirds of P17,2	Comments to P16
End of P17,2; core of P19 (Acts of Shelomo)	Insertion of end of P17,2; composition of P18 – P20		Edits to P19 (treaty chest, Meeting Tent, Moses); additions to P20		Addition to P19	Glosses to P17; glosses to end of P17,2; comments/ glosses/edits to P19

Pre-Compositional Stage Source Documents (ca. 950 – 600 BCE)	First Stage Josianic Study Books (ca. 640 – 630 BCE)	Second Stage Exilic Expansion (ca. 580 – 550 BCE)	Third Stage Harmonization with Books of the Torah and Joshua (ca. 500 – 350 BCE)	Fourth Stage Prophetic Expansions (ca. 450 – 300 BCE)	Fifth Stage Other Expansions (ca. 500 – 200 BCE)	Sixth Stage Canonical Scripture (ca. 640 – 100 BCE)
		First third of P20,1			Last two-thirds of P20,1; all of P20,2 – P20,3; first half of P21	
	Second half of P21	Final sentence of P21; first two-thirds of P22	Last third of P22		Additions to second half of P21; first sentence of P22	
Possibly core of P23 (Acts of Shelomo)	P23					
Cores of first half of P24 and of P24,1 (Acts of Shelomo)	First half of P24 plus all of P24,1				Second half of P24	
Cores of P26 and of P27,1 (Acts of Shelomo)	Second half of P26; first two-thirds of P27; all of P27,1				P25; addition to P25	Comments to P25
	P28				First half of P26; last one-third of P27	
	P29		Comments to P28		P28,1	Comments to P28
P30 (Acts of Shelomo + NK: Yarov'am)	P30 – P30,1		Addition to P30,1		P29,1 plus addition to P29,1	Comments to P29,1
P30,2 (NK: Yarov'am); detail in P30,3? (Acts of Shelomo)	P30,2 – P30,3					Comment to P30,1

SCHEMA FOR THE COMPOSITION HISTORY OF KINGS

Pre-Compositional Stage Source Documents (ca. 950 – 600 BCE)	First Stage Josianic Study Books (ca. 640 – 630 BCE)	Second Stage Exilic Expansion (ca. 580 – 550 BCE)	Third Stage Harmonization with Books of the Torah and Joshua (ca. 500 – 350 BCE)	Fourth Stage Prophetic Expansions (ca. 450 – 300 BCE)	Fifth Stage Other Expansions (ca. 500 – 200 BCE)	Sixth Stage Canonical Scripture (ca. 640 – 100 BCE)
Beginning of P30,4; core of P31 and beginning of P31,1 (NK: Yarov'am)	P30,4 – P31; first half of P31,1			Second half of P31,1; all of P32		Edits to P30,4
Fragments of P32,1 (NK: Yarov'am)	P32,1 – P33		Edit to P32,1	Addition to P33; all of P34 – P35		Edits to P32,1; addition to P33; comment to P35
	P36 – P38					Comment to P38
Details in P39; core of P40 (SK: Rehav'am)	First half of P39; all of P40					Correction and additions to P39; addition to P40
Core of P41 (SK: Aviyyam)	P41				Comment to P41	Correction to P41
Core of P42 – P42,1 (SK: Asa)	P42 – P42,1					
Fragment of P43 (NK: Nadav)	P43					Addition to P43
Fragments of P44 – P44,1 (NK: Ba'sha)	P44 and second half of P44,1			First half of P44,1		
Core of P45 (NK: Elah)	P45					
Core of P46 (NK: Zimriy)	P46					
P47	Insertion of P47					Gloss to P47
Core of P48 (NK: Omriy)	P48					Comment to P48

403

Pre-Compositional Stage Source Documents (ca. 950 – 600 BCE)	First Stage Josianic Study Books (ca. 640 – 630 BCE)	Second Stage Exilic Expansion (ca. 580 – 550 BCE)	Third Stage Harmonization with Books of the Torah and Joshua (ca. 500 – 350 BCE)	Fourth Stage Prophetic Expansions (ca. 450 – 300 BCE)	Fifth Stage Other Expansions (ca. 500 – 200 BCE)	Sixth Stage Canonical Scripture (ca. 640 – 100 BCE)
Beginning of P49; end of P59,1 (NK: Ah'av)	P49 plus end of P59,1			Eliyyahu: P49.1 – P51,2, P55 – P58 Other prophetic material: P52 – P54; P54,1; P59 plus all of P59,1 but end Other: addition to P51,1 (theophany) plus variant; addition to first half of P51,2; repair of P56; end of P58		Correction and addition to P49; gloss to P49,1; comment to P51,1; gloss to P51,2; glosses to P52; gloss to P54; variants to P55; comments to P56
Core of P60 (SK: Yehoshaphat)	First half of P60 plus end	Addition to P60				
Details in P60,1 (NK: Ahazyahu)	P60,1; beginning of P60,2; all of P60,3 but beginning			All of P60,2 but beginning; beginning of P60,3		
	P61 – P61,1			Eliysha: P62 – P63		
Details in P64 (NK: Yehoram)	P64			Eliysha: P65 – P74		Gloss to P69
Core of P75 (SK: Yehoram)	P75					Gloss to P75
Core of P76 (SK: Ahazyahu)	P76			First half of P77		Edits to first half of P77
	Second half of P77; P78 – P79			Comments to second half of P77		Comment to second half of P77; additions to P78; gloss to P78,1; gloss to P79
Core of P80 (NK: Yehu)	P80		Possible edits to P80			Edits to P80

Pre-Compositional Stage Source Documents (ca. 950 – 600 BCE)	First Stage Josianic Study Books (ca. 640 – 630 BCE)	Second Stage Exilic Expansion (ca. 580 – 550 BCE)	Third Stage Harmonization with Books of the Torah and Joshua (ca. 500 – 350 BCE)	Fourth Stage Prophetic Expansions (ca. 450 – 300 BCE)	Fifth Stage Other Expansions (ca. 500 – 200 BCE)	Sixth Stage Canonical Scripture (ca. 640 – 100 BCE)
	P81 – P82,2					Edits to P82, P82,1, and P82,2
P82,3; details in P83; core of P85 (SK: Yeho'ash)	P82,3 – P85					Gloss to P83; comment to P84
Details in P86 (NK: Yeho'ahaz)	P86				Addition to P86	Possible edit to P86 (synchronism)
Details in P87 (NK: Yeho'ash)	P87			Eliysha: P88 – P89 Other: P90		Possible edit to P87 (synchronism)
Core of P91 – P93 (SK: Amatzyahu)	P91 – P93		Comment to P91			Comment to P91; possible comment to P93
Details in P94 (NK: Yarov'am)	P94					Correction to P94
Core of P95 (SK: Azaryah)	P95					Edit to P95 (synchronism)
Details in P96 (NK: Zekaryahu)	P96					
Details in P97 (NK: Shallum)	P97					
Core of P98 (NK: Menahem)	P98					Comment to P98
Core of P99 (NK: Peqahyah)	P99					
Core of P100 (NK: Peqah)	P100					Edit (synchronism) and gloss to P100
Details in P101 (SK: Yotham)	P101	Possible edit to P101				Edit to P101 (synchronism)

Pre-Compositional Stage Source Documents (ca. 950 – 600 BCE)	First Stage Josianic Study Books (ca. 640 – 630 BCE)	Second Stage Exilic Expansion (ca. 580 – 550 BCE)	Third Stage Harmonization with Books of the Torah and Joshua (ca. 500 – 350 BCE)	Fourth Stage Prophetic Expansions (ca. 450 – 300 BCE)	Fifth Stage Other Expansions (ca. 500 – 200 BCE)	Sixth Stage Canonical Scripture (ca. 640 – 100 BCE)
Core of P102 (SK: Ahaz)	P102		Comment to P102			Edit (synchronism) and comments to P102
Details in P103? (NK: Hoshea)	P103; end of P104		All of P104 but end			Comments and gloss to P104
	First two-thirds of P105; end of P105		Addition to P105			Edits to P105
Core of P106 – P108; details at end of P112 (SK: Hizqiyyah)	P106 – P107; end of P112	Insertion of P108	Possible comments to P106; comment at end of P107	Yeshaʿyahu: P109 – P111,1; all of P112 but end; addition to P109; additions to P110,1 and P110,2		Comments to P106; comment and edit (date) to P108; additions to P111,1
Details in P113 and at the end of P113,1 (SK: Manasseh)	First half of P113; end of P113,1	End of P113; first half of P113,1	Additions to P113 and comment to 113,1			Comments to P113 and P113,1
Core of P114 (SK: Amon)	P114					
Details in P115; small parts of P116, including end (SK: Yoshiyyahu)		P115; middle part of P116; material near end of P116	First part of P116 and addition to latter part of P116	Addition to P116	End of P116	Comment(s) and gloss to P116
Core of P117? (SK: Yehoʾahaz)		P117				
Details in P117,1 (SK: Yehoyaqiym)		P117,1				Comment to P117,1?
		P118 – P120,1			Additions to P118 and P119,2	Gloss to P118; glosses to P119,2; gloss (or variant) to P120,1

Appendix: Chronology of the kingdoms of Israel and Judah

The authors of the earliest version of Kings adopted a chronicle format for their book, excerpting and commenting on material from two royal chronicles—one from Israel and one from Judah—to create what I believe was a "study book" for the young king Josiah. This book taught him about the Davidic kings who were his ancestors, it taught him about the rulers of the former kingdom of Israel (a territory on which Josiah was told the Davidic king had a historical claim), and it taught him the importance of the king's "pleasing Yahweh" through proper management of the cult. Today the book of Kings provides a rich mine of material for scholars to delve into and to deepen our understanding of the history and religious practices of the kingdoms of Israel and Judah. The study of history naturally involves questions of chronolology, and one especially interesting aspect of Kings is that its chronicle format offers scholars the opportunity to reconstruct the chronology of the kingdoms of Israel and Judah.

With respect to the chronology that we find in Kings, the authors of the book employed a system in which each king's accession to the throne is dated by reference to the regnal year of his counterpart in the neighboring kingdom. (Scholars refer to the dates in this system as "synchronisms.") For example, the book's authors state that Ahav's reign over Israel began in the thirty-eighth year of Judah's king Asa, and then later in the book they tell us that Jehoshaphat's reign over Judah began in Ahav's fourth year.[1] Scholars have long debated whether this chrononological system was devised by the authors of Kings or whether they adopted it from the system they found in their two primary source documents, *The Chronicles of the Kings of Israel* and *The Chronicles of the Kings of Judah*. My own belief is that some of the quirks we find in the synchronisms in Kings are easier to explain if the book's authors adopted the system from their source documents.[2] Given my view that the system appeared in the source

---

1 See Kgs P49 and P60.
2 The clearest example of this is found in P107, which is based on the account of Samaria's fall as it appeared in *The Chronicles of the Kings of Judah*. See the discussion in note 107a above.

documents, I thought it would be an interesting exercise to reconstruct the chronology of the kingdoms of Israel and Judah on the assumption that the synchronisms we see in Kings are, with a few exceptions, accurate. What follows is my attempt to do so. Perhaps unsurprisingly, my reconstruction differs only in minor details with reconstructions produced by other scholars.[3]

**

The starting point of any reconstruction of the chronology of Israel and Judah must be to look for "anchors" from non-biblical sources that allow us to date specific events in either Israel or Judah with a high degree of certainty. There are five synchronisms with Mesopotamian history based on the regnal years of Assyrian and Babylonian kings that scholars use as anchors for their reconstructions:[4]

> (1) Shalmaneser III's battle against a coalition of kings that included Israel's king Ahav, which is dated to 853 BCE. The Assyrian source in which Ahav's name appears is known as the Kurkh Monolith.
>
> (2) Shalmaneser III's receipt of tribute from Israel's king Yehu, which is dated to 841 BCE. The Assyrian source mentioning Yehu is known as the Black Obelisk.[5]
>
> (3) Shalmaneser III's receipt of tribute from Israel's king Yehoash, which is dated to 796 BCE. The Assyrian source mentioning Yehoash is known as the Rimah Stele.
>
> (4) Sennacherib's campaign against Judah, including his capture of Lachish and his attack on Hezekiah in Jerusalem, events which are dated to 701 BCE. The earliest Assyrian

---

[3] For good recent discussions of some of the issues in reconstructing the chronologies of Israel and Judah, see K. van Bekkum, "Competing Chronologies, Competing Histories: Ancient Israel and the Chronology of the Southern Levant, ca. 1200 – 587 BCE," in K. Heimer and G. Pierce (eds.), *The Ancient Israelite World* (London: Routledge, 2023), pp. 34-53 and W. Zwickel, "Chronological Data and Mid-Ninth Century BC Israel," in P. van der Veen, R. Wallenfels, and P. James (eds.), *Assyria and the West: A Fresh Look at the Unshakeable Pillars of Late Bronze and Iron Age Chronology in the Eastern Mediterranean World* (Oxfordshire: Archaeopress, 2025), pp. 265-277. Both papers helpfully contain lists of synchronisms with significant events associated with Assyrian and Babylonian kings and reproduce widely used scholarly reconstructions of the chronologies of Israel and Judah.

[4] See van Bekkum, p. 41, and Zwickel, p. 266.

[5] See note 80d and figure 1 above.

source mentioning these events is known as the Rassam Cylinder (a later version of this source is known as the Taylor Prism).[6]

(5) Nebuchadnezzar II's conquest of Jerusalem and installation of a new king, which is dated to 597 BCE. The Babylonian source mentioning these events is known as the Jerusalem Chronicle.

There are six other mentions of Israel or Judah in Assyrian and Babylonian sources where the dates are slightly less certain, but which nonetheless serve as useful additional anchors for our chronological reconstruction:[7]

(1) Tiglash Pileser III's receipt of tribute from Menahem King of Israel, which is dated to either 740 or 738 BCE. The Assyrian source for this is known as the Iran Stele.

(2) Tiglath Pileser III's receipt of tribute from Ahaz King of Judah, which is dated to sometime between 734 and 732 BCE. The Assyrian source for this is known as Summary Inscription 7.

(3) Three inscriptions of Tiglath Pileser III mention the death of Peqah King of Israel and the tribute paid by Peqah's successor Hoshea. Based on Assyrian synchronisms, these events are dated to sometime between 733 and 731 BCE. The sources for these events are Summary Inscriptions 4, 9, and 13.

(4) Inscriptions of Shalmaneser V and Sargon II mention the conquest of Samaria and the deportation of its inhabitants. Assyrian sources mentioning these events are the Sargon II Display Inscriptions, the Nimrud Prism, the Assur Charter, and the Babylonian Chronicle I. Based on synchronisms in these sources, the fall of Samaria is dated to sometime between 722 and 720 BCE.

(5) Manasseh King of Judah's sending of corvée laborers to Esarhaddon. This event is mentioned in the Esarhaddon Prism B, and Assyrian synchronisms suggest a date of around 676 BCE.

---

6 See note 108c above.
7 See van Bekkum, pp. 41f.

(6) Ashurbanipal's receipt of tribute from Manasseh King of Judah. The event is mentioned in the Rassam Cylinder and in the Ashurbanipal Cylinder C. Assyrian synchronisms suggest a date of 667 BCE.

These two lists give us eleven anchors for our chronological reconstruction. The dates for the first five anchors are very firm, and the dates for the other six anchors are less certain but still of high confidence. The eleven anchors are as follows:

(1) Ahav's reign, which lasted 22 years, must have included 853 BCE.

(2) Yehu's reign, which lasted 28 years, must include 841 BCE.

(3) Yehoash of Israel's reign, which lasted 16 years, must include 796 BCE.

(4) Hezekiah's reign, which lasted 29 years, must include 701 BCE.

(5) Jehoiachin's reign must have ended in 597 BCE and Zedekiah's reign must have begun in that same year.

(6) Menahem's reign, which lasted ten years, must include either or both of 740 and 738 BCE.

(7) Ahaz's reign, which lasted 16 years, must include at least one of the years from 734 to 732 BCE.

(8) Peqah's death and the accession of his successor Hoshea must have happened in the period from 733 to 731 BCE.

(9) The fall of Samaria and deportation of its inhabitants must have happened in the period from 722 to 720 BCE.

(10) and (11) Manasseh's reign, which lasted 55 years, must include both 676 and 667 BCE.

**

With the anchor dates in place, one might expect the process of reconstructing the chronology for Israel and Judah to be a relatively straightforward matter of using the regnal lengths and synchronisms in Kings to fill in the regnal dates before and after each of the anchors. While that is true for the reigns of many kings, it is unfortunately the case that the chronological data in Kings is quite messy in several places. Consequently, the reconstruction process requires one to make a number of assumptions and, at times, arbitrary decisions. To manage this process in a consistent way, I have adopted the following methodological rules for my reconstruction:

> (1) The regnal lengths are more reliable than the synchronisms. When the two cannot be reconciled, the regnal length should take precedence.
>
> (2) Because the calendar used by ancient Israel and Judah was "lunisolar" and required the intercalation of an extra month every few years, one should not expect to be able to reconstruct a chronology in perfect agreement with the regnal lengths and synchronisms in Kings. The rule I held myself to in the reconstruction was that my proposed regnal lengths and synchronisms could vary by no more than one year from the numbers we find in Kings.
>
> (3) In order to reconcile synchronisms with regnal lengths and arrange them to fit the eleven anchor dates that we have from Assyrian insciptions, it is acceptable to propose co-regencies. Because this solution is quite arbitrary, I employed it only as a last resort.
>
> (4) Proposed accession and ending dates of a reign should match the regnal length in Kings if possible; because of the practice of intercalation, accession and ending dates that imply a regnal length that is one year shorter than the number in Kings is acceptable.
>
> (5) When one calculates a regnal length from synchronisms, there are three possible outcomes because of differences in timing within the year: the regnal length is equal to the difference between the two synchronisms, the regnal length is one more than the difference between the two synchronisms, or the regnal length is one less than the difference between the two synchronisms.[8]
>
> (6) Synchronisms are calculated as the accession year of the new king subtracted from the accession year of that king's counterpart. One then has the option to increase

---

8   Consider, for example, a king whose reign is said to begin in the eleventh year of his counterpart and end in the sixteenth year of his counterpart. If his reign began late in the eleventh year and ended early in the sixteenth year, that would imply a regnal length of four years, whereas if his reign began early in the eleventh year and ended late in the sixteenth year, that would imply a regnal length of six years.

this number by one to reflect differences in timing within the year.[9]

(7) In reconciling my proposed chronology with the synchronisms and regnal lengths given in Kings, I used the flexibility provided in rules (5) and (6) to match my numbers as closely as possible to the numbers found in Kings.[10]

**

A convenient place to start our reconstruction is with the earliest anchor that we have: the year 853 BCE, which is tied to the reign of Ahav. Our first decision is where to end Ahav's reign. We know from one of our anchors that Yehu was king of Israel in 841 BCE; furthermore, Kings tells us that the two kings between Ahav and Yehu ruled, respectively, for two and twelve years. In order to squeeze these fourteen years into the twelve-year gap between 853 and 841, I have thought it best to assume that Ahav's reign must have ended no later than 853 BCE and that he had a co-regency with with his son Ahazyahu. Kings P49 tells us Ahav ruled for 22 years, which puts his accession year at 876/875 BCE. Moving on to Ahav's father Omri, we run into our next problem: in P48, we are told Omri ruled for twelve years; however, the synchronisms with Asa King of Judah suggest his rule was only seven years.[11] In such situations, the easiest—if somewhat ad hoc and arbitrary—solution is to propose a co-regency. In this case, I propose that Ahav began a co-regency with his father Omri beginning in Omri's seventh or eighth year. This would put the beginning of Omri's reign as 883/882 BCE.

With Omri, we run into another problem with the early chronology of Israel: the narrative of Kings portrays him as becoming king after his coup against Zimri. Given that Zimri ruled for only seven days,

---

9   Consider the case of Jehoshaphat. In the reconstruction below, I propose an accession date of 871 BCE for him; his counterpart was Ahav, for whom I propose an accession date of 875 BCE. If Ahav assumed the throne in late 875 and Jehoshaphat in early 871, then the beginning of Jehoshaphat's reign would be dated to the fourth year of Ahav's rule; however, if Ahav assumed the throne in early 875 and Jehoshaphat in late 871, then the beginning of Jehoshaphat's reign would be dated to the fifth year of Ahav's rule.

10 Again, consider the example of Jehoshaphat: his proposed accession year is 871 BCE and his counterpart Ahav's proposed accession year is 875 BCE. In my reconstruction, I had the option of selecting either the fourth year of Ahav or the fifth year of Ahav as the synchronism for Jehoshaphat; I chose the fourth year of Ahav in order to match the number given in Kings.

11 In P48, Omri is said to become king of Israel in Asa's thirty-first year, and in P49, Ahav is said to become king of Israel in Asa's thirty-eighth year.

the synchronism for Omri and Zimri should be the same. But in fact Zimri's synchronism with the king of Judah is four years earlier than Omri's (the twenty-seventh year of Asa vs. the thirty-first year of Asa). Again, if we assume the synchronisms are accurate, the only solutions at our disposal are somewhat arbitrary and ad hoc. In this situation, one option is to propose that *The Chronicles of the Kings of Israel* included an account of Tivni's reign (see P46), and that this source counted Omri's reign as beginning after the end of Tivni's reign, which I would conjecture lasted two years. There are no problems with the synchronisms of the kings that precede Zimri. Once we fill in the dates of Zimri's predecessors using the synchronisms found in Kings, we can use synchronisms to infer to the dates of all the kings of Judah up to our first anchor date of 853 BCE. These actions produce the following tables for the kings of Israel from Jeroboam through Ahav and for the kings of Judah from Rehoboam through Jehoshaphat:

Table 1. The kings of Israel from Jeroboam to Ahav

Kings of Israel	Length of reign (years)	Estimated reign (BCE)	Accession to co-regency	Synchronism in the book of Kings	Synchronism based on Whitt reconstruction
Jeroboam	22	932 – 911		1st of Rehoboam	1st of Rehoboam
Nadav	2	911 – 909		2nd of Asa	2nd of Asa
Baasha	24	909 – 886		3rd of Asa	3rd of Asa
Elah	2	886 – 884		26th of Asa	26th of Asa
Zimri	7 days	884		27th of Asa	28th of Asa
Tivni	2?	884 – 882 (?)		None given	N.A.
Omri	12	882 – 871		31st of Asa	31th of Asa
Ahav	22	875 – 853	8th of Omri	38th of Asa	38th of Asa

Table 2. The kings of Judah from Rehoboam to Jehoshaphat

Kings of Judah	Length of reign (years)	Estimated reign (BCE)	Accession to co-regency	Synchronism in the book of Kings	Synchronism based on Whitt reconstruction
Rehoboam	17	932 – 915		1st of Jeroboam	1st of Jeroboam
Aviyyam	3	915 – 912		18th of Jeroboam	18th of Jeroboam
Asa	41	912 – 871		20th of Jeroboam	20th of Jeroboam
Jehoshaphat	25	871 – 846		4th of Ahav	4th of Ahav

**

For the second step in my reconstruction, I look at the next earliest anchor date, which is 841 BCE, when Yehu presented tribute to Shalmaneser III. If 841 represents the beginning of Yehu's reign, then—as stated above—we must squeeze the reigns of his two predecessors (who ruled for fourteen years) into the twelve years from 853 to 841 BCE. To solve this problem, I assume a short co-regency between Ahav and his son Ahazyahu. This gives us dates of 854 to 852 for Ahazyahu's two-year reign, followed by 852 to 841 for Yehoram's twelve-year reign and 841 to 813 for Yehu's 28-year reign. For the corresponding time period in Judah, I use regnal lengths and synchronisms to fill in the kings from Yehoram through Yoash. Note that for the kings of Judah, I propose a short co-regency between Yoram and Jehoshaphat based on the synchronisms given for Yehoram of Judah and his counterpart Yehoram of Israel.[12] These actions produce the following tables:

Table 3. The kings of Israel from Ahazyahu to Yehu

Kings of Israel	Length of reign (years)	Estimated reign (BCE)	Accession to co-regency	Synchronism in the book of Kings	Synchronism based on Whitt reconstruction
Ahazyahu	2	854 – 852	21st of Ahav	17th of Jehoshaphat	17th of Jehoshaphat
Yehoram	12	852 – 841		18 Jehosh. / 2 Yehoram	19th of Jehoshaphat
Yehu	28	841 – 813		None given	1st of Ahazyahu

Table 4. The kings of Judah from Yoram to Yoash

Kings of Judah	Length of reign (years)	Estimated reign (BCE)	Accession to co-regency	Synchronism in the book of Kings	Synchronism based on Whitt reconstruction
Yoram	8	848 – 841	23rd of Jehosh.	5th of Yehoram	5th of Yehoram
Ahazyahu	1	842 – 841	7th of Yoram	12th/11th of Yehoram	12th of Yehoram
Athalyahu	6	841 – 834		None given	1st of Yehu
Yoash	40	834 – 793		7th of Yehu	7th of Yehu

**

---

[12] Yehoram of Israel is said to become king in Jehoshaphat's eighteenth year. (In my reconstruction, this is Jehoshaphat's nineteenth year.) Conversely, Yoram of Judah is said to become king in Yehoram of Israel's fifth year. This would imply Jehoshaphat ruled for 23 years. However, the authors of P60 state that Jehoshaphat ruled for 25 years. This discrepancy may be reconciled through a co-regency between Jehoshaphat and his son Yoram beginning in Jehoshaphat's twenty-third year, which is what I have proposed in my reconstruction.

We turn next to the reigns of two kings for whom we have multiple anchor dates: Israel's last king, Hoshea, and Hezekiah, whose reign overlapped with Hoshea's. There are two anchor dates for Hoshea; as discussed above, these imply that his reign must have begun between 733 and 731 BCE and must have ended between 722 and 720 BCE. If we accept the comment in P103 that he ruled for nine years, then the only regnal period that fits the two anchor dates is 731 - 722 BCE.

The reconstruction of Hezekiah's reign is more challenging, as it is impossible to find a regnal period that aligns the anchor dates and the synchronisms that we have for him. First, in P106, the authors state that Hezekiah became king in Hoshea's third year. If Hoshea became king in 731, as determined above, then this synchronism would imply that Hezekiah became king in 729 or 728. Second, in P107, we are told that Samaria fell in the sixth year of Hezekiah's reign. Based on the anchor date for Samaria's fall of sometime between 722 and 720, this would imply Hezekiah's reign began sometime between 728 and 725 BCE. Third, in P108, the authors tell us Sennacherib besieged Jerusalem in the fourteenth year of Hezekiah's reign. Based on the anchor date for Sennacherib's invasion of Judah listed above, this would imply that Hezekiah's reign began in 715 or 714 BCE.

Clearly one of the synchronisms for Hezekiah must be incorrect, even though—as I suggest in the notes and comments—the source of all three synchronisms is the *The Chronicles of the Kings of Judah*. The most likely explanation, in my opinion, is that the synchronism in P108 originally read "in the twenty-eighth year" of Hezekiah and that late in Kings' transmission process—most likely the Hellenistic period—this was changed by an editor to read "in the fourteenth year" on the basis of the story in P111,1, which states that Hezekiah would live fifteen years after Sennacherib's invasion. The editor knew that Hezekiah ruled for twenty-nine years, and thus "corrected" the synchronism in P108 to state that Sennacherib's siege of Jerusalem occurred in Hezekiah's fourteenth year. If we accept that the synchronism in P108 is in error, then the synchronisms in P106 and P107 suggest that Hezekiah's reign began in 728 BCE.

**

For the next step in my reconstruction, I look at the last kings of Judah. This step is a very simple process of using the latest anchor date—Nebuchadnezzar's conquest of Jerusalem in 597 BCE and his replacement of Jehoiachin with Zedekiah—and then filling in the prior and succeeding kings based on the lengths of the reigns we find in Kings. In this process, the logical beginning date for Manasseh's reign is 696 BCE, whereas the logical end date for Hezekiah's reign based on the discussion above is 699 BCE. To close this gap, I have "stretched" the reigns of Hezekiah, Josiah, and Yehoyaqim by one year each.[13] This process produces the following table:

Table 5. The kings of Judah from Hezekiah to Zedekiah

Kings of Judah	Length of reign (years)	Estimated reign (BCE)
Hezekiah	29	728 – 698
Manasseh	55	698 – 643
Amon	2	643 – 641
Josiah	31	641 – 609
Yehoahaz	3 months	609
Yehoyaqim	11	609 – 597
Jehoiachin	3 months	597
Zedekiah	11	597 – 586

**

The final task is to fill in the final nine kings of Israel from Yehoahaz to Hoshea (whose reign we already determined must have been from 731 to 722 BCE), and to fill in the four kings of Judah from Amatzyah through Ahaz. The anchor dates for this period are that Ahaz's reign must include either or both of 734 and 732 BCE and that Peqah died and Hoshea succeeded him sometime between 733 and 731 BCE.

With respect to the final nine kings of Israel, it was only possible to make synchronisms for the final seven kings of Israel fit the numbers in Kings by beginning Jeroboam II's reign in 789 BCE. This, however, introduces a problem with the reigns of the two preceding kings, Yehoahaz and Yehoash: if Jeroboam II's reign began in 789, then the period between the beginning of his reign and the end of Yehu's reign is twenty-four years, yet Yehoahaz and Yehoash ruled for a total of thirty-three years. As a solution, I propose a co-regency for Yehoahaz beginning in Yehu's twenty-second year and a co-regency for Yehoash beginning in Yehoahaz's fourteenth year.[14] While this solution is

---

13 It is theoretically possible that Hezekiah could have ruled for twenty-nine years while beginning his rule in 728 and ending his rule in 698. Likewise Josiah could have ruled for thirty-one years while beginning his rule in 641 and ending it in 609, and Yehoyaqim could have ruled for eleven years while beginning his rule in 609 an ending it in 597.

14 Alternatively, one could propose a co-regency for Yehoahaz beginning in Yehu's nineteenth year, and no co-regency for Yehoash.

arbitrary and implies that the synchonisms in Kings for Yehoahaz and Yehoash must be erroneous, it allows all the synchonisms of the succeeding kings of Israel to fit what Kings records for their reigns. Moreover, there is a plausible explanation for how the erroneous synchonisms might have been introduced into Kings: a later editor who was unaware of the co-regency of Yehoahaz with Yehu (but was aware of the co-regency between Yehoash with Yehoahaz) may have "corrected" the synchonisms for these two kings in P86 and P87 by moving their synchonisms with Yoash of Judah forward by nine years. In fact, it is tempting to think that the same editor who "corrected" the synchonisms for the kings of Judah discussed above in note 100a may also have "corrected" the synchonisms given for Yehoahaz and Yehoash. These actions produce the following table:

Table 6. The kings of Israel from Yehoahaz to Hoshea

Kings of Israel	Length of reign (years)	Estimated reign (BCE)	Accession to co-regency	Synchronism in the book of Kings	Synchronism based on Whitt reconstruction
Yehoahaz	17	819 – 802	22nd of Yehu	23rd of Yoash of Jud.	14th of Yoash of Jud.
Yehoash	16	805 – 789	14th Yehoahaz	37th of Yoash of Jud.	28th of Yoash of Jud.
Jeroboam II	41	789 – 748		15th of Amatzyahu	15th of Amatzyahu
Zekaryahu	6 months	748		38th of Azaryahu	38th of Azaryahu
Shallum	1 month	747		39th of Azaryahu	39th of Azaryahu
Menahem	10	747 – 737		39th of Azaryahu	39th of Azaryahu
Peqahyah	2	737 – 735		50th of Azaryahu	50th of Azaryahu
Peqah	4	735 – 731		52nd of Azaryahu	52nd of Azaryahu
Hoshea	9	731 – 722		12 Ahaz/20 Yotham	13th of Ahaz
Fall of Sam.		722		6th of Hezekiah	6th of Hezekiah

The reconstruction of the reigns of the four kings of Judah in this period is challenging because there are clear errors in synchronisms for three of them: Azaryahu, Yotham, and Ahaz. I proposed in my notes and comments that these erroneous synchronisms are due to changes made by a later editor who was unaware of the co-regency between Yotham and Azaryah.[15] The reigns of three of the four Judean kings of this period—Amatzyahu, Azaryahu, and Ahaz—are cited as synchronisms in the accounts of the kings of Israel. In my reconstruction, I assumed these synchronisms were correct, and I used these to determine the years each king ruled. In order to make the synchronisms and regnal lengths for these kings agree with one another and

---

15   See note 100a above; see also notes 95a, 100d, 101a, and 102a.

to fit them within the known anchor dates, it was necessary for me to propose co-regencies for each of the four kings of Judah in this period. These actions produce the following table:

Table 7. The kings of Judah from Amatzyahu to Ahaz

Kings of Judah	Length of reign (years)	Estimated reign (BCE)	Accession to co-regency	Synchronism in the book of Kings	Synchronism based on Whitt reconstruction
Amatzyahu	29	803 – 774	30th of Yoash	2nd of Yoash	2nd of Yoash
Azaryahu	52	786 – 734	17th Amatzyah	27th of Jeroboam II	4th of Jeroboam II
Yotham	16	760 – 744	26th Azaryah	2nd of Peqah	31st of Jeroboam
Ahaz	16	744 – 728	42rd Azaryah	17th of Peqah	4th of Menahem

**

I conclude with the three summary tables shown on the following pages. The first table shows all the kings of Israel, the second shows all the kings of Judah, and the third shows the kings of Israel and Judah together.

Table 8. The kings of Israel, 932 to 722 BCE

Kings of Israel	Length of reign (years)	Estimated reign (BCE)	Accession to co-regency	Synchronism in the book of Kings	Synchronism based on Whitt reconstruction
Jeroboam	22	932 – 911		1st of Rehoboam	1st of Rehoboam
Nadav	2	911 – 909		2nd of Asa	2nd of Asa
Baasha	24	909 – 886		3rd of Asa	3rd of Asa
Elah	2	886 – 884		26th of Asa	26th of Asa
Zimri	7 days	884		27th of Asa	28th of Asa
Tivni	2 (?)	884 – 882 (?)		None given	N.A.
Omri	12	882 – 871		31st of Asa	31th of Asa
Ahav	22	875 – 853	8th of Omri	38th of Asa	38th of Asa
Ahazyahu	2	854 – 852	21st of Ahav	17th of Jehoshaphat	17th of Jehoshaphat
Yehoram	12	852 – 841		18 Jehosh. / 2 Yehoram	19th of Jehoshaphat
Yehu	28	841 – 813		None given	1st of Ahazyahu
Yehoahaz	17	819 – 802	22nd of Yehu	23rd of Yoash of Jud.	14th of Yoash of Jud.
Yehoash	16	805 – 789	14th Yehoahaz	37th of Yoash of Jud.	28th of Yoash of Jud.
Jeroboam II	41	789 – 748		15th of Amatzyahu	15th of Amatzyahu
Zekaryahu	6 months	748		38th of Azaryahu	38th of Azaryahu
Shallum	1 month	747		39th of Azaryahu	39th of Azaryahu
Menahem	10	747 – 737		39th of Azaryahu	39th of Azaryahu
Peqahyah	2	737 – 735		50th of Azaryahu	50th of Azaryahu
Peqah	4	735 – 731		52nd of Azaryahu	52nd of Azaryahu
Hoshea	9	731 – 722		12th Ahaz/20th Yotham	13th of Ahaz

Table 9. The kings of Judah, 932 to 586 BCE

Kings of Judah	Length of reign (years)	Estimated reign (BCE)	Accession to co-regency	Synchronism in the book of Kings	Synchronism based on Whitt reconstruction
Rehoboam	17	932 – 915		1st of Jeroboam	1st of Jeroboam
Aviyyam	3	915 – 912		18th of Jeroboam	18th of Jeroboam
Asa	41	912 – 871		20th of Jeroboam	20th of Jeroboam
Jehoshaphat	25	871 – 846		4th of Ahav	4th of Ahav
Yoram	8	848 – 841	23rd of Jehosh.	5th of Yehoram	5th of Yehoram
Ahazyahu	1	842 – 841	7th of Yoram	12th/11th of Yehoram	12th of Yehoram
Athalyahu	6	841 – 833		None given	1st of Yehu
Yoash	40	834 – 793		7th of Yehu	7th of Yehu
Amatzyahu	29	803 – 774	30th of Yoash	2nd of Yoash	2nd of Yoash
Azaryahu	52	786 – 734	17th Amatzyah	27th of Jeroboam II	4th of Jeroboam II
Yotham	16	760 – 744	26th Azaryah	2nd of Peqah	31st of Jeroboam
Ahaz	16	744 – 728	42nd Azaryah	17th of Peqah	4th of Menahem
Hezekiah	29	728 – 698		3rd of Hoshea	3rd of Hoshea
Manasseh	55	698 – 643			
Amon	2	643 – 641			
Josiah	31	641 – 609			
Yehoahaz	3 months	609			
Yehoyaqim	11	609 – 597			
Jehoiachin	3 months	597			
Zedekiah	11	597 – 586			

Table 10. The kings of Israel and Judah*

Kings of Israel	Estimated Reign (BCE)	Record of Reign
Yarovam (I)	932 – 911	P32,1 – P38
Nadav	911 – 909	P43
Baasha	909 – 886	P44 – P44,1
Elah	886 – 884	P45
Zimriy	884	P46
Tivniy	884 – 882 (?)	P47
Omri	882 – 871	P48
Ahav	875 – 853	P49 – P59,1
Ahazyahu	854 – 852	P60,1 – P61,1
Yehoram	852 – 841	P64 – P65,1; P77
Yehu	841 – 813	P77 – P80
Yehoahaz	819 – 802	P86
Yehoash	805 – 789	P87
Yarovam (II)	789 – 748	P94
Zekaryah	748	P96
Shallum	747	P97
Menahem	747 – 737	P98
Peqahyah	737 – 735	P99
Peqah	735 – 731	P100
Hoshea	731 – 722	P103

Kings of Judah	Estimated Reign (BCE)	Record of Reign
Rehavam	932 – 915	P30,4 – P32; P39 – P40
Aviyyam	915 – 912	P41
Asa	912 – 871	P42 – P42,1
Yehoshaphat	871 – 846	P60
Yoram	848 – 841	P75
Ahazyahu	842 – 841	P76 – P77
Athalyahu	841 – 834	P81 – P82,1
Yehoash	834 – 793	P82,3 – P85
Amatzyahu	803 – 774	P91 – P93
Azaryahu / Uzziyahu	786 – 734	P95
Yotham	760 – 744	P101
Ahaz	744 – 728	P102
Hizqiyyahu	728 – 698	P106 – P112
Menashsheh	698 – 643	P113 – P113,1
Amon	643 – 641	P114
Yoshiyyahu	641 – 609	P115 – P116
Yehoahaz	609	P117
Yehoyaqim	609 – 597	P117 – P117,1
Yehoyakin	597	P118
Tzidqiyyahu	597 – 586	P119 – P119,1

* Please note that for ease of reference with the *parashot* in the translation, in this table I have not used any traditional anglicized spellings of the names of the kings.

www.ingramcontent.com/pod-product-compliance
Lightning Source LLC
Chambersburg PA
CBHW081828170426
43199CB00017B/2677